W9-AQZ-126

The Revolution in America 1754-1788

The Revolution in America 1754–1788

Documents and Commentaries

EDITED BY
J. R. POLE
Reader in American History and Government at the University of Cambridge and Fellow of Churchill College

Stanford University Press
Stanford, California
1970

Stanford University Press

Stanford, California

Originating publisher: Macmillan and Co., Ltd,
London and Basingstoke, 1970

Printed in Great Britain

ISBN 0 8047 0755 3
LC 70–126037

Contents

PART 1: *The Problem of Continental Government*

I

Towards Political Independence

II

Public Finance and the Continental Congress

III

Economic Proposals and Policies Affecting the Articles of Confederation

IV

Towards a New Constitution

V

The Convention and the Constitution

PART 2: *Wealth, Wages and Prices: Congressional and State Economic Policies*

PART 3 : *Public Lands: Congress, The States and The People*

III

Virginia

IV

Pennsylvania

PART 5: *America After the Revolution*

General Editor's Preface

Historical perception demands immediacy and depth. These qualities are lost in attempts at broad general survey; for the reader of history, depth is the only true breadth. Each volume in this series, therefore, explores an important historical problem in depth. There is no artificial uniformity; each volume is shaped by the problem it tackles. The past bears its own witness; the core of each volume is a major collection of original material (translated into English where necessary) as alive, as direct and as full as possible. The reader should feel the texture of the past. The volume editor provides interpretative notes and introduction and a full working bibliography. The volume will stand in its own right as a 'relived experience' and will also serve as a point of entry into a wider area of historical discourse. In taking possession of a particular historical world, the reader will move more freely in a wider universe of historical experience.

*

In this volume Dr J. R. Pole explores the American Revolution as a revolution in America and has produced a book which is unique in its character and unprecedented in its scope. The struggle for home rule, said Charles Becker, was also a struggle over who was to rule at home, but it is precisely this central theme of the American Revolution which is ill-served by most existing collections of documents, which concentrate on the quarrel between Britain and the colonies or examine the problem in purely constitutional terms.

Not only is there a certain dissociation in the presentation of the original evidence; there is a disjuncture between published collections of original material and the major historiographical controversy which characterises historical writing on the period. For this is one of the rich and brilliant sectors of American history; the generation of Charles Beard, Becker, Turner which placed social and constitutional conflict at the centre of their interpretation, which saw a revolutionary impulse checked and reversed by the 'counter-revolution' of the Constitution, has been succeeded by a generation of 'revisionists' who subjected their work to minute and critical examination, who reasserted an older consensual tradition in modern terms or developed new, tougher socio-constitutional interpretations, and who were, in turn, confronted by historians working in a more sophisticated manner within the Beard tradition, by men who brought to bear the preoccupations of the New Left, by writers who sought to apply the techniques of econometrics to problems considered political and ethical in character.

In short, the problem examined in this volume has called into existence a whole *œuvre* of historical work which in quality ranks equal with the finest produced anywhere at any time. But between this splendid historiographical provision and the provision of published evidence, there has been a dissociation. That dissociation Dr J. R. Pole has now annulled.

The central problem for this study was the imbalanced provision of already published evidence. He has resolved it in a striking and percussant manner. He closes in first on the problem of continental government, which the patriots inherited, supplying the essential material on state-making, from the Albany Plan of 1754, through the institutions of revolution to the Articles of Confederation. He then provides the missing dimension in a crucial section on public finance, currency, debts, which were the raw material of political conflict in the period, fully explores the crucial period of Robert Morris's financial 'dictatorship', which was a decisive formative factor in the history of the new state and carries the story through to the overthrow of the Articles and the creation of the Constitution.

Since political and even constitutional problems in this period were inextricably intermingled with conflicts of economic interest, since the disposal of public lands, the activities of speculators, currency problems, settlement and expansion, constitution-making at state and continental level, even the elaboration of political ideologies were inseparable from each other, the core of the volume is devoted to a detailed examination of state and continental policies on public lands, wealth, wages and prices and of the process of constitution-making within the states themselves, with the rich and complex history of Massachusetts (test-case for a major controversy) given pride of place. The collection ends with an examination of the processes of social and political change detonated by the Revolution – Bernard Bailyn's 'contagion of liberty' – and with the first attempt of new Americans to define themselves.

This extraordinarily rich and unusual volume is designed to be read in conjunction with the central works of interpretation, but it stands in its own right as a concrete and vivid reconstruction of the day-to-day problems of a community, largely English in its intellectual and spiritual make-up, which had made the leap into a principled independence and which strove to create a principled polity in a thoroughly un-English environment. The collection is particularly strong in economic materials, statutes, resolutions, statistical tables, commentary in private correspondence, the reports of Robert Morris; it documents in detail, official and private, the struggle to create states and to create a nation; it conveys the crisis of conscience over slavery in a land whose official doctrine was that all men were created equal. Every single historical controversy finds concrete expression here, and the reader, through the complexities of local and national conflict, can sense throughout the search for a viable national identity, epitomised in Noah Webster's characteristic and heroic attempt to create a new American language.

This book echoes. The issues debated with such passion and often with such unrivalled felicity of language in this period are not only central to American history; they are central to the experience of any community rooted in the sovereignty of the people. In this rich, complex, tough-textured book the reader can himself re-live the experience of the first political community to ground itself explicitly on a principle, a doctrine, whose history has been, and still is, an arduous struggle to make the ideal reality.

GWYN A. WILLIAMS

Acknowledgements

The publishers wish to thank Brown University Press, for extracts from *The King's Friends*, by Wallace Brown (© 1966); Alfred A. Knopf Inc., for the extract from *The Declaration of Independence*, by Carl Becker; the Institute of Early American History and Culture and the University of North Carolina Press for the extracts from *The Power of the Purse*, by E. James Ferguson; the Belknap Press of Harvard University Press, for the extracts from *The Diary and Autobiography of John Adams*, vol. II, edited by Lyman H. Butterfield, Leonard C. Faber and Wendell D. Garrett (© 1961 by Massachusetts Historical Society); Ceceila M. Kenyon, for extracts from *The Antifederalists*, edited by Cecelia M. Kenyon (© 1966).

Introduction

When the Americans seized their independence they at once made themselves responsible for a wide range of complex and dangerous operations, including the waging of war, the conduct of international diplomacy, the making of new governments, the responsibility for economic and social order and the advancement of private business. The American Revolution was bound to be much more than a War of Independence, for the struggle was for survival, and because both of its intensity and its long duration it resulted in much domestic upheaval and re-ordering of political and economic life.

The documents in this collection are intended to illustrate the domestic side of these events; except incidentally, they do not deal either with relations between the Americans and Crown or Parliament, or with military operations; even such records as the *Declarations of the Stamp Act Congress* and the *Declaration of Independence* are included as indications of opinion, and action, looking towards self-government, rather than for their bearing on the imperial question.[1]

Taken together, these documents provide the outlines of an answer to questions about the internal consequences of the separation from Britain, and therefore offer some of the material needed for a discussion of how far the Revolution was, in the domestic sense, a revolution, and how deep a reconstruction of American society resulted from it. The principles of the selection are explained by the division of the book into five parts. Each part deals with a major theme; and the themes selected are in general (not exclusively) those which fell within the area of governmental action. This, in other words, is a selection dealing with issues of policy on which governments were called on to act, rather than an illustration of the quality of private life; but many of the documents do in fact throw light on such aspects of the Revolution, and a few in Part 5 have been selected for their comment on the fast-changing American scene that the Revolution left behind – or opened up.

Part 1, which is much the longest and which falls into five sections,

[1] *Sources and Documents Illustrating the American Revolution 1764–1788 and the Formation of the Constitution*, ed. S. E. Morison (Oxford, 1923; new ed., 1962) gives fuller cover to the dispute with Britain.

assembles documents on the great problem of continental government. It follows the Continental Congress through the vicissitudes of establishing its own authority, of laying down economic policies, and of bringing into existence a permanent Confederation, and it concludes with an outline of the Federal Constitution.

Part 2 takes up economic problems in greater detail and follows both Congress and the States in their attempts to regulate the economy.

Part 3 deals with the problem of the public lands. Here the documents reveal the struggles of private interests to influence the Congress, and the gradual development of a general policy, culminating in the Northwest Ordinance of 1787.

Part 4 is devoted to the theme of the making of state constitutions. It concentrates on the Constitution of Massachusetts, but includes materials from other states to show comparisons and variations.

In Part 5, an attempt has been made to illustrate the state of the country; the materials included here are mainly opinions – and the fact that they are well-informed opinions does not prevent them from affording ground for sharply differing views of the prospects before America following the Revolution.

The problem of setting up an inter-colonial Congress with some authority over the separate provinces was, of course, inseparable from that of the actual questions over which its authority would be exercised. It proved also to be inseparable from questions of procedure in the Congress itself, as was discovered as soon as the delegates confronted the question of how they were to vote – as individuals, or delegations; as representatives of equal units, or as representatives of differing amounts of wealth and population? Extracts from John Adams' *Diary* and from the *Journals of the Continental Congress* show the complexity of the problem and how it was handled. The Congress decided to proceed with voting by states, not because it was felt that the states were or ought to be counted as equals but more simply because no satisfactory procedure for ascertaining their wealth and population could be found. It was Congress that took the decisive steps towards Independence, recommending the several colonies to form separate governments in May 1776 and voting its own Declaration – on the basis of an earlier resolution moved by Richard Henry Lee – on 2 July and 4 July.

The constitutional questions of the Continental Congress were never really settled. The Articles of Confederation, drafted in 1776, were held up until 1781 by disagreements over the relative powers of Congress and the states and, most important, over the ownership of the public lands. But the Congress was obliged to provide the means of fighting and financing the war while the interminable wrangles about its own constitution went on; and the need for public finance, which takes up the second section of Part I, called forth a decision to issue continental currency as early as June 1775. The means of war finance were provided by home borrowings, foreign loans, and paper money; the repeated emissions and rapid depreciation of the congressional money – which were the fate of similar policies in most of the states – gravely weakened the credit of the Congress. The inflation also reverberated through the private as well as the official sectors of the economy. The colonies had not developed a wide variety of choices of investment, and for the merchant or farmer or even the prosperous artisan who had saved a little money, the simplest means of making more was to lend at interest. All these creditors were adversely affected by the decline in the value of money. The alarm generated by this collapse of credit can be clearly seen in the desperate but unsuccessful efforts both of Congress and states to arrest the process. However, it is easier to document the efforts to stabilise prices and wages and to set standards, and to find expressions of anxiety, than it is to register the continual slipping away of the standards set. Economic regulations, of which there are plenty in these pages, are obviously expressions of public policy but the reader should remind himself that they record intentions, not achievements.

If the Congress was to survive, it had to be able to pay its own debts and finance its own operations. Financial and economic policies provide the materials for Section III of Part I. Robert Morris, as Superintendent of Finance, acted the central part in planning and holding together the economic operation of Congress, and his statements offer some of the most penetrating and forthright analyses ever made of the nature of the problem, which was inseparably linked with the constitutional questions of congressional power. Unfortunately Morris's private financial operations, which were not always easy to separate from his public actions, aroused deep misgivings (see **I** III 3); the opposition did not, however, prevent the founding in Philadelphia, under congressional charter, of the Bank of North America. The importance of this step to the advancement of business interests is obvious from the fact that other banks began to spring up in other states within the following few years. The political weakness of the Congress, under the Articles of Confederation, lay particularly in its want of power to raise taxes, or to enforce its requisitions on the states; and an ominous development began when the states themselves undertook the responsibility for paying the debts of Congress. This process belongs to State Policy, and is therefore recorded in Part 2. Before this theme is taken up, Part I goes on in Sections IV and V to the conclusion of the main issue of continental government by noting the principal steps to the Constitutional Convention at Philadelphia.

Since that Convention lasted some four months, and the process of ratification continued sporadically in the several states for more than a further year, a collection on the internal aspects of the American Revolution can treat them only in outline. The Constitution and its first ten amendments may be said to round off the theme of continental government first raised at Albany in 1754.[1]

The economic questions tackled by Congress as seen in the documents in Part I are basic questions of public finance; on them depended the very existence of Congress, its ability to wage war and assert its own power.

Part 2 takes up actual economic development, and shows the attempts of state governments, as well as Congress, to exercise some control. It must be emphasised that the documents are illustrative but in no sense do they claim to be conclusive. Pennsylvania and New York are shown here in the act of authorising their own paper currencies. These measures came in response to powerful alliances of farmers and merchants and were not evidence of control of the legislatures by mobs of debtors; actually five other states, Georgia, South Carolina, North Carolina, New Jersey and Rhode Island issued paper currencies in the same post-war period, and some of these currencies held up very well even after the adoption of the Federal Constitution.[2] On the other hand, the remaining state governments resisted all pressure for paper money. In Massachusetts, hard-money policies, combined with trade depression and a number of local grievances, produced a minor

[1] For a useful selection from the Convention, see *The Federal Convention and the Formation of the Union*, ed. Winton U. Solberg (Indianapolis and New York, 1958); for a valuable collection of Antifederalist tracts, *The Antifederalists*, ed. Cecelia M. Kenyon (Indianapolis and New York, 1966).

[2] Merrill Jensen, *The New Nation* (New York, 1950) ch. 16. Forrest McDonald, *We the People* (Chicago, 1958) p. 296; pp. 388–9.

rebellion – Shays's Rebellion of 1786. The outbreak was of much more than minor significance, because it frightened many influential people in other states into believing that the whole social order was threatened. After all, if a government based on consent was to be the victim of a rebellion, what hope could be held out for the success of the American principles of republican government?

The attempts of some of the states to regulate prices and wages give us some useful information about the costs of living. The tables of prices may not in fact have held up very long, but they register in some detail the commodity prices that were expected to prevail and they give a comparable idea of the standards of living that different skills and trades could, under the same dispensation, expect to attain. Some of the opportunities for gain under war-time conditions are also illustrated in this Part.

The problem of western lands, which form the subject matter of Part 3, had occupied the more ambitious American business minds since long before the specific events leading to the break with Britain. The first document in this series might be the Albany Plan of 1754 (which actually appears as the first in the book) because Benjamin Franklin, the chief architect of that plan, envisaged that the lands claimed by Virginia would fall under the sovereignty of the proposed inter-colonial government.[1] Before the War, the rival American land companies had to exert their influence wherever it was most likely to be effective, and this often meant in London rather than in the colonial governments; but after Independence, the whole of this pressure was transferred to the American continent. For those who were most closely concerned, the outcome of these land claims took precedence over all other issues, including the future of the American attempt at confederate government. It seems reasonably clear that unless the interests in the middle states, especially Maryland, had been satisfied in their demands, they would have been willing to go on indefinitely blocking the formation of a permanent inter-state system of government. As it was, Maryland refused to ratify the Articles of Confederation until Virginia had made a formal offer to cede all of her western claims beyond Kentucky, so that the Articles date technically only from 1781, although the Continental Congress had acted as a form of government almost from its first meetings in 1774.

[1] T. P. Abernethy, *Western Lands and the American Revolution* (New York, 1937) pp. 14–15.

As a result of the cessions of New York and Virginia, the struggle of land companies for concessions in the Northwestern territories was transferred to Congress, where general policies for the formation of the new states had been already outlined in October 1780 (**3** 3). The final document in this series is the famous Northwest Ordinance of 1787; that measure reflected the successful lobbying of the Ohio Company, though its detailed provisions include earlier policies, on which Thomas Jefferson, a member of the committee that produced the first set of specific plans in 1784, had impressed his ideas about the distribution of equal lots of land in fee simple to freeholding farmers.[1] In a very strong sense, the American Revolution is inseparable from the land question. Looking to the possibilities of alternative courses of history, one can no doubt see that, eventually, the British colonists were destined to push westward into the Mississippi Valley, and in that sense the Revolution did not alter the trend of probabilities; but it did alter both the timing and the manner in which settlement proceeded. The seizure of power by the Americans led to an acceleration of the western movement so violent as to be almost revolutionary in itself. Within a generation of the beginning of the War, the territories of the Ohio Valley had qualified for statehood, a process whose speed no one had anticipated in the 1770s; the upheaval involved vast transferences of population, which often left older settlements depleted or even deserted, weakening both the wealth in real property values, and the political influence, of the New England states. During the War itself, the redistribution of landed property began with the expropriation of the estates of Loyalists. The small farmer was not the first to benefit, however; wealthier speculators were better equipped to bid, leaving in the outcome a pattern of ownership that may not have differed very sharply from what had existed before. It should be noted that the decision of Congress to reimburse officers of the continental armies by land grants in the Ohio Valley did represent a redistributive move both in real property and in the areas of settlement. Not until near the end of the nineteenth century would the land question cease to raise issues of public policy and private interest.

When the Continental Congress recommended the provinces to form independent governments it took a step leading directly to political separation from Britain. Every province had its own constitutional history, and each had the responsibility for forming a new

[1] Jensen, *The New Nation*, p. 358.

government of its own. American history can never be understood by excessive concentration on the central government; as Part 2 showed state action on economic policy, Part 4 takes up the making of new state constitutions. Much the most profuse documentation of these processes is available in Massachusetts, where the towns were drawn into the making of the new constitution and where they actually rejected a frame of government offered to them by the Legislature in 1778. The present collection illustrates the case of Massachusetts in some detail. After the holding of a convention, through the winter of 1779–80, the towns were again asked to ratify, and the returns of the town meetings give a great deal of comment on the various clauses of the new constitution. There has been no room to include this second set of returns in this volume, but the tenor of the political thinking of the state is amply reflected in the preceding town meeting reports, in the *Address* circulated by the Convention to explain its handiwork, and by the Constitution itself. Extracts from the influential pamphlet known as *The Essex Result*, which 'resulted' from a convention of the gentry of Essex County in 1778, have been included to indicate the problems of reconciling the interests of property with the commitment of the whole state to representative government and a fairly advanced form of popular rule. It is one of the strongest conservative statements of the period; many provisions of state constitutions reflected similar thinking.

The making of the state constitution in Massachusetts differs significantly from the process in the other states, however. In Massachusetts, the Whig idea that legitimate power is derived from the people led straight to the ratification of the constitution by the town meetings. This was taking Whig theory more literally than was felt necessary, or safe, by other state governments. In all other states (except New Hampshire, which formed a constitution, ratified by the people, in 1784) the legislatures kept the whole responsibility in their own hands, without submitting the constitution for popular ratification. Two states, Connecticut and Rhode Island, retained their existing governments unaltered, on the grounds that they had been contending for their charter rights throughout the dispute with Britain, and saw no reason for reform.

Although every state had its own peculiarities, so that the full process of the making of the revolutionary constitutions could be documented only in a large volume devoted exclusively to that theme, these separate instruments of government had a great deal in common. They were all products of a common body of Whig political thought and of similar inheritances of political institutions and law. Most of the specific differences represent variations on a theme rather than differences of principle. The guiding principles were suggested by John Adams, who composed his *Thoughts on Government* partly to assist constitutional deliberations going forward in Virginia. This pamphlet was probably the most influential of the publications that aimed specifically to affect the thinking of those who were engaged in designing new constitutions, but expressions of other and sometimes more radical, or democratic, opinion were also advanced in the press, and can be glimpsed in some of the town opinions on the proposed Massachusetts constitution of 1778.[1]

The most democratic constitution actually adopted was that of Pennsylvania, where a Radical party, which had arisen rapidly in the early 1770s, rode into power on the divisions between the older rulers created by the imperial crisis. The unicameral legislature of Pennsylvania under the Constitution of 1776 closely resembled the system set up by the Charter of 1701 and in that sense was not novel; but the extension of the suffrage to tax-payers was a marked advance on previous practice and gave the State a far more democratic base than that adopted by other states. In general, the state constitutions were built up in a carefully graded hierarchy of rights, each level being connected with the ownership of specified values of property; equally important, in the eyes of contemporaries, was the privileged protection afforded in some states to the Protestant religion. Religious qualifications were widely attached to the exercise of political rights.[2]

Political right was conceived of in the Whig tradition. The Bill of Rights adopted in Virginia and Pennsylvania (which shared several identical clauses) stand here as representative, along with that of

[1] For tracts illustrating the development of political thought, see *Pamphlets of the American Revolution*, ed. Bernard Bailyn, vol. 1 and volumes in continuation; *Tracts of the American Revolution, 1763–1776*, ed. Merrill Jensen (Indianapolis and New York, 1967). Although the present volume contains comparatively few tracts, political institutional ideas are constantly apparent throughout these selections.

[2] The Whig ideas of representative government in relation to the social order, both in America and England, are discussed in some detail in J. R. Pole, *Political Representation in England and the Origins of the American Republic* (London and New York, 1966).

Massachusetts. But these declarations did not mean the same thing in all places. In Massachusetts, the affirmation of human equality was held by the Supreme Court of the Commonwealth to amount to the abolition of slavery without further legislative procedure; no such inference was drawn from that affirmation in the states which held any large numbers of slaves.

Slavery was much the most important institution that was in fact left, in its main strongholds, largely untouched by the passage of the Revolution. It is true that the rhetoric of American Independence was highly adaptable to libertarian causes; gradually, the middle and Northeastern states did away with slavery by legislative acts, while the Northwest Ordinance banned slavery from the territories and future states of the Ohio Valley. The debates in the Constitutional Convention produced some sharp exchanges on the question, and resulted in a compromise under which the slave-holding states were allowed to count three-fifths of their slaves as population for the enumeration of representatives, and the African slave trade was allowed to continue for a further twenty years; after which time the Congress was empowered to ban all further slave importation. The slave population was greatly increased, and the slave-holding interests correspondingly strengthened, before the restrictive arm of this compromise was brought into effect in 1808.

At the end of the War there was room for differences of opinion about the aims of American government and the existing or probable character of society. The histories of some of the individual states reveal intense struggles for power and the sources of wealth. These, again, have had to be largely omitted from a single volume; but Part 5 brings together some leading views of outstanding social problems.

In several directions, social and political improvements not only followed the separation from Britain, but were clearly a result of it. Extensions of suffrage, reforms that brought the branches of governments closer to the electorate, liberations of the press (whose freedom in some ways had been restricted under colonial governments) and much wider religious tolerance, were among the movements that Americans freely initiated when the power was theirs. In Virginia, a small and distinguished committee codified and humanised the laws, abolishing or modifying most of the cruelties of the penal code; in Virginia also, Thomas Jefferson promoted the passage of the Act for Religious Liberty which is one of the three achievements recorded on his tombstone. The aftermath of Independence also saw the abolition of primogeniture and entail where they survived, as in Virginia, and these measures undoubtedly had some liberating effect on the economic dispositions of landowners. However, it is doubtful whether primogeniture and entail could have exerted a definitive influence on the social structure; primogeniture applied, in any case, only to cases of intestate deaths; and entail often proved a nuisance to the estate that it was meant to strengthen, restricting the owner's freedom to take advantage of the land market. The abolition of this relic of English land law (which, in Virginia, had been adopted as it happened in 1705) may well have gratified many of the more ambitious planters.

The overthrow of the rule of Parliament liberated American commerce from the Acts of Trade and the Navigation and American manufacture from the Restraining Acts. The documents collected in Part 2 show that the American governments, upon whom British authority had devolved, had very soon to accept the responsibility for economic policies; in face of hard necessity they were hardly less mercantilist than Britain. American trade gradually expanded beyond the old grooves worn by British rules but did not abandon those grooves. The new nation continued to depend on British imports and British capital; the overall trade pattern for many years showed little reflection of the political revolution. American manufactures were stimulated by the War of Independence, but could make relatively little headway against the competition from cheap British goods, for which a big demand made itself felt immediately after the War. One result was the outflow of hard money and a serious depression in the American economy. American manufacturing and commerce both revived, and gained strength during the European wars in the wake of the French Revolution; but these gradual developments would be difficult to indicate by the reprinting of specific documents. Readers should note these limitations. Most of the economic documents are public papers; productivity, employment patterns, the gradually altering courses of American overseas trade and the American balance of payments *vis-à-vis* Europe, though sometimes the subject of comment, are not specifically illustrated in the present collection. Whether or not these secular developments should be attributed to or considered as part of the 'American Revolution' is in itself a somewhat difficult question to resolve. Political liberation from Britain certainly accelerated them but can hardly have been their mainspring.

Meanwhile Noah Webster, inspired by American Independence, began soon after the war his great work, a sort of codification of the American language. His *Dictionary* appeared in 1828, but his spellers and tracts had long made him the exemplar of uniformity and correctness in the writing of the English language in America, and the Preface here printed shows the force of a basically conservative view of American language. It is significant, however, that Webster found differences of usage belonging to American speech, which it was the duty of an American Dictionary to indicate.

The collection closes with an extract from Dr David Ramsay's contemporary history of the American Revolution, an account that will help to explain much that has gone before. This passage has been placed at the end because of its summary and explanatory character, but it might almost as well have been put at the beginning. Readers who choose to read it first will thereby give themselves a helpful preview; they will probably want to come back to it more than once.

Churchill College
Cambridge

J. R. POLE

PART I

The Problem of Continental Government

I Towards Political Independence

I.I.I THE ALBANY PLAN OF UNION, JULY 10, 1754[1]

Works of Benjamin Franklin, ed. Jared Sparks (1856) III 36 *et seq.*

It is proposed that humble application be made for an act of Parliament of Great Britain, by virtue of which one general government may be formed in America, including all the said colonies, within and under which government each colony may retain its present constitution, except in the particulars wherein a change may be directed by the said act, as hereafter follows.

1. That the said general government be administered by a President-General, to be appointed and supported by the Crown; and a Grand Council, to be chosen by the representatives of the people of the several Colonies met in their respective assemblies.

2. That within – months after the passing such act, the House of Representatives that happen to be sitting within that time, or that shall be especially for that purpose convened, may and shall choose members for the Grand Council, in the following proportion, that is to say,

Massachusetts Bay	7
New Hampshire	2
Connecticut	5
Rhode Island	2
New York	4
New Jersey	3
Pennsylvania	6
Maryland	4
Virginia	7
North Carolina	4
South Carolina	4
	48

[1] The Albany Congress was attended by delegates from New England, New York, Pennsylvania and Maryland, and was summoned to negotiate a treaty with the Iroquois in view of the outbreak of new hostilities with the French.

The Plan of Union offered by this Congress was designed by Benjamin Franklin, one of the delegates from Pennsylvania. Thomas Hutchinson of Massachusetts Bay probably proposed some additions which were accepted. The Plan made no headway either among the American colonies or in Britain.

3. – who shall meet for the first time at the city of Philadelphia, being called by the President-General as soon as conveniently may be after his appointment.

4. That there shall be a new election of the members of the Grand Council every three years; and, on the death or resignation of any member, his place should be supplied by a new choice at the next sitting of the Assembly of the Colony he represented.

5. That after the first three years, when the proportion of money arising out of each Colony to the general treasury can be known, the number of members to be chosen for each Colony shall, from time to time, in all ensuing elections, be regulated by that proportion, yet so that the number to be chosen by any one province be not more than seven, nor less than two.

6. That the Grand Council shall meet once in every year, and oftener if occasion require, at such time and place as they shall adjourn to at the last preceding meeting, or as they shall be called to meet at by the President-General on any emergency; he having first obtained in writing the consent of seven of the members to such call, and sent duly and timely notice to the whole.

7. That the Grand Council have power to choose their speaker; and shall neither be dissolved, prorogued, nor continued sitting longer than six weeks at one time, without their own consent or the special command of the Crown.

8. That the members of the Grand Council shall be allowed for their service ten shillings sterling per diem, during their session and journey to and from the place of meeting; twenty miles to be reckoned a day's journey.

9. That the assent of the President-General be requisite to all acts of the Grand Council, and that it be his office and duty to cause them to be carried into execution.

10. That the President-General, with the advice of the Grand Council, hold or direct all Indian treaties, in which the general interest of the Colonies may be concerned; and make peace or declare war with Indian nations.

11. That they make such laws as they judge necessary for regulating all Indian trade.

12. That they make all purchases from Indians, for the Crown, of lands not now within the bound of particular Colonies, or that shall

not be within their bounds when some of them are reduced to more convenient dimensions.

13. That they make new settlements on such purchases, by granting lands in the King's name, reserving a quitrent to the Crown for the use of the general treasury.

14. That they make laws for regulating and governing such new settlements, till the Crown shall think fit to form them into particular governments.

15. That they raise and pay soldiers and build forts for the defense of any of the Colonies, and equip vessels of force to guard the coasts and protect the trade on the ocean, lakes, or great rivers; but they shall not impress men in any Colony, without the consent of the Legislature.

16. That for these purposes they have power to make laws, and lay and levy such general duties, imposts, or taxes, as to them shall appear most equal and just (considering the ability and other circumstances of the inhabitants in the several Colonies), and such as may be collected with the least inconvenience to the people; rather discouraging luxury, than loading industry with unnecessary burdens.

17. That they may appoint a General Treasurer and Particular Treasurer in each government when necessary; and, from time to time, may order the sums in the treasuries of each government into the general treasury; or draw on them for special payments, as they find most convenient.

18. Yet no money to issue but by joint orders of the President-General and Grand Council; except where sums have been appropriated to particular purposes, and the President-General is previously empowered by an act to draw such sums.

19. That the general accounts shall be yearly settled and reported to the several Assemblies.

20. That a quorum of the Grand Council, empowered to act with the President-General, do consist of twenty-five members; among whom there shall be one or more from a majority of the Colonies.

21. That the laws made by them for the purposes aforesaid shall not be repugnant, but, as near as may be, agreeable to the laws of England, and shall be transmitted to the King in Council for approbation, as soon as may be after their passing; and if not disapproved within three years after presentation, to remain in force.

22. That, in case of the death of the President-General, the Speaker of the Grand Council for the time being shall succeed, and be vested

with the same powers and authorities, to continue till the King's pleasure be known.

23. That all military commission officers, whether for land or sea service, to act under this general constitution, shall be nominated by the President-General; but the approbation of the Grand Council is to be obtained, before they receive their commissions. And all civil officers are to be nominated by the Grand Council, and to receive the President-General's approbation before they officiate.

24. But in case of vacancy by death or removal of any officer, civil or military, under this constitution, the Governor of the Province in which such vacancy happens may appoint, till the pleasure of the President-General and Grand Council can be known.

25. That the particular military as well as civil establishments in each Colony remain in their present state, the general constitution notwithstanding; and that on sudden emergencies any Colony may defend itself, and lay the accounts of expense thence arising before the President-General and General Council, who may allow and order payment of the same, as far as they judge such accounts just and reasonable.

1.1.2 DECLARATIONS OF THE STAMP ACT CONGRESS, OCTOBER 7–24, 1765

Proceedings of the Congress at New York (Annapolis, 1766) pp. 15–16

The Members of this Congress, sincerely devoted, with the warmest Sentiments of Affection and Duty to his Majesty's Person and Government, inviolably attached to the present happy Establishment of the Protestant Succession, and with Minds deeply impressed by a Sense of the present and impending Misfortunes of the *British* Colonies on this Continent; having considered as maturely as Time will permit, the Circumstances of the said Colonies, esteem it our indispensable Duty, to make the following Declarations of our humble Opinion, respecting the most Essential Rights and Liberties of the Colonists, and of the Grievances under which they labour, by Reason of several late Acts of Parliament.

I. That his Majesty's Subjects in these Colonies, owe the same Allegiance to the Crown of *Great-Britain*, that is owing from his

Subjects born within the Realm, and all due Subordination to that August Body the Parliament of *Great-Britain.*

II. That his Majesty's Liege Subjects in these Colonies, are entitled to all the inherent Rights and Liberties of his Natural born Subjects, within the Kingdom of *Great-Britain.*

III. That it is inseparably essential to the Freedom of a People, and the undoubted Right of *Englishmen,* that no Taxes be imposed on them, but with their own Consent, given personally, or by their Representatives.

IV. That the People of these Colonies are not, and from their local Circumstances cannot be, Represented in the House of Commons in *Great-Britain.*

V. That the only Representatives of the People of these Colonies, are Persons chosen therein by themselves, and that no Taxes ever have been, or can be Constitutionally imposed on them, but by their respective Legislatures.

VI. That all Supplies to the Crown, being free Gifts of the People, it is unreasonable and inconsistent with the Principles and Spirit of the *British* Constitution, for the People of *Great-Britain,* to grant to his Majesty the Property of the Colonists.

VII. That Trial by Jury, is the inherent and invaluable Right of every *British* Subject in these Colonies.

VIII. That the late Act of Parliament, entitled, *An Act for granting and applying certain Stamp Duties, and other Duties, in the* British *Colonies and Plantations in* America, *&c.* by imposing Taxes on the Inhabitants of these Colonies, and the said Act, and several other Acts, by extending the Jurisdiction of the Courts of Admiralty beyond its ancient Limits, have a manifest Tendency to subvert the Rights and Liberties of the Colonists.

IX. That the Duties imposed by several late Acts of Parliament, from the peculiar Circumstances of these Colonies, will be extremely Burthensome and Grievous; and from the scarcity of Specie, the Payment of them absolutely impracticable.

X. That as the Profits of the Trade of these Colonies ultimately center in *Great-Britain,* to pay for the Manufactures which they are obliged to take from thence, they eventually contribute very largely to all Supplies granted there to the Crown.

XI. That the Restrictions imposed by several late Acts of Parliament, on the Trade of these Colonies, will render them unable to purchase the Manufactures of *Great-Britain*.

XII. That the Increase, Prosperity, and Happiness of these Colonies, depend on the full and free Enjoyment of their Rights and Liberties, and an Intercourse with *Great-Britain* mutually Affectionate and Advantageous.

XIII. That it is the Right of the *British* Subjects in these Colonies, to Petition the King, or either House of Parliament.

Lastly, That it is the indispensable Duty of these Colonies, to the best of Sovereigns, to the Mother Country, and to themselves, to endeavour by a loyal and dutiful Address to his Majesty, and humble Applications to both Houses of Parliament, to procure the Repeal of the Act for granting and applying certain Stamp Duties, of all Clauses of any other Acts of Parliament, whereby the Jurisdiction of the Admiralty is extended as aforesaid, and of the other late Acts for the Restriction of *American* Commerce.

The petition to the House of Commons; ibid. pp. 21–4

To the Honourable the Knights, Citizens, and Burgesses of Great-Britain, *in Parliament assembled.*

The PETITION of his Majesty's dutiful and loyal Subjects, the Freeholders and other Inhabitants of the Colonies of the *Massachusetts-Bay*, *Rhode-Island*, and *Providence* Plantations,
, *New-Jersey*, *Pennsylvania*, the Government of the Counties of *New-Castle*, *Kent*, and *Sussex*, upon *Delaware*, *Maryland*,

Most humbly Sheweth,

That the several late Acts of Parliament imposing divers Duties and Taxes on the Colonies, and laying the Trade and Commerce thereof under very Burthensome Restrictions, but above all the Act for granting and applying certain Stamp Duties, &c. in *America*, have fill'd them with the deepest Concern and Surprize; and they humbly conceive the Execution of them will be attended with Consequences very Injurious to the Commercial Interest of *Great-Britain* and her Colonies, and must terminate in the eventual Ruin of the latter.

Your Petitioners therefore most ardently implore the Attention of the Honourable House, to the united and dutiful Representation of their Circumstances, and to their earnest Supplications for Relief, from those Regulations which have already involv'd this Continent in Anxiety, Confusion, and Distress.

We most sincerely recognize our Allegiance to the Crown, and acknowledge all due Subordination to the Parliament of *Great-Britain*, and shall always retain the most grateful Sense of their Assistance and Protection. It is from and under the *English* Constitution, we derive all our Civil and Religious Rights and Liberties: We Glory in being Subjects of the best of Kings, and having been Born under the most perfect Form of Government; but it is with most ineffable and humiliating Sorrow, that we find ourselves, of late, deprived of the Right of Granting our own Property for his Majesty's Service, to which our Lives and Fortunes are entirely devoted, and to which, on his Royal Requisitions, we have ever been ready to contribute to the utmost of our Abilities.

We have also the Misfortune to find, that all the Penalties and Forfeitures mentioned in the Stamp Act, and in divers late Acts of Trade extending to the Plantations, are, at the Election of the Informer, Recoverable in any Court of Admiralty in *America*. This, as the newly erected Court of Admiralty has a general Jurisdiction over all *British America*, renders his Majesty's Subjects in these Colonies, liable to be carried, at an immense Expence, from one End of the Continent, to the other.

It gives us also great Pain, to see a manifest Distinction made therein, between the Subjects of our Mother Country, and those in the Colonies, in that the like Penalties and Forfeitures recoverable there only in his Majesty's Courts of Record, are made cognizable here by a Court of Admiralty: By these Means we seem to be, in Effect, unhappily deprived of Two Privileges essential to Freedom, and which all *Englishmen* have ever considered as their best Birthrights, that of being free from all Taxes but such as they have consented to in Person, or by their Representatives, and of Trial by their Peers.

Your Petitioners further shew, That the remote Situation, and other Circumstances of the Colonies, render it impracticable that they should be Represented, but in their respective subordinate Legislature; and they humbly conceive, that the Parliament, adhering strictly to the Principles of the Constitution, have never hitherto Tax'd any, but those who were actually therein Represented; for this Reason, we humbly apprehend, they never have Tax'd *Ireland*, or any other of the Subjects without the Realm.

But were it ever so clear, that the Colonies might in Law, be reasonably deem'd to be Represented in the Honourable House of Commons, yet we conceive, that very good Reasons, from Inconvenience, from the Principles of true Policy, and from the Spirit of the *British* Constitution, may be adduced to shew, that it would be for the real Interest of *Great-Britain*, as well as her Colonies, that the late Regulations should be rescinded, and the several Acts of Parliament imposing Duties and Taxes on the Colonies, and extending the Jurisdiction of the Courts of Admiralty here, beyond their ancient Limits, should be Repeal'd.

We shall not Attempt a minute Detail of all the Reasons which the Wisdom of the Honourable House may suggest, on this Occasion, but would humbly submit the following Particulars to their Consideration.

That Money is already become very scarce in these Colonies, and is still decreasing by the necessary Exportation of Specie from the Continent, for the Discharge of our Debts to *British* Merchants.

That an immensly heavy Debt is yet due from the Colonies for *British* Manufactures, and that they are still heavily burthen'd with Taxes to discharge the Arrearages due for Aids granted by them in the late War.

That the Balance of Trade will ever be much against the Colonies, and in Favour of *Great-Britain*, whilst we consume her Manufactures, the Demand for which must ever Increase in Proportion to the Number of Inhabitants settled here, with the Means of Purchasing them. We therefore humbly conceive it to be the Interest of *Great-Britain*, to increase, rather than diminish, those Means, as the Profits of all the Trade of the Colonies ultimately center there to pay for her Manufactures, as we are not allowed to purchase elsewhere; and by the Consumption of which, at the advanced Prices the British Taxes oblige the Makers and Venders to set on them, we eventually contribute very largely to the Revenue of the Crown.

That from the Nature of *American* Business, the Multiplicity of Suits and Papers used in Matters of small Value, in a Country where Freeholds are so minutely divided, and Property so frequently transferr'd, a Stamp Duty must ever be very Burthensome and Unequal.

That it is extremely improbable that the Honourable House of Commons, shou'd at all Times, be thoroughly acquainted with our

Condition, and all Facts requisite to a just and equal Taxation of the Colonies.

It is also humbly submitted, Whether there be not a material Distinction in Reason and sound Policy, at least, between the necessary Exercise of Parliamentary Jurisdiction in general Acts, for the Amendment of the Common Law, and the Regulation of Trade and Commerce through the whole Empire, and the Exercise of that Jurisdiction, by imposing Taxes on the Colonies.

That the several subordinate Provincial Legislatures have been moulded into Forms, as nearly resembling that of their Mother Country, as by his Majesty's Royal Predecessors was thought convenient; and their Legislatures seem to have been wisely and graciously established, that the Subjects in the Colonies might, under the due Administration thereof, enjoy the happy Fruits of the *British* Government, which in their present Circumstances, they cannot be so fully and clearly availed of, any other Way under these Forms of Government we and our Ancestors have been Born or Settled, and have had our Lives, Liberties, and Properties, protected. The People here, as every where else, retain a great Fondness for their old Customs and Usages, and we trust that his Majesty's Service, and the Interest of the Nation, so far from being obstructed, have been vastly promoted by the Provincial Legislatures.

That we esteem our Connections with, and Dependance on *Great-Britain*, as one of our greatest Blessings, and apprehend the latter will appear to be sufficiently secure, when it is considered, that the Inhabitants in the Colonies have the most unbounded Affection for his Majesty's Person, Family, and Government, as well as for the Mother Country, and that their Subordination to the Parliament, is universally acknowledged.

We therefore most humbly entreat, That the Honourable House would be pleased to hear our Counsel in Support of this Petition, and take our distressed and deplorable Case into their serious Consideration, and that the Acts and Clauses of Acts, so grievously restraining our Trade and Commerce, imposing Duties and Taxes on our Property, and extending the Jurisdiction of the Court of Admiralty beyond its ancient Limits, may be repeal'd; or that the Honourable House would otherwise relieve your Petitioners, as in your great Wisdom and Goodness shall seem meet.

And your Petitioners as in Duty bound shall ever pray.

1.1.3 THE DEBATE ON VOTING IN THE CONTINENTAL CONGRESS

September 5, 1774, *Diary of John Adams*, ed. L. M. Butterfield (Cambridge, Mass., 1961) II 122–4

At Ten, The Delegates all met at the City Tavern, and walked to the Carpenters Hall, where they took a View of the Room, and of the Chamber where is an excellent Library. There is also a long Entry, where Gentlemen may walk, and a convenient Chamber opposite to the Library. The General Cry was, that this was a good Room, and the Question was put, whether We were satisfyed with this Room, and it passed in the Affirmative. A very few were for the Negative and they were chiefly from Pensylvania and New York.[1]

Then Mr Lynch arose, and said there was a Gentleman present who had presided with great Dignity over a very respectable Society, greatly to the Advantage of America, and he therefore proposed that the Hon. Peytoun Randolph Esqr., one of the Delegates from Virginia, and the late Speaker of their House of Burgesses, should be appointed Chairman and he doubted not it would be unanimous. – The Question was put and he was unanimously chosen.

Mr Randolph then took the Chair, and the Commissions of the Delegates were all produced and read.[2]

[1] 'The City have offered us the Carpenters Hall, so called, to meet in, and Mr Galloway offers the State House and insists on our meeting there, which he says he has a right to offer as Speaker of that House. The last is evidently the best place, but as *he* offers, the other party oppose' (Silas Deane to Mrs Deane, September 1–3, 1774, *Letters of Members*, ed. Burnett (1921–36) I 4–5; see also pp. 8–10).

Carpenters' Hall was so new that some details in it were not yet completed. The second floor had, however, been rented and occupied by the Library Company of Philadelphia since 1773. The most authoritative historical and descriptive account of Carpenters' Hall is by Charles E. Peterson, in *Historic Philadelphia* (American Philosophical Society, *Transactions*, vol. 43 (1953) 96–128), which is copiously illustrated.

[2] Printed in full in *Journals of the Continental Congress*, I 15–24. The North Carolina delegates had not yet come in, and Georgia sent no delegates to the first Continental Congress.

Then Mr Lynch proposed that Mr Charles Thompson a Gentleman of Family, Fortune, and Character in this City should be appointed Secretary, which was accordingly done without opposition, tho Mr Duane and Mr Jay discovered at first an Inclination to seek further.[1]

Mr Duane then moved that a Committee should be appointed, to prepare Regulations for this Congress. Several Gentlemen objected. I then arose and asked Leave of the President to request of the Gentleman from New York, an Explanation, and that he would point out some particular Regulations which he had in his Mind. He mentioned particularly the Method of voting – whether it should be by Colonies, or by the Poll, or by Interests.

Mr Henry then arose, and said this was the first general Congress which had ever happened – that no former Congress could be a Precedent – that We should have occasion for more general Congresses, and therefore that a precedent ought to be established now. That it would be great Injustice, if a little Colony should have the same Weight in the Councils of America, as a great one, and therefore he was for a Committee.

Major Sullivan observed that a little Colony had its All at Stake as well as a great one.

This is a Question of great Importance. – If We vote by Colonies, this Method will be liable to great Inequality and Injustice, for 5 small Colonies, with 100,000 People in each may outvote 4 large ones, each of which has 500,000 Inhabitants. If We vote by the Poll, some Colonies have more than their Proportion of Members, and others have less. If We vote by Interests, it will be attended with insuperable Difficulties, to ascertain the true Importance of each Colony. – Is the Weight of a Colony to be ascertained by the Number of Inhabitants, merely – or by the Amount of their Trade, the Quantity of their Exports and Imports, or by any compound Ratio of both. This will lead us into such a Field of Controversy as will greatly perplex us. Besides I question whether it is possible to ascertain, at this Time, the Numbers of our People or the Value of our Trade. It will not do in

[1] For an account of Thomson's assumption of his duties, supposedly written by Thomson himself, see *Letters of Members*, ed. Burnett, I 10, note. Galloway's unhappy comments on the selection of both the meeting place and the secretary are in his letter of this date to Gov. William Franklin (*Archives of the State of New Jersey*, 1st series, vol. 10 (1886) 477–8).

such a Case, to take each other's Words. It ought to be ascertained by authentic Evidence, from Records.[1]

Notes of Debates in the Continental Congress, September 6, 1774,[2] ibid. 124–6

Mr Henry. Government is dissolved. Fleets and Armies and the present State of Things shew that Government is dissolved. – Where are your Land Marks? your Boundaries of Colonies.

We are in a State of Nature, Sir. I did propose that a Scale should be laid down. That Part of N. America which was once Mass. Bay, and that Part which was once Virginia, ought to be considered as having a Weight. Will not People complain, 10,000 (*People*) Virginians have not outweighed 1000 others.

I will submit however. I am determined to submit if I am overruled.

A worthy Gentleman (Ego)[3] near me, seemed to admit the Necessity of obtaining a more Adequate Representation.

I hope future Ages will quote our Proceedings with Applause. It is one of the great Duties of the democratical Part of the Constitution to keep itself pure. It is known in my Province, that some other Colonies are not so numerous or rich as they are. I am for giving all the Satisfaction in my Power.

The Distinctions between Virginians, Pensylvanians, New Yorkers and New Englanders, are no more.

I am not a Virginian, but an American.

Slaves are to be thrown out of the Question, and if the freemen can be represented according to their Numbers I am satisfyed.

Mr Lynch. I differ in one Point from the Gentleman from Virginia, that is in thinking that Numbers only ought to determine the Weight of Colonies. I think that Property ought to be considered, and that it ought to be a compound of Numbers and Property, that should determine the Weight of the Colonies.

[1] This speech was unquestionably made by J.A. himself.

[2] First entry in D/JA/22A, a collection of loose folded sheets of various sizes in which from time to time J.A. entered minutes of the debates in the first Continental Congress. These entries are mostly undated but have been inserted below under their most likely dates. Burnett, who prints the present notes in full, gives the evidence for assigning them to September 6 (*Letters of Members*, 1 14–15).

[3] This word inserted above the line in MS. Parentheses have been supplied by the editors.

I think it cannot be now settled.

Mr Rutledge. We have no legal Authority and Obedience to our Determinations will only follow the reasonableness, the apparent Utility, and Necessity of the Measures We adopt. We have no coercive or legislative Authority. Our Constitutents are bound only in Honour, to observe our Determinations.

Govr Ward. There are a great Number of Counties in Virginia, very unequal in Point of Wealth and Numbers, yet each has a Right to send 2 Members.

Mr Lee. But one Reason, which prevails with me, and that is that we are not at this Time provided with proper Materials. I am afraid We are not.

Mr Gadsden. I cant see any Way of voting but by Colonies.

Coll. Bland. I agree with the Gentleman (Ego)[3] who spoke near me, that We are not at present provided with Materials to ascertain the Importance of each Colony. The Question is whether the Rights and Liberties of America shall be contended for, or given up to arbitrary Power.

Mr Pendleton. If the Committee should find themselves unable to ascertain the Weight of the Colonies, by their Numbers and Property, they will report this, and this will lay the Foundation for the Congress to take some other Steps to procure Evidence of Numbers and Property at some future Time.

Mr Henry. I agree that authentic Accounts cannot be had – if by Authenticity is meant, attestations of officers of the Crown.

I go upon the Supposition, that Government is at an End. All Distinctions are thrown down. All America is all thrown into one Mass. We must aim at the Minutiæ of Rectitude.

Mr Jay. Could I suppose, that We came to frame an American Constitution, instead of indeavouring to correct the faults in an old one – I cant yet think that all Government is at an End. The Measure of arbitrary Power is not full, and I think it must run over, before We undertake to frame a new Constitution.

To the Virtue, Spirit, and Abilities of Virginia We owe much – I should always therefore from Inclination as well as Justice, be for giving Virginia its full Weight.

I am not clear that We ought not to be bound by a Majority tho ever so small, but I only mentioned it, as a Matter of Danger, worthy of Consideration.

1.1.4 THE CONTINENTAL CONGRESS: RESOLUTION ON VOTING

September 6, 1774, *Journals of the Continental Congress, 1774–89*, ed. W. C. Ford *et al.* (Washington, 1904) I 25

At 10 o'clock a.m.

The Congress met according to adjournment.

Present: The same members as yesterday, and moreover, from the colony of Virginia, Richard Henry Lee, Esqr., from counties of Newcastle, Kent and Sussex on Delaware, Thomas McKean, Esqr.

The Congress, resuming the consideration of appointing a Committee to draw up rules of conduct to be observed in debating and determining the questions, that come under consideration, after a good deal of debate the motion was diverted to facts

1. Shall a Committee be appointed to draw up rules for the proceedings of this Congress. Carried in the Negative.

2. Shall a Committee be appointed to fix the mode of voting by allowing to each province one or more votes, so as to establish an equitable representation according to the respective importance of each Colony. Carried in the negative.

Upon motion the Question was put and

Resolved, That in determining questions in this Congress, each Colony or Province shall have one Vote. – The Congress not being possess'd of, or at present able to procure proper materials for ascertaining the importance of each Colony.[1]

[1] The 'debate' printed in *Works of John Adams,* II 366, must have taken place also on the 6th, and not wholly on the 5th as printed. Patrick Henry favored numbers of freemen as a basis of representation; Lynch wished the weight of each Colony to be determined by numbers and property. Richard Henry Lee raised the proper objection of a want of information to make any scale, in which John Adams agreed with him. Gadsden favored voting by Colonies. The difficulty to be met was raised by Virginia, who claimed a prominence that the delegates from other Colonies were unwilling to concede. It was finally decided that each Colony should have 'one voice; but as this was objected to as unequal, an entry was made on the journals to prevent its being drawn into a precedent'.

1.1.5 RESOLUTIONS OF THE CONTINENTAL CONGRESS ON GRIEVANCES AGAINST BRITAIN

October 14, 1774, *Journals of the Continental Congress*, I 63–73

The Congress met according to adjournment, & resuming the consideration of the subject under debate – came into the following Resolutions:[1]

Whereas, since the close of the last war, the British parliament, claiming a power of right to bind the people of America, by statute in all cases whatsoever, hath in some acts expressly imposed taxes on them, and in others, under various pretences, but in fact for the purpose of raising a revenue, hath imposed rates and duties payable in these colonies, established a board of commissioners, with unconstitutional powers, and extended the jurisdiction of courts of Admiralty, not only for collecting the said duties, but for the trial of causes merely arising within the body of a county.

And whereas, in consequence of other statutes, judges, who before held only estates at will in their offices, have been made dependant on the Crown alone for their salaries, and standing armies kept in times of peace:

And it has lately been resolved in Parliament, that by force of a statute, made in the thirty-fifth year of the reign of king Henry the eighth, colonists may be transported to England, and tried there upon accusations for treasons, and misprisions, or concealments of treasons committed in the colonies; and by a late statute, such trials have been directed in cases therein mentioned.

And whereas, in the last session of parliament, three statutes were made; one, intituled 'An act to discontinue, in such manner and for such time as are therein mentioned, the landing and discharging, lading, or shipping of goods, wares & merchandise, at the town, and within the harbour of Boston, in the province of Massachusetts-bay, in

[1] The fourth article as adopted (p. 21) was prepared by John Adams, and caused much debate in committee and in Congress. Galloway, and his followers, thought it aimed at independence, and sought to have it amended. It was left unaltered in its essentials, and the final form of the report was the work of John Adams.

North-America'; another, intituled 'An act for the better regulating the government of the province of the Massachusetts-bay in New-England'; and another, intituled 'An act for the impartial administration of justice, in the cases of persons questioned for any act done by them in the execution of the law, or for the suppression of riots and tumults, in the province of the Massachusetts-bay, in New-England'. And another statute was then made, 'for making more effectual provision for the government of the province of Quebec, &c.' All which statutes are impolitic, unjust, and cruel, as well as unconstitutional, and most dangerous and destructive of American rights.

And whereas, Assemblies have been frequently dissolved, contrary to the rights of the people, when they attempted to deliberate on grievances; and their dutiful, humble, loyal, & reasonable petitions to the crown for redress, have been repeatedly treated with contempt, by his majesty's ministers of state:

The good people of the several Colonies of New-hampshire, Massachusetts-bay, Rhode-island and Providence plantations, Connecticut, New-York, New-Jersey, Pennsylvania, Newcastle, Kent and Sussex on Delaware, Maryland, Virginia, North Carolina, and South Carolina, justly alarmed at these arbitrary proceedings of parliament and administration, have severally elected, constituted, and appointed deputies to meet and sit in general congress, in the city of Philadelphia, in order to obtain such establishment, as that their religion, laws, and liberties may not be subverted:

Whereupon the deputies so appointed being now assembled, in a full and free representation of these Colonies, taking into their most serious consideration, the best means of attaining the ends aforesaid, do, in the first place, as Englishmen, their ancestors in like cases have usually done, for asserting and vindicating their rights and liberties, declare,

That the inhabitants of the English Colonies in North America, by the immutable laws of nature, the principles of the English constitution, and the several charters or compacts, have the following Rights:

Resolved, N. C. D. 1. That they are entitled to life, liberty, & property, and they have never ceded to any sovereign power whatever, a right to dispose of either without their consent.

Resolved, N. C. D. 2. That our ancestors, who first settled these colonies, were at the time of their emigration from the mother country, entitled to all the rights, liberties, and immunities of free and natural-born subjects, within the realm of England.

Resolved, N. C. D. 3. That by such emigration they by no means forfeited, surrendered, or lost any of those rights, but that they were, and their descendants now are, entitled to the exercise and enjoyment of all such of them, as their local and other circumstances enable them to exercise and enjoy.

Resolved, 4. That the foundation of English liberty, and of all free government, is a right in the people to participate in their legislative council: and as the English colonists are not represented, and from their local and other circumstances, cannot properly be represented in the British parliament, they are entitled to a free and exclusive power of legislation in their several provincial legislatures, where their right of representation can alone be preserved, in all cases of taxation and internal polity, subject only to the negative of their sovereign, in such manner as has been heretofore used and accustomed. But, from the necessity of the case, and a regard to the mutual interest of both countries, we cheerfully consent to the operation of such acts of the British parliament, as are bona fide, restrained to the regulation of our external commerce, for the purpose of securing the commercial advantages of the whole empire to the mother country, and the commercial benefits of its respective members; excluding every idea of taxation, internal or external, for raising a revenue on the subjects in America, without their consent.

Resolved, N. C. D. 5. That the respective colonies are entitled to the common law of England, and more especially to the great and inestimable privilege of being tried by their peers of the vicinage, according to the course of that law.

Resolved, 6. That they are entituled to the benefit of such of the English statutes as existed at the time of their colonization; and which they have, by experience, respectively found to be applicable to their several local and other circumstances.

Resolved, N. C. D. 7. That these, his majesty's colonies, are likewise entitled to all the immunities and privileges granted & confirmed to them by royal charters, or secured by their several codes of provincial laws.

Resolved, N. C. D. 8. That they have a right peaceably to assemble, consider of their grievances, and petition the King; and that all prosecutions, prohibitory proclamations, and commitments for the same, are illegal.

Resolved, N. C. D. 9. That the keeping a Standing army in these colonies, in times of peace, without the consent of the legislature of that colony, in which such army is kept, is against law.

Resolved, N. C. D. 10. It is indispensably necessary to good government, and rendered essential by the English constitution, that the constituent branches of the legislature be independent of each other; that, therefore, the exercise of legislative power in several colonies, by a council appointed, during pleasure, by the crown, is unconstitutional, dangerous, and destructive to the freedom of American legislation.

All and each of which the aforesaid deputies, in behalf of themselves and their constituents, do claim, demand, and insist on, as their indubitable rights and liberties, which cannot be legally taken from them, altered or abridged by any power whatever, without their own consent, by their representatives in their several provincial legislatures.

In the course of our inquiry, we find many infringements and violations of the foregoing rights, which, from an ardent desire, that harmony and mutual intercourse of affection and interest may be restored, we pass over for the present, and proceed to state such acts and measures as have been adopted since the last war, which demonstrate a system formed to enslave America.

Resolved, N. C. D. That the following acts of Parliament are infringements and violations of the rights of the colonists; and that the repeal of them is essentially necessary in order to restore harmony between Great-Britain and the American colonies, viz:

The several acts of 4 Geo. 3. ch. 15, & ch. 34. – 5 Geo. 3. ch. 25. – 6 Geo. 3. ch. 52. – 7 Geo. 3. ch. 41, & ch. 46. – 8 Geo. 3. ch. 22, which impose duties for the purpose of raising a revenue in America, extend the powers of the admiralty courts beyond their ancient limits, deprive the American subject of trial by jury, authorize the judges' certificate to indemnify the prosecutor from damages, that he might otherwise be liable to, requiring oppressive security from a claimant of ships and goods seized, before he shall be allowed to defend his property, and are subversive of American rights.

Also the 12 Geo. 3. ch. 24, entituled 'An act for the better securing his Majesty's dock-yards, magazines, ships, ammunition, and stores', which declares a new offence in America, and deprives the American subject of a constitutional trial by a jury of the vicinage, by authorizing the trial of any person, charged with the committing any offence described in the said act, out of the realm, to be indicted and tried for the same in any shire or county within the realm.

Also the three acts passed in the last session of parliament, for stopping the port and blocking up the harbour of Boston, for altering the charter & government of the Massachusetts-bay, and that which is entituled 'An act for the better administration of Justice', &c.

Also the act passed in the same session for establishing the Roman Catholick Religion in the province of Quebec, abolishing the equitable system of English laws, and erecting a tyranny there, to the great danger, from so total a dissimilarity of Religion, law, and government of the neighbouring British colonies, by the assistance of whose blood and treasure the said country was conquered from France.

Also the act passed in the same session for the better providing suitable quarters for officers and soldiers in his Majesty's service in North-America.

Also, that the keeping a standing army in several of these colonies, in time of peace, without the consent of the legislature of that colony in which such army is kept, is against law.

To these grievous acts and measures, Americans cannot submit, but in hopes that their fellow subjects in Great-Britain will, on a revision of them, restore us to that state in which both countries found happiness and prosperity, we have for the present only resolved to pursue the following peaceable measures:

⟨*Resolved*, unanimously, That from and after the first day of December next, there be no importation into British America, from Great Britain or Ireland of any goods, wares or merchandize whatsoever, or from any other place of any such goods, wares or merchandize.⟩[1]

1st. To enter into a non-importation, non-consumption, and non-exportation agreement or association.

2. To prepare an address to the people of Great-Britain, and a memorial to the inhabitants of British America, &

3. To prepare a loyal address to his Majesty; agreeable to Resolutions already entered into.

[1] Matter in ⟨ ⟩ indicates that it was deleted.

1.1.6 THE ASSOCIATION

October 20, 1774, *Journals of the Continental Congress*, I 75–80

The Congress met.

The association being copied, was read and signed at the table, and is as follows:

Here insert the Association.

We, his majesty's most loyal subjects, the delegates of the several colonies of New-Hampshire, Massachusetts-Bay, Rhode-Island, Connecticut, New-York, New-Jersey, Pennsylvania, the three lower counties of New-Castle, Kent and Sussex, on Delaware, Maryland, Virginia, North-Carolina, and South-Carolina, deputed to represent them in a continental Congress, held in the City of Philadelphia, on the 5th day of September, 1774, avowing our allegiance to his majesty, our affection and regard for our fellow-subjects in Great-Britain and elsewhere, affected with the deepest anxiety, and most alarming apprehensions, at those grievances and distresses, with which his Majesty's American subjects are oppressed; and having taken under our most serious deliberation, the state of the whole continent, find, that the present unhappy situation of our affairs is occasioned by a ruinous system of colony administration, adopted by the British ministry about the year 1763, evidently calculated for inslaving these colonies, and, with them, the British empire. In prosecution of which system, various acts of parliament have been passed, for raising a revenue in America, for depriving the American subjects, in many instances, of the constitutional trial by jury, exposing their lives to danger, by directing a new and illegal trial beyond the seas, for crimes alleged to have been committed in America: and in prosecution of the same system, several late, cruel, and oppressive acts have been passed, respecting the town of Boston and the Massachusetts-Bay, and also an act for extending the province of Quebec, so as to border on the western frontiers of these colonies, establishing an arbitrary government therein, and discouraging the settlement of British subjects in that wide extended country; thus, by the influence of civil principles and ancient prejudices, to dispose the inhabitants to act with hostility against the free Protestant colonies, whenever a wicked ministry shall chuse so to direct them.

To obtain redress of these grievances, which threaten destruction to the lives, liberty, and property of his majesty's subjects, in North America, we are of opinion, that a non-importation, non-consumption, and non-exportation agreement, faithfully adhered to, will prove the most speedy, effectual, and peaceable measure: and, therefore, we do, for ourselves, and the inhabitants of the several colonies, whom we represent, firmly agree and associate, under the sacred ties of virtue, honour and love of our country, as follows:

1. That from and after the first day of December next, we will not import, into British America, from Great-Britain or Ireland, any goods, wares, or merchandise whatsoever, or from any other place, any such goods, wares, or merchandise, as shall have been exported from Great-Britain or Ireland; nor will we, after that day, import any East-India tea from any part of the world; nor any molasses, syrups, paneles,[1] coffee, or pimento, from the British plantations or from Dominica; nor wines from Madeira, or the Western Islands; nor foreign indigo.

2. We will neither import nor purchase, any slave imported after the first day of December next;[2] after which time, we will wholly discontinue the slave trade, and will neither be concerned in it ourselves, nor will we hire our vessels, nor sell our commodities or manufactures to those who are concerned in it.

3. As a non-consumption agreement, strictly adhered to, will be an effectual security for the observation of the non-importation, we, as above, solemnly agree and associate, that, from this day, we will not purchase or use any tea, imported on account of the East-India company, or any on which a duty hath been or shall be paid; and from and after the first day of March next, we will not purchase or use any East-India tea whatever; nor will we, nor shall any person for or under us, purchase or use any of those goods, wares, or merchandise, we have agreed not to import, which we shall know, or have cause to suspect, were imported after the first day of December, except such as come under the rules and directions of the tenth article hereafter mentioned.

4. The earnest desire we have, not to injure our fellow-subjects in

[1] Brown unpurified sugar.

[2] In the pamphlet edition this sentence reads: 'That we will neither import, nor purchase any slave imported, after the first day of December next.'

Great-Britain, Ireland, or the West-Indies, induces us to suspend a non-exportation, until the tenth day of September, 1775; at which time, if the said acts and parts of acts of the British parliament herein after mentioned are not repealed, we will not, directly or indirectly, export any merchandise or commodity whatsoever to Great-Britain, Ireland, or the West-Indies, except rice to Europe.

5. Such as are merchants, and use the British and Irish trade, will give orders, as soon as possible, to their factors, agents and correspondents, in Great-Britain and Ireland, not to ship any goods to them, on any pretence whatsoever, as they cannot be received in America; and if any merchant, residing in Great-Britain or Ireland, shall directly or indirectly ship any goods, wares or merchandise, for America, in order to break the said non-importation agreement, or in any manner contravene the same, on such unworthy conduct being well attested, it ought to be made public; and, on the same being so done, we will not, from thenceforth, have any commercial connexion with such merchant.

6. That such as are owners of vessels will give positive orders to their captains, or masters, not to receive on board their vessels any goods prohibited by the said non-importation agreement, on pain of immediate dismission from their service.

7. We will use our utmost endeavours to improve the breed of sheep, and increase their number to the greatest extent; and to that end, we will kill them as seldom[1] as may be, especially those of the most profitable kind; nor will we export any to the West-Indies or elsewhere; and those of us, who are or may become overstocked with, or can conveniently spare any sheep, will dispose of them to our neighbours, especially to the poorer sort, on moderate terms.

8. We will, in our several stations, encourage frugality, economy, and industry, and promote agriculture, arts and the manufactures of this country, especially that of wool; and will discountenance and discourage every species of extravagance and dissipation, especially all horse-racing, and all kinds of gaming, cock-fighting, exhibitions of shews, plays, and other expensive diversions and entertainments; and on the death of any relation or friend, none of us, or any of our families, will go into any further mourning-dress, than a black crape or ribbon on the arm or hat, for gentlemen, and a black ribbon and

[1] The pamphlet says *sparingly*.

necklace for ladies, and we will discontinue the giving of gloves and scarves at funerals.

9. Such as are venders of goods or merchandise will not take advantage of the scarcity of goods, that may be occasioned by this association, but will sell the same at the rates we have been respectively accustomed to do, for twelve months last past. – And if any vender of goods or merchandise shall sell any such goods on higher terms, or shall, in any manner, or by any device whatsoever violate or depart from this agreement, no person ought, nor will any of us deal with any such person, or his or her factor or agent, at any time thereafter, for any commodity whatever.

10. In case any merchant, trader, or other person,[1] shall import any goods or merchandise, after the first day of December, and before the first day of February next, the same ought forthwith, at the election of the owner, to be either re-shipped or delivered up to the committee of the county or town, wherein they shall be imported, to be stored at the risque of the importer, until the non-importation agreement shall cease, or be sold under the direction of the committee aforesaid; and in the last-mentioned case, the owner or owners of such goods shall be reimbursed out of the sales, the first cost and charges, the profit, if any, to be applied towards relieving and employing such poor inhabitants of the town of Boston, as are immediate sufferers by the Boston port-bill; and a particular account of all goods so returned, stored, or sold, to be inserted in the public papers; and if any goods or merchandises shall be imported after the said first day of February, the same ought forthwith to be sent back again, without breaking any of the packages thereof.

11. That a committee be chosen in every county, city, and town, by those who are qualified to vote for representatives in the legislature, whose business it shall be attentively to observe the conduct of all persons touching this association; and when it shall be made to appear, to the satisfaction of a majority of any such committee, that any person within the limits of their appointment has violated this association, that such majority do forthwith cause the truth of the case to be published in the gazette; to the end, that all such foes to the rights of British-America may be publicly known, and universally contemned as the enemies of American liberty; and thenceforth we respectively will break off all dealings with him or her.

[1] Persons is used in the pamphlet.

12. That the committee of correspondence, in the respective colonies, do frequently inspect the entries of their custom-houses, and inform each other, from time to time, of the true state thereof, and of every other material circumstance that may occur relative to this association.

13. That all manufactures of this country be sold at reasonable prices, so that no undue advantage be taken of a future scarcity of goods.

14. And we do further agree and resolve, that we will have no trade, commerce, dealings or intercourse whatsoever, with any colony or province, in North-America, which shall not accede to, or which shall hereafter violate this association, but will hold them as unworthy of the rights of freemen, and as inimical to the liberties of their country.

And we do solemnly bind ourselves and our constituents, under the ties aforesaid, to adhere to this association, until such parts of the several acts of parliament passed since the close of the last war, as impose or continue duties on tea, wine, molasses, syrups, paneles, coffee, sugar, pimento, indigo, foreign paper, glass, and painters' colours, imported into America, and extend the powers of the admiralty courts beyond their ancient limits, deprive the American subject of trial by jury, authorize the judge's certificate to indemnify the prosecutor from damages, that he might otherwise be liable to from a trial by his peers, require oppressive security from a claimant of ships or goods seized, before he shall be allowed to defend his property, are repealed. – And until that part of the act of the 12 G. 3. ch. 24, entitled 'An act for the better securing his majesty's dock-yards, magazines, ships, ammunition, and stores,' by which any persons charged with committing any of the offences therein described, in America, may be tried in any shire or county within the realm, is repealed – and until the four acts, passed the last session of parliament, viz. that for stopping the port and blocking up the harbour of Boston – that for altering the charter and government of the Massachusetts-Bay – and that which is entitled 'An act for the better administration of justice, &c.' – and that 'for extending the limits of Quebec, &c.' are repealed. And we recommend it to the provincial conventions, and to the committees in the respective colonies, to establish such farther regulations as they may think proper, for carrying into execution this association.

The foregoing association being determined upon by the Congress, was ordered to be subscribed by the several members thereof; and thereupon, we have hereunto set our respective names accordingly.

IN CONGRESS, PHILADELPHIA, *October 20, 1774.*

Signed, PEYTON RANDOLPH, *President.*

New Hampshire	Jno. Sullivan Nathel. Folsom	New Jersey	J. Kinsey Wil: Livingston Stepn. Crane Richd. Smith John De Hart
Massachusetts Bay	Thomas Cushing Saml. Adams John Adams Robt. Treat Paine	Pennsylvania	Jos. Galloway John Dickinson Cha Humphreys Thomas Mifflin E. Biddle John Morton Geo: Ross
Rhode Island	Step. Hopkins Sam: Ward	The Lower Counties New Castle	Cæsar Rodney Tho. M: Kean Geo: Read
Connecticut	Elipht Dyer Roger Sherman Silas Deane	Maryland	Mat Tilghman Ths. Johnson Junr. Wm. Paca Samuel Chase
New York	Isaac Low John Alsop John Jay Jas. Duane Phil. Livingston Wm. Floyd Henry Wisner S: Boerum		

I.I.7 CONGRESS RECOMMENDS THE COLONIES TO FORM INDEPENDENT STATE GOVERNMENTS, MAY 10–15, 1776

Journals of the Continental Congress, IV 352, 357

Whereas, His Britannic Majesty, in conjunction with the Lords and Commons of Great Britain, has, by a late Act of Parliament, excluded the inhabitants of these United Colonies from the protection of his Crown; and whereas, no answer whatever to the humble petitions of the colonies for redress of grievances and reconciliation with Great

Britain has been or is likely to be given; but the whole force of that kingdom, aided by foreign mercenaries, is to be exerted for the destruction of the good people of these colonies; and whereas, it appears absolutely irreconcileable to reason and good conscience for the people of these colonies now to take the oaths and affirmations necessary for the support of any government under the Crown of Great Britain, and it is necessary that every kind of authority under the said Crown should be totally suppressed, and all the powers of government exerted, under the authority of the people of these colonies, for the preservation of internal peace, virtue, and good order, as well as for the defence of their lives, liberties, and properties against the hostile invasions and cruel depredations of their enemies; therefore

Resolved, That it be recommended to the respective Assemblies and Conventions of the United Colonies, where no government sufficient to the exigencies of their affairs have been hitherto established, to adopt such a government as shall, in the opinion of the representatives of the people, best conduce to the happiness and safety of their constituents in particular, and America in general.

I.I.8 THE DECLARATION OF INDEPENDENCE

(i) *In draft form (as it reads in the Lee copy, which is probably the same as the report of the Committee of Five, with parts omitted by Congress here shown ⟨ ⟩ and the parts added, in italics)*

'A Declaration by the Representatives of the United States of America in General Congress assembled', in Carl L. Becker, *The Declaration of Independence* (New York, 1922) pp. 174–93

When in the course of human events it becomes necessary for one people to dissolve the political bands which have connected them with another, and to assume among the powers of the earth the separate and equal station to which the laws of nature and of nature's god entitle them, a decent respect to the opinions of mankind requires that they should declare the causes which impel them to the separation.

We hold these truths to be self-evident; that all men are created equal; that they are endowed by their Creator with ⟨inherent and inalienable> *certain unalienable*[1] rights; that among these are life, liberty, and the pursuit of happiness; that to secure these rights, governments are instituted among men, deriving their just powers from the consent of the governed; that whenever any form of government becomes destructive of these ends, it is the right of the people to alter or to abolish it, and to institute new government, laying it's foundation on such principles, and organizing it's powers in such form as to them shall seem most likely to effect their safety and happiness. prudence indeed will dictate that governments long established should not be changed for light & transient causes. and accordingly all experience hath shewn that mankind are more disposed to suffer, while evils are sufferable, than to right themselves by abolishing the forms to which they are accustomed. but when a long train of abuses and usurpations, <begun at a distinguished period &> pursuing invariably the same object, evinces a design to reduce them under absolute despotism, it is their right, it is their duty, to throw off such government, & to provide new guards for their future security. such has been the patient sufferance of these colonies, & such is now the necessity which constrains them to <expunge> *alter* their former systems of government. the history of the present king of Great Britain is a history of <unremitting> *repeated* injuries and usurpations, <among which appears no solitary fact to contradict the uniform tenor of the rest, but> all <have> *having* in direct object the establishment of an absolute tyranny over these states. to prove this let facts be submitted to a candid world, <for the truth of which we pledge a faith yet unsullied by falsehood>.

He has refused his assent to laws the most wholesome and necessary for the public good.

he has forbidden his governors to pass laws of immediate & pressing importance, unless suspended in their operation till his assent should be obtained; and when so suspended, he has *utterly* neglected <utterly> to attend to them.

[1] The Rough Draft reads '<inherent &> *certain* inalienable'. There is no indication that Congress changed 'inalienable' to 'unalienable'; but the latter form appears in the text in the rough Journal, in the corrected Journal, and in the parchment copy. John Adams, in making his copy of the Rough Draft, wrote 'unalienable'. Adams was one of the committee which supervised the printing of the text adopted by Congress, and it may have been at his suggestion that the change was made in printing. 'Unalienable' may have been the more customary form in the eighteenth century.

he has refused to pass other laws for the accomodation of large districts of people, unless those people would relinquish the right of representation in the legislature; a right inestimable to them, & formidable to tyrants only.

he has called together legislative bodies at places unusual, uncomfortable, & distant from the depository of their public records, for the sole purpose of fatiguing them into compliance with his measures.

he has dissolved Representative houses repeatedly ⟨& continually⟩ for opposing with manly firmness his invasions on the rights of the people.

he has refused for a long time after such dissolutions to cause others to be elected whereby the legislative powers, incapable of annihilation, have returned to the people at large for their exercise, the state remaining in the meantime exposed to all the dangers of invasion from without, & convulsions within.

he has endeavored to prevent the population of these states; for that purpose obstructing the laws for naturalization of foreigners; refusing to pass others to encourage their migrations hither; & raising the conditions of new appropriations of lands.

he has ⟨suffered⟩ *obstructed* the administration of justice ⟨totally to cease in some of these states⟩, *by* refusing his assent to laws for establishing judiciary powers.

he has made ⟨our⟩ judges dependent on his will alone, for the tenure of their offices, and the amount & paiment of their salaries.

he has erected a multitude of new offices ⟨by a self assumed power⟩, & sent hither swarms of officers to harrass our people, and eat out their substance.

he has kept among us, in times of peace, standing armies ⟨and ships of war⟩, without the consent of our legislatures.

he has affected to render the military independent of, & superior to, the civil power.

he has combined with others to subject us to a jurisdiction foreign to our constitutions and unacknoleged by our laws; giving his assent to their acts of pretended legislation for quartering large bodies of armed troops[1] among us;

for protecting them by a mock-trial from punishment for any murders which they should commit on the inhabitants of these states;

[1] The text in the corrected Journal reads 'bodies of troops'.

for cutting off our trade with all parts of the world;

for imposing taxes on us without our consent;

for depriving us *in many cases* of the benefits of trial by jury;

for transporting us beyond seas to be tried for pretended offenses;

for abolishing the free system of English laws in a neighboring province, establishing therein an arbitrary government, and enlarging it's boundaries so as to render it at once an example & fit instrument for introducing the same absolute rule into these states;

for taking away our charters, abolishing our most valuable laws, and altering fundamentally the forms of our governments;

for suspending our own legislatures, & declaring themselves invested with power to legislate for us in all cases whatsoever.

he has abdicated government here, ⟨withdrawing his governors, &⟩ *by* declaring us out of ⟨his allegiance and protection⟩ *and waging war against us.*

he has plundered our seas, ravaged our coasts, burnt our towns, & destroyed the lives of our people.

he is at this time transporting large armies of foreign mercenaries, to compleat the works of death, desolation & tyranny, already begun with circumstances of cruelty & perfidy *scarcely paralleled in the most barbarous ages and totally* unworthy the head of a civilized nation.

he has *excited domestic insurrection amongst us and has* endeavored to bring on the inhabitants of our frontiers the merciless Indian savages, whose known rule of warfare is an undistinguished destruction of all ages, sexes, & conditions ⟨of existence⟩.

⟨he has incited treasonable insurrections of our fellow citizens, with the allurements of forfeiture & confiscation of property.⟩

he has constrained *our fellow citizens* ⟨others⟩ taken captives on the high seas to bear arms against their country, to become the executioners of their friends & brethren, or to fall themselves by their hands.

⟨he has waged cruel war against human nature itself, violating it's most sacred rights of life & liberty in the persons of a distant people, who never offended him, captivating and carrying them into slavery in another hemisphere, or to incur miserable death in their transportation thither. this piratical warface, the opprobrium of *infidel* powers, is the warfare of the *Christian* king of Great Britain. determined to keep open a market where MEN should be bought &

sold, he has prostituted his negative for suppressing every legislative attempt to prohibit or to restrain this execrable commerce: and that this assemblage of horrors might want no fact of distinguished die, he is now exciting those very people to rise in arms among us, and to purchase that liberty of which *he* has deprived them, by murdering the people upon whom *he* also obtruded them: thus paying off former crimes committed against the *liberties* of one people, with crimes which he urges them to commit against the *lives* of another.⟩

In every stage of these oppressions, we have petitioned for redress in the most humble terms; our repeated petitions have been answered only by repeated injury. a prince whose character is thus marked by every act which may define a tyrant, is unfit to be the ruler of a *free* people ⟨who mean to be free. future ages will scarce believe that the hardiness of one man adventured within the short compass of twelve years only to build a foundation, so broad and undisguised, for tyranny over a people fostered and fixed in principles of freedom⟩.

Nor have we been wanting in attentions to our British brethren. we have warned them from time to time of attempts by their legislature to extend ⟨a⟩ *an unwarrantable* jurisdiction over *us*. ⟨these our states⟩. we have reminded them of the circumstances of our emigration and settlement here, ⟨no one of which could warrant so strange a pretension: that these were effected at the expence of our own blood and treasure, unassisted by the wealth or the strength of Great Britain: that in constituting indeed our several forms of government, we had adopted one common king, thereby laying a foundation for perpetual league and amity with them: but that submission to their parliament was no part of our constitution. nor ever in idea, if history may be credited: and⟩ we *have* appealed to their native justice & magnanimity, ⟨as well as to⟩ *and we have conjured them by* the tyes of our common kindred, to disavow these usurpations, which ⟨were likely to⟩ *would inevitably* interrupt our connection*s* & correspondence. they too have been deaf to the voice of justice and of consanguinity;[1] ⟨and when occasions have been given them, by the regular course of their laws, of removing from their councils the disturbers of our harmony, they have by their free election re-established them in power. at this very time too, they are permitting their chief magistrate to send over not only soldiers of our common blood, but Scotch and foreign mercenaries

[1] The text in the corrected Journal reads 'and consanguinity'.

to invade and destroy us. these facts have given the last stab to agonizing affection; and manly spirit bids us to renounce forever these unfeeling brethren⟩. we must *therefore* ⟨endeavor to forget our former love for them, and to hold them as we hold the rest of mankind, enemies in war, in peace friends. we might have been a free & a great people together; but a communication of grandeur and of freedom, it seems, is below their dignity. be it so, since they will have it. the road to happiness and to glory is open to us too; we will climb it apart from them, and⟩ acquiesce in the necessity which denounces our ⟨eternal⟩ separation *and hold them, as we hold the rest of mankind, enemies in war, in peace friends.* [!]

We therefore the Representatives of the United states of America in General Congress assembled, *appealing to the supreme judge of the world for the rectitude of our intentions* do, in the name & by authority of the good people of these *colonies, solemnly publish and declare, that these united colonies are and of right ought to be free and independent states; that they are absolved from all allegiance to the British Crown, and that* ⟨states, reject and renounce all allegiance and subjection to the kings of Great Britain, & all others who may hereafter claim by, through, or under them; we utterly dissolve⟩ all political connection ⟨which may heretofore have subsisted⟩ between ⟨us⟩ *them* and the *state* ⟨people or parliament⟩ of Great Britain *is & ought to be totally dissolved;* ⟨and finally we do assert and declare these colonies to be free and independent states⟩ & that as free & independent states, they have full power to levy war, conclude peace, contract alliances, establish commerce, & to do all other acts and things which independent states may of right do. And for the support of this declaration, *with a firm reliance on the protection of divine providence,* we mutually pledge to each other our lives, our fortunes, and our sacred honor.

Contrary to a tradition early established and long held, the Declaration was not signed by the members of Congress on July 4. Neither the rough nor the corrected Journal shows any signatures, except that the printed copy in the rough Journal closes with these words, of course in print: 'Signed by order and in behalf of the Congress, John Hancock, President.' The secret domestic Journal for July 19 contains the following entry: 'Resolved that the Declaration passed on the 4th be fairly engrossed.' And in the margin there is added: 'Engrossed on parchment with the title and stile of "The Unanimous Declaration of the 13 United States of America", and that the same when engrossed be signed by every member of Congress.' On August 2 occurs the following entry: 'The Declaration of Independence being engrossed and compared at the table was signed by the members.' Certain members, being absent on the 2 of August, signed the engrossed copy at a later date. The engrossed parchment copy, carefully preserved at Washington, is identical in phraseology with the copy in the rough Journal. The paragraphing, except in one instance, is indicated by dashes; the capitalization and punctuation, following neither previous copies, nor reason, nor the custom of any age known to man, is one of the irremediable evils of life to be accepted with becoming resignation. Two slight errors in engrossing have been corrected by interlineation.

(ii) *Final Version: 'The unanimous declaration of the thirteen United States of America'*

When in the Course of human events, it becomes necessary for one people to dissolve the political bands, which have connected them with another, and to assume among the powers of the earth, the separate and equal station to which the Laws of Nature and of Nature's God entitle them, a decent respect to the opinions of mankind requires that they should declare the causes which impel them to the separation. – We hold these truths to be self-evident, that all men are created equal, that they are endowed by their Creator with certain unalienable Rights, that among these are Life, Liberty and the pursuit of Happiness. – That to secure these rights, Governments are instituted among Men, deriving their just powers from the consent of the governed, – That whenever any Form of Government becomes destructive of these ends, it is the Right of the People to alter or to abolish it, and to institute new Government, laying its foundation on such principles and organizing its powers in such form, as to them shall seem most likely to effect their Safety and Happiness. Prudence, indeed, will dictate that Governments long established should not be changed for light and transient causes; and accordingly all experience hath shewn, that mankind are more disposed to suffer, while evils are sufferable, than to right themselves by abolishing the forms to which they are accustomed. But when a long train of abuses and usurpations, pursuing invariably the same Object evinces a design to reduce them under absolute Despotism, it is their right, it is their duty, to throw off such

Government, and to provide new Guards for their future security. – Such has been the patient sufferance of these Colonies; and such is now the necessity which constrains them to alter their former Systems of Government. The history of the present King of Great Britain is a history of repeated injuries and usurpations, all having in direct object the establishment of an absolute Tyranny over these States. To prove this, let Facts be submitted to a candid world. – He has refused his Assent to Laws, the most wholesome and necessary for the public good. – He has forbidden his Governors to pass Laws of immediate and pressing importance, unless suspended in their operation till his Assent should be obtained; and when so suspended, he has utterly neglected to attend to them. – He has refused to pass other Laws for the accommodation of large districts of people, unless those people would relinquish the right of Representation in the Legislature, a right inestimable to them and formidable to tyrants only. – He has called together legislative bodies at places unusual, uncomfortable, and distant from the depository of their public Records, for the sole purpose of fatiguing them into compliance with his measures. – He has dissolved Repres*en*tative Houses repeatedly, for opposing with manly firmness his invasions on the rights of the people. – He has refused for a long time, after such dissolutions, to cause others to be elected; whereby the Legislative powers, incapable of Annihilation, have returned to the People at large for their exercise; the State remaining in the meantime exposed to all the dangers of invasion from without, and convulsions within. – He has endeavoured to prevent the population of these States; for that purpose obstructing the Laws for Naturalization of Foreigners; refusing to pass others to encourage their migrations hither, and raising the conditions of new Appropriations of Lands. – He has obstructed the Administration of Justice, by refusing his Assent to Laws for establishing Judiciary powers. – He has made Judges dependent on his Will alone, for the tenure of their offices, and the amount and payment of their salaries. – He has erected a multitude of New Offices, and sent hither swarms of Officers to harrass our people, and eat out their substance. – He has kept among us, in times of peace, Standing Armies without the Consent of our legislatures. – He has affected to render the Military independent of and superior to the Civil power. – He has combined with others to subject us to a jurisdiction foreign to our constitution, and unacknowledged by our laws; giving his Assent to their Acts of pretended Legislation. – For quartering large bodies of armed troops among us: – For protecting them, by a mock Trial, from punishment for any Murders which they should commit on the Inhabitants of these States: – For cutting off our Trade with all parts of the world: – For imposing Taxes on us without our Consent: – For depriving us in many cases, of the benefits of Trial by Jury: – For transporting us beyond Seas to be tried for pretended offenses: – For abolishing the free System of English Laws in a neighboring Province, establishing therein an Arbitrary government, and enlarging its Boundaries so as to render it at once an example and fit instrument for introducing the same absolute rule into these Colonies: – For taking away our Charters, abolishing our most valuable Laws, and altering fundamentally the Forms of our Governments: – For suspending our own Legislatures, and declaring themselves invested with power to legislate for us in all cases whatsoever. – He has abdicated Government here, by declaring us out of his Protection and waging War against us. – He has plundered our seas, ravaged our Coasts, burnt our towns, and destroyed the lives of our people. – He is at this time transporting large Armies of foreign Mercenaries to compleat the works of death, desolation and tyranny, already begun with circumstances of Cruelty & perfidy scarcely paralleled in the most barbarous ages, and totally unworthy the Head of a civilized nation. – He has constrained our fellow Citizens taken Captive on the high Seas to bear Arms against their Country, to become the executioners of their friends and Brethren, or to fall themselves by their Hands. – He has excited domestic insurrections amongst us, and has endeavoured to bring on the inhabitants of our frontiers, the merciless Indian Savages, whose known rule of warfare, is an undistinguished destruction of all ages, sexes and conditions. In every stage of these Oppressions We have Petitioned for Redress in the most humble terms: Our repeated Petitions have been answered *only* by repeated injury. A Prince whose character is thus marked by every act which may define a Tyrant, is unfit to be the ruler of a free people. Nor have We been wanting in attentions to our Brittish brethren. We have warned them from time to time of attempts by their legislature to extend an unwarrantable jurisdiction over us. We have reminded them of the circumstances of our emigration and settlement here. We have appealed to their native justice and magnanimity, and we have conjured them by the ties of our common kindred to disavow these usurpations, which would inevitably interrupt our connections and correspondence. They too have been deaf to the voice of justice and of consanguinity. We must, therefore, acquiesce in the necessity, which denounces our Separation, and hold them, as we hold the rest of mankind, Enemies in War, in Peace Friends. –

We, therefore, the Representatives of the united States of America, in General Congress, Assembled, appealing to the Supreme Judge of the world for the rectitude of our intentions do, in the Name, and by Authority of the good People of these Colonies, solemnly publish and declare, That these United Colonies are, and of Right ought to be Free and Independent States; that they are Absolved from all Allegiance to the British Crown, and that all political connection between them and the State of Great Britain, is and ought to be totally dissolved: and that as Free and Independent States, they have full Power to levy War, conclude Peace, contract Alliances, establish Commerce, and to do all other Acts and Things which Independent States may of right do. – And for the support of this Declaration, with a firm reliance on the protection of divine Providence, we mutually pledge to each other our Lives, our Fortunes and our sacred Honor.

The signatures on the parchment copy, of which only a few are now legible, are given below.

John Hancock.
Samuel Chase.
Wm. Paca.
Thos. Stone.
Charles Carroll of Carrollton.
George Wythe.
Richard Henry Lee.
Th Jefferson.
Benja. Harrison.
Thos. Nelson jr.
Francis Lightfoot Lee.
Carter Braxton.
Robt. Morris.
Benjamin Rush.
Benja. Franklin.
John Morton.
Geo Clymer.
Jas. Smith.

Frans. Lewis.
Lewis Morris.
Richd. Stockton.
Jno. Witherspoon.
Fras. Hopkinson.
John Hart.
Abra Clark.
Josiah Bartlett.
Wm. Whipple.
Saml. Adams.
John Adams.
Robt. Treat Paine.
Elbridge Gerry.
Step Hopkins.
William Ellery.
Roger Sherman.
Saml. Huntington.
Wm. Williams.

Geo. Taylor.
James Wilson.
Geo. Ross.
Caesar Rodney.
Geo Read.
Tho M: Kean.
Wm. Floyd.
Phil. Livingston.
Arthur Middleton.
Button Gwinnett.
Oliver Wolcott.
Matthew Thornton.
Wm. Hooper.
Joseph Hewes.
John Penn.
Edward Rutledge.
Thos. Heyward Junr.
Thomas Lynch Junr.
Lyman Hall.
Geo Walton.

1.1.9 THE ARTICLES OF CONFEDERATION, AS DRAFTED IN 1776

Journals of the Continental Congress, v 674–90

Congress resolved itself into a committee of the whole to take into their farther consideration the Articles of Confederation; and after some time, the president resumed the chair, and Mr [John] Morton reported, that the committee having had under consideration the articles of Confederation, had gone through the same, [and] have agreed to sundry articles, which he was ordered to submit to Congress.

The report of the committee being read,

Articles[1] *of Confederation and Perpetual Union, between the Colonies*[2] *of*

New-Hampshire,
Massachusetts-Bay,
Rhode-Island,
The counties of New-Castle,
Kent and Sussex on Delaware,
Maryland,

[1] A copy of this second printed issue of the Articles of Confederation is in the *Papers of the Continental Congress*, no. 47, folio 29. In order to show more clearly the changes made in the text while under consideration, the first printed form is printed in parallel with the second reported this day.

A copy of the first issue is in Jefferson Papers, with manuscript changes in the writing of Thomas Jefferson. These changes, except in the cases mentioned in the notes, follow those that are made by Thomson during the consideration of the Articles before August 20, and are thus embodied in the second printed form.

[2] This word was changed to 'States' in the second printed form of the Articles.

Connecticut,
New-York,
New-Jersey,
Pennsylvania,
Virginia,
North-Carolina,
South-Carolina, and
Georgia.

FIRST PRINTED FORM

Art. I. THE Name of this Confederacy shall be 'The United States of America'.

Art. II. The said Colonies unite themselves so as never to be divided by any Act whatever, and hereby severally enter into a firm League of Friendship with each other, for their common Defence, the Security of their Liberties, and their mutual and general Welfare, binding the said Colonies to assist one another against all Force offered to or attacks made upon them or any of them, on Account of Religion, Sovereignty, Trade, or any other Pretence whatever.

Art. III. Each Colony shall retain and enjoy as much of its present Laws, Rights and Customs, as it may think fit, and reserves to itself the sole and exclusive Regulation and Government of its internal police, in all matters that shall not interfere with the Articles of this Confederation.

Art. IV. No Colony or Colonies, without the Consent of the United States assembled, shall send any Embassy to or receive any

SECOND PRINTED FORM

Art. I. THE name of this Confederacy shall be 'The United States of America'.

Art. II. The said States hereby severally enter into a firm league of friendship with each other, for their common defence, the security of their liberties, and their mutual and general welfare, binding themselves to assist each other against all force offered to or attacks made upon them or any of them, on account of religion, sovereignty, trade, or any other pretence whatever.[1]

Art. III. Each State reserves to itself the sole and exclusive regulation and government of its internal police, in all matters that shall not interfere with the articles of this Confederation.

Art. IV. No State, without the consent of the United States in Congress Assembled, shall send any Embassy to or receive any

[1] The Jefferson copy here adds 'by any power foreign to this confederacy'.

Embassy from, or enter into any Treaty, Convention or Conference with the King or Kingdom of Great-Britain, or any foreign Prince or State; nor shall any Colony or Colonies, nor any Servant or Servants of the United States, or of any Colony or Colonies, accept of any Present, Emolument, Office, or Title of any Kind whatever, from the King or Kingdom of Great-Britain, or any foreign Prince or State; nor shall the United States assembled, or any Colony grant any Title of Nobility.

embassy from, or enter into any conference, agreement, alliance or treaty with any King, Prince or State; nor shall any person holding any office of profit or trust under the United States or any [of] them, accept of any present, emolument, office, or title of any kind whatever, from any King, Prince or foreign State; nor shall the United States Assembled, or any of them, grant any title of nobility.

Art. V. No two or more Colonies shall enter into any Treaty, Confederation or Alliance whatever between them, without the previous and free Consent and Allowance of the United States assembled, specifying accurately the Purposes for which the same is to be entered into, and how long it shall continue.

Art. V. No two or more States shall enter into any treaty, confederation or alliance whatever between them without the Consent of the United States in Congress Assembled, specifying accurately the purposes for which the same is to be entered into, and how long it shall continue.

Art. VI. The Inhabitants of each Colony shall henceforth always have the same Rights, Liberties, Privileges, Immunities and Advantages, in the other Colonies, which the said Inhabitants now have, in all Cases whatever, except in those provided for by the next following Article.

Art. VII. The Inhabitants of each Colony shall enjoy all the Rights, Liberties, Privileges, Immunities, and Advantages, in

Trade, Navigation, and Commerce, in any other Colony, and in going to and from the same from and to any Part of the World, which the Natives of such Colony enjoy.

ART. VIII. Each Colony may assess or lay such Imposts or Duties as it thinks proper, on Importations or Exportations, provided such Imposts or Duties do not interfere with any Stipulations in Treaties hereafter entered into by the United States assembled, with the King or Kingdom of Great-Britain, or any foreign Prince or State.

ART. IX. No standing Army or Body of Forces shall be kept up by any Colony or Colonies in Times of Peace, except such a Number only as may be requisite to garrison the Forts necessary for the Defence of such Colony or Colonies: But every Colony shall always keep up a well regulated and disciplined Militia, sufficiently armed and accoutred; and shall provide and constantly have ready for Use in Public Stores, a due Number of Field Pieces and Tents, and a proper Quantity of Ammunition, and Camp Equipage.

ART. VI. No State shall lay any imposts or duties which may interfere with any stipulations in treaties hereafter entered into by the United States Assembled with any King, Prince or State.

ART. VII. No vessels of war shall be kept up in time of peace by any State, except such number only as shall be deemed necessary by the United States Assembled for the defence of such state or its trade, nor shall any body of forces be kept up by any State in time of peace, except such number only as in the judgment of the United States in Congress Assembled shall be deemed requisite to garrison the forts necessary for the defence of such State, but every State shall always keep up a well regulated and disciplined Militia, sufficiently armed and accoutred, and shall provide and constantly have ready for use in public stores a due number of field pieces and tents and a proper quantity of ammunition and camp equipage.

ART. X. When Troops are raised in any of the Colonies for the common Defence, the Commission Officers proper for the Troops raised in each Colony, except the General Officers, shall be appointed by the Legislature of each Colony respectively or in such manner as shall by them be directed.	ART. VIII. When land forces are raised by any State for the common defence, all officers of or under the rank of Colonel, shall be appointed by the legislatures of each State respectively, by whom such forces shall be raised, or in such manner as such State shall direct, and all vacancies shall be filled up by the State which first made the appointment.
ART. XI (postponed). All Charges of Wars and all other Expences that shall be incurred for the common Defence, or general Welfare, and allowed by the United States assembled, shall be defrayed out of a common Treasury, which shall be supplied by the several Colonies in Proportion to the Number of Inhabitants of every Age, Sex and Quality except Indians not paying Taxes, in each Colony, a true Account of which, distinguishing the white Inhabitants shall be triennially taken and transmitted to the Assembly of the United States. The Taxes for paying that Proportion shall be laid and levied by the Authority and Direction of the Legislatures of the several Colonies, within the Time agreed upon by the United States assembled.	ART. IX. All charges of war and all other expences that shall be incurred for the common defence, or general welfare, and allowed by the United States Assembled, shall be defrayed out of a common treasury, which shall be supplied by the several States in proportion to the number of inhabitants of every age, sex and quality except Indians not paying taxes, in each State, a true account of which, distinguishing the white inhabitants shall be triennially taken and transmitted to the Assembly of the United States. The taxes for paying that proportion shall be laid and levied by the authority and direction of the legislatures of the several States, within the time agreed upon by the United States Assembled.
ART. XII. Every colony shall abide by the Determinations of the United States assembled, concerning the Services performed	ART. X. Every State shall abide by the determinations of the United States in Congress Assembled, on all questions which by

and Losses or Expences incurred by every Colony for the common Defence or general Welfare, and no Colony or Colonies shall in any Case whatever endeavor by Force to procure Redress of any Injury or Injustice supposed to be done by the United States to such Colony or Colonies in not granting such Satisfactions, Indemnifications, Compensations, Retributions, Exemptions, or Benefits of any Kind, as such Colony or Colonies may think just or reasonable.

this Confederation are submitted to them.

ART. XIII. No Colony or Colonies shall engage in any War without the previous Consent of the United States assembled, unless such Colony or Colonies be actually invaded by Enemies, or shall have received certain Advice of a Resolution being formed by some Nations of Indians to invade such Colony or Colonies, and the Danger is so imminent, as not to admit of a Delay, till the other Colonies can be consulted: Nor shall any Colony or Colonies grant Commissions to any Ships or Vessels of War, nor Letters of Marque or Reprisal, except it be after a Declaration of War by the United States assembled, and then only against the Kingdom or State and the Subjects thereof, against which War has been so declared, and under such Regulations as shall be

ART. XI. No State shall engage in any war without the consent of the United States in Congress Assembled, unless such State be actually invaded by enemies, or shall have received certain advice of a resolution being formed by some nation of Indians to invade such State, and the danger is so imminent, as not to admit of a delay, till the other States can be consulted: Nor shall any State grant commissions to any ships or vessels of war, nor letters of marque or reprisal, except it be after a declaration of war by the United States Assembled, and then only against the Kingdom or State and the subjects thereof against which war has been so declared and under such regulations as shall be established by the United States Assembled.

established by the United States assembled.

Art. XIV (postponed). No Purchases of Lands, hereafter to be made of the Indians by Colonies or private Persons before the Limits of the Colonies are ascertained, to be valid: All Purchases of Lands not included within those Limits, where ascertained, to be made by Contracts between the United States assembled, or by Persons for that Purpose authorized by them, and the great Councils of the Indians, for the general Benefit of all the United Colonies.

Art. XV (postponed). When the Boundaries of any Colony shall be ascertained by Agreement, or in the Manner herein after directed, all the other Colonies shall guarantee to such Colony the full and peaceable Possession of, and the free and entire Jurisdiction in and over the Territory included within such Boundaries.

Art. XVI. For the more convenient Management of the general Interests of the United States, Delegates should be annually appointed in such Manner as the Legislature of each Colony shall direct, to meet at the City of Philadelphia, in the Colony of Pennsylvania, until otherwise ordered by the United States assembled; which Meeting shall be on

Art. XII. For the more convenient management of the general interests of the United States, Delegates shall be annually appointed in such manner as the legislature of each State shall direct, to meet at the city of Philadelphia, in Pennsylvania, until otherwise ordered by the United States in Congress Assembled; which meeting shall be the first Monday of November in every Year, with a Power reserved to those who appointed the said Delegates, respectively to recal them or any of them at any time within the Year, and to send new Delegates in their stead for the Remainder of the Year. Each Colony shall support its own Delegates in a Meeting of the States, and while they act as Members of the Council of State, herein after mentioned.

Art. XVII. In determining Questions each Colony shall have one Vote.

Art. XVIII. The United States assembled shall have the sole and exclusive Right and Power of determining on Peace and War, except in the Cases mentioned in the thirteenth Article – Of establishing Rules for deciding in all Cases, what Captures on Land or Water shall be legal – In what Manner Prizes taken by land or naval Forces in the Service of the United States shall be divided or appropriated – Granting Letters of Marque and Reprisal in Times of Peace – Appointing Courts for the Trial of all Crimes, Frauds and Piracies committed on the High Seas, or on any navigable River, not within the Body of a County or Parish – Establishing Courts for receiving and determining finally Appeals in all Cases of Captures – Sending and

on the first Monday in November in every year, with a power reserved to each State to recal its Delegates or any of them at any time within the year, and to send others in their stead for the remainder of the year. Each State shall support its own Delegates in a meeting of the States, and while they act as members of the Council of State, herein after mentioned.

Art. XIII. In determining questions each State shall have one vote.

Art. XIV. The United States Assembled shall have the sole and exclusive right and power of determining on peace and war, except in the cases mentioned in the eleventh article – Of establishing rules for deciding in all cases, what captures on land or water shall be legal – In what manner prizes taken by land or naval forces in the service of the United States shall be divided or appropriated – granting letters of marque and reprisal in times of peace – appointing Courts for the trial of piracies and felonies committed on the high seas – establishing Courts for receiving and determining finally appeals in all cases of captures – sending and recieving Ambassadors – entering into treaties and alliances – deciding all disputes and differences receiving ambassadors under any character – Entering into Treaties and Alliances – Settling all Disputes and Differences now subsisting, or that hereafter may arise between two or more Colonies concerning Boundaries, Jurisdictions, or any other Cause whatever – Coining Money and regulating the Value thereof – Regulating the Trade, and managing all Affairs with the Indians[1] – Limiting the Bounds of those Colonies, which by Charter or Proclamation, or under any Pretence, are said to extend to the South Sea, and ascertaining those Bounds of any other Colony that appear to be indeterminate – Assigning Territories for new Colonies, either in Lands to be thus separated from Colonies and heretofore purchased or obtained by the Crown of Great-Britain from the Indians, or hereafter to be purchased or obtained from them – Disposing of all such Lands for the general Benefit of all the United Colonies – Ascertaining Boundaries to such new Colonies, within which Forms of Government are to be established on the Principles of Liberty – Establishing and regulating Post-Offices throughout all the United Colonies, on the Lines of Com-

now subsisting, or that hereafter may arise between two or more States concerning boundaries, jurisdictions, or any other cause whatever – coining money and regulating the value thereof – fixing the standard of weights and measures throughout the United States – regulating the trade, and managing all affairs with the Indians, not members of any of the States – Establishing and regulating Post-Offices from one State to another throughout all the United States, and exacting such postage on the papers passing through the same, as may be requisite to defray the expences of said office – appointing general Officers of the land forces in the service of the United States – commissioning such other officers of the said forces as shall be appointed by virtue of the eighth article – appointing all the officers of the naval forces in the service of the United States – making rules for the government and regulation of the said land and naval forces, and directing their operations.

[1] On the Dickinson manuscript Thompson has written 'agreed' against the first part of this article, and 'postponed' against the part from 'Limiting' to 'Principles of Liberty'.

munication from one Colony to another – Appointing General Officers of the Land Forces in the Service of the United States – Commissioning such other Officers of the said Forces as shall be appointed by Virtue of the tenth Article – Appointing all the Officers of the Naval Forces in the Service of the United States – Making Rules for the Government and Regulation of the said Land and Naval Forces – Appointing a Council of State, and such Committees and civil Officers as may be necessary for managing the general Affairs of the United States, under their Direction while assembled, and in their Recess, of the Council of State – Appointing one of their number to preside, and a suitable Person for Secretary – And adjourning to any Time within the Year.

The United States assembled shall have Authority for the Defence and Welfare of the United Colonies and every of them, to agree upon and fix the necessary Sums and Expences – To emit Bills, or to borrow Money on the Credit of the United Colonies – To raise Naval Forces – To agree upon the Number of Land Forces to be raised, and to make Requisitions from the Legislature of each Colony, or the Persons therein authorized by the Legislature

The United States in Congress Assembled shall have authority to appoint a Council of State, and such Committees and Civil Officers as may be necessary for managing the general affairs of the United States, under their direction while assembled, and in their recess under that of the Council of State – to appoint one of their number to preside, and a suitable person for Secretary – And to adjourn to any time within the year, and to any place to execute such Requisitions, for the Quota of each Colony, which is to be in Proportion to the Number of white Inhabitants in that Colony, which Requisitions shall be binding and thereupon the Legislature of each Colony or the Persons authorized as aforesaid, shall appoint the Regimental Officers, raise the Men, and arm and equip them in a soldier-like Manner; and the Officers and Men so armed and equiped, shall march to the Place appointed, and within the Time agreed on by the United States assembled.

But if the United States assembled shall on Consideration of Circumstances judge proper, that any Colony or Colonies should not raise Men, or should raise a smaller Number than the Quota or Quotas of such Colony or Colonies, and that any other Colony or Colonies should raise a greater number of men than the Quota or Quotas thereof, such extra-numbers shall be raised, officered, armed and equiped in the same Manner as the Quota or Quotas of such Colony or Colonies, unless the Legislature of such Colony or Colonies respectively, shall judge, that such extra-

within the United States – to agree upon and fix the necessary sums and expences – to borrow Money or emit bills on the credit of the United States – to build and equip a navy – to agree upon the number of land forces, and to make requisitions from each State, for its quota in proportion to the number of white inhabitants in such State, which requisitions shall be binding, and thereupon the legislature of each State shall appoint the regimental officers, raise the men, and arm and equip them in a soldier-like manner; and the officers and men so armed and equipped, shall march to the place appointed, and within the time agreed on by the United States Assembled.

But if the United States in Congress Assembled shall on consideration of circumstances judge proper, that any State or States should not raise men, or should raise a smaller number than the quota or quotas of such State or States, and that any other State or States should raise a greater number of men than the quota or quotas thereof, such extra-numbers shall be raised, officered, armed and equipped in the same Manner as the quota or quotas of such State or States, unless the legislature of such State or States respectively, shall judge, that such extra-numbers cannot numbers cannot be safely spared out of the same, in which Case they shall raise, officer, arm and equip as many of such extra-numbers as they judge can be safely spared; and the Officers and Men so armed and equiped shall march to the Place appointed and within the Time agreed on by the United States assembled.

To establish the same Weights and Measures throughout the United Colonies.

But the United States assembled shall never impose or levy any Taxes or Duties, except in managing the Post-Office, nor interfere in the internal Police of any Colony, any further than such Police may be affected by the Articles of this Confederation. The United States assembled shall never engage the United Colonies in a War, nor grant Letters of Marque and Reprisal in Time of Peace, nor enter into Treaties or Alliances, nor coin Money nor regulate the Value thereof, nor agree upon nor fix the Sums and Expences necessary for the Defence and Welfare of the United Colonies, or any of them, nor emit Bills, nor borrow Money on the Credit of the United Colonies, nor raise Naval Forces, nor agree upon the Number of Land Forces to be raised, unless the Delegates of nine Colonies freely assent to the same: Nor shall a Question on

be safely spared out of the same, in which case they shall raise, officer, arm and equip as many of such extra-numbers as they judge can be safely spared; and the officers and men so armed and equipped shall march to the place appointed, and within the time agreed on by the United States Assembled.

The United States in Congress Assembled shall never engage in a war, nor grant letters of marque and reprisal in time of peace, nor enter into any treaties or alliances except for peace, nor coin money nor regulate the value thereof, nor agree upon nor fix the sums and expences necessary for the defence and welfare of the United States, or any of them, nor emit bills, nor borrow money on the credit of the United States, nor appropriate money, nor agree upon the number of vessels of war to be built or purchased, or the number of land or sea forces to be raised, nor appoint a Commander in Chief of the army or navy, unless nine States assent to the same: Nor shall a question on any other point, except for adjourning from day to day be determined, unless by the votes of a majority of the United States.

any other Point, except for adjourning be determined, unless the Delegates of seven Colonies vote in the affirmative.

No Person shall be capable of being a Delegate for more than three Years in any Term of six Years.

No Person holding any Office under the United States, for which he, or another for his Benefit, receives any Salary, Fees, or Emolument of any Kind, shall be capable of being a Delegate.

The Assembly of the United States to publish the Journal of their Proceedings monthly, except such Parts thereof relating to Treaties, Alliances, or military Operations, as in their Judgment require Secrecy – The Yeas and Nays of the Delegates of each Colony on any Question to be entered on the Journal, where it is desired by any Delegate; and the Delegates of a Colony, or any of them, at his or their Request, to be furnished with a Transcript of the said Journal, except such Parts as are above excepted, to lay before the Legislatures of the several Colonies.

Art. XIX. The Council of State shall consist of one Delegate from each Colony, to be named annually by the Delegates of each Colony, and where they cannot agree, by the United States assembled.

No person shall be capable of being a Delegate for more than three years in any term of six years.

No person holding any office under the United States, for which he, or another for his benefit, receives any salary, fees, or emolument of any kind, shall be capable of being a Delegate.

The Assembly of the United States to publish the Journal of their Proceedings monthly, except such parts thereof relating to treaties, alliances, or military operations, as in their judgment require secrecy, the yeas and nays of the Delegates of each State on any question to be entered on the Journal, when it is desired by any Delegate; and the Delegates of a State, or any of them, at his or their request, to be furnished with a transcript of the said Journal, except such parts as are above excepted, to lay before the legislatures of the several States.

Art. XV. The Council of State shall consist of one Delegate from each State, to be named annually by the Delegates of each State, and where they cannot agree, by the United States assembled.

This Council shall have Power to receive and open all Letters directed to the United States, and to return proper Answers; but not to make any Engagements that shall be binding on the United States – To correspond with the Legislature of every Colony, and all Persons acting under the Authority of the United States, or of the said Legislatures – To apply to such Legislatures, or to the Officers in the several Colonies who are entrusted with the executive Powers of Government, for occasional Aid whenever and wherever necessary – To give Counsel to the Commanding Officers, and to direct military Operations by Sea and Land, not changing any Objects or Expeditions determined on by the United States assembled, unless an Alteration of Circumstances which shall come to the Knowledge of the Council after the Recess of the States, shall make such Change absolutely necessary – To attend to the Defence and Preservation of Forts and strong Posts, and to prevent the Enemy from acquiring new Holds – To procure Intelligence of the Condition and Designs of the Enemy – To expedite the Execution of such Measures as may be resolved on by the United States assembled, in Pursuance of the Powers hereby given to them

This Council shall have power to receive and open all Letters directed to the United States, and to return proper Answers; but not to make any engagements that shall be binding on the United States – To correspond with the legislature of every State, and all persons acting under the authority of the United States, or of the said legislatures – To apply to such Legislatures, or to the Officers in the several States who are entrusted with the executive powers of government, for occasional aid whenever and wherever necessary – To give counsel to the Commanding Officers, and to direct military operations by sea and land, not changing any objects or expeditions determined on by the United States Assembled, unless an alteration of circumstances which shall come to the knowledge of the Council after the recess of the States, shall make such change absolutely necessary – To attend to the defence and preservation of forts and strong posts – To procure intelligence of the condition and designs of the enemy – To expedite the execution of such measures as may be resolved on by the United States Assembled, in pursuance of the powers hereby given to them – To draw upon the treasurers for such sums as may be appropriated by the United States Assembled,

To draw upon the Treasurers for such Sums as may be appropriated by the United States assembled, and for the Payment of such Contracts as the said Council may make in Pursuance of the Powers hereby given to them – To superintend and controul or suspend all Officers civil and military, acting under the Authority of the United States – In Case of the Death or Removal of any Officer within the Appointment of the United States assembled, to employ a Person to fulfill the Duties of such Office until the Assembly of the States meet – To publish and disperse authentic Accounts of military Operations – To summon an Assembly of the States at an earlier Day than that appointed for their next Meeting, if any great and unexpected Emergency should render it necessary for the Safety or Welfare of the United Colonies or any of them – To prepare Matters for the Consideration of the United States, and to lay before them at their next Meeting all Letters and Advices received by the Council, with a Report of their Proceedings – To appoint a proper Person for their Clerk, who shall take an Oath of Secrecy and Fidelity, before he enters on the Exercise of his Office – Seven Members shall have Power to act – In Case of the Death of any Member, the Council shall

and for the payment of such contracts as the said Council may make in pursuance of the powers hereby given to them – To superintend and controul or suspend all Officers civil and military, acting under the authority of the United States – In case of the death or removal of any Officer within the appointment of the United States Assembled, to employ a person to fulfill the Duties of such Office until the Assembly of the States meet – To publish and disperse authentic accounts of military operations – To summon an Assembly of the States at an earlier day than that appointed for their next meeting, if any great and unexpected emergency should render it necessary for the safety or welfare of the United States or any of them – To prepare matters for the consideration of the United States, and to lay before them at their next meeting all letters and advices received by the Council, with a report of their proceedings – To appoint a proper person for their Clerk, who shall take an oath of secrecy and fidelity, before he enters on the exercise of his office – seven Members shall have power to act – In case of the death of any Member, the Council shall immediately apply to his surviving colleagues to appoint some one of themselves to be a Member immediately apply to his surviving Colleagues to appoint some one of themselves to be a Member thereof till the Meeting of the States, and if only one survives, they shall give immediate Notice, that he may take his Seat as a Councilor till such Meeting.

thereof till the meeting of the States, and if only one survives, they shall give immediate notice, that he may take his seat as a Councillor till such meeting.

Art. XX. Canada acceding to this Confederation, and entirely joining in the Measures of the United Colonies, shall be admitted into and entitled to all the Advantages of this Union: But no other Colony shall be admitted into the same, unless such Admission be agreed to by the Delegates of nine Colonies.

Art. XVI. Canada acceding to this Confederation, and entirely joining in the measures of the United States,[1] shall be admitted into and entitled to all the advantages of this Union: But no other Colony shall be admitted into the same, unless such admission be agreed to by nine States.

These Articles shall be proposed to the Legislatures of all the United Colonies, to be by them considered, and if approved by them, they are advised to authorize their Delegates to ratify the same in the Assembly of the United States, which being done, the Articles of this Confederation shall inviolably be observed by every Colony, and the Union is to be perpetual: Nor shall any Alteration be at any Time hereafter made in these Articles or any of them, unless such Alteration be agreed to in an Assembly of the United States, and be afterwards confirmed by the Legislatures of every Colony.

These Articles shall be proposed to the legislatures of all the United States, to be by them considered, and if approved by them, they are advised to authorize their Delegates to ratify the same in the Assembly of the United States, which being done, the Articles of this Confederation shall inviolably be observed by every State, and the Union is to be perpetual: Nor shall any alteration at any time hereafter be made in these Articles or any of them, unless such alteration be agreed to in an Assembly of the United States, and be afterwards confirmed by the Legislatures of every State.

[1] The Jefferson copy here inserts: 'and all new colonies to be established by the United States assembled'.

Ordered, That eighty copies of the Articles of Confederation, as reported from the committee of the whole, be printed under the same injunctions as the former articles were printed, and delivered to the members under the like restrictions as formerly.

Resolved, That Mr Hamilton Young be permitted to reside in Pensylvania, till the farther orders of Congress.

The committee appointed to prepare a device for a great seal for the United States, brought in the same, with an explanation thereof:

The great Seal sh'd on one side have the Arms of the United States of America, which Arms should be as follows: The Shield has six Quarters, parti one, coupé two. The 1st. Or, a Rose enammelled gules and argent for England: the 2d. argent, a Thistle proper, for Scotland: the 3d. Verd, a Harp Or, for Ireland: the 4th. Azure a Flower de Luce Or for France: the 5th. Or, the Imperial Eagle Sable for Germany: and the 6th. Or, the Belgic Lion gules for Holland, pointing out the Countries from which these States have been peopled. The Shield within a Border Gules entoire of thirteen Scutcheons argent linked together by a chain Or, each charged with initial Letters Sable as follows: 1st. N. H. 2d. M. B. 3d. R. I. 4th. C. 5th. N. Y. 6th. N. J. 7th. P. 8th. D. C. 9. M. 10th. V. 11th. N. C. 12th. S. C. 13 G. for each of the thirteen independent States of America.

Supporters, dexter the Goddess Liberty in a corselet of armour alluding to the present Times, holding in her right Hand the Spear and Cap, and with her left supporting the Shield of the States; sinister, the Goddess Justice bearing a Sword in her right hand, and in her left a Balance.

Crest. The Eye of Providence in a radiant Triangle whose Glory extends over the Shield and beyond the Figures.

Motto. E PLURIBUS UNUM.

Legend, round the whole Atchievement. Seal of the United States of America MDCCLXXVI.

On the other side of the said Great Seal should be the following Device. Pharoah sitting in an open Chariot, a Crown on his head and a Sword in his hand passing through the divided Waters of the Red Sea in pursuit of the Israelites: Rays from a Pillow of Fire in the Cloud, expressive of the divine Presence and Command, beaming on Moses who stands on the Shore, and extending his hand over the Sea causes it to overwhelm Pharoah.

Motto. Rebellion to Tyrants is Obedience to God.

II Public Finance and the Continental Congress

I.II.I CONGRESS RESOLVES TO ISSUE ITS OWN MONEY

June 22, 1775, *Journals of the Continental Congress*, II 103.

Deleted material indicated thus, ⟨ ⟩.

The Congress met according to adjournment.

Resolved, That a sum not exceeding two millions of Spanish milled dollars be emitted by the Congress in bills of Credit, for the defence of America.

Resolved, That the twelve confederated colonies be pledged for the redemption of the bills of credit, now directed to be emitted.[1]

⟨Resolved, That the pay of the aids de camp of the majors general be increased to thirty-three dollars per month.⟩

June 23, 1775, ibid. pp. 105–6

Agreeable to the order of the day the Congress resolved itself into a committee of the whole, to take into further consideration the state of America, and after some time spent therein, the president resumed the chair, and Mr [Samuel] Ward reported that the committee had come into certain resolutions which they desired him to report, but not having yet finished, they had ordered him to move for leave to sit again.

The report of the Committee being read,

Resolved, That the Number and denomination of the bills to be emitted be as follows, viz:

49,000 bills	of 8 dollars each	392,000
49,000 do.	of 7 dollars each	343,000
49,000 do.	of 6 dollars each	294,000
49,000 do.	of 5 dollars each	245,000
49,000 do.	of 4 dollars each	196,000
49,000 do.	of 3 dollars each	147,000
49,000 do.	of 2 dollars each	98,000
49,000 do.	of 1 dollars each	49,000
11,800 do.	of 20 dollars each	236,000
403,800		2,000,000

[1] The list of Brigadiers and the resolution on bills of credit were printed in the *Pennsylvania Packet*, December 11, 1775.

Resolved, That the form of the bills be as follows, viz:

CONTINENTAL CURRENCY

No. Dollar.

THIS bill entitles the bearer to receive
Spanish Milled dollars, or the value thereof in gold or silver, according to the resolutions of the Congress, held at Philadelphia, on the 10th day of May, A. D. 1775.

Resolved, That Mr J[ohn] Adams, Mr J[ohn] Rutledge, Mr [James] Duane, Doctor [Benjamin] Franklin, and Mr [James] Wilson, be a committee to get proper plates engraved, to provide paper, and to agree with printers to print the above bills.

I.II.2 CONGRESS PROVIDES A SCALE FOR ARMY PAY; APPOINTS TREASURERS; AND REQUIRES THE COLONIES TO RAISE TAXES ON A QUOTA BASED ON POPULATION, TO ABSORB CONTINENTAL CURRENCY

July 29, 1775, *Journals of the Continental Congress*, II 220–3

Met according to adjournment.

The Congress resumed the consideration of the report from the Committee of the whole,

Resolved, That the pay of the commissary general of musters be 40 dollars per month.

That the pay of the deputy commissary genl. of stores and provisions be 60 dollars ditto.

Deputy adjutant general, 50 do.
Deputy muster master general, 40 do.
Brigade Major, 33 do.
Commissary of Artillery, 30 do.
Judge advocate, 20 do.
Colonel, 50 do.
Lieutenant colonel, 40 do.
Major, 33⅓.
Captain, 20.

Lieutenant, $13\frac{1}{3}$.
Ensign, 10.
Serjeant, 8.
Corporal, drummer, and fifer, each $7\frac{1}{3}$.
Private, $6\frac{2}{3}$.
Adjutant, $18\frac{1}{3}$.
Quarter master, $18\frac{1}{3}$.
Chaplain, 20.

That the pay of the light infantry be the same as that in the Regiment from a captain to a private, and both included.

That in the artillery, the pay of captain be $26\frac{2}{3}$ dollars per month.
Captain lieutenant, 20.
First and second lieutenants, each $18\frac{1}{3}$.
Lieutenant fire worker, $13\frac{1}{3}$.
Serjeant, $8\frac{1}{3}$.
Corporals, $7\frac{1}{2}$.
Bombardiers, 7.
Matrosses, $6\frac{5}{6}$.

That the appointment of provost Marshal, waggon master, and master carpenter, be left to the commander in chief of the army, who is to fix their pay, having regard to the pay such receive in the ministerial army, and the proportion that the pay of the Officers in said army bears to the pay of our Officers.

William Tudor, Esqr. was elected Judge Advocate of the army.

Resolved, That Michael Hillegas, and George Clymer, Esqrs be, and they are hereby appointed, joint treasurers of the United Colonies: that the Treasurers reside in Philadelphia, and that they shall give bond, with surety, for the faithful performance of their office, in the sum of 100,000 Dollars, to John Hancock, Henry Middleton, John Dickinson, John Alsop, Thomas Lynch, Richard Henry Lee, and James Wilson, Esqrs and the survivor of them, in trust for the United Colonies.

That the provincial Assemblies or conventions do each chuse a treasurer for their respective colonies, and take sufficient security for the faithful performance of the trust.

That each colony provide ways and means to sink its proportion of the bills ordered to be emitted by this Congress, in such manner as may be most effectual and best adapted to the condition, circumstances, and usual mode of levying taxes in such colony.

That the proportion or quota of each colony be determined according to the number of Inhabitants, of all ages, including negroes and mulattoes in each colony; But, as this cannot, at present, be ascertained, that the quotas of the several colonies be settled for the present, as follows, to undergo a revision and correction, when the list of each colony is obtained.

New Hampshire,	124,069½	Delaware,	37,219½
Massachusetts bay,	434,244	Maryland,	310,174½
Rhode Island,	71,959½	Virginia,	496,278
Connecticut,	248,139	North Carolina,	248,139
New York,	248,139	South Carolina,	248,139
New Jersey,	161,290½		
Pennsylvania,	372,208½		3,000,000

That each Colony pay its respective quota in four equal annual payments, the first payment to be made on or before the last day of November, which will be in the year of our Lord, one thousand seven hundred and seventy nine; the second, on or before the last day of November, 1780; the third, on or before the last day of November, 1781; and the fourth or last, on or before the last day of November, 1782. And that for this end, the several provincial assemblies, or conventions, provide for laying and levying taxes in their respective provinces or colonies, towards sinking the continental bills: That the said bills be received by the collectors in payment of such taxes, and be by the sd. collectors pd. into the hands of the provincial treasurers, with all such other monies as they may receive in lieu of the continental bills, which other monies the sd. provincial treasurers shall endeavour to get exchanged for continental bills, and where that cannot be done, shall send to the continental treasurers the deficiency in silver or gold, with the bills making up the quota to be sunk in that year, taking care to cut, by a circular punch, of an Inch diameter, an hole in each bill, and to cross the same, thereby to render them unpassable, though the sum or value is to remain fairly legible: And the continental treasurers, as fast as they receive the said quotas, shall, with the assistance of a committee of five persons, to be appointed by the Congress, if sitting, or by the assembly or convention of the province of Pensylvania, examine and count the continental bills, and in the presence of the said committee, burn and destroy them. And the silver and gold sent them to make up the deficiencies of quotas, they shall retain in their hands until demanded in redemption of continental bills, that may be brought to them for that purpose, which bills so redeemed, they shall also burn and destroy in presence of the said committee. And the treasurers, whenever they have silver or gold in their hands for the redemption of continental bills, shall advertise the same, signifying that they are ready to give silver or gold for such bills, to all persons requiring it in exchange.

The provincial treasurers and collectors are to have such allowances for their respective services, as shall be directed by the several assemblies or conventions, to be paid by their respective province or colony,

That the continental treasurers be allowed for their service this year, five hundred dollars each.

I.II.3 CONGRESS RESOLVES TO EMIT $3 MILLION IN BILLS OF CREDIT

November 29, 1775, *Journals of the Continental Congress*, III 390

The Congress then took into consideration the report of the Committee on the state of the treasury, and came to the following resolutions thereon:

Resolved, That a quantity of bills of Credit be emitted by Congress amounting to 3,000,000 of Dollars.

Resolved, That it be referred to the Committee to consult with the printer, and report the number and denomination of the bills to be emitted, and that they contract for proper paper for this purpose.

I.II.4 CONGRESS REQUIRES EACH COLONY TO FIND WAYS TO ABSORB ITS PROPORTION OF THE BILLS OF CREDIT

December 26, 1775, *Journals of the Continental Congress*, III 457–9

The Congress took into consideration the report of the committee on the state of the treasury, and thereupon came to the following resolutions:

Whereas an estimate hath lately been formed of the public expence already arisen, and which may accrue in the defence of America, to the 10 day of June next, in pursuance whereof this Congress, on the 29 day of November, resolved that a farther sum of three millions of dollars be emitted in bills of credit,

Resolved, Therefore that the thirteen United Colonies be pledged for the redemption of the bills of credit so directed to be emitted.

That each colony provide ways and means to sink its proportion of the said bills, in such manner as may be most effectual, and best adapted to the condition, circumstances, and equal mode of levying taxes in each colony.

That the proportion or quota of each respective colony be determined according to the number of inhabitants, of all ages, including negroes and mulattoes in each colony.

That it be recommended to the several assemblies, conventions, or councils, or committees of safety of the respective colonies, to ascertain, by the most impartial and effectual means in their power, the number of inhabitants in each respective colony, taking care that the lists be authenticated by the oaths of the several persons who shall be entrusted with this service; and that the said assemblies, conventions, councils, and committees of safety, do respectively lay before this Congress a return of the number of inhabitants of their respective colonies, as soon as the same shall be procured.

That each colony pay its respective quota in four equal payments; the first to be made on or before the last day of November, 1783; the second, on or before the last day of November, 1784; the third, on or before the last day of November, 1785; and the fourth or last, on or before the last day of November, 1786; and that, for this end, the several assemblies or conventions provide for laying and levying taxes in their respective colonies, towards sinking the continental bills; that the said bills be received by the collectors in payment of such taxes, and be by the collectors paid into the hands of the provincial treasurers, with all such other monies as they may receive in lieu of the continental bills; which other monies the provincial treasurers shall endeavour to get exchanged for continental bills; and when that cannot be done, shall send to the continental treasurers the deficiency in gold and silver, with the bills, making up the quota to be sunk in that year; taking care to cut, by a circular punch of an inch diameter, an hole in such bills, and to cross the same, thereby to render them unpassable, tho the sum or value is to remain fairly legible; and the continental treasurers, as fast as they receive the said quotas, shall, with the assistance of a committee of five persons, to be appointed by the Congress, if sitting, or by the assembly or convention of the province of Pensylvania, examine and count the continental bills, and, in the presence of the said committee, burn and destroy them; and the silver and gold sent them to make up the deficiencies of quotas, they shall retain in their hands, until demanded in redemption of continental bills, that may be brought to them for that purpose; which bills, so redeemed, they shall also burn and destroy in the presence of the said committee; and the treasurers, whenever they have silver or gold in their hands for the redemption of continental bills, shall advertise the same, signifying that they are ready to give gold or silver for such bills, to all persons requiring it in exchange.

I.II.5 CONGRESS DECIDES TO RAISE $5 MILLION ON LOAN

October 3, 1776, *Journals of the Continental Congress*, V 485

Congress took into consideration the report of the Board of Treasury, on the ways and means for raising a farther sum of money; Whereupon,

Resolved, That five millions of continental dollars be immediately borrowed for the use of the United States of America, at the annual interest of four per cent. per annum:

That the faith of the United States be pledged to the Lenders for the payment of the sums to be borrowed, and the interest arising thereon, and that certificates be given to the lenders in the form following:

The United States of America acknowledge the receipt of dollars from , which they promise to pay to the said , or bearer, on the day of , with interest annually, at the rate of four per cent. per annum, agreeable to a resolution of the United States, passed the third day of October, 1776. Witness the hand of the treasurer, this day of , A. D.

'Countersigned' by the commissioners of one of the loan offices hereafter mentioned.

That for the convenience of the lenders, a loan office be established in each of the United States, and a commissioner, to superintend such office, be appointed by the said states respectively, which are to be responsible for the faithful discharge of their duty in the said offices.

I.II.6 CONGRESS RECOMMENDS THE STATES TO TAKE STEPS TO SUPPLY THE ARMY

October 31, 1776, *Journals of the Continental Congress*, VI 914–16

Whereas, it has been represented to Congress, that sundry inhabitants of these United States, to keep supplies from the army, or promote their own interest, have purchased considerable quantities of cloathing, and refuse to dispose of the same, unless upon extravagant or unreasonable terms;

Resolved, That it be recommended to the assemblies, conventions, councils or committees of safety of the several states, forthwith to take suitable measures for obtaining, for the use of the army, such necessary articles, as being thus engrossed in their respective states, cannot be otherwise immediately procured, allowing to the owners reasonable prices for the same; and that laws be provided in each of the states, for effectually preventing monopolies of necessaries for the army, or inhabitants of the same.[1]

I.II.7 CONGRESS ATTEMPTS TO MAINTAIN VALUE OF ITS CURRENCY AGAINST DEPRECIATION

January 14, 1777, *Journals of the Continental Congress*, VII 35–7

Deleted matter indicated thus, ⟨ ⟩.

The report from the committee of the whole being read, ⟨was taken into consideration, Whereupon,⟩ was agreed to as follows, viz.

[1] Printed in the *Pennsylvania Gazette*, November 6, 1776.

Whereas the continental money ought to be supported, at the full value expressed in the respective bills, by the inhabitants of these States, for whose benefit they were issued, and who stand bound to redeem the same, according to the like value; and the pernicious artifices of the enemies of American liberty to impair the credit of the said bills, by raising the nominal value of gold and silver, or any other species of money whatsoever, ought to be guarded against and prevented:

Resolved, That all bills of credit, emitted by authority of Congress, ought to pass current in all payments, trade, and dealings, in these States, and be deemed in value equal to the same nominal sum in Spanish milled dollars; and that whosoever shall offer, ask, or receive more in the said bills for any gold or silver coins, bullion, or any other species of money whatsoever, than the nominal sum or amount thereof in Spanish milled dollars, or more, in the said bills, for any lands, houses, goods, or commodities whatsoever, than the same could be purchased at of the same person or persons in gold, or silver, or any other species of money whatsoever; or shall offer to sell any goods or commodities for gold or silver coins, or any other species of money whatsoever, and refuse to sell the same for the said continental bills; every such person ought to be deemed an enemy to the liberties of these united States, and to forfeit the value of the money so exchanged, or house, land, or commodity so sold or offered to sale. And it is recommended to the legislatures of the respective States, to enact laws inflicting such forfeitures and other penalties on offenders as aforesaid, as will prevent such pernicious practices:

That it be recommended to the legislatures of the united States, to pass laws to make the bills of credit, issued by the Congress, a lawful tender, in payment of public and private debts; and a refusal thereof an extinguishment of such debts: that debts payable in sterling money be discharged with continental dollars, at the rate of 4/6 sterling per dollar; and that in discharge of all other debts and contracts, continental dollars pass at the rate fixed by the respective States for the value of Spanish milled dollars:

Resolved, That it be recommended to the legislatures of the several united States to pass resolutions that they will make provision for drawing in and sinking their respective quotas of the bills emitted by Congress at the several periods fixed, or that shall be fixed by Congress:

That it be recommended to the legislatures of the several States, to raise, by taxation, in the course of the current year, and remit to the treasury, such sums of money as they shall think will be most proper in the present situation of the inhabitants; which sums shall be carried to their credit, and accounted for in the settlement of their proportion of the public expences and debts, for which the united States are jointly bound:

That an additional sum of two millions of dollars be borrowed at the loan offices, on certificates of 200 dollars each:

That the commissioners of the loan office be directed to receive the bills of credit heretofore emitted by the States in which they respectively hold their offices, for such sums as ⟨they⟩ shall be ordered by the commissioners of the treasury, or continental treasurer, from time to time, ⟨to pay⟩ for continental purposes, within such States respectively.

I.II.8 CONGRESS FIXES RATE OF INTEREST ON ITS LOANS

February 26, 1777, *Journals of the Continental Congress*, VII 158

Deleted matter indicated thus, ⟨ ⟩.

Congress resumed the consideration of the ⟨report of the Committee on Ways and Means⟩ rate of interest to be allowed on the sums of money ordered to be ⟨paid⟩ borrowed; Whereupon,

Resolved, That an interest of 6 per cent. per annum be allowed on all sums of money already borrowed, and directed to be borrowed on loan office certificates, although such certificates mention an interest of 4 per centum per annum.

Resolved, That the interest on the prizes, drawn in the continental lottery, shall remain at 4 per centum.

Resolved, That it be recommended to the legislatures of the several States, not to offer or give more than at the rate of 6 per centum per annum upon any monies to be borrowed in their respective loan offices.

I.II.9 CONGRESS RECOMMENDS STATES TO RAISE $5 MILLION BY TAXES AND LAYS DOWN QUOTAS

November 1777, *Journals of the Continental Congress*, IX 955–7

Deleted material indicated thus, 〈 〉.

1. *Resolved*, That it be most earnestly recommended to the respective states to raise in the course of the year 1778, commencing on the first day of January next, by quarterly payments, the sum of five millions of dollars, by taxes, to be levied on the inhabitants of the respective states, in the proportions following, viz.

New Hampshire	200,000 dollars	Pennsylvania	620,000 dollars
Massachusetts Bay	820,000	Delaware	60,000
Rhode Island & Providence Plantations	100,000	Maryland	520,000
		Virginia	800,000
		North Carolina	250,000
Connecticut	600,000	South Carolina	500,000
New York	200,000	Georgia	60,000
New Jersey	270,000		
			5,000,000

That the sum so assessed and to be raised shall not be considered as the proportion of any State, but being paid into the treasury shall be placed to their respective credit, bearing an interest of six per cent. per annum, from the time of payment until the quotas shall be finally ascertained and adjusted by the Congress of the United States, agreeable to the confederation hereafter to be adopted and ratified by the several states. And if it shall then appear that any State is assessed more than its just quota of the said tax, it shall continue to receive interest on the surplus, and if less it shall be charged with interest on the deficiency, until by a future tax such surplus or deficiency shall be properly adjusted.

2. *Resolved*, That it be earnestly recommended to the legislatures of the several states to refrain from further emissions of bills of credit, and where there is a sufficient quantity of continental bills of credit for the purposes of a circulating medium, forthwith to call in by loans or taxes and to cancel the paper money, small bills for change under a dollar excepted, which such Ssate has already emitted; and, for the

future, to provide for the exigencies of war, and the support of government by taxes to be levied within the year, or such other expedients as may produce a competent supply.

3. And whereas the obstruction of the course of justice in any State may not only prove injurious to its ⟨inhabitants⟩ citizens, but also to the circulation and credit of the currency of such State and of the United States:

Resolved, therefore, That it be recommended to the several states, forthwith to take effectual care that justice be duly administered within their respective jurisdictions, as well for the recovery of debts as for the punishment of crimes and misdemeanors; provided, that no suit or actions shall be maintainable for the benefit of the enemies of these United States.

4. And whereas signal advantages have arisen from the establishment of continental loan offices, on which Congress continue to place great dependence; in order, therefore, as far as it is practicable, to ascertain the supplies for the war ⟨for the next four months⟩ which may be raised in the several states upon loan office certificates;

Resolved, That it be recommended to the legislatures, or, in the recess of any of them, to the executive authority of the respective states, to cause subscriptions to be opened under the inspection of one or more respectable ⟨inhabitants⟩ citizens within each town or district, specifying the names of the lenders, and the sums they are willing to lend, and that copies of such subscription papers shall, from time to time, be delivered to the respective commissioners of the said loan offices, and by them transmitted to Congress; provided, that no certificate shall issue for less than two hundred dollars.

5. *Resolved,* That it be recommended to the legislatures, or, in their recess, to the executive power of the respective states of New Hampshire, Massachusetts bay, Rhode Island and Providence Plantations, Connecticut, New York, New Jersey, Pensylvania, and Delaware, respectively, to appoint commissioners to convene at New Haven, in Connecticut, on the 15 day of January next; and to the states of Virginia, Maryland, and North Carolina, respectively, to appoint commissioners to convene at Fredericksburg, in Virginia, on the said 15 day of January; and to the states of South Carolina and Georgia, respectively, to appoint commissioners to convene at Charleston, on the 15 day of February next; in order to regulate and ascertain the price of labour, manufactures, internal produce, and commodities

imported from foreign parts, military stores excepted; and also to regulate the charges of inn-holders; and that, on the report of ⟨such⟩ the commissioners, each of the respective legislatures enact ⟨such⟩ suitable laws, as well for enforcing the observance of such of the regulations as they shall ratify, and enabling such inn-holders to obtain the necessary supplies, as to authorize the purchasing commissaries for the army, or any other person whom the legislature may think proper, to take from any engrossers, forestallers, or other person possessed of a larger quantity of any such commodities or provisions than shall be competent for the private annual consumption of their families, and who shall refuse to sell the surplus at the prices to be ascertained as aforesaid, paying only such price for the same.

6. And in order to introduce immediate œconomy in the public expence, the spirit of sharping and extortion, and the rapid and excessive rise of every commodity being confined within no bounds; and considering how much time must unavoidably elapse before the plan directed by the preceding resolution can be carried into effect,

Resolved, That it be earnestly recommended to the respective legislatures of the United States, without delay, by their separate authority, to adopt and effectually enforce a temporary regulation of the prices of provisions and other commodities for the supply of the army, in such manner as they shall judge reasonable; and to continue in force until the general regulation before proposed shall be adopted.

I.II.10 CONGRESS RESOLVES ON ARMY OFFICERS' PAY

December 1, 1779, *Journals of the Continental Congress*, XV, 1335–7

The committee, to whom was referred the memorial of the general officers &c. brought in a report.

The Committee appointed to take into consideration what allowance ought to be made to officers in the different Departments of the army, to whom the provision made by the Resolutions of Congress of the 18th August last doth not extend, and to whom was also referred the Memorial of the general officers, beg leave to report:

Whereas some of the legislatures of the United States, have already passed laws to extend the half pay which Congress 'resolved should be given to the officers in the army of the United States for and during the term of seven years next after the conclusion of the present war', for and during life to such officers as belong to the Battalions raised in such States respectively; and whereas Congress hath recommended to all the States and some have already entered into measures for making good the deficiency in pay occasioned by the depreciation of the bills of credit; and whereas the principle of equal distributive justice clearly point out, that such officers of the army who in point of such provision do not belong to any State should be provided for by the United States in general in the same manner. It is therefore,

Resolved, That all the General officers and officers of the military and civil staff of the army, now bearing commissions from Congress, or who may here after engage to serve in the Army of the United States under such commissions, and who are not by any former resolutions of Congress recommended to the attention of the States in general or any of them in particular, shall have their pay as the same hath heretofore been established made good by a liquidation of the different rates of depreciation from the time of such establishments, and that all monies which such officers may have received as pay, shall be charged to them, and the true value thereof liquidated in manner aforesaid.

That all such officers as aforesaid (general officers excepted) for whom no provision has been made in point of subsistence in lieu of rations withheld shall be allowed at the rate of one hundred dollars per month for every ration so withheld since the 18th day of August last, and a like sum for every ration that shall so be withheld in future.

That all such officers as aforesaid, General officers included, who shall continue to serve during the present war, shall from the conclusion thereof be entitled to and receive half pay for life, to be computed on the pay established for such officers next before the 1st day of January, 1777; and that the half pay of such officers who hold or may hold offices established since the said 1st day of January, 1777, shall be computed on the full pay reduced to real value, according to the rate of depreciation, when the office was established and the pay appointed. Provided always, that if less than a majority of the Legislatures of the several United States should only provide half pay for life, that then the provision hereby extended for life shall cease and determine at the end of seven years next after the conclusion of the present war.

And whereas Congress wish to afford a durable testimony of public gratitude to those virtuous Citizens, who braving the danger and distress incident on the military life, generously flew to the banners of freedom to support the just rights and liberties of their Country threatened with destruction by an unfeeling and unrelenting Tyrant, it is resolved:

That provision shall be made to give unto the present, or any future Commander in Chief of the Army of the United States, who shall serve as such before the conclusion of the present war, the quantity of ten thousand acres of land.

To every Major General so serving as aforesaid three thousand acres.

To every Brigadier general so serving as aforesaid 2000 acres, and to every other officer, noncommissioned officer and soldier, in the military and civil Departments of the Army, the quantity of 100 acres for every five dollars of monthly pay reduced to real value at the rate of depreciation when their appointments and pay were respectively established. Provided always that officers holding more than one commission shall only be allowed subsistence money, half pay and land on the Commission they hold in the military line of the army.

That all officers serving in the civil Departments of the army, and who now receive commissions on the money by them paid out, in lieu of pay, and who shall continue to serve during the war, shall be entitled to all the immunities, granted by the foregoing resolutions to officers bearing commissions under Congress, and on the like limitations and restrictions.

That if any of the officers and soldiers to whom lands are to be granted by these resolutions shall die before the conclusion of the war, their heirs or legal representatives respectively shall be entitled to the lands designed for them.

That the heirs or legal representatives of all such officers, as were in the army of the United States on the first of January, 1777, and who have since died whilst in the service, shall be entitled to the lands such officers would have respectively been entitled to if they had lived to the conclusion of the present war.

That the widows of all such officers aforesaid, and all officers of the

Line, who have died or may die in the service of the United States, before the conclusion of the war, shall be entitled to the half pay such officers would have been entitled to had they lived to the end of the war.

I.II.11 CONGRESS REQUIRES STATES TO SUPPORT THE ARMY

December 14, 1779, *Journals of the Continental Congress*, XV 1376–7

The Committee to whom was referred General Washington's letter of the 18 Nov: last, and other matters relative to recruiting the army, Beg leave further to report:

That for the ensuing campaign the several States be required to furnish by draught or otherwise, on or before the first day of April next, the Deficiency of their respective quotas of 80 Battalions of Infantry, as apportioned by a resolution of Congress of the 9th of March, 1779. (Passed.)

That the non-commissioned Officers and soldiers that are or may be enlisted in the several military Corps of the army, not included in the said 80 Battalions, be considered as part of the said quota and credited to the States to which such officers and soldiers respectively do or may belong. (Passed.)

That it be recommended to each State to make like provision for officers, and for the soldiers enlisted for the war, in the said Corps who shall continue in service until the establishment of Peace, and belong to the said State, as may be made for other officers and soldiers of its Battalion, pursuant to a Resolution of Congress of the 17th August last. (Passed.)

That the letter from General Washington of the 18 November last, and the abstract of the army enclosed therein, be referred to the Board of War, who are directed forthwith to report to Congress a list of the deficiencies of Troops to be furnished by the first of April next, and at other periods during the next campaign, by the several States, agreeable to the preceeding Resolves.

The Committee desire leave to sit again.

And the committee on supplies, brought in reports; which were read:

Resolved, That the committee on the letter of 18 November, have on their request leave to sit again.

Congress took into consideration the report of the committee on supplies, and thereupon came to the following resolution:

Whereas the aid of the several states is necessary in furnishing provisions for the army, and other supplies for carrying on the war; and justice requires that they be called upon to furnish their respective quotas at equitable prices:

Resolved, That all the states shall be called upon to furnish their quotas of such supplies as may, from time to time, be wanted for carrying on the war; and in making the requisitions, due care shall be taken to suit the convenience of the several states; and the articles by them respectively furnished shall be credited towards their quotas of the monies which they are called upon to raise for the United States, at equal prices for articles of the same kind and quality, and for others in due proportion; and the accounts shall be finally compared and adjusted so as to do equity to all the states.

On passing the foregoing resolution, the yeas and nays being required by Mr [James] Forbes,

State / Member	Vote	State vote
Massachusetts Bay,		
Mr Gerry,	ay	ay
Lovell,	ay	
Holten,	ay	
Partridge,	ay	
Rhode Island,		
Mr Ellery,	ay	ay
Connecticut,		
Mr Huntington,	ay	ay
Sherman,	ay	
New York,		
Mr Livingston,	ay	ay
Floyd,	ay	
L'Hommedieu,	ay	
New Jersey,		
Mr Fell,	ay	ay
Houston,	ay	

I.II.12 LOAN OFFICE ACCOUNTS

April 18, 1781, *Journals of the Continental Congress*, XIX 402–5

The committee consisting of Mr Duane, Mr Sharpe, Mr Wolcott appointed to 'estimate and state the amount of the debts due from the United States, with the necessary estimates for the current year as near as can be done, in order that the same may be laid before the respective legislatures' brought in a report;

That they have attended to this business; but from the unsettled condition of the publick accounts they can only give a general view of the publick debts.

By returns made to the Board of Treasury up to February 16, 1781, it appears that from the opening of the loan offices to the first day of March, 1778, there has

		Dollars		An. interest [Specie][1]
been borrowed, the sum of		7,313,306	Int. payable in bills on France	438,798 $\frac{31}{90}$
From last February, 1778, to dates of last returns, 53,245,138, valued [by the table of depreciation] at		4,962,172		297,703 $\frac{29}{90}$
Amount of bills of exchange drawn on commissioners and ministers at the Court of France, for payment of three years interest	1,316,394			
Do. drawn on ministers at that and other courts for supplies, and to answer pressing emergencies on account of deficiencies in the publick treasury	2,165,578			
Supplies by them purchased and sent over, for which payment has not been made, and of which no exact returns have yet been obtained, together with expences of commissioners and ministers abroad, estimated at	2,518,208	6,000,000		360,000
		18,275,478		
		Dollars	Int. payable in bills on France	An. interest [Specie]
Deduct for depreciation on money borrowed from 1st Sept. 1777, to 1st March, 1778		883,914		
Principal sum specie		17,391,564	An. Interest	1,096,528 $\frac{60}{90}$
Due to the army for pay and subsistance, up to the last of December, 1780, estimated		1,000,000		
		18,391,564		
Due to the civil officers of government		98,927		

[1] The words in brackets are in the report but not in the *Journal*.

Besides the above, there are large debts contracted by the quartermaster and commissary, for part of which they have settled with the persons who have furnished the supplies, and given them certificates, bearing interest, viz:		
The late quartermaster has returned debts settled	20,758,850	
Unsettled, (excluding those contracted in North Carolina, South Carolina and Georgia) estimated at	27,149,870	
The present quartermaster has not made returns; but as it is well known that he has not been supplied with money, whatever exertions have been made or supplies furnished in that department must have been on credit. It is to be presumed that the debts by him contracted up to 1 Jan. 1781, amount in specie to		500,000
The commissary of purchases has made returns of debts due in his department, amounting to	11,388,903	
To this is to be added what yet remains of the old currency unredeemed, suppose	160,000,000	
To which may be added for navy debts, &c., for debts due in the departments of the Board [of War], of the commissary general of military stores and the cloathier general, estimated at	10,702,377	
Total in continental at 75 for 1	230,000,000 is	3,066,666$\frac{2}{3}$
To which adding the new money issued in lieu of the old which is called in and destroyed		2,000,000
[Deficiency of civil list debts		8,927]
Total debts in specie		24,057,157$\frac{2}{3}$

I.II.13 CONGRESS LIMITS EMISSIONS OF PAPER MONEY

September 3, 1779, *Journals of the Continental Congress*, XV 1019

Congress proceeded to consider the second clause of the resolution moved the 1st instant, and the same being set aside; in lieu thereof,

On motion of Mr [Henry] Laurens, seconded by Mr [Elbridge] Gerry,

Congress came to the following resolution:

And whereas the sum emitted by Congress and now in circulation, amounts to 159,948,880 dollars, and the sum of 40,051,120 dollars remains to complete the two hundred million dollars above mentioned:

Resolved, That Congress will emit such part only of the said sum of forty millions fifty one thousand one hundred and twenty dollars, as shall be absolutely necessary for public exigencies before adequate supplies can be otherwise obtained, relying for such supplies on the exertions of the several states.

I.II.14 TREASURY DISBURSEMENTS AND ALLOCATIONS TO THE END OF 1781 IN OLD CONTINENTAL CURRENCY

E. James Ferguson, *The Power of the Purse* (Chapel Hill, 1961) pp. 28–9

		Specie Value (arbitrary valuation)
1775–1776	$ 20,064,666	$20,064,666
1777	26,426,333	24,986,646
1778	66,965,269	24,289,438
1779	149,703,856	10,794,620
	$263,160,124	$80,135,370
1780	$82,908,320	$2,500,000
	891,236 (new emission)	500,000
		$3,000,000
1781	$11,408,095	$ 285,202
	1,179,249 (new emission)	589,624
	320,049 specie	320,049
	747,590 (expended by financier)	747,590
		$1,942,465

I.II.15 DEPRECIATION OF OLD CONTINENTAL CURRENCY: CURRENCY REQUIRED TO PURCHASE $1·00 SPECIE

Ibid., p. 32

1777		*1778*		*1779*		*1780*		*1781*	
January	1·25	January	4·00	January	8·00	January	42·50	January	100·00
April	2·00	April	6·00	April	16·00	April	60·00	April	167·50
July	3·00	July	4·00	July	19·00	July	62·50		
October	3·00	October	5·00	October	30·00	October	77·50		

I.II.16 RECEIPTS AND EXPENDITURES, NOVEMBER 1, 1784–9

Ibid., pp. 236–7

November 1, 1784 (end of Morris's administration) to *December 31, 1784*

RECEIPTS

Balance in Treasury, Nov. 1		21,986	
Payments from or credits to states		54,740	
Other domestic incomes		2,758	
			79,484

EXPENDITURES

Administrative expenses		16,245	
Army		6,275	
Others		6,145	
Anticipations		32,379	
Balance in Treasury		18,440	
			79,484

1785

RECEIPTS

Balance in Treasury, Jan. 1		18,440	
Domestic incomes:			
Payments from or credits to states	378,866		
Others	26,278		
		405,144	
Foreign incomes:			
Dutch loan, etc.		208,802	
			632,386

EXPENDITURES

Domestic:			
Administration	85,715		
Army	132,372		
Others	65,084		
Debts and anticipations	97,439		
Balance in Treasury	41,902		
		422,512	
Foreign:			
Interest on Dutch loan		209,874	
			632,386

1786

RECEIPTS

Balance in Treasury, Jan. 1		41,902	
Domestic incomes:			
Payments from or credits to states	328,872		
Others	9,249		
		338,121	
Foreign incomes:		None	
Payments over receipts:		59,571	
			439,594

EXPENDITURES

Domestic:			
Administration	117,430		
Army	145,530		
Others	24,223		
Credit to South Carolina for supplies	27,730		
Past debts	49,681		
		364,594	
Foreign:			
Interest on Dutch loan		75,000	
			439,594

Domestic incomes:				Accumulated deficit:		59,571	
Payments from or credits to state	276,639			*Domestic:*			
Others	41,931			Administration	128,332		
		318,570		Army	160,406		
Foreign incomes:		4,909		Others	39,675		
				Payment of old accounts	9,318		
						337,731	
Payments over receipts and accumulated deficit:		105,815		*Foreign:*			
				Interest on Dutch loan		31,992	
			429,294				429,294

1788

Domestic incomes:				Accumulated deficit:		105,815	
Payments from or credits to states	261,679			*Domestic:*			
Others	77,909			Administration	94,610		
		339,588		Army	196,404		
Foreign incomes:		1,645		Others	96,104		
Payments over receipts and accumulated deficit:		174,189		Payment of old accounts	10,248		
						397,366	
				Foreign:		None	
				Discrepancy in indent account:		12,241	
			515,422				515,422

1789 (*incomplete*)

Domestic incomes:				Accumulated deficit:		174,189	
Payments from or credits to states	127,837			*Domestic:*			
Others	14,432			Administration	55,741		
		142,269		Army	78,311		
Foreign incomes:		None		Others	23,339		
Payments over receipts and accumulated deficit:		189,906		Payment of old accounts	595		
						157,986	
			332,175				332,175

I.II.17 CONGRESS REPUDIATES OLD CURRENCY AND ISSUES NEW

March 18, 1780, *Journals of the Continental Congress*, XVI 261–7

Deleted matter indicated thus, ⟨ ⟩.

Congress resumed the consideration of the report of the Committee of the Whole, and a motion being made by Mr [Thomas] Burke, seconded by Mr [Allen] Jones,

That the states be requested to pass laws enabling Congress to levy an impost of one per cent on all exports and imports, as a fund for sinking the emissions for carrying on the present war, to continue until a sum equal to the whole of the said emissions shall be collected.

Congress proceeded to the consideration of the report, which being debated by paragraphs was agreed to, as follows:

These United States having been driven into this just and necessary war, at a time when no regular civil governments were established, of sufficient energy to enforce the collection of taxes, or to provide funds for the redemption of such bills of credit as their necessities obliged them to issue; and before the powers of Europe were sufficiently convinced of the justice of their cause, or of the probable event of the controversy, to afford them aid or credit, in consequence of which, their bills increasing in quantity beyond the sum necessary for the purpose of a circulating medium, and wanting, at the same time, specific funds to rest on for their redemption, they have seen them daily sink in value, notwithstanding every effort that has been made to support the same; insomuch that they are now passed, by common consent, in most parts of these United States, at least 39-40ths below their nominal value, and still remain in a state of depreciation, whereby the community suffers great injustice, the public finances are deranged, and the necessary dispositions for the defence of the country are much impeded and perplexed; and whereas, as effectually to remedy these evils, for which purpose the United States are now become competent, their independence being well assured, their civil governments established and vigorous, and the spirit of their citizens ardent for exertion, it is necessary speedily to reduce the quantity of the paper medium in circulation, and to establish and appropriate funds that shall ensure the punctual redemption of the bills; therefore,

Resolved, That the several states continue to bring into the continental treasury, by taxes or otherwise, their full quotas of fifteen million dollars monthly, as assigned them by the resolution of the 7th of October, 1779; a clause in the resolution of the 23d of February last, for relinquishing two-thirds of the said quotas, to the contrary notwithstanding; and that the states be further called on to make provision for continuing to bring into the said treasury their like quotas monthly, to the month of April, 1781, inclusive:

That silver and gold be receivable in payment of the said quotas, at the rate of one Spanish milled dollar in lieu of 40 dollars of the bills now in circulation.

That the said bills, as paid in, except for the months of January and February past, which may be necessary for the discharge of past contracts, be not re-issued, but destroyed. <That the specie paid in on said quotas be appropriated solely to sinking the outstanding bills>. [Rejected.]

That as fast as the said bills shall be brought in to be destroyed, and funds shall be established, as hereafter mentioned, for other bills, other bills be issued, not to exceed, on any account, one-twentieth part of the nominal sum of the bills brought in to be destroyed.

That the bills which shall be issued, be redeemable in specie, within six years after the present, and bear an interest at the rate of five per centum per annum, to be paid also in specie at the redemption of the bills, or, at the election of the holder, annually, at the respective continental loan offices, in sterling bills of exchange, drawn by the United States on their commissioners in Europe, at four shillings and six pence sterling per dollar.

That the said new bills issue on the funds of individual states, for that purpose established, and be signed by persons appointed by them, and that the faith of the United States be also pledged for the payment of the said bills, in case any State on whose funds they shall be emitted, should, by the events of war, be rendered incapable to redeem them; which undertaking of the United States, and that of drawing bills of exchange, for payment of interest as aforesaid, <if demanded>, shall be endorsed on the bills to be emitted, and signed by a commissioner to be appointed by Congress for that purpose.

That the face of the bills to be emitted read as follows, viz.

The possessor of this bill shall be paid   Spanish milled dollars, by the 31 day of December, 1786, with interest, in like money, at the rate of five per cent. per annum, by the State of   , according to an act of the legislature of the said State, of the   day of   , 1780.

And the endorsement shall be as follows, viz.

⟨'The United States of America will pay this bill according to the face of it, if the State of should by any means fail of its redemption; and will also pay the interest annually in bills of exchange on their commissioners in Europe, at four shillings, six pence sterling, per dollar, if desired, – agreeable to a resolution of Congress of the day of March, 1780.'⟩ [Postponed.]

The United States ensure the payment of the within bill, and will draw bills of exchange for the interest annually, if demanded, according to a resolution of Congress of the 18 day of March, 1780.

That the said new bills shall be struck under the direction of the Board of Treasury, in due proportion for each State, according to their said monthly quotas, and lodged in the continental loan offices in the respective states, where the commissioner to be appointed by Congress, in conjunction with such persons as the respective states appoint, shall attend the signing of the said bills; which shall be compleated no faster than in the aforesaid proportion of one to twenty of the other bills brought in to be destroyed, and which shall be lodged for that purpose in the said loan offices.

That as the said new bills are signed and compleated, the states respectively, on whose funds they issue, receive six-tenths of them, and that the remainder be subject to the orders of the United States, and credited to the states on whose funds they are issued, the accounts whereof shall be adjusted agreeably to the resolution of the 6th of October, 1779.

That the said new bills be receivable in payment of the said monthly quotas, at the same rate as aforesaid of specie; the interest thereon to be computed to the respective states, to the day the payment becomes due.

That the respective states be charged with such parts of the interest on their said bills, as shall be paid by the United States, in bills of exchange; and the accounts thereof shall be adjusted agreeably to the resolution aforesaid, of the 6th of October, 1779.

That whenever interest on the bills to be emitted shall be paid prior to their redemption, such bills shall be thereupon exchanged for others of the like tenor, to bear date from the expiration of the year for which such interest is paid.

That the several states be called on to provide funds for their quotas of the said new bills, to be so productive as to sink or redeem one sixth part of them annually, after the 1st. day of January next.

That nothing in the foregoing resolutions shall be construed to ascertain the proportions of the expence incurred by the war, which each state on a final adjustment ought to be charged with, or to exclude the claims of any State to have the prices at which different states have furnished supplies for the army hereafter taken into consideration and equitably adjusted.

That the foregoing resolutions, with a letter from the President, be despatched to the executive of the several states, and that they be requested to call their assemblies, if not already convened, as speedily as possible, to take them into immediate consideration, to establish ample and certain funds for the purposes therein mentioned, and to take every other measure necessary to carry the same into full and vigorous effect, and that they transmit their acts for that purpose to Congress without delay.

On passing the foregoing resolutions, the yeas and nays were required by Mr [Allen] Jones,

New Hampshire,		
Mr Peabody,	no	div.
Folsom,	ay	
Massachusetts Bay,		
Mr Lovell,	ay	ay
Holten,	ay	
Partridge,	ay	
Rhode Island,		
Mr Ellery,	ay	ay
Collins,	ay	
Connecticut,		
Mr Huntington,	ay	ay
Sherman,	ay	
Ellsworth,	ay	
New York,		
Mr Livingston,	ay	ay
Floyd,	ay	
L'Hommedieu,	ay	
Schuyler,	ay	
Scott,	ay	
New Jersey,		
Mr Fell,	no	ay
Houston,	ay	
Clark,	ay	
Pennsylvania,		
Mr Searle,	ay	ay
Muhlenberg,	ay	
McLene,	ay	
Shippen,	ay	
Delaware,		
Mr McKean,	no	no
Maryland,		
Mr Plater,	no	*
Virginia,		
Mr Griffin,	no	no
North Carolina,		
Mr Burke,	no	no
Jones,	no	
South Carolina,		
Mr Mathews,	no	no

So it passed in the affirmative.

I.II.18 EXPRESSIONS OF ANXIETY ABOUT SPECULATION AND DEPRECIATION OF THE CURRENCY

James Madison to Joseph Jones, Philadelphia, October 24, 1780, in *Letters of the Continental Congress*, ed. E. C. Burnett (Washington, D.C., 1931) V 427–8

Dear Sir: Your favor of the 9th which ought to have come on Monday last did not arrive till thursday. That of the 17th came yesterday according to expectation.

I wish it was in my power to enable you to satisfy the uneasiness of people with respect to the disappointment in foreign succour. I am sensible of the advantage which our secret enemies take of it. I am persuaded, also that those who ought to be acquainted with the cause are sensible of it; and as they give no intimations on the subject it is to be inferred they are unable to give any that would prevent the mischief. It is so delicate a subject, that with so little probability of succeeding, it would perhaps be hardly prudent to suggest it. As soon as any solution comes out you shall be furnished with it. . . .

We continue to receive periodical alarms from the Commissary's and Quarter Master's departments. The season is now arrived when provision ought to be made for a season that will not admit of transportation, and when the monthly supplies must be subject to infinite disappointments even if the States were to do their duty. But instead of Magazines being laid in our army is living from hand to mouth, with a prospect of being soon in a condition still worse. How a total dissolution of it can be prevented in the course of the winter is for any resources now in prospect utterly inexplicable, unless the States unanimously make a vigorous and speedy effort to form magazines for the purpose. But unless the States take other methods to procure their specific supplies than have prevailed in most of them, the utmost efforts to comply with the requisitions of Congress can be only a temporary relief. This expedient as I take it was meant to prevent the emission of money. Our own experience as well as the example of other Countries made it evident that we could not by taxes draw back to the treasury the emissions as fast as they were necessarily drawn out. We could not follow the example of other Countries by borrowing, neither our own Citizens nor foreigners being willing to lend as far as our wants extended. To continue to emit *ad infinitum.* was thought more dangerous than an absolute occlusion of the press. Under these circumstances the expedient of specific requisitions was adopted for supplying the necessities of the war. But it is clear the success of this expedient depends on the mode of carrying it into execution. If instead of executing it by specific taxes, State emissions or Commissary's and Q. Master's certificates which are a worse species of emissions are recurred to, what was intended for our relief will only hasten our destruction. . . .

James Madison to the Governor of Virginia (Thomas Jefferson), Philadelphia, May 5, 1781, ibid. (1933) VI 79–80

Sir: The Executive of New Jersey in consequence of authority vested in them by the Legislature for that purpose, by an Act of the 27th Ulto. established the rate of exchange between the old continental currency and the bills issued pursuant to the Act of Congress of the 18th of March 1780, to be 150 for 1. The Speculation arising from this measure to the prejudice of this State with the other reasons stated in the inclosed publication by the Executive Council led to their act of the 2d instant therein referred to declaring the rate between the two kinds of money above mentioned to be 175 for 1. The effect of this declaration has been a confusion among the people of this City approaching nearly to tumult, a total Stop to the circulation of the old money, and a considerable stagnation and increased depreciation of the new.[1] The difference between the latter and hard money is at present vibrating

[1] The following appeared in the *Royal Gazette*, May 13: THE CONGRESS'S FINAL BANKRUPTCY: 'By a person arrived from Philadelphia, we are informed that last Saturday [i.e., May 5] a large body of the inhabitants with paper dollars in their hats by way of cockades, paraded the streets of Philadelphia, carrying colours flying, with a DOG TARR'D, and instead of the usual appendage and ornament of feathers, his back was covered with the Congress's paper Dollars, this example of disaffection immediately under the eyes of the rulers of the revolted provinces in solemn session at the State House assembled, was directly followed by the Jailor, who refused accepting bills in purchase of a glass of rum, and afterwards by the traders of the city, who shut up their shops, declining to sell any more goods but for gold or silver; it was declared also by the popular voice, that if the opposition to Great Britain was not in future carried on by solid money instead of paper bills, all further resistance to the mother country were in vain, and must be given up. . . .'

from 4 to 1 downwards. Should the Circulation of the former therefore revive, its value can not exceed 1/700 of that of hard money. The opportunity which this circumstance gives and which we have reason to believe many are already taking measures to improve, of fraudulent speculation not only on the Citizens of Virginia, but on the State itself, is so obvious and alarming that we thought it our duty to set an Express in immediate motion to put you on your guard against the mischief.

The Virginia delegates to the Governor of Virginia (Thomas Jefferson), Philadelphia, May 8, 1781, ibid., p. 80

S'r: Having so lately and so often wrote to your Excellency we have little new to Communicate at present; the confusion respecting money still continues in this City, tho with less commotion than could be expected as in a few days the old Continental money has depreciated from two hundred to seven, eight, and some say nine Hundred for one. the new money has of course suffered in proportion – what this Convulsion will end in, it is difficult to surmise. in the mean time we are in infinite distress as may be easily supposed; the Currency of the old money has been sto[pped] for some days past and it is said to day that the new is about to share the same fate.

Daniel Carroll to the Governor of Maryland (Thomas Sim Lee), Philadelphia, May 8, 1781, ibid. p. 81

Dear Sir: I wrote you a few lines last saturday informing you that large Sums of the old Continental money were sent to the Southward to be got rid of immediately in consequence of the Step taken by the Executive of this State. The enclosed paper contains a publication of the President and Council explaining their motives. The confusion still subsists in this city. I believe little or nothing can be bought here at present for the old money at any rate.[1]

[1] James Swan wrote to Dr John Witherspoon, from Boston, May 24: 'I received yours of the 8th instant. . . . The immense sums forced in here from your quarter, has entirely stopped the circulation and value of the old paper currency. The new is going fast – there has been most horrible doings by speculators from Philadelphia. I am very fortunate in being but slightly effected by the wreck.' *Royal Gazette*, June 13, 1781.

Samuel Johnston to James Iredell, Philadelphia, May 8, 1781, ibid. pp. 81–2

Dear Sir: . . . The great and sudden fall of the old Continental money, has occasioned very great convulsions and Dissatisfaction in this city, and has reduced all paper currency to a very doubtful state, very many refusing to have anything to do with it. We have no official accounts from General Greene or the Southern Army since the beginning of last month. Report says he has turned his face towards Camden – if so, I doubt not he had good reason for his conduct. Mr Robert Morris is appointed to superintend the finances of the United States. Great matters are expected from this gentleman's abilities. The finances of no country were at any time more deranged or more in want of wisdom and political knowledge to make them effectual.

James Lovell to Samuel Holten, May 8, 1781,[1] ibid. p. 83

Dear Sir: Your Favor of the 26. of April reached me yesterday. Your Troops are coming on 'in large numbers'. The General informs you that Tents etc. will be much wanted; and the Court will make their 'usual Exertions'. Indeed Doctor I am persuaded that in a Comparative View Massachusetts will appear to have been among the most vigorous States; but we are at this moment in the most disgraceful and hazardous Situation from the Backwardness of every individual State. Foreign Troops are to garison West Point because foreign Troops *can* feed themselves, and *are* paid. Our Quar'r Mast'r genl. has been obliged to sell some of his provision to enable himself to *transport* the rest to a Skeliton of an Army in Want of the very Pounds of meat or Flour which he has been forced to part with. If you know of a Compliance with one Requisition of Congress, *in Time and Quantity*, do let me have it that I may show it to the Delegates of the 12 States who cannot produce a single Instance.

We are in an Uproar here about the Money. Sailors with Clubs parade the Streets instead of working for Paper. The Beer houses demand hard for a Pot of Drink; and all this because the Council have

[1] Preceding this letter in the volume named is a brief letter of the same date, evidently written later in the day, and touching upon some of the same matters. Then follows this remark: 'I scratched a Letter and would not trust it to the Post. Perhaps I shall send it by Mr Payne who goes tomorrow.' It was, no doubt, the letter here printed that he was unwilling to trust to the post.

published that the difference between Silver and old Continental was 174, the latter having been sold 180 and 200 for one several Days. Did Massachusetts sink its Quota by the 1st of April? Some States had not then begun to sink a Shilling.

You say Mr Partridge and Mr Osgood are coming on: I ask with what money in their Pockets? That of our State is not counted money here. The old continental is dying by Yards not Inches. . . .

The Connecticut delegates to the Governor of Connecticut (Jonathan Trumbull), Philadelphia, July 12, 1781, ibid. p. 142

Sir: We were honored with your Excellency's letter of the 18th of last month, and are well pleased with the measures taken by the Hon. General Assembly, therein mentioned. It is the wish of Congress, as well as of the people in general this way, to get rid of paper currency; it greatly embarasses our affairs; it is but little used here in any trade or dealing, and not at all in the market; the prices of many articles of country produce are near as low for hard money (as) they were before the war. The new continental and State bills are not better than five for one specie; the issuing them at that rate, if they are to be redeemed at par, must be a very great loss to the public. We are glad that the State we have the honor to represent has determined to issue no more bills of credit, and that those now outstanding are likely to be soon redeemed in a way that will do justice to the possessors and the public.

. . . No Journals of Congress have been printed since December for want of money to pay the expence. The regulation of the clothing department has been lately altered, and the several States excused from procuring any account of the United States after the first day of September next. We opposed the measure, being of opinion that the army will suffer for want of clothing, if not supplied by the particular States, also that many articles of clothing can be provided by the people easier than they can raise hard money to purchase them. We have the satisfaction to find that General Washington has the same apprehensions with us as to the first particular, which will probably induce Congress to reconsider it.

The State of Massachusetts has applied to Congress for justice with respect to the old continental bills in that State, whose currency is now at an end; the matter is under the consideration of a Committee. . . .

III Economic Proposals and Policies Affecting the Articles of Confederation

I.III.1 PLANS FOR A CONTINENTAL IMPOST

November 8, 1780, *Journals of the Continental Congress*, XVIII 1033–5

Deleted matter indicated thus, ⟨ ⟩

The Committee of Estimates and of Ways and Means delivered in a report.

The Committee of Ways and Means, Report,

Whereas it is necessary in order to provide funds for the discharge of such foreign debts as the United States have already contracted and to enable them to make such further loans as the public Exigencies may require That certain stated revenues be assigned for ⟨that⟩ those purpose[s]:

Resolved, That it be recommended to the Legislatures of each of the United States to impose without delay a duty of two and one half per cent on all exports being of the growth or manufacture of ⟨either⟩ any of the said States or the produce of the fisheries and a similar duty upon all imports except military stores and except also cloathing ⟨imported⟩ on account of the United States.

Resolved, That in order to prevent frauds in the collection of such duties it be recommended to the several States to vest the appointment of the officers necessary for that purpose in Congress.

Resolved, That all such duties be paid in specie *or in kind*.

Resolved, That the money raised by such duties be applied to the discharge of such debts as have been or may be hereafter contracted with foreign powers and to no other use whatever.

Resolved, That Books containing a true state of such debts be open at the Treasury Board for the inspection of the Delegates or Agents of the respective States ⟨to the inspection of the legislatures of every State by their respective committees⟩ and that the said duties cease when the said foreign debts are discharged.

Resolved, That ⟨a committee be appointed to⟩ the Board of Treasury adjust a tariff of all exports and imports and ⟨to⟩ form a plan for the collection of such duties that the same being adopted by the respective Legislatures may render the system equal and uniform.

Resolved, That it be recommended to every State that shall have passed laws ⟨above recommended⟩ for the purposes aforesaid to repeal all ⟨laws containing⟩ embargoes and restrictions on trade ⟨and embargoes now in force in such state⟩ taking care at the same time that their several quota of supplies for the Army be ⟨provided⟩ effectually secured.

Resolved, That the Treasury take immediate measures to ascertain the value of the exports and imports from and into the several ⟨ports of the United⟩ States and lay before Congress an estimate thereof.

Resolved, That copies of such estimates be transmitted to the Minister of the United States at the Court of Versailles and Madrid, and that they be empowered to enter into stipulations for the repayment ot such sums of money as they may borrow, out of the said funds and pledge the faith of the United States to make up any deficiency in the same.

And whereas Congress have recommended to the States of Virginia and Maryland to raise by Assessment upon their respective Inhabitants a certain quantity of Tobacco amounting to –

And whereas it appears by a return from Virginia that they will have on hand 4000 hogsheads by the 1st. day of Jany. next.

Resolved, That ⟨Dr Franklin⟩ the minister at the Court of Versailles of these States be directed to pledge the same for the repayment of a sum of Money equal to its value with 5 pr. Cent interest the same to be ⟨paid⟩ delivered at some port in Chesapeake Bay.

Resolved, That it be recommended to the said States of Virginia and Maryland to take the necessary measures for the delivery of the Tobacco assessed on the said States to the order of the Minister of the United States at the Court of ⟨his most Christian Majesty⟩ Versailles.

⟨*Resolved,* That Bills of Exchange to the Amt. of £100,000 sterg. be drawn on Mr Jay at 6 months sight and disposed of under the directions of the Board of Treasury at par for specie or *new Bills* of Credit issued agreeable to the resolutions of the 18th. March last or for the highest exchange in the Bills of Credit emitted by Congress.

Resolved, That Bills of Exchange to the Amt. of £30,000 sterlg. be drawn on Doctr. [Franklin] to be disposed of on like condition as above by the Board of Treasury,⟩

And whereas it is absolutely necessary to assign some fixed and stated revenue to be applied to the use of the navy that ⟨they may be enabled⟩ more effectual ⟨ly to protect⟩ protection may be afforded to the trade of these United States.

Resolved, That it be recommended to the Legislatures of the respective States to impose a duty of 5 pr. Cent on the value of all prizes ⟨taken from the enemy⟩ to be collected by officers of the United States empowered by each State for that purpose which impost shall be applied solely to the use of the navy of the United States.

Congress took into consideration the draught of the circular letter; and after debate,

Ordered, That it be re-committed.

Adjourned to 10 o'Clock to Morrow.

December 18, 1780, ibid. 1157–65

The committee appointed to prepare instructions;

The committee for regulating the finances of the United States; and

The Committee for regulating the Finances of America &c. &c beg leave to report.

That to establish the national credit furnish a proper circulating medium support the credit of the bills issued by the States in pursuance of the act of Congress passed the 18th. of March last it will be necessary for the Confederation to be ratified.

The exclusive right to duties arising on certain imported articles herein after mentioned to be vested in Congress.

The old Continental Bills taken out of circulation.

The States called upon to establish funds for redemption of the new Bills.

That every reasonable encouragement be given to exportation. High duties laid upon all articles of luxury imported.

That Congress be vested with a power of laying Embargoes in time of war.

And that a loan be solicited from the Inhabitants of these States to the amount of six millions of dollars in specie to supply the deficiency of a circulating medium which has happened by some of the States being unable to call in their Quotas of the old Emissions and establishing funds to support the credit of Bills of the new Emission.

That the specie so obtained be deposited in a Bank for the purpose of effectually supporting the credit of the New Bills and redeeming such Bank notes as may be issued thereon agreeable to the plan hereafter proposed.

Your Committee therefore beg leave to submit the following resolutions viz.

Resolved, That the State of Maryland be requested to accede to the Confederation on or before the last day of March next, and in case of neglect or refusal that the other twelve States be called upon to confederate independent of that State.

That it be recommended to the States respectively to pass laws establishing funds for paying the interest and redeeming the Bills emitted in consequence of the act of the 18th. of March last [Postponed.] ⟨which funds are not to be altered or the laws establishing the same repealed but by advice or consent of Congress until the redemption of said Bills is compleated.

That for enabling Congress to restrain the importation of Foreign articles of luxury; being the ballance of trade in favor of the United States, and support the credit of a paper medium.⟩ It be recommended to the respective States as indispensibly necessary that they pass laws granting to Congress for the use of the United States from the first day of May next four pr cent upon the value of all goods, as well prize goods as others at the time and place of importation, duties upon all articles of Foreign growth or manufacture which may be imported into either of the States from any Foreign Port Island or Plantation after the said first day of May 1781. [Agreed.]

⟨Madeira wine 8d. per Gallon

Port Lisbon and Teneriffe wine 6d. per Gallon.

Porter 6d. per Gallon

Rum 6d. per Gallon

Green Tea 2s. per pound

Bohea Tea 1s. per pound.

Jewellry 100 pr cent.

China 50 pr cent

Silks of all kinds for garments or ornaments 5/– per yard.

Broad cloaths above 12/– sterling price, 5/– per yard.

Narrow cloaths above 5/– Sterlg 2/– per yard.

Gilt Furniture 100 pr cent.

Mahogany furniture of all kinds 100 pr cent.

Linnens above 2/6 Sterlg. 1 shilling per yard.

Gold and silver ornaments for men and women 100 per cent.

Hats above 15/– Sterlg cost 5/

Double and Treble refined sugar 6do. per lb

Gaming Tables of all kinds 100 per cent.
Carriages of all kinds 100 per cent.
Stuffs woolen and silk and silk and woolen 1/ pr yard.
Men's and women's silk hose 5/ per pair.
Silk Gloves 2/6 per pair
Silk Handkerchiefs 2/6 per pc
Gauze 3/ per yard.
Lawns and Muslins 4/ per yard
Silk velvet 5/ per yard.
Cotton do 3/ per yard.
Cambricks 5/ per yard.
Carpeting 100 per cent
Wrought marble 100 per cent
Playing cards 1/ per pack
Dice 1/ per sett.
Spices of all kinds 2/6 per lb
Tobacco pipes 6/ per groce
Cheese 1/ per pound.
6 pence per ton on all vessels of more than 20 Tons burthen.⟩

Resolved, that the above duties be paid in specie at the rate of six shillings per Dollar or coined silver at six shillings and eight pence per ounce which shall be the standard of calculation throughout the United States. [Postponed.]

Resolved, That it be recommended to the Legislatures of the several States, to take effectual measures for calling in and cancelling their Quotas of the Bills of credit issued by Congress previous to the 18th. day of March last agreeable to and by the time mentioned in the act of Congress of that date or sooner if possible in order that such Bills may have no further circulation in any State after its Quota shall be called in and cancelled. And to establish permanent and substantial funds (where it is not already done) for redemption of the new Bills, issued agreeable to the before mentioned act. And to take every possible measure for supporting the credit of the new Bills. [Postponed.]

And that it be further recommended to the respective Legislatures to call out of circulation as soon as shall be consistent with their public faith pledged by their acts for emitting the same all their State emissions and not to issue any more but by advice or consent of Congress that the paper bills in circulation flowing from one source may be readily ascertained. [Agreed.]

⟨That in all debts due to or from the United States Congress will receive and pay the bills of credit emitted pursuant to the act of the 18th. of March last equal with silver and gold.⟩

Resolved, That it be recommended to the respective Legislatures, to pass laws impowering Congress to lay Embargoes in time of war and that when Embargoes are not laid they give all just and reasonable encouragement to exportation and use all means in their power to prevent the importation of Foreign Articles of luxury. [Postponed.]

That in order to procure a Loan of six millions of dollars in specie: a subscription be immediately opened in the respective States for coined and uncoined Gold, Silver and Copper to that amount which is to be received by the Treasurers of the respective States at its real value, viz. Coined Gold, silver and copper at its present current value. [Postponed.]

New wrought silver plate.

Old silver plate at six shillings and eight pence per ounce.

That the money, bullion and copper so received be forwarded by the respective States to the seat of Congress, where a bank is to be established and supported in which the same is to be deposited. [Postponed.]

That all the plate and copper so received and deposited be coined into such pieces of money as Congress may from time to time direct.

Resolved, That Congress proceed to appoint a Director and other proper officers to manage and transact the business of the Bank.

Resolved, that a share in the Bank shall be fifty dollars, and that the respective Treasurers issue no receipt for less than half a share which if made up by divers persons shall be receipted for to one of them only, who is to be accountable to the other proprietors interested.

Resolved that the respective Treasurers keep a fair register of all money and plate received, of all receipts given and of the names of the persons to whom given, and transmit the same to the Director of the Bank, who is to enter the same in the Bank Books that such persons may be known and considered as proprietors in the Bank.

Resolved, That the receipt given be in the following form viz.

Resolved, That the receipt given and entry made as aforesaid shall entitle the lender to receive his interest and one twelfth part of his principal annually if demanded, which is to be paid only to the original lender or his order unless the stock is by him transferred by Testament,

Bill of Sale, Letter of Attorney or Entry in the Books with a delivery over the receipt which shall entitle the purchaser or legatee to have the stock transferred to him on the Books, and to receive the advantages thereof.

Resolved, that if any proprietor of the Bank, shall die intestate his interest in the Bank shall be vested in his administrator in the same manner as other personal estate.

Resolved, that as security for payment of the principal and interest of the sums lent as aforesaid the several States be and are hereby requested to pass acts: laying duties upon exports, tonnage, or upon such other articles as may be found most convenient for raising annually in specie their respective quotas of the interest and a twelfth part of the principal as aforesaid in the proportion in the annexed calculation, (Vide paper No. 1) which sums are to be forwarded by the respective States and deposited in the Bank by the first day of September annually for the purposes aforesaid.

Resolved, That as a farther security for the punctual payment of the sums lent as aforesaid: The duties collected upon imported articles be also lodged in the Bank and appropriated to the payment of said notes so far as will make up any deficiency that may happen by the States not forwarding their respective Quotas, in due time for discharging the interest and twelfth part of the principal as aforesaid.

And that the surplus of said duties on imports be appropriated to the redemption of the Bills issued in pursuance of the Act of Congress passed the 18th. day of March last.

Resolved, that upon the money so borrowed and deposited in Bank, as well as upon all public monies the property of the United States; arising from Loans, the sale of Lands or other public property the surplus of imposts or taxes Congress may strike Bank notes signed by the Director payable at the Bank in specie on demand: in different sums from one hundred dollars to one eighth of a dollar which notes are to be redeemed at the Bank on sight.

Resolved, that Congress may issue the whole or any part of the money in specie, or may issue notes on part, and reserve such part for negotiations as may from time to time appear necessary, but are in no case to draw specie from the Bank so as to leave a less sum in stock than will pay the whole of the Bank notes in circulation.

Resolved, That when stock receipts shall be lost in any case, or when Bank notes shall be lost consumed or destroyed where silver and gold would not have been liable to the same accident: upon proper evidence thereof being given to the satisfaction of the managers of the Bank, or a major part of them: the owners shall receive other receipts or notes, of the same tenor and date.

Resolved, that the Bank notes be in the following form viz.

Whereas, The Congress of the United States have recommended to the several and respective Legislatures to pass laws for restraining the importation of Foreign articles of luxury; as the most effectual means for encouraging industry, bringing the ballance of trade in favor of the United States and increasing the national wealth –

Be it therefore enacted by –, That from and after the first day of April 1781 there shall be raised levied collected and paid within this State for the purposes of redeeming the paper Bills of Credit issued for defraying the public expence and to remain at the disposal of Congress for the aforesaid purposes the several Rates and Duties herein after mentioned for and upon all articles of foreign growth or manufacture hereafter mentioned which may be imported into this State from any foreign port market Island or Plantation viz.

Upon Madeira wine 8d. per Gal
Port, Lisbon and Teneriffe wine 6d. per do
Porter 6d. per Gallon
Rum 6d. per Gallon
Green Tea 2/ per lb
Bohea Tea 1/ pr lb
Jewellry 100 pr cent
China 50 per cent.
Silks of all kinds for garments or ornaments 5/ p yard.
Broad Cloth above 12/ Stg. pr yard 5/ per yard.
Narrow do above 5/ Sterling 2/ per yard
Gilt furniture of all kinds 100 pr cent.
Mahogany furniture of all sorts 100 pr cent
Linnens above 2/6 Sterg. 1/ per yard
Gold and silver ornaments for men and women 100 per cent.
Hats above 15/ Sterg. 5/
Double and Treble refined sugar 6d. per lb
Gaming tables of all kinds 100 per cent
Stuffs woolen and silk and silk and woollen 1/ per yard
Carriages of all kinds 100 per cent.
Men's and women's silk hose 5/ per pair.

Silk Gloves 2/6 pr pair	Carpeting 100 per cent
Silk Handkerchiefs 2/6.	Wrought marble 100 per cent
Gauze 3/ per yard	Playing cards 1/ per pack
Lawns and muslins 4/ pr yd.	Dice 1/ per sett
Silk velvet 5/ per yd.	Spices of all kinds 2/6 per lb.
Cotton do 3/ per yd.	Tobacco Pipes 6/ per groce
Cambricks 5/ per yd.	Cheese 1/ per lb.

Six pence per ton on all vessels of more than 20 Tons burthen.

The above duties to be paid in specie at the rate of 6/8d. pr ounce for coined silver.

And be it further enacted that the Congress of the United States may from time to time establish within this State such Custom Houses and appoint such officers to collect said duties as may appear necessary, and that every aid protection and assistance shall be given to such officers in the execution of their office.

And be it further enacted that when any of the before mentioned articles of Foreign Growth or manufacture shall be imported into any port or Haven in this State an entry thereof shall be made by the master or commander of the ship or vessel importing the same within forty eight hours after arrival of said vessel in port and the duties paid thereon or bond given therefor before breaking bulk.

And be it further enacted by the authority aforesaid, that all articles of Foreign Growth or manufactures before enumerated which shall be shipped at any Foreign Port Island or Plantations and landed or attempted to be landed at any Port or place within this State not having been cleared out for some Port in the United States and entered at the Custom House as aforesaid the same shall be forfeited together with the vessel importing the same with all her tackle furniture and cargo for the use of the United States.

And be it further enacted by the authority aforesaid, that all articles before enumerated which shall be imported from ports for any Port or Haven in this State shall be entered at the Custom House within forty eight hours under penalty of vessel and cargo.

And be it further enacted that the secretaries and other officers of the customs appointed by Congress shall have liberty to enter and search all vessels coming into any Port in this State without molestation, and in case of resistance may apply to any justice of the Peace within said State who shall forthwith order proper assistance for searching the vessels and securing the person making such resistance, and the Justice is hereby directed to bind such offender over to the next court of sessions who upon conviction shall sentence him to pay a fine not exceeding one thousand pounds.

And be it further enacted that all articles imported into this State for and on account of the United States shall be free from imposts, and the vessel importing the same exempted from paying tonnage provided said vessel so exempted from paying tonnage shall be principally freighted with articles for the use of the United States.

And be it further enacted that any officer of the Customs appointed by Congress in this State may sue for and recover in the name and for the use of the United States the several penalties fines and forfeitures aforesaid in any court proper to try the same.

This act to remain in force for the term of twelve years unless sooner repealed by advice or consent of Congress.

Resolved, That in order to facilitate the aforesaid Loans the following address to the Inhabitants of the United States be forwarded to the respective Legislatures to be by them communicated to the people.

And that it be recommended to them to use all the influence in their power to promote and forward the same. (Vide paper No. 2.)

February 3, 1781, ibid. XIX 112–13

The report from the Committee of the Whole, being amended, was agreed to as follows:

Resolved, That it be recommended to the several states, as indispensably necessary,[1] that they <pass laws granting to> vest a power in Congress, to levy for the use of the United States, a duty of five per cent. *ad valorem,* at the time and place of importation, upon all goods, wares and merchandises of foreign growth and manufactures, which may be imported into any of the said states from any foreign port, island or plantation, after the first day of May, 1781; except arms, ammunition, cloathing and other articles imported on account of the United States, or any of them; and except wool-cards and cotton-cards, and wire for making them; and also, except salt, during the war:

Also, a like duty of five per cent. on all prizes and prize goods <taken on the high seas and brought into any of the said states and

[1] From this point the entries are by George Bond.

libelled and⟩ condemned in the court of admiralty of any of these states as lawful prize:

⟨That the monies arising from the said duties be paid quarterly into the hands of such persons as Congress shall appoint to receive the same.⟩

That the monies arising from the said duties be appropriated to the discharge of the principal and interest of the debts already contracted, or which may be contracted, on the faith of the United States, for supporting the present war:

That the said ⟨laws be continued in force and the⟩ duties ⟨aforesaid collected and paid as aforesaid⟩ be continued until the said debts shall be fully and finally discharged.[1]

I.III.2 ROBERT MORRIS AS SUPERINTENDENT OF FINANCE

Morris to the President of Congress, Philadelphia, May 17, 1781, *Revolutionary Diplomatic Correspondence of the United States*, ed. F. Wharton (Washington, 1889) IV 421

Sir: I beg to submit the enclosed plan for establishing a national bank in these United States and the observations on it to the perusal and consideration of Congress.

Anticipation of taxes and funds is all that ought to be expected from any system of paper credit. This seems as likely to rise into a fabric equal to the weight as any I have yet seen or thought of; and I submit

[1] At this point Charles Thomson resumed the entries. A copy of this report, in the writing of Charles Thomson, is in the *Papers of the Continental Congress*, no. 36, IV, folio 43. The following is indorsed 'Motion for amendment'. It is in James Madison's writing, and is in the *Papers of the Continental Congress*, no. 36, IV, folio 263:

That it be earnestly recommended to the States, as indespensably necessary to the support of public credit and the prosecution of the War immediately to pass laws laying an impost of 5 pr. cent ad valorem on all goods wares and merchandises imported into them respectively after the 1st. day of May next from any foreign port Island or plantation; to vest Congress with full power to collect and to appropriate the same to the discharge of the principal and interest of all debts already contracted or which may be contracted on the faith of the United States during the present war, and to give to the officers which shall be appointed by Congress to collect the said impost all the legal authorities necessary to the ⟨punctual⟩ execution of his duty.

whether it may not be necessary and proper that Congress should make immediate application to the several States to invest them with the powers of incorporating a bank, and for prohibiting all other banks or bankers in these States, at least during the war.

Morris to the Governors of the States, Philadelphia, July 25, 1781, ibid. 601–4

Sir: I had the honor to write to you on the – instant, enclosing a certified copy of the account of your State as it stands in the treasury books of the United States. I now pray leave to recall your attention to it.

It gives me very great pain to learn that there is a pernicious idea prevalent among some of the States that their accounts are not to be adjusted with the continent. Such an idea can not fail to spread listless languor over all our operations. To suppose this expensive war can be carried on without joint and strenuous efforts is beneath the wisdom of those who are called to the high offices of legislation. Those who inculcate maxims which tend to relax these efforts most certainly injure the common cause, whatever may be the motives which inspire their conduct. If once an opinion is admitted that those States who do the least and charge most will derive the greatest benefit and endure the smallest evils, your excellency must perceive that shameless inactivity must take the place of that noble emulation which ought to pervade and animate the whole Union. It is my particular duty, while I remind my fellow-citizens of the tasks which it is incumbent on them to perform, to remove, if I can, every impediment which lies in the way, or which may have been raised by disaffection, self-interest, or mistake. I take, therefore, this early opportunity to assure you that all the accounts of the several States with the United States shall be speedily liquidated if I can possibly effect it, and my efforts for that purpose shall be unceasing. I make this assurance in the most solemn manner, and I entreat that the consequences of a contrary assertion may be most seriously weighed and considered before it is made or believed.

These accounts naturally divide themselves into two considerable branches, viz, those which are subsequent to the resolutions of Congress of the 18th of March, 1780.[1] The former must be adjusted as

[1] It stands thus in the manuscript, but there seems to be an omission of what is meant by the *first branch* of the accounts. – Sparks.

soon as proper officers can be found and appointed for the purpose and proper principles established, so as that they may be liquidated in an equitable manner. I say, sir, in an equitable manner; for I am determined that justice shall be the rule of my conduct as far as the measure of abilities which the Almighty has been pleased to bestow shall enable me to distinguish between right and wrong. I shall never permit a doubt that the States will do what is right; neither will I ever believe that any one of them can expect to derive advantage from doing what is wrong. It is by being just to individuals, to each other, to the Union, to all; by generous grants of solid revenue, and by adopting energetic methods to collect that revenue; and not by complainings, vauntings, or recriminations, that these States must expect to establish their independence and rise into power, consequence, and grandeur. I speak to your excellency with freedom, because it is my duty so to speak, and because I am convinced that the language of plain sincerity is the only proper language to the first magistrate of a free community.

The accounts I have mentioned as subsequent to the resolutions of the 18th of March, 1780, admit of an immediate settlement. The several States have all the necessary materials. One side of this account consists of demands made by resolutions of Congress long since forwarded; the other must consist of the compliances with those demands. This latter part I am not in a capacity to state, and for that reason I am to request the earliest information which the nature of things will permit of the moneys, supplies, transportation, &c., which have been paid, advanced, or furnished by your State, in order that I may know what remains due. The sooner full information can be obtained the sooner shall we know what to rely on, and how to do equal justice to those who have contributed and those who have not; to those who have contributed at one period and those who have contributed at another.

I enclose an account of the specific supplies demanded of your State, as extracted from the journals of Congress, but without any mention of what has been done in consequence of those resolutions; because, as I have already observed, your excellency will be able to discover the balance much better than I can.

I am further to entreat, sir, that I may be favored with copies of the several acts passed in your State since the 18th of March, 1780, for the collection of taxes and the furnishing supplies or other aids to the United States, the manner in which such acts have been executed, the times which may have been necessary for them to operate, and the consequences of their operation. I must also pray to be informed of so much of the internal police of your State as relates to the laying, assessing, levying, and collecting taxes. I beg leave to assure your excellency that I am not prompted either by an idle curiosity or by any wish to discover what prudence would dictate to conceal. It is necessary that I should be informed of these things, and I take the plain, open, candid method of acquiring information. To palliate or conceal any evils or disorders in our situation can answer no good purpose; they must be known before they can be cured. We must also know what resources can be brought forth, that we may proportion our efforts to our means and our demands to both. It is necessary that we should be in condition to prosecute the war with ease before we can expect to lay down our arms with security, before we can treat of peace honorably, and before we can conclude it with advantage. I feel myself fettered at every moment and embarrassed in every operation from my ignorance of our actual state and of what is reasonably to be asked or expected. Yet when I consider our real wealth and numbers, and when I compare them with those of other countries, I feel a thorough conviction that we may do much more than we have yet done, and with more ease to ourselves than we have yet felt, provided we adopt the proper modes of revenue and expenditure.

Your excellency's good sense will anticipate my observations on the necessity of being informed what moneys are in your treasury and what sums you expect to have there, as also the times by which they must probably be brought in. In addition to this, I must pray you to communicate the several appropriations.

A misfortune peculiar to America requires that I entreat your excellency to undertake one more task, which, perhaps, is far from being the least difficult. It is, sir, that you will write me very fully as to the amount of the several paper currencies now circulating in your State, the probable increase or decrease of each, and the respective rates of depreciation.

Having now stated the several communications which are most indispensable, let me entreat of your excellency's goodness that they may be made as speedily as possible, to the end that I may be early prepared with those propositions which, from a view of all circumstances, may be most likely to extricate us from our present difficulties. I am also to entreat that you will inform me when your legislature is to meet.

My reason for making this request is, that any proposals to be made to them may arrive in season for their attentive deliberation.

I know that I give you much trouble, but I also know that it will be pleasing to you, because the time and labor will be expended in the service of your country. If, sir, my feeble but honest efforts should open to us the prospect of American glory, if we should be enabled to look forward to a period when, supported by solid revenue and resources, this war should have no other duration or extent than the wisdom of Congress might allow, and when its object should be the honor and not the independence of our country; if with these fair views the States should be roused, excited, animated, in the pursuit and unitedly determining to be in that happy situation find themselves placed there by the very determination – if, sir, these things should happen, and what is more if they should happen soon, the reflection that your industry has principally contributed to effect them would be the rich reward of your toils, and give to your best feelings their amplest gratification.

Duties of the Superintendent; September 7 and October 23, 1781, *Journals of the Continental Congress*, XXI 943 and 1070

On motion of Mr [James Mitchell] Varnum, seconded by Mr [James] Duane,

Resolved, That until an agent of marine shall be appointed by Congress, all the duties, powers and authority assigned to the said agent, be devolved upon and executed by the superintendant of finance:

That as soon as the said superintendant of finance shall take upon him the execution of the duties, powers and authority hereby devolved upon him, the functions and appointments of the Board of Admiralty, the several navy boards, agents, and all civil officers under them, shall cease and determine:

Resolved, That the registers, books, and papers, belonging to the admiralty and navy boards, or in their custody, be delivered over to the said superintendant of finance, and preserved by him.

On motion of Mr [Edmund] Randolph, seconded by Mr [Roger] Sherman,

Resolved, That the superintendant of finance be, and hereby is authorised to correspond with the several foreign ministers of these

United States, as often as there shall be occasion, upon subjects relating to his department.

[Adjourned to 10 o'Clock to-morrow.]

Morris to the Governors of North Carolina, South Carolina, and Georgia, Office of Finance, December 19, 1781, *Revolutionary Diplomatic Correspondence*, ed. Wharton, v 56–9

Sir: In my circular letter on that subject I have already had the honor to transmit the requisitions of Congress, contained in their acts of the 30th of October and 2d of November last, by which the quota of your State for the year 1782 is – dollars, payable in quarterly payments, commencing the 1st day of April next.

The distresses which your State has lately suffered will not, I fear, permit the collection of this quota in hard money, although the subsistence of the army will naturally call for an expenditure to a great amount in such articles as the State can furnish. The mode hitherto pursued of granting receipts and certificates by every one empowered or employed to impress or purchase can not but be attended with much confusion and difficulty, if not with oppression and fraud. It is the duty of those who are entrusted with the management of the public affairs to prevent as much as possible these evils, and as much as possible to equalise and diminish those burdens which the people must bear. It would give me great pleasure to be put in such a situation as that I might at once contract for the supplies of the southern army; but I have not specie for the purpose, nor do I find that taxes are yet laid in the southern States to procure it. Wherefore I must wait yet some time until the public treasury is replenished, until the hard money now in America gets somewhat more diffused, and until I have prospect of receiving back from those States in hard money their quota of the public taxes.

In this situation of things I have devised and proposed to the delegates of the three southern States the following plan: To appoint a receiver of the taxes in each State, agreeably to the act of Congress, and to empower such receiver to issue notes on the warrants of the General, payable in those taxes, or from the amount of them when collected. By which means those articles necessary for the consumption of the army may be purchased, and the quota of the State be thereby paid.

The delegates of North and South Carolina thought the plan eligible, but one of the delegates of Georgia was disinclined to that part of it which requires the previous passing of a law to raise the quota of taxes called for by the United States. I am this morning informed that, upon a reconsideration of the matter, a majority of the delegates of South Carolina are also of opinion that it would be better not to make the enacting such a law an indispensable part of the system. I am very sorry for this circumstance, because, as all the delegates from the three States mentioned approve of the plan in other respects, I did expect their warm recommendation of it to their respective legislatures, for your excellency will perceive at a single glance that it originated in the sincere desire of relieving those States, and has that relief for its object as far as the public service of the United States will possibly permit.

Those gentlemen who object to making a tax bill the preliminary to any issues of the notes have proposed, as an expedient, a law promising the payment of the notes when taxation shall become practicable, compelling the receipt of them in payment as specie, and limiting the prices of those articles which the army may want. This is done to obviate two objections which are supposed to be against taxation—that the state of the country will not admit of the collection, and that those who have no property left but lands can not pay the taxes without extreme distress.

Before I go into any detailed observations on these subjects I beg leave to state on general reason why I must insist on the tax law, even if in other respects I should have no material objections to the expedient proposed. As superintendent of the finances of the United States, it is my duty to urge a compliance with the requisitions of Congress, and therefore to facilitate that compliance; but I should betray the trust reposed in me if by any expedient whatever I assisted in eluding those requisitions. With me, therefore, the propriety of passing the tax bill can admit of no question; and, in consequence, my orders are precise to prevent the issue of a single note until such bills shall have been enacted and effectual provision made for the collection.

I shall now take the liberty of trespassing on your patience with some observations as to the two laws proposed. And, first, as to the expediency of taxing and the weight of the objections against it. When it is considered that the expenditures of the army (supposing the war to be carried on in the southern States) must greatly exceed the amount of the sums called for from those States, one position is clear, that by complying with the requisitions of Congress a balance of money must necessarily be brought in from the other States to supply the deficiency of the whole revenue in those particular States, when compared with the amount of the whole expenditure. But by neglecting to comply with the requisitions of Congress (as it will be impossible to supply the army in the same regular manner which prevails elsewhere), the whole cost of the expenditure will fall in the first instance on those who are near the seat of war, subject to a future settlement of accounts. Besides which, it is demonstrable that this latter mode of supply, which is at present practised, is very wasteful and expensive. Nor is this the only objection, though certainly a very strong one. We must further consider that, according to the present mode of taking supplies, the burden falls very unequally on the inhabitants, and, of course, very unjustly. I fear that with truth it may be added that, in some instances, it is attended with strong circumstances of distress.

Hence, then, I conclude that the propriety of taxation is evident, unless the reasons against it are of weight sufficient to counterbalance the inconveniences which would result from neglecting it. I proceed, therefore to examine them. And, first, as to the state of the country and the means of collection. It is clear that within the enemy's lines taxes can not be collected; but out of them they certainly may be. For surely it is as easy to compel a man to pay money by seizing his property as it is to seize that property for the subsistence of the troops. There is, however, this additional advantage in taxing, that those may be compelled to pay who have not articles useful for the army as well as those who have. The objection that those who have land only will be distressed by the sale of it will have just as much weight as the legislature may choose to give it; for if no taxes are raised on land the objection will vanish, and certainly the legislature will be in capacity to determine whether any tax should be laid on it and what that tax should be.

But, further, it appears that the objection is calculated to favor the rich, who are great land holders, in preference to the poor, who labor on a small plantation; and how far this may be either wise or just is not for me to determine. I will, however, suggest an expedient, that, as the taxes are payable quarterly, the first two quarters' tax should be raised on the polls, the slaves, and other personal property in the State, and the land tax be paid on the last quarterly installments. This will give the several land holders room to turn themselves so as to provide for their several appropriations in season. I will just add under this head, that if (as there is some reason to hope) the southern States should be totally evacuated, the extension of their commerce will soon obviate every objection which can possibly be in the way of taxation.

I must observe, further, that those States which delay the levying of taxes to answer present requisitions will become totally incapable of complying with future calls, and consequently we shall always be dealing in doubts and uncertainties, instead of establishing that confidence and vigor which alone can perfect our independence.

I come now to the proposed law for compelling the receipt of the notes and regulating the prices of articles. My opinion of all such laws is decidedly fixed. I know both from reason and experience that they injure the credit of the paper they appear designed to support. They show doubts in the mind of the legislature, they communicate those doubts to the breasts of the people, the credit of the paper is then destroyed before it is issued, and all the after operation of the law is one continued scene of fraud and iniquity. If, therefore, such tax bill shall be passed as will permit issuing the notes in question, I entreat that on no representation, nor for any cause whatever, any law be passed making the notes a tender, valuing the price of goods, or anything of that sort. I ask for no embargo, no regulations. On the contrary, I wish and pray that the whole detestable tribe of restrictions may be done away, and the people be put in possession of that freedom for which they are contending. I have no system of finance except that which results from the plain self-evident dictates of moral honesty. Taxation and economy are the two pillars by which that system is supported, and if the several States will provide the former, I will pledge myself for the latter as far as my abilities will permit.

To return then, sir, to the plan I have to propose. It is simply this: I expect that the legislature of your State will immediately pass laws to collect by the days named the sums called for from them for the service of the year 1782. To facilitate the collection and payment of the taxes I consent to receive the notes signed by the receiver of the continental taxes for your State. If, therefore, the legislature approve of my plan, they will merely add a clause rendering those notes receivable by their collectors as specie in the continental taxes. They will, I doubt not, provide the ways and means by which the receiver shall compel the several collectors to pay over whatever sums, either of those notes or of hard money, they may have received. This will leave it purely optional with the people to take the notes or to let them alone, If the taxes are collected, they must either pay those notes or hard money. If they pay hard money, the notes will not be necessary. If they pay the notes, the public will already have received the value of them in the articles for which they are first paid.

I enclose the form of the notes and the denominations, and I will appoint the receiver of the continental taxes for your State as soon as I can fix on a proper person and prepare the necessary instructions. In the mean time the law may easily be passed with a clause directing the mode in which the appointment of such receiver shall be announced to the public.

Morris to the Governors of the States, Office of Finance, January 3, 1782, ibid. pp. 84–5

Sir: Although it is now eleven months since Congress recommended an impost of five per cent. on goods imported and on prizes and prize goods, the States of Massachusetts, Rhode Island, and Maryland have not yet complied with that recommendation.

I will not repeat the arguments to induce a compliance which are contained either in my letter of the 27th of July or elsewhere; that is unnecessary. The object of this letter is to make a representation which can no longer be delayed consistently with the duties I owe either to myself or my country. And although it is principally designed for those three States just mentioned, yet I transmit it to the other States (in a letter of which the copy is enclosed), because all ought to know what is interesting to all.

Convinced that the impost recommended was not sufficient, I had devised some additional funds for the payment of our debts and the support of our credit. These I should have submitted to the consideration of Congress had the States complied with their former recommendations.

In a circular letter dated the 19th of October last I had the honor to mention an order prohibiting loan officers from issuing certificates in payment of interest, together with the reasons for which it was made. That order has already produced much clamor among the public creditors. This I expected, and I still expect that it will occasion much more.

The public debt is considerable, and the public credit must be lost if the interest of it be not provided for. Congress have done their duty in requesting revenue, and I have done mine in soliciting a compliance with their request. It only remains for me to bear testimony against those who oppose that compliance, and to declare that they, and they only, must be responsible for the consequences. They are answerable to the other States, to their fellow-citizens, to the public creditors, and to the whole world.

I must speak plainly on this subject. I must point out from time to time the reason of those things which have produced murmurs and complaints against the representative body of America. I must direct those who suffer to those who occasion their sufferings, and those who are injured to those who have done them wrong. Let me then once more entreat that this great object be seriously considered. Let me repeat that the hope of our enemy is in the derangement of our finances; let me add, that when revenue is given that hope must cease. He, therefore, who opposes the grant of such revenue not only opposes himself to the dictates of justice, but he labors to continue the war, and, of consequence, to shed more blood, to produce more devastation, and to extend and prolong the miseries of mankind.[1]

Robert Morris on the public credit, Office of Finance, July 29, 1782; August 5, 1782, *Journals of the Continental Congress*, XXII 429–47

Sir: The reference which Congress were pleased to make, of a Remonstrance and Petition from Blair McClenaghan and others, has induced me to pray their Indulgence, while I go somewhat at large into the subject of that Remonstrance. The propriety and utility of public Loans have been subjects of much controversy. Those who find themselves saddled with the Debts of a preceding Generation, naturally exclaim against Loans, and it must be confessed, that when such Debts are accumulated by Negligence, Folly or Profusion, the complaint is well founded. But it would be equally so against Taxes when

[1] January 7. This day the National Bank of North America opens to transact business. This institution, I am persuaded, will flourish under the management of honest men and honest measures. The present directors are such men, and the present system of measures are founded in principles of justice and equity. Therefore, I shall most cheerfully assist all in my power to establish and support this bank. And, as a beginning, I have this day issued my warrant on the Treasury for two hundred thousand dollars in part of the shares which I have subscribed on behalf of the public. – *Diary*.

wasted in the same way. The difference is, that the weight of Taxes being more sensible, the waste occasions greater Clamour, and is therefore more speedily remedied; but it will appear that the eventual evils which Posterity must sustain from heavy Taxes are greater than from Loans. Hence may be deduced this conclusion, that in Governments liable to a vicious administration it would be better to raise the current expence by Taxes; but when an honest and wise appropriation of money prevails it is highly advantageous to take the benefit of Loans. Taxation to a certain point is not only proper but useful, because by stimulating the industry of Individuals it increases the Wealth of the Community. But when Taxes go so far as to intrench on the subsistence of the People, they become burthensome and oppressive. The expenditure of money ought in such case to be (if possible) avoided, and if unavoidable it will be most wise to have recourse to Loans.

Loans may be of two kinds either domestic or foreign. The relative advantages and disadvantages of each as well as those which are common to both will deserve attention. Reasonings of this kind (as they depend on rules of arithmetic) are best understood by numerical positions. For the purposes of elucidation therefore it may be supposed that the annual Tax of any particular Husbandman were fifteen Pounds during a ten years' war, and that his net Revenue were but fifteen Pounds, so that (the whole being regularly consumed in payment of Taxes) he would be no richer at the end of the war, than he was at the beginning. It is at the same time notorious that the profits made by Husbandmen on funds which they borrowed were very considerable. In many instances their plantations, as well as the cattle and farming utensils have been purchased on credit, and the bonds given for both have shortly been paid by sales of produce. It is therefore no exaggeration to state the profits at twelve per cent. The enormous usury which people in trade have been induced to pay, and which will presently be noticed demonstrates that the profits made by other professions are equal to those of the Husbandmen. The instance therefore taken from that, which is the most numerous class of Citizens, will form no improper standard for the whole. Let it then be farther supposed in the case already stated that the party should annually borrow the sum of ten Pounds to pay part of his Tax of fifteen Pounds at 6 pr. cent, on this Sum then he would make a profit of twenty four shillings, and have to pay an interest of twelve shillings. The enclosed calculation will shew that in ten years he would be indebted one hundred Pounds, but his additional improvements would be worth near one hundred and fifty, and his net Revenue be increased near twelve after deducting the interest of his debt; whereas if he had not borrowed, his revenue would have continued the same as has already been observed. This mode of reasoning might be pursued farther; but what has been said is sufficient to show that he would have made a considerable advantage from the yearly loan. If it be supposed that every person in the community made such loan a similar advantage would arise to the community. And lastly if it be supposed that the Government were to make a loan and ask so much less in Taxes the same advantage would be derived. Hence also may be deduced this position, that in a society where the average profits of stock are double to the Interest at which money can be obtained, every public loan for necessary expenditures provides a fund in the aggregate of national wealth equal to the discharge of its own interest. Were it possible that a society should exist in which every member would of his own accord, industriously pursue the increase of national property without waste or extravagance the public wealth would be impaired by every species of taxation. But there never was, and unless human nature should change, there never will be such a society. In any given number of men there will always be some who are idle, and some who are extravagant. In every society also there must be some taxes, because the necessity of supporting Government and defending the State always exist. To do these on the cheapest terms is wise, and when it is considered how much men are disposed to indolence and profusion, it will appear that (even if these demands did not require the whole of what could be raised) still it would be wise to carry taxation to a certain amount, and expend what should remain after providing for the support of Government and the national defence in works of public utility, such as the opening of roads and navigation. For Taxes operate two ways towards the increase of national wealth. First they stimulate industry to provide the means of payment. Secondly, they encourage economy so far as to avoid the purchase of unnecessary things, and keep money in readiness for the Tax-gatherer. Experience shews that those exertions of industry and economy grow by degrees into Habit. But in order that taxation may have these good effects, the sum which every man is to pay, and the period of payment, should be certain and unavoidable.

This digression opens the way to a comparison between foreign and domestic Loans. If the loan be domestic, money must be diverted from those channels in which it would otherwise have flowed, and therefore either the public must give better terms than Individuals, or there must be money enough to supply the wants of both. In the latter case, if the Public did not borrow, the quantity of money would exceed the demand, and the interest would be lowered; borrowing by the Public therefore would keep up the rate of interest, which brings the latter case within the reason of the former. If the Public outbid Individuals, those Individuals are deprived of the means of extending their industry. So that no case of a domestic loan can well be supposed where some public loss will not arise to counterbalance the public gain, except when the creditor spares from his consumption to lend to the Government, which operates a national economy. It is however an advantage peculiar to domestic loans, that they give stability to Government by combining together the interests of moneyed men for its support, and consequently in this Country a domestic debt, would greatly contribute to that Union, which seems not to have been sufficiently attended to, or provided for, in forming the national compact. Domestic loans are also useful from the farther consideration, that as taxes fall heavy on the lower orders of a community, the relief obtained for them by such loans more than counterbalances the loss sustained by those, who would have borrowed money to extend their commerce or tillage. Neither is it a refinement to observe, that since a plenty of money and consequent ease of obtaining it, induce men to engage in speculations which are often unprofitable, the check which these receive is not injurious, while the relief obtained for the poor is highly beneficial.

By making foreign Loans the Community (as such) receive the same extensive benefits, which one Individual does in borrowing of another. This Country was always in the practice of making such Loans. The Merchants in Europe trusted those of America. The American Merchants trusted the Country Storekeepers, and they the People at large. This advance of credit may be stated at not less than twenty million of dollars; and the want of that credit is one principal reason of those usurious contracts mentioned above. These have been checked by the institution of the Bank; but the funds of that Corporation not permitting those extensive advances which the views of different people require, the price given for particular accommodations of money continues to be enormous, and that again shews, that to make domestic Loans would be difficult if not impracticable. The merchants not having now that extensive credit in Europe, which they formerly had, the obtaining such credit by the Government becomes in some sort necessary. But there remains an objection with many against foreign loans which (though it arises from a superficial view of the subject) has no little influence. This is that the Interest will form a balance of trade against us, and drain the country of specie, which is only saying in other words, that it would be more convenient to receive money as a present than as a Loan, for the advantages derived by the Loan exist, notwithstanding the payment of Interest. To shew this more clearly, a case may be stated which in this City is very familiar. An Island in the Delaware overflowed at Highwater has for a given sum – suppose a thousand Pounds – been banked in, drained and made to produce, by the hay sold from it at Philadelphia, a considerable sum annually, for instance two hundred Pounds. If the owner of such an Island had borrowed (in Philadelphia) the thousand Pounds to improve it, and given six pr. cent Interest he would have gained a nett revenue of one hundred and forty Pounds. This certainly would not be a balance of trade against his Island, nor the draining it of specie. He would gain considerably, and the city of Philadelphia also would gain by bringing to market an increased quantity of a necessary article. In like manner, money lent by the City of Amsterdam to clear the forests of America would be beneficial to both. Draining marshes and bringing forests under culture are beneficial to the whole human race; but most so to the Proprietor. But at any rate, in a Country and in a situation like ours to lighten the weight of present burthens (by Loans) must be good policy. For as the Governments acquire more stability, and the people more wealth, the former will be able to raise and the latter to pay much greater sums than can at present be expected.

What has been said on the general nature and benefit of Public Loans as well as their particular utility to this Country, contains more of detail than is necessary for the United States in Congress, tho' perhaps not enough for many of those to whose consideration this subject must be submitted. It may seem superfluous to add that credit is necessary to the obtaining of loans. But among the many extraordinary conceptions which have been produced during the present Revolution, it is neither the least prevalent nor the least pernicious that Foreigners will trust us with millions, while our own citizens will not trust us with a shilling. Such an opinion must be unfounded and will appear to be false at the first glance. Yet men are (on some occasions) so willing to deceive themselves, that the most flattering expectations will be formed from the acknowledgement of American Independence by the State General. But surely no reasonable hope can be raised on that circumstance, unless something more be done by ourselves. The loans made to us hitherto have either been by the Court of France, or on their credit. The Government of the United Netherlands are so far from being able to lend, that they must borrow for themselves. The most therefore which can be asked from them, is to become security for America to their own subjects; but it cannot be expected, that they will do this, until they are assured and convinced that we will punctually pay. This follows necessarily from the nature of their Government, and must be clearly seen by the several States, as well as by Congress, if they only consider what conduct they would pursue on a similar occasion. Certainly Congress would not put themselves in a situation which might oblige them to call on the several States for money to pay the debts of a foreign power. Since then no aid is to be looked for from the Dutch Government without giving them sufficient evidence of a disposition and ability to pay both the principal and interest of what we borrow, and since the same evidence which would convince the Government must convince the Individuals who compose it, asking the aid of Government must either be unnecessary or ineffectual. Ineffectual before the measures taken to establish our credit, and unnecessary afterwards.

We are therefore brought back to the necessity of establishing public credit, and this must be done at home before it can be extended abroad. The only question which can remain is with respect to the means, and here it must be remembered that a free Government whose natural offspring is public credit, cannot have sustained a loss of that credit unless from particular causes, and therefore those causes must be investigated and removed before the effects will cease. When the Continental money was issued, a greater confidence was shown by America, than any other people ever exhibited. The general promise of a body not formed into, nor claiming to be a Government, was accepted as current coin and it was not until long after an excess of quantity had forced on depreciation that the validity of these promises was questioned. Even then the public credit still existed in a degree, nor was it finally lost until March, 1780, when an idea was entertained that Government had committed injustice. It is useless to enter into the reasons for and against the resolutions of that Period. They were adopted, and are now to be considered only in relation to their effects. These will not be altered by saying that the Resolutions were misunderstood, for in those things which depend on public opinion, it is no matter (as far as consequences are concerned) how that opinion is influenced. Under present circumstances, therefore, it may be considered as an uncontrovertible proposition that all paper money ought to be absorbed by taxation (or otherwise) and destroyed before we can expect our public credit to be fully reestablished. For so long as there be any in existence the holder will view it as a monument of national perfidy.

But this alone would be taking only a small step in the important business of establishing national credit. There are a great number of individuals in the United States who trusted the public in the hour of distress, and who are impoverished, and even ruined by the confidence they reposed. There are others whose property has been wrested from them by force to support the war, and to whom certificates have been given in lieu of it which are entirely useless. It needed not inspiration to show that justice establisheth a nation; neither are the principles of religion necessary to evince that political injustice will receive political chastisement. Religious men will cherish these maxims in proportion to the additional force they derive from divine Revelation. But our own experience will shew, that from a defect of justice this nation is not established, and that her want of honesty is severely punished by the want of credit. To this want of credit must be attributed the weight of taxation for support of the war, and the continuance of that weight by continuance of the war. It is, therefore, with the greatest propriety your Petitioners already mentioned have stated in their memorial, that both policy and justice require a solid provision for funding the public debts. It is with pleasure, Sir, that I see this numerous, meritorious and oppressed body of men, who are creditors of the Public, beginning to exert themselves for the obtaining of justice. I hope they may succeed, not only because I wish well to a righteous pursuit, but because this success will be the great groundwork of a credit which will carry us safely through the present just, important and necessary war, which will combine us closely together on the conclusion of a peace, which will always give to the Supreme Representative of America a means of acting for the

General Defence on sudden emergencies and which will of consequence procure the third of those great objects for which we contend – *Peace, Liberty, and Safety.*

Such, Sir, are the cogent principles by which we are called on to provide solid funds for the national debt. Already Congress have adopted a plan for liquidating all past accounts, and if the States shall make the necessary grants of Revenue, what remains will be a simple executive operation which will presently be explained. But however powerful the reasons in favor of such grants over and above those principles of moral justice which none however exalted can part from with impunity, still there are men who (influenced by penurious selfishness) will grumble at the Expence, and who will assert the impossibility of sustaining it. On this occasion the sensations with respect to borrowing are reversed. All would be content to relieve themselves by Loan from the weight of Taxes; but many are unwilling to take up as they ought the weight of Debt. Yet this must be done before the other can happen, and it is not so great but that we should find immediate relief by assuming it, *even if it were a foreign Debt.* I say if it were a *foreign* Debt, because I shall attempt to shew first that being *a domestic Debt*, to fund it will cost the community nothing, and secondly that it will produce (on the contrary) a considerable advantage; and as to the first point, one observation will suffice. The expenditure has been made, and a *part* of the community have sustained it. If the Debt were to be paid, by a single effort of taxation, it could only create a transfer of property from one Individual to another and the aggregate wealth of the whole community would be precisely the same. But since nothing more is attempted than merely to fund the debt by providing for the interest (at 6 per cent) the question of ability is resolved to this single point, whether it is easier for *a part of the people* to pay one hundred dollars, than for the *whole people* to pay six dollars. It is equally clear, tho' not equally evident that a considerable advantage would be produced by funding our debts, over and above what has been already mentioned as the consequence of national credit. This advantage is threefold. First many persons by being Creditors of the Public, are deprived of those funds which are necessary to the full exercise of their skill and industry, consequently the community are deprived of the benefits which would result from that exercise, whereas if these debts, which are in a manner dead, were brought back to existence, monied men would purchase them up (tho' perhaps at a considerable discount) and thereby restore to the public many useful members, who are now entirely lost, and extend the operations of many more to considerable advantage. For altho' not one additional shilling would be by this means brought in, yet by distributing property into those hands which could render it most productive, the Revenue would be increased while the original stock continued the same. Secondly, many foreigners who make speculations to this Country would, instead of ordering back remittances, direct much of the proceeds of their cargoes to be invested in our public funds; which according to principles already established would produce a clear advantage with this addition (from peculiar circumstances) that it would supply the want of credit to the mercantile Part of Society. The last but not least advantage is that in restoring ease, harmony and confidence, not only the Government (being more respectable) would be more respected and consequently better obeyed; but the mutual dealings among men on private credit would be facilitated. The horrors which agitate people's minds from an apprehension of depreciating paper would be done away. The secret hoards would be unlocked. In the same moment the necessity of money would be lessened and the quantity increased. By these means the collection of taxes would be facilitated, and thus instead of being obliged to give valuable produce for useless minerals, that produce would purchase the things we stand in need of, and we should obtain a sufficient circulating medium by giving the people what they have always a right to demand, solid assurance in the integrity of their rulers.

The next consideration which offers is the amount of the public Debt, and every good American must lament that confusion in public affairs, which renders an accurate state of it unattainable. But it must continue to be so, until all accounts both at home and abroad be finally adjusted. The enclosed is an estimate furnished by the Comptroller of the Treasury, from which it appears that there is already an acknowledged Debt, bearing interest to the amount of more than twelve millions of dollars. On part of this also there is a large arrearage of interest, and there is a very considerable Debt unsettled, the evidence whereof exists in various certificates given for property applied to the public service. This (including pay due to the army previous to the present year) cannot be estimated at less than between seven and eight millions. Our Debt to his Most Christian Majesty is above five millions. The nearest guess therefore, which can be made at the sum total, is from twenty five to twenty seven millions of dollars, and if to this we add what it may be necessary to borrow for the year 1783, the amount will be (with interest) by the time proper revenues are obtained considerably above thirty millions. Of course the Interest will be between eighteen hundred thousand and two million dollars. And here, previous to the consideration of proper revenues for that amount, it may not be amiss to make a few general observations, the first of which is, that it would be injurious to the United States to obtain money on loan, without providing beforehand the necessary funds. For if those who are now so deeply engaged to support the war, will not grant such funds to procure immediate relief, certainly those who came after them will not do it, to pay a former Debt. Remote objects dependent on abstract reasoning never influence the mind like immediate sensibility. It is therefore the province of wisdom to direct towards proper objects that sensibility which is the only motive to action among the mass of mankind. Should we be able to get money from the Dutch, without first providing funds, which is more than doubtful, and should the several States neglect afterwards making provision to perform the engagements of Congress, which is more than probable, the credit of the United States abroad would be ruined forever. Very serious discussions also might be raised among Foreign Powers. Our creditors might have recourse to arms, and we might dishonorably be compelled to do, what dishonestly we had left undone. Secondly the idea which many entertain of soliciting Loans abroad to pay the Interest of domestic Debts, is a measure pregnant with its own destruction. If the States were to grant revenues sufficient only to pay the Interest of present Debts, we might perhaps obtain new credit upon a general opinion of our justice, tho' that is far from certain. But when we omit paying by Taxes the interest of Debts already contracted, and ask to borrow for the purpose, making the same promises to obtain the new loans, which had been already made to obtain the old, we shall surely be disappointed. Thirdly, it will be necessary not only that revenues be granted, but that those revenues be amply sufficient for the purpose because (as will presently appear) a deficiency would be highly pernicious while an excess would be not only unprejudicial but very advantageous. To perceive this with all necessary clearness, it must be remembered that the revenues asked for on this occasion must be appropriated to the purposes for which they are asked, and in like manner the sums required for current expenditure must be appropriated to the current service. If then the former be deficient the latter cannot be brought in to supply the deficiencies, and of course the public credit would be impaired; but should there be an excess of Revenue, it could be applied in payment of a part of the Debt immediately and in such case if the credits should have depreciated, they would be raised to par and if already at par, the offer of payment would induce Creditors to lower the interest. Thus in either case, the means of making new loans on good terms would be extended, and the necessity of asking more Revenues obviated. Lastly these Revenues ought to be of such a nature naturally and necessarily to increase, for creditors will have a greater confidence when they have a clear prospect of being repaid, and the people will always be desirous to see a like prospect of relief from the Taxes. Besides which it will be necessary to incur some considerable expence after the war in making necessary establishments for a permanent naval force, and it will always be least objectionable to borrow for that purpose on funds already established.

The requisition of a five per cent impost made on the 3rd. day of February 1781, has not yet been complied with by the State of Rhode Island; but as there is reason to believe that their compliance is not far off, this Revenue may be considered as being already granted. It will however be very inadequate to the purposes intended. If goods be imported and prizes introduced to the amount of twelve millions annually, the five per cent would be six hundred thousand, from which at least one sixth must be deducted as well for the cost of collection, as for the various defalcations, which will necessarily happen, and which it is unnecessary to enumerate. It is not safe therefore to estimate this Revenue at more than half a million of dollars, for tho' it may produce more, yet probably it will not produce so much. It was in consequence of this, that on the 27th. day of February last I took the liberty to submit the propriety of asking the States for a Land Tax of one dollar for every hundred acres of land, a Poll Tax of one dollar on all freemen, and all male slaves between 16 and 60 (excepting such as are in the federal army, and such as are by wounds or otherwise rendered unfit for service) and an excise of one eighth of dollar per gallon, on all distilled spirituous liquors. Each of these may be estimated at half a million, and should the product be equal to the estimation, the sum total of Revenues for funding the public

Debts would be equal to two millions. What has been the fate of these propositions I know not; but I will beg leave on this occasion, not only to renew them but also to state some reasons in their favor and answer some objections against them.

And first, as to a Land Tax. The advantages of it are, that it can be reduced to a certainty as to the amount and time. That no extraordinary means are necessary to ascertain it. And that land being the Ultimate object of human avarice, and that particular species of permanent property which so peculiarly belongs to a Country as neither to be removed nor concealed, it stands foremost for the object of taxation and ought most particularly to be burthened with those Debts which have been incurred by defending the freedom of its Inhabitants. But besides these general reasons, there are some which are in a manner peculiar to this Country; the land of America may, as to the proprietors be divided into two kinds, that which belongs to the great Landholder and that which is owned and occupied by the industrious cultivator. This latter class of citizens is generally speaking the most numerous and most valuable part of a community. The artisan may under any government minister to the luxuries of the Rich, and the Rich may under any government obtain the luxuries they covet; but the free husbandman is the natural Guardian of his Country's freedom. A Land Tax will probably at the first mention, startle this order of men, but it can only be from the want of reflection, or the delusion must be kept up by the artifice of others. To him who cultivates from one to five hundred acres, a dollar per hundred is a trifling object; but to him who owns an hundred thousand it is important. Yet a large proportion of America is the property of great landholders, they monopolize it without cultivation, they are (for the most part) at no expence either of money or personal service to defend it, and keeping the price higher by monopoly than otherwise it would be they impede the settlement and culture of the Country. A Land Tax, therefore, would have the salutary operation of an agrarian law without the iniquity. It would relieve the indigent and aggrandize the State by bringing property into the hands of those who would use it for the Benefit of Society. The objections against such a Tax are twofold first that it is unequal, and secondly, that it is too high. To obviate the inequality some have proposed an estimate of the value of different kinds of lands; but this would be improper, because first it would be attended with great delay expence and inconvenience.

Secondly it would be uncertain and therefore improper, particularly when considered as a fund for public Debts. Thirdly there is no reason to believe that any estimate would be just, and even if it were it must be annually varied, or else come within the force of the objection as strongly as ever; the former would cost more than the Tax, and the latter would not afford the remedy asked for. Lastly such valuations would operate as a tax upon industry, and promote that land monopoly which every wise Government will study to repress. But further the true remedy for any inequality will be obtained in the apportioning other taxes of which there will always be enough to equalize this. Besides the Tax being permanent and fixed it is considered in the price of land on every transfer of property, and that produces a degree of equality which no valuation could possibly arrive at. In a word, if exact numerical proportion be sought after in taxes there would be no end to the search. Not only might a Poll Tax be objected to as too heavy on the poor and too light on the rich, but when that objection was obviated, the physical differences in the human frame would alone be as endless a source of contention, as the different qualities of land. The second objection that the Tax is too high, is equally futile with the former. Land which is so little worth that the owner will not pay annually one penny per acre for the defence of it, ought to belong to the society by whom the expence of defending it is defrayed. But the truth is that this objection arises from and is enforced by those men, who can very well bear the expence, but who wish to shift it from themselves to others. I shall close this subject by adding, that as such a Tax would besides the benefits to be derived from the objects of it, have the farther advantage of encouraging settlements and population, this would redound not only to the national good, but even to the particular good of the landholders themselves.

With respect to the Poll Tax, there are many objections against it; but in some of the States a more considerable Poll Tax already exists without inconvenience. The objections are principally drawn from Europe, by men who do not consider that a difference of circumstances makes a material difference in the nature of political operations. In some parts of Europe where nine-tenths of the people are exhausted by continual labor to procure bad cloathing and worse food, this Tax would be extremely oppressive; but in America where three days of labor produce sustenance for a week, it is not unreasonable to ask two days out of a year as a contribution to the payment of public Debts. Such a Tax will on the Rich be next to nothing, on the middling ranks it will be of little consequence, and it cannot affect the poor, because such of them as are unable to labor will fall within the exception proposed. In fact, the situation of America differs so widely from that of Europe as to the matter now under consideration, that hardly any maxim which applies to one will be alike applicable to the other. Labor is in such demand among us, that the Tax will fall on the consumer. An able bodied man who demands one hundred dollars bounty to go into military service for three years, cannot be oppressed by the annual payment of one dollar, while not in that service. This Tax also will have the good effect of placing before the eyes of Congress the number of men in the several States, an information always important to Government.

The excise proposed is liable to no other objection than what may be made against the mode of collection; but it is conceived that this may be such as can produce no ill consequences. Excise laws exist, and have long existed in the several States. Of all Taxes those on the consumption of articles are most agreeable, because being mingled with the price, they are less sensible to the people. And without entering into a discussion, with which speculative men have amused themselves on the advantages and disadvantages of this species of taxation, it may be boldly affirmed that no inconvenience can arise from laying a heavy Tax on the use of ardent Spirits. These have always been equally prejudicial to the constitutions and morals of the people. The Tax will be a means of compelling vice to support the cause of virtue, and like the Poll Tax will draw from the idle and dissolute that contribution to the public service which they will not otherwise make.

Having said thus much on the propriety of these Taxes, I shall pray leave to assure you of my ready acquiescence in the choice of any others which may be more agreeable to the United States in Congress, praying them nevertheless to consider, that as the situation of the respective States is widely different, it will be wise to adopt a variety of Taxes because by that means the consent of all will be more readily obtained, than if such are chosen as will fall heavy only on particular States. The next object is the collection, which for the most obvious reasons ought to be by authority derived from the United States. The collecting of a Land Tax as has been observed above will be very simple. That of the Poll Tax may be equally so, because certificates of the payment may annually be issued to the Collectors, and they be bound to return the certificates or the money, and empowered to compel a payment by every man not possessed of a certificate. If in addition to this, those who travel from one State to another be obliged to take out and pay for a new certificate in each State, that would operate an useful regulation of police, and a slight distinction between those and the common certificates, would still preserve their utility in numbering the people. It is not necessary to dwell on the mode of collecting these branches of Revenue, because (in reason) a determination on the propriety of the Taxes should precede it. I will only take the liberty to drop one idea with respect to the impost already required. It is conceived that laws should be so formed as to leave little or nothing to the discretion of those by whom they are executed. That Revenue laws in particular should be guarded in this respect from odium being (as they are) sufficiently odious in themselves, and therefore, that it would have been well to have stipulated the precise sum payable on different species of commodities. The objection is, that the list (to be accurate) must be numerous; but this accuracy is unnecessary. The description ought to be very short and general so as to comprise many commodities under one head, and the duty ought to be fixed according to their average value. The objection against this regulation is, that the Tax on fine commodities would be trivial, and on coarse commodities great. This indeed is true; but it is desirable for two reasons. First that coarse and bulky commodities *could* not be smuggled to evade the *heavy* duty, and that fine commodities *would* not be smuggled to evade the *light* duty. Secondly that coarse commodities (generally speaking) minister to the demands of necessity or convenience, and fine commodities to those of Luxury. The heavy duty on the former would operate an encouragement to produce them at home, and by that means a stoppage of our commerce in time of war would be most felt by the wealthy, who have always the most abundant means of procuring relief.

I shall now, Sir, take the liberty to suppose, that the Revenues I have mentioned or some others to the amount of at least two millions nett annual produce were asked for and obtained, as a pledge to the public creditors, to continue until the principal and interest of the Debts contracted, or to be contracted should be finally paid. This supposition is made that I may have an opportunity (thus early) to express my sentiments on the mode of appropriation. It would be as follows – Any one of the Revenues being estimated, a loan should be opened on the credit of it by subscription to a certain amount and public debts of a particular description (or specie) be received in payment of the Subscriptions. This funded Debt should be transferable under particular forms calculated for the prevention of fraudulent and facilitating of honest negotiations. In like manner on each of these Revenues should subscriptions be opened proceeding by degrees so as to prevent any sudden revolutions in money matters, such revolutions being always more or less injurious. I should farther propose, that the surplus of each of these Revenues (and care should be taken that there would be a surplus) should be carried to a sinking fund on the credit of which, and of the general promises of Government new loans should be opened when necessary, the Interest should be paid half yearly, which would be convenient to the Creditors and to the Government, as well as useful to the people at large; because by this means, if four different loans were opened at different times, the Interest would be payable eight times in the year, and thus the money would be paid out of the treasury as fast as it came in, which would require fewer officers to manage the business, keep them in more constant and regular employment, dispense the Interest so as to command the confidence and facilitate the views of the creditors and returned speedily the wealth obtained by Taxes into the common stock. I know it will be objected, that such a mode of administration would enable speculators to perform their operations. A general answer to this would be, that any other mode would be more favorable to them. But farther I conceive first that it is much beneath the dignity of Government to intermeddle in such considerations. Secondly that speculators always do least mischief where they are left most at liberty. Thirdly, that it is not in human prudence to counteract their operations by laws, whereas when left alone they invariably counteract each other; and fourthly that even if it were possible to prevent speculation, it is precisely the thing which ought not to be prevented, because he who wants money to commence pursue or extend his business is more benefited by selling stock of any kind (even at considerable discount) than he could be by the rise of it at a future period. Every man being able to judge better of his own business and situation than the Government can for him. So much would not perhaps have been said on the head of this objection, if it did not naturally lead to a position, which has been ruinous' and might prove fatal. There are many men (and some of them honest men) whose zeal against speculation leads them to be sometimes unmindful not only of sound policy, but even of moral justice. It is not uncommon to hear, that those who have bought the public Debts for small sums, ought only to be paid their purchase money. The reasons given are, that they have taken advantage of the distressed creditors, and shewn a diffidence in the public faith. As to the first, it must be remembered that in giving the creditor money for his Debt, they have at least afforded him some relief, which he could not obtain elsewhere and if they are deprived of the expected benefit, they never will afford such relief again. As to the second, those who buy up the public Debts shew at least as much confidence in the public faith, as those who sell them; but allowing (for argument's sake) that they have exhibited the diffidence complained of, it would certainly be wiser to remove than to justify it. The one mode tends to create establish and secure Public Credit, and the other to sap overturn and destroy it. Policy is therefore on this (as I believe it to be on every other occasion) upon the same side of the question with honesty. Honesty tells us, that the duty of the public to pay is like the same duty in an Individual. Having benefited by the advances, they are bound to replace them to the party or to his Representatives. The Debt is a species of property, and whether disposed of for the whole nominal value, or the half, for something or for nothing is totally immaterial. The right of receiving, and the duty of paying must always continue the same. In a word, that Government which can (through the intervention of its Courts) compel the payment of private Debts and performance of private contracts on principles of distributive justice but refuse to be guided by those principles as to their own contracts and Debts, merely because they are not amenable to human laws, shews a flagitious contempt of moral obligations, which must necessarily weaken, as it ought to do, their authority over the people.

Before I conclude this long letter it would be unpardonable not to mention a fund which has long since been suggested and dwells still in the minds of many. You doubtless, Sir, anticipate my naming of what are called the Back Lands. The question as to the property of those lands, I confess myself utterly incompetent to decide, and shall not for that reason presume to enter on it. But it is my duty to mention, that the offer of a pledge, the right to which is contested, would have ill consequences and could have no good ones. It could not strengthen our credit, because no one would rely on such a pledge, and the recurrence to it would give unfavorable impressions of our political sagacity; but admitting that the right of Congress is clear, we must remember also, that it is disputed by some considerable members of the Confederacy. Dissensions might arise from hasty decisions on this subject, and a Government torn by intestine commotions is not likely to acquire or maintain credit at home or abroad. I am not however the less clear in my opinion that it would be alike useful to the whole nation and to those very constituent parts of it, that the entire disposition of these lands should be in Congress. Without entering therefore into the litigated points, I am induced to believe, and for that reason to suggest, the proposing this matter to the States as an amicable arrangement. I hope to be pardoned when I add that considering the situation of South Carolina and Georgia, it might be proper to ask their consent to matters of the clearest right. But that supposing the right to be doubtful, urging a decision in the present moment might have a harsh and ungenerous appearance. But if we suppose this matter to be arranged either in the one mode or in the other so that the right of Congress be rendered indisputable (for that is a previous point of indispensible necessity) the remaining question will be as to the appropriation of that fund. And I confess it does not appear to me, that the benefits resulting from it are such as many are led to believe. When the imagination is heated in pursuit of an object, it is generally overrated. If these lands were now in the hands of Congress, and they were willing to mortgage them to their present creditors, unless they were accompanied with a due provision for the Interest it would bring no relief. If these lands were to be sold for the public Debts, they would go off for almost nothing. Those who want money could not afford to buy land. Their certificates would be bought up for a trifle. Very few moneyed men would become possessed of them, because very little money would be invested in so remote a speculation. The small number of purchasers would easily and readily combine. Of consequence they would acquire the lands for almost nothing, and effectually defeat the intentions of government, leaving it still under the necessity of making farther provision, after having needlessly squandered an immense property. This reasoning is not new. It has been advanced on similar occasions before, and the experience which all America has had of the sales of confiscated estates, and the like will now shew that it was well founded.

The Back Lands then will not answer our purpose without the necessary Revenues. But those Revenues will alone produce the desired effect. The Back Lands may afterwards be formed into a fund for opening new loans in Europe on a low Interest redeemable within a future period (for instance, twenty years) with a right reserved to the creditors of taking portions of those lands on the nonpayment of their Debts, at the expiration of that term. Two modes would offer for Liquidation of those Debts. First to tender payment during the term, to those who would not consent to alter the nature of the Debt, which (if our credit be well established) would place it on the general footing of national faith, and secondly to sell portions of the land (during the term) sufficient to discharge the mortgage. I persuade myself that the consent of the reluctant States might be obtained, and that this fund might hereafter be converted to useful purposes. But I hope that, in a moment when the joint effort of all is indispensible, no causes of altercation may be mingled unnecessarily in a question of such infinite magnitude as the restoration of public credit. Let me add, Sir, that unless the money of foreigners be brought in for the purpose, sales of public land would only absorb that surplus wealth, which might have been extracted by taxes, so that in fact no new resource is produced, and that while (as at present) the demand for money is so great as to raise Interest to five per cent per month, public lands must sell extremely low were the title ever so clear. What then can be expected, when the validity of that title is one object of the war?[1]

The Committee [Mr Samuel Osgood, Mr Abraham Clark, Mr Arthur Lee] to whom was referred the letter of the Superintendant of Finance on the establishment of a fund for discharging debts due from the United States to individuals for supplies furnished the Army, beg leave to report:

That the Committee are of opinion, the mode pointed out in the letter referred, for raising a revenue for the purposes therein mentioned, is in general too exceptionable to meet with the approbation

[1] This report is in the *Papers of the Continental Congress*, no. 137, I, fos. 677–705, and the calculation enclosed is on fo. 707*a*. The indorsement shows that it was referred, on this day, to the Grand Committee. Committee book no. 186 shows that this was the Grand Committee appointed July 22, 'to take into consideration and report the most effectual means of supporting the credit of the United States' and that, on September 25, Mr [Joseph] Montgomery was appointed on the committee, in place of Mr [George] Clymer.

of Congress; as it would operate very unequally, as well with respect to the different States, as to the inhabitants of each State.

That a revenue for the purpose of discharging the claims of individuals in the several States for supplies furnished the Army when liquidated; may become necessary: But inasmuch, as Congress by their resolution of the 2nd. of Novr. last agreed to accept certificates of such debts from the several States on account of deficiencies on former requisitions, whereby it may happen that if not the whole of those debts may be discharged, it will be proper to defer going into measures for providing such revenue until a final settlement shall ascertain the sums that remain to be discharged.[1]

The Committee [Mr John Rutledge, Mr Arthur Lee, Mr Abraham Clark] to whom was referred the report of the Superintendant of Finance submit the following report:

Whereas, it appears, that the money appropriated as a fund in Europe for payment of bills of exchange for the interest of loan office certificates issued before the 1st. of March 1778 will be exhausted by discharging the interest due thereon antecedent to the 10th. day of March last, and no other fund having yet been established, either for paying such interest, or the interest due on certificates of a later date, owing to the backwardness of the States in complying with the requisition of Congress to lay an import duty of five per cent on imported goods; and it being equally just to provide, as well for the latter, as former loans, Whereupon,

Resolved, That no more bills for interest due on any loan office certificate since the 10th. day of March last, be drawn until the further order of Congress.

I.III.3 THE POLITICAL IMPLICATIONS OF ROBERT MORRIS

Samuel Osgood to John Adams, Annapolis, December 7, 1783, *Letters of the Continental Congress*, ed. Burnett, VII 378–81

I should have done myself the Pleasure of writing to you before this Time: But since Joining Congress, we have been in an unsettled Posture – little other Business has been done than that of determining

[1] This report is in the *Papers of the Continental Congress*, no. 19, IV, fo. 351. It is in the writing of Abraham Clark and was referred on this day, as the indorsement states, to the Grand Committee.

a Place, or Places, for the future Residence of Congress. The Discussion of these Questions bro't into view many others, of great Importance. The Decissions of Congress, you are undoubtedly acquainted with, respecting their future Residences. But you may probably be uninform'd, as to the Motives and Reasons, that operated in the Minds of the Delegates of several of the States, to agree to Measures, that seem to be attended with no inconsiderable Inconveniency on several Accounts. . . .[1] There are several Weighty Reasons to support the late Decissions of Congress. It was necessary to accomodate the several Parts of the Continent, some of which were greatly agitated, and dissatisfied with the first Determination of Congress. It was necessary in Order to destroy Systems, which would finally have ended in absolute Aristocracy, the Effects of which have been too apparent for several Years past. It would not have been possible that Congress should ever have been a free and independent Body in the City of P——a. Plans for absolute Government, for deceiving the lower Classes of People, for introducing undue Influence, for any Kind of Government, in which Democracy has the least possible share, originate, are cherished and disseminated from thence.

With Respect to accomodating the several States in the Union, it is a Matter of absolute Necessity. The seven eastern States may, by the Iron Hand of voting, carry the Seat of Congress much more Northward than it really ought to be, and accomodate themselves very well. But it is unnatural to suppose that the Southern states would chearfully submit to such a Decission; they openly declare that they cannot, and will not; and as a foederal Town cannot be erected without their Concurrence; the final Event must have been, that Congress would have again fallen into the City P——a, and there remained, until the several States for Want of Confidence in them, should have voluntarily put an End to their Existence, which, without pretending to have the Gift of Prophesying, one might easily foresee would not be a very distant Period. As to the Matter of travelling one or two hundred Miles farther, it is of no Weight. The Climate has some. But if Congress can dispatch all their Business in the Fall and Winter, which they certainly may do in future, Our pointed Objection against a southern

[1] There follows a discussion of motives, probable and possible, and the 'systematical intrigue of a few'. For an explanation of motives, on the one side and on the other, see Jefferson's statement of November 11 (*Letters of the Continental Congress*, vol. VII, letter 444).

Climate will not exist at those Seasons of the Year. I am therefore fully of the Opinion that public Harmony and Concord are Objects of no small Consequence in the Union and that private Inconvenience ought always to give Way to them.

That Systems of Intrigue and Influence have been laid, that, they are too strongly rooted already, is but too well known to those who have had a share in public Business for these several Years past. . . .[1]

The System of Influence began, when the United States were reduced to the most deplorable Situation, on Account of their Finances; when the virtuous Spirit of the People began to Subside, and when among many an Indifference to the Cause began to be too manifest. At this fatal Moment the eagle eyed Politican of our great Ally, discovered the absolute Importance of the Aid of his Master, and the critical Situation of the United States. It was then he ventured to propose that Congress should subject their Peace Commissioners to the absolute controul of a foreign court. . . .[2]

In this Situation was Congress, when the great Officers of State commenced. The Financier and Secretary for foreign Affairs were admirably well adapted to support, and not only so, but to become the principal Engines of Intrigue. The first mentioned Officer, is a Man of inflexible Perseverance. He Judges well in almost all Money Matters; and mercantile Transactions. He well knows what is necessary to support public Credit. But never thinks it necessary to secure the Confidence of the People, by making Measures palatable to them. A Man destitute of every Kind of theoretic Knowledge; but from extensive mercantile Negociations, he is a good practical Merchant; more than this cannot be said with Justice. He Judges generally for himself; and acts with great Decision. He has many excellent Qualities for a Financier, which however do not comport so well with Republicanism, as Monarchy. Ambitious of becoming the first Man in the united States, he was not so delicate in the Choice of Means, and Men for his

[1] Some further general comments on the system of intrigue and 'manoeuvres' are here omitted.

[2] Osgood next launches into a bitter denunciation of French influence in Congress, particularly as exerted through the 'Ministers of State', set up, he assumes, primarily in the interest of France and at her dictation. That he could have imagined the establishment of executive departments to have been a manoeuvre of the minister of France for his own purposes show how deep an obsession had taken hold of a group in Congress against French influence and particularly against the superintendent of finance.

Purpose, as is indispensably necessary in a free Government. The good Ally of the United States could assist him in Money, and he was heartily dispos'd to make her very grateful Returns. The United States abound with Men absolutely devoted. With such a Financier and with such Materials, it is easy to conceive what an amazing Power he would soon acquire. He stood in need of foreign Support, and *they* stood in need of him: thus far the political Machinery was in Unison; and republicanism grated harsh Discords.

The Secretary for foreign Affairs was a Man of more acquired Knowledge, and less natural Ability. A Person as completely devoted to promote all the Views and Wishes of our good Ally, as his Minister and Secretary could possibly be. His Office was misterious, and secret to all those, who ought to have a perfect Knowledge of all it contain'd. It was undoubtedly public to all those, to whom it ought to have been a profound Secret. Two foreigners were private Secretaries in that Office; one of which it is probable was educated a Jesuit,[1] the other had been a french Priest. With this Arrangement, it is impossible to suppose that any Thing of Importance, would not be communicated immediately to such as the Interest of the united States required, should not know it. More real Injury resulted from this Arrangement, than could possibly have done, if there had been no Office and no pretended Secrets. It was a Snare to our faithful foreign Ministers, and a secure Asylum, to such as were dispos'd to prostrate the Honor and Dignity of the United States, before the polluted Shrine of Monarchy. In this Situation it was impossible to support an honest Man; All our foreign Ministers, excepting one, have felt very severely the Effects of this unaccountable System. It is strange that so many, who seem to be republicans, were so easily drawn into the Snare, and that they either could not, or would not see, that it was giving up at once, all the Priviledges for the Preservation of which we had freely lavish'd our Blood and Treasure.

It was fortunate for the United States, that the Secretary at War,[2]

[1] Osgood first wrote 'a Disciple of the Sorbonne'. These were Peter S. Duponceau and Rev. John P. Tetard. The former, having served under Steuben before being made an under secretary in Livingston's office, became a distinguished attorney and writer in Philadelphia. Concerning the latter see Livingston to Congress December 2, 1782 (*Revolutionary Diplomatic Correspondence*, ed. Wharton, VI 100), and the *Journals of the Continental Congress*, May 16, 1783.

[2] Gen. Benjamin Lincoln of Massachusetts.

was a true Republican, and totally oppos'd to Intrigue and aristocratical Measures. had Genl. Schuyler, who nearly carried the Choice, been plac'd in that Office, It is a great Question in my Mind, whether it would have been practicable for Congress, to have disbanded their Army. The Financier only wanted a Person in that Office who would go any Lengths with him: a Number of Officers as well as Citizens were ripe for the Measure. It had undoubtedly been deliberately digested, And the Finance Office was probably the Center of Motion. I am well informed that an Attempt was made to draw in the late Secretary at War, But he checkd it with a Firmness, that will always do him Honor. such a Triumvirate, would have been too powerful for the United States; and Heaven only knows what Kind of a Form our foederal Government would have assum'd. The present, by that Party, is held in the utmost Detestation, and they will persevere inflexibly in their Attempts for any Alteration, by Intrigue, and by open Force, when Matters are matured, and promise more Success, than at present.

These Plans, in which our good Allies, were undoubtedly more than idle Spectators, originated in the Beginning of the year 1781 and operated fully before the End of the Year.

Samuel Osgood to John Adams, Annapolis, December 14, 1783 [January 14, 1784], ibid. pp. 414–16

Sir: I had the Pleasure of seeing Mr Thaxter your late private Secretary at Philadelphia. Congress were then on their Way to this Place. He being anxious to return to Mass'tts it was not tho't expedient for him to come on here, as he delivered his Dispatches to the President of Congress in Philadel'a and as it did not seem probable that Congress would be soon assembled at this Place. This is the first Day we have had nine States assembled. About fifteen Days since, having then no Prospect of nine States, it was moved that seven States should proceed to ratify the Definitive Treaty. The Competency of seven States, was urged upon these Grounds, that Nine States had ratified the Provisional Treaty, the Articles of which constituted the definitive. That Nine States did in October last instruct our Ministers commissioned to make Peace to adopt the Provisional Articles as a definitive Treaty unless farther Advantages for the United States could be obtain'd. That the Ratification had become mere Matter of Form. That seven States might expedite it and the United States would be bound thereby.

That the Time for exchanging Ratifications would expire on the 3d of March. That if not exchanged on or before that Time, the Provisional Treaty would be at an End, and it would be in the Option of G. B'n after that Time to accept it, or not as she should think proper. These Assertions, excepting the Matters of Fact, were very warmly opposed, and Congress being pretty equally divided the Matter was of Course delayed till this Day. I hope Colo. Hermer who is entrusted with the Ratification will arrive before the Time expires for exchanging it.

In some of your Letters you seem to be in Opinion that there is an absolute Necessity of braceing up the Confederation. That Funds are necessary for supporting the Credit of the United States. I cannot collect your Ideas precisely. But I am apprehensive that if you were here, you would find it very difficult to establish Funds that would not have a Tendency to destroy the Liberties of this Country. Our Embarassments are very great. Our Danger lies in this – That if permanent Funds are given to Congress, the aristocratical Influence, which predominates in more than a Major Part of the United States will finally establish an arbitrary Government in the United States. I do most heartily wish there was no continental Treasury and that our Debt was equitably divided among the several States. In the Way of this, lays our foreign Debt. perhaps it would be better to establish Funds for this alone. But it is impossible to say what the States will do as to Funds. Congress have none as yet and I am apprehensive they will not have any permanent ones. many of the States are very jealous. Every State imagines or pretends to imagine that they have very large Demands against the United States. The Accounts are unadjusted and I fear it is the Policy of some States to keep them forever in that Situation. This becomes every Day more and more serious. Our State is very deeply interested in it. She is now uneasy about it and that Uneasiness must encrease, for her Delegates however powerful and Eloquent will never be able to argue the Money out of the Pockets of the Citizens of another State into those of our own. At least Appearances are against it at present. Time will discover whether our Union is natural; or rather whether the Dispositions and Views of the several Parts of the Continent are so similar as that they can and will be happy under the same Form of Government. There is too much Reason to believe they are not.

I have been in Congress sometime and intend to leave it forever in four or five Weeks. I have not done myself the Honor to write you from Time to Time; for which Omission I hold myself inexcuseable, Tho I don't know of any Information I could have communicated, which would have essentially altered any Thing. I have seen the Days of Servility, if not of Corruption and I weep over them.

Congress, I think will certainly adjourn the Beginning of May next to the first Monday in November following The Business has greatly diminished since Peace took Place. There are a few Objects of great Magnitude which require the Assent of Nine States. Our Army is dismissed saving about five hundred Men. It now remains with Congress to determine whether they will maintain any Men at the Expence of the United States. The Question has been warmly debated in Congress, but no Decision. The Opponents say that the Confederation gives Congress no Power to keep up Troops in a Time of Peace. There is an inconquerable Aversion in many to any Thing that looks like a standing Army in Time of Peace. They will therefore have no Nest Egg, and why may not every State provide for its own Garrisons. The Confederation speaks this Language. The Question will not obtain in the present Congress. The Civil List must be put upon a new footing before Congress Adjourn. A very important Report respecting the future Negociations with the Indians is now before Congress and will require very close Attention. This is a very delicate Business as it respects the several States. I expect N – Y – – k will purchase all our western Territory of the Indians, before we know it. They are really to cunning for M——tts in Matters of Land.

A general Plan for entering into Commercial Treaties must be matured and adopted before the Recess, And I think by the present Appearance in Congress the Interest of the United States will be the governing Principle. Last November bro't about a capital Revolution in Congress – the Limitation of three Years, struck off a Number indeed all the prime Actors in the late strange and unnatural System of our foreign Affairs. Our State have instructed us to urge a new Arrangement of the Office of Finance. They seem to apprehend that such an Office in the Hands of one Person is incompatible with the Liberties of this Country. A Board in Commission is their Object. The one and the other have very weighty Objections. I wish there was no Occasion for either. I understand the united Netherlands have no public Chest.

Our late Officers having formed themselves into a Society by the Name of the Cincinnati, the Institution begins to be attended to and by many judicious Persons it is tho't that in Time it will be very dangerous. It is suggested that the Idea did not originate on this Side the Atlantic – *Latent Anguis in Herba* – surely this Country will not consent to a Race of Hereditary Patricians. There are many others besides the Officers whose Names ought and will be immortalized for their Conduct during the late War.

I.III.4 SETTLEMENT OF ARMY PAY: OFFICERS AFTER DISCHARGE TO BE SECURED TO FEDERAL INTEREST AS PUBLIC CREDITORS

March 22, 1783, *Journals of the Continental Congress*, XXIV 206–10

Deleted matter indicated thus, ⟨ ⟩.

The committee, consisting of Mr [Nathaniel] Gorham, Mr [John] Collins and Mr [Thomas] Fitzsimmons, to whom was re-committed the Ordinance on the memorial from the inhabitants of Nantucket, reported the draught of a passport, which was read and agreed to.

On the report of a committee, consisting of Mr [Alexander] Hamilton, Mr [Eliphalet] Dyer and Mr [Gunning] Bedford, to whom was referred a motion of Mr [Eliphalet] Dyer, together with the memorial of the officers of the army, and the report of the committee thereon; Congress came to the following resolutions:

Whereas the officers of the several lines under the immediate command of his Excellency General Washington, did, by their late memorial transmitted by their committee, represent to Congress, that the half-pay granted by sundry resolutions, was regarded in an unfavourable light by the citizens of some of these states, who would prefer a compensation for a limited term of years, or by a sum in gross, to an establishment for life; and did, on that account, solicit a commutation of their half pay for an equivalent in one of the two modes above-mentioned, in order to remove all subject of dissatisfaction from the minds of their fellow-citizens: and whereas Congress are desirous, as well of gratifying the reasonable expectations of the officers of the army, as of removing all objections which may exist in any part of the United States, to the principle of the half pay establishment, for which the faith of the United States hath been pledged; persuaded that those objections can only arise from the nature of the compensation, not from any indisposition to compensate those whose services, sacrifices and sufferings, have so just a ⟨claim⟩ title to the approbation and rewards of their country:

Therefore, *Resolved*, That such officers as are now in service, and shall continue therein to the end of the war, shall be entitled to receive the amount of five years' full pay in money, or securities on interest at six per cent. per annum, as Congress shall find most convenient, instead of the half pay promised for life, by the resolution of the 21 day of October, 1780; the said securities to be such as shall be given to other creditors of the United States, provided that it be at the option of the lines of the respective states, and not of officers individually in those lines, to accept or refuse the same; and provided also, that their election shall be signified to Congress through the Commander in Chief, from the lines under his immediate command, within ⟨one month⟩ two months, and through the commanding officer of the southern army, from those under his command, within ⟨three⟩ six months from the date of this resolution:

That the same commutation shall extend to the corps not belonging to the lines of particular states, [and who are entitled to half pay for life as aforesaid]; the acceptance or refusal to be determined by corps, and to be signified in the same manner, and within the same time as abovementioned:

That all officers belonging to the hospital department, who are entitled to half pay by the resolution of the 17th day of January, 1781, may collectively agree to accept or refuse the aforesaid commutation, signifying the same through the Commander in Chief within six months from this time: that ⟨the deranged⟩ such officers ⟨who⟩ as have retired at different periods, entitled to half pay for life, ⟨shall be entitled to the same commutation⟩ may collectively, in each State of which they are inhabitants, accept or refuse the same; their acceptance or refusal to be signified by agents authorised for that purpose, within six months from this period; that with respect to ⟨the deranged officers who have retired on half-pay for life⟩ such retiring officers, the commutation, if accepted by them, shall be in lieu of whatever may be now due to them since the time of their retiring from service, as well as of what might hereafter become due; and that so soon as their acceptance shall be signified, the Superintendant of finance be, and he is hereby directed to take measures for the settlement of their accounts accordingly, and to issue to them certificates bearing interest at six per cent ⟨for what shall be found due to them⟩. That all officers entitled to half pay for life not included in the preceding resolution, may also collectively agree to accept or refuse the aforesaid commutation, signifying the same ⟨by their agents authorised for that purpose⟩ within six months from this time.[1]

[Motion of Mr Oliver Wolcott, seconded by Mr Jonathan Arnold]

Whereas an application has been made by a committee of officers from the army, requesting the United States in Congress Assembled, that a composition should be made for the half pay of such officers as shall be entitled thereto for life, after the expiration of the present war.

And whereas it is the opinion of Congress that five years full pay would be on an average an adequate compensation for the half pay of such officers, as are by sundry acts of Congress entitled thereto as aforesaid.

And whereas it would probably be a matter of convenience to some of the States to settle and discharge the half pay due to the officers of their respective lines, which if it should be effected by them, might prevent those demands upon the funds of the United States which otherwise it would probably be difficult to discharge, it is, therefore,

Resolved, that any State which shall by composition or other satisfactory security settle with the officers of their line, including those who have retired or been deranged therefrom, and who are by acts of Congress entitled to half pay for life after the expiration of the present war, such State shall not be holden to contribute anything on account of said half pay or any composition therefor, to the officers of any other line, excepting only to the line of any State which shall be disabled by the events of the war from making composition or settlement as aforesaid.[2]

[1] This report, in the writing of Alexander Hamilton, except the words in square brackets, which are in the writing of Elias Boudinot, is in the *Papers of the Continental Congress*, no. 21, folios 315 and 332. The vote was transcribed by Thomson on the report.

[2] This motion, in the writing of Oliver Wolcott, is in the *Papers of the Continental Congress*, no. 21, folio 331. It is indorsed: 'Motion of Mr Wolcott seconded by Mr Arnold to postpone the report of the committee on a commutation to the army for their half pay and to take into consideration.'

On the question to agree to the foregoing act, the yeas and nays being required by Mr [Silas] Condict,

State / Member	Vote	State vote
New Hampshire,		
Mr Gilman,	no	no
White,	no	
Massachusetts,		
Mr Holten,	ay	ay
Osgood,	ay	
Gorham,	ay	
Higginson,	ay	
Rhode Island,		
Mr Arnold,	no	*
Connecticut,		
Mr Wolcott,	ay	ay
Dyer,	ay	
New York,		
Mr Floyd,	ay	ay
Hamilton,	ay	
New Jersey,		
Mr Boudinot,	ay	no
Clark,	no	
Condict,	no	
Pennsylvania,		
Mr Fitzsimmons,	ay	ay
Wilson,	ay	
Montgomery,	ay	
Peters,	ay	
Delaware,		
Mr McComb,	ay	ay
Bedford,	ay	
Maryland,		
Mr T. S. Lee,	ay	ay
Hemsley,	ay	
Virginia,		
Mr Madison,	ay	ay
Bland,	ay	
A. Lee,	ay	
Mercer,	ay	
North Carolina,		
Mr Hawkins,	ay	ay
Williamson,	ay	
South Carolina,		
Mr Rutledge,	ay	ay
Izard,	ay	
Gervais,	ay	

So it was resolved in the affirmative.[1]

[1] On this day, according to the indorsement, was read a letter from General Washington, dated March 18, giving the result of the proceedings of the meeting of officers at Newburgh. It is in the *Papers of the Continental Congress*, no. 152, XI, folios 131–6, and is printed in the *Writings of Washington* (Ford), X 178. According to the record in Committee Book no. 186, it was referred, March 22, together with Washington's letter of March 12, and the Proceedings of the Officers, March 15, to Mr [Samuel] Osgood, Mr [Theodorick] Bland, Mr [Alexander] Hamilton, Mr [Oliver] Wolcott, and Mr [Richard] Peters, who delivered a report April 1.

I.III.5 FINANCIAL EXIGENCIES OF CONGRESS

February 13, 1786, *Journals of the Continental Congress*, XXX 62–8

The Committee, consisting of Mr. [Rufus] King, Mr. [Charles] Pinckney, Mr. [John] Kean, Mr. [James] Monroe, and Mr. [Charles] Pettit, to whom were referred several Reports and Documents, concerning the system of General Revenue, recommended by Congress on the 18th of April 1783, Report:

That in pursuance of the above Reference, they have carefully examined the acts of the several States, relative to the general system of Revenue recommended by Congress on the 18th. of April, 1783, and find that the states of Delaware and North Carolina, have passed acts in full conformity with the several parts thereof; the former of which states has inserted a proviso in their act, restraining the operation thereof; until each of the other states shall have made a like and equally extensive Grant; that the States of New Hampshire, Massachusetts, Connecticut, New Jersey, Virginia and South Carolina, have each passed acts complying with that part of the system, which recommends a general impost, but have come to no decision on the other part, which proposes the establishment of Funds, supplementary to, and in aid of the general impost; that the state of Pennsylvania has passed an act complying with the recommendation of the general impost; and in the same act has declared, that their proportion or Quota of the supplementary Funds, shall be raised and levied on the persons and Estates of the inhabitants of that state, in such manner as the Legislature thereof shall from time to time direct, with this proviso, that if any of the annual proportion of the supplementary funds shall be otherwise raised and paid to the U. S. then such annual levy or Tax shall be discontinued: The committee conceive that this clause is rather an Engagement that Pennsylvania will provide adequate supplementary funds, than an actual establishment thereof; nevertheless, the act contains a proviso restraining its operation, until each of the other states shall have passed laws in full conformity with the whole of the Revenue system aforesaid: The committee farther find that the state of R. Island has passed an Act on this Subject, but so different from the plan recommended, and so wholly insufficient that it cannot be considered as a compliance with any part of the system submitted for their adoption; that the State of Maryland passed an act in 1782, and a supplement thereof in 1784, complying with the *recommendation* of Congress of the 3d of February, 1781, which *recommendation* is not compatible with, and was relinquished by the resolves of Congress of the 18th. of April, 1783; but that neither the state of Maryland, New York, nor Georgia, has passed any Act in pursuance of the system of the 18th. of April, 1783.

From this Statement it appears that Seven States, viz. New Hampshire, Massachusetts, Connecticut, New Jersey, Virginia, North Carolina, and South Carolina, have granted the Impost in such manner, that if the other Six States had made similar Grants, the plan of the general impost might immediately begin to operate; that two other states, viz. Pennsylvania and Delaware, have also granted the impost, but have connected their grants with proviso's, which will suspend their operation until all the other states shall have passed laws in full conformity with the whole of the Revenue system aforesaid; that two only of these nine states, viz. Delaware and North Carolina, have fully acceeded to that system in all its parts; and that the four other states, viz. R. Island, New York, Maryland and Georgia have not decided in favor of any part of the system of Revenue aforesaid, so long since, and so repeatedly presented by Congress for their Adoption.

The Committee have thought it their Duty candidly to examine the principles of this System, and to discover if possible the Reasons which have prevented its adoption; they cannot learn that any member of the confederacy has stated or brought forth any objections against it, and the result of their impartial Enquiries into the nature and Operation of the plan, has been a clear and decided Opinion, that the system itself is more free from well founded exceptions, and is better calculated to receive the approbation of the several States than any other that the wisdom of Congress can devise.

In the course of this enquiry it most clearly appeared, that the Requisitions of Congress for Eight years past have been so irregular in their operation, so uncertain in their collection, and so evidently unproductive, that a Reliance on them in future, as a Source from whence monies are to be drawn, to discharge the engagements of the confederacy, definite as they are in time and amount, would be not less dishonorable to the Understandings of those, who entertain such confidence, than it would be dangerous to the welfare and peace of the Union. The committee are therefore seriously impressed with the indispensible Obligation that Congress are under of representing to the immediate and impartial consideration of the several States, the utter impossibility of maintaining and preserving the Faith of the federal government, by temporary Requisitions on the states, and the consequent necessity of an early and complete accession of all the States to the Revenue system of the 18th of April, 1783.

Although in a business of this magnitude, and importance to the respective States, it was natural to expect a due degree of caution, and a thorough investigation of the system recommended, yet the committee cannot forbear to remark, that this plan has been under Reference for nearly three years; that during that period numerous changes have taken place in the Delegations of every State, but that this system has received the repeated approbation of each successive congress, and that the urgency of the public engagements at this time, renders it the unquestionable Duty of the several States to adopt, without farther delay, those measures, which alone in the Judgment of the committee, can preserve the sacred faith of this Confederacy.

The following state of facts must convince the States of the propriety of urging this system with unusual anxiety at this period.

	Dollars
That the sum necessary to discharge the interest on loans of the King of France, to January 1, 1787, is	240,740·60
For interest on Certificates to foreign Officers made payable in France to January 1, 1787	22,370
For interest on the Spanish Loan, to March 21, 1787	48,596·55
For interest on the Dutch Loans, to June 1, 1787	265,000
	577,307·25

That although some of the Objects of Disbursement are in the year 1787, the periods at which they become due, will shew the absolute necessity of an immediate provision for them.

That notwithstanding some of the above sums do not fall due until 1787, yet there will be due exclusive of the same, in that year, 1,252,938 Dollars and 57/90 and during the nine succeeding years that is until the year 1797, including the payment of the interest and the partial reimbursements of the Capitals of the French and Dutch Loans, the average sum of near one million of Dollars annually; for the certain obtaining of which, at fixed periods, effectual measures can no longer be delayed. More fully to illustrate this subject, the committee annex a schedule of the French and Dutch Loans, shewing the periods of their Redemption, with the annual interest payable thereon, until their final Extinction. In addition to the above foreign demands, the interest on the Spanish Loan, and on the Debts due to foreign Officers, must be provided for and annually paid. The amount of these annual Demands will be greatly increased by adding the annual interest on the domestic Debt, the whole of which is not yet liquidated, and the aggregate whereof, will consequently be enlarged beyond its last Estimate.

The committee contemplate, with great satisfaction, the prospect of extinguishing a part of the domestic Debt, by the sales of the western Territory of the United States; but a considerable Time must elapse before that Country can be surveyed and disposed of; and the domestic creditors, until that Event, must depend for support on the Justice of their Country: The Revenue system, if adopted, would afford this support, and enable Congress to fulfill the public Engagements with their Foreign Creditors. The whole product of this System is appropriated for the payment of the principal and interest of the national Debt, and no part thereof can be diverted to other purposes.

That it has been the earnest wish of congress to prevent the vast accumulation of foreign interest that now exists, appears from their Estimates and Requisitions of the 27th of April, 1784, and the 27th Sept. 1785; and the following Abstract, taken from the books of the Treasury, of the amount of monies brought into the federal Treasury in the course of the last four years, viz. between the 1st November, 1781, and the 1st January, 1786, will shew the little success of Requisitions, and demonstrate the inadequacy of their products to maintain the federal Government, and at the same time to discharge the annual public Engagements:

	Dollars
The Receipts of Taxes from the 1st November, 1781, to the 1st November, 1784, amount to	2,025,089·34
From the 1st November, 1784, to the 1st January, 1786	432,897·81
Total	2,457,987·25

Thus it is evident that the sum of 2,457,987 Dollars and 25/90th only, was received in a space of more than four years, when the Requisitions in the most forcible manner, pressed on the States the payment of much larger sums, and for purposes of the highest national importance. It should be here observed, that the Receipts of the last fourteen months of the above period, amount only to 432,897 Dollars and 81/90 which is at the rate of 371,052 Dollars per annum, a sum short of what is essentially necessary for the bare maintenance of the federal Government on the most economical Establishment, and in time of profound peace.

The committee observe, with great concern, that the security of the navigation and commerce of the Citizens of these States from the Barbary powers, the protection of the Frontier inhabitants from the Savages, the immediate establishment of military magazines in different parts of the Union, rendered indispensable by the principles of public Safety, the maintenance of the federal Government at home, and the support of the public Servants abroad, each, and all, depend upon the contributions of the States under the annual Requisitions of Congress. The monies essentially necessary for these important Objects, will so far exceed the Sums formerly collected from the States by Taxes, that no Hope can be indulged of being able, from that Source, to make any Remittances for the discharge of foreign Engagements.

Thus circumstanced, after the most solemn deliberation, and under the fullest conviction that the public embarrassments are such as above represented, and that they are daily encreasing, the committee are of opinion, that it has become the Duty of Congress to declare most explicitly, that the Crisis has arrived, when the people of these United States, by whose will, and for whose benefit the federal Government was instituted, must decide, whether they will support their Rank as a nation, by maintaining the public faith at home, and abroad; or whether, for want of a timely exertion in establishing a General Revenue, and thereby giving strength to the confederacy, they *will hazard not only the existence of the Union, but of those great and invaluable privileges, for which they have so arduously and so honorably contended.*

And to the end that Congress may remain wholly acquitted from every imputation of a want of attention to the interest and welfare of those whom they represent, the committee submit the following Resolves –

Resolved, That the Requisitions of congress of the 27th of April, 1784, and the 27th of September, 1785, cannot be considered as the establishment of a System of General Revenue, in opposition to that recommended to the several states by the resolves of congress of the 18th of April, 1783: That the said Requisitions were adopted for the exigencies of Government, and as a temporary provision for the payment of the interest of the National Debt; and that Congress have ever trusted that the Good Sense and Experience of the several States, would impress on them the necessity of adopting, in the fullest manner, the Resolves above mentioned.

Resolved, That the Resolves of congress of the 18th of April, 1783, recommending a system of general Revenue, be again presented to the consideration of the Legislatures of the several States, which have not fully complied with the same. That it be earnestly recommended to the Legislatures of New Hampshire, Massachusetts, Connecticut, New Jersey, Pensylvania, Virginia and South Carolina, which have complied only in part with the said system, completely to adopt the same; and to the Legislatures of the States of Rhode Island, New York, Maryland, and Georgia, which have not adopted the said system, either in whole or in part, to pass Laws without further Delay, in full conformity with the same. But as it is highly necessary that every possible aid should in the most expeditious manner be obtained to the Revenue of the United States, it is therefore recommended to the several states that in adopting the said system they enable the United States in Congress assembled to carry into effect that part which relates to the imposts so soon as it shall be acceeded to.

Resolved, That whilst the United States in Congress, are denied the means of satisfying those Engagements which they have constitutionally entered into for the common Benefit of the Union; they cannot be responsible for those fatal Evils which will inevitably flow from a breach of Public faith, pledged by solemn contract, and a violation of those principles of Justice, which are the only solid Basis of the honor and prosperity of Nations.

August 16, 1786, ibid. XXXI 521–3
Deleted matter indicated thus, ⟨ ⟩.

The Committee consisting of Mr [William Samuel] Johnson, Mr [Charles] Pinckney and Mr [Charles] Pettit to whom was referred a motion of Mr Pinckney, Report:

That in examining the several provisions which have been intended by Congress for the security and payment of the domestic debt, they find that such has been the inattention of the several states to the annual requisition of Congress and so few of them have passed acts in conformity with that part of the Revenue system of the 18 April, 1783, which proposes the establishment of funds supplementary to and in aid of the general impost, that no reasonable hope can be indulged of effectual provision being made by either of the means above mentioned.

That it appears to your committee expedient some mode should be established for the speedy extinguishment of the said domestic debt and which would tend to equalize its burden by drawing from the several members of the confederacy their full and just proportions of the same.

After the fullest investigation there appears no mode so reasonable or so probable of success as that of apportioning upon the several states their quota's of the domestic debt as far as the same is at present liquidated and requiring them to pay the same into the federal treasury at a stated period.

Whereupon the Committee submit to Congress the following resolutions:

Resolved, That the Board of Treasury be and they are hereby directed to report a requisition on the several states for their respective quotas of the domestic debt as far as the same is at present liquidated and ascertained.

That the said states be required to pay their respective quotas of the said debt into the federal treasury on or before the day of in continental loan office certificates and other certificates of debts due from the United States liquidated and ascertained according to the direction of the United States in Congress assembled, the Loan office certificates bearing date after the last day of february, 1778, to be liquidated by the scale of June, 1780.

That if any state shall offer in payment Certificates, whereon interest has not been paid up to the 31st December, 1785, such state shall be credited on account of the facility part of the requisitions of 1785 and 1786 for the amount of such interest as may remain due on such certificates to the said 31 december 1785.

That any state which shall have paid its quota of such certificates shall at any time after the Expiration of the said Day of be permitted to pay in any farther sum in certificates of the like kind to be passed to the credit of such state and be allowed in the settlement of the general account of such state with the United States.

That the vacant territory of the U. S. to be sold in the respective states Pursuant to the Ordinance of the 20th May, 1785, may be paid for in the mode therein mentioned or in such certificates of debts due from the state in which the lands are as aforesaid to be sold as such state shall direct, – provided such state shall be paid into the treasury of the U. S. the quota of certificates demanded by the said requisition.

That the states shall respectively have Credit on account of the supplementary funds recommended by the system of 18 April, 1783, or on account of such requisition as may hereafter be made for the purpose of paying the interests of the domestic debt, for the amount of the interests which shall from time to time become due from and after the 31st December, 1785, on such certificates of liquidated debts as any state shall have paid in, pursuant to the said requisition.

The Committee consisting of Mr [William Samuel] Johnson, Mr [Charles] Pinckney and Mr Pettit to whom was referred a motion of Mr [Charles] Pinckney, Report in part:

That in pursuance of the above reference they have carefully examined the acts passed by the several states relative to the general system of revenue recommended by Congress on the 18 April, 1783, and find that only the states of Massachusetts, Pennsylvania, Delaware, Maryland, and North Carolina have passed acts in pursuance of that part of the recommendation which proposes the establishment of funds supplementary to, and in aid of the general impost.

That it appears to your committee indispensably necessary to the restoration of public credit – the honourable and punctual discharge of the debts of the United States and the equalising the said system of revenue, that this part of the recommendation should be speedily and fully complied with by all the members of the Confederacy.

Whereupon the committee ⟨recommend⟩ submit to Congress the following resolution:

Resolved, That it be again earnestly recommended to the legislatures of the states of New Hampshire, Rhode Island, Connecticut, New York, New Jersey, Virginia, South Carolina, and Georgia which have not yet complied with that part of the system of general revenue recommended by Congress on the 18 April, 1783, which proposes the establishment of funds supplementary to and in aid of the general impost to pass laws ⟨without further delay⟩ in full conformity with the same at their session next succeeding the date of these resolutions and not further delay the completion of a system so essential to the assertion of the public credit and the honourable and punctual discharge of the debts of the U. S.

I.III.6 CONGRESS PROPOSES AMENDMENTS TO THE ARTICLES OF CONFEDERATION

August 7, 1786, *Journals of the Continental Congress*, XXXI 494–8

Deleted matter indicated thus, ⟨ ⟩.

The Grand Committee consisting of Mr [Samuel] Livermore, Mr [Nathan] Dane, Mr [James] Manning, Mr [William Samuel] Johnson, Mr [Melancton] Smith, Mr [John Cleves] Symmes, Mr [Charles] Pettit, Mr [William] Henry, Mr [Henry] Lee, Mr [Timothy] Bloodworth, Mr [Charles] Pinckney and Mr [William] Houstoun appointed to report such amendments to the confederation, and such resolutions as it may be necessary to recommend to the several states for the purpose of obtaining from them such powers as will render the federal government adequate to the ends for which it was instituted.

Beg leave to submit the following Report to the consideration of Congress:

Resolved, That it be recommended to the Legislatures of the several States to adopt the following Articles as Articles of the Confederation, and to authorise their Delegates in Congress to sign and ratify the same severally as they shall be adopted, to wit:

ART. 14. The United States in Congress Assembled shall have the sole and exclusive power of regulating the trade of the States as well with foreign Nations as with each other and of laying such prohibitions and such Imposts and duties upon imports and exports as may be Necessary for the purpose; provided the Citizens of the States shall in no instance be subjected to pay higher duties and Imposts that those imposed on the subjects of foreign powers, provided also, that all such duties as may be imposed shall be collected under such regulations as the united States in Congress Assembled shall establish consistent with the Constitutions of the States Respectively and to accrue to the use of the State in which the same shall be payable; provided also, that the Legislative power of the several States shall not be restrained from laying embargoes in time of Scarcity and provided lastly that every Act of Congress for the above purpose shall have the assent of Nine States in Congress Assembled, and in that proportion when there shall be more than thirteen in the Union.

ART. 15. That the respective States may be induced to perform the several duties mutually and solemnly agreed to be performed by their federal Compact, and to prevent unreasonable delays in any State in furnishing her just proportion of the common Charges of the Union when called upon, and those essential evils which have heretofore often arisen to the Confederacy from such delays, it is agreed that whenever a requisition shall be made by Congress upon the several States on the principles of the Confederation for their quotas of the common charges or land forces of the Union Congress shall fix the proper periods when the States shall pass Legislative Acts complying therewith and give full and compleat effect to the same and if any State shall neglect, seasonably to pass such Acts such State shall be charged with an additional sum to her quota called for from the time she may be required to pay or furnish the same, which additional sum or charge shall be at the rate of ten per Cent pr. annum on her said Quota, and if the requisition shall be for Land forces, and any State shall neglect to furnish her quota in time the average expence of such quota shall be ascertained by Congress, and such State shall be charged therewith, or with the average expence of what she may be deficient and in addition thereto from the time her forces were required to be ready to act in the field with a farther sum which sum shall be at the rate of twelve per Cent per Annum on the amount of such expences.

ART. 16. And that the resources of any State which may be negligent in furnishing her just proportion of the Common expence of the Union may in a reasonable time be applied, it is further agreed that if any State shall so Neglect as aforesaid to pass laws in compliance with the said Requisition and to adopt measures to give the same full effect for the space of Ten months, and it shall then or afterwards be found that a Majority of the States have passed such laws and adopted such measures the United States in Congress Assembled shall have full power and authority to levy, assess, and collect all sums and duties with which any such state so neglecting to comply with the requisition may stand charged on the same by the Laws and Rules by which the last State tax next preceeding such requisition in such State was levied, assessed and Collected, to apportion the sum so required on the Towns or Counties in such State to order the sums so apportioned to be assessed by the assessors of such last State tax and the said assessments to be committed to the Collector of the same last

State tax to collect and to make returns of such assessments and Commitments to the Treasurer of the United States who by himself or his deputy, when directed by Congress shall have power to recover the monies of such Collectors for the use of the United States in the same manner and under the same penalties as State taxes are recovered and collected by the Treasurers of the respective States and the several Towns or Counties respectively shall be responsible for the conduct of said Assessors and Collectors and in case there shall be any vacancy in any of said Offices of Assessors or Collectors by death, removal, refusal to serve, resignation or otherwise, then other fit persons shall be chosen to fill such Vacancies in the usual manner in such Town or County within Twenty days after Notice of the assessment, and in case any Towns or Counties, any assessor, Collectors or Sheriffs shall Neglect or refuse to do their duty Congress shall have the same rights and powers to compel them that the State may have in assessing and collecting State Taxes.

And if any state by any Legislative Act shall prevent or delay the due Collection of said sums as aforesaid, Congress shall have full power and authority to appoint assessors and Collectors thereof and Sheriffs to enforce the Collections under the warrants of distress issued by the Treasurer of the United States, and if any further opposition shall be made to such Collections by the State or the Citizens thereof, and their conduct not disapproved of by the State, such conduct on the part of the State shall be considered as an open Violation of the federal compact.

ART. 17. And any State which from time to time shall be found in her payments on any Requisition in advance on an average of the payments made by the State shall be allowed an interest of ⟨six⟩ – per Cent pr. annum on her said advanced sums or expences and the State which from time to time shall be found in arrear on the principles aforesaid shall be charged with an Interest of ⟨six⟩ – per Cent pr. annum on the sums in which she may be so in arrear.

ART. 18. In case it shall hereafter be found Necessary by Congress to establish any new Systems of Revenue and to make any new regulations in the finances of the U. S. for a limited term not exceeding fifteen years in their operation for supplying the common Treasury with monies for defraying all charges of war, and all other expences that shall be incurred for the common defence or general welfare, and such new Systems or regulations shall be agreed to and adopted by the United States in Congress Assembled and afterwards be confirmed by the Legislatures of eleven States and in that proportion when there shall be more than thirteen States in the Union, the same shall become binding on all the States, as fully as if the Legislatures of all the States should confirm the same.

ART. 19. The United States in Congress Assembled shall have the sole and exclusive power of declaring what offences against the United States shall be deemed treason, and what Offences against the same Mis-prison of treason, and what Offences shall be deemed piracy or felony on the high Seas and to annex suitable punishments to all the Offences aforesaid respectively, and power to institute a federal Judicial Court for trying and punishing all officers appointed by Congress for all crimes, offences, and misbehaviour in their Offices and to which Court an Appeal shall be allowed from the Judicial Courts of the several States in all Causes wherein questions shall arise on the meaning and construction of Treaties entered into by the United States with any foreign power, or on the Law of Nations, or wherein any question shall arise respecting any regulations that may hereafter be made by Congress relative to trade and Commerce, or the Collection of federal Revenues pursuant to powers that shall be vested in that body or wherein questions of importance may arise and the United States shall be a party – provided that the trial of the fact by Jury shall ever be held sacred, and also the benefits of the writ of *Habeas Corpus;* provided also that no member of Congress or officer holding any other office under the United States shall be a Judge of said Court, and the said Court shall consist of Seven Judges, to be appointed from the different parts of the Union to wit, one from New Hampshire, Rhode Island, and Connecticut, one from Massachusetts, one from New York and New Jersey, one from Pennsylvania, one from Delaware and Maryland, one from Virginia, and one from North Carolina, South Carolina and Georgia, and four of whom shall be a quorum to do business.

ART. 20. That due attention may be given to the affairs of the Union early in the federal year, and the sessions of Congress made as short as conveniently may be each State shall elect her Delegates annually before the first of July and make it their duty to give an Answer before the first of September in every year, whether they accept their appointments or not, and make effectual provision for filling the places of those who may decline, before the first of October yearly, and to transmit to Congress by the tenth of the same month, the names of the Delegates who shall be appointed and accept their appointments, and it shall be the indispensable duty of Delegates to make a representation of their State in Congress on the first Monday in November annually, and if any Delegate or Delegates, when required by Congress to attend so far as may be Necessary to keep up a Representation of each State in Congress, or having taken his or their Seat, shall with-draw without leave of Congress, unless recalled by the State, he or they shall be proceeded against as Congress shall direct, provided no punishment shall be further extended than to disqualifications any longer to be members of Congress, or to hold any Office of trust or profit under the United States or any individual State, and the several States shall adopt regulations effectual to the attainment of the ends of this Article.[1]

[1] This report, the preamble in the writing of Charles Pinckney and the rest in the writing of Henry Remsen Jr., is in the *Papers of the Continental Congress*, no. 24, folio 179. According to indorsement it was read August 7 and Monday the 14th assigned.

IV Towards a New Constitution

I.IV.1 RESOLUTION OF THE GENERAL ASSEMBLY OF VIRGINIA, JANUARY 21, 1786

Documents illustrative of the Formation of the Union (Washington, D.C., 1927) p. 38

Resolved, That Edmund Randolph, James Madison, jun., Walter Jones, Saint George Tucker, and Meriwether Smith, Esquires, be appointed commissioners, who, or any three of whom, shall meet such commissioners as may be appointed by the other States in the Union, at a time and place to be agreed on, to take into consideration the trade of the United States; to examine the relative situations and trade of the said States; to consider how far a uniform system in their commercial regulations may be necessary to their common interest and their permanent harmony; and to report to the several States, such an act relative to this great object, as, when unanimously ratified by them, will enable the United States in Congress, effectually to provide for the same.

I.IV.2 PROCEEDINGS OF COMMISSIONERS TO REMEDY DEFECTS OF THE FEDERAL GOVERNMENT, ANNAPOLIS IN THE STATE OF MARYLAND, SEPTEMBER 11, 1786

Ibid. pp. 39–43

At a meeting of Commissioners, from the States of New York, New Jersey, Pennsylvania, Delaware and Virginia –

Present

ALEXANDER HAMILTON EGBERT BENSON	*New York*
ABRAHAM CLARKE WILLIAM C. HOUSTON JAMES SCHUARMAN	*New Jersey*
TENCH COXE	*Pennsylvania*
GEORGE READ JOHN DICKINSON RICHARD BASSETT	*Delaware*
EDMUND RANDOLPH JAMES MADISON, Junior SAINT GEORGE TUCKER	*Virginia*

Mr Dickinson was unanimously elected Chairman.

The Commissioners produced their Credentials from their respective States; which were read.

After a full communication of Sentiments, and deliberate consideration of what would be proper to be done by the Commissioners now assembled, it was unanimously agreed: that a Committee be appointed to prepare a draft of a Report to be made to the States having Commissioners attending at this meeting . . .

September 14, 1786
. . . the Report . . . was unanimously agreed to, and is as follows, to wit.

To the Honorable, the Legislatures of Virginia, Delaware, Pennsylvania, New Jersey, and New York –

The Commissioners from the said States, respectively assembled at Annapolis, humbly beg leave to report.

That, pursuant to their several appointments, they met, at Annapolis in the State of Maryland, on the eleventh day of September Instant, and having proceeded to a Communication of their powers; they found that the States of New York, Pennsylvania, and Virginia, had, in substance, and nearly in the same terms, authorised their respective

Commissioners 'to meet such Commissioners as were, or might be, appointed by the other States in the Union, at such time and place, as should be agreed upon by the said Commissioners to take into consideration the trade and Commerce of the United States, to consider how far an uniform system in their commercial intercourse and regulations might be necessary to their common interest and permanent harmony, and to report to the several States such an Act, relative to this great object, as when unanimously ratified by them would enable the United States in Congress assembled effectually to provide for the same.'

That the State of Delaware, had given similar powers to their Commissioners, with this difference only, that the Act to be framed in virtue of those powers, is required to be reported 'to the United States in Congress assembled, to be agreed to by them, and confirmed by the Legislatures of every State'.

That the State of New Jersey had enlarged the object of their appointment, empowering their Commissioners, 'to consider how far an uniform system in their commercial regulations and *other important matters*, might be necessary to the common interest and permanent harmony of the several States', and to report such an Act on the subject, as when ratified by them 'would enable the United States in Congress assembled, effectually to provide for the exigencies of the Union'.

That appointments of Commissioners have also been made by the States of New Hampshire, Massachusetts, Rhode Island, and North Carolina, none of whom however have attended; but that no information has been received by your Commissioners, of any appointment having been made by the States of Connecticut, Maryland, South Carolina, or Georgia.

That the express terms of the powers to your Commissioners supposing a deputation from all the States, and having for object the Trade and Commerce of the United States, Your Commissioners did not conceive it advisable to proceed on the business of their mission, under the Circumstance of so partial and defective a representation.

Deeply impressed however with the magnitude and importance of the object confided to them on this occasion, your Commissioners cannot forbear to indulge an expression of their earnest and unanimous wish, that speedy measures may be taken, to effect a general meeting, of the States, in a future Convention, for the same, and such other purposes, as the situation of public affairs, may be found to require.

If in expressing this wish, or in intimating any other sentiment, your Commissioners should seem to exceed the strict bounds of their appointment, they entertain a full confidence, that a conduct, dictated by an anxiety for the welfare, of the United States, will not fail to receive an indulgent construction.

In this persuasion, your Commissioners submit an opinion, that the Idea of extending the powers of their Deputies, to other objects, than those of Commerce, which has been adopted by the State of New Jersey, was an improvement on the original plan, and will deserve to be incorporated into that of a future Convention; they are the more naturally led to this conclusion, as in the course of their reflections on the subject, they have been induced to think, that the power of regulating trade is of such comprehensive extent, and will enter so far into the general System of the fœderal government, that to give it efficacy, and to obviate questions and doubts concerning its precise nature and limits, may require a correspondent adjustment of other parts of the Fœderal System.

That there are important defects in the system of the Fœderal Government is acknowledged by the Acts of all those States, which have concurred in the present Meeting; That the defects, upon a closer examination, may be found greater and more numerous, than even these acts imply, is at least so far probable, from the embarrassments which characterise the present State of our national affairs, foreign and domestic, as may reasonably be supposed to merit a deliberate and candid discussion, in some mode, which will unite the Sentiments and Councils of all the States. In the choice of the mode, your Commissioners are of opinion, that a Convention of Deputies from the different States, for the special and sole purpose of entering into this investigation, and digesting a plan for supplying such defects as may be discovered to exist, will be entitled to a preference from considerations, which will occur, without being particularised.

Your Commissioners decline an enumeration of those national circumstances on which their opinion respecting the propriety of a future Convention, with more enlarged powers, is founded; as it would be an useless intrusion of facts and observations, most of which have been frequently the subject of public discussion, and none of which can have escaped the penetration of those to whom they would in this instance be addressed. They are however of a nature so serious, as, in the view of your Commissioners to render the situation of the

United States delicate and critical, calling for an exertion of the united virtue and wisdom of all the members of the Confederacy.

Under this impression, Your Commissioners, with the most respectful deference, beg leave to suggest their unanimous conviction, that it may essentially tend to advance the interests of the union, if the States, by whom they have been respectively delegated, would themselves concur, and use their endeavours to procure the concurrence of the other States, in the appointment of Commissioners, to meet at Philadelphia on the second Monday in May next, to take into consideration the situation of the United States, to devise such further provisions as shall appear to them necessary to render the constitution of the Fœderal Government adequate to the exigencies of the Union; and to report such an Act for that purpose to the United States in Congress assembled, as when agreed to, by them, and afterwards confirmed by the Legislatures of every State, will effectually provide for the same.

Though your Commissioners could not with propriety address these observations and sentiments to any but the States they have the honor to Represent, they have nevertheless concluded from motives of respect, to transmit Copies of this Report to the United States in Congress assembled, and to the executives of the other States.

I.IV.3 RESOLUTION OF GENERAL ASSEMBLY OF VIRGINIA TO APPOINT DELEGATES TO A CONVENTION IN PHILADELPHIA, OCTOBER 16, 1786

Records of the Federal Convention of 1787, ed. Max Farrand (New Haven, 1937) III 559–60

Whereas the Commissioners who assembled at Annapolis on the fourteenth day of September last for the purpose of devising and reporting the means of enabling Congress to provide effectually for the Commercial Interests of the United States have represented the necessity of extending the revision of the fœderal System to all it's defects and have recommended that Deputies for that purpose be appointed by the several Legislatures to meet in Convention in the

City of Philadelphia on the second [Mon]day of May next, a provision which was preferable to a discussion of the subject in Congress where it might be too much interrupted by the ordinary business before them and where it would besides be deprived of the valuable Counsels of sundry Individuals who are disqualified by the Constitution or Laws of particular States or restrained by peculiar circumstances from a Seat in that Assembly: And Whereas the General Assembly of this Commonwealth, taking into view the actual situation of the Confederacy as well as reflecting on the alarming representations made from time to time by the United States in Congress particularly in their Act of the fifteenth day of February last can no longer doubt that the Crisis is arrived at which the good People of America are to decide the solemn question whether they will by wise and magnanimous Efforts reap the just fruits of that Independence which they have so gloriously acquired and of that Union which they have cemented with so much of their common Blood, or whether by giving way to unmanly Jealousies and Prejudices or to partial and transitory Interests they will renounce the auspicious blessings prepared for them by the Revolution, and furnish to its Enemies an eventual Triumph over those by whose virtue and valor it has been accomplished: And Whereas the same noble and extended policy and the same fraternal and affectionate Sentiments which originally determined the Citizens of this Commonwealth to unite with their Bretheren of the other States in establishing a Fœderal Government cannot but be Felt with equal force now as motives to lay aside every inferior consideration and to concur in such farther concessions and Provisions as may be necessary to secure the great Objects for which that Government was instituted and to render the *United States* as happy in peace as they have been glorious in War: Be it therefore enacted by the General Assembly of the Commonwealth of Virginia that seven Commissioners be appointed by joint Ballot of both Houses of Assembly who, or any three of them, are hereby authorized as Deputies from this Commonwealth to meet such Deputies as may be appointed and authorized by other States to assemble in Convention at Philadelphia as above recommended and to join with them in devising and discussing all such Alterations and farther Provisions as may be necessary to render the Fœderal Constitution adequate to the Exigencies of the Union and in reporting such an Act for that purpose to the United States in Congress as when agreed to by them and duly confirmed by the several States will effectually provide for the same... AND the Governor is requested to transmit forthwith a Copy of this Act to the United States in Congress and to the Executives of each of the States in the Union.

I.IV.4 CONGRESS RESOLVES TO SUMMON A CONVENTION IN PHILADELPHIA

February 21, 1787, *Journals of the Continental Congress*, XXXII 71–4

The report of a grand com'ee . . . was called up and which is contained in the following resolution viz

'Congress having had under consideration the letter of John Dickinson esqr. chairman of the Commissioners who assembled at Annapolis during the last year also the proceedings of the said commissioners and entirely coinciding with them as to the inefficiency of the federal government and the necessity of devising such farther provisions as shall render the same adequate to the exigencies of the Union do strongly recommend to the different legislatures to send forward delegates to meet the proposed convention on the second Monday in May next at the city of Philadelphia.'

The delegates for the state of New York thereupon laid before Congress Instructions which they had received from their constituents, and in pursuance of the said instructions moved to postpone the farther consideration of the report in order to take up the following proposition to wit:

'That it be recommended to the States composing the Union that a convention of representatives from the said States respectively be held at on for the purpose of revising the Articles of Confederation and perpetual Union between the United States of America and reporting to the United States in Congress assembled and to the States respectively such alterations and amendments of the said Articles of Confederation as the representatives met in such convention shall judge proper and necessary to render them adequate to the preservation and support of the Union.'

On the question to postpone for the purpose above mentioned . . . the question was lost.

A motion was then made by the delegates for Massachusetts to postpone the farther consideration of the report in order to take into consideration a motion which they read in their place; this being agreed to, the motion of the delegates for Massachusetts was taken up and being amended was agreed to as follows

Whereas there is provision in the Articles of Confederation and perpetual Union for making alterations therein by the assent of a Congress of the United States and of the legislatures of the several States; And whereas experience hath evinced that there are defects in the present Confederation, as a mean to remedy which several of the States and particularly the State of New York, by express instructions to their delegates in Congress have suggested a convention for the purposes expressed in the following resolution, and such convention appearing to be the most probable mean of establishing in these states a firm national government.

Resolved that in the opinion of Congress it is expedient that on the second Monday in May next a Convention of delegates who shall have been appointed by the several states be held at Philadelphia for the sole and express purpose of revising the Articles of Confederation and reporting to Congress and the several legislatures such alterations and provisions therein as shall, when agreed to in Congress and confirmed by the states render the federal constitution adequate to the exigencies of Government and the preservation of the Union.

V The Convention and the Constitution

I.V.I THE VIRGINIA PLAN

Records of the Federal Convention of 1787, I 18–23

Mr. RANDOLPH then opened the main business . . .

He expressed his regret, that it should fall to him, rather than those, who were of longer standing in life and political experience, to open the great subject of their mission. But, as the convention had originated from Virginia, and his colleagues supposed that some proposition was expected from them, they had imposed this task on him.

He then commented on the difficulty of the crisis, and the necessity of preventing the fulfilment of the prophecies of the American downfal.

He observed that in revising the fœderal system we ought to inquire 1. into the properties, which such a government ought to possess, 2. the defects of the confederations, 3. the danger of our situation & 4. the remedy.

1. The Character of such a government ought to secure *1.* against foreign invasion: *2.* against dissentions between members of the Union, or seditions in particular states: *3.* to procure to the several States various blessings, of which an isolated situation was incapable: *4.* to be able to defend itself against incroachment: & *5.* to be paramount to the state constitutions.

2. In speaking of the defects of the confederation he professed a high respect for its authors, and considered them, as having done all that patriots could do, in the then infancy of the science, of constitutions, & of confederacies, – when the inefficiency of requisitions was unknown – no commercial discord had arisen among any states – no rebellion had appeared as in Massts. – foreign debts had not become urgent – the havoc of paper money had not been foreseen – treaties had not been violated – and perhaps nothing better could be obtained from the jealousy of the states with regard to their sovereignty.

He then proceeded to enumerate the defects: *1.* that the confederation produced no security against foreign invasion; congress not being permitted to prevent a war nor to support it by their own authority – Of this he cited many examples; most of which tended to shew, that they could not cause infractions of treaties or of the law of nations, to be punished: that particular states might by their conduct provoke war without controul; and that neither militia nor draughts being fit for defence on such occasions, inlistments only could be successful, and these could not be executed without money.

2. that the fœderal government could not check the quarrels between states, nor a rebellion in any, not having constitutional power nor means to interpose according to the exigency:

3. that there were many advantages, which the U. S. might acquire, which were not attainable under the confederation – such as a productive impost – counteraction of the commercial regulations of other nations – pushing of commerce ad libitum – &c &c.

4. that the fœderal government could not defend itself against the incroachments from the states.

5. that it was not even paramount to the state constitutions, ratified, as it was in ma[n]y of the states.

3. He next reviewed the danger of our situation, appealed to the sense of the best friends of the U. S. – the prospect of anarchy from the laxity of government every where; and to other considerations.

4. He then proceeded to the remedy; the basis of which he said must be the republican principle.

He proposed as conformable to his ideas the following resolutions, which he explained one by one . . .

1. Resolved that the Articles of Confederation ought to be so corrected & enlarged as to accomplish the objects proposed by their institution; namely, 'common defence, security of liberty, and general welfare'.

2. Resd. therefore that the rights of suffrage in the National Legislature ought to be proportioned to the Quotas of contribution, or to the number of free inhabitants, as the one or the other rule may seem best in different cases.

3. Resd. that the National Legislature ought to consist of two branches.

4. Resd. that the members of the first branch of the National Legislature ought to be elected by the people of the several States every   for the term of   ; to be of the age of   years at least, to receive liberal stipends by which they may be compensated for the devotion of their time to public service; to be ineligible to any office established by a particular State, or under the authority of the United States, except those peculiarly belonging to the functions of the first branch, during the term of service, and for the space of after its expiration; to be incapable of reelection for the space of after the expiration of their term of service, and to be subject to recall.

5. Resold. that the members of the second branch of the National Legislature ought to be elected by those of the first, out of a proper number of persons nominated by the individual Legislatures, to be of the age of years at least; to hold their offices for a term sufficient to ensure their independency; to receive liberal stipends, by which they may be compensated for the devotion of their time to public service; and to be ineligible to any office established by a particular State, or under the authority of the United States, except those peculiarly belonging to the functions of the second branch, during the term of service, and for the space of after the expiration thereof.

6. Resolved that each branch ought to possess the right of originating Acts; that the National Legislature ought to be impowered to enjoy the Legislative Rights vested in Congress by the Confederation & moreover to legislate in all cases to which the separate States are incompetent, or in which the harmony of the United States may be interrupted by the exercise of individual Legislation; to negative all laws passed by the several States, contravening in the opinion of the National Legislature the articles of Union;[1] and to call forth the force of the Union agst. any member of the Union failing to fulfill its duty under the articles thereof.

7. Resd. that a National Executive be instituted; to be chosen by the National Legislature for the term of years, to receive punctually at stated times, a fixed compensation for the services rendered, in which no increase or diminution shall be made so as to affect the Magistracy, existing at the time of increase or diminution, and to be ineligible a second time; and that besides a general authority to execute the National laws, it ought to enjoy the Executive rights vested in Congress by the Confederation.

8. Resd. that the Executive and a convenient number of the National Judiciary, ought to compose a Council of revision with authority to examine every act of the National Legislature before it

1 (The phrase 'of any treaty subsisting under the authority of the Union' is here added in the transcript.)

shall operate, & every act of a particular Legislature before a Negative thereon shall be final; and that the dissent of the said Council shall amount to a rejection, unless the Act of the National Legislature be again passed, or that of a particular Legislature be again negatived by of the members of each branch.

9. Resd. that a National Judiciary be established to consist of one or more supreme tribunals, and of inferior tribunals to be chosen by the National Legislature, to hold their offices during good behaviour; and to receive punctually at stated times fixed compensation for their services, in which no increase or diminution shall be made so as to affect the persons actually in office at the time of such increase or diminution; that the jurisdiction of the inferior tribunals shall be to hear & determine in the first instance, and of the supreme tribunal to hear and determine in the dernier resort, all piracies & felonies on the high seas, captures from an enemy, cases in which foreigners or citizens of other States applying to such jurisdictions may be interested, or which respect the collection of the National revenue; impeachments of any National officers, and questions which may involve the national peace and harmony.

10. Resolvd. that provision ought to be made for the admission of States lawfully arising within the limits of the United States, whether from a voluntary junction of Government & Territory or otherwise, with the consent of a number of voices in the National legislature less than the whole.

11. Resd. that a Republican Government & the territory of each State, except in the instance of a voluntary junction of Government & territory, ought to be guarantied by the United States to each State.

12. Resd. that provision ought to be made for the continuance of Congress and their authorities and privileges, until a given day after the reform of the articles of Union shall be adopted, and for the completion of all their engagements.

13. Resd. that provision ought to be made for the amendment of the Articles of Union whensoever it shall seem necessary, and that the assent of the National Legislature ought not to be required thereto.

14. Resd. that the Legislative Executive & Judiciary powers within the several States ought to be bound by oath to support the articles of Union.

15. Resd. that the amendments which shall be offered to the Confederation, by the Convention ought at a proper time, or times, after the approbation of Congress to be submitted to an assembly or assemblies of Representatives, recommended by the several Legislatures to be expressly chosen by the people, to consider & decide thereon.

He concluded with an exhortation, not to suffer the present opportunity of establishing general peace, harmony, happiness and liberty in the U. S. to pass away unimproved.

It was then Resolved – That the House will tomorrow resolve itself into a Committee of the Whole House to consider of the state of the American Union. – and that the propositions moved by Mr Randolph be referred to the said Committee . . .

I.V.2 THE NEW JERSEY PLAN

June 14, In Convention, *Records of the Federal Convention of 1787*, I 240

Mr Patterson, observed to the Convention that it was the wish of several deputations, particularly that of N. Jersey, that further time might be allowed them to contemplate the plan reported from the Committee of the Whole, and to digest one purely federal, and contradistinguished from the reported plan. He said they hoped to have such an one ready by tomorrow to be laid before the Convention: And the Convention adjourned that leisure might be given for the purpose.

June 15, 1787, ibid. 242–5

Mr Patterson, laid before the Convention the plan which he said several of the deputations wished to be substituted in place of that proposed by Mr Randolp. After some little discussion of the most proper mode of giving it a fair deliberation it was agreed that it should be referred to a Committee of the Whole, and that in order to place the two plans in due comparison, the other should be recommitted. At the earnest desire of Mr Lansing & some other gentlemen, it was also agreed that the Convention should not go into Committee of the whole on the subject till tomorrow, by which delay the friends of the plan proposed by Mr Patterson wd. be better prepared to explain & support it, and all would have an opportuy of taking copies.[1]

The propositions from N. Jersey moved by Mr Patterson were in the words following.

1. Resd. that the articles of Confederation ought to be so revised, corrected & enlarged, as to render the federal Constitution adequate to the exigences of Government, & the preservation of the Union.

2. Resd. that in addition to the powers vested in the U. States in Congress, by the present existing articles of Confederation, they be authorized to pass acts for raising a revenue, by levying a duty or duties on all goods or merchandizes of foreign growth or manufacture, imported into any part of the U. States, by Stamps on paper, vellum or parchment, and by a postage on all letters or packages passing through the general post-Office, to be applied to such federal purposes as they shall deem proper & expedient; to make rules & regulations for the collection thereof; and the same from time to time, to alter & amend in such manner as they shall think proper: to pass Acts for the regulation of trade & commerce as well with foreign nations as with each other: provided that all punishments, fines, forfeitures & penalties to be incurred for contravening such acts rules and regulations shall be adjudged by the Common law Judiciarys of the State in which any offence contrary to the true intent & meaning of such Acts rules & regulations shall have been committed or perpetrated, with liberty of commencing in the first instance all suits & prosecutions for that purpose in the superior Common law Judiciary in such State, subject

[1] This plan had been concerted among the deputations or members thereof, from Cont. N. Y. N. J. Del. and perhaps Mr Martin from Maryd. who made with them a common cause on different principles. Cont. and N. Y. were agst. a departure from the principle of the Confederation, wishing rather to add a few new powers to Congs. than to substitute, a National Govt. The States of N. J. and Del. were opposed to a National Govt. because its patrons considered a proportional representation of the States as the basis of it. The eagourness displayed by the Members opposed to a Natl. Govt. from these different ⟨motives⟩ began now to produce serious anxiety for the result of the Convention. – Mr Dickenson said to Mr Madison you see the consequence of pushing things too far. Some of the members from the small States wish for two branches in the General Legislature, and are friends to a good National Government; but we would sooner submit to a foreign power, than submit to be deprived of an equality of suffrage, in both branches of the legislature, and thereby be thrown under the domination of the large States.

nevertheless, for the correction of all errors, both in law & fact in rendering judgment, to an appeal to the Judiciary of the U. States

3. Resd. that whenever requisitions shall be necessary, instead of the rule for making requisitions mentioned in the articles of Confederation, the United States in Congs. be authorized to make such requisitions in proportion to the whole number of white & other free citizens & inhabitants of every age sex and condition including those bound to servitude for a term of years & three fifths of all other persons not comprehended in the foregoing description, except Indians not paying taxes; that if such requisitions be not complied with, in the time specified therein, to direct the collection thereof in the non complying States & for that purpose to devise and pass acts directing & authorizing the same; provided that none of the powers hereby vested in the U. States in Congs. shall be exercised without the consent of at least States, and in that proportion if the number of Confederated States should hereafter be increased or diminished.

4. Resd. that the U. States in Congs. be authorized to elect a federal Executive to consist of persons, to continue in office for the term of years, to receive punctually at stated times a fixed compensation for their services, in which no increase or diminution shall be made so as to affect the persons composing the Executive at the time of such increase or diminution, to be paid out of the federal treasury; to be incapable of holding any other office or appointment during their time of service and for years thereafter; to be ineligible a second time, & removeable by Congs. on application by a majority of the Executives of the several States; that the Executives besides their general authority to execute the federal acts ought to appoint all federal officers not otherwise provided for, & to direct all military operations; provided that none of the persons composing the federal Executive shall on any occasion take command of any troops, so as personally to conduct any enterprise as General, or in other capacity.

5. Resd. that a federal Judiciary be established to consist of a supreme Tribunal the Judges of which to be appointed by the Executive, & to hold their offices during good behaviour, to receive punctually at stated times a fixed compensation for their services in which no increase or diminution shall be made, so as to affect the persons actually in office at the time of such increase or diminution; that the Judiciary so established shall have authority to hear & determine in the first

instance on all impeachments of federal officers, & by way of appeal in the dernier resort in all cases touching the rights of Ambassadors, in all cases of captures from an enemy, in all cases of piracies & felonies on the high seas, in all cases in which foreigners may be interested, in the construction of any treaty or treaties, or which may arise on any of the Acts for regulation of trade, or the collection of the federal Revenue: that none of the Judiciary shall during the time they remain in Office be capable of receiving or holding any other office or appointment during their time of service, or for   thereafter.

6. Resd. that all Acts of the U. States in Congs. made by virtue & in pursuance of the powers hereby & by the articles of confederation vested in them, and all Treaties made & ratified under the authority of the U. States shall be the supreme law of the respective States so far forth as those Acts or Treaties shall relate to the said States or their Citizens, and that the Judiciary of the several States shall be bound thereby in their decisions, any thing in the respective laws of the Individual States to the contrary notwithstanding; and that if any State, or any body of men in any State shall oppose or prevent ye. carrying into execution such acts or treaties, the federal Executive shall be authorized to call forth ye power of the Confederated States, or so much thereof as may be necessary to enforce and compel an obedience to such Acts, or an Observance of such Treaties.

7. Resd. that provision be made for the admission of new States into the Union.

8. Resd. the rule for naturalization ought to be the same in every State.

9. Resd. that a Citizen of one State committing an offence in another State of the Union, shall be deemed guilty of the same offence as if it had been committed by a Citizen of the State in which the Offence was committed.[1]

[1] This copy of Mr Patterson's propositions varies in a few clauses from that in the printed Journal furnished from the papers of Mr Brearley a Colleague of Mr Patterson. A confidence is felt, notwithstanding, in its accuracy. That the copy in the Journal is not entirely correct is shewn by the ensuing speech of Mr Wilson (June 16) in which he refers to the mode of removing the Executive by impeachment & conviction as a feature in the Virga. plan forming one of its contrasts to that of Mr Patterson, which proposed a removal on the application of a majority of the Executives of the States. In the copy printed in the Journal, the two modes are combined in the same clause; whether through inadvertence, or as a contemplated amendment does not appear.

Adjourned

June 16, in Committee of the whole, ibid. pp. 249–53

Mr LANSING called for the reading of the 1st. resolution of each plan, which he considered as involving principles directly in contrast; that of Mr Patterson says he sustains the sovereignty of the respective States, that of Mr Randolph distroys it: the latter requires a negative on all the laws of the particular States; the former, only certain general powers for the general good. The plan of Mr R. in short absorbs all power except what may be exercised in the little local matters of the States which are not objects worthy of the supreme cognizance. He grounded his preference of Mr P.'s plan, chiefly on two objections agst. that of Mr R. 1. want of power in the Convention to discuss & propose it. 2. the improbability of its being adopted . . .

Mr PATTERSON, said as he had on a former occasion given his sentiments on the plan proposed by Mr R. he would now avoiding repetition as much as possible give his reasons in favor of that proposed by himself. He preferred it because it accorded 1. with the powers of the Convention, 2. with the sentiments of the people. If the confederacy was radically wrong, let us return to our States, and obtain larger powers, not assume them of ourselves . . . Our object is not such a Governmt. as may be best in itself, but such a one as our Constituents have authorized us to prepare, and as they will approve. If we argue the matter on the supposition that no Confederacy at present exists, it can not be denied that all the States stand on the footing of equal sovereignty. All therefore must concur before any can be bound. If a proportional representation be right, why do we not vote so here? If we argue on the fact that a federal compact actually exists, and consult the articles of it we still find an equal Sovereignty to be the basis of it. He reads the 5th. art: of Confederation giving each State a vote – & the 13th. declaring that no alteration shall be made without unanimous consent. This is the nature of all treaties. What is unanimously done, must be unanimously undone. It was observed (by Mr Wilson) that the larger States gave up the point, not because it was right, but because the circumstances of the moment urged the concession. Be it so. Are they for that reason at liberty to take it back. Can the donor resume his gift without the consent of the donee. This doctrine may be convenient, but it is a doctrine that will sacrifice the lesser States. The large States acceded readily to the confederacy. It was the small ones that came in reluctantly and slowly. N. Jersey & Maryland were the two last, the former objecting to the want of power in Congress over trade: both of them to the want of power to appropriate the vacant territory to the benefit of the whole. – If the sovereignty of the States is to be maintained, the Representatives must be drawn immediately from the States, not from the people: and we have no power to vary the idea of equal sovereignty. The only expedient that will cure the difficulty, is that of throwing the States into Hotchpot. To say that this is impracticable, will not make it so. Let it be tried, and we shall see whether the Citizens of Massts. Pena. & Va. accede to it. It will be objected that Coercion will be impracticable. But will it be more so in one plan than the other? Its efficacy will depend on the quantum of power collected, not on its being drawn from the States, or from the individuals; and according to his plan it may be exerted on individuals as well as according that of Mr R. A. distinct executive & Judiciary also were equally provided by his plan. It is urged that two branches in the Legislature are necessary. Why? for the purpose of a check. But the reason of the precaution is not applicable to this case. Within a particular State, where party heats prevail, such a check may be necessary. In such a body as Congress it is less necessary, and besides, the delegations of the different States are checks on each other. Do the people at large complain of Congs.? No, what they wish is that Congs. may have more power. If the power now proposed be not eno', the people hereafter will make additions to it. With proper powers Congs. will act with more energy & wisdom than the proposed Natl. Legislature; being fewer in number, and more secreted & refined by the mode of election. The plan of Mr R. will also be enormously expensive. Allowing Georgia & Del. two representatives each in the popular branch the aggregate number of that branch will be 180. Add to it half as many for the other branch and you have 270. members coming once at least a year from the most distant as well as the most central parts of the republic. In the present deranged state of our finances can so expensive a system be seriously thought of? By enlarging the powers of Congs. the greatest part of this expence will be saved, and all purposes will be answered. At least a trial ought to be made.

Mr Wilson entered into a contrast of the principal points of the two plans so far he said as there had been time to examine the one last proposed. These points were 1. in the Virga. plan there are 2 & in some degree 3 branches in the Legislature: in the plan from N. J. there is to be a *single* legislature only – 2. Representation of the people at large is the basis of the one: – the State Legislatures, the pillars of the other – 3. proportional representation prevails in one: – equality of suffrage in the other – 4. A single Executive Magistrate is at the head of the one: – a plurality is held out in the other. – 5. in the one the majority of the people of the U. S. must prevail: – in the other a minority may prevail. 6. the Natl. Legislature is to make laws in all cases to which the separate States are incompetent & – : – in place of this Congs. are to have additional power in a few cases only – 7. A negative on the laws of the States: – in place of this coertion to be substituted – 8. The Executive to be removeable on impeachment & conviction; – in one plan: in the other to be removeable at the instance of majority of the Executives of the States – 9. Revision of the laws provided for in one: – no such check in the other – 10. inferior national tribunals in one: – none such in the other. 11. In ye. one jurisdiction of Natl. tribunals to extend &c – ; an appellate jurisdiction only allowed in the other. 12. Here the jurisdiction is to extend to all cases affecting the Nationl. peace & harmony: there, a few cases only are marked out. 13. finally ye. ratification is in this to be by the people themselves: – in that by the legislative authorities according to the 13 art: of Confederation . . .

I.v.3 THE CONSTITUTION OF THE UNITED STATES

(from the Convention's Draft)
Records of the Federal Convention of 1787, II 651–5

We the People of the United States, in Order to form a more perfect Union, establish Justice, insure domestic Tranquility, provide for the common defence, promote the general Welfare, and secure the Blessings of Liberty to ourselves and our Posterity, do ordain and establish this Constitution for the United States of America.

Article I

Section 1. All legislative Powers herein granted shall be vested in a Congress of the United States, which shall consist of a Senate and House of Representatives.

Section 2. The House of Representatives shall be composed of Members chosen every second Year by the People of the several States, and the Electors in each State shall have ∧the Qualifications requisite for Electors of the most numerous Branch of the State Legislature.

No person shall be a Representative who shall not have attained to the Age of twenty five Years, and been seven Years a Citizen of the United States, and who shall not, when elected, be an Inhabitant of that State in which he shall be chosen.

Representatives and direct Taxes shall be apportioned among the several States which may be included within this Union, according to their respective Numbers, which shall be determined by adding to the whole Number of free Persons, including those bound to Service for a Term of Years, and excluding Indians not taxed, three fifths of all other Persons. The actual Enumeration shall be made within three Years after the first Meeting of the Congress of the United States, and within every subsequent Term of ten Years, in such Manner as they shall by Law direct. The Number of Representatives shall not exceed one for every thirty Thousand, but each State shall have at Least one Representative; and until such enumeration shall be made, the State of New Hampshire shall be entitled to chuse three, Massachusetts eight, Rhode-Island and Providence Plantations one, Connecticut five, New-York six, New Jersey four, Pennsylvania eight, Delaware one, Maryland six, Virginia ten, North Carolina five, South Carolina five, and Georgia three.

When vacancies happen in the Representation from any State, the Executive Authority thereof shall issue Writs of Election to fill such Vacancies.

The House of Representatives shall chuse their Speaker and other Officers; and shall have the sole Power of Impeachment.

Section 3. The Senate of the United States shall be composed of two Senators from each State, chosen by the Legislature thereof, for six Years; and each Senator shall have one Vote.

Immediately after they shall be assembled in Consequence of the first Election, they shall be divided as equally as may be into three Classes. The Seats of the Senators of the first Class shall be vacated at the Expiration of the second Year, of the second Class at the Expiration of the fourth Year, and of the third Class at the Expiration of the sixth Year, so that one third may be chosen every second Year; and if Vacancies happen by Resignation, or otherwise, during the Recess of the Legislature of any State, the Executive thereof may make temporary Appointments until the next Meeting of the Legislature, which shall then fill such Vacancies.

No Person shall be a Senator who shall not have attained to the Age of thirty Years, and been nine Years a Citizen of the United States, and who shall not, when elected, be an Inhabitant of that State for which he shall be chosen.

The Vice President of the United States shall be President of the Senate, but shall have no Vote, unless they be equally divided.

The Senate shall chuse their other Officers, and also a President pro tempore, in the Absence of the Vice President, or when he shall exercise the Office of President of the United States.

The Senate shall have the sole Power to try all Impeachments. When sitting for that Purpose, they shall be on Oath or Affirmation.
is tried
When the President of the United States ∧ the Chief Justice shall preside: And no Person shall be convicted without the Concurrence of two thirds of the Members present.

Judgment in Cases of Impeachment shall not extend further than to removal from Office, and disqualification to hold and enjoy any Office of honor, Trust or Profit under the United States: but the Party convicted shall nevertheless be liable and subject to Indictment, Trial, Judgment and Punishment, according to Law.

Section 4. The Times, Places and Manner of holding Elections for Senators and Representatives, shall be prescribed in each State by the Legislature thereof; but the Congress may at any time by Law make or alter such Regulations, except as to the Places of chusing Senators.

The Congress shall assemble at least once in every Year, and such Meeting shall be on the first Monday in December, unless they shall by Law appoint a different Day.

Section 5. Each House shall be the Judge of the Elections, Returns and Qualifications of its own Members, and a Majority of each shall constitute a Quorum to do Business; but a smaller Number may adjourn from day to day, and may be authorized to compel the Attendance of absent Members, in such Manner, and under such Penalties as each House may provide.

Each House may determine the Rules of its Proceedings, punish its Members for disorderly Behaviour, and, with the Concurrence of two thirds, expel a Member.

Each House shall keep a Journal of its Proceedings, and from time to time publish the same, excepting such Parts as may in their Judgment require Secrecy; and the Yeas and Nays of the Members of either House on any question shall, at the Desire of one fifth of those Present, be entered on the Journal.

Neither House, during the Session of Congress, shall, without the Consent of the other, adjourn for more than three days, nor to any other Place than that in which the two Houses shall be sitting.

Section 6. The Senators and Representatives shall receive a Compensation for their Services, to be ascertained by Law, and paid out of the Treasury of the United States. They shall in all Cases, except Treason, Felony and Breach of the Peace, be privileged from Arrest during their Attendance at the Session of their respective Houses, and in going to and returning from the same; and for any Speech or Debate in either House, they shall not be questioned in any other Place.

No Senator or Representative shall, during the Time for which he was elected, be appointed to any civil Office under the Authority of the United States, which shall have been created, or the Emoluments whereof shall have been encreased during such time; and no Person holding any Office under the United States, shall be a Member of either House during his Continuance in Office.

Section 7. All Bills for raising Revenue shall originate in the House of Representatives; but the Senate may propose or concur with Amendments as on other Bills.

Every Bill which shall have passed the House of Representatives and the Senate, shall, before it become a Law, be presented to the President of the United States; If he approve he shall sign it, but if not he shall return it, with his Objections to that House in which it shall have originated, who shall enter the Objections at large on their Journal, and proceed to reconsider it. If after such Reconsideration two thirds of that House shall agree to pass the Bill, it shall be sent, together with the Objections, to the other House, by which it shall likewise be reconsidered, and if approved by two thirds of that House, it shall become a Law. But in all such Cases the Votes of both Houses shall be determined by yeas and Nays, and the Names of the Persons voting for and against the Bill shall be entered on the Journal of each House respectively. If any Bill shall not be returned by the President within ten days (Sundays excepted) after it shall have been presented to him, the Same shall be a Law, in like Manner as if he had signed it, unless the Congress by their Adjournment prevent its Return in which Case it shall not be a Law.

Every Order, Resolution, or Vote to which the Concurrence of the Senate and House of Representatives may be necessary (except on a question of Adjournment) shall be presented to the President of the United States; and before the Same shall take Effect, shall be approved by him, or being disapproved by him, shall be repassed by two thirds of the Senate and House of Representatives, according to the Rules and Limitations prescribed in the Case of a Bill.

Section 8. The Congress shall have Power To lay and collect Taxes, Duties, Imposts and Excises, to pay the Debts and provide for the common Defence and general Welfare of the United States; but all Duties, Imposts and Excises shall be uniform throughout the United States;

To borrow Money on the credit of the United States;

To regulate Commerce with foreign Nations, and among the several States, and with the Indian Tribes;

To establish an uniform Rule of Naturalization, and uniform Laws on the subject of Bankruptcies throughout the United States;

To coin Money, regulate the Value thereof, and of foreign Coin, and fix the Standard of Weights and Measures;

To provide for the Punishment of counterfeiting the Securities and current Coin of the United States;

To establish Post Offices and post Roads;

To promote the Progress of Science and useful Arts, by securing for limited Times to Authors and Inventors the exclusive Right to their respective Writings and Discoveries;

To constitute Tribunals inferior to the supreme Court;

To define and punish Piracies and Felonies committed on the high Seas, and Offences against the Law of Nations;

To declare War, grant Letters of Marque and Reprisal, and make Rules concerning Captures on Land and Water;

To raise and support Armies, but no Appropriation of Money to that Use shall be for a longer Term than two Years;

To provide and maintain a Navy;

To make Rules for the Government and Regulation of the land and naval Forces;

To provide for calling forth the Militia to execute the Laws of the Union, suppress Insurrections and repel Invasions;

To provide for organizing, arming, and disciplining, the Militia, and for governing such Part of them as may be employed in the Service of the United States, reserving to the States respectively, the Appointment of the Officers, and the Authority of training the Militia according to the discipline prescribed by Congress;

To exercise exclusive Legislation in all Cases whatsoever, over such District (not exceeding ten Miles square) as may, by Cession of particular States, and the Acceptance of Congress, become the Seat of the Government of the United States, and to exercise like Authority over all Places purchased by the Consent of the Legislature of the State in which the Same shall be, for the Erection of Forts, Magazines, Arsenals, dock-Yards, and other needful Buildings; – And

To make all Laws which shall be necessary and proper for carrying into Execution the foregoing Powers, and all other Powers vested by this Constitution in the Government of the United States, or in any Department or Officer thereof.

Section 9. The Migration or Importation of such Persons as any of the States now existing shall think proper to admit, shall not be prohibited by the Congress prior to the Year one thousand eight hundred and eight, but a Tax or duty may be imposed on such Importation, not exceeding ten dollars for each Person.

The Privilege of the Writ of Habeas Corpus shall not be suspended, unless when in Cases of Rebellion or Invasion the public Safety may require it.

No Bill of Attainder or ex post facto Law shall be passed.

No Capitation, or other direct, Tax shall be laid, unless in Proportion to the Census or Enumeration herein before directed to be taken.

No Tax or Duty shall be laid on Articles exported from any State.

No Preference shall be given by any Regulation of Commerce or Revenue to the Ports of one State over those of another: nor shall Vessels bound to, or from, one State, be obliged to enter, clear, or pay Duties in another.

No Money shall be drawn from the Treasury, but in Consequence of Appropriations made by Law; and a regular Statement and Account of the Receipts and Expenditures of all public Money shall be published from time to time.

No Title of Nobility shall be granted by the United States: And no Person holding any Office or Profit or Trust under them, shall, without the Consent of the Congress, accept of any present, Emolument, Office, or Title, of any kind whatever, from any King, Prince, or foreign State.

Section 10. No State shall enter into any Treaty, Alliance, or Confederation; grant Letters of Marque and Reprisal; coin Money; emit Bills of Credit; make any Thing but gold and silver Coin a Tender in Payment of Debts; pass any Bill of Attainder, ex post facto Law, or Law impairing the Obligation of Contracts, or grant any Title of Nobility.

No State shall, without the Consent of $\overset{\text{the}}{\wedge}$ Congress, lay any Imposts or Duties on Imports or Exports, except what may be absolutely necessary for executing it's inspection Laws: and the net Produce of all Duties and Imposts, laid by any State on Imports or Exports, shall be for the Use of the Treasury of the United States; and all such Laws shall be subject to the Revision and Controul of $\overset{\text{the}}{\wedge}$ Congress.

No State shall, without the Consent of Congress, lay any Duty of Tonnage, keep Troops, or Ships of War in time of Peace, enter into any Agreement or Compact with another State, or with a foreign Power, or engage in War, unless actually invaded, or in such imminent Danger as will not admit of delay.

Article II

Section 1. The executive Power shall be vested in a President of the United States of America. He shall hold his Office during the Term of four Years, and, together with the Vice President, chosen for the same Term, be elected as follows

Each State shall appoint, in such Manner as the Legislature thereof may direct, a Number of Electors, equal to the whole Number of Senators and Representatives to which the State may be entitled in the Congress: but no Senator or Representative, or Person holding an Office of Trust or Profit under the United States, shall be appointed an Elector.

The Electors shall meet in their respective States, and vote by Ballot for two Persons, of whom one at least shall not be an Inhabitant of the same State with themselves. And they shall make a List of all the Persons voted for, and of the Number of Votes for each; which List they shall sign and certify, and transmit sealed to the Seat of the Government of the United States, directed to the President of the Senate. The President of the Senate shall, in the Presence of the Senate and House of Representatives, open all the Certificates, and the Votes shall then be counted. The Person having the greatest Number of Votes shall be the President, if such Number be a Majority of the whole Number of Electors appointed; and if there be more than one who have such Majority, and have an equal Number of Votes, then the House of Representatives shall immediately chuse by Ballot one of them for President; and if no Person have a Majority, then from the five highest on the List the said House shall in like Manner chuse the President. But in chusing the President, the Votes shall be taken by States, the Representation from each State having one Vote; A quorum for this Purpose shall consist of a Member or Members from two thirds of the States, and a Majority of all the States shall be necessary to a Choice. In every Case, after the Choice of the President, the Person having the greatest Number of Votes of the Electors shall be the Vice President. But if there should remain two or more who have equal Votes, the Senate shall chuse from them by Ballot the Vice President.

The Congress may determine the Time of chusing the Electors, and the Day on which they shall give their Votes; which Day shall be the same throughout the United States.

No Person except a natural born Citizen, or a Citizen of the United States, at the time of the Adoption of this Constitution, shall be eligible to the Office of President; neither shall any Person be eligible to that Office who shall not have attained to the Age of thirty five Years, and been fourteen Years a Resident within the United States.

In Case of the Removal of the President from Office, or of his Death, Resignation, or Inability to discharge the Powers and Duties of the said Office, the Same shall devolve on the Vice President, and the Congress may by Law provide for the Case of Removal, Death, Resignation or Inability, both of the President and Vice President, declaring what Officer shall then act as President, and such Officer shall act accordingly, until the Disability be removed, or a President shall be elected.

The President shall, at stated Times, receive for his Services, a Compensation, which shall neither be encreased nor diminished during the Period for which he shall have been elected, and he shall not receive within that Period any other Emolument from the United States, or any of them.

Before he enter on the Execution of his Office, he shall take the following Oath or Affirmation: – 'I do solemnly swear (or affirm) that I will faithfully execute the Office of President of the United States, and will to the best of my Ability, preserve, protect and defend the Constitution of the United States.'

Section 2. The President shall be Commander in Chief of the Army and Navy of the United States, and of the Militia of the several States, when called into the actual Service of the United States; he may require the Opinion, in writing, of the principal Officer in each of the executive Departments, upon any Subject relating to the Duties of their respective Offices, and he shall have Power to grant Reprieves and Pardons for Offences against the United States, except in Cases of Impeachment.

He shall have Power, by and with the Advice and Consent of the Senate, to make Treaties, provided two thirds of the Senators present concur; and he shall nominate, and by and with the Advice and Consent of the Senate, shall appoint Ambassadors, other public Ministers and Consuls, Judges of the supreme Court, and all other Officers of the United States, whose Appointments are not herein otherwise provided for, and which shall be established by Law: but the Congress may by Law vest the Appointment of such inferior Officers, as they think proper, in the President alone, in the Courts of Law, or in the Heads of Departments.

The President shall have Power to fill up all Vacancies that may happen during the Recess of the Senate, by granting Commissions which shall expire at the End of their next Session.

Section 3. He shall from time to time give to the Congress Information of the State of the Union, and recommend to their Consideration such Measures as he shall judge necessary and expedient; he may, on extraordinary Occasions, convene both Houses, or either of them, and in Case of Disagreement between them, with Respect to the Time of Adjournment, he may adjourn them to such Time as he shall think proper; he shall receive Ambassadors and other public Ministers; he shall take Care that the Laws be faithfully executed, and shall Commission all the Officers of the United States.

Section 4. The President, Vice President and all civil Officers of the United States, shall be removed from Office on Impeachment for, and Conviction of, Treason, Bribery, or other high Crimes and Misdemeanors.

Article III

Section 1. The judicial Power of the United States, shall be vested in one supreme Court, and in such inferior Courts as the Congress may from time to time ordain and establish. The Judges, both of the supreme and inferior Courts, shall hold their Offices during good Behaviour, and shall, at stated Times, receive for their Services, a Compensation, which shall not be diminished during their Continuance in Office.

Section 2. The judicial Power shall extend to all Cases, in Law and Equity, arising under this Constitution, the Laws of the United States, and Treaties made, or which shall be made, under their Authority; – to all Cases affecting Ambassadors, other public Ministers and Consuls; – to all Cases of admiralty and maritime Jurisdiction; – to Controversies to which the United States shall be a Party; – to Controversies between two or more States; – between a State and Citizens of another State; – between Citizens of different States, – between Citizens of the same state claiming Lands under Grants of different States, and between a State, or the Citizens thereof, and foreign States, Citizens or Subjects.

In all Cases affecting Ambassadors, other public Ministers and Consuls, and those in which a State shall be Party, the supreme Court shall have original Jurisdiction. In all the other Cases before mentioned, the supreme Court shall have appellate Jurisdiction, both as to Law and Fact, with such Exceptions, and under such Regulations as the Congress shall make.

The Trial of all Crimes, except in Cases of Impeachment, shall be by Jury; and such Trial shall be held in the State where the said Crimes shall have been committed; but when not committed within any State, the Trial shall be at such Place or Places as the Congress may by Law have directed.

Section 3. Treason against the United States, shall consist only in levying War against them, or in adhering to their Enemies, giving them Aid and Comfort. No person shall be convicted of Treason unless on the Testimony of two Witnesses to the same overt Act, or on Confession in open Court.

The Congress shall have Power to declare the Punishment of Treason, but no Attainder of Treason shall work Corruption of Blood, or Forfeiture except during the Life of the Person attainted.

Article IV

Section 1. Full Faith and Credit shall be given in each State to the public Acts, Records, and judicial Proceedings of every other State. And the Congress may by general Laws prescribe the Manner in which such Acts, Records and Proceedings shall be proved, and the Effect thereof.

Section 2. The Citizens of each State shall be entitled to all Privileges and Immunities of Citizens in the several States.

A Person charged in any State with Treason, Felony, or other Crime, who shall flee from Justice, and be found in another State, shall on Demand of the executive Authority of the State from which he fled, be delivered up, to be removed to the State having Jurisdiction of the Crime.

No Person held to Service or Labour in one State, under the Laws thereof, escaping into another, shall, in Consequence of any Law or Regulation therein, be discharged from such Service or Labour, but shall be delivered up on Claim of the Party to whom such Service or Labour may be due.

Section 3. New States may be admitted by the Congress into this Union; but no new State shall be formed or erected within the Jurisdiction of any other State; nor any State be formed by the Junction of two or more States, or Parts of States, without the Consent of the Legislatures of the States concerned as well as of the Congress.

The Congress shall have Power to dispose of and make all needful Rules and Regulations respecting the Territory or other Property belonging to the United States; and nothing in this Constitution shall be so construed as to Prejudice any Claims of the United States, or of any particular State.

Section 4. The United States shall guarantee to every State in this Union a Republican Form of Government, and shall protect each of them against Invasion; and on Application of the Legislature, or of the Executive (when the Legislature cannot be convened) against domestic Violence.

Article V

The Congress, whenever two thirds of both Houses shall deem it necessary, shall propose Amendments to this Constitution, or, on the Application of the Legislatures of two thirds of the several States, shall call a Convention for proposing Amendments, which, in either Case, shall be valid to all Intents and Purposes, as Part of this Constitution, when ratified by the Legislatures of three fourths of the several States, or by Conventions in three fourths thereof, as the one or the other Mode of Ratification may be proposed by the Congress; Provided that no Amendment which may be made prior to the Year One thousand eight hundred and eight shall in any Manner affect the first and fourth Clauses in the Ninth Section of the first Article; and that no State, without its Consent, shall be deprived of it's equal Suffrage in the Senate.

Article VI

All Debts contracted and Engagements entered into, before the Adoption of this Constitution, shall be as valid against the United States under this Constitution, as under the Confederation.

This Constitution, and the Laws of the United States which shall be made in Pursuance thereof; and all Treaties made, or which shall be made, under the Authority of the United States, shall be the supreme Law of the Land; and the Judges in every State shall be bound thereby, any Thing in the Constitution or Laws of any State to the Contrary notwithstanding.

The Senators and Representatives before mentioned, and the Members of the several State Legislatures, and all executive and judicial Officers, both of the United States and of the several States, shall be bound by Oath or Affirmation, to support this Constitution; but no religious Test shall ever be required as a Qualification to any Office or public Trust under the United States.

Article VII

The Ratification of the Conventions of nine States, shall be sufficient for the Establishment of this Constitution between the States so ratifying the Same.

The Word, 'the', being interlined between the seventh and eighth Lines of the first Page, The Word 'Thirty' being partly written on an Erazure in the fifteenth Line of the first Page, The Words 'is tried' being interlined between the thirty second and thirty third Lines of the first Page and the Word 'the' being interlined between the forty third and forty fourth Lines of the second Page.
Attest WILLIAM JACKSON
Secretary

done in Convention by the Unanimous Consent of the States present the Seventeenth Day of September in the Year of our Lord one thousand seven hundred and Eighty seven and of the Independance of the United States of America the Twelfth In witness whereof We have hereunto subscribed our Names,

GO. WASHINGTON – Presidt. and deputy from Virginia

New Hampshire	John Langdon Nicholas Gilman
Massachusetts	Nathaniel Gorham Rufus King
Connecticut	Wm Saml Johnson Roger Sherman
New York . .	Alexander Hamilton
New Jersey	Wil: Livingston David Brearley. Wm Paterson. Jona: Dayton
Pensylvania	B Franklin Thomas Mifflin Robt Morris Geo. Clymer Thos FitzSimons Jared Ingersoll James Wilson Gouv Morris
Delaware	Geo: Read Gunning Bedford jun John Dickinson Richard Bassett Jaco: Broom
Maryland	James McHenry Dan of St Thos Jenifer Danl Carroll
Virginia	John Blair – James Madison Jr.
North Carolina	Wm Blount Richd Dobbs Spaight. Hu Williamson
South Carolina	J. Rutledge Charles Cotesworth Pinckney Charles Pinckney Pierce Butler.
Georgia	William Few Abr Baldwin

I.V.4 GEORGE MASON OBJECTS TO THE PROPOSED FEDERAL CONSTITUTION

From proceedings of the Virginia Ratifying Convention, *The Anti-Federalists*, ed. Cecelia M. Kenyon (Indianapolis, 1966) 192–5

There is no declaration of rights: and the laws of the general government being paramount to the laws and constitutions of the several states, the declarations of rights, in the separate states, are no security. Nor are the people secured even in the enjoyment of the benefit of the common law, which stands here upon no other foundation than its having been adopted by the respective acts forming the constitutions of the several states.

In the House of Representatives there is not the substance, but the shadow only of representation; which can never produce proper information in the legislature, or inspire confidence in the people. – The laws will, therefore, be generally made by men little concerned in, and unacquainted with their effects and consequences.[1]

The Senate have the power of altering all money-bills, and of originating appropriations of money, and the salaries of the officers of their appointment, in conjunction with the President of the United States – Although they are not the representatives of the people, or amenable to them. These, with their other great powers, (viz. their powers in the appointment of ambassadors, and all public officers, in making treaties, and in trying all impeachments) their influence upon, and connection with, the supreme executive from these causes, their duration of office, and their being a constant existing body, almost continually sitting, joined with their being one complete branch of the legislature, will destroy any balance in the government, and enable them to accomplish what usurpations they please, upon the rights and liberties of the people.

The judiciary of the United States is so constructed and extended, as to absorb and destroy the judiciaries of the several states; thereby rendering laws as tedious, intricate, and expensive, and justice as

[1] This objection has been in some degree lessened, by an amendment, often before refused, and at last made by an erasure, after the engrossment upon parchment, of the word forty, and inserting thirty, in the third clause of the second section of the first article.

unattainable by a great part of the community, as in England; and enabling the rich to oppress and ruin the poor.

The President of the United States has no constitutional council (a thing unknown in any safe and regular government.) he will therefore be unsupported by proper information and advice; and will generally be directed by minions and favorites – or he will become a tool to the Senate – or a council of state will grow out of the principal officers of the great departments – the worst and most dangerous of all ingredients for such a council, in a free country; for they may be induced to join in any dangerous or oppressive measures, to shelter themselves, and prevent an inquiry into their own misconduct in office. Whereas, had a constitutional council been formed (as was proposed) of six members, viz., two from the eastern, two from the middle, and two from the southern states, to be appointed by vote of the states in the House of Representatives, with the same duration and rotation of office as the Senate, the executive would always have had safe and proper information and advice; the president of such a council might have acted as Vice-President of the United States, *pro tempore*, upon any vacancy or disability of the chief magistrate; and long continued sessions of the Senate, would in a great measure have been prevented. From this fatal defect of a constitutional council, has arisen the improper power of the Senate, in the appointment of the public officers, and the alarming dependence and connexion between that branch of the legislature and the supreme executive. Hence, also, sprung that unnecessary officer, the Vice-President, who, for want of other employment, is made President of the Senate; thereby dangerously blending the executive and legislative powers; besides always giving to some one of the states an unnecessary and unjust pre-eminence over the others.

The President of the United States has the unrestrained power of granting pardon for treason; which may be sometimes exercised to screen from punishment those whom he had secretly instigated to commit the crime, and thereby prevent a discovery of his own guilt. By declaring all treaties supreme laws of the land, the executive and the Senate have, in many cases, an exclusive power of legislation, which might have been avoided, by proper distinctions with respect to treaties, and requiring the assent of the House of Representatives, where it could be done with safety.

By requiring only a majority to make all commercial and navigation laws, the five southern states (whose produce and circumstances are totally different from those of the eight northern and eastern states) will be ruined: for such rigid and premature regulations may be made, as will enable the merchants of the northern and eastern states not only to demand an exorbitant freight, but to monopolize the purchase of the commodities, at their own price, for many years, to the great injury of the landed interest, and the impoverishment of the people: and the danger is the greater, as the gain on one side will be in proportion to the loss on the other. Whereas, requiring two-thirds of the members present in both houses, would have produced mutual moderation, promoted the general interest, and removed an insuperable objection to the adoption of the government.

Under their own construction of the general clause at the end of the enumerated powers, the Congress may grant monopolies in trade and commerce, constitute new crimes, inflict unusual and severe punishments, and extend their power as far as they shall think proper; so that the state legislatures have no security for the powers now presumed to remain to them; or the people for their rights. There is no declaration of any kind for preserving the liberty of the press, the trial by jury in civil cases, nor against the danger of standing armies in time of peace.

The state legislatures are restrained from laying export duties on their own produce – the general legislature is restrained from prohibiting the further importation of slaves for twenty odd years, though such importations render the United States weaker, more vulnerable, and less capable of defence. Both the general legislature, and the state legislatures are expressly prohibited making *ex post facto* laws, though there never was, nor can be, a legislature, but must and will make such laws, when necessity and the public safety require them, which will hereafter be a breach of all the constitutions in the union, and afford precedents for other innovations.

This government will commence in a moderate aristocracy; it is at present impossible to foresee whether it will, in its operation, produce a monarchy, or a corrupt oppressive aristocracy; it will most probably vibrate some years between the two, and then terminate in the one or the other.

I.V.5 MELANCTON SMITH OBJECTS TO THE PROPOSED FEDERAL CONSTITUTION

From the New York Ratifying Convention. *The Anti-Federalists*, ed. Cecelia M. Kenyon (Indianapolis, 1966) 370–89

The Hon. Mr SMITH said, he conceived that the Constitution ought to be considered by paragraphs. An honorable gentleman yesterday had opened the debate with some general observations; another honorable gentleman had just answered him by general observations. He wished the Constitution to be examined by paragraphs. In going through it, he should offer his objections to such parts of it as he thought defective.

The first section of the first article was then read, and passed by without remark.

The second section being read,

Mr SMITH again rose. He most heartily concurred in sentiment with the honorable gentleman who opened the debate, yesterday, that the discussion of the important question now before them ought to be entered on with a spirit of patriotism; with minds open to conviction; with a determination to form opinions only on the merits of the question, from those evidences which should appear in the course of the investigation.

How far the general observations made by the honorable gentleman accorded with these principles, he left to the house to determine.

It was not, he said, his intention to follow that gentleman through all his remarks. He should only observe that what had been advanced did not appear to apply to the subject under consideration.

He was as strongly impressed with the necessity of a union as any one could be. He would seek it with as much ardor. In the discussion of this question, he was disposed to make every reasonable concession, and, indeed, to sacrifice every thing for a union, except the liberties of his country, than which he could contemplate no greater misfortune. But he hoped we were not reduced to the necessity of sacrificing, or even endangering, our liberties, to preserve the Union. If that was the case, the alternative was dreadful. But he would not now say that the adoption of the Constitution would endanger our liberties; because that was the point to be debated, and the premises should be laid down previously to the drawing of any conclusion. He wished that all observations might be confined to this point, and that declamations and appeals to the passions might be omitted.

Why, said he, are we told of our weakness? of the defenceless condition of the southern parts of our state? of the exposed situation of our capital? of Long Island, surrounded by water, and exposed to the incursions of our neighbors in Connecticut? of Vermont having separated from us, and assumed the powers of a distinct government? and of the north-west parts of our state being in the hands of a foreign enemy? Why are we to be alarmed with apprehensions that the Eastern States are inimical, and disinclined to form alliances with us? He was sorry to find that such suspicions were entertained. He believed that no such disposition existed in the Eastern States. Surely it could not be supposed that those states would make war upon us for exercising the rights of freemen, deliberating and judging for ourselves, on a subject the most interesting that ever came before any assembly. If a war with our neighbors was to be the result of not acceding, there was no use in debating here; we had better receive their dictates, if we were unable to resist them. The defects of the old Confederation needed as little proof as the necessity of a union. But there was no proof in all this that the proposed Constitution was a good one. Defective as the old Confederation is, he said, no one could deny but it was possible we might have a worse government. But the question was not whether the present Confederation be a bad one, but whether the proposed Constitution be a good one.

It had been observed, that no example of federal republics had succeeded. It was true that the ancient confederated republics were all destroyed; so were those which were not confederated; and all ancient governments, of every form, had shared the same fate. Holland had, no doubt, experienced many evils from the defects in her government; but, with all these defects, she yet existed: she had, under her confederacy, made a principal figure among the nations of Europe, and he believed few countries had experienced a greater share of internal peace and prosperity. The Germanic confederacy was not the most pertinent example to produce on this occasion. Among a number of absolute princes, who consider their subjects as their property, whose will is law, and to whose ambition there are no bounds, it was no difficult task to discover other causes from which the convulsions in that country rose, than the defects of their confederation. Whether a confederacy of states, under any form, be a practicable government, was a question to be discussed in the course of investigating the Constitution.

He was pleased that, thus early in debate, the honorable gentleman had himself shown that the intent of the Constitution was not a confederacy, but a reduction of all the states into a consolidated government. He hoped the gentleman would be complaisant enough to exchange names with those who disliked the Constitution, as it appeared from his own concessions, that they were federalists, and those who advocated it were anti-federalists. He begged leave, however, to remind the gentleman, that Montesquieu, with all the examples of modern and ancient republics in view, gives it as his opinion, that a confederated republic has all the internal advantages of a republic, with the external force of a monarchical government. He was happy to find an officer of such high rank recommending to the other officers of government, and to those who are members of the legislature, to be unbiased by any motives of interest or state importance. Fortunately for himself, he was out of the verge of temptation of this kind, not having the honor to hold any office under the state. But, then, he was exposed, in common with other gentlemen of the Convention, to another temptation, against which he thought it necessary that we should be equally guarded. If, said he, this Constitution is adopted, there will be a number of honorable and lucrative offices to be filled; and we ought to be cautious lest an expectancy of some of them should influence us to adopt without due consideration.

We may wander, said he, in the fields of fancy without end, and gather flowers as we go. It may be entertaining, but it is of little service to the discovery of truth. We may, on one side, compare the scheme advocated by our opponents to *golden images, with feet part of iron and part of clay;* and on the other, *to a beast dreadful and terrible, and strong exceedngly, having great iron teeth, – which devours, breaks in pieces, and stamps the residue with his feet;* and after all, said he, we shall find that both these allusions are taken from the same *vision*; and their true meaning must be discovered by sober reasoning.

He would agree with the honorable gentlemen that perfection in any system of government was not to be looked for. If that was the object, the debates on the one before them might soon be closed. But he would observe, that this observation applied, with equal force, against changing any system, especially against material and radical changes. Fickleness, and inconstancy, he said, were characteristic of a free people; and, in framing a constitution for them, it was, perhaps, the most difficult thing to correct this spirit, and guard against the evil effects of it. He was persuaded it could not be altogether prevented without destroying their freedom. It would be like, attempting to correct a small indisposition in the habit of the body, fixing the patient in a confirmed consumption. This fickle and inconstant spirit was the more dangerous in bringing about changes in the government. The instance that had been adduced by the gentleman from sacred history, was an example in point to prove this. The nation of Israel, having received a form of civil government from Heaven, enjoyed it for a considerable period; but, at length, laboring under pressures which were brought upon them by their own misconduct and imprudence, instead of imputing their misfortunes to their true causes, and making a proper improvement of their calamities, by a correction of their errors, they imputed them to a defect in their constitution; they rejected their divine Ruler, and asked Samuel to make them a king to judge them, like other nations. Samuel was grieved at their folly; but still, by the command of God, he hearkened to their voice, though not until he had solemnly declared unto them the manner in which the king should reign over them. 'This (says Samuel) shall be the manner of the king that shall reign over you. He will take your sons, and appoint them for himself, for his chariots, and for his horsemen, and some shall run before his chariots; and he will appoint him captains over thousands, and captains over fifties, and will set them to ear his ground, and to reap his harvest, and to make his instruments of war, and instruments of his chariots. And he will take your daughters to be confectionaries, and to be cooks, and to be bakers. And he will take your fields, and your vineyards, and your olive-yards, even the best of them, and give them to his servants. And he will take the tenth of your seed, and of your vineyards, and give to his officers and to his servants, and he will take your men-servants, and your maid-servants, and your goodliest young men, and your asses, and put them to his work. He will take the tenth of your sheep; and ye shall be his servants. And ye shall cry out in that day, because of your king which ye have chosen you; and the Lord will not hear you in that day!' How far this was applicable to the subject, he would not now say, it could be better judged of when they had gone through it. On the whole, he wished to take up this matter with candor and deliberation.

He would now proceed to state his objections to the clause just read, (section 2, of article 1, clause 3.) His objections were comprised under three heads: 1st, the rule of apportionment is unjust; 2d, there is no precise number fixed on, below which the house shall not be reduced; 3d, it is inadequate. In the first place, the rule of apportionment of the representatives is to be according to the whole number of the white inhabitants, with three fifths of all others; that is, in plain English, each state is to send representatives in proportion to the number of freemen, and three fifths of the slaves it contains. He could not see any rule by which slaves were to be included in the ratio of representation. The principle of a representation being that every free agent should be concerned in governing himself, it was absurd in giving that power to a man who could not exercise it. Slaves have no will of their own. The very operation of it was to give certain privileges to those people who were so wicked as to keep slaves. He knew it would be admitted that this rule of apportionment was founded on unjust principles, but that it was the result of accommodation; which, he supposed, we should be under the necessity of admitting, if we meant to be in union with the Southern States, though utterly repugnant to his feelings. In the second place, the number was not fixed by the Constitution, but left at the discretion of the legislature; perhaps he was mistaken; it was his wish to be informed. He understood, from the Constitution, that sixty-five members were to compose the House of Representatives for three years; that, after that time, the census was to be taken, and the numbers to be ascertained by the legislature, on the following principles: 1st, they shall be apportioned to the respective states according to numbers; 2d, each state shall have one, at least; 3d, they shall never exceed one to every thirty thousand. If this was the case, the first Congress that met might reduce the number below what it now is – a power inconsistent with every principle of a free government, to leave it to the discretion of the rulers to determine the number of representatives of the people. There was no kind of security except in the integrity of the men who were intrusted; and if you have no other security, it is idle to contend about constitutions. In the third place, supposing Congress should declare that there should be one representative for every thirty thousand of the people, in his opinion, it would be incompetent to the great purposes of representation. It was, he said, the fundamental principle of a free government, that the people should make the laws by which they were to be governed. He who is controlled by another is a slave; and that government which is directed by the will of any one, or a few, or any number less than is the will of the community, is a government for slaves.

The new point was, How was the will of the community to be expressed? It was not possible for them to come together; the multitude would be too great: in order, therefore, to provide against this inconvenience, the scheme of representation had been adopted, by which the people deputed others to represent them. Individuals entering into society became one body, and that body ought to be animated by one mind; and he conceived that every form of government should have that complexion. It was true, notwithstanding all the experience we had from others, it had appeared that the experiment of representation had been fairly tried; there was something like it in the ancient republics, in which, being of small extent, the people could easily meet together, though, instead of deliberating, they only considered of those things which were submitted to them by their magistrates. In Great Britain, representation had been carried much further than in any government we knew of, except our own; but in that country it now had only a name. America was the only country in which the first fair opportunity had been offered. When we were colonies, our representation was better than any that was then known: since the revolution; we had advanced still nearer to perfection. He considered it as an object, of all others the most important, to have it fixed on its true principle; yet he was convinced that it was impracticable to have such a representation in a consolidated government. However, said he, we may approach a great way towards perfection by increasing the representation and limiting the powers of Congress. He considered that the great interests and liberties of the people could only be secured by the state governments. He admitted that, if the new government was only confined to great national objects, it would be less exceptionable; but it extended to every thing dear to human nature. That this was the case, would be proved without any long chain of reasoning; for that power which had both the purse and the sword had the government of the whole country, and might extend its powers to any and to every object. He had already observed that, by the true doctrine of representation, this principle was established – that the representative must be chosen by the free will of the majority of his constituents. It therefore followed that the representative should be chosen from small districts. This being admitted, he would ask, Could 65 men for

3,000,000, or 1 for 30,000, be chosen in this manner? Would they be possessed of the requisite information to make happy the great number of souls that were spread over this extensive country? There was another objection to the clause: if great affairs of government were trusted to few men, they would be more liable to corruption. Corruption, he knew, was unfashionable amongst us, but he supposed that Americans were like other men; and though they had hitherto displayed great virtues, still they were men; and therefore such steps should be taken as to prevent the possibility of corruption. We were now in that stage of society in which we could deliberate with freedom; how long it might continue, God only knew! Twenty years hence, perhaps, these maxims might become unfashionable. We already hear, said he, in all parts of the country, gentlemen ridiculing that spirit of patriotism, and love of liberty, which carried us through all our difficulties in times of danger. When patriotism was already nearly hooted out of society, ought we not to take some precautions against the progress of corruption?

He had one more observation to make, to show that the representation was insufficient. Government, he said, must rest, for its execution, on the good opinion of the people; for, if it was made [in] heaven, and had not the confidence of the people, it could not be executed; that this was proved by the example given by the gentleman of the Jewish theocracy. It must have a good setting out, or the instant it takes place, there is an end of liberty. He believed that the inefficacy of the old Confederation had arisen from that want of confidence; and this caused, in a great degree, by the continual declamation of gentlemen of importance against it from one end of the continent to the other, who had frequently compared it to a rope of sand. It had pervaded every class of citizens; and their misfortunes, the consequences of idleness and extravagance, were attributed to the defects of that system. At the close of the war, our country had been left in distress; and it was impossible that any government on earth could immediately retrieve it; it must be time and industry alone that could effect it. He said, he would pursue these observations no further at present, – and concluded with making the following motion: –

'*Resolved*, That it is proper that the number of representatives be fixed at the rate of one for every twenty thousand inhabitants, to be ascertained on the principles mentioned in the 2d section of the 1st article of the Constitution, until they amount to three hundred; after which they shall be apportioned among the states, in proportion to the number of inhabitants of the states respectively; and that, before the first enumeration shall be made, the several states shall be entitled to choose double the number of representatives, for that purpose mentioned in the Constitution.'

[Deletion of a speaker other than Smith]

Mr M. SMITH. I had the honor, yesterday, of submitting an amendment to the clause under consideration, with some observations in support of it. I hope I shall be indulged in making some additional remarks in reply to what has been offered by the honorable gentleman from New York.

He has taken up much time in endeavoring to prove that the great defect in the old Confederation was, that it operated upon states instead of individuals. It is needless to dispute concerning points on which we do not disagree. It is admitted that the powers of the general government ought to operate upon individuals to a certain degree. How far the powers should extend, and in what cases to individuals, is the question.

As the different parts of the system will come into view in the course of our investigation, an opportunity will be afforded to consider this question. I wish, at present, to confine myself to the subject immediately under the consideration of the committee. I shall make no reply to the arguments offered by the honorable gentleman to justify the rule of apportionment fixed by this clause; for, though I am confident they might be easily refuted, yet I am persuaded we must yield this point, in accommodation to the Southern States. The amendment therefore proposes no alteration to the clause in this respect.

The honorable gentleman says, that the clause, by obvious construction, fixes the representation. I wish not to torture words or sentences. I perceive no such obvious construction.

I see clearly that, on one hand, the representatives cannot exceed one for thirty thousand inhabitants; and, on the other, that whatever larger number of inhabitants may be taken for the rule of apportionment, each state shall be entitled to send one representative. Every thing else appears to me in the discretion of the legislature. If there be any other limitation, it is certainly implied. Matters of moment should not be left to doubtful construction. It is urged that the number of representatives will be fixed at one for thirty thousand, because it will be the interest of the larger states to do it. I cannot discern the force of this argument. To me it appears clear, that the relative weight of influence of the different states will be the same, with the number of representatives at sixty-five as at six hundred, and that of the individual members greater; for each member's share of power will decrease as the number of the House of Representatives increases. If, therefore, this maxim be true, that men are unwilling to relinquish powers which they once possess, we are not to expect the House of Representatives will be inclined to enlarge the numbers. The same motive will operate to influence the President and Senate to oppose the increase of the number of representatives; for, in proportion as the House of Representatives is augmented, they will feel their own power diminished. It is, therefore, of the highest importance that a suitable number of representatives should be established by the Constitution.

It has been observed, by an honorable member, that the Eastern States insisted upon a small representation, on the principles of economy. This argument must have no weight in the mind of a considerate person. The difference of expense, between supporting a House of Representatives sufficiently numerous, and the present proposed one, would be twenty or thirty thousand dollars per annum. The man who would seriously object to this expense, to secure his liberties, does not deserve to enjoy them. Besides, by increasing the number of representatives, we open a door for the admission of the substantial yeomanry of our country, who, being possessed of the habits of economy, will be cautious of imprudent expenditures, by which means a greater saving will be made of public money than is sufficient to support them. A reduction of the numbers of the state legislatures might also be made, by which means there might be a saving of expense much more than sufficient for the purpose of supporting the general legislature; for as, under this system, all the powers of legislation, relating to our general concerns, are vested in the general government, the powers of the state legislatures will be so curtailed as to render it less necessary to have them so numerous as they now are.

But an honorable gentleman has observed, that it is a problem that cannot be solved, what the proper number is which ought to compose the House of Representatives, and calls upon me to fix the number. I admit that this is a question that will not admit of a solution with mathematical certainty; few political questions will; yet we may determine with certainty that certain numbers are too small or too large. We may be sure that ten is too small, and a thousand too large a number.

Every one will allow that the first number is too small to possess the sentiments, be influenced by the interests of the people, or secure against corruption; a thousand would be too numerous to be capable of deliberating.

To determine whether the number of representatives proposed by this Constitution is sufficient, it is proper to examine the qualifications which this house ought to possess, in order to exercise their power discreetly for the happiness of the people. The idea that naturally suggests itself to our minds, when we speak of representatives, is, that they resemble those they represent. They should be a true picture of the people, possess a knowledge of their circumstances and their wants, sympathize in all their distresses, and be disposed to seek their true interests. The knowledge necessary for the representative of a free people not only comprehends extensive political and commercial information, such as is acquired by men of refined education, who have leisure to attain to high degrees of improvement, but it should also comprehend that kind of acquaintance with the common concerns and occupations of the people, which men of the middling class of life are, in general, more competent to than those of a superior class. To understand the true commercial interests of a country, not only requires just ideas of the general commerce of the world, but also, and principally, a knowledge of the productions of your own country, and their value, what your soil is capable of producing, the nature of your manufactures, and the capacity of the country to increase both. To exercise the power of laying taxes, duties, and excises, with discretion, requires something more than an acquaintance with the abstruse parts of the system of finance. It calls for a knowledge of the circumstances and ability of the people in general – a discernment how the burdens imposed will bear upon the different classes.

From these observations results this conclusion – that the number of representatives should be so large, as that, while it embraces the men of the first class, it should admit those of the middling class of life. I am convinced that this government is so constituted that the representatives will generally be composed of the first class in the community, which I shall distinguish by the name of the *natural aristocracy* of the country. I do not mean to give offence by using this term. I am sensible this idea is treated by many gentlemen as chimerical. I shall be asked what is meant by the *natural aristocracy*, and told that no such distinction of classes of men exists among us. It is true, it is our singular felicity that we have no legal or hereditary distinctions of this kind; but still there are real differences. Every society naturally divides itself into classes. The Author of nature has bestowed on some greater capacities than others; birth, education, talents, and wealth, create distinctions among men as visible, and of as much influence, as titles, stars, and garters. In every society, men of this class will command a superior degree of respect; and if the government is so constituted as to admit but few to exercise the powers of it, it will, according to the natural course of things, be in their hands. Men in the middling class, who are qualified as representatives, will not be so anxious to be chosen as those of the first. When the number is so small, the office will be highly elevated and distinguished; the style in which the members live will probably be high; circumstances of this kind will render the place of a representative not a desirable one to sensible, substantial men, who have been used to walk in the plain and frugal paths of life.

Besides, the influence of the great will generally enable them to succeed in elections. It will be difficult to combine a district of country containing thirty or forty thousand inhabitants, – frame your election laws as you please, – in any other character, unless it be in one of conspicuous military, popular, civil, or legal talents. The great easily form associations; the poor and middling class form them with difficulty. If the elections be by plurality, – as probably will be the case in this state, – it is almost certain none but the great will be chosen, for they easily unite their interests: the common people will divide, and their divisions will be promoted by the others. There will be scarcely a chance of their uniting in any other but some great man, unless in some popular demagogue, who will probably be destitute of principle. A substantial yeoman, of sense and discernment, will hardly ever be chosen. From these remarks, it appears that the government will fall into the hands of the few and the great. This will be a government of oppression. I do not mean to declaim against the great, and charge them indiscriminately with want of principle and honesty. The same passions and prejudices govern all men. The circumstances in which men are placed in a great measure give a cast to the human character. Those in middling circumstances have less temptation; they are inclined by habit, and the company with whom they associate, to set bounds to their passions and appetites. If this is not sufficient, the want of means to gratify them will be a restraint: they are obliged to employ their time in their respective callings; hence the substantial yeomanry of the country are more temperate, of better morals, and less ambition, than the great. The latter do not feel for the poor and middling class; the reasons are obvious – they are not obliged to use the same pains and labor to procure property as the other. They feel not the inconveniences arising from the payment of small sums. The great consider themselves above the common people, entitled to more respect, do not associate with them; they fancy themselves to have a right of preëminence in every thing. In short, they possess the same feelings, and are under the influence of the same motives, as an hereditary nobility. I know the idea that such a distinction exists in this country is ridiculed by some; but I am not the less apprehensive of danger from their influence on this account. Such distinctions exist all the world over, have been taken notice of by all writers on free government, and are founded in the nature of things. It has been the principal care of free governments to guard against the encroachments of the great. Common observation and experience prove the existence of such distinctions. Will any one say that there does not exist in this country the pride of family, of wealth, of talents, and that they do not command influence and respect among the common people? Congress, in their address to the inhabitants of the province of Quebec, in 1775, state this distinction in the following forcible words, quoted from the Marquis Beccaria: 'In every human society there is an essay continually tending to confer on one part the height of power and happiness, and to reduce the other to the extreme of weakness and misery. The intent of good laws is to oppose this effort, and to diffuse their influence universally and equally.' We ought to guard against the government being placed in the hands of this class. They cannot have that sympathy with their constituents which is necessary to connect them closely to their interests. Being in the habit of profuse living, they will be profuse in the public expenses. They find no difficulty in paying their taxes, and therefore do not feel public burdens. Besides, if they govern, they will enjoy the emoluments of the government. The middling class, from their frugal habits, and feeling themselves the public burdens, will be careful how they increase them.

But I may be asked, Would you exclude the first class in the community from any share in legislation? I answer, By no means. They would be factious, discontented, and constantly disturbing the government. It would also be unjust. They have their liberties to protect, as well as others, and the largest share of property. But my idea is, that the Constitution should be so framed as to admit this class, together with a sufficient number of the middling class to control them. You will then combine the abilities and honesty of the community, a proper degree of information, and a disposition to pursue the public good. A representative body, composed principally of respectable yeomanry, is the best possible security to liberty. When the interest of this part of the community is pursued, the public good is pursued, because the body of every nation consists of this class, and because the interest of both the rich and the poor are involved in that of the middling class. No burden can be laid on the poor but what will sensibly affect the middling class. Any law rendering property insecure would be injurious to them. When, therefore, this class in society pursue their own interest, they promote that of the public, for it is involved in it.

In so small a number of representatives, there is great danger from corruption and combination. A great politician has said that every man has his price. I hope this is not true in all its extent; but I ask the gentleman to inform me what government there is in which it has not been practised. Notwithstanding all that has been said of the defects in the constitution of the ancient confederacies in the Grecian republics, their destruction is to be imputed more to this cause than to any imperfection in their forms of government. This was the deadly poison that effected their dissolution. This is an extensive country, increasing in population and growing in consequence. Very many lucrative offices will be in the grant of the government, which will be objects of avarice and ambition. How easy will it be to gain over a sufficient number, in the bestowment of offices, to promote the views and the purposes of those who grant them! Foreign corruption is also to be guarded against. A system of corruption is known to be the system of government in Europe. It is practised without blushing; and we may lay it to our account, it will be attempted amongst us. The most effectual as well as natural security against this is a strong democratic branch in the legislature, frequently chosen, including in it a number of the substantial, sensible yeomanry of the country. Does the House of Representatives answer this description? I confess, to me they hardly wear the complexion of a democratic branch; they appear the mere shadow of representation. The whole number, in both houses, amounts to ninety-one; of these forty-six make a quorum; and twenty-four of those, being secured, may carry any point. Can the liberties of three millions of people be securely trusted in the hands of twenty-four men? Is it prudent to commit to so small a number the decision of the great questions which will come before them? Reason revolts at the idea.

The honorable gentleman from New York has said, that sixty-five members in the House of Representatives are sufficient for the present situation of the country; and, taking it for granted that they will increase as one for thirty thousand, in twenty-five years they will amount to two hundred. It is admitted, by this observation, that the number fixed in the Constitution is not sufficient without it is augmented. It is not declared that an increase shall be made, but is left at the discretion of the legislature, by the gentleman's own concession; therefore the Constitution is imperfect. We certainly ought to fix, in the Constitution, those things which are essential to liberty. If any thing falls under this description, it is the number of the legislature. To say, as this gentleman does, that our security is to depend upon the spirit of the people, who will be watchful of their liberties, and not suffer them to be infringed is absurd. It would equally prove that we might adopt any form of government. I believe, were we to create a despot, he would not immediately dare to act the tyrant; but it would not be long before he would destroy the spirit of the people, or the people would destroy him. If our people have a high sense of liberty, the government should be congenial to this spirit, calculated to cherish the love of liberty, while yet it had sufficient force to restrain licentiousness. Government operates upon the spirit of the people, as well as the spirit of the people operates upon it; and if they are not conformable to each other, the one or the other will prevail. In a less time than twenty-five years, the government will receive its tone. What the spirit of the country may be at the end of that period, it is impossible to foretell. Our duty is to frame a government friendly to liberty and the rights of mankind, which will tend to cherish and cultivate a love of liberty among our citizens. If this government becomes oppressive, it will be by degrees: it will aim at its end by disseminating sentiments of government opposite to republicanism, and proceed from step to step in depriving the people of a share in the government. A recollection of the change that has taken place in the minds of many in this country in the course of a few years, ought to put us on our guard. Many, who are ardent advocates for the new system, reprobate republican principles as chimerical, and such as ought to be expelled from society. Who would have thought, ten years ago, that the very men, who risked their lives and fortunes in support of republican principles, would now treat them as the fictions of fancy? A few years ago, we fought for liberty; we framed a general government on free principles; we placed the state legislatures, in whom the people have a full and a fair representation, between Congress and the people. We were then, it is true, too cautious, and too much restricted the powers of the general government. But now it is proposed to go into the contrary, and a more dangerous extreme – to remove all barriers, to give the new government free access to our pockets, and ample command of our persons, and that without providing for a genuine and fair representation of the people. No one can say what the progress of the change of sentiment may be in twenty-five years. The same men who now cry up the necessity of an energetic government, to induce a compliance with this system, may, in much less time, reprobate this in as severe terms as they now do the Confederation, and may as strongly urge the necessity of going as far beyond this as this is beyond the Confederation. Men of this class are increasing: they have influence, talents, and industry. It is time to form a barrier against them. And while we are willing to establish a government adequate to the purposes of the Union, let us be careful to establish it on the broad basis of equal liberty.

I.v.6 JAMES MADISON DEFENDS THE PROPOSED CONSTITUTION

'The Federalist no. 39'[1]

To the People of the State of New York: The last paper having concluded the observations which were meant to introduce a candid survey of the plan of government reported by the Convention, we now proceed to the execution of that part of our undertaking. The first question that offers itself is, whether the general form and aspect

[1] From *The Independent Journal*, January 16, 1788. This essay appeared on the same day in *The Daily Advertiser*, on January 18 in *The New-York Packet*, and on January 30 in *The New-York Journal*. It was numbered 39 in the McLean edition and 38 in the newspapers, with the exception of *The New-York Journal* where it was numbered 37 and was the last essay to appear.

of the government be strictly republican? It is evident that no other form would be reconcileable with the genius of the people of America; with the fundamental principles of the revolution; or with that honorable determination, which animates every votary of freedom, to rest all our political experiments on the capacity of mankind for self-government. If the plan of the Convention therefore be found to depart from the republican character, its advocates must abandon it as no longer defensible.

What then are the distinctive characters of the republican form? Were an answer to this question to be sought, not by recurring to principles, but in the application of the term by political writers, to the constitutions of different States, no satisfactory one would ever be found. Holland, in which no particle of the supreme authority is derived from the people, has passed almost universally under the denomination of a republic. The same title has been bestowed on Venice, where absolute power over the great body of the people, is exercised in the most absolute manner, by a small body of hereditary nobles. Poland, which is a mixture of aristocracy and of monarchy in their worst forms, has been dignified with the same appellation. The government of England, which has one republican branch only, combined with a hereditery aristocracy and monarchy, has with equal impropriety been frequently placed on the list of republics. These examples, which are nearly as dissimilar to each other as to a genuine republic, shew the extreme inaccuracy with which the term has been used in political disquisitions.

If we resort for a criterion, to the different principles on which different forms of government are established, we may define a republic to be, or at least may bestow that name on, a government which derives all its powers directly or indirectly from the great body of the people; and is administered by persons holding their offices during pleasure, for a limited period, or during good behaviour. It is *essential* to such a government, that it be derived from the great body of the society, not from an inconsiderable proportion, or a favored class of it; otherwise a handful of tyrannical nobles, exercising their oppressions by a delegation of their powers, might aspire to the rank of republicans, and claim for their government the honorable title of republic. It is *sufficient* for such a government, that the persons administering it be appointed, either directly or indirectly, by the people; and that they hold their appointments by either of the tenures just specified; otherwise every government in the United States, as well as every other popular government that has been or can be well organized or well executed, would be degraded from the republican character. According to the Constitution of every State in the Union, some or other of the officers of government are appointed indirectly only by the people. According to most of them the chief magistrate himself is so appointed. And according to one, this mode of appointment is extended to one of the coordinate branches of the legislature. According to all the Constitutions also, the tenure of the highest offices is extended to a definite period, and in many instances, both within the legislative and executive departments, to a period of years. According to the provisions of most of the constitutions, again, as well as according to the most respectable and received opinions on the subject, the members of the judiciary department are to retain their offices by the firm tenure of good behaviour.

On comparing the Constitution planned by the Convention, with the standard here fixed, we perceive at once that it is in the most rigid sense conformable to it. The House of Representatives, like that of one branch at least of all the State Legislatures, is elected immediately by the great body of the people. The Senate, like the present Congress, and the Senate of Maryland, derives its appointment indirectly from the people. The President is indirectly derived from the choice of the people, according to the example in most of the States. Even the judges, with all other officers of the Union, will, as in the several States, be the choice, though a remote choice, of the people themselves. The duration of the appointments is equally conformable to the republican standard, and to the model of the State Constitutions. The House of Representatives is periodically elective as in all the States: and for the period of two years as in the State of South-Carolina. The Senate is elective for the period of six years; which is but one year more than the period of the Senate of Maryland; and but two more than that of the Senates of New-York and Virginia. The President is to continue in office for the period of four years; as in New-York and Delaware, the chief magistrate is elected for three years, and in South-Carolina for two years. In the other States the election is annual. In several of the States however, no constitutional provision is made for the impeachment of the Chief Magistrate. And in Delaware and Virginia, he is not impeachable till out of office. The President of the United States is impeachable at any time during his continuance in office. The tenure by which the Judges are to hold their places, is, as it unquestionably ought to be, that of good behaviour. The tenure of the ministerial offices generally will be a subject of legal regulation, conformably to the reason of the case, and the example of the State Constitutions.

Could any further proof be required of the republican complextion of this system, the most decisive one might be found in its absolute prohibition of titles of nobility, both under the Federal and the State Governments; and in its express guarantee of the republican form to each of the latter.

But it was not sufficient, say the adversaries of the proposed Constitution, for the Convention to adhere to the republican form. They ought, with equal care, to have preserved the *federal* form, which regards the union as a *confederacy* of sovereign States; instead of which, they have framed a *national* government, which regards the union as a *consolidation* of the States. And it is asked by what authority this bold and radical innovation was undertaken. The handle which has been made of this objection requires, that it should be examined with some precision.

Without enquiring into the accuracy of the distinction on which the objection is founded, it will be necessary to a just estimate of its force, first to ascertain the real character of the government in question; secondly, to enquire how far the Convention were authorised to propose such a government; and thirdly, how far the duty they owed to their country, could supply any defect of regular authority.

First. In order to ascertain the real character of the government it may be considered in relation to the foundation on which it is to be established; to the sources from which its ordinary powers are to be drawn; to the operation of those powers; to the extent of them; and to the authority by which future changes in the government are to be introduced.

On examining the first relation, it appears on one hand that the Constitution is to be founded on the assent and ratification of the people of America, given by deputies elected for the special purpose; but on the other, that this assent and ratification is to be given by the people, not as individuals composing one entire nation; but as composing the distinct and independent States to which they respectively belong. It is to be the assent and ratification of the several States, derived from the supreme authority in each State, the authority of the people themselves. The act therefore establishing the Constitution, will not be a *national* but a *federal* act.

That it will be a federal and not a national act, as these terms are understood by the objectors, the act of the people as forming so many independent States, not as forming one aggregate nation, is obvious from this single consideration that it is to result neither from the decision of a *majority* of the people of the Union, nor from that of a *majority* of the States. It must result from the *unanimous* assent of the several States that are parties to it, differing no other wise from their ordinary assent than in its being expressed, not by the legislative authority, but by that of the people themselves. Were the people regarded in this transaction as forming one nation, the will of the majority of the whole people of the United States, would bind the minority; in the same manner as the majority in each State must bind the minority; and the will of the majority must be determined either by a comparison of the individual votes; or by considering the will of a majority of the States, as evidence of the will of a majority of the people of the United States. Neither of these rules has been adopted. Each State in ratifying the Constitution, is considered as a sovereign body independent of all others, and only to be bound by its own voluntary act. In this relation then the new Constitution will, if established, be a *federal* and not a *national* Constitution.

The next relation is to the sources from which the ordinary powers of government are to be derived. The house of representatives will derive its powers from the people of America, and the people will be represented in the same proportion, and on the same principle, as they are in the Legislature of a particular State. So far the Government is *national* not *federal*. The Senate on the other hand will derive its powers from the States, as political and co-equal societies; and these will be represented on the principle of equality in the Senate, as they now are in the existing Congress. So far the government is *federal*, not *national*. The executive power will be derived from a very compound source. The immediate election of the President is to be made by the States in their political characters. The votes allotted to them, are in a compound ratio, which considers them partly as distinct and co-equal societies; partly as unequal members of the same society. The eventual election, again is to be made by that branch of the Legislature which consists of the national representatives; but in this particular act, they are to be thrown into the form of individual delegations from so many distinct and co-equal bodies politic. From this aspect of the Government, it appears to be of a mixed character presenting at least as many *federal* as *national* features.

The difference between a federal and national Government as it relates to the *operation of the Government* is supposed to consist in this, that in the former, the powers operate on the political bodies composing the confederacy, in their political capacities: In the latter, on the individual citizens, composing the nation, in their individual capacities. On trying the Constitution by this criterion, it falls under the *national*, not the *federal* character; though perhaps not so compleatly, as has been understood. In several cases and particularly in the trial of controversies to which States may be parties, they must be viewed and proceeded against in their collective and political capacities only. So far the national countenance of the Government on this side seems to be disfigured by a few federal features. But this blemish is perhaps unavoidable in any plan; and the operation of the Government on the people in their individual capacities, in its ordinary and most essential proceedings, may on the whole designate it in this relation a *national* Government.

But if the Government be national with regard to the *operation* of its powers, it changes its aspect again when we contemplate it in relation to the *extent* of its powers. The idea of a national Government involves in it, not only an authority over the individual citizens; but an indefinite supremacy over all persons and things, so far as they are objects of lawful Government. Among a people consolidated into one nation, this supremacy is compleatly vested in the national Legislature. Among communities united for particular purposes, it is vested partly in the general, and partly in the municipal Legislatures. In the former case, all local authorities are subordinate to the supreme; and may be controuled, directed or abolished by it at pleasure. In the latter the local or municipal authorities form distinct and independent portions of the supremacy, no more subject within their respective spheres to the general authority, than the general authority is subject to them, within its own sphere. In this relation then the proposed Government cannot be deemed a *national* one; since its jurisdiction extends to certain enumerated objects only, and leaves to the several States a residuary and inviolable sovereignty over all other objects. It is true that in controversies relating to the boundary between the two jurisdictions, the tribunal which is ultimately to decide, is to be established under the general Government. But this does not change the principle of the case. The decision is to be impartially made, according to the rules of the Constitution; and all the usual and most effectual precautions are taken to secure this impartiality. Some such tribunal is clearly essential to prevent an appeal to the sword, and a dissolution of the compact; and that it ought to be established under the general, rather than under the local Governments; or to speak more properly, that it could be safely established under the first alone, is a position not likely to be combated.

If we try the Constitution by its last relation, to the authority by which amendments are to be made, we find it neither wholly *national*, nor wholly *federal*. Were it wholly national, the supreme and ultimate authority would reside in the *majority* of the people of the Union; and this authority would be competent at all times, like that of a majority of every national society, to alter or abolish its established Government. Were it wholly federal on the other hand, the concurrence of each State in the Union would be essential to every alteration that would be binding on all. The mode provided by the plan of the Convention is not founded on either of these principles. In requiring more than a majority, and particularly, in computing the proportion by *States*, not by *citizens*, it departs from the *national*, and advances towards the *federal* character: In rendering the concurrence of less than the whole number of States sufficient, it loses again the *federal*, and partakes of the *national* character.

The proposed Constitution therefore is in strictness neither a national nor a federal constitution; but a composition of both. In its foundation, it is federal, not national; in the sources from which the ordinary powers of the Government are drawn, it is partly federal, and partly national: in the operation of these powers, it is national, not federal: In the extent of them again, it is federal, not national: And finally, in the authoritative mode of introducing amendments, it is neither wholly federal, nor wholly national.

PUBLIUS

I.V.7 THE FIRST TEN AMENDMENTS TO THE CONSTITUTION, FORMALLY ADOPTED DECEMBER 15, 1791

Article I. Congress shall make no law respecting an establishment of religion, or prohibiting the free exercise thereof; or abridging the freedom of speech, or of the press; or the right of the people peaceably to assemble, and to petition the Government for a redress of grievances.

Article II. A well regulated Militia, being necessary to the security of a free State, the right of the people to keep and bear Arms, shall not be infringed.

Article III. No Soldier shall, in time of peace be quartered in any house, without the consent of the Owner, nor in time of war, but in a manner to be prescribed by law.

Article IV. The right of the people to be secure in their persons, houses, papers, and effects, against unreasonable searches and seizures, shall not be violated, and no Warrants shall issue, but upon probable cause, supported by Oath or affirmation, and particularly describing the place to be searched, and the persons or things to be seized.

Article V. No person shall be held to answer for a capital, or otherwise infamous crime, unless on a presentment or indictment of a Grand Jury, except in cases arising in the land or naval forces, or in the Militia, when in actual service in time of War or public danger; nor shall any person be subject for the same offence to be twice put in jeopardy of life or limb; nor shall be compelled in any criminal case to be a witness against himself, nor be deprived of life, liberty, or property, without due process of law; nor shall private property be taken for public use, without just compensation.

Article VI. In all criminal prosecutions, the accused shall enjoy the right to a speedy and public trial, by an impartial jury of the State and district wherein the crime shall have been committed, which district shall have been previously ascertained by law, and to be informed of the nature and cause of the accusation; to be confronted with the witnesses against him; to have compulsory process for obtaining witnesses in his favor, and to have the Assistance of Counsel for his defence.

Article VII. In Suits at common law, where the value in controversy shall exceed twenty dollars, the right of trial by jury shall be preserved, and no fact tried by a jury, shall be otherwise re-examined in any Court of the United States, than according to the rules of common law.

ARTICLE VIII. Excessive bail shall not be required, nor excessive fines imposed, nor cruel and unusual punishments inflicted.

ARTICLE IX. The enumeration in the Constitution, of certain rights, shall not be construed to deny or disparage others retained by the people.

ARTICLE X. The powers not delegated to the United States by the Constitution, nor prohibited by it to the States, are reserved to the States respectively, or to the people.

PART 2

Wealth, Wages and Prices: Congressional and State Economic Policies

2.1 ECONOMIC OPPORTUNITIES ADVANCED BY WAR

September 25, 1775, *Journals of the Continental Congress*, III 473–4

Monday. An uneasiness among some of the members, concerning a contract with Willing and Morris for powder,[1] by which the House, without any risk at all, will make a clear profit of twelve thousand pounds at least. Dyer and Deane spoke in public; Lewis, to me, in private, about it. All think it exorbitant.

S. Adams desired that the Resolve of Congress, upon which the contract was founded might be read: he did not recollect it.

De Hart. One of the contractors, Willing, declared to this Congress, that he looked upon the contract to be, that the first cost should be insured to them, not the fourteen pounds a barrel for the powder.

R. R. Livingston. I never will vote to ratify the contract in the sense that Morris understands it.

Willing. I am, as a member of the House, a party to that contract, but was not privy to the bargain. I never saw the contract, until I saw it in Dr Franklin's hand. I think it insures only the first cost; my partner thinks it insures the whole. He says that Mr Rutledge said, at the time, that Congress should have nothing to do with sea risk. The committee of this city offered nineteen pounds. I would wish to have nothing to do with the contract, but to leave it to my partner, who is a man of reason and generosity, to explain the contract with the gentlemen who made it with him.

J. Rutledge. Congress was to run no risk, only against men-of-war and custom-house officers. I was surprised, this morning, to hear that Mr Morris understood it otherwise. If he won't execute a bond, such as we shall draw, I shall not be at a loss what to do.

Johnson. A hundred tons of powder was wanted. *Ross.* In case of its arrival, Congress was to pay fourteen pounds; if men-of-war or custom-house officers should get it, Congress was to pay first cost only, as I understood it. *Zubly.* We are highly favored; fourteen pounds we are to give, if we get the powder, and fourteen pounds, if we don't get it. I understand, persons enough will contract to supply powder at fifteen pounds and run all risks.

Willing. Sorry any gentleman should be severe. Mr. Morris's character is such that he cannot deserve it.

[1] See *Journals of Congress*, September 18, 1775.

Lynch. If Morris will execute the bond, well; if not, the committee will report.

Deane. It is very well that this matter has been moved, and that so much has been said upon it.

Dyer. There are not ten men, in the Colony I came from, who are worth so much money as will be made, clear, by this contract. *Ross*. What has this matter to (do with) the present debate, whether Connecticut men are worth much or no; it proves there are no men there whose capital or credit is equal to such contracts; that is all. *Harrison*. The contract is made, and the money paid. How can we get it back?

Johnson. Let us consider the prudence of this contract. If it had not been made, Morris would have got nineteen pounds, and not have set forward a second adventure. *Gadsden* understands the contract as Morris does, and yet thinks it a prudent one, because Morris would have got nineteen pounds.

J. Adams. &c. &c. &c.

Cushing. I move that we take into consideration a method of keeping up an army in the winter.

Richard Adams to Thomas Adams, Williamsburg, June 1, 1778, *Virginia Historical Magazine*, v 293–4

Dear Bror.: From the present pleasing Prospect, I hope our Public affairs will soon be put on a better footing, and to prevent Foreigners as much as Possible from Engrossing the Trade as heretofore, I think nothing will contribute more to the Interest of this Country than for the Principal Gentn. immediately to form themselves into Compys. & to have some Capitol Stores at the Heads of the Rivers, to supply the People at large on the best terms, and to receive consignments &c. I have had some conversation with our Friend, Mr Jno. Harvie on the subject, he is desirous of engaging in Trade himself, and thinks he can form some connextions to the Northwd. that may be of advantage. Probably Mr Robt. Morriss may be willing to take a Share with us, his connextions & Influence might be of the greatest service. I have therefore refer'd Mr Harvie to you, as from the oppty. you have had, you may form a better Opinion than myself, and shall rely on your Judgement, whether suppose Mr Morriss, Mr Harvie, Mr Banister, Mr J. Southall with you & my self, should form ourselves into a Compy. to employ such a sum of money that would be necessary on our own accts. and to receive consignmts. from all others that can be procured, at Richmd. & Petersburg, those two places have the advantage of all others, as Tobo., wheat, & Flour are the Principal articles of our Export. If Mr Bannister should incline to come into our scheme, I think you might contrive to fix matters on a Permanent footing, and any Terms you make for me or Col. Southall, we shall Gladly confirm. Pray let me know your opinion of this matter as soon as Possible, & whether you approve of this scheme, or can point out a better. We have lately had a large Importation of Goods from France, a 50 Gunn Ship is arrived in Jas. River wth. about £50,000 Sterlings worth, & two other vessels, a Brigg & Schooner all private Property. Mr. Francey now with you at Yorke I understand has an Interest in the Goods. I hope you have made an acquaintance with him, as I am informed he is a valuable man. Our assembly will rise to-Day, we have determined to raise 350 Horse & 2,000 foot, to reinforce our Grand Army immediately, & have Elected our members to Congress for the Ensueing year, as below.

Richmond Hill, July 4, 1778, ibid. pp. 294–5

Dear Bror.: I rec'd your letter of the 22 June, wch. Confirmed the agreeble News of the enemy's evacuating Philadelphia, this great event is, I hope, a Prelude to their leaving us altogether, and at last make a virtue of Necessity, by declaring us Independent. The Conduct of the Congress, in regard to the Commissioners, gives general satisfaction. We are Impatient to hear the fate of the Enemy on their retreat through the Jerseys. I hope our Noble General will give a good acct. of them. Pray continue to send me the News Papers, they afford great Satisfaction to all Friends here.

As to the Plan of Trade I mentioned to you, you certainly did not think I meant to be either a forestaller or Engrosser in order to make an advantage of the distresses of my Country Men, you must know I have always had the greatest abhorence to such a practice, or might have made my Thousands as others have done, no, I mean to form a Compy. of a few Principal Gentn. of the first fortunes & Characters, who will Carry on Trade, on a fair, open, Liberal Plan, as well for their own Advantage as the Benefit of the Country at large, and to accommodate all Foreigners that may Come among us, may We not expect a great Number of Such, who are Ignorant of the Language & Customs of the Country & who may fall into such Hands as may deter them from Coming a Second Time, will it not therefore be Convenient to them, to find Houses founded by Gentn. of Fortune & who Act from Principles of Honour, to Commit the Transactions of their affairs to, and where they are such their property will be safe. This I think would be the first object (while things remained in this unsettled state), to engage all the Consignments we Possibly could from foreigners & to see that they are fairly dealt by, & the best despatch given their Ships, &c., this would Endear us to them, & fix them in our Trade, & of course throw most of their Business into such Capital Houses I would have Established at the heads of all the Rivers.

2.2 BOSTON ATTEMPTS, UNSUCCESSFULLY, TO REGULATE PRICES AND WAGES

Boston Town Records, August 16, 1779, in *Report of the Record Commissioners of the City of Boston: Records Relating to the Early History of Boston* (1876–1909) vol. 35

[301.] The Committee appointed to affix the Pricies of the Several Articles mentioned in the 4th. and 5th. Resolves of the Convention held at Concord July 14th. 1779 Reported

Whereas the Goods and wares imported from Europe are so various in their kinds and qualities as to render it quite impracticable to determine the exact Price at which every Article ought to sold and it is necessary the Pricies of those kinds of Goods, should be reduced in the same proportion as the West India Imports

Therefore Resolved that all Holders and Retailers of Europian Wares and Merchandize shall from time to time forward sell all such Articles at twenty pct. or one fifth part less than the Prices at which the same Articles were sold in the Month of July last, that being the avarige deduction in the Prices of West India Goods

And in Order that the aforegoing Resolve may be more effectually complyed with, and that all those who wish to enrich themselves at the Expence of their Neighbours, and who on all Occasions are disposed to take Advantage of our Friends in the Country may be prevented in future from Preying upon their more worthy fellow citizens and Country Bretheren

Be it Resolved, that William Cooper Esqr. Mr. Gibbens Sharp, Capt. Isaac Phillips, Colo. Edward Procter, Capt. Gustavus Fellows Major Thomas Melvill, Mr. Henry Prentice, Mr. William Hoskins [302.] Capt. Alexr. Willson Dr. Nathl. Noyes Mr. Samuel Ruggles, Mr. Joshua Pulling and Dr. Charles Jarvis, be a Committee with whom may be lodg'd Complaints of all Violations and evasions of the above Resolve, who are hereby impowered and directed to enquire into all Such complaints and to Publish the Names of those who upon good and Satisfactory Evidence may be convicted of Violating or evading said Resolves, as Enemies to their Country as they may be delt with according to their Demerit and all Persons whether from the Town or Country, who may think themselves imposed upon by any Person in the Town in not Complying with the aforegoing Resolve are hereby desired to lodge a Complaint with aforementioned Committee that the Matter may be enquired into

Resolved that the following Prices for Labourers and Manufactures &c. be the highest that shall be demanded or given for the future Labourers 60/ p Day they finding themselves Ship-Carpenters, Carpenters, caulkers, Riggers Ship Joiners Housewrights and Masens 78/ p Day they finding themselves – Blacksmiths Block makers, Carvers, Cabinet makers Peiwtarers shall reduce their Prices at Least 10 p Ct. from the Preasent Prices – Printers Ropemakers Boat Builders Coopers Cordwainers and Tinmen shall reduce their Prices at least twenty pc from the Present Prices – Saillmakers shall not have more than £1.8/ p Bolt for working New Canvas and for old Work in Proportion [303.] Tanners 18/ p Pound for Sole Leather and other Leather in proportion – Leather Dressers for a pr. Dearskin Breeches of the very best sort – £35 and other Articles in proportion – Hatters for best Beaver Hatts £35. beaveretts £24 and felt Hatts £4 each, Barbers and hair Dressers shall reduce their Prices from the present rates at least 15/ Tailors shall not have more than £18 p Suit for plain Cloaths £22. 10/ for half trimed, and other Work in proportion – Painters shall reduce their Prices from the present rate 15 p Ct. Ship Chandlers shall reduce their prices from the present Rate 20 p Ct. execept Pitch which shall not exceed £35 p Barrell and Tar and Turpentine £30. each Truckman for truckage of a Large Hogshead of Sugar 18/ Molasses Rum &c 15/ tierces 9/ Barrel 4/ by the Load and Other Work in proportion – Wharfingers for Wharfage, Cording, Sealing and carrying off Wood £3. 12/ p Cord Farriers for Shoeing a Horse all round £6 and for shifting a set of Shoes 48/ – Refined Iron £37. 10/ p Ct. Card makers £36 p dozn. for Cards and 66/ a single pair. Glaziers for setting Glass and finding the putty shall not have more than 4/6 p square, Inholders and Victuallers shall reduce their Prices of Victualling and Horse Keeping in proportion to the Reduction of the Prices of Provisions and Hay – Hucksters shall not take more than Six-pence advance upon the shilling – Fishmongers shall not take more than 12d. p pound for Cod, 3d. for Haddock and 1/3 for Hallybut, without entrails, Goldsmiths shall not demand of the Purchaser no more than the weight of the Plate they Manufacture and twenty Times what they had for their Labour in Manufacturing before the year 1775 (304.] All Other Tradesmen not mentioned shall reduce their Prices in an Average proportion with those of their Bretheren, and the Article of Consumption

ISAAC SMITH p Order

Which Report having been read and taken up, Paragraph by Paragraph the Question was put Vizt. Whether such Report as amended by the said Town be accepted passed in the Affermative and so far as relates to regulating prices of Goods unanimously

Adjourned to 5. O.Clock P.M.

5. OClock Met according to Adjournment A Committee Appointed to consider and report the most effectual and Speedy Measures for carrying the Resolves of the Convention and of the Town into Effect reported as follows

Whereas the carrying into effect the Resolutions of the Convention at Concord and the subsequent Resolves of this Town in Conformity thereto is of the last importance to the Community and the Violation of them in the present scituation of Publick Affairs a crime of the deepest dye

Voted, that any Person directly or indirectly either by himself or any Person for and under him who shall buy or sell, or Offer to give or take an higher price at publick Market or private Sale or who may withhold any Article except from Persons who may be Inhabitants of such places as have not Adopted simaler measures or in any [305.] Other Way whatever Violate the said Resolutions shall have his or her Names Published by the Committee hereafter Appointed in the News Papers in this Town that the Publick knowing may Abstain from all Trade And Conversation with them and the People at Large inflict upon them that Punishment which such Wretches deserve to trade or hold any intercourse or conversation with such Persons

Voted, that it is the duty of every Citizen to keep a Vigilant Eye upon his Neighbour that Any infrindgements upon the Resolutions aforesaid may be prevented and where it may unhappely take place to give immediate information to the Committee, Appointed to receive such Complaints

Voted, that William Cooper Esqr. Deacon Gibbens Sharp, Capt. Isaac Phillips, Colo. Edwd. Procter, Capt. Gustavus Fellows, Majr. Thomas Melvill, Mr. Henry Prentice, Mr. William Hoskins, Capt. Alexr. Wilson Doctr. Nathl. Noyes, Mr. Saml. Ruggles, Capt. John Pulling and Doctr. Charles Jarvis, be a Committee for the purpose aforesaid, In as much as sending Servants to the Market Ferries to the Neck, and to the Neighbouring Towns with discretionary Orders has a direct tendency to counteract the Resolves of the Convention and of this Town

Therefore it is repeatedly and especially Resolved that if any Person who shall by his Servant or any Person under him presume either directly or indirectly to Offer or give either in Town [306.] Or out of it for any Article of Consumption an higher Price than is Stipulated therefore in the Resolves aforesaid incure the higest Resentment of the People and be proceeded against as in the first preceeding Resolves, And the Committee of Twelve Appointed to Aid the Civil Magistrate in the Execution of the Monopoly Act, are hereby appointed a Committee to Advance and Assist the Committee of thirteen aforesaid in carrying this Resolve into the fullest Execution

The Committee further Report that the Inhabitants in all their Purchases of Meat, buy by the Pound and not by the quarter as the latter Mode is an Inlet to great evasions and may elude the salutary Purpose in View

That it be earnestly recommended to the Committee of the Neighbouring Towns to Meet together as Speedialy as possible at any Town which they may think proper to fix the Prices which Vegetables and other Articles not already regulated as usually brought to this Market shall be sold and delivered in this Town and make returne to the Committee of the State Convention in order that the same may be Published for the Government of its Inhabitants

NATHANIEL APPLETON p Order

The foregoing Report having been considered and amended, it was Voted unanimously that the Town do accept the same

Boston Town Records, November 9, 1779, ibid.

Tuesday November 9. 10 O.Clock Forenoon Met according to Adjournment

Samuel Adams Esqr. the Moderator and Stephen Higginson Esqr. Moderator Pro Temo.:

The Honble. Samuel Adams Esqr. the Moderator and Mr. Higginson the Moderator Pro Temo. being out of Town the Inhabitants were directed to withdraw and bring in their Votes, for a Moderator Pro Temo. and the same being brought in and sorted it appeared that

John Tudor Esqr.

was chosen Moderator of the Meeting Pro Temo.

[347.] The Committee appointed to affix the prices of European Merchandize &c &c

Reported verbally – That they had spent considerable time in considering the Buisiness Assigned them by the Town, and found it to be impracticable to affix particular prices to the various Articles of European Merchandize, or to do any thing more than the Late Convention at Concord had done in that matter

On a Motion made Voted, that the Honble. Thomas Cushing Esqr. and James Gorham Esqr. who were of the Number of Commissioners from the New England Colonies who lately met at Hartford in order to consider the expediency of Stating Prices &c – be desired to Attend this Meeting, and that a Committee be now chosen to wait upon them for that purpose

Voted, that Mr. Christopher Clark be a Committee to waite upon those Gentleman

Mr. Cushing and Mr. Gorham at the disire of the Town attended accordingly, and at the request of the Inhabitants acquainted them with the Proceedings of the Convention at Hartford relative to the consideration of the expediency of stating prices &c.

2.3 CONGRESS DEBATES PRICE REGULATION

Benjamin Rush, Diary, February 14, 1777, from *Letters of the Continental Congress*, ed. Burnett, II 250–3

Upon the question whether the Congress should recommend to the States to adopt the plan for reducing and regulating the price of labor, Manufactures, imports, and provisions which had been adopted in the four new England States.

It was said in the negative by *Mr Jas Smith*. That such a recommendation would interfere with the domestic police of each State which were of too delicate a nature to be touched by the Congress.

Dr Rush. I am against the whole of the resolution. It is founded in the contrary of justice, policy and necessity as has been declared in the resolution. The wisdom and power of goverment have been employed in all ages to regulate the price of necessaries to no purpose. It was attempted in Engd. in the reign of Edward II by the English parliament but without effect. The laws for limiting the price of every thing were repealed, and Mr Hume who mentions this fact records even the very attempt as a monument of human folly. The congress with all its authority have failed in a former instance of regulating the price of goods. You have limited Bohea tea to ¾ of a dollar, and yet it is daily sold before your eyes for 30/. The Committee of Philada limited the price of West India goods about a year ago. But what was the consequence? The merchents it is true sold their rum, sugar and molasses at the price limited by the committee, but they charged a heavy profit upon the barrel, or the paper which contained the rum or the sugar. Consider Sir the danger of failing in this experiment. The Salvation of this continent depends upon the Authority of this congress being held as sacred as the cause of liberty itself. Suppose we should fail of producing the effects we wish for by the resolution before you. Have we any charecter to spare? Have we committed no mistakes in the management of the public Affairs of America? We have Sir. It becomes us therefore to be careful of the remains of our Authority and charecter. It is a common thing to cry aloud of the rapacity and extortion in every branch of business etc. among every class of men. This has led some people to decry the *public Virtue* of this country. True Sir there is not so much of it as we could wish, but there is much more than is sometimes allowed on this floor. We estimate our Virtue by a false barometer when we measure it by the price of goods. The extortion we complain off arises only from the excessive quantity of our money Now Sir a failure in this Attempt to regulate the price of goods will encrease the clamors against the rapacity of dealers, and thus depreciate our public virtue. Consider Sir the consequence of measuring our virtue by this false standard. You will add weight to the Arguments used at St. James's to explode patriotism altogether, and by denying its existence in this country destroy it forever. Persuade a Woman that there is no such thing as chastity, and if there is that She does not possess it, and She may be easily seduced if She was as chaste as Diana. Sir, The price of goods may be compared to a number of light substances in a bason of water. The hand may keep them down for a while, but nothing can detain them on the bottom of the bason but an Abstraction of the Water. The continent labours under a universal malady. From the crown of her head to the Soal of her feet She is full of disorders. She requires the most powerful tonic medicines. The resolution before you is Nothing but an *Opiate*. It may compose the continent for a night, but She will soon awaken again to a fresh sense of her pain and misery.

Col: Richd Henry Lee, in the affirmative. Mr President, The learned Doctor has mistook the disorder of the continent. She labours under a spasm, and Spasms he knows require *palliative* medicines. I look upon the resolution before you only as a temporary remedy. But it is absolutely necessary. It is true the regulations formerly recommended by Congress were not faithfully carried into execution, but this was owing to the want of regular governments. New and regular goverments have been instituted in every part of America, and these will enable all classes of people to carry the resolutions into execution.

Mr Saml Chase, in the Affirmative. Mr President This is a necessary resolution. It is true it failed formerly in Philada. because it abounded with tories. But it succeeded in Maryland. It must be done. The mines of Peru would not support a war at the present high price of the necesaries of life. your Soldiers cannot live on their pay. It must be raised unless we limit the price of the cloathing and other articles necessary for them.

Mr Seargant – Negative. The price of goods cannot be regulated while the quantity of our money and the articles of life are allowed to fluctuate. This is and must be the case with us, therefore we cannot regulate the price of anything.

Col James Wilson, Negative. Mr President, I differ from the gentleman from Virginia about the possibility of carrying the resolution before you into execution. The modern goverments I am sure have not half the vigilance or authority that the conventions and committees formerly had, and yet these failed in this business. *Connecticut* where the influence of good laws prevail greatly, adopted this plan with diffidence. There are certain things Sir which Absolute power cannot do. The whole power of the Roman Emperors could not add a single letter to the Alphabet. Augustus could not compel old batchelors to marry. He found out his error, and wisely repealed his edict least he should bring his Authority into contempt. Let us recommend the resolution to the *consideration* of the States only without giving our Opinion on it, that they may discuss it with unbiassed minds. Foreign trade is absolutely necessary to enable us to carry on the war. This resolution will put an end to it, for it will hang as a dead weight upon all the operations of external commerce.

Dr Witherspoon, Negative. Sir, It is a wise maxim to avoid those things which our enemies wish us to practise. Now I find that our enemies have published the Act of the Asembly of Connecticut for regulating the price of necessaries in the New York paper in order to shew our distress from that Quarter. I believe the regulations would be just, if the quantity of money and the scarcity of goods bore an exact proportion to each Other. But the price of goods is by no means proportioned to the quantity of money in every thing. The encrease of price began 1st upon the *Luxuries* 2ly Necessaries, 3rd Manufactories and 4ly grain, and Other produce of the earth. Now the reason why it has reached the grain etc last, is owing to thier quantity being plentiful and to an overproportion of money. Remember laws are not almighty. It is beyond the power of despotic princes to regulate the price of goods. Tea and Salt are higher in proportion than any Other Articles of trade owing entirely to thier price being limited. In Pensylvania salt was limited to 15/ but was sold for 60/ per bushel, while at the same time it was sold in Virginia where there was no limitation for 10/ a bushel. I fear if we fail in this measure we shall weaken the Authority of Congress. We shall do mischief by teaching the continent to *rest* upon it. If we limit *one* article, we must limit *every* thing, and this is impossible.

Mr John Adams, Negative. Perhaps I may here speak agst. the sense of my constitutents, but I cannot help it, I much doubt the justice, policy and necessity of the resolution. Its policy and necessity depend upon its practicability, and if it is practicable, I beleive it will be *unjust*. It amounts to the same as raising the value of your money to double its present value and this experiment was tried in vain even in the absolute goverment of France. The high price of many Articles arises from their scarcity. If we regulate the price of imports we shall immediately put to [*sic*] stop to them for ever.

Dr Rush. Sir, It has been said that the high price of goods in Philada. arose from the monoplies, and extortion of the tories. Here I must say the tories are blamed without cause. A similar Spirit of Speculation prevails among the Whigs in Philada. They are disposed to realise thier money in lands, or goods, But this is not owing to any timidity or disaffection among them. They fear the further depreciation of your money by future emissions. Stop your emissions of money and you will stop Speculation, and fill your treasury from the loan Offices. I beg leave to inform Congress that the committee of Philada. was supported by the country people in thier Attempt to regulate the price of West India goods, but were notwithstanding unsuccessful. Now Sir, the country people are equally concerned with the merchants in keeping Up the price of every thing, and in eluding laws for reducing them. I am not apt to reply to *words* much less to *play* upon them. The gentleman from Virginia has miscalled the malady of the continent. It is not a spasm, but a dropsy. I beg leave to prescribe two remedies for it. 1 Raising the interest of the money we borrow to 6 per cent. this like a cold bath will give an immediate *Spring* to our affairs – and 2 *taxation*. This like *tapping*, will diminish the Quantity of our Money, and give a proper value to what remains.

The resolution was amended. The plan of the 4 New England States was *referred* only to the Other States, to act as they tho't proper.[1]

Thomas Burke, Abstract of Debate, ibid. 253

Feb. 15th. Yesterday was consumed in desultory debates upon a report of a special committee upon the proceedings of the four New England Governments above mentioned, and it was recommitted. This day it was brought in under a form agreeable to what was the sense of the House on what was yesterday considered. At first it expressed the

[1] The resolve in its final form was passed February 15.

opinion of Congress, that the proceedings were founded in justice, policy and necessity, and merited the warmest approbation. The second declared neither approbation or opinion, except particularly relating to the New England Governments, because of their peculiar circumstances, but proposed laying it before the other States for their imitation if they thought proper, avoiding as much as possible any expression that might suggest to the States that Congress approved or disapproved. In this form it passed without a negative, and it was voted that several States should be advised to confer with each other on this subject: viz: New York, New Jersey, Pennsylvania, Maryland and Virginia: North Carolina, South Carolina and Georgia.

February 15, 1777, *Journals of the Continental Congress*, VII 124–5

Resolved, That considering the situation of the New England States, Congress approve of the measures adopted and recommended by the committee from the four New England States, for the defence of the State of Rhode Island; and also of the measures to be taken for preventing the depreciation of their currency, except that part which recommends the striking bills bearing interest, which, being a measure tending to depreciate the continental and other currencies, ought not to be adopted, and it is so recommended by Congress to the said New England states:

That the plan for regulating the price of labour, of manufactures and of internal produce within those states, and of goods imported from foreign parts, except military stores, be referred to the consideration of the other united States: and that it be recommended to them, to adopt such measures, as they shall think most expedient to remedy the evils occasioned by the present fluctuating and exorbitant prices of the articles aforesaid:

That, for this purpose, it be recommended to the legislatures, or, in their recess, to the executive powers of the States of New York, New Jersey, Pensylvania, Delaware, Maryland, and Virginia, to appoint commissioners to meet at York town, in Pensylvania, on the 3d Monday in March next, to consider of, and form a system of regulation adapted to those States, to be laid before the respective legislatures of each State, for their approbation:

That, for the like purpose, it be recommended to the legislatures, or executive powers in the recess of the legislatures of the States of North

Carolina, South Carolina, and Georgia, to appoint commissioners to meet at Charlestown, in South Carolina, on the first Monday in May next:

That it be recommended to the legislatures of the several States, to take the most effectual measures for manning the continental frigates, fitted for the sea in their respective States:

That it be earnestly recommended to the united States, to avoid, as far as possible, further emissions of paper money, and to take the most effectual measures for speedily drawing in and sinking their paper currency already emitted:

That such parts of the proceedings of the said committees from the four New England states, as relate to the price of labour and other things, be published and transmitted to the other States, together with these resolutions . . .

2.4 CONGRESS RECOMMENDS STATES TO ADOPT PRICE REGULATION

November 19, 1779, *Journals of the Continental Congress*, XV 1288–93

Your Committee to whom was referred the ways and means for supplying the Treasury, report:

1st. That Bills of Exchange be drawn on Mr. Jay to the amount of £100,000 Sterling and on Mr. Lawrence [Laurens] to the amount of £100,000 Sterling, payable at six months sight, and that the same be sold at the current rate of exchange.

2ly. That a loan be opened on the following terms to wit, that for every sum of 8,000 Dollars paid into the Treasury before the 1st. day of February, the person paying the same shall be entitled to £100 Sterling payable at the end of ten years, with 6 p. c. interest. The principal and interest to be paid either in Bills of Exchange, specie or current money at the rate of Exchange.

3ly. That an annuity office be opened on the following terms to wit: that for every sum of 100,000 Dollars paid into the Treasury, before the 1st. day of February, the person paying the same shall be entitled to receive £100 Sterling annually for 22 Years, either in Bills of Exchange, specie or current money at the rate of Exchange.

That a Committee be appointed to report on the manner of carrying the above Resolutions into effect.

Congress resumed the consideration of the report of the committee on the representation of the legislative council and general assembly of New Jersey, and the proceedings of the convention of commissioners from the five eastern states, and thereupon came to the following resolutions:

Whereas Congress by their resolution of 1 September last, did determine not to emit any Bills of Credit above the amount in the said resolution limited, relying for the further means of prosecuting the War, on Taxes and Loans, and considering that the ascertainment of the greatest possible sum which could come into circulation, would prevent the depreciation of the said Bills of Credit beyond the degree which the surplus of quantity, and some other causes of less influence, would naturally produce; and

Whereas there is reason to believe that the continued and disproportionate advance of prices is to be attributed, in a considerable measure, to the arts of unprincipled and disaffected people, who still cherish the Hopes of defeating by this means the establishment of the Liberty and Independence of the United States, and to the credulity of such as suffer themselves to be imposed upon by these arts and Management; and,

Whereas the fluctuating state of prices not only causes inequality and injustice in private dealings, and in furnishing the public supplies from the several states, but renders it impracticable to make the proper estimates for future expences, and to fix equitable salaries for those employed in the service of the United States: and whereas the estimates according to which the requisitions for the taxes of the succeeding year have been made by the resolution of the 6th of October last, have been formed on the principle that the prices of commodities necessary for the public use would not exceed twenty fold of the former prices, and should they rise above that rate, the taxes must be accordingly increased, but should they fall below it, the surplus of the sum raised may be applied to the sinking fund: therefore

And whereas, although the collection of Taxes and the natural course of trade might, in time, reduce the prices to a proper standard, and remedy the mischiefs which prevail, yet these being too slow in their operation to give that relief which the present exigencies of affairs require, unless aided by proper expedients for fixing prices in some uniformity throughout the various States, and in juster proportion to the effect of the quantity of money emitted, together with that of other natural causes of depreciation;

Resolved, That it be earnestly recommended to the several states forthwith to enact laws for establishing and carrying into execution a general limitation of prices throughout their respective jurisdictions, on the following principles, and to commence in their operation from the first day of February next:

Articles of domestic produce, farming and common labor, the wages of tradesmen and mechanics, water and land carriage, not to exceed twenty fold of the prices current through the various seasons of the year 1774.

Articles imported from foreign parts to be in due proportion with labor and the articles as above stated, making a proper allowance for freight, insurance, and other charges.[1]

Salt and military stores, whether of home manufacture or imported from abroad, to be excepted from limitation of price.

Resolved, That it be recommended to the several states to enact strict laws against engrossing and withholding, and to take the necessary measures for having the same carried into full execution.

Resolved, That the voluntary agreements and associations formed in divers parts of these States by the merchants, traders and other citizens, for adopting, by general consent, and under the authority of the laws, proper expedients to prevent the advance of prices, and to appreciate the paper currency, are highly laudable. (Previous question.)

Resolved, That the proceedings of the commissioners from the eastern states to New York inclusive, at their meeting in Hartford, in Connecticut, on the 20th of October last, discover a generous attention to the public good, and are well calculated to promote the same: it is nevertheless expected that no time will be lost in giving effect to these resolutions, as the same general purpose may thereby be attained, and at an earlier period.

And whereas, it is hereby recommended that the article of Salt be left unlimited in the price, which is of indispensible necessity to all ranks of people, and often difficult to be procured;

[1] This paragraph was postponed, but passed after amendment in language.

Resolved, That it be recommended to the well disposed and publick spirited citizens of these States, who are blessed with plenty and affluence, and particulary to those who inhabit in or near to towns, cities and other places of trade, to form voluntary associations for procuring a plentiful supply of the said article, and for reducing the price thereof, that the poor may be furnished therewith on the most reasonable terms. (Previous question carried.)

Resolved, That all officers and agents employed in making purchases for the United States, be directed to conform strictly to all regulations that are or may be established in the several states:

That all such as purchase on commission be allowed the same on such sums only as the articles by them purchased would amount to at the rated prices; and that they be allowed a commission of five per cent on all savings made by purchasing under such prices. (Previous question carried.)

That accounts be kept and returns made by all persons employed to make purchases in behalf of the United States, or to hire vessels, carriages, or men, for the service of the same, of the prices by them respectively given in such states as shall not, before the first day of February, 1780, pass laws for the limitation of prices agreeable to the recommendation contained in the foregoing resolutions; to the intent that such states as shall have neglected to pass laws for the purposes aforesaid, may respectively be charged in the public accounts with the aggregate amount of the difference of prices paid from and after the said first day of February, 1780, in such states and those in which such laws may have been enacted.

The last resolution reported by the committee being read, viz.

'That it be recommended to the legislatures of the several states to revise their laws for making the paper currency a tender in the payment of debts, and so to frame them that injustice to creditors or debtors may be prevented;' and an amendment being moved by Mr [John] Witherspoon, seconded by Mr [James] Forbes, by adding the words 'and that the injustice which has already taken place may be remedied, as far as may be practicable:'

A motion was made by Mr [Elbridge] Gerry, seconded by Mr [John] Mathews, that the consideration of that part of the report and the amendment be postponed;

On which the yeas and nays being required by Mr [James] Forbes,

New Hampshire,		
Mr Peabody,	ay	div.
Langdon,	no	
Massachusetts Bay,		
Mr Gerry,	ay	ay
Lovell,	ay	
Holten,	ay	
Partridge,	ay	
New Jersey,		
Mr Witherspoon,	ay	ay
Scudder,	ay	
Fell,	no	
Houston,	ay	
Pennsylvania,		
Mr Searle,	ay	ay
Muhlenberg,	ay	
Shippen,	ay	
Maryland,		
Mr Plater	ay	div.
Forbes,	no	
Rhode Island,		
Mr Marchant,	no	no
Connecticut,		
Mr Huntington,	no	no
Sherman,	no	
Root,	no	
New York,		
Mr Schuyler,	ay	div.
Lewis,	no	
Virginia,		
Mr Griffin,	no	*
North Carolina,		
Mr Harnett,	ay	ay
Sharpe,	ay	
South Carolina,		
Mr Mathews,	ay	ay

So it was resolved in the affirmative.

Resolved, That the report of the Medical Committee on the hospital staff be postponed till to morrow, and that the same be taken into consideration immediately after reading the journal.

Adjourned to 10 o'Clock to Morrow.

2.5 NEW YORK STATE LEGISLATES TO REGULATE WAGES AND PRICES

'An act to regulate the wages of mechanicks and labourers, the prices of goods and commodities and the charges of innholders, within this State, and for other purposes therein mentioned.' PASSED the 3rd April, 1778; *Laws of New York*, 1778, vol. 1 (Albany, 1886) First Session, ch. 34

Whereas the honorable the congress of the United States of *America* by certain resolutions bearing date the twenty second day of *November* in the year of our Lord one thousand seven hundred and seventy seven, did among other things therein mentioned recommend to the legislatures of the respective states of *New-Hampshire*, *Massachusetts-Bay*, *Rhode-Island* and *Providence Plantations Connecticut*, *New-York*, *New-Jersey*, *Pennsylvania* and *Delaware* respectively to appoint commissioners to convene at *New-Haven* in *Connecticut* on the fifteenth day of *January* then next in order to regulate and ascertain the price of labor manufactures, internal produce and commodities imported from foreign parts, military stores excepted, and also to regulate the charges of innholders and that on the report of the commissioners each of the legislatures should enact suitable laws, as well for enforcing the observance of such of the regulations as they should ratify and enabling such innholders to obtain the necessary supplies, as to authorize the purchasing commissaries of the army or any other person whom the legislatures may think proper, to take from any engrossers, forestallers or any other person, possessed of a larger quantity of any such commodities or provisions than shall be competent for the private annual consumption of their families, and who shall refuse to sell the surplus at the prices to be ascertained as aforesaid, paying only such price for the same.

And Whereas in pursuance of the said resolutions, commissioners in behalf of the several States of *New-Hampshire*, *Massachusetts-Bay*, *Rhode-Island* and *Providence-Plantations*, *Connecticut*, *New-York*, *New-Jersey* and *Pennsylvania* did convene at *New-Haven* in *Connecticut* and after sundry adjournments did on the thirtieth day of the said month of *January*, resolve and agree as follows, to wit.

First, That the various kinds of labor of farmers, mechanics and others be set and affixed, at rates not exceeding seventy-five per centum advance from what the prices of their respective labor were in the same places, in the several States aforesaid, through the various seasons of the year of our Lord one thousand seven hundred and seventy-four.

Secondly, That the price of teaming and all land transportation should not exceed the rate of five twelfths of a continental dollar for the carriage of twenty hundred neat weight per mile including all expences attending the same.

Thirdly, That all kinds of American manufactures, and internal produce not particularly mentioned and regulated by the said convention be estimated at rates not exceeding seventy-five per centum advance from the prices they were usually sold at in the several parts of the respective States aforesaid in the year one thousand seven hundred and seventy-four.

Fourthly, That the price of hemp, flax, sheep's wool, all kinds of linnen and woolen clothes hosiery of all kinds, felt hats, wire and wool cards manufactured in *America* shall not exceed the rate of centum per centum advance from the price they severally were at in the several parts of the States aforesaid in the year of our Lord one thousand seven hundred and seventy four.

Fifthly, That the prices of all kinds of European goods wares and merchandizes imported from foreign parts or brought into the respective States by capture or otherwise shall not exceed the rate of one continental dollar for each shilling sterling of prime cost of the same respectively in Europe, exclusive of all other charges when sold by the importer or captor, excepting only the following articles, *viz*. All kinds of woolen and linnen goods and checks suitable for the army, drugs and medicines, duck of all kinds, cordage, tin plates, copperas, files, alum, brimstone, felt hats, nails, window-glass, salt, steel, wire, wool cards, cotten cards, and naval and military stores.

Sixthly, That all woolen clothes, blankets, linnen, shoes, stockings, hats and other articles of cloathing suitable for the army theretofore imported, which are or shall be seized and taken by lawful authority of the respective States, for the use of the army shall be estimated at the above rates with the addition of the stated allowance for land carriage, if any there be, to the place where taken.

Seventhly, That the price of the following articles at the first port of delivery or place of manufacture within the respective States shall not exceed the rates to them affixed respectively *viz*. Good *West-India* rum three dollars per gallon by wholesale, good merchantable *New-England* rum two dollars per gallon, by wholesale, best *Muscovado* sugar, thirty three dollars and one third of a dollar per hundred, gross weight and all other sugars in usual proportion according to quality; best molasses one dollar and an half per gallon, by wholesale; coffee three fourths of a dollar per pound by the hundred weight; good merchantable geneva two dollars per gallon. Good merchantable brandy two dollars per gallon. Good merchantable whisky, one dollar and one sixth of a dollar per gallon. All other distilled spirits, not therein enumerated, not to exceed two dollars per gallon.

Eighthly. That no trader, retailer or vendor of foreign goods wares or merchandizes shall be allowed more than at the rate of twenty-five per cent. advance upon the price such goods wares and merchandizes are or shall be sold for by the importer or captor agreeable to the regulations therein prescribed and fixed with the addition only of the cost and charge of transportation by land at the rate of five twelfths of a dollar per mile for transporting twenty hundred neat weight from the first port of delivery to the place where the same shall be sold and delivered by retail.

Ninthly. That innholders be not allowed more than fifty per centum advance on the wholesale prices of all liquors or other foreign articles therein stated and by them sold in small quantities allowing as aforesaid for charges of transportation, and for all other articles of entertainment refreshment and forage not exceeding seventy five per centum advance on the prices which the same were sold at in the same places in the year one thousand seven hundred and seventy four.

Tenthly. That the following enumerated articles shall not be sold at higher prices within the respective States than are set down and affixed to such articles respectively with the addition only for the stated allowance for land carriage if any there shall be; the said sums being estimated at six shillings lawful money per dollar.

And whereas the said sums, as far as they respect this State, converted into lawful money of *New-York* are as follows; that is to say.

Good merchantable wheat, pease and white beans, thirteen shillings per bushel. Good merchantable wheat flour one pound sixteen shillings per hundred gross weight. Good merchantable rye or rye meal eight shillings and eight pence per bushel. Good merchantable Indian corn or Indian meal six shillings per bushel. Pork, well fatted, and weighing from one hundred to one hundred and fifty pounds per hog, seven pence one farthing per pound. Pork, well fatted and weighing from one hundred and fifty to two hundred pounds per hog, eight pence per pound. Pork, well fatted and weighing more than two hundred pounds per hog, eight pence three farthings per pound. American cheese of the best quality one shilling per pound. Merchantable oats, four shillings per bushel. Best grass fed beef with hide and tallow two pounds six shillings and eight pence for every hundred pounds weight and so in proportion for that of inferior quality. Best stall fed beef with the hide and tallow three pounds four shillings for every hundred pounds weight and so in proportion for that of inferior quality. Good butter by the firkin or cask one shilling and eight pence per pound and by the single pound or small quantity one shilling and nine pence half penny. Raw hides six pence per pound and other skins in the proportion of price they usually bore to raw hides. Good well tanned soal leather two shillings and eight pence per pound; and all kinds of curried leather in the proportions of price they usually bore to well tanned soal leather. Common sort of mens shoes made of neat leather sixteen shillings per pair. Mens calf skin shoes of the best quality twenty shillings per pair; and womens and childrens shoes in due proportion. Bloomery iron at the place of manufacture sixty four pounds per ton; and in that proportion for a lesser quantity. Refined iron at the place of manufacture seventy four pounds thirteen shillings and four pence per ton, pig iron at the place of manufacture twenty four pounds per ton. Best manufactured American steel fit for edged tools two shillings and eight pence per pound; and common American manufactured steel one shilling and nine pence half penny per pound.

Be it therefore enacted by the People of the State of New-York *represented in Senate and Assembly, and it is hereby enacted by the authority of the same* That no person or persons whatsoever shall ask demand, have receive take offer give pay or allow, either in money or in barter or exchange either directly or indirectly for any of the articles of labor or mechanical work, provisions, produce, manufactures, goods, commodities, wares or merchandizes, salt excepted and also except as is above excepted, or for refreshments of other supplies for man horse or cattle at any inn or inns within this State, the respective rates and prices whereof have been severally fixed and ascertained as aforesaid, any greater sum or sums, rate or rates, price or prices for the same respectively than those at which the same have been severally and respectively fixed and ascertained as aforesaid. *Provided always* that nothing herein contained shall extend to hinder or prevent bartering or exchanging between neighbours according to the several usages and customs in this State in the year one thousand seven hundred and seventy four for their own and families' use and consumption only.

And be it enacted by the authority aforesaid. That no person or persons having any greater quantity or number of the above mentioned enumerated or non enumerated articles, except as above excepted, than shall be sufficient for the necessary use and consumption of himself or themselves or his or their family or families respectively, being demanded to sell, shall refuse to sell the surplus thereof respectively or any part thereof, and in case of such refusal any one of the judges of the county court of common pleas, or a justice of the peace of the county, shall at the request of the party to whom such refusal shall be made determine whether the cause of such refusal shall have been sufficient to justify such refusal consistently with the true intent and meaning of this law. And if any person or persons whatsoever shall wittingly or knowingly offend in any matter or thing whatsoever against the tenor or true intent and meaning of this law he she or they so offending shall be subject to prosecution by information or indictment for the offence and moreover shall forfeit and pay for every offence treble the value or price as above rated and ascertained of every article which he she or they shall so sell barter or exchange or refuse to sell, or for which he she or they shall offer give pay or allow or ask or demand any greater price than is above ascertained, to be recovered with costs of suit, in a summary way before a justice of the peace of the county where the offence shall have been committed if such treble value shall not exceed five pounds, and if it shall be greater than five pounds, in any court of record within this State having cognizance thereof, by any person who shall sue and prosecute for the same to his own use, in an action of debt by bill plaint or information; in which suit in a court of record the defendant shall be held to bail, as in actions of debt on specialty and have no essoin, protection or wager of law nor more than one imparlance. And if the plaintif in any such suit or suits as aforesaid shall become non suit or discontinue or withdraw his suit or if judgment therein shall be rendered for the defendant that then and in every such case the defendant shall have execution for his costs to be taxed. *Provided always* That no such determination as aforesaid by any judge or justice shall be given in evidence or any such information or indictment or in any such popular action as aforesaid.

And be it further enacted by the authority aforesaid That in case any person or persons whatsoever shall refuse to sell to any person or persons appointed to the commissary or quarter masters department of the army of the United States of *America* or of any other forces imployed by the said United States or either of them, for the use of such forces only, any of the articles herein before rated, that in such case it shall and may be lawful to and for such commissary or quarter master to apply to two of the nearest justices of the peace who are hereby authorized and required immediately to inquire into the cause of such refusal and to issue their warrant under their hands and seals without delay authorizing such commissary or quarter master to take from such person or persons so refusing such articles the prices whereof are hereby respectively rated, as the said person or persons so refusing shall in their judgment be able reasonably to spare to such commissary or quarter master, he paying therefor at the price or prices hereinbefore regulated; *provided always* That no person shall be deemed or esteemed as belonging to the commissary's or quarter master's department for the purposes above mentioned unless regularly appointed thereto and such appointment be approved by the person administring the government by writing under his hand.

And be it further enacted by the authority aforesaid That this law, unless sooner repealed by the legislature of this State, shall be and continue in full force and effect during the present war between the United States of *America* and *Great-Britain* and no longer. *Provided always* That this law shall not take effect in the county of *Dutchess* until six days after the passing thereof, nor in the counties of *Ulster* and *Orange* or either of them until ten days after the passing thereof, nor in the county of *Albany* until twelve days after the passing thereof nor in the county of *Tryon* until sixteen days after the passing thereof, nor in the county of *Charlotte* until twenty days after the passing thereof, nor in the counties of *Cumberland* and *Gloucester* or either of them until twenty-five days after the passing thereof, nor in the county of *Westchester* until eight days after the passing thereof.

'An act more effectually to provide supplies of flour, meal and wheat for the army.' Passed the 31st of October, 1778, ibid., Second Session, ch. 5

Whereas on suggestion of congress, and other due information it appears that by the wicked arts of speculators, forestallers and engrossers, in this and others of the United States, it is rendered difficult to obtain timely and sufficient supplies for the operations of the army and navy unless the most vigorous measures are without delay adopted to restrain practices so destructive to the publick weal. Therefore

Be it enacted by the People of the State of New York, represented in Senate and Assembly and it is hereby enacted by the authority of the same, That all flour, meal or wheat purchased or which may be purchased with intent to be sold again, or to be exchanged or bartered for any goods, wares or merchandize or to be exported out of this State, shall be subject to be seized and taken by the commissary general of purchases for the American army, or any of his deputies or agents, to and for the use of the said army, the person seizing and taking the same paying for such flour meal and wheat, at and after the rate following to wit, For wheat at the rate of five dollars per bushel, for flour at the rate of fifteen dollars per hundred weight and a proportional price for meal.

And to the end that such seizures may be conducted with the greater order and to prevent abuses in the same

Be it further enacted by the authority aforesaid, That no person either as deputy or agent to the said commissary general, shall be authorized to seize or take any such flour, meal or wheat unless he shall be properly appointed by writing under the hand of the said commissary general or under the hand of the commander in chief of the said army, for the time being, or under the hand of a commandant of a department being a general officer, or under the hand of a deputy commissary general of purchases, in a department, and which said appointment shall be confirmed by the person administring the government of this State for the time being – That where any deputy or agent so appointed as aforesaid, shall suspect that any flour, meal or wheat purchased with such intent as aforesaid is in the possession of any person or persons, he shall thereupon apply to a justice of the peace of the county where such flour, meal or wheat shall be, who is hereby upon such application authorized and required, forthwith to make enquiry respecting the same, by examining any witness or witnesses on oath touching the said flour, meal or wheat, whether the same was purchased and if purchased, whether it was purchased with such intent as aforesaid, and if upon such enquiry and examination it shall either from the quantity purchased by any individual or from other circumstances in evidence appear probable to the said justice, that the said flour, meal or wheat was purchased with such intent as aforesaid, he shall thereupon by writing under his hand authorise the said deputy or agent, to seize the said flour meal or wheat, specifying the quantity, as near as can be discovered, for the use aforesaid. The said deputy or agent paying for the same at the rate aforesaid, but if on such enquiry as aforesaid such intent as aforesaid shall remain doubtful and if any person or persons in whose possession such flour, meal or wheat shall be, shall not upon being summoned to appear, before the said justice to be examined on oath as aforesaid, appear upon such summons, and due proof made of the service of such summons, by leaving a copy thereof at the usual place of his, her or their abode, and no sufficient excuse appearing to the said justice for such non appearance or appearing shall refuse to answer to interrogatories upon oath aforesaid, or on such oath, shall not declare himself ignorant of the intent, for which the said flour, meal or wheat was purchased, or shall declare, that the same was purchased with such intent as aforesaid, the said justice, shall in either of the cases above mentioned adjudge the said flour, meal or wheat to be purchased with such intent as aforesaid, and the same shall be subject to be seized in like manner, as it would have been, had the person, in whose possession the same shall be, appeared before the said justice, and confessed that the same was purchased, with such intent as aforesaid.

And whereas many farmers within this State, with various intentions injurous to the common cause of America, have with held their wheat of the crops of the last and preceeding years To the end therefore that such farmers, may be compelled to part with such wheat for the use of the army.

Be it further enacted by the authority aforesaid That where any person or persons shall be possessed of any wheat of their own raising, either threshed or in straw of the crop, of the year, one thousand seven hundred and seventy seven, or any preceeding year, such wheat shall be, and is hereby made subject to seizure by virtue of this act, in like manner as wheat purchased with such intent as aforesaid, and the same powers and authorities are hereby granted to the commissary general, his deputy or agent, with respect to such wheat, and the same proceedings, shall be had respecting the same, as in cases of wheat purchased with intent to be sold, bartered, exchanged or exported as aforesaid. Provided always That in every such case, a sufficient quantity of wheat, shall be left for the necessary support of the family of every such farmer.

And be it further enacted by the authority aforesaid, That if any person shall attempt to remove any flour, meal or wheat, suspected to be purchased with such intent as aforesaid, the justice shall upon such application as aforesaid, cause such flour, meal or wheat to be seized and detained, until such enquiry as aforesaid, respecting the same can be made.

And be it further enacted by the authority aforesaid, That when any wheat hereby made subject to seizure shall be unmerchantable, that the justice shall in such case, cause the same to be appraised by three freeholders upon oath, who shall have regard in such appraisement, to the price hereby fixed for good and merchantable wheat, and the person seizing such unmerchantable wheat, shall pay for the same, only such price, as the same shall be appraised at, by any two, of the three freeholders, any thing herein contained, notwithstanding, and where any wheat subject to seizure by virtue of this act shall be in the straw, that the person seizing the same, shall be permitted to retain, out of the price hereby allowed for the same, the expence of threshing and cleaning the same, and may enter into the barn of the person possessing such wheat, and use the same together with the flails or other implements, for the purpose of threshing and cleaning such wheat.

And be it further enacted by the authority aforesaid, That if any justice of the peace upon such application as aforesaid shall refuse to perform the duties required of him by this act, he shall for every offence forfeit the sum of fifty pounds, to be recovered in an action of debt, with costs by any person, who will sue for the same, and every justice shall, for his services in making such enquiry in each distinct case be entitled to demand and receive, from the person requiring such enquiry to be made, the sum of three dollars per day, for every day he shall be actually employed therein, and every constable serving a summons or subpœna in the execution of this act, shall be allowed and paid by the person requesting such service mileage at the rate of one shilling per mile, going and the like for returning.

And be it further enacted by the authority aforesaid That all flour, meal or wheat which shall after the twentieth day of November next be purchased with intent to be sold again, bartered or exchanged as aforesaid, such intent to be enquired into and adjudged in manner as aforesaid, shall be taken and seized by virtue of such authority as aforesaid the person so taking and seizing the same, applying the same to the use of the army and paying to such justice, authorizing the seizure, for the same at and after the price above fixed, and the said justice is hereby required to pay the monies thence arising into the treasury of and for the use of this State.

And be it further enacted by the authority aforesaid, That it shall be lawful for the commissary general and his deputies or agents, and every person who shall be aiding them therein, to break and enter any house, mill, barn, store or other place, where any flour, meal or wheat so adjudged liable to seizure, shall be deposited, in order to seize and take the same, and it shall in like manner be lawful, for any justice of the peace to break and enter into any place where any such flour, meal or wheat, subject to seizure by virtue of this act shall be suggested to be, in order to view or ascertain the quantity of the same.

2.6 NEW YORK SETTLES MILITIA ACCOUNTS WITH PAY CERTIFICATES

'An act for the settlement of the pay of the levies and militia for their services in the late war, and for other purposes therein mentioned', passed April 27, 1784, *Laws of New York*, 1784, vol. I, ch. 45

Be it enacted by the People of the State of New York represented in Senate and Assembly and it is hereby enacted by the authority of the same, That all brigadiers, colonels or commanding officers of regiments or corps of levies and militia respectively, who have been called into actual service during the late war, and to whom payment has not been made, shall as soon as possible after the passing of this act, deliver the abstracts and pay-rolls for all such services, to the auditor of this State for the time being, to the end that the same may be examined and liquidated agreable to law; The said auditor shall charge all such officers, non commissioned officers and privates respectively, for the amount of such certificates which they have respectively received of the auditors appointed to liquidate and settle the accounts of the troops of this State in the service of the United States, for the depreciation of their pay, for the time he or they were captivated, and also with such monies as may have been advanced to them respectively on account of this State, ascertaining the value thereof, if in Continental currency, agreable to the Continental scale of depreciation, and the said abstracts and pay-rolls being so examined and certified, and also all such which have heretofore been audited by the said State auditor, or by the late auditor general of the State, and which have not been paid, shall be delivered to the treasurer of the State for the time being, in order that certificates may be issued for the amount of the sums due to the persons respectively, named in such abstracts and pay-rolls.

And be it further enacted by the authority aforesaid, That the said state treasurer shall as soon as may be, cause a competent number of certificates to be printed, of such form and manner, as he shall deem best calculated to prevent frauds and counterfeits, and with blanks for the name of the creditor and the sum due to him, and purporting that the person named in such certificate, or his assigns, shall be entitled to receive from the treasury of this State, the sum specified in such certificate in current lawful money of this State, with the interest at five per cent per annum from the date of such pay-rolls or abstracts of the regiment or corps of levies and militia respectively for which such certificate shall be given in payment as aforesaid.

And be it further enacted by the authority aforesaid, That the treasurer of the said State, for the time being upon the application of any of brigadiers, colonels or commanding officers of any regiment or corps of levies and militia, or by any one of the officers of any of the said regiments or corps respectively, and as often as they or any one of them shall exhibit his or their pay-roll or abstract, examined and liquidated as by this act is required, the said treasurer shall proceed to fill up the blanks with the persons name and sum due, and sign his name to such number of certificates, as there shall appear names and sums expressed in such pay-rolls subsistance rolls or abstracts respectively, and shall take a receipt from such officer for the sum or sums issued to him in certificates for the purpose of discharging the amount of such pay-roll, subsistance roll or abstract respectively, and the said treasurer is to charge the said amount to the United States. And it shall be the duty of such officer to pay or deliver to each officer non-commissioned officers and privates belonging to his regiment or corps, a certificate for such sum as is mentioned in such abstract, pay-roll or subsistance roll which he hath exhibited to the state treasurer for settlement.

And be it further enacted by the authority aforesaid, That it shall not be lawful for such officer who shall receive the certificates from the state treasurer, to deliver such certificate to any person or persons but such as shall apply in their own person for that purpose, or upon the order or assignment witnessed, made by any person or persons to whom pay shall appear to be due, or to the legal representatives of such person, always retaining in his possession such order or assignment and at the same time takeing a receipt for such payment; and the said officer to whom the said treasurer shall pay, or deliver the certificates for the amount of the said abstract, pay-roll or subsistance roll shall within nine months after the receipt of the certificates, render a just and true account of the delivery of the same with vouchers of payment, and in case any shall remain in his hands, shall return the same to the said treasurer.

And be it further enacted by the authority aforesaid, That all the said certificates, signed by the said state treasurer by virtue of this act, shall be receivable in payment upon the purchases of all forfeited estates and also in payment for the waste and unappropriated lands for the amount thereof.

And be it further enacted by the authority aforesaid, That all such persons to whom pay may be due for military services as aforesaid, who may be deprived of the opportunity of settling with such officer to whom his certificate may be given, within the time above by this act appointed for settlement, shall and may thereafter apply to the treasurer, at the treasury office of the State, and the treasurer, in such case is hereby directed and authorized to examine the abstracts, pay rolls or subsistance rolls where the name of the person or persons so applying shall be said to be contained, and also the vouchers of payment made on account of such pay-roll, subsistance roll or abstract and if upon such examination it shall appear that a sum is due, he shall issue certificates therefor in the same manner as is ordered and directed by this act.

And whereas in the course of the late war, it has frequently been necessary for his excellency the governor the brigadier general or commanding officers of regiments or corps, to order out detachments of the levies and militia for the defence of the frontiers before any means could be provided for their regular subsistance, upon which emergencies such detachments have subsisted themselves or have been subsisted by the inhabitants and for which no recompence hath hitherto been made.

Be it therefore enacted by the authority aforesaid, That when any person or persons shall produce to the auditor for the State for the time being, a certificate attested on the oath of and signed by the commanding officer of any such detachment of levies or militia who may have been subsisted in manner aforesaid, specifying the number of men and the number of days they were subsisted as aforesaid, and also specifying that no provisions were drawn from any public magazine for the time therein mentioned, the said auditor shall and is hereby authorized and required to allow the person or persons named in such certificate at and after the rate of one shilling for every day each person in such detachment was employed, and the auditor shall give a certificate to the person or persons with whom he has so settled, purporting that this State is indebted to such person or persons in the sum therein mentioned, and shall charge the same to the United States.

And whereas many of the citizens of this State are now or hereafter may be possessed of accounts audited by the auditor-general of this State or by the auditor thereof for articles delivered or services performed for the use of the United States or of this State.

Be it further enacted by the authority aforesaid, That the treasurer of this State is hereby authorised and required upon the application of any person or persons possessed of an account or accounts audited as aforesaid or on the application of the legal representative of such person, to receive such accounts, and to deliver in lieu thereof and to alike amount one or more certificates as are by this act directed to be granted to the levies and militia with interest in like manner as by this act is directed, reducing the same to specie value by the Continental scale of depreciation, if not already so reduced, and which account the treasurer is further directed to retain in his hands with a discharge thereon and at the same time numbering with equal numbers the certificate so to be given and the account for which the same is given from number one progressively.

And be it further enacted by the authority aforesaid, That the said auditor shall keep an exact and true account of the number of persons contained in the abstracts or pay rolls by him audited in virtue of this act and the said treasurer shall have the certificates he is hereby authorised to issue bound in a book or books by him to be procured for that purpose, and in filling up the same as directed by this act, cut the same thereout, and leave a part thereof in the said book and number such certificates, as also the parts left in the book from number one progressively, and the sum in each certificate, as also the persons name to whom such certificate issues shall be inserted in the part of such certificate left in the book as aforesaid.

2.7 VIRGINIA ATTEMPTS ECONOMIC REGULATION

'An act to amend the act for preventing forestalling, regrating, engrossing, and publick vendues', October, 1778, *Laws of Virginia*, W. W. Hening (comp.), vol. IX, ch. 42, pp. 581–3

Whereas by an act of general assembly passed in the year one thousand seven hundred and seventy seven, intituled 'An act to prevent forestalling, regrating, engrossing, and publick vendues', it was enacted.

that if any person should buy within this commonwealth to sell again in this or any of the United States, any victual raised within this state, except such purchase was from the original owner or maker thereof, he should be declared an engrosser; under cover of which exception a practice hath prevailed of buying up great quantities of victual from those who make and raise the same, and withholding it from the poor and from the publick, until they have agreed to give a very advanced price for the same, which practice is found to be mischievous and oppressive:

Be it therefore enacted by the General Assembly, That if any person shall buy within this commonwealth to sell again in this or any of the United States, any victual raised within this state, he is hereby declared an engrosser, and as such shall be subject to the pains and penalties inflicted by the said act on engrossers; but this act shall not extend to the managers of any iron works purchasing victual necessary for the use of those employed about such iron works, and selling them to such persons, nor to ordinary keepers purchasing victual to be retailed in their ordinaries, or persons keeping private houses for lodging or entertainment, who may buy any kind of victual and retail the same in their respective houses after it is prepared and dressed for the table, nor to persons purchasing wheat to grind into flour, nor to bakers purchasing flour and selling the same in bread, nor to butchers purchasing live stock and retailing the same after slaughter, nor to brewers purchasing barley and converting the same into beer.

And it is also enacted, That so much of the same act as prohibits the sale of any articles, except such as are therein excepted at publick vendue, shall not be construed to extend to the sale of any vessel whether for sea or inland navigation.

And the more effectually to enforce the said act to prevent forestalling, regrating, engrossing, and publick vendues, and also so much of this act as is herein before contained, the same shall be particularly given in charge to all grand juries, and it shall be made a part of their oath specially that they will present all offences against the same coming to their knowledge; which presentments shall be tried in a summary way by a jury to be empannelled and charged at the next court, unless the said court, for very good cause to them shewn, shall continue the same.

And where any person hath heretofore bought within this commonwealth, to sell again in this or any of the United States, any victual raised within this state, the same shall be subject in his hands to seizure in the same manner, for the same time and purposes, and under the same conditions and directions as victual in the hands of forestallers, regraters, and engrossers, is directed to be seized by an act of general assembly passed at this present session, intituled 'An act to enable the governour and council to supply the armies and navies of the United States and of their allies with grain and flour'.

And whereas by an exception in the said act for preventing forestalling, regrating, engrossing, and publick vendues, it was provided that the said act should not extend to any agent of this commonwealth, or of the United States, or any of them purchasing necessaries really and bona fide for the use of the army or navy, and not dealing in such articles on account of himself or any other private persons; and moreover many good people of this commonwealth are disposed to sell their victual cheaper when for the use of the armies or navy of these states than when for the use of private individuals, certain persons thereupon intending to pervert to their own gain the purposes of the said exception, and the disposition of the good people of this commonwealth have feigned themselves to be agents for the United States, or some one of them, when in truth they were not, and in that character have engrossed great quantities of victual at low prices, and sold the same high to their own great and unrighteous profit, and to the oppression of the people of these states, *Be it therefore enacted*, That if any person pretending to be an agent of this commonwealth, or of the United States, or any of them, for the purchase of victual, shall buy within this commonwealth any victual raised therein, and shall refuse or omit to produce to any citizen of the same sufficient proof whenever called for by such citizen of his acting under authority from the United States, or some one of them, it shall be lawful for such citizen, and all others, forthwith to apprehend and carry him before any justice of the peace, or for any justice of the peace to apprehend or cause him to be apprehended in the first instance, whereupon if he still refuse or omit to produce such proof, he shall by the said justice be committed to jail without bail or mainprise, there to remain until the next court to be held for the county, when a jury shall be empannelled and charged to try whether he pretended himself to be such publick agent, and whether in truth he was so, and if they find that he did so pretend, and it shall not appear to them that he was in truth such an agent, he shall be adjudged to forfeit all the victual he shall have bought under such feigned character, and to be imprisoned one month, counting as a part thereof the time he shall have remained in close jail before judgment rendered; such forfeiture to enure, the one moiety to him who shall have apprehended the offender, the other to the vestry of the parish for the use of the poor thereof.

This act shall continue in force until the first day of November next.

'An Act to enable the Governour and Council to supply the armies and navies of the United States, and of their allies, with grain and flour', ibid. ch. 43, pp. 584–5

Sound policy requiring, and the necessities of the fleets and armies of the United States, and the squadrons of our faithful allies, demanding the utmost exertions of this commonwealth for the supplying them with provisions, and there being but little prospect of procuring a competency for this purpose unless they can be wrested out of the hands of the forestallers and engrossers, who have purchased up great quantities of flour and grain in this state:

Be it therefore enacted by the General Assembly, That it shall be lawful for the governour, by and with the advice of the council, and he is hereby authorised and empowered, to commission such and so many persons as he shall judge proper to seize upon and take for the use of the United States all grain and flour that shall be deemed necessary for the support of the American armies and navies, and the French squadron, that may have been or shall hereafter be purchased up by any forestaller, engrosser, or monopoliser, paying for the same such prices as shall be allowed therefor by three reputable freeholders within the county wherein the same shall be seized, they being first sworn by some magistrate in the said county to value and appraise the same according to their skill and judgment.

And to enable such persons, commissioned as aforesaid, to carry this act fully into execution, *Be it farther enacted*, That where any forestaller, engrosser, or monopoliser, shall refuse to deliver up his grain or flour, on complaint thereof made to any justice of the peace in the county where such grain or flour is or shall be purchased up, it shall be lawful for the said justice, and he is hereby required, to issue his warrant, directed to the sheriff or any constable in the said county, empowering either of them to break open in the day time any house or houses where such grain or flour shall be stored.

And be it farther enacted, That any person against whom an action may be commenced, for what he shall lawfully do in the execution of this act, may plead the general issue, and give this act in evidence; and if a verdict be found, or a judgment be given for him, he shall recover double costs.

This act shall continue and be in force until the end of the next session of assembly, unless the governour, with the advice of the council, shall, by proclamation, declare that the publick wants are sufficiently provided for, and no longer.

'An act to revive an act entitled An act to amend an act for preventing forestalling, regrating, engrossing, and publick vendues', 1779, ibid., vol. x, ch. 20, pp. 157–8

Whereas the act of assembly passed in the year one thousand seven hundred and seventy eight, entitled 'An act to amend an act for preventing, forestalling, regrating, engrossing, and publick vendues', expired on the first day of November last, and it is expedient and necessary that the same should be revived: *Be it therefore enacted*, That so much of the act entitled 'An act to amend an act for preventing forestalling, regrating, engrossing, and publick vendues', so far as it relates to forestalling, regrating, and engrossing, be revived, and shall continue and be in force from and after the passing of this act, for and during the term of one year, and from thence to the end of the next session of assembly.

And whereas it is thought expedient to impose a tax on goods, wares, and merchandizes, imported from other states and countries which shall be exposed to publick auction: *Be it therefore enacted*, That a tax of two and a half per centum on all goods, wares, and merchandizes, hereafter imported from other states and countries exposed to publick auction that shall not have been imported nine months before such sale, shall be paid into the publick treasury of this state in the months of April and October annually, by the vendue master, who at the same time shall render an account upon oath, of all sales made by him, unto the auditors. And whereas a practice has prevailed among vendue masters and owners of goods, wares, and merchandizes, that have been exposed to sale, to bid on the goods either with a view of enhancing the prices of the same, or of fixing the prices of goods of a similar kind; to prevent such practice, *Be it farther enacted*, That it shall not be lawful for the vendue master or person acting under him, either directly or indirectly, to bid for any goods, wares, or merchandizes subject to the tax aforesaid, which he may expose to publick sale, unless he shall openly declare that he intends to purchase the same bona fide for the use and consumption of himself and family; nor shall it be lawful for the owner or owners of any goods, wares, or merchandizes exposed to publick sale, either by himself, herself, or themselves or agents, directly or indirectly to bid on such goods, wares, or merchandizes; and in case any such vendue master, owner, or owners shall presume to violate or bid contrary to this act, on conviction thereof, he or they shall forfeit and pay three times the value of the goods, wares, and merchandizes so bid for, to be recovered in any court of record in this state, by action of debt, bill, or plaint, one half of the forfeiture to the informer, the other to the commonwealth.

And be it farther enacted, That the court of each county, where it may be necessary, shall appoint a vendue master, who shall give bond and security, in the sum of five thousand pounds, for the payment of all taxes arising from the sales of goods, wares, and merchandizes which he shall sell, into the publick treasury, and shall take an oath for the faithful discharge of his office, which oath may be administered by any justice.

2.8 PENNSYLVANIA ATTEMPTS ECONOMIC REGULATION

An act for the more effectually preventing engrossing and forestalling, for the encouragement of commerce and the fair trader, and for other purposes therein mentioned', *Statutes at Large of Pennsylvania 1779*, James T. Mitchell and Henry Flanders, comp. (1903) vol. IX, ch. 859, pp. 420–32

(Section I, P. L.) Whereas the evil practice of monopolizing and forestalling has a natural tendency to produce an artificial scarcity and to enhance the prices as well of foreign merchandise as country produce whereby the consumers are very much injured and the importer or merchant, who has run the risk receives not the least advantage:

(Section II, P. L.) And whereas such merchandise or country produce being often sold by one speculator to another, before it comes into the hands of the consumer, has a tendency equally injurious to the public good:

(Section III, P. L.) And whereas it is absolutely necessary in the most effectual manner by law to discourage such evil practices:

[Section I.] (Section IV, P. L.) Be it therefore enacted, and it is hereby enacted by the Representatives of the Freemen of the Commonwealth of Pennsylvania in General Assembly met, and by the authority of the same, That if any person shall buy, or cause to be bought any goods, wares or merchandise coming to any market or fair within this state, to be sold in such market or fair, or coming to any city, town, port, harbor, haven, or creek within this state to be sold, or shall make any bargain, contract or promise for the having or buying of any goods, wares or merchandise or any part thereof so coming as aforesaid, before the same shall be in the market, fair, city, town, port, harbor, haven or creek, ready there to be sold, or shall induce any person coming to this state or to any market or fair therein, to abstain or forbear to bring any goods, wares or merchandise [to this state] or any part thereof, shall be adjudged a forestaller; and on conviction thereof in any court of record in this state, shall be fined by the said court in any sum not exceeding five thousand pounds, or imprisoned, not exceeding one year, or both, at the discretion of the court:

(Section V, P. L.) Provided, That the buying any goods, wares, and merchandise (except provisions coming to the market of the city of Philadelphia), carrying to market by any person for the use and consumption of himself or family for six months, shall not be deemed forestalling.

[Section II.] (Section VI, P. L.) And be it further enacted by the authority aforesaid, That if any person within this commonwealth shall buy to sell again within this state, or in any of the adjoining states, any butter, beef, pork, wool, flax, woolens, hemp, tallow, raw hides, tanned leather or shoes, of the produce or growth of this state, or raised or manufactured in this state, or if any person within this state shall obtain or get into his hands by buying, contracting, or promise, any goods, wares or merchandise within this state, except from the original importer or his consignee, and except as is herein after excepted, with intent to sell the same again within this state, or in any of the adjoining states, such person shall be adjudged an engrosser; and on conviction thereof as aforesaid, shall forfeit the articles aforesaid so brought or got into his possession or the value thereof, one half to the state, and the other half to the informer, and may be fined in any sum not exceeding five thousand pounds, or imprisoned for any time not exceeding one year, or both, at the discretion of the court: Provided, That the buying of any goods, wares or merchandise by any agent of this or the United States for the public use, or the purchasing materials for the carrying on manufactories, and so converted by, or for the use of the purchaser, or the buying provisions by any licensed tavern-keeper for the use of his tavern, or the buying cattle by butchers to kill, which they shall kill accordingly, or the buying cattle by any grazer and fattened on his own farm and sold again by him, shall not be deemed engrossing within this act.

[Section III.] (Section VII, P. L.) And be it further enacted by the authority aforesaid, That no person or persons shall purchase any goods imported into or manufactured within this state, to sell, barter or exchange again, unless he shall purchase the same from the original importer, or his consignee, or manufacturer, under the penalty of forfeiting the goods so purchased one-half to the state, and the other half to the informer, and under the further penalty of any sum not exceeding one thousand pounds for each offense, and the onus probandi shall lie on such purchaser that such goods were bought as by this act is allowed; but this restraint shall not extend to licensed tavern-keepers, so as to prohibit them from purchasing liquors and other necessaries for the common use of their taverns only.

[Section IV.] (Section VIII, P. L.) And be it further enacted by the authority aforesaid, That every retailer shall sell goods purchased of the importer (or his consignee) or manufacturer for ready money if required, at not more than at the rate of twenty-five per centum on the purchase money paid to the importer (or his consignee) or manufacturer, and the charges of transportation or carriage to the place where exposed to sale, to be ascertained as herein after directed, except the articles of salt and brown sugar, which shall be sold at not more than thirty per centum profit on the purchase money and charges aforesaid.

[Section V.] (Section IX, P. L.) And be it further enacted by the authority aforesaid, That no person or persons within this commonwealth (except the original importer, consignee, or manufacturer, and except as is herein excepted) shall from and after the [twentieth] day of [October instant] presume to sell or expose to sell any goods, wares or merchandise before he, she or they shall obtain a permit for so doing from some one of the commissioners of trade hereinafter named of the proper county where such seller resides.

(Section X, P. L.) And to the end that the good purposes of this act may be the more effectually answered:

[Section VI.] Be it further enacted by the authority aforesaid, That before any person shall obtain such permit, he, she or they shall take the following oath or affirmation, which such commissioner is hereby required to administer before he shall grant such permit, viz.: I, A. B., do swear (or solemnly, sincerely and truly declare and affirm), that I will not directly or indirectly ask, demand, take or receive, any greater or other profits on any of the goods, wares and merchandise which I shall sell during the continuance of an act, entitled 'An act for the more effectually preventing engrossing and forestalling, for the encouragement of commerce and the fair trader and for other purposes therein mentioned, than is allowed in and by the said act; that I will not knowingly, either directly or indirectly buy, contract for, or get into my possession any such goods, wares or merchandise from any other person or persons than the original importer, consignee or manufacturer with intent to sell the same again within this state; and that I will in all things to the utmost of my power comply with the directions of the said act'. And if any person or persons except as aforesaid, shall sell or expose to sale any goods, wares or merchandise before he, she or they shall obtain such permit and before he, she or they shall take the oath or affirmation aforesaid, every person so offending shall forfeit double the value of the goods so sold or offered for sale, one-half thereof to the informer and the other half to the use of the state.

(Section XI, P. L.) And whereas the venders of goods in this state may still have on their hands goods, wares and merchandise, by them purchased before the publication of this act, under pretext and color of which they may abuse the good people of this state, by demanding and receiving extravagant and enormous prices for the same, as also for goods hereafter to be purchased:

For prevention whereof:

[Section VII.] (Section XII, P. L.) Be it further enacted by the authority aforesaid, That every person and persons having goods, wares or merchandise in his, her or their hands or possession before the publication of this act, shall and is hereby required on demand to sell the same for ready money, at the same rate which other goods of the same kind and quality are sold for at the same time.

[Section VIII.] (Section XIII, P. L.) And be it enacted by the authority aforesaid, That no person or persons shall purchase any goods, wares or merchandise condemned in the court of admiralty, from the original purchaser thereof, to sell, barter or exchange again and the original purchaser shall sell the same again, reserving sufficient for the use of himself and his family for six months if required, at not more than the rate of twenty-five per centum profit on the original purchase money, and the charges of transportation or carriage to the place where exposed to sale, except the articles of salt brown sugar which shall be sold at not more than thirty per centum profit on the purchase money with charges as aforesaid.

[Section IX.] (Section XIV, P. L.) And be it further enacted by the authority aforesaid, that if any such purchaser of condemned goods shall refuse to sell the same at the prices above limited for ready money, if required, he shall forfeit and pay the sum of one thousand pounds for every such refusal.

(Section XV, P. L.) And whereas the wicked arts of speculators, forestallers and engrossers, who infest every part of the country and are industriously purchasing up grain, flour and salt, at the most exorbitant prices, render it impracticable to obtain timely and sufficient supplies for the army and navy, unless the most rigorous measures are adopted without delay:

[Section X.] (Section XVI, P. L.) Be it therefore enacted, That it shall and may be lawful for any justice of the peace in any county of this state, and he is hereby authorized and required on information being given on oath or affirmation, of any quantity of grain, flour or salt being purchased by or in the possession of, any individual, inhabiting, residing or being within this state, who may have engrossed the same or having the care, custody or possession thereof, being engrossed, to issue his warrant empowering the informer or informers to seize the same for the use of the United States; and such justice of the peace shall forthwith call to his assistance two other justices of the peace of the same city or county, who (if the seizure shall be approved of by them or a majority of them), shall retain the flour or grain, or salt so seized, for the use of the said states; and shall, as soon as may be, transmit a certificate from under their hands of the quantity of grain, flour or salt so seized to the president and council, who shall cause the substance of such certificate to be entered on their proceedings; and the said justices, or any two of them, shall have full power and authority to call on the sheriff of the county, or his deputy, to aid and assist them in carrying this act into effect, which said sheriff, or deputy shall, and is hereby required to aid and assist such justices accordingly.

[Section XI.] (Section XVII, P. L.) And be it further enacted by the authority aforesaid, That the said justices, or any two of them shall and they are hereby required, as soon as may be, after determining the grain or flour aforesaid to be liable to seizure, to cause the same to be delivered to the commissary general, quarter master general, or either of their deputies or assistants, he or they paying or tendering the current price to the owner or person entitled to receive the same; and if there shall be any diversity of opinion respecting the current price between the owner or persons entitled to receive the same and the commissary general, quarter master general, his or their deputies or assistants, the justices of the peace aforesaid or any two of them are hereby authorized and required to fix and ascertain what the current price shall be deemed to be; and the said justices, or any two of them, shall and they are hereby required immediately on determining the grain, flour or salt so seized to have been engrossed, to bind over the said engrosser or engrossers if present, by recognizance, with good security, to appear at the next court of general quarter sessions of the proper city or county where the said grain, flour or salt shall be so engrossed, there to answer for the offense aforesaid, or in default of such security to commit the said offender or offenders to gaol there to remain until delivered by a due course of law; and if such engrosser or engrossers be absent, or shall reside in any other county within this state, the said justices or any two of them, shall issue their warrant, directed to the sheriff of the county where the party or parties reside or may be found, to apprehend him or them, and when apprehended such sheriff shall carry the party or parties before some justice of the county where apprehended, who shall bind him or them over as aforesaid.

[Section XII.] (Section XVIII, P. L.) And be it further enacted by the authority aforesaid, That in case any justice of the peace or sheriff, being duly called upon, shall refuse or neglect to do his duty as by this law required, he or they shall forfeit and pay the sum of five hundred pounds for each refusal or neglect.

[Section XIII.] (Section XIX, P. L.) And be it enacted by the authority aforesaid, That if any action or suit shall be commenced against any person or persons for anything done in pursuance of this act, the defendant or defendants, in any such action or suit, may plead the general issue, and give this act, and the special matter in evidence at any trial to be had thereupon, and that the same was done in pursuance and by the authority of this act; and if it shall appear so to have been done, the jury shall find for the defendant or defendants, and if the plaintiff shall become non-suit or discontinue his action after the defendant or defendants have appeared, or if judgment shall be given upon any verdict or demurrer against the plaintiff, the defendant or defendants shall and may recover treble costs.

(Section XX, P. L.) And whereas the salutary laws heretofore made to prevent and punish forestalling and engrossing, have not been duly executed or productive of all the good consequences which the good people of this state hath reason to expect from them; by reason whereof, and by the destructive practices of speculators and domestic enemies, our currency hath been depreciated to an incredible degree, when we consider that the Almighty Ruler of the universe hath in the course of his providence, blest our arms with such uncommon success, that it will be owing to our own want of public virtue if we are not soon a free, independent and happy people; and because in the tumult of war the laws of civil society often lose their force, it is thought necessary in order that this act may be the more effectually put into execution, to appoint commissioners of trade in the city of Philadelphia and in each county within this commonwealth:

Therefore:

[Section XIV.] (Section XXI, P. L.) [Commissioners appointed . . .]

[Section XV.] (Section XXII, P. L.) [Meetings of commissioners, oath of office and procedure . . .]

[Section XVI.] (Section XXIII, P. L.) And be it further enacted by the authority aforesaid, That if any person shall use insulting or abusive language to any such commissioner when in the execution of his office, upon conviction thereof, in the court of quarter sessions of the proper county, shall be fined by the said court in any sum not exceeding one hundred pounds.

[Section XVII.] (Section XXIV, P. L.) And be it further enacted by the authority aforesaid, That if any commissioner appointed by this act, shall refuse to serve, not having a lawful excuse in the opinion of the court of general quarter sessions of the proper county, such commissioner for such refusal shall forfeit any pay any sum not exceeding five hundred pounds, lawful money of Pennsylvania; and the other commissioners or a majority of them shall upon the refusal of any commissioner to act as aforesaid, or should any commissioner die, or be otherwise rendered incapable to discharge the duties of this act, proceed to choose some fit person to act in his room, who shall, previous to his acting, take the oath or affirmation aforesaid.

[Section XVIII.] (Section XXV, P. L.) And be it enacted by the authority aforesaid, That the said commissioners and every of them shall have full power and authority, and they are hereby directed and required to make diligent inquiry throughout their city or county of all breaches against this act, and shall have all the power and authority of justices of the peace, to call all persons before them against whom information shall be made on oath or affirmation as offenders against this act, and may bind them over with sufficient security to appear at the next court of general quarter sessions to be held for the proper city or county, or for default of such security may commit the offender to gaol, there to remain till delivered by a due course of law; and if the commissioners aforesaid, or any of them, shall have reason to believe that any person or persons can give information of any offense being committed against this act, they shall immediately cause such person or persons to come before them, who shall be examined on oath or affirmation, and if need be shall compel such person or persons to enter into recognizance for his, her or their appearance, to testify against such offenders.

(Section XXVI, P. L.) And whereas millers by being allowed to buy wheat, and to manufacture the same into flour, may, under color thereof, hoard the same up contrary to the true meaning and intent of this act; for prevention whereof:

[Section XIX.] (Section XXVII, P. L.) Be it enacted by the authority aforesaid, That every miller who shall purchase wheat, shall manufacture the same into flour, and expose such flour to sale as soon as may be, and if any miller shall purchase or get into his possession any quantity of wheat (besides what shall be deemed necessary for the support of himself and family for one year,) and shall not manufacture the said wheat into flour within six weeks after the same came into his possession, except he is prevented by some unavoidable cause, or having manufactured the same into flour shall refuse to expose such flour to sale at the current price, every such person shall be adjudged an engrosser, and shall be punished as engrossers are directed to be punished by this act.

(Section XXVIII, P. L.) And whereas merchants and others may, under pretence of purchasing flour or grain for exportation, engross large quantities thereof and elude this act:

For prevention wherof:

[Section XX.] (Section XXIX, P. L.) Be it further enacted, That if any merchant, exporter or any person on his or their behalf, shall purchase any flour or grain, except what may be necessary for the support and consumption of himself and family for six months, every such person or persons shall bona fide export the same according to the true intent and meaning of this act, within six weeks after the same shall be purchased by him or them as aforesaid, unless prevented by some unavoidable cause or accident: And if any merchant, importer, or other persons, shall buy or get into his possession any quantity of flour or grain, except as aforesaid, under pretence that the same was bought for exportation, and shall not export the same as aforesaid, except prevented as aforesaid, every such person shall be adjudged an engrosser and liable to the like punishment.

[Section XXI.] (Section XXX, P. L.) And be it further enacted by the authority aforesaid, That the naval officer shall, and he is hereby required to publish in one of the English and German newspapers, monthly and every month, a list of all vessels which shall arrive in the port of Philadelphia, with a list of their cargo, and to whom they belong or to whom consigned.

[Section XXII.] (Section XXXI, P. L.) And be it further enacted by the authority aforesaid, That the importers of goods, wares, or merchandise shall expose the same to sale within the space of two weeks after the same shall arrive at the Port of Philadelphia; and if any importer or his agent shall neglect or refuse to expose to sale any goods or merchandise, except what may be necessary for the use of himself and family for six months, on being tendered the current price therefor in ready money; every person so offending shall be adjudged an engrosser, and punished as by this act is directed.

Passed October 8, 1779. See the note to the Act of Assembly passed January 2, 1778, Statutes at large of Pennsylvania, ch. 779. The act in the text was repealed by the Act of Assembly passed March 22, 1780, ibid. ch. 779.

2.9 PENNSYLVANIA ISSUES PAPER CURRENCY

'An act for furnishing the quota of this state towards paying the annual interest of the debts of the United States; and for funding and paying the interest of the public debts of this state'.[1] March 16,

[1] By the former part of this act, which has been repealed, the revenues of the state were formed into an aggregate fund, for the purpose of discharging the following engagements: – 1st. The installments of the legislative grant to the late proprietaries, as they became due (see *Laws of the Commonwealth of Pennsylvania*, pages 205 and 240.) – 2d. The state's estimated quota of the annual interest of the aggregate debt of the United States, contracted during the late war, amounting to £123,932, which sum was directed to be transferred by the Executive into the hands of the continental Loan-Officer, yearly, and every year, after the termination of the year 1784, to be applied to the payment of the interest on such continental certificates as were originally issued to the citizens of this state, or to the officers and soldiers of the Pennsylvania line, or quota of troops, &c. – 3d. The interest for one year on all debts due from, and assumed by, this state, and liquidated, ascertained and certified, according to law (debts funded on the excise, and other certificates of depreciation of pay, excepted) to be paid by the Treasurer, yearly, and every year. – 4th. The arrearages of interest on the state debts, whenever there remained in the aggregate fund a residuary sum of £15,000. And, in order to strengthen and establish the aggregate fund, thus created, the act also provided that a tax of £76,945 17 6 should be assessed, raised and levied, from the estates real and personal, and persons, in the city and counties, yearly, and every year, successively, after the year 1785. By an act of the 1st of March, 1786, a loan was opened to receive continental in exchange for state certificates, commonly called New Loan Certificates (which was the origin of the funding system of Pennsylvania) and providing for the payment of the interest on such new loan certificates, &c. By an act of the 8th of March, 1786, so much of the law in the text, as related to the paying of the £123,932, annually, to the continental Loan-Officer, and his distribution of the same, was repealed, and a provision made to pay the balances due on the pecuniary requisitions of Congress. By an act of the 28th of March, 1787, the Comptroller was directed to receive, on loan, the continental Loan-Office certificates issued in the states of New-Jersey and Delaware, upon loans made by persons who were, at the time of making the same, and continue, citizens of Pennsylvania; and the parties claiming that benefit are required to make oath or affirmation, that the certificates offered are, *bona fide*, the property of the persons to whom they were originally granted. By an act of the 27th of March, 1789, it was declared, that the interest on the new loan certificates should be paid, so as to compleat the payment of interest to four years; but that so much of every act, as directs or secures the payment of the principal or interest of such certificates, beyond the term of four years, shall be void; the Executive

1785, *Laws of the Commonwealth of Pennsylvania*, ed. A. J. Dallas (Philadelphia, 1793) ch. 183, pp. 252–62

---

was authorised, on application of the holders, to direct the re-exchange of the continental for new loan certificates, the interest being first equalised on the respective certificates, and the balance paid in indents; but which, by an act of the 30th day of September, 1791, was allowed to be done in three per cent. stock. By an act of the 1st of April, 1790, further regulations were made respecting the re-exchange of the continental and new loan certificates. By an act of the 8th of December, 1789, the annual tax of £76,945 17 6 was suspended for one year; the suspension was protracted for another year by an act of the 6th of April, 1791; and by an act of the 9th of the same month, so much of the act in the text, (including all but the 33d, from the 22d to the 51st section) and of every other act, as authorised the assessing, levying and collecting the tax, was repealed, with a proviso, that the repeal should not prevent the collection of the arrearages due on the 31st of December, 1790, or prevent the levying and collecting county rates and levies, taxes for the relief of the poor, and taxes for opening and keeping in repair roads and highways. From the report of the officers of the department of accounts to the Governor, on the 30th of November, 1791, it appears, that the arrearages of the funding tax, due the 31st of October, 1791, inclusive, amounted to £61,133 10 11. – See the appendix to the *Journal of the House of Representatives* for the session, which commenced on the 6th of December, 1791.

In pursuance of an act of the 9th day of April, 1791, the legislative grant to the late Proprietaries of Pennsylvania has been discharged. – See *Laws of the Commonwealth of Pennsylvania*, page 240 (*q.*) And by an act of the 10th day of April, 1792, effectual provision is made for paying all the debts of the state of the following descriptions: – 1st. All the certificates issued by this state, upon which an interest of six per cent. per annum is payable, by virtue of any existing laws of this commonwealth, at their nominal value: – 2d. All the certificates which were issued by this state, bearing an interest of six per cent. as an equivalent for the loss sustained upon the deferred stock of the United States by the creditors of this state, who subscribed to the loan proposed by Congress, at the rate of thirty-nine pounds, in gold or silver money, for every hundred pounds in the nominal amount of the certificates of deferred stock, on which such additional six per cent. certificates were respectively granted by the state as aforesaid: – 3d. All the certificates which were issued by this state, bearing an interest of three per cent. as an equivalent for the loss sustained upon the three per cent. stock of the United States by the creditors of this state, who subscribed to the loan proposed by Congress, at such rate as the same may be purchased; provided the same does not exceed the rate of fifty pounds, in gold or silver, for every hundred pounds in the nominal amount of the certificates of three per cent. stock, on which such additional three per cent. certificates were, respectively, granted by the state as aforesaid: – 4th. All and every the bills of credit, commonly called Dollar Money, remaining in circulation, together with the interest due thereon, at the nominal value and amount of such bills, and of the interest due thereon.

. . . SECT. LI. And whereas, from the scarcity of gold and silver money in the country, the inhabitants of this commonwealth are suffering much inconvenience for want of a sufficient circulating medium of internal commerce, and it is deemed expedient that a moderate sum in bills of credit should be issued, and that their punctual redemption should be secured by the funds herein before established:

SECT. LII. *Be it further enacted by the authority aforesaid*, That bills of credit to the amount or value of one hundred and fifty thousand pounds, and of the several denominations herein after mentioned, shall be prepared and printed on good strong paper, as soon as conveniently may be after the passing of this act, under the care and direction of the trustees herein after mentioned and appointed; which bills of credit shall severally be prepared and printed in the words following; that is to say, 'This bill by law shall pass current for within the commonwealth of Pennsylvania, according to an act of the General Assembly, passed at Philadelphia, the day of *Anno Domini* one thousand seven hundred and eighty-five'. And each of the said bills shall have the arms of the state, as an escutcheon, in the margin thereof, together with such other device or devices as the said trustees shall think proper, as well to prevent counterfeits, as to distinguish their several denominations: And the said bills shall be of the several denominations, and in the quantities following; that is to say,

Fifty-four thousand five hundred and forty-five of twenty shillings each.

Fifty-four thousand five hundred and forty-six of fifteen shillings each.

Fifty-four thousand five hundred and forty-five of ten shillings each.

Fifty-four thousand five hundred and forty-six of five shillings each.

Fifty-four thousand five hundred and forty-six of two shillings and six-pence each.

Fifty-four thousand five hundred and forty-six of one shilling and six-pence each.

Fifty-four thousand five hundred and forty-six of nine-pence each.

And fifty-four thousand five hundred and forty-six of three-pence each.

SECT. LIII. *And be it enacted by the authority aforesaid*, That the said trustees shall, severally, take the oath or affirmation following, before a Justice of the peace, and before they enter upon the said office; to wit . . .

SECT. LIV. And in order to perfect the said bills of credit, according to the true intent and meaning of this act, *Be it enacted by the authority aforesaid*, That every denomination of the said bills shall be numbered from number one, progressively, and that each and every of the said bills, of the denomination of ten shillings and upwards, shall be signed by three of the persons herein after named and appointed as signers; and that each and every of the said bills, of a smaller denomination, down to one shilling and six-pence, inclusive, shall be signed by two of the said signers; and that such of the said bills that are of a smaller denomination shall be signed by one of said signers; and the said Treasurer shall deliver out the said bills to the said signers, to be numbered and signed as aforesaid, in such manner, and in such quantities at a time, as he, in his discretion, shall think proper, taking proper receipts for such deliveries, and taking care that all such bills, so delivered out, be duly returned into the treasury, after being signed and numbered as aforesaid.

SECT. LV. *And be it enacted by the authority aforesaid*, That John Biddle, George Schlosser, Joseph Dean, and John Wharton, be, and they are hereby, appointed trustees, for procuring materials, and preparing the bills of credit aforesaid, and that each and every of the said trustees, who shall perform the duties herein required, shall be allowed and paid the sum of fifteen shillings for every day he shall be employed, *bona fide*, in the said service. And that John Chaloner, William Turnbull, George Lattimer, Reynold Keen, Andrew Tybout, Edward Fox, James Collins, Peter Baynton, William Smith, druggist, Samuel Murdoch, James Bayard, Joseph Redman, Robert Smith, merchant, John Rhea, William Gray, brewer, William Tilton, Francis Wade, Thomas Irwin, Charles Risk, Andrew Pettit, James M'Crea, John Taylor, Samuel Caldwell, Stacy Hepburn, and John Duffield,[1] be, and they are hereby, appointed signers of the said bills, according to the directions herein before mentioned, and shall be severally allowed and paid for the same, at and after the rate of ten shillings for every thousand of the said bills, which they shall respectively sign and number as aforesaid; all which wages, together with all other contingent expences of procuring materials, and preparing and perfecting the said bills of

[1] An additional number of signers was appointed by an act of the 10th of September, 1785.

credit, shall be paid out of the public treasury of this state, and charged on the fund herein before mentioned, the account of the said charges, respectively, being first adjusted and certified by the Comptroller-General, and approved by the Supreme Executive Council.

SECT. LVI. *And be it enacted by the authority aforesaid,* That when and so soon as the said bills of credit shall be perfected, and re-delivered to the Treasurer as aforesaid, they shall severally be taken, deemed, and accounted for, as money in his hands, according to the nominal value expressed in the said bills respectively, and appropriated accordingly in manner following, that is to say; the amount or value of fifty thousand pounds thereof shall be reserved, for the purpose of erecting and establishing a Loan-office in this state, in such manner as the legislature shall direct; and the residue of the said bills of credit shall be appropriated for and towards the payment of the sum and sums herein before directed to be paid into the hands of the continental Loan-Officer in this state, and for and towards the payment of the interest due on the debts of this state, as herein before mentioned.[1]

SECT. LVII. *And be it enacted by the authority aforesaid,* That the bills of credit, herein before directed to be made and issued, shall be taken, deemed, and received as equal to gold and silver money, for the sums mentioned in each bill, respectively, in all payments to this state, for lands purchased or to be purchased within the same, and for arrearages due on lands already located or warranted, and also for the arrearages of all general taxes heretofore assessed, and for the taxes herein directed to be assessed and collected; and for the debts due to the state; and for all customs, imposts, duties and debts whatsoever, which shall hereafter arise and become due to this state, by virtue of this act, or of any act or law heretofore made; and the several officers and persons, appointed and authorised to receive and collect the same, are hereby, directed to receive such bills of credit accordingly, any law, usage or custom, to the contrary, in any wise notwithstanding.

SECT. LVIII. *And be it enacted by the authority aforesaid,* That if any person or persons shall presume to counterfeit any of the bills of credit, herein directed to be prepared, perfected and issued, by printing, or procuring to be printed, any such bills, of the likeness and similitude of any of the said genuine bills of credit, and if any person or persons

[1] The loan-office, here provided for, is established by an act of the 4th of April 1785. – See the act of that date, and the acts there cited.

shall forge, or procure to be forged, the name or names of any of the signers of such genuine bills of credit, to any such counterfeit bill or bills, whether such counterfeiting or forging be done within this state, or elsewhere, or shall utter any such bill or bills, knowing the same to be so counterfeited as aforesaid, every such person, so offending, and being thereof legally convicted, by confession, standing mute, or by verdict of a jury in the Supreme Court, or court of Oyer and Terminer, shall suffer death, without benefit of clergy. And if any person or persons shall counterfeit any of the said bills of credit, by altering the denomination thereof, with design to encrease the value of the same, or shall utter any of the said bills, knowing them to be so counterfeited or altered as aforesaid, and shall be legally convicted thereof as aforesaid, every such person, so convicted, shall be sentenced to the pillory, and to have both his or her ears cut off, and nailed to the pillory; and moreover, every such offender shall forfeit the sum of one hundred pounds, to be levied on his or her lands and tenements, goods and chattles, one half thereof to the use of the commonwealth, and the other half to the use of the person or persons, who shall make discovery of such offence, and prosecute such offender to conviction.

SECT. LIX. And to the end that the bills of credit aforesaid may be fully and fairly redeemed and cancelled, *Be it enacted by the authority aforesaid*, That from and out of such of the said bills of credit, which shall be paid into the treasury of this state, in the year of our Lord one thousand seven hundred and eighty-six, by means of the taxes, debts and duties aforesaid, the Treasurer for the time being shall, and he is, hereby, authorised and directed to cancel, or cause to be cancelled, so many of the said bills, as shall amount to the sum of twenty thousand pounds, by punching or piercing a hole, not less than the size of one eighth of a dollar, through some part of each bill, near the center thereof; which bills, so cancelled, he shall report to the General Assembly, at their next meeting thereafter; and when a committee of the said Assembly, to be appointed for the purpose, shall have examined and counted the said cancelled bills, such bills shall be burned in their presence, and report thereof shall be made to the House, and entered on the journals of their proceedings. And the like sum of twenty thousand pounds, of the said bills of credit, shall be cancelled and burned, in like manner, in the year of our Lord one thousand seven hundred and eighty-seven, and the like sum in each succeeding year, until the whole of the said bills of credit shall have been so redeemed, cancelled and destroyed.[1]

SECT. LX. *And be it enacted by the authority aforesaid*, That the Treasurer of this state, for the time being, shall be allowed, by way of commission, for his trouble and expences in receiving such monies as he shall receive by virtue of this act, and for paying and cancelling the same, as herein before directed, eight shillings and four-pence for every hundred pounds he shall so receive and pay away, or cancel, as aforesaid, and no more.

2.10 PENNSYLVANIA ACTS TO RAISE MONEY TO PAY ITS QUOTA TO CONGRESS AND TO RELIEVE ITS OWN CITIZENS WHO ARE CREDITORS OF THE UNITED STATES[2]

'An act for providing the quota of federal supplies for the year one thousand seven hundred eighty and three, and for the relief of the citizens of this state who have become creditors of the United States of America by loans of money or other modes of furnishing public supplies'. 1783, *Statutes at Large of Pennsylvania*, vol. XI, ch. 1021, pp. 81–91

(Section I, P. L.) Whereas the United States of America in congress assembled by their act of the eighteenth day of October last, have required of the several states in union their respective quotas of the sum of two million of dollars for the service of the year one thousand seven hundred eighty and three, the proportion or quota whereof allotted to and required of this commonwealth is stated at three

[1] In addition to the sum here directed to be annually destroyed, an act of the 27th of November, 1787, provides for cancelling, in the same manner, all the bills of credit which shall be received into the Loan-office on account of mortgages. By the report which the officers of the department of accounts made to the Governor, on the 30th of November, 1791, it appears that the sum of £29,672, in the bills of credit emitted by this act, then remained in circulation.

[2] *Editor's note:* The importance of this step lies in the fact that the State government now assumed a liability which the Congress was felt to be incapable of discharging.

hundred thousand dollars, which requisition the representatives of the freemen of this state are desirous should be complied with:

(Section II, P. L.) And whereas a great number of the virtuous citizens of this state, from motives of patriotism and zeal in the common cause, and confiding in the public promises and plighted faith of the United States, have advanced large portions of their property by loans and otherwise to the public use at the more early and hazardous periods and gloomy seasons of this great contest for the liberties and independence of the United States:

(Section III, P. L.) And whereas it is highly expedient and proper as well from motives of good policy and a regard to the preservation of public credit as by an act of justice to enable those worthy citizens who have exhausted their substance by loans to the public to pay their proportion of taxes, and thereby to facilitate the collection of the requisite supplies for the current service, which the good citizens of this state are desirous to furnish, that provision be made for the payment of the interest on such of the said debts as are due to the citizens of this state, until the United States shall be enabled to appropriate adequate funds for that purpose:

(Section IV, P. L.) And whereas the said United States, in congress assembled, did by a certain act on the tenth day of September, one thousand seven hundred and eighty-two, require of the several states to raise their respective quotas of the sum of twelve hundred thousand dollars, for the purpose of paying the interest due on loan-office certificates and other ascertained debts of the United States, the proportion or quota whereof required of this state, is one hundred and eighty thousand dollars:

(Section V, P. L.) And whereas it appears that the said sum of one hundred and eighty thousand dollars will be insufficient to pay one year's interest on the debts due to the citizens of this state who are creditors of the United States to a much larger amount than the quota of this state of the whole of the public debts, and it being the desire of the legislature to raise and appropriate for this purpose, a sum sufficient to pay one years interest on all the ascertained debts due from the United States to the citizens of this state, which it is supposed will require the sum of one hundred and twenty thousand dollars in addition to the one hundred and eighty thousand dollars so required by congress, making in the whole three hundred thousand dollars over and beside the aforesaid three thousand dollars to be raised as the quota of this state for the current service of the year one thousand seven hundred eighty and three. To the end, therefore, that the quota of this state of the supplies required for the service of the year one thousand seven hundred eighty and three may be the more speedily and certainly raised and furnished and the public creditors at the same time receive temporary relief:

[Section I.] (Section VI, P. L.) Be it enacted by the Representatives of the Freemen of the Commonwealth of Pennsylvania in General Assembly met, and by the authority of the same, That the sum of two hundred and twenty-five thousand pounds, being equal in value to six hundred thousand Spanish milled dollars, shall be assessed, raised and levied, in gold and silver moneys, and in the notes hereinafter mentioned, upon the estates real and personal, and persons, as hereinafter directed, within the city and several counties of this state, by four equal proportions or payments, whereof the first shall be collected and made on or before the first day of July next; the second proportion in three months after the first; and so of the other two proportions; each to be collected and paid three months after the other, so that the whole of the said sum of two hundred and twenty-five thousand pounds shall become due and be levied, collected and paid, within one year from and after the said first day of July next, according to the method and in the proportions following, that is to say,

Upon the estates real and personal and persons within the city and county of Philadelphia, the sum of seventy-four thousand five hundred and forty-three pounds.

Upon the estates real and personal and persons within the county of Bucks, the sum of fourteen thousand seven hundred and forty-four pounds.

Upon the estates real and personal and persons within the county of Chester, the sum of twenty-three thousand six hundred and sixty-eight pounds.

Upon the estates real and personal and persons within the county of Lancaster, the sum of thirty-two thousand and thirty-two pounds.

Upon the estates real and personal and persons within the county of York, the sum of seventeen thousand eight hundred and forty-six pounds.

Upon the estates real and personal and persons within the county of Cumberland, the sum of sixteen thousand seven hundred and seventy-four pounds.

Upon the estates real and personal and persons within the county of Berks, the sum of sixteen thousand one hundred and eleven pounds.

Upon the estates real and personal and persons within the county of Northampton, the sum of nine thousand two hundred and seventy-four pounds.

Upon the estates real and personal and persons within the county of Bedford, the sum of five thousand and eighty-four pounds.

Upon the estates real and personal and persons within the county of Northumberland, the sum of six thousand two hundred and eighty pounds.

Upon the estates real and personal and persons within the county of Westmoreland, the sum of four thousand three hundred and twenty-two pounds.

And upon the estates real and personal and persons within the county of Washington, the sum of four thousand three hundred and twenty-two pounds.

[Section II.] (Section VII, P. L.) That the several directions, authorities and powers, rewards, penalties and sanctions, appeals, remedies and allowances contained in and provided by an act of the general assembly of this commonwealth, passed on the twenty-seventh day of March last, entitled 'An act to raise effective supplies for the year one thousand seven hundred and eighty-two',[1] or the purposes there set forth (the same being accommodated to the intent and design of this act, by altering the dates in the oaths and affirmations of office thereby directed to the year of our Lord one thousand seven hundred and eighty-three, and otherwise adapting the said act to the purposes of this act) shall be and the same hereby are extended to the raising, levying, collecting and securing the payment of the aforesaid sum of two hundred and twenty-five thousand pounds; and all fines, forfeitures and penalties which may thereby accrue and become due and payable according to the repartition of the taxes aforesaid upon the city and several counties of this state respectively, in manner aforesaid; and the said recited act shall be accordingly applied and enforced to the execution of this act in such manner as to bring into the treasury of this state the taxes directed by this act, except in such cases and instances wherein special provision is made or as in and by this act is otherwise directed.

[1] Passed March 27, 1782, *Statutes at Large of Pennsylvania*, ch. 961.

(Section VIII, P. L.) And whereas it is designed that a sum not exceeding three hundred thousand dollars, part of the taxes by this act to be raised and levied as aforesaid, should be appropriated and paid to the public creditors herein before mentioned as a temporary relief till more permanent and certain provision can be made for them: And whereas it may improve and hasten such relief and facilitate the payment of the taxes aforesaid, if notes be prepared and issued to the said public creditors, which notes shall be received in payment of the said taxes:

[Section III.] (Section IX, P. L.) That the treasurer of this state be authorized and empowered and he is hereby authorized, empowered and directed to prepare at the public expense notes respectively payable to the bearer thereof to the amount of three hundred thousand dollars of the following denominations; that is to say,

Five thousand and sixty-three notes of twenty dollars each.
Five thousand and sixty-three notes of fifteen dollars each.
Five thousand and sixty-four notes of twelve dollars each.
Five thousand and sixty-three notes of six dollars each.
Five thousand and sixty-four notes of three dollars each.
Five thousand and sixty-four notes of two dollars each.
Five thousand and sixty-three notes of one dollar each.
Five thousand and sixty-four notes of one quarter dollar each.

Which notes shall be printed in such form and with such devices and checks as the said treasurer shall devise and the president or vice-president and council shall approve; and the said notes of each denomination shall be numbered from number one progressively and shall be signed by the said treasurer, and by him delivered to Thomas Smith, esquire, continental loan-officer for this state at such times and in such quantities as the president or vice president by warrant under his hand in council shall from time to time direct, which warrant shall be registered in the office of the comptroller-general of this state; and thereupon the said loan-officer shall become answerable for the sum mentioned in every such warrant; and the said loan-officer, previous to his issuing or paying away the said notes in manner herein after directed, shall countersign each and every note he shall issue or pay.

[Section IV.] (Section X, P. L.) That it shall and may be lawful for the said loan-officer to pay, with and out of such notes as aforesaid, the lawful interest for one year on all such certificates of moneys loaned to the United States, or other certificates of debts due from the United States, liquidated, ascertained and certified, according to the directions of the United States in congress assembled (other than certificates for pay or other personal demands of officers, civil or military, or of soldiers or seamen) as shall be demanded by the holders or possessors of the said certificates, and such payment shall be endorsed thereon; provided that such certificates as aforesaid were originally issued from the loan-office of this state, or given or granted for articles furnished or services done and performed by the citizens of this state, except as before excepted and in the name and for the use of any person or persons who at the time of such issuing was or were, or since have been a citizen or citizens of this state and actually resident within the same, or in the name or for the use of a body politic or corporate within this state; and provided also that there be the interest for one year at least due thereon, and if any difficulty shall arise in determining whether the person holding or possessing any such certificate shall be entitled to receive the interest thereon within the meaning of this act, it shall be incumbent on the claimant to produce the proof necessary to establish the claim, and if the evidence offered by the claimant be not sufficient to satisfy the said loan-officer, the same shall be referred to the president or vice-president in council, whose determination and order thereon shall be conclusive.

(Section XI, P. L.) And whereas the principal sum mentioned in the said certificates, or some of them, may be described in continental money:

[Section V.] That the value thereof in specie shall be computed and ascertained according to the directions of the United States in congress assembled, in and by their act of the twenty-eighth day of June in the year of our Lord one thousand seven hundred and eighty. And to the end that a fair and proper account may be kept of all the moneys paid for interest by virtue of this act, and that this state may have proper credit therefor with the United States, the said loan officer is hereby directed to keep a fair and exact account of such payments as he shall make in which shall be specified the date and number of the certificate on which payment shall be made, the amount of the principal sum mentioned therein, and the name of the person to whom it was issued, as well as the sum paid thereon, and shall take receipts from the persons to whom the moneys shall be paid as vouchers for the said account; and on producing such account and vouchers and the same being approved and allowed by the comptroller-general of this state, it shall be admitted in discharge for the amount thereof of the notes he shall have received from the treasury as aforesaid. And if any of the said notes shall remain in his hands on the first day of July which will be in the year of our Lord one thousand seven hundred and eighty-four, the said loan-officer may pay them into the hands of the treasurer of this state, taking his receipt therefor, the amount of which shall be allowed him in discharge of the residue of the said notes which shall as aforesaid have been delivered to him:

(Section XII, P. L.) And to the end that the payment of the said notes for interest may the more certainly answer the good purposes hereby intended,

[Section VI.] That it shall and may be lawful to and for each and every person on whom the taxes to be raised by virtue of this act shall be levied, or from whom the same or any part thereof shall be demanded, to pay any part not exceeding one-half thereof in the said notes signed by the treasurer and countersigned by the loan-officer as aforesaid, and the said notes are hereby declared to be a legal tender in the payment of any such proportion of the said tax, or of the said proportion of any one of the quarterly payments thereof herein directed to be made; provided that the said residue of such tax, or of the quarterly payment thereof then due, be tendered or offered to be paid at the same time in gold or silver money; and the collectors of taxes, and all others whom it may concern, are hereby empowered and directed to receive the said notes in payment accordingly.

(Section XIII, P. L.) And to the end that the moneys hereby intended to be raised may be faithfully appropriated and applied to the purposes hereby intended, as speedily as possible:

[Section VII.] That it shall and may be lawful for the treasurer of this state, when and as often as any moneys to be levied and raised by virtue of this act shall be paid into his hands, to divide the same into equal moieties or half parts and to pay one of the said moieties to the treasurer of the United States, or to such other person or persons as shall be duly authorized by the said United States to receive the same for their use, and the receipt of the said treasurer, or other person authorized as aforesaid, shall be a sufficient voucher to the treasurer of this state for such payment and payments; and the other moiety of the said moneys, in which shall be included all the said notes which shall have been paid in for taxes as aforesaid, shall be disposed in the following manner; that is to say, such of the said notes as shall be paid in as aforesaid shall be by the said treasurer marked, by punching or piercing a hole, not less than the size of one-eighth of a dollar, through some part of each note near the center thereof; and the quantity of such notes in the treasury at the commencement of each session of the general assembly shall be reported to the house by the treasurer, to be cancelled and destroyed in such manner as the house shall direct, until the whole shall have been destroyed. And such gold and silver money as shall belong to this moiety of the taxes as aforesaid, shall be given in exchange for such notes by the said treasurer to such person and persons as shall apply for the same at any time after the last payment of the taxes hereby directed to be raised shall have become due; and if at the end of six months after the said time any such money shall remain in the treasury unapplied for in exchange for such notes, it shall be lawful for the treasurer to pay the same or any part thereof to the aforesaid loan-officer on his producing such warrant as aforesaid, to be applied to the payment of such interest due in manner aforesaid as may remain unpaid; provided that not more than one year's interest be paid on any one debt or certificate by virtue of this act.

[Section VIII.] (Section XIV, P. L.) That all fines and penalties imposed and made recoverable by this act, other than such as are otherwise specially appropriated by the act herein before recited and referred to, shall be paid in gold or silver money, and applied towards defraying the extraordinary expenses and charges of executing this act. And that the treasurer of this state shall be allowed and paid for his labor and trouble in numbering and signing the said notes two shillings for every hundred thereof; and that the said loan-officer shall be allowed and paid for his labor and trouble in countersigning and issuing the said notes and accounting for the same in the manner herein directed, at the rate of four shillings and six pence for every hundred notes he shall so sign, issue and account for, over and besides the allowance he is entitled to receive from the United States for the payment of the interest on loans; which payment to the said loan-officer is to be made by the treasurer on a warrant to be produced under the hand of the president or vice-president in council, and entered in the office of the comptroller-general. And the treasurer of this state and the loan-officer aforesaid shall be, and they are hereby severally made accountable to the general assembly for all moneys and notes which shall come to their hands respectively by virtue of this act, and for all other transactions under the same and shall at all proper times and seasons submit their books, papers and accounts, relative thereto, to the inspection and examination of the president or vice-president in council, or to such persons as they shall appoint to inspect the same.

[Section IX.] (Section XV, P. L.) That if any person or persons shall counterfeit any one or more of the notes directed to be emitted by this act, by printing or procuring the same to be printed in the likeness and similitude of the said genuine notes; and also if any person or persons shall forge the name or names of the said treasurer or loan-officer, or either of them, to such counterfeit notes, whether the counterfeiting the said notes or names be done within this state or elsewhere, or shall utter such note, knowing it to be counterfeit as aforesaid, and shall be thereof legally convicted in any court of oyer and terminer within this state, he or they so offending shall suffer death without benefit of clergy.

(Section XVI, P. L.) And if any person or persons shall counterfeit any of the said notes by altering the denomination thereof with design to increase the value of such notes, or shall utter the same knowing them to be so counterfeited or altered as aforesaid, and shall be thereof legally convicted in any court of record in this state, such person or persons shall be sentenced to the pillory, and have both his or her ears cut off and nailed to the pillory, and be publicly whipped on his or her bare back with thirty-nine lashes well laid on; and moreover, every such offender shall forfeit the sum of two thousand pounds, lawful money of Pennsylvania, to be levied on his or her lands and tenements, goods and chattels, the one moiety to the use of the state and the other moiety to the discoverer.

[Section X.] (Section XVII, P. L.) That every single freeman who at the time of assessing the tax imposed by this act shall be of the age of twenty-one years or upwards, and shall be out of his apprenticeship six months, shall pay a sum not exceding four pounds and not under the sum of twenty shillings over and above the sum to be levied on the estate of such single freeman by virtue of this act, anything in any law heretofore made to the contrary in anywise notwithstanding.

(Section XVIII, P. L.) And whereas the United States in congress assembled by their resolve of the seventeenth of February last did require the legislature of each state to take such measures as shall appear to them most effectual for obtaining a just and accurate account of the quantity of land in such state granted to or surveyed for any person, the number of buildings thereon distinguishing dwelling houses from other buildings, and the number of its inhabitants distinguishing white from black, and cause the said account to be transmitted and delivered to congress on or before the first day of March one thousand seven hundred and eighty-four.

[Section XI.] (Section XIX, P. L.) That the commissioners of the city and county of Philadelphia and of every county of this state shall in their warrants to the township, ward or district assessors of their respective counties, direct the said assessors to make a full and true return of the several quantities of land in the district or township, granted to, or surveyed for any person, the number of buildings thereon, distinguishing dwelling houses from other buildings, and the number of its inhabitants, distinguishing white from black, and the said commissioners shall cause the said returns to be transmitted to the general assembly of this state on or before the first day of November next ensuing the date hereof.

Passed March 21, 1783. Recorded L. B. No. 2, p. 79, etc. See the Acts of Assembly passed September 25, 1783, Statutes at Large of Pennsylvania, *ch. 1052; April 5, 1785, ibid., ch. 1161; March 8, 1786, ibid., ch. 1209.*

2.11 PENNSYLVANIA LEGISLATES TO MEET ITS OBLIGATIONS TOWARDS THE CONGRESS AND ITS OWN CITIZENS

'An act for furnishing the quota of this state towards paying the annual interest of the debts of the United States and for finding and paying the interest of the public debts of this state.' 1785, *Statutes at Large of Pennsylvania,* vol. XI, ch. 1137, pp. 454–62

(Section I, P. L.) Whereas the United States in congress assembled by their act of the eighteenth day of April, one thousand seven hundred and eighty-three did resolve that it be recommended to the several states as indispensably necessary to the restoration of public credit and to the punctual and honorable discharge of the public debts to invest the said United States in congress assembled with power to levy and collect for the use of the United States certain duties on goods therein enumerated and also a duty of five per centum ad valorem on all other goods at the time and place of importation provided that none of the said duties should be applied to any other purpose than the discharge of the interest or principal of the debts contracted on the faith of the United States for supporting the war nor be continued for a longer term than twenty-five years.

(Section II, P. L.) And whereas the said United States by their same act did further resolve that it be also recommended to the several states, to establish substantial and effectual revenues for a term limited to twenty-five years of such nature as they should severally judge most convenient for supplying their respective proportions of one million five hundred thousand dollars annually as necessary in addition to the sum to be raised by the duties aforesaid, for the restoration of the public credit and the punctual and honorable discharge of the aforesaid public debts. And whereas the legislature of this commonwealth, desirous to promote and facilitate the good intentions of the United States in the manner set forth in the said recommendation, did, on the twenty-third day of September in the year of our Lord one thousand seven hundred and eighty-three by law enact and declare that the said United States should be and they were fully authorized and empowered to levy and collect the several duties mentioned and required in and by the said recommendation, and did also further enact and declare in and by the same act that the sum of two hundred and five thousand one hundred and eighty-nine dollars (being the estimated proportion of this state, of the aforesaid one million five hundred thousand dollars) shall be annually for the term of twenty-five years raised and levied on the persons and estates of the inhabitants of this state for the uses and purposes aforesaid in such manner as the legislature of this commonwealth should from time to time thereafter direct.

(Section III, P. L.) Provided, That the said act should not take effect, until each and every of the thirteen United States should make laws conformably to the acts of congress on which the said act was founded.

(Section IV, P. L.) And whereas one or more of the said thirteen states have hitherto declined to comply with the said recommendations of the United States whereby the said act of this state is yet suspended and rendered ineffectual and the aforesaid plan of the United States for the discharge of their debts and the restoration of public credit is frustrated and yet remains impracticable.

(Section V, P. L.) And whereas considerable time may elapse before a general and effective plan for the good purposes aforesaid may be formed and ratified by the several states so as to be put in execution whereby the public credit may be farther impaired.

(Section VI, P. L.) And whereas a large portion of the aforesaid debts of the United States are due to the citizens of this state, many of whom are laboring under grievous hardships and inconveniences and some are suffering the extremeties of want by the withholding of the annual interest and the consequent depreciation in value of the principal of their just demands.

(Section VII, P. L.) And whereas it is the desire of the legislature of this commonwealth to grant relief to the suffering citizens thereof, in such manner as may tend to strengthen and establish public credit, and at the same time, be most likely to accord with such federal measures as the United States in their wisdom may adopt by contributing the full amount of the proportion of this state towards paying the annual interest of the whole debt of the United States, as well foreign as domestic, which proportion, according to the late estimation of congress, will require the sum of one hundred and twenty-three thousand nine hundred and thirty-two pounds, annually.

(Section VIII, P. L.) And whereas large sums of money are due and owing from this commonwealth to divers citizens thereof as well as to other persons, and it is just and reasonable that such creditors should receive interest for their respective demands until the funds of the state shall be sufficient to discharge the principal.

(Sections IX, P. L.) And whereas in and by an act of the general assembly of this commonwealth made and passed the twenty-seventh day of November, Anno Domini one thousand seven hundred and seventy-nine, entitled 'An act for vesting the estates of the late proprietaries of Pennsylvania in this commonwealth',[1] it is among other things enacted and declared that the sum of one hundred and thirty thousand pounds sterling money of Great Britain be paid out of the treasury of this state to the devisees and legatees of Thomas Penn and Richard Penn, late proprietaries of Pennsylvania respectively, and to the widow and relict of the said Thomas Penn in annual payments not exceeding twenty thousand nor less than fifteen thousand pounds sterling in any one year and that the first annual payment thereof be made at the expiration of one year after the termination of the war, and it is just and necessary that due provision should be made for effecting the said annual payments.

(Section X, P. L.) And whereas the United States in congress assembled by their act of the twenty-seventh day of April last setting forth

[1] Passed November 27, 1779, *Statutes at Large of Pennsylvania*, ch. 874.

that it would not be expedient to call into payment the whole balances of their requisitions on the several states of eight millions of dollars for the service of the year one thousand seven hundred and eighty-two and of two millions of dollars for the service of the year one thousand seven hundred and eighty-three did thereupon resolve in substance as follows, to-wit, that the states be required to furnish within the course of the present year (one thousand seven hundred and eighty-four) such part of their deficiencies under the requisition of eight millions as with their payments to the close of the year one thousand seven hundred and eighty-three would make up one-half of their original quoto thereof and that before any further demand should be made upon the states under the requisition for two millions of dollars or the requisition for eight millions of dollars congress would revise the quotas of the several states mentioned in the said requisitions respectively and make them agreeable to justice on the best information congress might have when such demand should be made. And whereas it appears that the payments so as aforesaid required for one-half of the quota of this state of the said requisition of eight millions of dollars will amount to the sum of five hundred and sixty thousand three-hundred and ninety-seven dollars which payments are already made and compleated or nearly so. And whereas large sums remain due and in arrears from divers citizens, inhabitants and estates within this commonwealth on account of the several taxes assessed by virtue of the acts of the general assembly in consequence of the said requisitions and it is proper that an appropriation should now be made of the residue of the said taxes after payment of the aforesaid five hundred and sixty thousand three hundred and ninety-seven dollars to the use of the United States.

(Section XI, P. L.) Therefore, in order to provide an adequate fund for the payment of the annual interest aforesaid and for making the said annual payment to the representatives of the said Thomas Penn and Richard Penn,

[Section I.] Be it enacted and it is hereby enacted by the Representatives of the Freemen of the Commonwealth of Pennsylvania in General Assembly met, and by the authority of the same, That all and singular the moneys which [have] arisen from and since the first day of November last past, and which shall hereafter arise and be received by virtue and in pursuance of a certain act of the general assembly of this commonwealth made and past the twenty-third day of December, Anno Domini one thousand seven hundred and eighty, entitled 'An act for an impost on goods, wares and merchandize imported into this state',[1] and by virtue and in pursuance of one other act of the [said] general assembly, passed the twenty-fifth day of September, one thousand seven hundred and eighty-three, entitled 'A supplement to an act, entitled "An act for an impost on goods, wares and merchandize imported into this state",'[2] and by virtue and in pursuance of one other act of the said general assembly, passed the fifteenth day of March, one thousand seven hundred and eighty-four, entitled 'An act for raising a further impost or duty on all goods, wares or merchandize imported into this state',[3] together with the annual taxes hereinafter directed to be levied and collected, and the residue of the taxes which have been heretofore assessed by virtue of other acts of the general assembly enacted since the first day of January, one thousand seven hundred and eighty-two, and which now remain due and in arrears from divers citizens, inhabitants and estates in this commonwealth so far as the same are released from former appropriations as aforesaid, be and the said revenues and sources of revenue are hereby severally and respectively appropriated for and towards a fund for the purposes aforesaid and for such other purposes as are and shall be hereinafter mentioned and so shall remain, continue and be applied and to no other use, intent or purpose whatsoever, any former or other appropriation thereof or of any part thereof or any law, usage or custom to the contrary notwithstanding.

(Section XII, P. L.) And whereas some provision hath been made for making the first of the aforesaid annual payments to the representatives of the said Thomas Penn and Richard Penn, and to the widow of the said Thomas Penn:

[Section II.] Be it enacted by the authority aforesaid, That when and so often as the second and other subsequent payments shall become due to the said representatives it shall and may be lawful for the supreme executive council to cause such payments to be made out of the treasury of this state in gold or silver money at the rate or value in British sterling money of the coin in which such payments shall be made to such person or persons as shall apply for the same being authorized to receive such payments and to give the proper acquittance

[1] Passed December 23, 1780, *Statutes at Large of Pennsylvania*, ch. 925.
[2] Passed September 25, 1783, ibid. ch. 1051.
[3] Passed March 15, 1784, ibid. ch. 1076.

according to the tenor, true intent and meaning of the before recited act directing such payments to be made.

[Section III.] (Section XIII, P. L.) And be it further enacted by the authority aforesaid, That there shall be paid into the hands of the continental loan officer in this state yearly and every year from and after the termination of the year of our Lord one thousand seven hundred and eighty-four out of the treasury of this state at such times and in such quantities as the president or vice-president by warrant under his hand in council shall from time to time direct the sum of one hundred and twenty-three thousand nine hundred and thirty-two pounds, being the estimated quota of this state of the annual interest of the aggregate debt of the United States contracted during the late war or such other sum as shall from time to time appear to be the true proportion or quota of this state of the said annual interest during the continuance of the said debt, which warrants shall respectively be registered in the office of the comptroller-general of this state and the said loan-officer shall thereupon become answerable for the sums respectively mentioned in every such warrant.

[Section IV.] (Section XIV, P. L.) And be it further enacted by the authority aforesaid, That the said loan-officer shall and may pay with and out of such money's as he shall receive in each year as aforesaid, the lawful interest for one year on all such certificates of moneys loaned to the United States or other certificates of debts due from the United States, liquidated, ascertained and authenticated according to the directions of the United States in congress assembled or according to the laws of this state, as shall be demanded by the holders or possessors of such certificates respectively and such payments shall be indorsed on every such certificate: Provided always, That such certificates respectively were originally issued from the said loan-office or given or granted for articles furnished or for services done and performed during the late war by the citizens of this state or by officers or soldiers admitted and adopted as of the Pennsylvania line or quota of the troops of this state and in the name and for the use of such person or persons or some other who at the time of such issuing was or were or since hath [or have] been a citizen or citizens of this state by actual residence within the same, or in the name or for the use of a body politic or corporate within this state, and that there be the interest for one year at least due thereon. . . . And provided also, That loan-office certificates, received by any citizen of this state in payment for services performed or articles furnished for the use of the United States from any quarter-master, commissary or other officer of the United States, to whom the same were issued for that purpose in lieu of money shall also be entitled to the payment of interest by virtue of this act in whosoever name or names the same may have issued from the said loan-office. And provided also, That such of the aforesaid certificates as shall have been issued for the pay, arrearages of pay or commutation to the officers and soldiers aforesaid commonly called 'final settlements' shall not have been alienated or transferred but shall remain at the time of making the first demand of interest by virtue of this act really and bona fide the property of such person or persons in whose name or for whose use such certificates respectively were originally issued, or the property of the heirs, executors, administrators or legatees of such person or persons or the property by donation or legacy of a body politic or corporate or charitable institution which property shall be proved by the oath or affirmation of the person making such demand or the person in whose right the demand shall be made before the prothonotary of some one of the countries in this state (which oath or affirmation the said prothonotaries are hereby severally authorized to administer) within ninety days next before the making of such demand, which oath or affirmation shall be in writing signed by the party making the same and shall specify the date, number and sum mentioned in the certificate to which it relates, the name of the person or persons to whom issued, the name of the officer or commissioner who signed and issued the same and shall be delivered to the loan-officer to be filed at the time of making such demand of interest for which oath or affirmation and certificate the said prothonotary shall be entitled to demand and receive one shilling and no more. And provided also, That no certificate issued or to be issued by or from the office of the treasury of the United States commonly called the comptroller-general, register-general or auditor-general's office shall be entitled to draw interest by virtue of this act, unless it shall appear by the attestation of the said comptroller-general, register-general, auditor-general or other officer, who shall have signed and issued any such certificate, that neither the consideration on which such certificate was issued, nor any part thereof hath arisen from any debt or certificate of a debt which would not have entitled the bearer thereof to have drawn interest by virtue of this act. . . .

2.12 PENNSYLVANIA ESTABLISHES A LOAN OFFICE

'An act for erecting and opening a loan office for the sum of fifty thousand pounds.' 1785, *Statutes at Large of Pennsylvania*, vol. XI, ch. 1159, pp. 560–72

(Section I, P. L.) Whereas the inhabitants of this commonwealth have for a considerable time, labored, and yet do labor under great difficulties for want of a sufficient circulating medium of commerce, whereby agriculture, population and improvement are much obstructed, and many people [are] reduced to great distress:

(Section II, P. L.) And whereas by the happy termination of the late war the people of this state are in quiet possession of very extensive and valuable tracts of land, which require cultivation and improvement; and it is conceived that the institution of a loan office upon just and proper principles would greatly tend to promote and establish the interests of internal commerce, agriculture and mechanic arts, and the welfare of the people in general, within this state:

(Section III, P. L.) And whereas the sum of fifty thousand pounds of the bills of credit directed to be made and prepared by an act, entitled 'An act for furnishing the quota of this state towards paying the annual interest of the debts of the United States, and for funding and paying the interest of the public debts of this state';[1] are by the said act set apart, and appropriated for the purpose of erecting and establishing a loan office as the legislature should thereafter direct:

Therefore,

[Section IV, P. L.] Be it enacted and it is hereby enacted by the Representatives of the Freeman of the Commonwealth of Pennsylvania in General Assembly met, and by the authority of the same, That the said sum of fifty thousand pounds shall be paid into the hands of the commissioners of the loan-office herein after mentioned, at such times and in such quantities as the president or vice-president by warrant under his hand in council shall from time to time direct, which warrants, respectively, shall be registered in the comptroller-general's office, and the said commissioners of the loan-office shall thereupon become chargeable with and answerable for the sums

[1] Passed March 16, 1785, *Statutes at Large of Pennsylvania*, chapter 1137.

mentioned in the said warrants, respectively, to be appropriated and accounted for as herein after is directed.

[Section II.] (Section V, P. L.) That Joseph Dean, George Schlosser and Robert Smith, esquires, be and they are hereby appointed trustees of the general loan-office of the state of Pennsylvania. [*Editor's note:* bond, sureties and oath . . .]

[Section IV.] (Section VII, P. L.) That the said trustees shall be one body politic and corporate in law, and by the name of 'The trustees of the general loan office of the commonwealth of Pennsylvania', are hereby authorized and empowered to receive applications from borrowers, judge of and determine the value of the lands and tenements, rents and hereditaments, offered in mortgage, and the validity of their titles, to take and receive mortgages, give receipts for money received, take, hold and enjoy, to them and their successors in their said trust, all such lands, tenements, rents and hereditaments, as shall be granted them in mortgage; sell and dispose of estates forfeited, to sue, be sued, and defend any suit or suits brought against them, and generally, to do, perform and execute all and every act, matter and thing, necessary for the just and due performance and execution of the trust reposed in them by virtue of this act.

[Section V.] (Section VIII, P. L.) Provided always nevertheless, That it shall not be lawful to and for the said trustees or any of them, to emit on loan any of the said bills of credit on any land security, which shall lie in any of the counties (other than such counties where any of the said trustees shall reside) before a certificate, under the hands of the commissioners of the county, or any two of them, where such landed security is situate, certifying the value thereof, shall be produced to them, which said certificate the said commissioners, on application to them made, shall make out and deliver to the person applying, but before the said commissioners shall grant such certificate, they, and each of them, shall, before some justice of the peace of their county, take an oath or affirmation, 'That they will certify under their hands the value of all such lands and other hereditaments, particularly setting forth the persons names whose lands bounds the same, to the best of their knowledge, within the said county (having regard to the last assessment thereof) as they shall be requested, to certify by any person or persons intending to mortgage, as directed by this act', which certificates they shall deliver to the person applying, to be by him produced to the trustees of the general loan office, which said qualification shall be certified and deposited by the said justice, with the clerks of the county court of quarter sessions for the county for which such commissioners are chosen, to be by him filed and preserved, and that the said commissioners shall have and be paid, out of the interest arising on the loans made in pursuance of this act, the sum of three shillings and nine pence for each certificate, and no more, and that the said certificates shall be duly filed and preserved by the said trustees, for the inspection of the assembly and their committees.

[Section VI.] (Section IX, P. L.) Provided also, That none of the trustees herein before appointed, or hereafter to be appointed, according to the direction of this act, or any of them, or any of their heirs, executors or administrators, or securities hereby directed to be given, be acquitted or discharged for anything done, or suffered, in or about the trust hereby committed to them, until they have accounted for, and paid and delivered up to the succeeding trustees, all bills of credit, moneys, securities, books of accounts, and other writings, relating or belonging to the said loan-office, and so from time to time during the continuance of this act, anything herein before contained to the contrary notwithstanding.

[Section VII.] (Section X, P. L.) That the trustees shall lend out of the aforesaid sum of fifty thousand pounds, in the proportions herein after mentioned, for and during the space, and up to the full end and term of eight years, from the first day of August in the year of our Lord one thousand seven hundred and eighty-five, all which loans, made by virtue of this act, shall be in sums not exceeding one hundred pounds, nor less than twenty-five pounds, to any one person, upon mortgages of messuages, lands, tenements, rents and hereditaments, in this state, whereof the borrower stands seized in fee-simple, in his or her own right, free from incumbrances, rent-charges, becoming due thereon, and discovered to the said trustees, only excepted; and that the said trustees shall inform themselves, the best they can, of the validity of the titles, and of the clear value of all messuages, lands and ground rents, offered in security, so as to be satisfied that the lands and ground rents are held in fee-simple, and are at least of the value of the sums requested to be lent; and that as to the messuages erected upon ground subject to the payment of ground rent, offered in mortgage, care shall be taken by the said trustees that there be no rent in arrear at the time of receiving the same in mortgage, and that the ground shall be near equal in value, above the ground rent, to the sum lent, yet so that the house and ground be of three times the value thereof, for the better security of the mortgage money: And thereupon, the said trustees, in pursuance of the trust hereby committed to them, shall, in the name and style of 'The trustees of the general loan office of the commonwealth of Pennsylvania', and not otherwise, take and receive deeds of mortgage in fee-simple, of such messuages, lands, tenements, rents and hereditaments, with the appurtenances, to secure the repayment of sums they lent, to be [made] yearly, on the first day of November, by equal payments with the whole interest accrued, at the rate of six per centum per annum.

[Section VIII.] (Section XI, P. L.) That the said sum of fifty thousand pounds shall be emitted on loan by the trustees aforesaid, in the manner herein before directed, to the inhabitants of the several and respective counties within this state, in the following proportions, viz:

Eight thousand pounds to the inhabitants of the city and county of Philadelphia.

Three thousand three hundred pounds to the inhabitants of the county of Bucks.

Five thousand eight hundred pounds to the inhabitants of the county of Chester.

Six thousand five hundred pounds to the inhabitants of the counties of Lancaster and Dauphin.

Four thousand eight hundred pounds to the inhabitants of the county of York.

Three thousand pounds to the inhabitants of the county of Cumberland.

Two thousand six hundred pounds to the inhabitants of the county of Northampton.

Three thousand six hundred pounds to the inhabitants of the county of Berks.

One thousand nine hundred pounds to the inhabitants of the county of Bedford.

One thousand eight hundred pounds to the inhabitants of the county of Northumberland.

One thousand two hundred and seventy pounds to the inhabitants of the county of Westmoreland.

Two thousand one hundred pounds to the inhabitants of the county of Washington.

One thousand three hundred and thirty pounds to the inhabitants of the county of Fayette.

Two thousand pounds to the inhabitants of the county of Franklin.

Two thousand pounds to the inhabitants of the county of Montgomery.

(Section XII, P. L.) Provided always, That if there shall not within the space of six months next after the first opening of the loan office by virtue of this act be applications for the said respective proportions of money from the inhabitants of the counties respectively, then and in such cases it shall and may be lawful for the said trustees to lend out the surplus thereof to such person or persons as shall apply for the same in the manner and on the sureties aforesaid.

(Section XIII, P. L.) Provided also, That if any mortgagor of any messuages, lands or rents, mortgaged in pursuance of this act, his heirs, executors, administrators or assigns, shall be inclined to pay off and discharge his mortgage and security, at any other time, than according to the time specified in his mortgage-deed, it shall be lawful for him or them so to do, by paying down the whole principal sums due, and to become due, together with the interest and charges then accrued, on the first day of November in any years, during the continuance of this Act.

[Section IX.] (Section XIV, P. L.) That the principal sums, and all and singular the parts, parcels and quotas thereof, or any of them, payable to the Trustees of the said General Loan Office, by any mortgagor or person whatsoever, shall not be paid into the Treasury of this state at any other time than by this present Act is directed, limited and appointed, any law, custom or usage to the contrary notwithstanding, but the same principal sums hereafter to be recovered or received by the said Trustees on or before the first day of November in the year of our Lord One thousand seven hundred and eighty-nine shall be, from time to time again lent out on securities, as hereinbefore directed for the residue of the aforesaid term of eight years; and also so often as any mortgage moneys, directed to be again lent out as aforesaid shall be recovered or received before the aforesaid first day of November One thousand seven hundred and eighty-nine, the principal moneys thence arising shall in like manner from time to time be lent out again on the like securities as aforesaid; and the said Trustees, or some of them, shall weekly attend at their office in Philadelphia on Tuesdays and Wednesdays until the aforesaid sum of fifty thousand pounds of the said bills of credit, hereby directed to be appropriated as aforesaid shall be wholly lent out as this act directs, and afterwards on the second Tuesday in October, December, February, April, June and August, and every year during the continuance of this act and at such other times as their duty and trust shall require.

[Section X.] (Section XV, P. L.) That all and every of the said deeds of mortgage shall be fairly entered in books of large paper, to be provided by the said trustees, attested copies of which deeds so entered and certified by the said trustees, or any of them, for the time being, shall be, and are hereby declared to be good evidence to prove the mortgages thereby mentioned to be made, and every of the aforesaid deeds of mortgage shall be indorsed or added an oath or affirmation, to be taken by the mortgagor or mortgagors, before some of the said trustees, or some justice of the peace, who are hereby empowered and required to administer the same, 'That he, she or they, is or are seized of the hereditaments and premises thereby granted, in his, her or their own right, and to his her or their own use, and that free from all arrearages of rent, and from any former gift, grant, sale, mortgage, judgment or any other encumbrance, to the knowledge of such mortgagor or mortgagors, except only such as are by him, hers or them, particularly mentioned and discovered to the trustees:' And the aforesaid deeds, being so executed and acknowledged, shall transfer the possession, and vest the inheritance, of and in such mortgaged premises, to and in the said trustees, and their successors, as fully and effectually as deeds of foeffment, with livery and seizin, or deeds enrolled in any of the courts of this state, may or can do; in all which deeds, the words grant, bargain and sell, shall be adjudged, in all places and courts whatsoever within this state, to have the force and effect of a covenant, that the mortgageor, notwithstanding any act done by him, was, at the time of execution of such deed, seized of the hereditaments and premises thereby granted, of an indefeasible estate of inheritance free from encumbrances, the rents, so as aforesaid discovered or to be discovered to the said trustees, only excepted.

Section XI. (Section XVI, P. L.) That together with every of the aforesaid mortgage deeds, the respective mortgagor shall execute a bond of double the mortgage money to the trustees aforesaid, conditioned for the payment of the money borrowed, with interest, according to the proviso or condition contained in each such mortgage deed, and also a warrant of attorney, empowering such person or persons as the said trustees shall appoint to confess or suffer judgment, which the said trustees are hereby required to cause their attorney to enter, in any of the courts of common pleas of this state, against such mortgagor as shall make default in payment of the mortgage moneys, or any part thereof, on the said bonds or mortgages, for non-performance of the conditions thereof, or in such actions of debt as the said trustees are required to bring for the value of the said bills of credit or moneys received by the mortgagors, whose titles shall happen to prove defective, together with the interest and costs of suits, in every which warrant of attorney, shall be inserted a release of errors by the mortgagor.

(Section XVII, P. L.) Provided [always] nevertheless, That until some default be made in payment of some part of the mortgage moneys, by the mortgagors respectively, it shall and may be lawful to and for them, and their heirs, to hold and enjoy the mortgaged premises, anything in this act, or in the mortgage deeds, to the contrary notwithstanding, but if default shall be made or suffered in payment of any part of the mortgage moneys aforesaid, whether of the principal or interest, which the mortgagors, their heirs, executors, administrators or assigns should or ought to pay according to the days of payment aforesaid, in their respective deeds of mortgage specified, the said trustees, after six months next following such default made as aforesaid, shall issue their precept to the sheriff of the county where the mortgaged premises shall lie, commanding him to enter upon the messuages, lands, rents and hereditaments, respectively, in the deeds of mortgage specified, and the same, or such part thereof as shall be sufficient to discharge and satisfy the mortgage moneys, with the interest thereof, and costs accruing on the sale, to sell on the premises, by public auction or vendue, and convey to the highest bidder, after at least thirty days' public notice given of such sale, by advertising them in the newspapers, and by affixing advertisements in some of the most public places in the county; and out of the moneys arising by such sale, to raise the principal sums due and to become due, with the interests, costs and charges accrued, returning the overplus, if any, to the owners of such lands and hereditaments, and also to pay and deliver the said principal sums and interest, to the said trustees, for the use of the state, which said precept the said sheriff is hereby enjoined and required fully and impartially to execute, for which he shall have the same fees for advertising and sale, as are allowed by law for like services where lands are sold by [a writ of] venditioni exponas, and no more.

[Section XII.] (Section XVIII, P. L.) That the mortgagor and mortgagors of all such lands, as shall be sold by virtue of this act, shall stand and be foreclosed of and from all right of redemption of the same.

[Section XIII.] (Section XIX, P. L.) That the said trustees shall indorse upon each mortgage deed, their receipts of all their yearly quotas, paid by the respective mortgagors, distinguishing the principal sum from the interest, which they shall also note on the counter parts to them produced, when required; and upon the last payment thereof, the said trustees shall enter in the margin of the enrolment of the mortgage deed, the time of the discharge thereof, for which they shall receive of the mortgagor one shilling, and no more: And the said trustees shall keep distinct, fair and true accounts of all the sums they receive by virtue of this act, and of what they lend, emit or pay, by virtue hereof, or by the orders of the assembly, in regular day-books, journals and ledgers, to be fairly kept for those purposes, and shall exhibit the same, together with their other vouchers, to the committees of assembly appointed for settling the public accounts, who shall settle and adjust the said accounts, and report the same to the house.

[Section XIV.] (Section XX, P. L.) That the said trustees shall have and receive, for the services enjoined and required of them by this act, the sum of four hundred and fifty pounds per annum, during the continuance of their re-emitting on mortgage as aforesaid, and the sum of one hundred and fifty pounds per annum, during the further continuance of this act, and no more, out of the interest money which shall come to their hands by virtue of this act.

[Section XV.] (Section XXI, P. L.) That if it shall appear on the settlement of the accounts of the said trustees by the said committees, and a confirmation thereof by the house of assembly, that any deficiency hath happened by any borrower or mortgagor not having right to the lands or tenements mortgaged, or in the value thereof, or by any other ways or means whatsoever, to pay the moneys and the interest accrued thereon, with the cost of such suits as shall be prosecuted for the same, then, and in every such case, the said trustees, having an order from the assembly for that purpose, shall draw an order on the treasurer of the county in which such deficiencies shall happen, for the payment of such deficiencies, if so much money shall be then in the treasury, and if not, the said trustees shall and they are hereby authorized and empowered to issue their precept to the commissioners and assessors of the said county, enjoining them to cause the said deficiencies so happening, with such costs and charges as shall accrue and be paid by the said trustees in endeavoring to recover the same, forthwith to be assessed, raised and levied, of and upon the county, in the same manner, by the same persons, and under the same pains, penalties and forfeitures, as other county rates are by law directed to be assessed, raised and levied, which the said commissioners and assessors are hereby enjoined and required to do, and the said deficiencies, when so levied, shall be paid to the said trustees, in order to replace the moneys so deficient.

[Section XVI.] (Section XXII, P. L.) [Penalty of £100 for neglect of duty.]

[Section XVII.] (Section XXIII, P. L.) [Accounts to be exhibited.]

(Section XXIV, P. L.) And the better to prevent inconveniences arising from indulging the mortgagors to be behind in their payments hereby directed to be made:

[Section XVIII.] That the trustees for the time being, shall, and they are hereby required to keep the mortgagors aforesaid up to their annual payments as by this act is directed and appointed, and the committees of assembly to be annually appointed to audit the said trustees' accounts, are hereby directed not to allow of any quotas in arrear and unpaid, which have been due twelve months at the time of settlement, but to consider and report the same as moneys in the hands of the said trustees for which the said trustees shall be accountable, excepting only such sums, for which the trustees have commenced suits, or otherwise have proceeded, according to the direction of this act, for the recovery of the money due.

[Section XIX.] (Section XXV, P. L.) That if any of the said trustees herein before appointed, or hereafter to be appointed by virtue of this act, shall neglect or refuse to act as trustee, or shall happen to die, or be removed for misfeasance in his office, some other fit person shall be appointed by the general assembly of this state in the place or places of such trustee or trustees unless such neglect, refusal, death or removal shall happen during the recess of assembly, in which case and not otherwise, some other fit person or persons shall be appointed by the supreme executive council of this state, and the said trustee or trustees, so to be appointed, shall have, hold and exercise the same powers and authorities to all intents and purposes as if he or they were appointed by this act.

(Section XXVI, P. L.) Provided always, That none of the said trustees, appointed in and by virtue of this act shall continue in the exercise of their said offices longer than the space of three years from the time of the commencement of their said trust, and from thence until a new nomination and appointment of the same or other trustees shall be made by the general assembly, anything in this act to the contrary notwithstanding.

[Section XX.] (Section XXVII, P. L.) That the said trustee shall, for the better regulating of their said office, choose and employ a fit and able person for their clerk, during their pleasure, for whom they shall be answerable, who shall prepare the deeds of mortgage, with the mortgageors' affidavits, bonds, warrants of attorney, and releases of errors, and shall have and receive the following fees, and no more, viz: For every mortgage deed, recording the same, the counterpart or copy thereof, the mortgagor's oath or affirmation indorsed on the mortgage deed, and the bond warrant of attorney and release of errors, the sum of twenty shillings, and no more, to be paid by the said mortgagor, and the said clerk shall keep true accounts of the names of all persons applying to borrow on securities, as this act directs, and shall record their deeds of mortgage, in the same order of time as they were executed, and shall once in each year, make out a list of the names of all mortgagors, with the sums they borrow, and date of their mortgage deeds, and the same lists shall transmit or deliver to the committees of assembly to be appointed to settle the said trustees accounts, but before any person so chosen to be clerk, shall enter upon the execution of his office, he shall take an oath or affirmation before some justice of the peace, 'That he will truly and faithfully perform the office and duty directed and required of him by this act, [wherein he will give] no undue preference or unnecessary delays, or be guilty of any fraudulent practice.'

Passed April 4, 1785. Recorded L. B. No. 2, p. 503. See the Acts of Assembly passed September 10, Statutes at Large of Pennsylvania, 1755, *ch. 1174; November 27, 1787, ibid. ch. 1328; April 1, 1790, ibid. ch 1506; April 7, 1791, ibid. ch. 1554.*

2.13 PENNSYLVANIA ENACTS A PROTECTIVE TARIFF, 1785

'An act to encourage and protect the manufactures of this state by laying additional duties on the importation of certain manufactures which interfere with them.' 1785, *Statutes at Large of Pennsylvania*, vol. XII, ch. 1188, pp. 99–104

(Section I. P. L.) Whereas divers useful and beneficial arts and manufactures have been gradually introduced into Pennsylvania, and the same have at length risen to a very considerable extent and perfection, insomuch that during the late war between the United States of America and Great Britain when the importation of European goods was much interrupted and often very difficult and uncertain, the artizans and mechanics of this state were able to supply in the hours of need not only large quantities of weapons and other implements but also ammunition and clothing, without which the war could not have been carried on, whereby their oppressed country was greatly assisted and relieved:

(Section II. P.L.) And whereas, although the fabrics and manufactures of Europe and other foreign parts imported into this country in times of peace may be afforded at cheaper rates than they can be made here yet good policy and a regard to the well being of divers useful and industrious citizens who are employed in the making of like goods in this state demand of us that moderate duties be laid on certain fabrics and manufacturers imported, which do most interfere with and which (if no relief be given) will undermine and destroy the useful manufacturers of the like kind in this country:

For this purpose:

[Section I.] (Section III. P.L.) Be it enacted and it is hereby enacted by the Representatives of the Freemen of the Commonwealth of Pennsylvania in General Assembly met and by the authority of the same, That further and additional duties as hereinafter specified shall be levied, collected and paid on the importation into this state of certain goods, wares and merchandise enumerated and particularized in this act, of foreign product, growth or manufacture; and the same duties shall be collected, secured and paid in like manner for like continuance as the impost of two and a half per centum is or shall be collected, secured and paid subject to like regulations, seizure[s] and forfeiture[s] and entitled to like drawbacks upon re-exportation, and the collector of the port of Philadelphia shall be subject to like account and responsibility for the same: That is to say:

Upon any coach, chariot or landau or other carriage having four wheels, the sum of twenty pounds.

Upon every chaise, chair, kittereen, curricle or other carriage having two wheels, ten pounds; and in the same proportion for any parts of such carriages.

Upon every clock, thirty shillings.

Upon every dozen packs of playing cards, seven shillings and six-pence.

Upon every dozen reaping hooks and sickles, twelve shillings.

Upon every dozen scythes, except dutch and german, fifteen shillings.

Upon every hundredweight of refined sugar, eight shillings and four pence.

Upon every gallon of beer, ale, porter and cider, six pence.

Upon every dozen bottles of beer, ale porter or cider, four shillings.

Upon all malted barley or other malted grain, five per centum ad valorem.

Upon all salted or dried fish, seven shillings and six pence for every hundred weight thereof.

Upon every hundredweight of cheese and butter, eight shillings and four pence.

Upon all beef, two per centum ad valorem.

Upon all pork, five per centum ad valorem.

Upon every pound of soap, except castile soap, one penny.

Upon every pound of chocolate, four pence.

Upon every pound of candles of tallow or wax, one penny.

Upon every pound of glue, two pence.

Upon every pound of starch and of hair powder, one penny.

Upon all hulled barley, dried peas and mustard, ten per centum ad valorem.

Upon all manufactured tobacco other than snuff, six pence for every pound thereof.

Upon every pound of snuff including the bottles, canister, or other package, one shilling.

Upon all lamp black, cotton and wool cards, manufactured leather, pasteboards, parchment, writing, printing, wrapping and sheathing paper, and paper hangings, ten per centum ad valorem.

Upon every pair of men's and women's leathern shoes, two shillings.

Upon every pair of women's silken shoes, or slippers, two shillings and six pence.

Upon every pair of women's stuff shoes or slippers, one shilling.

Upon every pair of boots, five shillings.

Upon every saddle for men's or women's use, twelve shillings and sixpence.

Upon every ounce of wrought gold, twenty shillings.

Upon every ounce of wrought silver, two shillings.

Upon all utensils and vessels of pewter, tin or lead, upon all wrought copper, brass, bell-metal, and cast iron, ten per centum ad valorem.

Upon all british steel, ten per centum ad valorem.

Upon all slit iron, nail rods, and sheet iron, ten per centum ad valorem.

Upon all garments ready made for men's or women's wear, including castor and wool hats, ten per centum ad valorem.

Upon every beaver hat, seven shillings and sixpence.

Upon all blank books, bound or unbound, ten per centum ad valorem.

Upon all tarred cordage, yarns, or fixed rigging, eight shillings and four pence, for every hundred weight thereof.

Upon all white ropes, log-lines, twine and seines, twelve shillings and sixpence, for every hundredweight thereof.

Upon all polished or cut stones in imitation of jewelry, chimney pieces and tables, and other polished marble; upon all cabinet and joiner's work, horsemen's whips, carriage whips, walking canes, musical instruments, and instruments used in surveying, ten per centum ad valorem.

Upon all stone and earthen ware, ten per centum ad valorem.

Upon all panes, plates, vessels and utensils of british glass, two and a half per centum ad valorem.

Upon all teas imported from Europe, or the west-indies, viz; upon every pound of hyson tea, sixpence, upon every pound of other tea, two pence.

Upon all rum imported in any vessel belonging to any foreign state or kingdom, sixpence for every gallon thereof, and the like sum upon all rum imported into this state by land or water from any of the

United States except it should be made [to] appear by the oath of the exporter, certified by the collector of the port from whence it may be last shipped, that it was distilled in the state from whence it be imported, or that it has been imported into that state by vessels belonging to the United States.

Upon all wines and fruit, being of the growth of the Kingdom of Portugal or of the territories thereunto belonging, viz; upon all wines, one shilling for every gallon thereof; upon every box of lemons, five shillings; upon every hundred weight of raisins or other fruit, seven shillings and six pence, the said duties to continue so long as the flour of America is prohibited from being imported into the kingdom and territories aforesaid.

Upon every ton of shipping belonging in whole or in part to any foreign nation or state whatever except such as the honorable the Congress of the United States have entered into treaties of commerce with, seven shillings and sixpence for every ton thereof, capenters measure, for each and every voyage.

Upon all ready made sails, ten per centum ad valorem.

Upon all testaments, psalters, spelling books and primers, in the english and german languages; upon all romances, novels and plays, to fifteen per centum ad valorem.

Upon all horn and tortoise-shell combs, five per centum ad valorem.

Upon all saddle-trees, ten per centum ad valorem.

Upon all linens made of flax, two and a half per centum ad valorem.

And the same imposts and every of them shall become due and payable to the commonwealth in manner as is herein before specified and directed from and after the first day of the year one thousand seven hundred and eighty-six.

[Section II.] (Section IV. P. L.) And be it further enacted by the authority aforesaid, That all tin in pigs and tinned plates, lead, pewter, brass, copper in pigs and in plates, cocoa, molasses, sheep's wool, cotton wool, hemp, flax, all dying woods and dying drugs, whale oil and other fish oil, skins and hides shall [be] from and after the passing of this act exonerated and discharged of all impost and duty upon the importation of them or any of them from any place whatsoever; and that the hundredweight herein before mentioned shall be deemed to be one hundred avoirdupois, containing one hundred and twelve pounds.

[Section III.] (Section V. P. L.) And be it further enacted by the authority aforesaid, That a separate account shall be kept of the product and amount of the revenue which shall become payable to the commonwealth out of and from the additional imposts declared and enacted by this act, and the same shall be rendered to the comptroller general of this state and to the general assembly and the president or vice-president in council, in like manner as the former impost laws have directed concerning the former impost revenue.

Section IV. (Section VI. P. L.) [sic.] And be it further enacted by the authority aforesaid, That an additional impost of five per centum ad valorem in like manner as is herein before directed shall be levied, collected and paid to the use of this commonwealth on the importation into this state by land or by water of all foreign manufactures of refined iron or of refined iron and steel or of steel not otherwise especially rated and charged in and by this act, except wire, files, tinned plates and [Dutch or] German scythes and cutting knives; and an impost in like manner of seven and an half per centum ad valorem on all foreign made carpenter's work, blocks for shipping and sheeves for ship use and upon all foreign leather as well tawed as tanned leather, not otherwise herein before rated and charged and upon all turner's work and turner's wares; and that the collector of the port of Philadelphia shall be responsible for the same and shall [pay] over the moneys which shall come to his hands therefrom to the treasurer of this commonwealth and that he shall account for the same in like manner and to like effect as is provided by law concerning the former impost revenues of this state.

Passed September 20, 1785. Recorded L. B. no. 3, p. 44, etc.

See the Act of Assembly passed December 24, 1785, Statutes at Large of Pennsylvania, *ch. 1198; April 8, 1786, ibid. ch. 1227; September 26, 1786, ibid. ch. 1254; March 15, 1787, ibid. ch. 1276; March 29, 1788, ibid. ch. 1346.*

2.14 PENNSYLVANIA ACTS FURTHER TO RELIEVE ITS CITIZENS WHO ARE CREDITORS OF THE UNITED STATES

'An act for the further relief of the public creditors who are citizens of this state by receiving on loan certain debts of the United States of America and for funding the same and for paying the annual interest of such loans and the interest of certain debts of this state every six months', *Statutes at Large of Pennsylvania*, 1786, vol. XII, ch. 1202, pp. 158–64

(Section I. P. L.) Whereas by an act of the general assembly of this commonwealth passed on the sixteenth day of March in the year of our Lord one thousand seven hundred and eighty-five, entitled 'An act for furnishing the quota of this state towards paying the annual interest of the debts of the United States and for funding and paying the interest of the public debts of this State',[1] provision was made amongst other things for enabling the continental loan officer in this state to pay the annual interest of certain debts of the United States due to the citizens of this state on the certificates in the said act set forth and described.

And whereas the United States in Congress Assembled by act bearing date the twenty-seventh day of September in the year of our Lord one thousand seven hundred and eighty-five have made such regulations concerning the payment of the said interest as to render it expedient to continue the payment of the same in the manner directed by the aforesaid act of this state.

And whereas it is just and proper that the patriotic citizens of this state who in the late arduous conflict yielded their property and their personal services to the public use and thereby eminently contributed to the establishment of the peace, liberty and safety of the United States of America should be relieved as far as circumstances will admit from bearing an undue proportion of the public burden which ought to rest equally on all citizens.

[Section I.] (Section II. P. L.) Be it therefore enacted and it is hereby enacted by the Representatives of the Freemen of the Commonwealth of Pennsylvania in General Assembly met and by the authority

[1] *Statutes at Large of Pennsylvania*, ch. 1137.

of the same, That the treasurer of this state be and he is hereby authorized and directed to procure at the public expense a competent number of blank certificates printed on thin paper resembling that of the continental loan office certificates with proper checks and devices to guard against counterfeits, and with a large margin or counterpart sufficient to contain a memorandum of the essential circumstances of the debts to be thereby secured respectively and of the annual payments of interest which shall have been made thereon, which certificates so to be procured shall severally be signed by the said treasurer and by him delivered to the comptroller general of this state to be filled up, numbered, registered, countersigned and delivered out as herein after is directed, and the said blank certificates shall severally contain the words following viz: The commonwealth of Pennsylvania hath received on loan from the sum of , to be paid to the said or bearer on or before the first day of March in the year of our Lord one thousand seven hundred and ninety-six with interest from the day of at the rate of six per centum per annum to be paid half yearly at the state treasury according to the directions of an act of the general assembly passed on the day of

Section II. (Section III. P. L.) And be it further enacted by the authority aforesaid, That the comptroller general of this state be and he is hereby authorized and directed to receive on loan in behalf of the state such certificates of the debts due from the United States of America as are herein after described, and no other and to issue and deliver in lieu thereof to the person or persons who shall before the first day of March which shall be in the year of our Lord one thousand seven hundred and eighty-eight voluntarily make such loan or loans a certificate or certificates (of those hereinbefore described) to the amount of or value of the sum or sums due as principal money on the certificate and certificates which he shall [so] receive on loan, expressing the period from which the said principal sum is entitled to draw interest according to the tenor and terms of the certificate or certificates so received on loan. . . .

[Section III.] (Section IV. P. L.) That the certificates so to be received on loan as aforesaid shall be such loan office certificates and other certificates of the debts of the United States of America and no other whereof the holders severally were entitled to receive the annual interest thereon respectively accruing from the loan office of the United States of America for this state by virtue of the act of the sixteenth day of March last hereinbefore recited.

(Section V. P. L.) Provided nevertheless, That no certificate of a debt or balance due to any person or persons on the books of the treasury of the United States now commonly called funded debts shall be received as aforesaid unless it be accompanied with a proper attestation from the register general of the United States of America or other proper officer having the custody of the said books that the consideration on which such debt did arise and every part thereof was originally of such kind and quality as is within the true intent and meaning of the debts hereinbefore described which are entitled to the benefit of this act nor unless such certificate be accompanied with a regular transfer or power to make such transfer to the commonwealth of Pennsylvania. And provided also, That such of the aforesaid Loan Office certificates as bear date on or after the first day of March in the year of our Lord one thousand seven hundred and seventy-eight shall be accounted and received for so much and no more as the sums expressed therein amount to in specie value according to the scale of depreciation established by the United States of America for ascertaining the value of such certificates.

(Section VI. P. L.) And whereas certain of the loan office certificates aforesaid which bear date between the first day of September in the year of our Lord one thousand seven hundred and seventy-seven and the first day of March in the year of our Lord one thousand seven hundred and seventy-eight are subject to liquidation by the aforesaid scale of depreciation on the final redemption and payment of the principal sums thereof respectively althought the possessors of the same certificates be entitled to receive the annual interest thereof at full value on the nominal sums therein expressed until such redemption and payment of the principal be made; and it may be necessary to distinguish and set forth this particularity on the certificates to be given for loans to be made as aforesaid in such certificates in order that the proper liquidation of the principal moneys thereof may be made on the final payment and discharge of the same.

[Section IV.] (Section VII. P. L.) That on every certificate which shall be issued as aforesaid for loans which shall be made in the continental loan office certificates last herein described shall be written the number, date and sum mentioned in every such continental loan office certificate as shall be received as the consideration for the certificates of this state so to be issued respectively, and such certificates shall be subject to such liquidation on the payment of the principal as the said continental certificates are now subject to.

[Section V.] (Section VIII. P. L.) That the treasurer of this state for the time being be and he is hereby authorized and required twice in every year to pay with and out of the aggregate fund provided by the aforesaid act of the sixteenth day of March in the year of our Lord one thousand seven hundred and eighty-five the interest for six months accrued on all such debts due from this state as shall be ascertained and established by certificates so as aforesaid to be made and issued by virtue of this act which payments of interest shall commence on the first day of April and October respectively in each year and be made to the holders or possessors of such certificates respectively, and the said treasurer is hereby required and directed to take receipts and account for such payments and to proceed in the payment of the arrearages of interest on the said certificates in such manner as is directed in and by the before recited act, enacted on the sixteenth day of March one thousand seven hundred and eighty-five, respecting the payments to be made by virtue of the said act. Provided that in the first of the said payments of interest on the certificates to be issued by virtue of this act the said treasurer shall and he is hereby directed to pay the interest for one whole year.

Section VI. (Section IX. P. L.) [Records of certificates issued to be kept by comptroller-general.]

Section VII. (Section X. P. L.) And be it further enacted by the authority aforesaid, That the said comptroller-general shall from time to time as occasion shall require present all such certificates of debts due from the United States of America as shall so as aforesaid or otherwise come into his hands and custody for the use of the state to the officer appointed by the United States of America to pay the interest which shall be due thereon in the manner after which the same interest is or shall be directed to be paid by the United States of America and on receipt of such interest in money or in certificates he shall note every such payment and registry aforesaid and pay the same over to the treasurer of the state taking the receipt of the said treasurer for and making him chargeable with the amount thereof and the said treasurer shall pay the same to the officer appointed and authorized to receive such payment in behalf of the United States of America in order that the same may be duly allowed and passed to the credit of this state.

[Section VIII.] (Section XI. P. L.) That the new certificates when procured and issued as hereinbefore is directed shall be and the same are hereby made and declared to be receivable in the land office of this state in the same manner, in similar cases and to like purposes and effect as the certificates of debts due by this state and as the certificates for debts due by the United States of America to the citizens of this state were receivable in the same office before the publication of this act except for lands especially appropriated for the redemption of depreciation certificates.

[Section IX.] (Section XII. P. L.) That the interest on all certificates of this state which have been issued by virtue of the act of the first of April in the year of our Lord one thousand seven hundred and eighty-four, entitled[1] 'An act to enable the comptroller-general to issue certificates for the balances due on the accounts of the ranging companies raised for the defense of the frontiers and other accounts due to the citizens of this state', and by one other act of the general assembly of the thirteenth day of March in the year of our Lord one thousand seven hundred and eighty-five, entitled 'An act for the relief of such persons as have debts due to them from the estates of persons attainted of treason and confiscated in the [late] war and for other purposes therein mentioned,'[2] and for the annual payment of which interest by the treasurer of this state provision hath been made by the said act of the sixteenth [day] of March in the year of our Lord one thousand seven hundred and eighty-five shall after the next annual payment of interest thereon be thenceforth paid half-yearly by the treasurer of this state in manner aforesaid and that the arrearages of interest due upon such certificates before the first of January next shall be paid by the said treasurer as directed by the same act of the sixteenth day of March in the year of our Lord one thousand seven hundred and eighty-five.

[Section X.] (Section XIII. P. L.) That the interest of the certificates which have been funded on the revenue arising from the excise on wines and spirituos liquors by the act of general assembly, entitled 'An act to appropriate certain moneys arising from the excise for the payment of the annual interest on unalienated certificates therein

[1] *Statutes at Large of Pennsylvania.* ch. 1100.

[2] Ibid., ch. 1149.

mentioned,'[1] of the twenty-first day of March in the year of our Lord one thousand seven hundred and eighty-three and other subsequent acts of assembly shall in like manner from and after the tenth day of April next be payable by the treasurer half-yearly to the holders of the said certificates respectively.

Passed 1st of March 1786. Recorded L. B. no. 3, p. 74.

2.15 NEW YORK ISSUES A PAPER CURRENCY: 1786

'An act for emitting the sum of two hundred thousand pounds in bills of credit for the purposes therein mentioned,' passed the 18th April, 1786, *Laws of New York State*, 1785–8, *Ninth Session*, vol. II, ch. 40, pp. 253–72

Whereas from the distresses occasioned by the late calamitous war the inhabitants of this State labour under great difficulties for want of a sufficient circulating medium.

I. *Be it enacted by the People of the State of New York represented in Senate and Assembly, and it is hereby enacted by the authority of the same,* That bills of credit to the value of two hundred thousand pounds current money of New York forthwith after the passing hereof be printed as follows (vizt.) Six thousand bills each of the value of ten pounds four thousand bills each of the value of five pounds six thousand bills each of the value of four pounds ten thousand bills each of the value of three pounds ten thousand bills each of the value of two pounds twenty four thousand bills each of the value of one pound twenty thousand bills each of the value of ten shillings and forty eight thousand bills each of the value of five shillings upon which bills shall be impressed the arms of the State of New York on the right side of every of the said bills; and the said bills shall be in the words following By a law of the State of New York this bill shall be received in all payments into the treasury for New York the day of , one thousand seven hundred and eighty six. Which bills shall be numbered by Evert Bancker, Henry Remsen Jonathan Lawrence John De Peyster and William Heyer and signed by any two of them and shall by such signers be delivered to the treasurer of this State.

[1] Ibid., ch. 1024.

II. *And be it further enacted by the authority aforesaid* That the said signers are hereby directed and empowered upon the delivery to them of the said bills by the printer thereof to administer to him and he is hereby directed to take an oath in the words following I do solemnly swear and declare that from the time the letters were set and fit to be put in the press for printing the bills of credit now delivered by me to you, until the bills were printed, and the letters afterwards distributed into the boxes I went at no time out of the room in which the said letters were without locking them up so as they could not be come at without violence a false key or other art unknown to me, and therefore, to the best of my knowledge, no copies were printed off but in my presence, and that all the blotters and other papers whatsoever impressed by the said letters whilst set for printing the said bills, to the best of my knowledge are here delivered to you together with the stamps; and in all things relating to this affair I have well and truly demeaned myself according to the true intent and meaning of the law in that case made and provided to the best of my knowledge and understanding, so help me God. Which printer shall have a copy of this oath at the time he gets orders to print the said bills that he may govern himself accordingly *provided always* that if any unforseen accident happens, such printer may have liberty to make an exception thereof in such oath declaring fully how such accident happened. And if any more of the said bills are printed than by this act is directed when the said Evert Bancker, Henry Remsen Jonathan Lawrence John De Peyster and William Heyer or any two of them, have signed the number hereby directed to be issued they shall immediately destroy all the remainder.

III. *And be it enacted by the authority aforesaid* That such person as the major part of the said signers of the said bills of credit shall agree with shall engrave according to the directions he shall receive from the majority of the said signers so many stamps for the sides of the said bills and for the arms of this State as the majority of the said signers shall deem necessary and shall deliver them to the treasurer who shall in the presence of the majority of the said signers deliver them unto Samuel Loudon printer, and take his receipt for the same: And when the said Samuel Loudon has finished and completed printing the bills hereby directed to be struck and issued he shall re-deliver the said stamps to the said signers who are hereby directed and required to seal them up with their several seals, and to deliver them to the treasurer who shall deposit the same in the treasury of this State there to remain until they shall be ordered to be made use of by any future act of the legislature and the receipt of the said treasurer to the said signers shall be a sufficient discharge for such delivery but in the case of the death, sickness or inability of the said Samuel Loudon to print the said bills, then the majority of the said signers shall appoint another printer for the service aforesaid in his place which printer so appointed shall take the oath as above directed.

IV. *And be it enacted by the authority aforesaid* That before the said signers do receive any of the said bills they shall (before any of the magistrates of the city of New York) respectively take an oath or (if of the people called Quakers) affirmation well and truly to perform what by this act they are enjoined as their duty and that they will not knowingly sign more bills of credit than such as are directed by this act.

V. *And be it further enacted by the authority aforesaid* That the said treasurer shall, out of the bills of credit so signed and numbered as aforesaid deliver to the loan officers herein after mentioned on producing the certificates of qualifications herein after directed the sums and quota's following to wit.

To the loan officers of the county of New York, to and for the purposes herein after mentioned the sum of thirty two thousand pounds.

To the loan officers of the county of Albany to and for the purposes herein after mentioned the sum of twenty two thousand pounds.

To the loan officers of Kings county to and for the purposes herein after mentioned the sum of four thousand five hundred pounds.

To the loan officers of Queens county to and for the purposes herein after mentioned the sum of eleven thousand five hundred pounds.

To the loan officers of Suffolk county to and for the purposes herein after mentioned the sum of ten thousand pounds.

To the loan officers of Richmond county to and for the purposes herein after mentioned the sum of four thousand five hundred pounds.

To the loan officers of West Chester county to and for the purposes herein after mentioned the sum of nine thousand five hundred pounds.

To the loan officers of Dutchess county to and for the purposes herein after mentioned the sum of seventeen thousand pounds.

To the loan officers of Orange county to and for the purposes herein after mentioned the sum of ten thousand pounds.

To the loan officers of Ulster county, to and for the purposes herein after mentioned the sum of fourteen thousand pounds.

To the loan officers of Montgomery county to and for the purposes herein after mentioned the sum of twelve thousand pounds.

To the loan officers of the county of Washington to and for the purposes herein after mentioned the sum of three thousand pounds.

For which respective sums, the said loan officers respectively shall give receipts to the said treasurer indorsed on the clerks certificate herein after directed: which receipts shall be to the said treasurer, his executors and administrators, a sufficient discharge if otherwise he has well and truly performed the duty enjoined by this act.

VI. *And be it further enacted by the authority aforesaid,* That before the said loan officers do respectively enter upon their said office, every of them shall give bond to the people of the State of New York, with such sufficient security, as shall be approved of by one or more of the judges of the inferior court of the county together with a majority of the supervisors of the same county, and in the city of New York, by any one, or more, of the judges of the supreme court, signified, by signing such his, or their approbation on the back of the said bond, which bond shall be in the full sum by this act committed to his charge, with condition for the true and faithful performance of his office and duty and that without favor malice or partiality.

VII. *And be it further enacted by the authority aforesaid* That each loan officer respectively shall take the following oath, or if of the people called Quakers affirmation (vizt.) 'I will according to the best of my skill and knowledge, faithfully, impartially, and truly, demean myself in discharge of the trust committed to me as one of the loan officers for the of by the act entitled "An act for emitting the sum of two hundred thousand pounds in bills of credit for the purposes therein mentioned", according to the purport, true intent and meaning of the said act, so as the public may not be prejudiced by my consent privity or procurement' which oath or affirmation shall be administered by any justice of the peace and indorsed on the back of the said bond and signed by such justice and the loan officer.

VIII. *And be it further enacted by the authority aforesaid,* That the aforesaid bond indorsed with the approbation and affidavit or affirmation aforesaid shall be lodged with the clerk of the county, who upon receipt thereof shall give the loan officer a certificate that such bond indorsed as aforesaid is lodged with him which certificate shall be delivered to the said treasurer on his delivering to the loan officer the bills of credit aforesaid; which bond and indorsements shall be recorded by the clerk, and in case of the forfeiture of the same bond the majority of the supervisors with any one or more of the judges of the inferior court of such county are hereby impowered to order the same to be put in suit; and the monies recovered by virtue thereof shall be applied to the use of the county.

IX. *And be it further enacted by the authority aforesaid* That on the second Tuesday in May next the judges of the inferior courts, or any one or more of them, together with the supervisors (or the majority of them) of the several counties respectively of this State, shall meet at the court house of the counties respectively, or if there be no court house in any county at the place at which the inferior court of common pleas has been held the term next preceding the passing this act at which place the majority of them shall elect two sufficient freeholders of their respective counties to be loan officers for the same county, except in the county of Orange in which county such meeting shall be at the court house in the new city.

X. *And be it further enacted by the authority aforesaid,* That the loan officers of the several counties, when elected appointed and qualified according to the directions of this act, shall respectively be bodies politic and corporate in fact and in law, by the name and stile of the loan officers of the county of which they are respectively loan officers with full power to every the said bodies politic, to use a common seal, and by the same seal and in the name of such body politic, to grant receipts, receive mortgages, and again to grant the same, to sue and be sued, and generally with all such powers as are necessary to be used for the due execution of the trust reposed in the said loan-officers by this act; any law, usage, or custom, to the contrary in any wise notwithstanding.

XI. *And be it further enacted by the authority aforesaid,* That when the said loan officers respectively have qualified themselves as by this act is directed, they shall receive the said bills of credit signed by two of the said signers which bills of credit so signed, shall be let out to such as shall apply for the same, and can and will give security to the said loan officers, by mortgage on lands lots or houses lying in the same county; they the said loan officers first giving public notice (as in other cases is by this act directed for notice) and by advertizement to be published in one of the newspapers printed in this State that on a certain day at least ten days after the said notice given they will be ready to receive borrowers qualified according to the directions of this act: And as on that day borrowers do offer, their names and sums they apply for shall be orderly entered in the minute book of proceedings; and every one shall be served according to the priority of application, if there be no reasonable objections against the title and value of the lands offered to be mortgaged, or some other sufficient reason, which shall be entered also in the minute book of proceedings. *Provided always* that if upon the first day so many borrowers do offer as to apply for a greater sum than the whole sum in that county to be lent out; then, and in such case every such borrower shall be abated of the sum applied for proportionably.

XII. *And be it further enacted by the authority aforesaid* That the said loan officers respectively before they accept of any lands, lots or houses in mortgage for any of the said bills, shall first view, what is so offered in mortgage, or make due enquiry respecting the value thereof, and shall examine the titles thereto, by perusing the deeds, patents, surveys, and other writings and conveyances by which the same are held, and by which the value and quantity may be better known; and the said loan officers respectively, are hereby empowered, and required to administer to all persons applying for any of the bills as aforesaid, the following oath or (if of the people called Quakers) affirmation to wit, 'I am bona fide seised in fee simple of the lands tenements and hereditaments, by me now offered to be mortgaged, in my own right, and to my own use, and the same were not conveyed to me in trust, to borrow any sum or sums of money upon the same, for the use of any other person or persons whatsoever; and the said premises are free and clear from any other or former gift, grant, sale mortgage judgment, extent, recognizance or other incumbrance whatsoever, to my knowledge.'

XIII. *And be it further enacted by the authority aforesaid,* That the loan officers of the said counties respectively, upon finding borrowers qualified, and the loan officers being satisfied as aforesaid, are hereby required, and by virtue of this act, have full power, to lend out the bills delivered to them as aforesaid at the interest of five per cent per annum for the term of fourteen years from the third Tuesday in June next to come, in sums not exceeding three hundred and not under twenty pounds, (unless the proportion as aforesaid be less) to any one person the said loan officers, taking security for the same by way of mortgage as aforesaid of at least double the value in lands tenements and hereditaments; and of at least three times the value in houses within the said respective counties, and administering an oath or affirmation to the borrower as aforesaid, and the said mortgage shall be executed before two or more witnesses signing thereto, and the substance thereof shall be minuted in a book to be by the said loan officers kept for the purpose in each respective county, for the making of which mortgage and minute the borrower shall pay to the said loan officers the sum of four shillings and no more; which mortgage and minute shall be and each of them are hereby declared to be matter of record; and an attested copy of the said mortgage, if in being, or of the said minute in case the said mortgage is lost, under the hands of the said loan officers and the seal of the loan office shall be good evidence of the said mortgage in any court within this State.

XIV. *And be it further enacted by the authority aforesaid* That the interest of the money lent out as aforesaid shall be payable yearly on the third Tuesday of June to the loan officers; and the principals of all the monies lent out as aforesaid shall be paid in again in the following manner; that is to say, one tenth part of the principal money on the third Tuesday of June which will be in the year of our Lord one thousand seven hundred and ninety one; one other tenth part thereof on the third Tuesday of June which will be in the year of our Lord one thousand seven hundred and ninety two . . .

XV. *And be it further enacted by the authority aforesaid* That in case any loan officer shall remove out of the county, die or neglect or refuse to perform the duty required or enjoined him by this act, or shall behave himself in his office with favor, affection partiality or malice, whereby the public, or any private person may be injured; upon report or complaint made thereof to any two or more of the judges aforesaid of the county for which he is loan officer the said judges are hereby required and commanded by summons to convene the judges and supervisors of the same county, to meet at such time and place, as in the said precept shall be appointed to hear and determine summarily upon the said report or complaint; and upon sufficient proof made to any one or more of the said judges with a major part of the said supervisors of any death, removal, neglect or refusal in the said office as aforesaid, then and in that case the said majority of the supervisors, with concurrence of one or more of the judges aforesaid, shall proceed in manner as herein before directed to elect and are hereby required and commanded to elect a loan officer in the room and stead of such deceased or absent person, or such person who shall have neglected or refused as aforesaid, which loan officer so elected as aforesaid having entered into bond and been qualified in like manner as other loan officers, are by this act directed, shall then have all the powers priviledges and advantages, and shall be subject to all the penalties, and forfeitures, which any of the loan officers of the county as aforesaid, are vested or charged with, entitled or subject to, by virtue of this act.

XVI. [Resignation of loan officer.]

XVII. [Person appointed to vacancy to receive books, etc., of predecessor.]

XVIII. *And be it further enacted by the authority aforesaid*, That if any borrower shall neglect to bring in and pay, or cause to be brought in and paid yearly and every year on the third Tuesday in June or within twenty two days thereafter, on one of the days, which the loan officers aforesaid are by this act directed to attend the respective loan offices, the yearly interest due by his mortgage, and also the part of the principal as it becomes payable, then, and in either of these cases, the loan officers to whom such mortgage was granted shall be seised of an absolute indefeazible estate, in the lands, houses, tenements and hereditaments thereby mortgaged, to them, their successors and assigns, to the uses in this act mentioned; and the mortgagor his or her heirs and assigns shall be utterly foreclosed and barred of all equity of redemption of the mortgaged premises; any law, usage, or custom, or practice in courts of equity, to the contrary notwithstanding.

XIX. *And be it further enacted by the authority aforesaid*, That the loan officers shall respectively attend the loan office every year to receive the monies by this act directed to be paid to them upon the third Tuesday of June and thereafter on the Tuesday in each week for the term of three weeks.

XX. *And be it further enacted by the authority aforesaid*, That the loan officers shall within eight days after the last of the Tuesdays aforesaid yearly and every year cause advertisements to be fixed at not less than three of the most public places, in three or more towns, precincts or districts, of the county where the premises are situated, describing the quantity and situation of the lands mentioned in the said mortgage and giving notice that on the third Tuesday in September in the same year they are to be sold at the court house of the respective counties where the lands lie, by way of public vendue to the highest bidder.

XXI. *And be it further enacted by the authority aforesaid*, That the loan officers of the respective counties aforesaid, shall on the said third

Tuesday of September yearly, expose the lands in the mortgages foreclosed as aforesaid, to sale at public vendue; and upon such sale shall convey the said lands to the highest bidder, or bidders, and the purchaser or purchasers shall and may hold and enjoy the same lands for such estate as was conveyed to the said loan officers by the mortgage executed by such mortgagor clearly discharged and freed from all benefit and equity of redemption and all other incumbrances made and suffered after the execution of such mortgage, by the mortgagor, his or her heirs or assigns and such purchaser or purchasers shall pay the loan officers for drawing and executing such conveyance the sum of five shillings.

XXII. *And be it further enacted by the authority aforesaid,* That the money for which the premises are sold, shall upon the sale thereof be paid to the said loan officers, out of which they shall retain in their hands, the amount of the principal then due together with the interest which would have been due thereon on the third Tuesday of June next thereafter if such sale had not been made, as also the expence of the advertizements, and of the sale, such expence not exceeding fifteen shillings and the remainder (if any be) the loan officers shall pay to the mortgagor, his, or her heirs or assigns. *Provided always,* that if any person or persons offer at the time of the sale to borrow (on sufficient security within this act) the whole principal that is to be retained out of the price, and lent out again, then and in that case the loan officers, shall not retain interest beyond the day of sale. *Provided also* that if the purchaser incline to borrow the principal sum or sums, that is, or are to be paid by him, and lent out again, and if the loan officers be satisfied with the security to be given by such purchaser in manner aforesaid, such purchaser shall be preferred to any other borrower. *Provided likewise* that the loan officers shall not be obliged to take notice of any assigns of the mortgagor unless they enter a notice of their right with the said loan officers at or before the time of sale; which notice the loan officers shall enter on the mortgage and minute thereof on demand, the assignee paying one shilling for the same; and assignees shall be preferred according to the priority of their entries of such notices.

XXIII. *And be it further enacted by the authority aforesaid* That after any lands houses tenements or hereditaments, are mortgaged according to the directions of this act, if it shall appear to the loan officers, upon good and sufficient grounds (which they shall insert in the minute book of their proceedings) that the mortgagor had no good right or title to the premises mortgaged, or has otherwise broken the covenant of his mortgage so that the public may be in danger of loosing the monies, or any part thereof advanced in loan upon the credit of the premises, it shall and may be lawful to and for the said loan officers, and they are hereby empowered, and required to commence an action or actions of debt or covenant, upon the said mortgage against the said mortgagor, his or her heirs executors or administrators and the same to prosecute to judgment by all lawful ways and means whatsoever in any court of record for the recovery of the whole monies lent upon the mortgages and the interest become due and that shall become due until the third Tuesday of June next following the judgment, with costs and charges in which action or actions the mortgagor shall be held to special bail and the court in which such action is brought, is, and the judges thereof in vacation are hereby authorized and directed to give such short day for the rules of pleading thereon, that judgment or a trial and final determination may be had the first court after the court at which the defendant first appeared to the same action.

XXIV. *And be it further enacted by the authority aforesaid,* That if any person or persons whatsoever shall presume to counterfeit any of the bills of credit to be issued by virtue of this act, or shall alter any of the said bills issued as aforesaid, so that they shall appear to be of greater value than by this act the same bill or bills so altered, were enacted signed or numbered to pass for, or shall knowingly pass or give in payment any of the bills aforesaid so counterfeited or altered, every person guilty of counterfeiting or altering any of the said bills as aforesaid, or of knowingly passing or giving in payment any such counterfeit or altered bill or bills, shall be guilty of felony, and being thereof convicted, shall forfeit all his or her estate both real and personal to the people of this State, and be committed to the bridewell of the city of New York for life, and there confined to hard labor, under the direction of the corporation of the said city, at the expence (if any should arise) of this State, and to prevent escape shall be branded on the left cheek with the letter C, with a red hot iron and though such counterfeiting, altering or knowingly passing counterfeit or altered bills, shall be done out of this State, yet any grand jury within this State, is hereby empowered to present the same and to set forth in the indictment, the place where, by their evidence it appeared that the fact was committed, which indictment is hereby declared good, notwithstanding that the place alledged be out of this State; and the petit jurors on the trial of all such foreign issues, shall be returned from the body of the county where the said supreme court shall be statedly held, any law usage or custom to the contrary notwithstanding.

XXV. *And be it enacted by the authority aforesaid,* That the respective loan offices in this State shall be kept at the court house of each respective county, or at some other convenient place near the same except that the loan officers for the county of Orange shall meet alternately at Goshen, and at the new city in the said county, and their first meeting to be at the court house in Goshen; and the said loan officers shall so soon as the said bills are signed and delivered to them, set up advertizements, of the first day of their attending the loan office, for the purposes herein before mentioned, and shall duly attend the same on that first day, and on every Tuesday and Wednesday in each week for the space of four weeks thereafter, if their be occasion of their sitting so long, and the said treasurer so soon as he can fix the day upon which he can deliver the said bills to the loan officers shall send notice by letter to them to come and receive the bills at that day.

XXVI. *And be it further enacted by the authority aforesaid* That the loan officers respectively shall retain in their hands so much of the interest monies paid into them as will pay them their respective salaries appointed by this act, any thing in this act to the contrary notwithstanding, and the remainder of the said interest monies shall be annually paid to the treasurer of this State on or before the last Tuesday of the month of August and the said treasurers receipt shall be to the said loan officers and every of them their heirs executors and administrators a sufficient discharge.

XXVII. *And be it further enacted by the authority aforesaid* That the yearly salary of the loan officers aforesaid for the services required of them by this act shall be as follows to wit

For every of the loan officers of the county of New York forty pounds
For every of the loan officers of the county of Albany thirty pounds
For every of the loan officers of Kings county ten pounds
For every of the loan officers of Queens county sixteen pounds
For every of the loan officers of Suffolk county fifteen pounds
For every of the loan officers of Richmond county ten pounds
For every of the loan officers of West Chester county fifteen pounds
For every of the loan officers of Dutchess county twenty pounds
For every of the loan officers of Orange county fifteen pounds

For every of the loan officers of Ulster county eighteen pounds
For every of the loan officers of Montgomery county sixteen pounds
For every of the loan officers of Washington county ten pounds

XXVIII. *And be it further enacted by the authority aforesaid* That the supervisors and judges aforesaid of the several counties of this State shall on the first Tuesday in October which will be in the year of our Lord one thousand seven hundred and eighty seven, and yearly thereafter on the first Tuesday in October meet together with the said loan officers at the court house of the county; and the majority of the supervisors with one or more of the judges aforesaid, shall carefully inspect and examine the mortgages, minutes and accounts of the loan officers and if it be found that any loan officer or loan officers has or have refused or neglected to perform the duties enjoined upon him or them by this act, the said judges and supervisors shall elect a loan officer or loan officers in the stead of such who shall so have refused or neglected as aforesaid and if any deficiency has happened by borrowers not having right to the lands mortgaged or by the selling thereof for a less price than what is before mentioned, or otherwise; then the said supervisors or a majority of them, with the concurrence of one or more of the said judges shall cause all such deficiencies to be assessed and levied in the county as other county charges, so that the whole of such deficiencies be paid to the said loan officers by the third Tuesday of June then next following.

XXIX. [Attendance of judges and supervisors, how enforced.]

XXX. *And be it further enacted by the authority aforesaid*, That all and every the sums of money which may at any time afterwards be recovered by the loan officers aforesaid, of such persons as have been the occasion of such deficiencies as aforesaid, shall be applied to the use of such county; and the judge or judges and supervisors are hereby empowered to take all lawfull ways and means in the name of the said loan officers to recover the same.

XXXI. *And be it further enacted by the authority aforesaid*, That it shall and may be lawful for the said loan officers to let out upon loan any of the said bills of credit in such manner as they shall think best upon security of good plate to be delivered to them at six shilling per ounce, to be paid to the said loan officers on the third Tuesday in June annually then next, with a years interest, at five per cent for the same, and in case of non payment at any of the three stated days of meeting of the loan officers, then the said loan officers are to sell the same plate in such manner, and upon the same day, as they are directed to sell the lands of the mortgagors forfeited as aforesaid; and they are to return the overplus if any be to the owner after payment of the principal and charges, with interest past and to come; until the third Tuesday of June then next, unless a borrower offers at the time of sale, as in case of lands herein before mentioned; any thing in this act to the contrary notwithstanding.

XXXII. *And be it further enacted by the authority aforesaid* That if any monies shall remain in the hands of the loan officers for want of borrowers, four weeks after the first day appointed for letting it out, it shall be lawful for them to let out the same on good security by mortgage of lands in the county, or on plate as aforesaid to any person who will borrow the same, in any sums, though they be upwards of three hundred pounds.

XXXIII. *And be it further enacted by the authority aforesaid,* That if any of the bills of credit shall remain four weeks over and above the four weeks aforesaid that is to say in all eight weeks, in the hands of the loan officers for want of borrowers, after the first day appointed for letting out as aforesaid, then and in that case the said loan officers or one of them by consent of the other to be entered and signed in the minute book of proceedings, shall carry it to the loan officers of the next county or counties, where there were more monies demanded in loan than there were monies to lend, and deliver it to the loan officers of such next county or counties, upon their receipts for the same, and their entering a memorandum of it in the minutes of their proceedings; which loan officers to whom such sum is brought, shall accept thereof and shall set up advertizements thereof, and therein assign a day in the next week for borrowers to offer, and shall proceed in the lending such further sum, in their county, as nearly as circumstances will admit, in the like manner as they proceeded in lending the first sum; of which transposition of those monies, the loan officers of the several counties, shall give notice in writing signed by them to the treasurer at the time of their paying to him the first interest monies thereafter, of which notices to him he shall enter memorandums in his books of accounts the better to ascertain the interest he is to receive yearly from the respective counties, and the principal sums that the counties are finally to cancel.

XXXIV. And to prevent frauds that may happen by executors in their nonpayment of any part of the money borrowed as aforesaid by their respective testators, *Be it further enacted by the authority aforesaid* That if any person or persons who shall become a borrower or borrowers of the bills issued by virtue of this act shall afterwards make his her or their last will and testament in due form of law, thereby devising the premises so mortgaged, to any other person or persons, leaving personal estate sufficient to pay his or her debts, with an overplus not otherwise in the said will disposed of, and not expressly providing in other manner by the said will; in such case it shall be understood, that the devisor intended that the mortgage money in arrear at the time of his death should be paid out of his personal estate, and his executor or executors shall accordingly be compelled to pay the same thereout in aid of such devisee or devisees: But in case the said last will was made before the premises were mortgaged, then it shall be understood that the testators intent was (unless otherwise expressed in such will) that the devisee or devisees should pay the residue of the mortgage money in arrear, at the time of such testators death; and in case any executor or executors contrary to the intent of this act, having effects sufficient, shall permit a sale to be made of the premises mortgaged; such devisee or devisees may immediately have his, her or their action either in proper person, or by guardian or next friend, if under age, against such executor, or executors, and recover double the damages sustained with costs of suit; and in case any executor or executors, shall in such case be a purchaser of the premises so mortgaged, or any other in trust for him, or for his use, he or they shall be deemed seised of the premises for the use of the devisee, or devisees; and such executor or executors and their trustee or trustees, are hereby disabled from making any conveyance thereof, from such devisee or devisees, and if any such conveyance is made, the same is hereby declared fraudulent and void against such devisee or devisees.

XXXV. *And be it further enacted by the authority aforesaid*, That if any person shall falsely swear or affirm in any of the cases where an oath or affirmation is required to be taken by this act, or shall wilfully or knowingly act contrary to the oath or affirmation, he has before taken, such offence is hereby declared to be perjury, and the offender being convicted thereof shall suffer the pains and penalties, of perjury.

XXXVI. *And be it further enacted by the authority aforesaid*, That the respective loan officers within this State for the time being, shall permit any person or persons at seasonable times to search and view the books of mortgages in their hands and custody, upon their paying one shilling for the search, and the entry of the respective mortgages in the books of the said loan offices shall have the like priority operation and effect as if such mortgages were registered in the clerks of the county in which the lands mortgaged lie.

XXXVII. *And be it further enacted by the authority aforesaid,* That for the greater uniformity in the securities to be taken in the loan offices for the money to be lent by virtue of this act; the mortgages shall be in the form following to wit . . .

XXXVIII. *And be it further enacted by the authority aforesaid,* That the said Samuel Loudon shall print eight thousand copies of the said mortgages, and bind so many of them in a book together with six leaves of clean paper for an alphabet for the use of the loan office of each county, that there may be a mortgage for every twenty pounds of bills of credit given to the loan office of that county, and the number remaining he shall give in loose sheets in the like proportion to each of the loan officers in order therewith (if there should be occasion) to give attested copies of the original mortgages to the purchasers of any of the mortgaged lands: Which books together with the said loose sheets, are to be delivered by the printer to the treasurer of this State; by him with the bills to be delivered to the loan officers of each county.

XXXIX. *And be it further enacted by the authority aforesaid* That no mortgage shall be taken in the loan offices but by filling up one of the blanks of the said book of mortgages; none of them shall be defaced or torn out, except the seals, when the mortgagor pays off the whole principal and interest of the mortgage: And the loan officers shall proceed in the taking the mortgages from the beginning of the book forward, numbering the mortgages as they are taken and inserting the mortgagors name and number in the alphabet under the letter answering the mortgagors sirname.

XL. [Additional books for loan officers.]

XLI. *And be it further enacted by the authority aforesaid* That the loan officers shall in one end of the last mentioned book minute the substance of each mortgage to wit, the number thereof the date, the mortgagors name, the sum lent and the boundaries of the lands mortgaged; and when the one loan officer, has the custody of the book of mortgages, the other shall have the custody of the other book, that fire or other accidents which might happen may be guarded against; and the printer shall make an alphabet to it like to that of the book of mortgages; and for the satisfaction of the mortgagor he may examine or see the minute examined with the original mortgage, and with the witness shall sign the same.

XLII. *And be it further enacted by the authority aforesaid,* That the loan officers beginning at the other end of the said book shall insert the minutes of their proceedings therein, to wit.

First, The day they meet, place, house and loan officers present.

Second, If any one is absent, they shall at their next meeting minute the cause of his absence.

Third, Shall enter the hour that every one applies for the loan of money, and the sum he applies for.

Fourth, Shall enter down the reason why a prior applicant had not the money according to his application, and the substance of examinations for clearing titles and value.

Fifth, Shall enter down the monies received from the treasurer, and the monies delivered to or received from the loan officers of another county, and the day when, with a copy of the notice thereof, to be delivered to the treasurer, and when that notice was delivered to the treasurer, and by whom.

Sixth, The last day of their four days of meeting, for receiving of monies yearly, they shall enter whose mortgages are forclosed, and the numbers and sums of them.

Seventh, Shall enter the orders for, and copies of the advertisements for sale, and places at which they are to be set up, and the persons names that are to set them up.

Eighth, Shall enter the names of the purchasers of lands, and prices sold for, and payment of the overplus to whom it belongs with the time and witnesses of such payment.

Ninth, In case any principals or part thereof are paid in before the times of payment in the mortgages, the whole amount of such principals so paid in, shall be entered in the said books –

Tenth, Shall enter the cause of all suits, and the informations they have received, and of whom at length, or if too long, refer to them in papers apart, minuting the substance.

Eleventh, Shall enter the meetings, with the judges, and supervisors, and persons present, together with the minutes of all proceedings of such judges and supervisors, particularly what were the deficiencies laid before them what measures were taken for assessing and levying such deficiencies and which of the said judges and supervisors were for assessing or for neglecting or delaying it.

XLIII. *And be it further enacted by the authority aforesaid,* That the printer shall also cause to be bound other twelve books of paper, one of them for the use of each loan office, about two thirds of the size of the book of mortgages for the same county, to be delivered as aforesaid with the book of mortgages and that therein shall be entered all the accounts of the loan office; that at the beginning there shall be an alphabet wherein shall be inserted every mans name, and the page wherein his account stands, and that this book be kept in the fairest and best method that the loan officers can, and it is to remain in the custody of him who has the minutes of the mortgages and proceedings.

XLIV *And be it further enacted by the authority aforesaid,* That the deeds to be granted by the loan officers for any lands to be sold by them, whereof the equity of redemption is foreclosed shall be in form following to wit . . .

To which deed the loan officers shall affix the seal of the loan office and respectively subscribe their names in the presence of two witnesses.

XLV. [On sale of land, copy of mortgage to be given purchaser. Form of bond of loan officers.]

XLVI. *And be it further enacted by the authority aforesaid,* That in case of the forfeiture of such bond as aforesaid the suit thereon shall be staid, on the defendants paying or tendering in court to pay the damage arisen by the breach of the condition of the said bond, with the costs to that time; and if judgment be had thereon a jury shall inquire of the damages according to law.

XLVII. *And be it further enacted by the authority aforesaid,* That for the better satisfaction of the loan officers, as to the title and value of what is offered in mortgage, by borrowers; the loan officers or either of them are hereby authorized and impowered to examine the borrower, and witnesses upon oath, or if of the people called Quakers, on affirmation, concerning the same, a brief minute of which examination, and the names of the persons so examined, they shall enter into their minute book of proceedings.

XLVIII. *And be it further enacted by the authority aforesaid* That the treasurer shall pay the expence of printing the said bills and the incidental expences which may arise in or about the same and to each of the same persons authorized to sign the bills to be emitted by virtue of this act at the rate of two shillings for every hundred of the said bills they may have respectively signed according to such accounts thereof as they shall respectively produce audited by the auditor of this State.

XLIX. *And be it further enacted by the authority aforesaid*, That the signers of the said bills or any three of them, shall meet at the treasury of this State on the first Monday in November which will be in the year one thousand seven hundred and eighty seven, and annually on every first Monday in November; and the treasurer of this State shall, when the said signers are so met as aforesaid, deliver unto them all such of the said bills of credit as shall then have come into his hands as treasurer of this State from any of the said loan officers, for principal and interest together with a list of the several denominations of the said bills, and having examined and compared the said bills, with such list, shall destroy the said bills, and shall certify that they have destroyed the bills mentioned and designated on such list, which list so certified shall be delivered to the said treasurer, and a copy thereof, so signed shall be kept by the said signers, or one of them, to be by him or them delivered to the legislature, when thereunto required.

L. *And be it further enacted by the authority aforesaid*, That whenever the said treasurer shall have received from the said loan officers a sum equal to one hundred and fifty thousand pounds in gold or silver, partly in gold and silver, and partly in the bills of credit aforesaid, it shall and may be lawful to and for the said treasurer and he is hereby required to exchange such of the said bills as may be then in circulation for the gold and silver, so received at the nominal value expressed on such bills, as may by any person be tendered to him for exchange; and the said treasurer is hereby required as soon as he shall have received to the said amount in manner aforesaid, to give public notice thereof by advertisement to be published in three of the newspapers printed in this State, and shall require all persons having any of the said bills of credit in possession, within sixty days from the date of such advertisement to bring the same into the treasury, and to receive gold or silver therefore, and if any such bills should be brought in, those remaining in circulation shall not be so exchanged, but shall be received in all payments into the treasury of this State.

LI. *And be it further enacted by the authority aforesaid* That the treasurer of this State be, and he is hereby authorized and required to procure at the expence of the people of this State a competent number of blank certificates with such checks and devices as he may deem proper to guard against counterfeits, and with a margin or counterpart sufficiently large to contain a memorandum of the annual payment of interest which may be made thereon; the blanks of which certificates so to be procured shall be filled up as to the numbers, sums, date, day and year of passing this act, and be delivered as herein after directed, and the said blank certificates shall severally contain the words following, vizt. Number

The people of the State of New York have received on loan from the sum of to be paid to the said or bearor on or before the first day of January which will be in the year of our Lord one thousand seven hundred and ninety with interest from the day of one thousand seven hundred and eighty five at the rate of per centum per annum to be paid annually at the treasury, according to a law of this State, passed on the day of

LII. *And be it further enacted by the authority aforesaid* That the said treasurer be and he is hereby authorized and required to receive on loan in behalf of the people of this State such public securities as are herein after described and to issue and deliver in lieu thereof to any person or persons who shall before the first day of May which will be in the year of our Lord one thousand seven hundred and eighty seven make such loan or loans a certificate or certificates at the election of the lender in the form herein before prescribed to the amount or value of the sum or sums due as principal money on the security and securities which he shall so receive on loan, and shall indorse on each certificate by him delivered, the amount of interest due to the first day of January one thousand seven hundred and eighty five and subscribe his name thereto. *Provided always* that no more than one certificate shall be issued by the said treasurer for a sum less than twenty pounds received from any one person.

LIII. [Blanks in certificates, how filled up.]

LIV. *And be it further enacted by the authority aforesaid* That the said treasurer shall be and he is hereby authorized and required to receive the following public securities on loan in manner aforesaid, vizt.

Loan office certificates issued by the Continental commissioner of loans in this State for monies lent to the United States, at the nominal value expressed therein if issued on or before the first day of September one thousand seven hundred and seventy seven.

Loan office certificates issued by the Continental commissioner of loans in this State for monies loaned to the United States since the said first day of September reduced to specie value by the scale of depreciation established by the United States in Congress assembled on the twenty eighth day of July one thousand seven hundred and eighty one.

Certificates issued, or to be issued by the Continental commissioner of accounts within this State for services performed or articles delivered by the inhabitants of this State for the use of the United States, commonly called Barbers notes.

Certificates issued by the treasurer of this State, for monies borrowed for the use of this State, and directed to be paid by an act entitled an act to provide for the payment of certain contingent expences of this State passed the 25th October 1779 reduced to specie value by the Continental scale of depreciation.

Certificates issued by the agent of this State, in pursuance of an act entitled an act to procure supplies for the use of the army and to prevent a monopoly of cattle within this State and more effectually to prevent supplies of cattle to the enemy passed the 24th of June 1780.

Certificates issued by the treasurer of this State in pursuance of an act entitled an act to provide for the payment of certain monies taken on loan by this State passed the 30th day of June 1780 at the rate of one dollar in silver for every forty of the nominal dollars specified in such certificates.

Warrants with receipts thereon indorsed given by virtue of the act entitled 'An act to compleat the Continental battalions raised under the direction of this State', passed the first day of July 1780, at the rate of one dollar in silver for every bushel of wheat specified in such warrants.

Certificates granted for horses, purchased by this State for the use of the armies of the United States in the year 1780.

Accounts liquidated and certified or certificates granted by the late auditor general of this State or the auditor of this State for the time being, reduced to specie value, if not already so reduced, by the Continental scale of depreciation.

Certificates issued by the auditors appointed in pursuance of the act entitled 'An act to liquidate and settle the accounts of the troops of this State in the service of the United States' passed the 4th day of October 1780.

Certificates given or which may be given, by virtue of the act entitled an act to empower the auditors appointed to liquidate and settle the accounts of the troops of this State in the service of the United States to grant certificates to the troops of this State in the service of the

United States for their pay accrued for the time therein mentioned passed the 6th day of April 1784.

Certificates issued or to be issued by virtue of an act entitled 'An act for the settlement of the pay of the levies and militia for their services in the late war and for other purposes therein mentioned' passed the 27th day of April 1784.

And all other certificates issued by the treasurer of this State for monies due by the people of this State to any person or persons whomsoever.

LV. *And be it further enacted by the authority aforesaid* That it shall and may be lawful to and for the said treasurer and he is hereby authorized and required immediately after completing any certificate or certificates and having signed and endorsed the same as herein directed to pay to the holder thereof the one fifth part of the interest endorsed thereon as aforesaid in the said bills entitled by virtue of this act remaining in the treasury; and for the residue of the said interest so endorsed as aforesaid to give unto such holder a certificate in the form following, to wit . . .

LVI. *And be it further enacted by the authority aforesaid* That the said treasurer shall make regular entries in a book or books to be kept for the purpose of the certificates for securities loaned as aforesaid which he shall issue by virtue of this act and which book or entries shall contain in convenient order the number and date of such certificates and the names of the persons to whom such certificate shall be issued, the principal sum, the interest paid thereon, the day to which it was paid and the annual interest to arise thereon and also a like entry of each and every security he shall receive on loan as aforesaid reducing in all cases the nominal sum to specie value as herein before directed.

And to the end that the credit of the bills to be emitted by virtue of this act may be most effectually established.

LVII. *Be it enacted by the authority aforesaid* That gold and silver and the bills of credit to be emitted by virtue of this act, shall be received by the collector for duties arising on goods wares and merchandize which shall be imported into this State after the passing of this act, and in the treasury of this State in payment arising from the duty on goods sold by public vendue by virtue of the act entitled 'An act for the regulation of sales by public auction'.

LVIII. *And be it further enacted by the authority aforesaid* That gold and silver and the bills of credit emitted in pursuance of this act and no other species of monies or bills shall be received by the loan officers in discharge of the principal and interest due on such mortgages.

LIX. *And be it further enacted by the authority aforesaid* That all the power and authority by this act given to and duties required to be done by the judges and the supervisors of the several counties of this State shall be vested in and exercised by the mayor aldermen and commonalty of the city of New York in common council convened, who shall be subject to like forfeitures so far forth as the manners and things in this act contained relate to the said city and county of New York; and that the word county in this act mentioned shall be construed to comprehend the said city and county of New York.

LX. *And be it further enacted by the authority aforesaid*, That the bills of credit to be emitted by virtue of this act shall be a legal tender in all cases where any suit is or shall be brought or commenced for any debt or damages and the costs of suit in any stage of the proceedings thereof. *Provided always* that nothing in this act shall extend to contravene any treaty between the United States of America and any foreign State or power.

LXI. *And be it further enacted by the authority aforesaid* That one of the loan officers of each respective county shall be allowed, in addition to the salaries herein before mentioned, the sum of six pence for every mile such loan officer shall be obliged to travel for the purpose of receiving the bills of credit in and by this act directed to be delivered to the loan officers, to be computed from the court house of the county for which such loan officer shall be appointed to the city of New York.

LXII. *And be it further enacted by the authority aforesaid* That the certificates to be issued by the treasurer by virtue of this act for securities taken on loan and also the certificates to be issued for part of the interest due thereon previous to the first day of January one thousand seven hundred and eighty five, shall be receiveable at the treasury of the State in payments for confiscated estates to be sold by the commissioners of forfeitures, and also in payment for the waste and unappropriated lands of this State.

2.16 PENNSYLVANIA PROTECTS MANUFACTURES AND DISCOURAGES THE EMIGRATION OF SKILLED WORKERS

'An act to encourage and protect the manufacturers of this state', 1788, *Statutes at Large of Pennsylvania*, vol. XIII, ch. 1347, pp. 58–62

(Section I, P. L.) Whereas it is necessary for the encouragement of the arts and manufacturers of this state that measures should be taken to prevent ill designing persons from exporting the tools, utensils and machines employed in the manufactures now established or likely so to be and from seducing artificers and manufacturers to leave this country.

[Section I.] (Section II, P. L.) Be it therefore enacted and it is hereby enacted by the Representatives of the Freemen of the Commonwealth of Pennsylvania in General Assembly met and by the authority of the same, That if any person or persons shall on any pretense whatever export, load or put on board or cause or procure to be exported, loaden or put on board or shall pack or cause or procure to be packed in order to be laden or put on board of any ship or vessel bound to any place beyond the sea or not within the United States of America or shall lade or cause or procure to be laden on board of any boat or other vessel or shall bring, or cause to be brought to any quay, wharf or other place in order to be so laden or put on board any such ship or vessel or shall wilfully and maliciously destroy or render useless any machine, engine, tool, press, utensil or implement whatever used in or proper for the woolen, cotton, linen, silk, iron or steel manufactures that now are or hereafter may be established in this state, or any part or parts of such machine, engine, tool, press, utensil or implement, or shall buy, purchase, collect or procure any such machine, engine, tool, press, utensil or implement or any part thereof for any of the purposes aforesaid, he or they so offending shall for every such offense not only forfeit and lose all such machines, engines, tools, presses, utensils and implement or parts or parcels thereof, together with the packages and all other goods packed therewith, if any there be, but upon complaint made thereof upon the oath or affirmation of one or more credible witness or witnesses it shall and may be lawful for any justice of the peace to issue his warrant to bring the person or persons so complained of before him or any other justice, and if such person or persons shall not thereupon give such an account of the use or purpose to which such machines, engines, tools, presses, utensils and implements or parts or parcels thereof are intended to be appropriated as shall be satisfactory to such justice it shall and may be lawful for such justice to bind the person or persons so charged to appear at the next court of oyer and terminer or quarter sessions of the peace to be held for the city or county in which the offense shall be committed with reasonable sureties for his or their appearance, or to commit such person or persons in default of giving such security until the next court of oyer and terminer or quarter sessions of the peace for the said city and county and in case such person or persons shall be convicted at such court of oyer and terminer or quarter sessions of the peace of any of the offenses aforesaid, he or they shall forfeit and pay for every such offense a fine of three hundred and fifty pounds and shall also suffer imprisonment in the common gaol of the city or county in which such offense shall have been committed for the space of twelve months without bail or mainprize and until such fine shall be paid together with the costs of prosecution.

[Section II.] (Section III, P. L.) And be it further enacted by the authority aforesaid, That it shall and may be lawful for any person or persons whatsoever to seize and secure all such machines, engines, tools, presses, utensils and implements or parts or parcels thereof as shall be found or discovered to be laden and put on board or intended to be laden and put on board of any ship, vessel or boat and intended to be exported contrary to the true intent and meaning of this act together with the packages and all other goods packed therewith if any such there be and after condemnation thereof in due course of law the same shall be publicly sold to the best bidder by the sheriff of the city or county in which the same shall be condemned and one moiety of the produce arising by the sale thereof after deducting the charges of the condemnation and sale shall be to the use of the commonwealth and the other moiety to the person who shall seize and prosecute the same as aforesaid.

[Section III.] (Section IV, P. L.) And be it further enacted by the authority aforesaid, That if any captain or master of any ship, boat or vessel, shall knowingly and designedly permit any such machine, engine, tool, press, utensil or implement or any part of parcel thereof to be put on board of his ship, boat or vessel, with design to export the same contrary to the meaning and intent of this act, such captain or master shall for every such offense forfeit and pay a fine of three hundred and fifty pounds and shall also suffer imprisonment in the common gaol of the city or county in which the said offense shall be committed for the space of twelve months, and until the said fine together with the costs of prosecution shall be paid.

[Section IV.] (Section V, P. L.) And be it further enacted by the authority aforesaid, That if any person or persons shall have in his or their custody, power or possession any such machine, engine, tool, press, utensil or implement or any part or parcel thereof with intention to export the same contrary to the intention of this act or to destroy the same or render it useless, upon complaint thereof made by the oath or affirmation of one or more credible witness or witnesses it shall and may be lawful for any justice of the peace to issue his warrant to seize such machine, engine, tool, press, utensil and implement or the parts or parcels thereof and to bring the person or persons so complained of before him or any other justice of the peace and if such person or persons shall not give a satisfactory account of the case or purposes to which such machines, engine, tool, press, utensil and implement or the parts or parcels thereof were intended to be applied, it shall and may be lawful for such justice to cause such machine, engine, tool, press, utensil or implement or the parts or parcels thereof to be detained and to bind the person or persons so charged to appear at the next court of oyer and terminer or quarter sessions of the peace for the county in which the offense shall have been committed, with reasonable sureties for his or their appearance and in default of such security to commit such person or persons to the common gaol of the city or county and in case any such person or persons shall be convicted at such court of oyer and terminer or quarter sessions of the peace of having in his or their custody, power or possession, any such machine, engine, tool, press, utensil or implement or any part or parcel thereof with such intent as aforesaid, the person or persons convicted thereof shall for every such offense forfeit and [lose] all such machines, engines, tools, presses, utensils and implements, and the parts and parcels thereof to the use of the commonwealth and of the prosecutor in manner aforesaid and shall also forfeit and pay a fine of three hundred and fifty pounds and shall suffer imprisonment in the common gaol of the city or county wherein he or they shall be convicted for the space of twelve months without bail or mainprize and until such fine shall be paid together with the costs of prosecution.

[Section V.] (Section VI, P. L.) And be it further enacted by the authority aforesaid, That if any person or persons shall contract with, entice, persuade or endeavor to seduce or encourage any artificer or workman concerned, skilled or employed in, or who shall have worked at or been employed in or who is skilled in the woolens, cotton, linen, silk, iron or steel manufactures which now are or hereafter may be established in this state, to go out of this state to parts beyond the sea or to any place not within the United States of America and shall be duly convicted thereof, every such person shall for every such offense forfeit and pay a fine of one hundred pounds and be committed to the common gaol aforesaid, there to remain without bail or mainprize for the space of four months and until such fine shall be paid together with the costs of prosecution.

[Section VI.] (Section VII, P. L.) And be it further enacted by the authority aforesaid, That if any suit or action shall be commenced against any person or persons for what he or they shall do in pursuance of this act such suit or action shall be commenced within six months next after the fact committed and the person or person so sued may plead the general issue and give this act and the special matter in evidence and if the plaintiff or prosecutor shall become non-suit or suffer a discontinuance or if a verdict shall be given against him or judgment entered against him on demurrer, the defendant shall recover double costs.

[Section VII.] (Section VIII, P. L.) And be it further enacted by the authority aforesaid, That nothing in this act contained shall be construed to prevent or prohibit the exportation of wool and cotton cards or of such other tools or implements as are or may be usually manufactured for sale and exportation within this state or any [of] the United States of America.

[Section VIII.] (Section IX, P. L.) And be it further enacted by the authority aforesaid, That this act shall be and continue in force for and during the term of two years from and after the publication thereof and from thence to the end of the then next session of the general assembly and no longer.

Passed March 29, 1788. Recorded L. B. no. 3, p. 368.

PART 3

Public Lands: Congress, the States and the People

3.1 LOYALIST ESTATES: NEW YORK ACT OF CONFISCATION

'An act, for the forfeiture and sale of the estates of persons who have adhered to the enemies of this State, and for declaring the sovereignty of the people of this State in respect to all property within the same', passed the 22d of October, 1779, *Laws of New York*, 1779, vol. 1 (Albany, 1886) third session, ch. 25, pp. 173–81

Whereas during the present unjust and cruel war waged by the king of Great Britain against this State, and the other United States of America, divers persons holding or claiming property within this State have voluntarily been adherent to the said king his fleets and armies, enemies to this State and the said other United States, with intent to subvert the government and liberties of this State and the said other United States, and to bring the same in subjection to the crown of Great Britain by reason whereof the said persons have severally justly forfeited all right to the protection of this State and to the benefit of the laws under which said property is held or claimed

And whereas the public justice and safety of this State absolutely require that the most notorious offenders should be immediately hereby convicted and attainted of the offence aforesaid in order to work a forfeiture of their respective estates and vest the same in the people of this State. *And whereas* the Constitution of this State hath authorized the legislature to pass acts of attainder, for crimes committed before the termination of the present war.

I. *Be it therefore enacted by the People of the State of New York represented in Senate and Assembly and it is hereby enacted by the authority of the same*, That, John Murray earl of Dunmore formerly governor of the colony of New York, William Tryon Esquire late governor of the said colony, John Watts, Oliver DeLancey, Hugh Wallace, Henry White, John Harris Cruger, William Axtell and Roger Morris Esquires late members of the council of the said colony; George Duncan Ludlow and Thomas Jones, late justices of the supreme court of the said colony, John Tabor Kempe, late attorney general of the said colony, William Bayard Robert Bayard and James DeLancey now or late of the city of New York Esquires David Matthews, late mayor of the said city, James Jauncey, George Foliot, Thomas White, William McAdam, Isaac Low, Miles Sherbrooke, Alexander Wallace and John Wetherhead, now or late of the said city merchants, Charles Inglis of the said city, clerk and Margaret his wife; Sir John Johnson late of the county of Tryon, knight and baronet, Guy Johnson, Daniel Claus and John Butler now or late of the said county, Esquires and John Joost Herkemer, now or late of the said county yeoman, Frederick Philipse and James DeLancey now or late of the county of Westchester Esquires, Frederick Philipse (son of Frederick) now or late of the said county gentleman, David Colden Daniel Kissam the elder, and Gabriel Ludlow now or late of Queens county Esquires, Philip Skeene, now or late of the county of Charlotte Esquire; and Andrew P. Skeene son of the said Philip Skeene and late of Charlotte county, Benjamin Seaman and Christopher Billop, now or late of the county of Richmond Esquires, Beverly Robinson, Beverly Robinson the younger and Malcom Morrison now or late of the county of Dutchess Esquires, John Kane now or late of the said county, gentleman, Abraham C. Cuyler now or late of the county of Albany Esquire, Robert Leake, Edward Jessup and Ebenezer Jessup now or late of the said county gentlemen, and Peter Dubois and Thomas H. Barclay now or late of the county of Ulster Esquires, Susannah Robinson, wife to the said Beverly Robinson and Mary Morris wife to the said Roger Morris, John Rapalje of Kings county Esquire; George Muirson, Richard Floyd and Parker Wickham of Suffolk county Esquires, Henry Lloyd the elder late of the State of Massachusetts Bay merchant and Sir Henry Clinton knight be and each of them are hereby severally declared to be *ipso facto* convicted and attainted of the offence aforesaid, and that all and singular the estate both real and personal held or claimed by them the said persons severally and respectively, whether in possession, reversion or remainder, within this State, on the day of the passing of this act, shall be and hereby is declared to be forfeited to, and vested in the people of this State.

II. *And be it further enacted by the authority aforesaid*, That the said several persons hereinbefore particularly named shall be and hereby are declared to be forever banished from this State, and each and every of them who shall at any time hereafter be found in any part of this State, shall be and are hereby adjudged and declared guilty of felony, and shall suffer death as in cases of felony without benefit of clergy.

And to the end That for the purpose aforesaid convictions and attainder for the offence aforesaid may in pursuance of this act, be had against other offenders than those hereinbefore particularly named.

III. *Be it further enacted by the authority aforesaid,* That it shall and may be lawful for the grand jurors at any supreme court of judicature to be held for this State, or at any court of oyer and terminer and general gaol delivery or general or quarter sessions of the peace to be held in and for any county of this State, whenever it shall appear to such grand jurors by the oath of one or more credible witness or witnesses, that any person or persons, whether in full life or deceased, generally reputed, if in full life to hold or claim, or if deceased, to have held or claimed at the time of their death respectively, real or personal estate within this State, hath or have been guilty of the offence aforesaid, to prefer bills of indictment against such persons as shall then be in full life for such offence, and in relation to the offence committed by such persons in their lives time as shall then be deceased severally and respectively, notwithstanding that such offence may have been committed elsewhere than in the county for which such grand jurors shall be summoned. That in every indictment to be taken in pursuance of this act, the offence or offences shall be charged to have been committed in the county where the indictment shall be taken, notwithstanding such offence or offences may have been committed elsewhere and it shall not be necessary to set forth specially whether the several persons charged in such indictment were respectively deceased or in full life or were reputed to hold or claim real or personal estate within this State. And on every such indictment shall be indorsed that the same was taken in pursuance of this act and the day when the same was preferred into court.

IV. *And be it further enacted by the authority aforesaid,* That whenever and as often as any such indictment shall be taken against any person or persons, the sherifs of the respective counties where such indictments shall be taken shall forthwith cause notices thereof agreeable to such form as is herein after mentioned to be published in one or more of the public news papers within this State, for at least four weeks,

V. *And be it further enacted by the authority aforesaid,* That in every case of a neglect to appear and traverse agreeable to the sherif's notice, the several persons charged in such indictment whether in full life or deceased shall respectively be and hereby are declared to be and shall be adjudged guilty of the offences charged against them respectively. And the several persons who shall in pursuance of this act either by reason of such default in not appearing and traversing as aforesaid or upon trial be convicted of the offence aforesaid shall forfeit all and singular the estate both real and personal, whether in possession reversion or remainder, held or claimed by them respectively within this State to the people of this State; and judgment shall accordingly be awarded in the supreme court of this State against the said persons respectively; and such forfeitures, as well of the estates, which were at the time of their death respectively of persons deceased, as of persons in full life, at the time of conviction, shall be deemed to have accrued and the estates accordingly attached to and vested in the people of this State as and from the day charged in each respective indictment most distant from the day of the taking thereof,

Provided nevertheless that where a trial shall be had upon any such indictment the forfeiture shall in such case be deemed to have accrued from the day to be found by the verdict of the jury, by which such persons shall be respectively convicted, most distant from the day of the taking of the indictment any other day to be charged in the indictment notwithstanding. And provided farther that the several persons who shall have been pardoned in pursuance of a declaration or ordinance of the convention of this State, passed the tenth day of May in the year of our Lord one thousand seven hundred and seventy seven 'offering free pardon to such of the subjects of the said State, as, having committed treasonable acts against the same, should return to their allegiance', or in consequence of any proclamation or proclamations heretofore issued by the commander in chief of the army of the United States of America, may respectively plead their pardons to indictments taken in pursuance of this act in like manner as they might or could do, to indictments for high treason taken in the ordinary course of law. And provided farther that each and every person who shall at any time before the fourth day of April in the year of our Lord one thousand seven hundred and seventy eight, have taken the oath of allegiance to this State, before the convention or councils of safety of this State or before the committee of the said convention appointed for enquiring into detecting and defeating all conspiracies which may be formed in this State against the liberties of America, or the commissioners appointed for the like purpose, or a county, district or precinct committee shall and may plead such taking the oath of allegiance in bar to any indictment to be taken in pursuance of this act for offences committed before the day on which they respectively took such oath.

VI. *And be it further enacted by the authority aforesaid* That all indictments to be from time to time taken in pursuance of this act at any court of oyer and terminer or general gaol delivery or general or quarter sessions of the peace shall by the clerks of the said courts respectively be returned under their respective hands and seals into the supreme court of this State, and shall be tried at the bar of the said court, and upon the trial of any such indictment, no greater number of witnesses shall be required than are required by law in cases of felony without benefit of clergy.

VII. *And be it further enacted by the authority aforesaid*, That the several sherifs shall from time to time respectively return under their hands and seals into the supreme court of this State, the several numbers of the news papers containing the notices published by them respectively there to remain as records of such notices until judgments shall be had against the several persons named in such notices respectively.

And to the end that in prosecutions for the offence aforesaid in pursuance of this act, no advantage may be taken of mere matters of form, and that the defendants may notwithstanding be fully apprized of the several matters charged against them in order to their defence.

VIII. *Be it further enacted by the authority aforesaid*, That it shall be sufficient in all indictments to be taken for the offence aforesaid in pursuance of this act, to charge generally, that the several persons therein charged did on the several days and at the several places therein mentioned adhere to the enemies of this State, and the grand jurors shall at the time they deliver any such indictment into court deliver into court the examinations or depositions of the witness or witnesses, upon whose testimony such indictment was found to be filed in court together with the indictment, and the defendants shall respectively upon application be entitled to copies of the indictments against them respectively and of such examinations or depositions; and the prosecutor on the part of the State shall not upon the trial be permitted to give evidence of any overt acts other than such as shall be charged in such examinations or depositions; and the clerks of the several courts of oyer and terminer and general gaol delivery and general or quarter sessions of the peace shall return such examinations or depositions into the supreme court in like manner as is hereinbefore directed with respect to indictment taken at the courts of oyer and terminer and general goal delivery, or general or quarter sessions of the peace.

IX. *And be it further enacted by the authority aforesaid*, That besides the several matters by the law of England declared to be evidence and overt acts of high treason in adhering to the king's enemies, and which are hereby declared to be evidence and overt acts of high treason in adhering to the enemies of the people of this State as sovereign thereof, the following matters shall be and are hereby declared to be evidence and overt acts of adhering to the enemies of the people of this State, whereon and for which persons may in pursuance of this act be indicted and convicted for the offence aforesaid, that is to say, being at any time since the ninth day of July in the year of our Lord one thousand seven hundred and seventy six (the day of the declaration of the independence of this State within the same) in any part of the United States, not in the power or possession of the fleets or armies of the king of Great Britain, and afterwards voluntarily withdrawing to any place within the power or possession of the king of Great Britain, his fleets or armies; or being apprehended by order of or authority from the commander in chief of the armies of the said United States, or of or from the provincial congress, or conventions or committees thereof, or councils of safety, of this State, or the commissioners above mentioned appointed for enquiring into detecting and defeating all conspiracies which may be formed in this State against the liberties of America, or county, district or precinct committees within this State, or by the supreme executive authority of this State, and confined within certain limits upon engagements by parole or otherwise, not to go beyond such limits, and breaking such engagements, and voluntarily escaping to any place in the power of the fleets or armies of Great Britain, or being so confined as aforesaid, and afterwards permitted by proper authority to go to any place in the power of the fleets or armies of Great Britain upon engagement to return within a certain given time, and not returning within such time but afterwards remaining at any place within the power or possession of the fleets or armies of Great Britain

And whereas divers persons inhabitants and well affected subjects of this State at the time of the declaration of the independence thereof, who had their fixed residence in the southern district of this State were obliged on the invasion of the said district by the enemy to fly before their superior force into parts of this or some other or others of the said United States, and some of them having thereby abandoned all or the greatest part of their property were so reduced as to have been respectively obliged through absolute necessity and the want of sufficient habitations and the necessary means of support and subsistence to return to their respective places of abode, and others of them for the same cause having deserted their habitations and fled in manner aforesaid have for particular reasons been permitted either by the commander in chief of the armies of the said United States, or other lawful authority in the places to which they respectively fled so returned within the power of the enemy where they also severally still do reside.

X. *Be it therefore further enacted by the authority aforesaid, and it is hereby provided,* That nothing in this act contained shall be construed to extend to or affect the said persons severally and respectively, or any or either of them except such of them as since his her or their return to any place or places within the power of the enemy has or have done any act or thing which in judgment of law would be construed, deemed and adjudged an adherence to the enemies of this State and high treason against the people thereof, had such person or persons respectively voluntarily and freely and without any such cause as aforesaid returned within the power of the enemy. In which case such return within the power of the enemy and such act or thing as aforesaid shall in judgment of law be construed deemed and is hereby declared to be adjudged an adherence to the enemies of the people of this State.

XI. *And be it further enacted by the authority aforesaid, and it is hereby provided* That no conviction or attainder in pursuance of this act, shall be construed to exempt any person or persons from being apprehended tried convicted attainted and executed for high treason according to the ordinary course of law.

XII. *And be it further enacted by the authority aforesaid* That all conveyances and assignments of any real or personal estate made or executed since the ninth day of July in the year of our Lord one thousand seven hundred and seventy six by any or either of the persons who are immediately convicted and attainted by this act or any or either of the persons who shall be convicted or attainted in persuance of this act or any or either of the persons who shall be convicted or attainted of high treason in the ordinary course of law for offences committed during the present war, shall be presumed to be fraudulent and to to have been made with intent to prevent a forfeiture of the estates by such conveyances or assignments respectively intended to be conveyed or assigned, and upon every trial, wherein any such conveyance or assignment shall come in question, the burthen of the proof shall lay upon the person or persons claiming under such conveyance or assignment, that the same was made and executed *bona fide,* for a valuable consideration, and not with intent to prevent a forfeiture as aforesaid.

XIII. *And be it further enacted by the authority aforesaid* That all titles estates and interests, by executory devise or contingent remainder, claimed by any person hereby, or by virtue of this law, to be convicted, shall on conviction be as fully forfeited to all intents, constructions and purposes in the law whatsoever to the people of this State as any other titles claims estates or interests whatsoever.

XIIII. *And be it further enacted by the authority aforesaid,* That the absolute property of all messuages lands tenements and hereditaments and of all rents royalties, franchises, prerogatives, priviledges, escheats, forfeitures, debts, dues duties and services by whatsoever names respectively the same are called and known in the law, and all right and title to the same, which next and immediately before the ninth day of July in the year of our Lord one thousand seven hundred and seventy six, did vest in, or belong, or was, or were due to the crown of Great Britain be, and the same and each and every of them hereby are declared to be, and ever since the said ninth day of July, in the year of our Lord one thousand seven hundred and seventy six, to have been, and for ever after shall be vested in the people of this State, in whom the sovereignty and seignory thereof, are and were united and vested, on and from the said ninth day of July, in the year of our Lord one thousand seven hundred and seventy six.

XV. *And be it further enacted by the authority aforesaid,* That the person administring the government of this State for the time being shall be, and he is hereby authorized and required by and with the advice and consent of the council of appointment to appoint, during the pleasure of the said council, and commission under the great seal of this State, three commissioners of forfeitures for each of the great districts of this State. That the said commissioners of a majority of them shall be, and hereby are authorized and required from time to time, to sell and dispose of all real estate within their respective districts, forfeited or to be forfeited to the people of this State, at public vendue to the highest bidder or bidders, and in such parcels as they shall from time to time think proper first giving eight weeks notice of each sale in one or more of the public news papers in this State containing a description as to the quantity by estimation of the lands or tenements to be sold, the situation thereof and the name or names of the person or persons by the conviction and attainder of whom the said lands or tenements are deemed to have become forfeited, and to make seal and deliver to the purchaser or purchasers respectively good and sufficient deeds and conveyances in the law, to vest the same in them respectively and their respective heirs and assigns upon such purchaser or purchasers respectively producing such receipt from the treasurer as is herein after mentioned. That every such purchaser and purchasers shall by virtue of such deeds and conveyances respectively be so vested in title seizin and possession of the lands and tenements so purchased as to have and maintain in his, her or their name or names any action for recovery thereof or damages relating thereto any actual seizin or possession thereof in any other person or persons notwithstanding. That every such deed and conveyance shall be deemed to operate as a warranty from the people of this State, to the purchaser or purchasers respectively and their respective heirs and assigns for the lands or tenements thereby respectively granted and conveyed against all claims titles and incumbrances whatsoever and such purchaser or purchasers respectively and their respective heirs or assigns shall in case of eviction have such remedy and relief upon such warranty in such manner as shall be more particularly provided for in such future act or acts of the legislature as are herein after mentioned

Provided that the said commissioners shall not be authorized to sell any lands in larger parcels than the quantity of five hundred acres in each parcel, that no more than one farm shall be included in one and the same sale, and that the sales shall be made in the county where the lands or tenements to be sold respectively lie.

And provided further that nothing in this law contained shall be construed deemed esteemed or adjudged to authorize the commissioners to be appointed by virtue hereof to make sale of any of the lands messuages tenements or hereditaments hereby forfeited or by virtue hereof to become forfeited before or until the first day of October next, and that all such sales shall be and the same hereby are wholly prohibited until that day.

And whereas it is impossible at present to form an estimate of what will be a proper compensation to the said commissioners, for their services and expences, in executing the business hereby committed to them.

XVI. *Be it therefore further enacted by the authority aforesaid*, That the publick faith of this State shall be and hereby is pledged to the said commissioners, for such allowance and compensation to them for their services and expences besides the expences of surveyors, clerks and other incidental charges, as shall hereafter by the legislature be deemed just and reasonable.

XVII. *And be it further enacted by the authority aforesaid,* That the treasurer of this State shall be, and he is hereby authorized out of the monies which now are, or hereafter may be in the treasury, to advance to the said commissioners for each district, a sum not exceeding two thousand pounds to defray the expence of the business hereby committed to them.

And whereas in many instances, lands, the reversion or remainder whereof is or may become forfeited to this State, are possessed by tenants who have at considerable expence made or purchased the improvements on the same, and which tenants have constantly, uniformly and zealously, since the commencement of the present war, endeavored to defend and maintain the freedom and independence of these United States.

XVIII. *Be it therefore further enacted by the authority aforesaid,* That where lands the reversion or remainder whereof is hereby or may become forfeited to the people of this State, shall be possessed by any tenant of the character above described, and who, or whose ancestor, testator or intestate, shall have made or purchased the improvements on the same, they shall continue in possession at their former rents and be at liberty as heretofore to transfer the improvements untill the fee simple of the said lands shall be sold, they paying their respective rents and the present arrearages thereof in money equal to the current prices of the articles of produce in which their rents were heretofore paid, into the treasury of this State, if such rents were reserved in produce, or if reserved in money then in so much money as will be equivalent to the price of wheat at seven shillings per bushel. And that when the fee simple of the said lands shall be sold by the commissioners to be appointed in pursuance of this act, they shall cause such lands to be appraised by three appraisers, at what shall be deemed the then present value thereof, exclusive of the improvements thereon, at the time of appraising; That one of the said appraisers shall be elected by the commissioners, another by the tenant claiming the benefit intended by this clause, and the third by the said other two appraisers; That the said appraisers previous to the making of such appraisements, shall each of them take an oath, and which oath the said commissioners are hereby authorized to administer well and truly to appraise the lands held by such tenant at what shall be deemed the then value thereof, exclusive of the improvements thereon; and upon payment into the treasury by such tenant of the sum at which such lands shall be so appraised, within three months after the making of such appraisement, together with all arrearages of rents, then due thereon, the commissioners shall convey the lands so appraised to such tenant, in like manner as if such lands had been sold at publick vendue, and such tenant had appeared and been the highest bidder for the same Provided that no person being a tenant himself or of affinity or consanguinity to the tenant requiring such appraisement to be made, shall be an appraiser.

And in order that the commissioners may be enabled to determine who are the proper objects of the benefit intended by the aforegoing clause.

XIX. *Be it further enacted by the authority aforesaid,* That no tenant shall be entitled to such benefit, unless he or she shall within one month after the same shall be required of him or her by the said commissioners, produce to them a certificate to be subscribed by at least twelve reputable inhabitants of the county of known and undoubted attachment to the American cause, to be approved of by the commissioners, and which inhabitants shall severally declare upon oath the truth of the matter by them certified, before a justice of the peace of the county, who is hereby authorized to administer such oath, certifying that such tenant had constantly and uniformly since the said ninth day of July, one thousand seven hundred and seventy six, demeaned himself, or herself, as a friend to the freedom and independence of the United States, and hath, as far forth as his or her circumstances would admit, taken an active and decisive part, to maintain and promote the same.

XX. *And be it further enacted by the authority aforesaid,* That whenever, the said commissioners shall within their respective districts, make sale of any lands either at publick vendue, or upon such appraisment as aforesaid, and the commissioners and the person or persons to whom such sale shall be made, having reciprocally subscribed a memorandom or note in writing of such sale, the commissioners shall immediately thereupon give to the person or persons to whom such sale shall be made, a certificate thereof, to contain the sum for which the lands purchased by such person or persons, were sold and if such sale was made upon such appraisement, then also of the arrearages of rent due on such lands. That the said person or persons to whom such certificates shall be given, shall within three months from the date thereof pay, into the treasury of the State the sums in such certificates respectively specified, and the treasurer is hereby required and authorized, to receive the same and to give to the said person or persons, paying, duplicate receipts for the monies by them respectively paid, and the several persons to whom such receipts shall be given, shall upon their respectively producing and lodging with the said commissioners one of the said receipts, be entitled to deeds and conveyances for the lands by them respectively purchased.

XXI. *And be it further enacted by the authority aforesaid,* That the commissioners for the respective districts shall and may in their own names commence and prosecute any suit upon a contract for the sale of any estate against any person or persons, who shall have subscribed such note or memorandom in writing thereof as aforesaid, and all damages which shall be recovered by the said commissioners in such suits, shall be by them paid into the treasury of this State.

XXII. *And be it further enacted by the authority aforesaid* That all purchases made at such vendues by the said commissioners, or any or either or them, or any other person to or for the use of them, or any or either of them, shall be null and void; and that each commissioner before he enter upon the execution of his office shall appear before one of the judges of any of the counties within the district for which such commissioner shall be appointed, and take and subscribe the following oath which such judge is hereby authorized and required to administer viz.

'I A B. appointed a commissioner of forfeitures, for the district, do solemnly and sincerely swear and declare in the presence of Almighty God, that I will faithfully and honestly execute the said office in such manner as I shall conceive most for the benefit and advantage of the people of this State, according to the true intent and meaning of an act entitled An act for the forfeiture and sale of the estates of persons who have adhered to the enemies of this State, and for declaring the sovereignty of the people of this State in respect of all property within the same.'

XXIII. *And be it further enacted by the authority aforesaid, and it is hereby provided,* That the said commissioners shall not be authorized to sell any lands which at the time of the sale thereof, shall be within the power of the enemy, any thing herein before mentioned notwithstanding.

XXIIII. *And be it further enacted by the authority aforesaid* That the treasurer of this State shall in his accounts of the monies arising by the sales of forfeited estates specify the names of the several persons to whom the several estates immediately before the forfeiture thereof were deemed to belong as the same shall appear from the certificate of the commissioners: To the end that when the legislature shall by future act or acts to be passed for the purpose, provide for the payment of the debts due from the said persons respectively the amount of the monies arising from the sales of their respective estates may with the greater ease be ascertained.

3.2 EFFECTS OF CONFISCATIONS ON LOYALISTS: CLAIMS FOR COMPENSATION OF LOYALISTS EXILED FROM MASSACHUSETTS, NEW YORK, PENNSYLVANIA AND SOUTH CAROLINA

Wallace Brown, *The King's Friends* (Providence, R.I., 1966) pp. 294–7; 306–9; 318–19; 338–9

MASSACHUSETTS

In the following tables 313 claims are analyzed. Two hundred and twenty-two were filed in London, ninety-one in Nova Scotia. Twenty-three London claimants returned to the United States, fifteen lived in Canada, one in the Bahamas, and one in Flanders. Ten of the Nova Scotia claimants returned to the United States.

National Origin (268 known)

Country of Birth	*Nova Scotia Claimants*	*London Claimants*	*Combined*		*% of Known*	
Great Britain (country unknown)	2	7	9	65	3·4	27·0
England	4	19	23		8·0	
Scotland	9	5	14		5·2	
Ireland	5	8	13		4·9	
Wales	0	2	2			
Germany	0	2	2			
Switzerland	1	0	1			
Sweden	0	1	1			
America	59	144	203			73·0
Unknown	11	34	45			
Total	91	222	313			100·00†

† In this and some other tables the percentages of very small numbers have not been calculated; hence the full 100 per cent is not always shown in the column above.

Date of Immigrants' Arrival in America (49 known)

	Nova Scotia	*London*	*Combined*
1763 and earlier	5	23	28
1764 and later	11	10	21
Unknown	4	12	16
Total	20	45	65

Occupations (302 known)

	Nova Scotia	*London*	*Combined*		*% of Known*	
Farmers and Landowners	20	17	37		11·5	
Commerce						
(a) Artisans and craftsmen	12†	15‡	27		9·1	
(b) Merchants and shopkeepers	39	67	106		35·0	
(c) Seamen and pilots	2	8	10	149		50·0
(d) Innkeepers	2	1	3			
(e) Shipbuilders	1	1	2			
(f) Auctioneer	0	1	1			
Professions						
(a) Anglican ministers	1	8	9			
Congregational minister	0	1	1			
(b) Lawyers	4	13	17			
(c) Schoolmasters	1	1	2			
(d) Doctors	1	16§	17			
(e) Surgeon's mate	0	1	1	51		17·0
(f) Dentist	0	1	1			
(g) Musician and organist	0	1	1			
(h) Limner and painter	0	1	1			
(i) Fencing master	1	0	1			
Office-Holders	6¶	58‖	64			21·5
Unknown	1	11	12			
Total	91	222	313			100·00

† One carpenter, one weaver, one tailor, one painter and glazier, two bakers, two mastmakers, two blacksmiths, one coppersmith, and one master builder.

‡ Two master builders, one painter, two printers, one barber, three tailors, one watchmaker, one silversmith, one farrier, one shoemaker, one tin-plate maker and one ropemaker.

§ Includes one doctor's apprentice.

¶ Four customs officers, one clerk of Common Pleas, and one surveyor of the king' woods.

‖ Thirty-nine customs officers, four judges of Common Pleas, one paymaster oi British troops in North America, two deputy surveyors of the king's woods, one registei of court of admiralty, one attorney-general, one advocate-general, one chief justice, three vice-admiralty court judges, one treasurer of Bahamas, one lieutenant-governor, one secretary of Massachusetts, one treasurer, and one deputy treasurer. (Fourteen oi these also merchants, one a doctor, and six lawyers.)

Amount of Claims (238 known)

	Nova Scotia	*London*	*Combined*	*% of Known*
£500 or less	24	27	51	21·2
£501–£1,000	17	17	34	14·5
£1,001–£2,000	14	30	44	18·6
£2,001–£5,000	12	44	56	23·5
£5,001–£10,000	9	22	31	13·0
Over £10,000	6	15	21	9·2
Unknown	7	51	58	
Claim for salary or income only	2	16	18	
Total	91	222	313	100·00

Service to the British
(London and Nova Scotia Claimants Combined)

Served in the armed forces including the militia	
In the ranks	3
Probably in the ranks	14
Officers	64
Probably officers	5
Status unknown	45
Total	131 or 42·0%
Served in some other official way	22 or 7·0%
Total who served in some way	153 or 49·0%
Claimants killed or wounded	16 or 4·8%
Claimants captured or imprisoned	59 or 19·0%

Geographic Distribution (299 known)

Berkshire County		9
New Ashford	5	
Lanesboro	1	
Pittsfield	1	
Stockbridge	1	
Gt. Barrington	1	
Bristol County		8
Taunton	6	
Freetown	1	
Berkley	1	
Cumberland County		14
Falmouth	14	
Essex County		24
Salem	12	
Marblehead	6	
Newbury	4	
Haverhill	1	
Ipswich	1	
Hampshire County		1
Deerfield	1	
Lincoln County		22
Penobscot and environs	15	
Deer Island nr. Penobscot	3	
Machias	2	
Pownal	1	
Woolwich	1	
Middlesex County		22
Cambridge	7	
Charlestown	5	
Groton	3	
Townsend	2	
Littleton	1	
Marlboro	1	
Medford	1	
Stow	1	
Middlesex County	1	

New York

In the following tables (which include Vermont) 1,106 claims are analyzed. Two hundred and twenty-five were filed in London, 881 in Nova Scotia. Ten London claimants returned to the United States, twenty-six were resident in Canada, one in the West Indies, and one in the East Indies. Eight Nova Scotia claimants returned to the United States.

National Origin (974 known)

Country of Birth	*Nova Scotia Claimants*	*London Claimants*	*Combined*		*% of Known*	
Great Britain (country unknown)	4	15	19		1·92	
England	43	38	81		8·3	
Scotland	191	23	214		21·5	
Ireland	65	32	97		10·0	
Wales	2	2	4	489		50·0
Germany	64	5	69		7·1	
Holland	1	2	3			
Minorca	0	1	1			
Alsace	1	0	1			
America	405	80	485			50·0
Unknown	105	27	132			
Total	881	225	1,106			100·00

Date of Immigrants' Arrival in America (438 known)

	Nova Scotia	*London*	*Combined*
1763 and earlier	111	87	198
1764 and later	209	31	240
Unknown	51	0	51
Total	371	118	489

Occupations (1,071 known)

	Nova Scotia	*London*	*Combined*			*% of Known*
Farmers and Landowners	742	58	800			74·7
Commerce						
(a) Artisans and craftsmen	65†	29‡	94		8·9	
(b) Merchants and shopkeepers	27	50	77		7·3	
(c) Seamen	1	8§	9	190		17·7
(d) Innkeepers	4	4	8			
(e) Boarding-house keepers	0	2	2			
Professions						
(a) Anglican ministers	0	9	9			
German Reformed	1	0	1			
Roman Catholic	0	1	1			
(b) Doctors	6	7	13			
(c) Lawyers	3	5	8			
(d) Surveyors	0	2	2	39		3·7
(e) Schoolmasters	0	2	2			
(f) King's College professors	0	2	2			
(g) Broker and vendue master	1	0	1			
Office-Holders	5¶	37‖	42			3·9
Unknown	26	9	35			
Total	881	225	1,106			100·00

† Nineteen blacksmiths, seven shoemakers, five tanners, five carpenters, four each: weavers, coopers, three millers, three tailors, two tinmen (one also a japanner), one each: silversmith, cordwainer, armorer, gardener, woodcutter, bricklayer, joiner, carter, ferryman, gunsmith, cutler, hatter, and millwright.

‡ Four watchmakers, three shoemakers, two each: tanner, hairdresser, one each: livery-stable keeper, saddler, cooper, silversmith, last-maker, brewer, carpenter and herring smoker, potash works and nailery, milkman, carter, baker, blacksmith, 'labourer', butcher, housekeeper, flaxdresser, waiter at a tavern, pavior.

§ Five masters of vessels and three mariners.

¶ Three sheriffs, one deputy commissary, one deputy surveyor-general.

‖ Six customs officials, four in Indian Department, three judges of Common Pleas, three sheriffs, two clerks of peace, two supreme court judges, one each: governor, chief justice, commander of sloop on Lake Champlain, deputy secretary of New York, mayor of New York, barrack-master, attorney-general, governor of Oswego, judge of admiralty, surveyor-general, secretary to Tryon, lieutenant-governor of Crown Point and Ticonderoga, chief engineer in America, master carpenter, land office, mayor and coroner of Albany, agent to Governor Skene.

Amount of Claims (1,025 known)

	Nova Scotia	*London*	*Combined*	*% of Known*
£500 or less	630	30	660	64·0
£501–£1,000	110	23	133	13·5
£1,001–£2,000	58	29	87	8·5
£2,001–£5,000	40	33	73	7·1
£5,001–£10,000	9	24	33	3·2
Over £10,000	2	37	39	3·7
Unknown	31	38	69	
Claim for salary or income only	1	11	12	
Total	881	225	1,106	100·00

Service to the British
(*London and Nova Scotia Claimants Combined*)

Served in the armed forces including the militia	
In the ranks	113
Probably in the ranks	70
Officers	160
Status unknown	390
Total	733 or 67·0%
Served in some other official way	87 or 8·0%
Total who served in some way	820 or 75·0%

Claimants killed or wounded		36 or 3·3%
Claimants captured or imprisoned		313 or 28·5%

Geographic Distribution (1,068 known)

Albany County		259
Albany and environs	32	
Arlington	10	
Balls Town	5	
Bennington	5	
Cambridge	12	
Hosack	8	
Manor of Livingston	3	
Manor of Rensselaer	7	
Pittstown	11	
Rensselaerwick	2	
Saratoga	43	
Schoharie	12	
Stillwater	10	
Albany County	99	
Charlotte County		143
Crown Point	11	
Fort Edward	10	
Kingsbury	20	
Skenesborough	13	
Ticonderoga	5	
Charlotte County	84	
Cumberland County		9
Rockingham	1	
Wethersfield	1	
Windsor	1	
Cumberland County	6	
Dutchess County		64
Fredericksburg	4	
Nine Partners	6	
Poughkeepsie	4	
Dutchess County	50	

Occupations (200 known)

	Nova Scotia	*London*	*Combined*		*% of Known*	
Farmers and Landowners	48	19	67			33·5
Commerce						
(a) Artisans and craftsmen	12†	29‡	41		20·5	
(b) Merchants and shopkeepers	13	20	33		16·5	
(c) Seamen and pilots	0	3	3	84		42·0
(d) Innkeepers	0	6	6			
(e) Shipbuilder	0	1	1			
Professions						
(a) Anglican ministers	0	7	7			
(b) Lawyers	0	4	4			
(c) Schoolmaster	0	1	1			
(d) Doctors	0	7	7			
(e) Newspaper printers	0	2	2	23		11·5
(f) Broker	0	1	1			
(g) Clerk to mayor of Philadelphia	0	1	1			
Office-Holders	4§	22¶	26			13·0
Unknown	1	5	6			
Total	78	128	206			100·00

† Five carpenters, two each: blacksmiths, millers, one each: millwright, leather-breeches maker, and whitesmith.

‡ Three blacksmiths, three tanners, two each: masons, weavers, whitesmiths, coach-makers, brewers, and carpenters, one each: snuff maker, silversmith, soap boiler, laborer, tailor, baker, watchmaker, millwright, livery stable, jeweler, and miller.

§ One each: deputy surveyor of Pennsylvania, customs official, Indian Department, and judge of Common Pleas.

¶ Ten customs officers, four judges of Common Pleas, one each: high constable of Philadelphia, judge of King's Bench, mayor of Philadelphia, attorney-general, clerk to the master of the rolls, military officer, lieutenant-governor, and marshal of admiralty court.

Amount of Claims (168 known)

	Nova Scotia	*London*	*Combined*	*% of Known*
£500 or less	35	23	58	35·0
£501–£1,000	14	16	30	18·0
£1,001–£2,000	15	19	34	20·0
£2,001–£5,000	5	19	24	14·0
£5,001–£10,000	3	9	12	7·0
Over £10,000	0	10	10	6·0
Unknown	2	24	26	
Claim for salary or income only	4	8	12	
Total	78	128	206	100·00

Service to the British
(*London and Nova Scotia Claimants Combined*)

Served in the armed forces including the militia	
In the ranks	7
Probably in the ranks	28
Officers	29
Probably officers	1
Status unknown	10
Total	75 or 36·0%
Served in some other official way	50 or 24·0%
Total who served in some way	125 or 60·0%
Claimants killed or wounded	10 or 4·9%
Claimants captured or imprisoned	59 or 28·0%

Occupations (317 known)

	Nova Scotia	*London*	*Combined*		*% of Known*	
Farmers and Landowners	67	77†	144			45·5
Commerce						
(a) Artisans and craftsmen	1‡	29§	30	101	9·3	31·5
(b) Merchants and shopkeepers	3	62	65		20·5	
(c) Seamen and pilots	0	2¶	2			
(d) Innkeepers	1	2	3			
(e) Ferry keeper	0	1	1			
Professions						
(a) Anglican ministers	0	6	6	36		11·5
Presbyterian minister	0	1	1			
(b) Lawyers	0	4	4			
(c) Doctors	1	10	11			
(d) Midwife	0	1	1			
(e) Schoolmasters	2	7	9			
(f) Artist	0	1	1			
(g) Organist	0	1	1			
(h) Fencing master	0	1	1			
(i) Surveyor	0	1	1			
Office-Holders	0	36‖	36			11·5
Unknown	1	2	3			
Total	76	244	320			100·00

† Includes three overseers.

‡ One blacksmith.

§ Four carpenters, three shoemakers, two each: millers, bakers, and blacksmiths, one each: tin-plate worker, jeweler, butcher, leather dresser, drayer, carter, weaver, tailor, gunsmith, distiller, saddler, coachmaker, shipwright, mantuamaker, upholsterer, and bricklayer.

¶ One master and one pilot.

‖ Ten customs officials, four in Indian Department, two receiver-generals of quit rents, one each: deputy to surveyor-general of woods, deputy surveyor-general, governor of Fort Johnson, treasurer, lieut.-governor, gunner at the fort, coxswain at the fort, judge of vice-admiralty, marshal of vice-admiralty court, chief justice, clerk of crown, deputy secretary of S.C., deputy register, clerk of council's office, harbor master of Charleston, sheriff, chief clerk of Common Pleas, secretary of S.C., and two attorney-generals.

Amount of Claims (293 known)

	Nova Scotia	*London*	*Combined*	*% of Known*
£500 or less	48	23	71	24·0
£501–£1,000	11	38	49	16·5
£1,001–£2,000	10	40	50	17·2
£2,001–£5,000	3	57	60	20·5
£5,001–£10,000	2	27	29	10·0
Over £10,000	1	33	34	11·8
Unknown	1	15	16	
Claim for salary or income only	0	11	11	
Total	76	244	320	100·00

Service to the British
(*London and Nova Scotia Claimants Combined*)

Served in the armed forces including the militia	
In the ranks	7
Probably in the ranks	57
Officers	82
Probably officers	3
Status unknown	12
Total	161 or 50·0%
Served in some other official way	24 or 7·5%
Total who served in some way	185 or 57·5%
Claimants killed or wounded	27 or 8·5%
Claimants captured or imprisoned	95 or 30·0%

3.3 MARYLAND OBJECTS TO VIRGINIA'S CLAIMS TO WESTERN LANDS

May 21, 1779, *Journals of the Continental Congress*, XIV 619–22

The delegates of Maryland informed Congress, that they have received instructions respecting the articles of confederation, which they are directed to lay before Congress, and to have entered on their journals; the instructions being read are as follows:

Instructions of the general assembly of Maryland, to George Plater, William Paca, William Carmichael, John Henry, James Forbes and Daniel of St Thomas Jenifer, esqrs;

GENTLEMEN, Having conferred upon you a trust of the highest nature, it is evident we place great confidence in your integrity, abilities and zeal to promote the general welfare of the United States, and the particular interest of this state, where the latter is not incompatible with the former; but to add greater weight to your proceedings in Congress, and to take away all suspicion that the opinions you there deliver, and the votes you give, may be the mere opinions of individuals, and not resulting from your knowledge of the sense and deliberate judgment of the state you represent, we think it our duty to instruct you as followeth on the subject of the confederation, a subject in which, unfortunately, a supposed difference of interest has produced an almost equal division of sentiments among the several states composing the union: We say a supposed difference of interests; for, if local attachments and prejudices, and the avarice and ambition of individuals, would give way to the dictates of a sound policy, founded on the principles of justice, (and no other policy but what is founded on those immutable principles deserves to be called sound,) we flatter ourselves this apparent diversity of interests would soon vanish; and all the states would confederate on terms mutually advantageous to all; for they would then perceive that no other confederation than one so formed can be lasting. Although the pressure of immediate calamities, the dread of their continuance from the appearance of disunion, and some other peculiar circumstances, may have induced some states to accede to the present confederation, contrary to their own interests and judgments, it requires no great share of foresight to predict, that when those causes cease to operate, the states which have thus acceded to the confederation will consider it as no longer binding, and will eagerly embrace the first occasion of asserting their just rights and securing their independence. Is it possible that those states, who are ambitiously grasping at territories, to which in our judgment they have not the least shadow of exclusive right, will use with greater moderation the increase of wealth and power derived from those territories, when acquired, than what they have displayed in their endeavours to acquire them? we think not; we are convinced the same spirit which hath prompted them to insist on a claim so extravagant, so repugnant to every principle of justice, so incompatible with the general welfare of all the states, will urge them on to add oppression to injustice. If they should not be incited by a superiority of wealth and strength to oppress by open force their less wealthy and less powerful neighbours, yet the depopulation, and consequently the impoverishment of those states, will necessarily follow, which by an unfair construction of the confederation may be stripped of a common interest in, and the common benefits derivable from, the western country. Suppose, for instance, Virginia indisputably possessed of the extensive and fertile country to which she has set up a claim, what would be the probable consequences to Maryland of such an undisturbed and undisputed possession? they cannot escape the least discerning.

Virginia, by selling on the most moderate terms a small proportion of the lands in question, would draw into her treasury vast sums of money, and in proportion to the sums arising from such sales, would be enabled to lessen her taxes: lands comparatively cheap and taxes comparatively low, with the lands and taxes of an adjacent state, would quickly drain the state thus disadvantageously circumstanced of its most useful inhabitants, its wealth; and its consequence in the scale of the confederated states would sink of course. A claim so injurious to more than one half, if not to the whole of the United States, ought to be supported by the clearest evidence of the right. Yet what evidences of that right have been produced? what arguments alleged in support either of the evidence or the right; none that we have heard of deserving a serious refutation.

It has been said that some of the delegates of a neighbouring state have declared their opinion of the impracticability of governing the extensive dominion claimed by that state: hence also the necessity was admitted of dividing its territory and erecting a new state, under the auspices and direction of the elder, from whom no doubt it would receive its form of government, to whom it would be bound by some alliance or confederacy, and by whose councils it would be influenced: such a measure, if ever attempted, would certainly be opposed by the other states, as inconsistent with the letter and spirit of the proposed confederation. Should it take place, by establishing a sub-confederacy, *imperium in imperio*, the state possessed of this extensive dominion must then either submit to all the inconveniences of an overgrown and unwieldy government, or suffer the authority of Congress to interpose at a future time, and to lop off a part of its territory to be erected into a new and free state, and admitted into the confederation on such conditions as shall be settled by nine states. If it is necessary for the happiness and tranquillity of a state thus overgrown, that Congress should hereafter interfere and divide its territory; why is the claim to that territory now made and so pertinaciously insisted on? we can suggest to ourselves but two motives; either the declaration of relinquishing at some future period a portion of the country now contended for, was made to lull suspicion asleep, and to cover the designs of a secret ambition, or if the thought was seriously entertained, the lands are now claimed to reap an immediate profit from the sale. We are convinced policy and justice require that a country unsettled at the commencement of this war, claimed by the British crown, and ceded to it by the treaty of Paris, if wrested from the common enemy by the blood and treasure of the thirteen states, should be considered as a common property, subject to be parcelled out by Congress into free, convenient and independent governments, in such manner and at such times as the wisdom of that assembly shall hereafter direct. Thus convinced, we should betray the trust reposed in us by our constituents, were we to authorize you to ratify on their behalf the confederation, unless it be farther explained: we have coolly and dispassionately considered the subject; we have weighed probable inconveniences and hardships against the sacrifice of just and essential rights; and do instruct you not to agree to the confederation, unless an article or articles be added thereto in conformity with our declaration: should we succeed in obtaining such article or articles, then you are hereby fully empowered to accede to the confederation.

That these our sentiments respecting the confederation may be more publicly known and more explicitly and concisely declared, we have drawn up the annexed declaration, which we instruct you to lay before Congress, to have it printed, and to deliver to each of the delegates of the other states in Congress assembled, copies thereof, signed by yourselves or by such of you as may be present at the time of the delivery; to the intent and purpose that the copies aforesaid may be communicated to our brethren of the United States, and the contents of the said declaration taken into their serious and candid consideration.

Also we desire and instruct you to move at a proper time, that these instructions be read to Congress by their secretary, and entered on the journals of Congress.

We have spoken with freedom, as becomes freemen, and we sincerely wish that these our representations may make such an impression on that assembly as to induce them to make such addition to the articles of confederation as may bring about a permanent union.

A true copy from the proceedings of December 15, 1778.

Test, J. Duckett, C. H. D.

3.4 POLICY OF VIRGINIA

'An act for more effectually securing to the officers and soldiers of the Virginia line, the lands reserved to them, for discouraging present settlements on the north west side of the Ohio river, and for punishing persons attempting to prevent the execution of land office warrants', October 1779, *Laws of Virginia*, W. W. Hening, comp. (Richmond, Virginia 1809–23), vol. x, ch. 21

I. WHEREAS all the lands lying between the Green river and the Tenissee river, from the Alleghany mountains to the Ohio river, except the tract granted unto Richard Henderson, esq and company, have been reserved for the officers and soldiers of the Virginia line, on continental and state establishment, to give them choice of good lands, not only for the publick bounty due to them for military service, but also in their private adventures as citizens; and no person was allowed by law to enter any of the said lands, until they shall have been first satisfied; and it is now represented to the general assembly, that several persons are, notwithstanding, settling upon the lands so reserved; whereby the said officers and soldiers may be in danger of losing the preference and benefit intended for them by the legislature: *Be it enacted by the General Assembly*, That every person hereafter settling upon the lands reserved for the officers and soldiers as aforesaid; or who having already settled thereon, shall not remove from the said lands within six months next after the end of this present session of assembly, shall forfeit all his or her goods and chattels to the commonwealth; for the recovery of which, the attorney for the state in the county of Kentuckey for the time being, is hereby required immediately after the expiration of the said term, to enter prosecution by way of information in the court of the said county on behalf of the commonwealth, and on judgment being obtained, immediately to issue execution and proceed to the sale of such goods and chattles; and if the person or persons so prosecuted shall not remove from off the said lands in three months after prosecution so entered, the said attorney shall certify to the governour the name or names of the person or persons so refusing to remove, who, with the advice of the council may, and he is hereby required to issue orders to the commanding officer of the said county, or to any other officer in the pay of this state, to remove such person or persons or any others that may be settled thereon, from off the said lands by force of arms, except such as were actually settled prior to the first day of January, one thousand seven hundred and seventy eight.

II. And whereas no law of this commonwealth hath yet ascertained the proportions or quantity of land to be granted, at the end of the present war, to the officers of the Virginia line on continental or state establishment, or to the officers of the Virginia navy, and doubts may arise respecting the particular quantity of land due to the soldiers and sailors, from the different terms of their enlistments; *Be it enacted*, That the officers who shall have served in the Virginia line on continental establishment, or in the army or navy upon state establishment to the end of the present war; and the non-commissioned officers, soldiers, and sailors upon either of the said establishments, their heirs or legal representatives, shall respectively be entitled to and receive the proportion and quantities of land following; that is to say, every colonel, five thousand acres; every lieutenant colonel, four thousand five hundred acres; every major, four thousand acres; every captain, three thousand acres; every subaltern, two thousand acres; every non-commissioned officer who having enlisted for the war, shall have served to the end thereof, four hundred acres; and every soldier and sailor under the like circumstances, two hundred acres; every non-commissioned officer, who having enlisted for the term of three years, shall have served out the same, or to the end of the present war, two hundred acres; and every soldier and sailor under the like circumstances, one hundred acres; every officer of the navy the same quantity of land as an officer of equal rank in the army.[1] And where any officer, soldier, or sailor shall have fallen or died in the service, his heirs or legal representatives shall be entitled to and receive the same quantity of land as would have been due to such officer, soldier, or sailor respectively, had he been living.

III. And whereas, although no lands were allowed by law to be entered or warrants to be located on the north west side of the Ohio river, until the farther order of the general assembly, several persons are notwithstanding removing themselves to and making new settlements on the lands upon the north west side of the said river, which will probably bring on an Indian war with some tribes still in amity with the United American States, and thereby involve the commonwealth in great expense and bring distress on the inhabitants of our western frontier: *Be it declared and enacted*, That no person so removing to and settling on the said lands on the north west side of the Ohio river, shall be entitled to or allowed any right of pre-emption or other benefit whatever, from such settlement or occupancy; and the governour is hereby desired to issue a proclamation, requiring all persons settled on the said lands immediately to remove therefrom, and forbidding others to settle in future, and moreover with the advice of the council, from time to time, to order such armed force as shall be thought necessary to remove from the said lands, such person or persons as shall remain on or settle contrary to the said proclamation: *Provided*, That nothing herein contained shall be construed in any

[1] See *Laws of Virginia*, vol. 9, pp. 179, 589, as to land bounty offered by congress. – See also *Laws of Virginia*, x 24, 34, as to land bounties promised to officers, soldiers, sailors and marines. – Ibid., p. 26, land bounties to volunteers, under *Col. George Rogers Clarke*, and to soldiers for the protection of the *Ilinois* country. – Ibid., p. 141, land bounties to chaplains, surgeons, and surgeons' mates. – See October, 1780, chap. 27, sec. 4, land bounties, for the first time, declared to general officers, and an addition of one third, to any former bounty, promised to officers. – November 1781, chap. 19, sec. 12, 13, 14, state officers entitled to the same bounty as continental; cavalry the same emoluments as infantry; and officers and seamen of the navy, the same as in land service. – May, 1782, chap. 47, sec. 9, 13, additional bounty for service over six years.

manner to injure or affect any French, Canadian, or other families, or persons heretofore actually settled in or about the villages near or adjacent to the posts reduced by the forces of this state.

IV. And whereas various reports have been industriously circulated by evil minded and designing men, of a combination to hinder by force and violence, the execution and survey of legal land warrants, whereby many people have been deterred from purchasing unappropriated lands upon the south east side of the Ohio river within this commonwealth, and the receipt of considerable sums of money at the treasury thereby prevented to the injury of the publick credit, and tending to destroy all confidence in the laws of the land: *Be it farther enacted*, That all and every person or persons who shall by force or violence, or by threats of force or violence, attempt to hinder or prevent the execution of any warrant from the register of the land office upon waste and unappropriated lands, or who shall by force or violence, or by threats of force or violence attempt to hinder, restrain, or prevent any surveyor, chain carriers, markers, or other persons necessary employed therein, from laying off, marking, or bounding any waste or unappropriated land according to law, by virtue of such warrant, and also all and every person or persons, aiding, abetting, or assisting in, or accessary to such force or violence, shall upon conviction thereof, forfeit and lose his, her, or their title to all ungranted land which he, she, or they, may or shall have acquired by settlement, preemption right, land office warrant, or any other means whatsoever, and shall moreover suffer twelve months imprisonment without bail or mainprize, and be rendered ineligible and incapable of being appointed to, or holding any office of trust or profit, civil or military within this commonwealth, for the space of seven years. And all justices of the peace and other civil officers, are hereby strictly enjoined and required to suppress all such force or violence, and to cause the offenders to be apprehended and brought to justice; and all and every person or persons rescuing or attempting to rescue any such offender, shall be deemed and are hereby declared accessaries, and subject to the same penalties and punishment as the principal.

3.5 CONGRESS DECLARES POLICY FOR PUBLIC LANDS AND FORMATION OF NEW STATES[1]

October 10, 1780, *Journals of the Continental Congress*, ed. G. Hunt, XVIII 915

Resolved, that the unappropriated lands that may be ceded or relinquished to the United States, by any particular States, pursuant to the recommendation of Congress of the 6 day of September last, shall be disposed of for the common benefit of the United States, and be settled and formed into distinct republican States, which shall become members of the Federal Union, and shall have the same rights of sovereignty, freedom and independence, as the other States: that each State which shall be so formed shall contain a suitable extent of territory, not less than one hundred nor more than one hundred and fifty miles square, or as near thereto as circumstances will admit;

That the necessary and reasonable expences which any particular State shall have incurred since the commencement of the present war, in subduing any of the British posts, or in maintaining forts or garrisons within and for the defence, or in acquiring any part of the territory that may be ceded or relinquished to the United States, shall be reimbursed;

That the said lands shall be granted and settled at such times and that under such regulations as shall hereafter be agreed on by the United States in Congress assembled, or any nine or more of them.

3.6 REMONSTRANCE FROM NEW JERSEY

June 1783, *Journals of the Continental Congress*, XXIV 408–9

To the United States in Congress Assembled.

The representation and remonstrance of the legislative council and general assembly of the State of New Jersey, sheweth,

That the legislature of this State is informed, that the important subject of the western, or what is commonly called crown lands, is

[1] A clause to the effect that no purchases from Indians within the ceded territory, 'which shall not have been ratified by lawful authority, shall be deemed valid or ratified by Congress', was lost on an even division. Cf. Constitution of Virginia, s. 21. [S. E. Morison's note.]

soon to be re-considered and finally determined by Congress, especially as far as relates to the cession made by the legislature of the State of Virginia, in January, 1781, of a part of the western country or vacant territory.

The legislature cannot but express their surprise on hearing that the consideration of the subject is resumed by Congress so speedily after its last discussion, as appears by an act of Congress of the eighteenth of April last past, which is contained in the following words:

'That as a further mean, as well of hastening the extinguishment of the debts, as establishing the harmony of the United States, it be recommended to the States, which have passed no acts towards complying with the resolutions of Congress of the sixth of September and tenth of October, 1780, relative to the cession of the territorial claims to make the liberal cessions therein recommended, and to the States which may have passed acts complying with the said resolutions, in part only, to revise and compleat such compliance;' which said act has been officially laid before us during the present sitting, and appears designed by Congress to be transmitted to every State in the union, not only to the legislatures thereof, but to the people at large: the legislature of this State must be of opinion, that the latter part of the said recommendation of Congress was expressly applicable to the act of the legislature of the Commonwealth of Virginia, as the cession thereby made has heretofore been deemed by Congress a partial one, and by this State, partial, unjust and illiberal.

The legislature, to avoid unnecessary repetition, beg leave in the most earnest manner, to call the attention of Congress to the records in their possession of the proceedings of the legislature of this State with regard to the present subject, beginning with their representation of the 16 of June, 1778, and at different periods since, in which are fully contained the just and uncontrovertible claims of this State to its full proportion of all vacant territory.

It is particularly disagreeable to have occasion to trouble Congress with so many applications on this head, but the importance of the subject, the danger of so much property being unjustly wrested from us, together with its being our indispensable duty, in justification and defence of the rights of the people we represent, must be our apology: we cannot be silent, while viewing one State aggrandizing herself by the unjust detention of that property, which has been procured by the common blood and treasure of the whole, and which on every principle of reason and justice, is vested in Congress for the use and general benefit of the Union they represent.

They doubt not the disposition of Congress to redress every grievance that may be laid before them, and are of opinion there can be no greater cause for complaint, nor more just reasons for redress, than in the present case.

They do therefore express their dissatisfaction with the cession of western territory made by the State of Virginia, in January, 1781, as being far short of affording that justice which is equally due to the United States at large, and request that Congress will not accept of the said cession, but that they will press upon the said State to make a more liberal surrender of that territory of which they claim so boundless a proportion.

The legislature place the utmost confidence in the wisdom and justice of Congress, and assure themselves that as far as it lies in the power of that august body, the union will be strictly maintained.

Council Chamber, June 14, 1783. House of Assembly, June 14, 1783.

By order of Council, By order of the House,

WIL. LIVINGSTON, *President.* EPHRAIM HARRIS, *Speaker.*

3.7 REPORT AND RESOLUTION OF CONGRESS ON THE QUESTION OF CONDITIONS OF THE VIRGINIA CESSION: INCLUDING THE TERMS OF THE VIRGINIA CESSION

September 13, 1783, *Journals of the Continental Congress,* XXV 554–64.

Deleted matter indicated thus, ⟨ ⟩

Congress resumed the consideration of the report of the committee on the Virginia cession, and the same being amended, a motion was made by Mr [Daniel] Carroll, seconded by Mr [James] McHenry, to postpone the further consideration of the report, in order to take up the following:

Whereas by the 6th article of the preliminary articles of peace between his Britannic Majesty, and their Most Christian and Catholic

Majesties, signed on the 3d day of November, 1762, and ratified the 10 day of February, 1763, it is stipulated and agreed, that, 'the confines between the dominions of Great Britain and France, on the continent of North America, shall be irrevocably fixed by a line drawn along the middle of the river Mississippi, from its source as far as the river Iberville, and from thence by a line drawn along the middle of this river, and of the lakes Maurepas and Pontchartrain to the sea'; and to this purpose the Most Christian king cedes in full right and guaranties to his Britannic Majesty the river and port of Mobile, and every thing that he possesses on the left side of the river Mississippi, except the town of New Orleans, and the island on which it is situated, which shall remain to France; provided that the navigation of the river Mississippi shall be equally free to the subjects of Great Britain and France, in its whole breadth and length from its source to the sea, and that part expressly which is between the said island of New Orleans, and the right bank of that river, as well as the passage both in and out of its mouth. And whereas by the nineteenth article of the said treaty, his Catholic Majesty cedes and guaranties in full right to his Britannic Majesty, all that Spain possesses in the continent of North America, to the east or to the southeast of the river Mississippi. And whereas by the articles of treaty between Great Britain and the United States, done at Paris the 30th day of November, 1782, the boundaries of the United States are set forth, described and agreed to be by the 2d article of the said treaty, viz. 'From the northwest angle of Nova Scotia, viz. that angle which is formed by a line drawn due north from the source of the St Croix river to the highlands which divide those rivers that empty themselves into the river St Lawrence, from those which fall into the Atlantic ocean, to the northwestermost head of Connecticut river, thence down along the middle of that river to the 45th degree of north latitude; from thence by a line due west on said latitude, until it strikes the river Iroquois or Cataraquy; thence along the middle of said river into lake Ontario, through the middle of said lake until it strikes the communication by water between that lake and lake Erie; thence along the middle of said communication into lake Erie, through the middle of said lake, until it arrives at the water communication between that lake and lake Huron; thence along the middle of said water communication into lake Huron; thence through the middle of the said lake to the water communication between that and lake Superior; thence through lake Superior northward of the isles Royal and Philipeaux, to the long lake; thence through the middle of said long lake and the water communication between it and the lake of the woods, to the said lake of the woods; thence through the said lake to the most northwestern point thereof, and from thence on a due west course to the river Mississippi; thence by a line to be drawn along the middle of the said river Mississippi, until it shall intersect the northermost part of the 31st degree of north latitude. South by a line to be drawn due east from the determination of the line last mentioned, in the latitude of 31 degrees north of the equator, to the middle of the river Apalachicola or Catahouche; thence along the middle thereof to its junction with the flint river; thence straight to the head of St Mary's river; and thence down along the middle of St Mary's river to the Atlantic ocean. East by a line to be drawn along the middle of the river St Croix, from its mouth in the bay of fundy to its source, and from its source directly north to the aforesaid highlands which divide the rivers that fall into the Atlantic ocean from those which fall into the river St Lawrence: comprehending all islands within twenty leagues of any part of the shores of the United States, and lying between lines to be drawn due east from the points where the aforesaid boundaries between Nova Scotia on the one part, and East Florida on the other, shall respectively touch the bay of Fundy, and the Atlantic ocean; excepting such islands as now are or heretofore have been within the limits of the said province of Nova Scotia.'

And whereas by the 6th and 11th articles of the treaty of alliance, eventual and ⟨definitive⟩ defensive, between the Most Christian King, and the United States, signed at Paris 6th February, 1778, and ratified by the United States in Congress assembled, the 4 day of May, 1778, the Most Christian King renounces for ever the possession of the islands of Bermudas, as well as of any part of the continent of North America, which before the treaty of Paris in 1763, or in virtue of that treaty, were acknowledged to belong to the Crown of Great Britain or to the United States, heretofore called British colonies, or which are at this time, or have lately been under the power of the King and Crown of Great Britain, and guarantees to the United States their possessions and the additions or conquests that their confederation may obtain during the war, from any of the dominions now or heretofore possessed by Great Britain in North America. And whereas the territory ceded and guarantied as aforesaid, comprehends a large extent of country lying without the lines, limits or acknowledged boundaries of any of the United States, over which, or any part of which, no State can or ought to exercise any sovereign, legislative or jurisdictional faculty, the same being acquired under the confederation, and by the joint and united efforts of all. And whereas ⟨more than a majority⟩ several of the states acceded to the confederation under the idea held forth by the State of Maryland, in her instructions to her delegates, entered on the Journals of Congress, May 21, 1779, viz. 'that a country unsettled at the commencement of this war, claimed by the British Crown, and ceded to it by the treaty of Paris, if wrested from the common enemy, by the blood and treasure of the thirteen states, should be considered as a common property, subject to be parcelled out by Congress, into free, convenient and independent governments, in such manner, and at such times, as the wisdom of that assembly shall hereafter direct'. And whereas the said State of Maryland, especially for herself, provides and declares, in 'An Act entered on the Journals of Congress, 12 February, 1781, entitled an act to empower the delegates of this State in Congress, to subscribe and ratify the Articles of Confederation', viz. 'that by acceding to the said confederation, this State doth not relinquish or intend to relinquish any right or interest she hath with the other united or confederated states, to the back country; but claims the same as fully as was done by the legislature of this State, in their declaration which stands entered on the Journals of Congress; this State relying on the justice of the several states hereafter, as to the said claim made by this State.'

And whereas the United States have succeeded to the sovereignty over the western territory, and are thereby vested as one undivided and independent nation, with all and every power and right exercised by the king of Great Britain, over the said territory, or the lands lying and situated without the boundaries of the several states, and within the limits above described; and whereas the western territory ceded by France and Spain to Great Britain, relinquished to the United States by Great Britain, and guarantied to the United States by France as aforesaid, if properly managed, will enable the United States to comply with their promises of land to their officers and soldiers; will relieve their citizens from much of the weight of taxation; will be a means of restoring national credit, and if cast into new states, will tend to increase the general happiness of mankind, by rendering the purchase of land easy, and the possession of liberty permanent; therefore

Resolved, That a committee be appointed to report the territory lying without the boundaries of the several states, and within the limits of the United States, and to report the most eligible part or parcels thereof, for one or more convenient and independent states; and also to report an establishment for a land-office.

On the question to postpone for the purpose aforesaid, the yeas and nays being required by Mr [Daniel] Carroll,

Delegate	Vote	State
New Hampshire,		
Mr Foster,	ay	*
Massachusetts,		
Mr Holten,	no	no
Higginson,	no	
Rhode Island,		
Mr Ellery,	no	no
Howell,	no	
Connecticut,		
Mr S. Huntington,	no	no
B. Huntington,	no	
New York,		
Mr Duane,	no	no
L'Hommedieu,	no	
New Jersey,		
Mr Boudinot,	ay	ay
Clark,	ay	
Pennsylvania,		
Mr Fitzsimmons,	no	no
Montgomery,	ay	
Peters,	no	
Maryland,		
Mr Carroll,	ay	ay
McHenry,	ay	
Virginia,		
Mr Jones,	no	no
Madison,	no	
Bland,	no	
Lee,	no	
Mercer,	no	
North Carolina,		
Mr Hawkins,	no	no
Williamson,	no	
South Carolina,		
Mr Rutledge,	no	no
Read,	no	
Beresford,	no	

So the question was lost.

The report as amended, is as follows:

The committee, consisting of Mr [John] Rutledge, Mr [Oliver] Ellsworth, Mr [Gunning] Bedford, Mr [Nathaniel] Gorham and Mr [James] Madison, to whom were referred the act of the legislature of Virginia, of the 2d of January, 1781, and the report thereon, report, that they have considered the several matters referred to them, and observe, that the legislature of Virginia, by their act of the 2d of January, 1781, resolved that they would yield to the Congress of the United States, for the benefit of the said states, all right, title and claim which the said Commonwealth hath to the lands northwest of the river Ohio, upon the following conditions, viz.

1. That the territory so ceded, should be laid out and formed into states, containing a suitable extent of territory, not less than one hundred nor more than one hundred and fifty miles square, or as near thereto as circumstances would admit: and that the states so formed, should be distinct republican states, and admitted members of the federal union; having the same rights of sovereignty, freedom and independence as the other states.

2. That Virginia should be allowed and fully reimbursed by the United States, her actual expences in reducing the British posts at the Kaskaskies and St. Vincents, the expence of maintaining garrisons and supporting civil government there, since the reduction of the said posts, and in general all the charge she has incurred on account of the country on the northwest side of the Ohio river, since the commencement of the present war.

3. That the French and Canadian inhabitants and other settlers of the Kaskaskies, St Vincents and the neighbouring villages, who have professed themselves citizens of Virginia, should have their possessions and titles confirmed to them, and should be protected in the enjoyment of their rights and liberties; for which purpose troops should be stationed there at the charge of the United States, to protect them from the encroachments of the British forces at Detroit or elsewhere, unless the events of the war should render it impracticable.

4. As Colonel George Rogers Clarke planned and executed the secret expedition by which the British posts were reduced, and was promised if the enterprize succeeded, a liberal gratuity in lands in that country, for the officers and soldiers who first marched thither with him; that a quantity of land not exceeding one hundred and fifty thousand acres, should be allowed and granted to the said officers and soldiers, and the other officers and soldiers that have been since incorporated into the said regiment, to be laid off in one tract, the length of which not to exceed double the breadth, in such place on the northwest side of the Ohio as the majority of the officers should choose, and to be afterwards divided among the said officers and soldiers, in due proportion according to the laws of Virginia.

5. That in case the quantity of good lands on the southeast side of the Ohio, upon the waters of Cumberland river, and between the Green river and Tennessee river, which have been reserved by law for

the Virginia troops upon continental establishment, should, from the North Carolina line, bearing in further upon the Cumberland lands than was expected, prove insufficient for their legal bounties, the deficiency should be made up to the said troops in good lands, to be laid off between the rivers Scioto and little Miamis, on the northwest side of the river Ohio, in such proportions as have been engaged to them by the laws of Virginia.

6. That all the lands within the territory so ceded to the United States, and not reserved for or appropriated to any of the before-mentioned purposes, or disposed of in bounties to the officers and soldiers of the American army, should be considered as a common fund for the use and benefit of such of the United American States, as have become or shall become members of the confederation or fœderal alliance of the said states, Virginia inclusive, according to their usual respective proportions in the general charge and expenditure, and should be faithfully and *bona fide* disposed of for that purpose, and for no other use or purpose whatsoever.

7. And therefore that all purchases and deeds from any Indian or Indians, or from any Indian nation or nations, for any lands within any part of the said territory which have been or should be made for the use or benefit of any private person or persons whatsoever, and royal grants within the ceded territory, inconsistent with the chartered rights, laws and customs of Virginia, should be deemed and declared absolutely void and of no effect, in the same manner as if the said territory had still remained subject to and part of the Commonwealth of Virginia.

8. That all the remaining territory of Virginia, included between the Atlantic ocean and the southeast side of the river Ohio, and the Maryland, Pensylvania and North Carolina boundaries, should be guarantied to the Commonwealth of Virginia, by the said United States.

Whereupon your committee are of opinion, that the first condition is provided for by the act of Congress of the 10th of October, 1780.

[That in order to comply with the second condition so far as has been heretofore provided for by the act of the 10th of October, 1780, it is agreed] that one commissioner should be appointed by Congress, one by the State of Virginia, and another by those two commissioners, who, or a majority of whom, should be authorised and empowered to adjust and liquidate the account of the necessary and reasonable expences incurred by the said State, [which they may judge to be comprised within the true intent and meaning of the said recited act.]

With respect to the third condition, the committee are of opinion, that the settlers therein described should have their possessions and titles confirmed to them, and be protected in the enjoyment of their rights and liberties.

Your committee are further of opinion, that the 4th, 5th and 6th conditions being reasonable, should be agreed to by Congress.

With respect to the 7th condition, your committee are of opinion, that it would be improper for Congress to declare the purchases and grants therein mentioned, absolutely void and of no effect; and that the 6th condition, engaging how the lands beyond the Ohio shall be disposed of, is sufficient on this point.

As to the last condition, your committee are of opinion, that Congress cannot agree to guarantee to the Commonwealth of Virginia, the land described in the said condition, without entering into a discussion of the right of the State of Virginia to the said land; and that by the acts of Congress it appears to have been their intention, which the committee cannot but approve, to avoid all discussion of the territorial rights of individual states, and only to ⟨require⟩ recommend and accept a cession of their claims, whatsoever they might be, to vacant territory. Your committee conceive this condition of a guarantee, to be either unnecessary or unreasonable; inasmuch as, if the land above-mentioned is really the property of the State of Virginia, it is sufficiently secured by the confederation, and if it is not the property of that State, there is no reason or consideration for such guarantee.

Your committee therefore upon the whole recommend, that if the legislature of Virginia make a cession conformable to this report, Congress ⟨should⟩ accept such cession.

⟨And that a committee be appointed to repair to the State of Virginia, make the proper representation to its legislature, and endeavor to obtain what may be necessary on the part of the State for carrying the views of Congress into effect,⟩[1]

[1] A printed copy of this report, which was the one considered, as the indorsement shows, is in the *Papers of the Continental Congress*, no. 30, folio 563. It was delivered June 6, debated June 20, and agreed to on September 13. The amendments in the printed copy, made in Congress, which are indicated by brackets, are in the writing of Elias Boudinot. It is indorsed as delivered June 6, entered and read and 'Monday next assigned'.

On the question to agree to this report, the yeas and nays being required by Mr [David] Howell,

New Hampshire,		
Mr Foster,	no	*
Massachusetts,		
Mr Gerry,	ay	ay
Holten,	ay	
Higginson,	ay	
Rhode Island,		
Mr Ellery,	ay	ay
Howell,	ay	
Connecticut,		
Mr S. Huntington,	ay	ay
B. Huntington,	ay	
New York,		
Mr Duane,	ay	ay
L'Hommedieu,	ay	
New Jersey,		
Mr Boudinot,	no	no
Clark,	no	
Pennsylvania,		
Mr Fitzsimmons,	ay	ay
Montgomery,	no	
Peters,	ay	
Maryland,		
Mr Carroll,	no	no
McHenry,	no	
Virginia,		
Mr Jones,	ay	ay
Madison,	ay	
Bland,	ay	
A. Lee,	ay	
Mercer,	ay	
North Carolina,		
Mr Hawkins,	ay	ay
Williamson,	ay	
South Carolina,		
Mr Rutledge,	ay	ay
Read,	ay	
Beresford,	no	

So it was resolved in the affirmative.

3.8 CONGRESSIONAL ORDINANCE ON PUBLIC LANDS, MAY 20, 1785

'An Ordinance for ascertaining the mode of disposing of Lands in the Western Territory', *Journals of the Continental Congress*, XXVIII 375–8

Be it ordained by the United States in Congress assembled, that the territory ceded by individual States to the United States, which has been purchased of the Indian inhabitants, shall be disposed of in the following manner:

A surveyor from each State shall be appointed by Congress or a Committee of the States, who shall take an oath for the faithful discharge of his duty, before the geographer of the United States, who . . . shall occasionally form such regulations for their conduct, as he shall deem necessary; and shall have authority to suspend them for misconduct in office, and shall make report of the same to Congress . . .

The surveyors, as they are respectively qualified, shall proceed to divide the said territory into townships of six miles square, by lines running due north and south, and others crossing these at right angles, as near as may be, unless where the boundaries of the late Indian purchases may render the same impracticable . . .

The first line, running due north and south as aforesaid, shall begin on the river Ohio, at a point that shall be found to be due north from the western termination of a line, which has been run as the southern boundary of the State of Pennsylvania; and the first line, running east and west, shall begin at the same point, and shall extend throughout the whole territory; provided, that nothing herein shall be construed, as fixing the western boundary of the State of Pennsylvania. The geographer shall designate the townships, or fractional parts of townships, by numbers progressively from south to north; always beginning each range with No. 1; and the ranges shall be distinguished by their progressive numbers to the westward. The first range, extending from the Ohio to the lake Erie, being marked No. 1. The geographer shall personally attend to the running of the first east and west line; and shall take the latitude of the extremes of the first north and south line, and of the mouths of the principal rivers.

The lines shall be measured with a chain; shall be plainly marked by chaps on the trees, and exactly described on a plat; whereon shall be noted by the surveyor, at their proper distances, all mines, salt-springs, salt-licks and mill-seats, that shall come to his knowledge; and all water-courses, mountains and other remarkable and permanent things, over and near which such lines shall pass, and also the quality of the lands.

The plats of the townships respectively, shall be marked by subdivisions into lots of one mile square, or 640 acres, in the same direction as the external lines, and numbered from 1 to 36; always beginning the succeeding range of the lots with the number next to that with which the preceding one concluded.

The board of treasury shall transmit a copy of the original plats, previously noting thereon the townships and fractional parts of townships, which shall have fallen to the several States, by the distribution aforesaid,[1] to the commissioners of the loan-office of the several States, who, after giving notice . . . shall proceed to sell the townships or fractional parts of townships, at public vendue, in the following manner, viz.: The township or fractional part of a township No. 1, in the first range, shall be sold entire; and No. 2, in the same range, by lots; and thus in alternate order through the whole of the first range . . . provided, that none of the lands, within the said territory, be sold under the price of one dollar the acre, to be paid in specie, or loan-office certificates, reduced to specie value, by the scale of depreciation, or certificates of liquidated debts of the United States, including interest, besides the expense of the survey and other charges thereon, which are hereby rated at 36 dollars the township . . . on failure of which payment, the said lands shall again be offered for sale.

There shall be reserved for the United States out of every township the four lots, being numbered 8, 11, 26, 29, and out of every fractional part of a township, so many lots of the same numbers as shall be found thereon, for future sale. There shall be reserved the lot No. 16, of every township, for the maintenance of public schools within the said township; also one-third part of all gold, silver, lead and copper mines, to be sold, or otherwise disposed of as Congress shall hereafter direct. . . .

3.9 ATTITUDES OF KENTUCKY SETTLERS, FROM THE *JOURNAL OF THE FIRST CONVENTION OF KENTUCKY*

Tuesday, January 4, 1785, *Journal of Southern History* (1935) I 75–6

The Convention resolved itself into a Committee of the whole on the Order of the day –

Whereupon Mr President quitted the Chair and Mr Shelby took the Chair of the Committee and after some time spent therein Mr

[1] One-seventh of the townships, chosen by lot, to be distributed by the States among their veterans.

President resumed the Chair and Mr Shelby reported That the Committee had come to sundry Resolutions which he read in his place and then delivered the same in at the Clerks Table where they were again twice read and agreed to as follows –

X Resolved that all Laws imposing partial Taxes either directly or in their operation are greevous and against the Fundamental rights of the People –

X Resolved That the Law imposing a Tax of Five Shillings per hundred on Lands exceeding fourteen hundred Acres whether the same be in one or more surveys provided the same be contiguous is a greevance, Because it is partial in its operation and in many instances a retrospective Law –

X The Yeas & Nays being required by Mr McDowell. For the Resolve Mr Anderson, Mr Campbell Mr Morrison, Mr Cox, Mr Phillips Mr Hinds Mr King Mr Greenup, Mr Harrod, Mr Hite, Mr Brooks & Mr Green against the Resolve Mr Kincheloe Mr John Logan, Mr William Kennedy Mr Wallace, Mr Moseby, Mr Moore Mr Shelby, Mr McDowell & Mr Benj.n Logan

[11] Resolved That the Law imposing a duty on Merchandize brought into this District by way of Pitsburg is a greevance Because such goods having paid a duty on their first importation are again subjected to an additional duty on their advanced price when so brought into the District

X Resolved That the Law restricting the payment of the Salleries of the Judges of the Supreme Court to certain duties and Taxes arising within the District and not out of the common Treasury is a Greevance, Because the Inhabitants not only pay their own Judges, but also their proportion for the support of the Judges for the Eastern part of the State –

Your Committee beg leave further to report That they have had under their consideration the Resolve proposed on Wednesday last. 'Declaring that power hath not been Delegated to any body of men to transferr the good People of the United States or any part of their Lands to any other State or to the United States and therefor ought not to be exercised without their consent. Nor ought they to be relinquished or denied protection by their own or the United States' Upon which Your Committee are of Opinion that it is a Case of a very serious consequence but can not conceive that it can come before this Convention as not being a grievance now [12] existing within the District But it is the Opinion of your Committee That should an attempt of this kind be made, The good People of this District ought to oppose it by every Just and Lawfull method in their power

X Resolved That to grant any Person a larger quantity of Land that he designs Bona Fide to seat himself or his Family on, is a greevance, Because it is subversive of the fundamental Principles of a free republican Government to allow any individual, or Company or Body of Men to possess such large tracts of Country in their own right as may at a future day give them an undue influence, and because it opens a door to speculation by which innumerable evils may ensue to the less opolent part of the Inhabitants and therefor ought not to be done in the future disposal of Lands in this District.

X Resolved That the Nonresidence of those who hold lucrative offices in this District is a greevance.

The Honorable the Judges of the Supreme Court have according to order delivered in their reasons as follows.–

[12] Mr Chairman

In Complyance with an order of Convention, we beg leave to submit to the Committee a short state of the reasons why the Judges of the Supreme Court for the District of Kentucky have not proceeded to the decision of suits depending in that Court –

We need only suggest that two of the Judges have been slain by the Savages and another having declined to accept the Office has occasioned repeated delays – and the Court not being furnished with a Copy legally attested of the records of the Court of Commissioners that adjusted the Claims to Lands of the first Adventurers which the Judges are informed by the Attorneys for the litigants will be the material Evidence in the greater number of Suits now on the Docket, has also been another delay – But the Funds allotted to the support of this Court having hitherto proved unfruitfull, a Court house, Prison and Jury rooms, could not be built, nor the Attendants, and Books of Law necessary for the Court be procured, And altho we are willing to discharge the duties of the Office with which we have been honoured, without having our expenses immediately reimbursed, and to forego the advantages we might derive if we were at Liberty to engage in other [13] in other [*sic*] employments without the prospect of an adequate compensation, yet if all other impediments were removed, we are decidedly of Opinion that the Judges would violate the Trust reposed in them were they to proceed to hear causes, many of which are weighty and intricate as a fair tryal & Just decision could seldome be obtained whilst the Court is destitute of the conveniences we have enumerated.–

Most Obt Hble Servts

The Committee of the State of the District

Saml McDowell
Caleb Wallace

3.10 NORTHWEST ORDINANCE OF 1787

July 13, 1787, 'An Ordinance for the government of the Territory of the United States northwest of the River Ohio', *Journals of the Continental Congress*, XXXII 334 and 343

Be it ordained by the United States in Congress assembled, That the said territory, for the purposes of temporary government, be one district, subject, however, to be divided into two districts, as future circumstances may, in the opinion of Congress, make it expedient.

Be it ordained by the authority aforesaid, That the estates, both of resident and non-resident proprietors in the said Territory, dying intestate, shall descend to, and be distributed among their children, and the descendants of a deceased child, in equal parts; the descendants of a deceased child or grandchild to take the share of their deceased parent in equal parts among them: And where there shall be no children or descendants, then in equal parts to the next of kin in equal degree; and among collaterals, the children of a deceased brother or sister of the intestate shall have, in equal parts among them, their deceased parents' share; and there shall in no case be a distinction between kindred of the whole and half-blood; saving, in all cases, to the widow of the intestate her third part of the real estate for life, and one-third part of the personal estate; and this law relative to descents and dower, shall remain in full force until altered by the legislature of the district. And until the Governor and Judges shall adopt laws as hereinafter mentioned, estates in the said Territory may be devised or bequeathed by wills in writing, signed and sealed by him or her in whom the estate may be (being of full age), and attested by three witnesses; and real estates may be conveyed by lease and release, or bargain and sale, signed sealed and delivered by the person, being of full age, in whom the estate may be, and attested by two witnesses, provided such wills be duly proved, and such conveyances be acknowledged, or the execution thereof duly proved, and be recorded within one year after proper magistrates, courts, and registers shall be appointed for that purpose; and personal property may be transferred by delivery; saving, however to the French and Canadian inhabitants, and other settlers of the Kaskaskies, St. Vincents and the neighboring villages who have heretofore professed themselves citizens of Virginia, their laws and customs now in force among them, relative to the descent and conveyance, of property.

Be it ordained by the authority aforesaid, That there shall be appointed from time to time by Congress, a Governor, whose commission shall continue in force for the term of three years, unless sooner revoked by Congress; he shall reside in the district, and have a freehold estate therein in 1,000 acres of land, while in the exercise of his office.

There shall be appointed from time to time by Congress, a Secretary, whose commission shall continue in force for four years unless sooner revoked; he shall reside in the district, and have a freehold estate therein in 500 acres of land, while in the exercise of his office; it shall be his duty to keep and preserve the Acts and Laws passed by the Legislature, and the public records of the district, and the proceedings of the governor in his Executive department; and transmit authentic copies of such acts and proceedings, every six months, to the Secretary of Congress: There shall also be appointed a Court to consist of three Judges, any two of whom to form a court, who shall have a common law jurisdiction, and reside in the district, and have each therein a freehold estate in 500 acres of land while in the exercise of their offices; and their commissions shall continue in force during good behavior.

The Governor and Judges, or a majority of them, shall adopt and publish in the district such laws of the original States, criminal and civil, as may be necessary and best suited to the circumstances of the district, and report them to Congress from time to time: which laws shall be in force in the district until the organization of the General Assembly therein, unless disapproved of by Congress; but afterwards the Legislature shall have authority to alter them as they shall think fit.

The Governor, for the time being, shall be commander-in-chief of the militia, appoint and commission all officers in the same below the rank of general officers; all general officers shall be appointed and commissioned by Congress.

Previous to the organization of the General Assembly, the Governor shall appoint such magistrates and other civil officers in each county or township, as he shall find necessary for the preservation of the peace and good order in the same: After the General Assembly shall be organized, the powers and duties of the magistrates and other civil officers shall be regulated and defined by the said Assembly; but all magistrates and other civil officers not herein otherwise directed, shall, during the continuance of this temporary government, be appointed by the Governor.

For the prevention of crimes and injuries, the laws to be adopted or made shall have force in all parts of the district, and for the execution of process, criminal and civil, the Governor shall make proper divisions thereof; and he shall proceed from time to time as circumstances may require, to lay out the parts of the district in which the Indian titles shall have been extinguished, into counties and townships, subject however to such alterations as may thereafter be made by the Legislature.

So soon as there shall be 5,000 free male inhabitants of full age in the district, upon giving proof thereof to the Governor, they shall receive authority, with time and place, to elect representatives from their counties or townships to represent them in the General Assembly: *Provided*, That, for every 500 free male inhabitants, there shall be one representative, and so on progressively with the number of free male inhabitants shall the right of representation increase, until the number of representatives shall amount to 25; after which, the number and proportion of representatives shall be regulated by the Legislature: *Provided*, That no person be eligible or qualified to act as a representative unless he shall have been a citizen of one of the United States three years, and be a resident in the district, or unless he shall have resided in the district three years; and, in either case, shall likewise hold in his own right, in fee simple, 200 acres of land within the same: *Provided, also*, That a freehold in 50 acres of land in the district, having been a citizen of one of the States, and being resident in the district, or the like freehold and two years residence in the district, shall be necessary to qualify a man as an elector of a representative.

The representatives thus elected, shall serve for the term of two years; and, in case of the death of a representative, or removal from office, the Governor shall issue a writ to the county or township for which he was a member, to elect another in his stead, to serve for the residue of the term.

The General Assembly or Legislature shall consist of the Governor, Legislative Council, and a House of Representatives. The Legislative Council shall consist of five members, to continue in office five years, unless sooner removed by Congress; any three of whom to be a quorum: and the members of the Council shall be nominated and appointed in the following manner, to wit: As soon as representatives shall be elected, the Governor shall appoint a time and place for them to meet together; and, when met, they shall nominate ten persons, residents in the district, and each possessed of a freehold in 500 acres of land, and return their names to Congress; five of whom Congress shall appoint and commission to serve as aforesaid; and, whenever a vacancy shall happen in the Council, by death or removal from office, the House of Representatives shall nominate two persons, qualified as aforesaid, for each vacancy, and return their names to Congress; one of whom Congress shall appoint and commission for the residue of the term. And every five years, four months at least before the expiration of the time of service of the members of Council, the said House shall nominate ten persons, qualified as aforesaid, and return their names to Congress; five of whom Congress shall appoint and commission to serve as members of the Council five years, unless sooner removed. And the Governor, Legislative Council, and House of Representatives, shall have authority to make laws in all cases, for the good government of the district, not repugnant to the principles and articles in this ordinance established and declared. And all bills, having passed by a majority in the House, and by a majority in the Council, shall be referred to the Governor for his assent; but no bill, or legislative act whatever, shall be of any force without his assent. The Governor shall have power to convene, prorogue, and dissolve the General Assembly, when, in his opinion, it shall be expedient.

The Governor, Judges, Legislative Council, Secretary, and such other officers as Congress shall appoint in the district, shall take an oath or affirmation of fidelity and of office; the Governor before the President of Congress, and all other officers before the Governor. As soon as a Legislature shall be formed in the district, the Council and House assembled in one room, shall have authority, by joint ballot, to elect a delegate to Congress, who shall have a seat in Congress, with a right of debating but not of voting during this temporary government.

And, for extending the fundamental principles of civil and religious liberty, which form the basis whereon these republics, their laws and constitutions are erected; to fix and establish those principles as the basis of all laws, constitutions, and governments, which forever hereafter shall be formed in the said territory: to provide also for the establishment of States, and permanent government therein, and for their admission to a share in the federal councils on an equal footing with the original States, at as early periods as may be consistent with the general interest:

It is hereby ordained and declared by the authority aforesaid, That the following articles shall be considered as articles of compact between the original States and the people and States in the said territory and forever remain unalterable, unless by common consent, to wit:

ART. 1st. No person, demeaning himself in a peaceable and orderly manner, shall ever be molested on account of his mode of worship or religious sentiments, in the said territory.

ART. 2d. The inhabitants of the said territory shall always be entitled to the benefits of the writ of habeas corpus, and of the trial by jury; of a proportionate representation of the people in the Legislature; and of judicial proceedings according to the course of the common law. All persons shall be bailable, unless for capital offences, where the proof shall be evident or the presumption great. All fines shall be moderate; and no cruel or unusual punishments shall be inflicted. No man shall be deprived of his liberty or property, but by the judgment of his peers or the law of the land; and, should the public exigencies make it necessary, for the common preservation, to take any person's property, or to demand his particular services, full compensation shall be made for the same. And, in the just preservation of rights and property, it is understood and declared, that no law ought ever to be made, or have force in the said territory, that shall, in any manner whatever, interfere with or affect private contracts or engagements, bona fide, and without fraud, previously formed.

ART. 3d. Religion, morality, and knowledge, being necessary to good government and the happiness of mankind, schools and the means of education shall forever be encouraged. The utmost good faith shall always be observed towards the Indians; their lands and property shall never be taken from them without their consent; and, in their property, rights, and liberty, they shall never be invaded or disturbed, unless in just and lawful wars authorized by Congress; but laws founded in justice and humanity, shall from time to time be made for preventing wrongs being done to them, and for preserving peace and friendship with them.

ART. 4th. The said Territory, and the States which may be formed therein, shall forever remain a part of this Confederacy of the United States of America, subject to the Articles of Confederation, and to such alterations therein as shall be constitutionally made; and to all the Acts and Ordinances of the United States in Congress assembled, conformable thereto. The inhabitants and settlers in the said Territory shall be subject to pay a part of the federal debts contracted or to be contracted, and a proportional part of the expenses of government, to be apportioned on them by Congress according to the same common rule and measure by which apportionments thereof shall be made on the other States; and the taxes for paying their proportion shall be laid and levied by the authority and direction of the Legislatures of the district or districts, or new States, as in the original States, within the time agreed upon by the United States in Congress assembled. The Legislatures of those districts or new States, shall never interfere with the primary disposal of the soil by the United States in Congress assembled, nor with any regulations Congress may find necessary for securing the title in such soil to the bona fide purchasers. No tax shall be imposed on lands the property of the United States; and, in no case, shall non-resident proprietors be taxed higher than residents. The navigable waters leading into the Mississippi and St Lawrence, and the carrying places between the same, shall be common highways and forever free, as well to the inhabitants of the said Territory as to the citizens of the United States, and those of any other States that may be admitted into the Confederacy, without any tax, impost, or duty therefor.

ART. 5th. There shall be formed in the said Territory, not less than three nor more than five States; and the boundaries of the States, as soon as Virginia shall alter her act of cession, and consent to the same, shall become fixed and established as follows, to wit: The Western State in the said territory, shall be bounded by the Mississippi, the Ohio, and Wabash rivers; a direct line drawn from the Wabash and Post Vincent's,[1] due North, to the territorial line between the United States and Canada; and, by the said territorial line, to the Lake of the

[1] Vincennes, Indiana. The State described includes Illinois, Wisconsin, and parts of Minnesota and Michigan.

Woods and Mississippi. The middle State[1] shall be bounded by the said direct line, the Wabash from Post Vincent's to the Ohio; by the Ohio, by a direct line, drawn due north from the mouth of the Great Miami, to the said territorial line, and by the said territorial line. The eastern State[2] shall be bounded by the last mentioned direct line, the Ohio, Pennsylvania, and the said territorial line: *Provided, however,* and it is further understood and declared, that the boundaries of these three States shall be subject so far to be altered, that, if Congress shall hereafter find it expedient, they shall have authority to form one or two States in that part of the said territory which lies north of an east and west line drawn through the southerly bend or extreme of lake Michigan. And, whenever any of the said States shall have 60,000 free inhabitants therein, such State shall be admitted, by its delegates, into the Congress of the United States, on an equal footing with the original States in all respects whatever, and shall be at liberty to form a permanent Constitution and State government: *Provided,* the Constitution and government so to be formed, shall be republican, and in conformity to the principles contained in these articles; and, so far as it can be consistent with the general interest of the Confederacy, such admission shall be allowed at an earlier period, and when there may be a less number of free inhabitants in the State than 60,000.

ART. 6th. There shall be neither slavery nor involuntary servitude in the said territory, otherwise than in the punishment of crimes whereof the party shall have been duly convicted: *Provided, always,* That any person escaping into the same, from whom labor or service is lawfully claimed in any one of the original States, such fugitive may be lawfully reclaimed and conveyed to the person claiming his or her labor or service as aforesaid.

Be it ordained by the authority aforesaid, That the resolutions of the 23rd of April 1784, relative to the subject of this ordinance, be, and the same are hereby repealed and declared null and void.

[1] Indiana and part of Michigan.
[2] Ohio and part of Michigan.

PART 4

State Constitution-making

I The Problem

4.1 JOHN ADAMS' *THOUGHTS ON GOVERNMENT*

In *Works of John Adams*, ed. Charles Francis Adams (Boston, 1851) IV 189–202

PREFACE

In the winter of 1776 there was much discussion in Congress concerning the necessity of independence, and advising the several States to institute governments for themselves under the immediate authority and original power of the people. Great difficulties occurred to many gentlemen in making a transition from the old governments to new, that is, from the royal to republican governments. In January, 1776, Mr George Wythe, of Virginia, passing an evening with me, asked me what plan I would advise a colony to pursue, in order to get out of the old government and into a new one. I sketched in words a scheme, which he requested me to give him in writing. Accordingly, the next day, I delivered to him the following letter. He lent it to his colleague, Richard Henry Lee, who asked me to let him print it; to which I consented, provided he would suppress my name; for if that should appear, it would excite a continental clamor among the tories, that I was erecting a battering-ram to demolish the royal government and render independence indispensable.

QUINCY, 21 July, 1811.

My dear Sir: If I was equal to the task of forming a plan for the government of a colony, I should be flattered with your request, and very happy to comply with it; because, as the divine science of politics is the science of social happiness, and the blessings of society depend entirely on the constitutions of government, which are generally institutions that last for many generations, there can be no employment more agreeable to a benevolent mind than a research after the best.

Pope flattered tyrants too much when he said,

> For forms of government let fools contest,
> That which is best administered is best.

Nothing can be more fallacious than this. But poets read history to collect flowers, not fruits; they attend to fanciful images, not the effects of social institutions. Nothing is more certain, from the history of nations and nature of man, than that some forms of government are better fitted for being well administered than others.

We ought to consider what is the end of government, before we determine which is the best form. Upon this point all speculative politicians will agree, that the happiness of society is the end of government, as all divines and moral philosophers will agree that the happiness of the individual is the end of man. From this principle it will follow, that the form of government which communicates ease, comfort, security, or, in one word, happiness, to the greatest number of persons, and in the greatest degree, is the best.

All sober inquirers after truth, ancient and modern, pagan and Christian, have declared that the happiness of man, as well as his dignity, consists in virtue. Confucius, Zoroaster, Socrates, Mahomet, not to mention authorities really sacred, have agreed in this.

If there is a form of government, then, whose principle and foundation is virtue, will not every sober man acknowledge it better calculated to promote the general happiness than any other form?

Fear is the foundation of most governments; but it is so sordid and brutal a passion, and renders men in whose breasts it predominates so stupid and miserable, that Americans will not be likely to approve of any political institution which is founded on it.

Honor is truly sacred, but holds a lower rank in the scale of moral excellence than virtue. Indeed, the former is but a part of the latter, and consequently has not equal pretensions to support a frame of government productive of human happiness.

The foundation of every government is some principle or passion in the minds of the people. The noblest principles and most generous affections in our nature, then, have the fairest chance to support the noblest and most generous models of government.

A man must be indifferent to the sneers of modern Englishmen, to mention in their company the names of Sidney, Harrington, Locke, Milton, Nedham, Neville, Burnet, and Hoadly. No small fortitude is necessary to confess that one has read them. The wretched condition of this country, however, for ten or fifteen years past, has frequently reminded me of their principles and reasonings. They will convince any candid mind, that there is no good government but what is republican. That the only valuable part of the British constitution is so; because the very definition of a republic is 'an empire of laws, and not of men.' That, as a republic is the best of governments, so that particular arrangement of the powers of society, or, in other words, that form of government which is best contrived to secure an impartial and exact execution of the laws, is the best of republics.

Of republics there is an inexhaustible variety, because the possible combinations of the powers of society are capable of innumerable variations.

As good government is an empire of laws, how shall your laws be made? In a large society, inhabiting an extensive country, it is impossible that the whole should assemble to make laws. The first necessary step, then, is to depute power from the many to a few of the most wise and good. But by what rules shall you choose your representatives? Agree upon the number and qualifications of persons who shall have the benefit of choosing, or annex this privilege to the inhabitants of a certain extent of ground.

The principal difficulty lies, and the greatest care should be employed, in constituting this representative assembly. It should be in miniature an exact portrait of the people at large. It should think, feel, reason, and act like them. That it may be the interest of this assembly to do strict justice at all times, it should be an equal representation, or, in other words, equal interests among the people should have equal interests in it. Great care should be taken to effect this, and to prevent unfair, partial, and corrupt elections. Such regulations, however, may be better made in times of greater tranquillity than the present; and they will spring up themselves naturally, when all the powers of government come to be in the hands of the people's friends. At present, it will be safest to proceed in all established modes, to which the people have been familiarized by habit.

A representation of the people in one assembly being obtained, a question arises, whether all the powers of government, legislative, executive, and judicial, shall be left in this body? I think a people cannot be long free, nor ever happy, whose government is in one assembly. My reasons for this opinion are as follow: –

1. A single assembly is liable to all the vices, follies, and frailties of an individual; subject to fits of humor, starts of passion, flights of enthusiasm, partialities, or prejudice, and consequently productive of hasty results and absurd judgments. And all these errors ought to be corrected and defects supplied by some controlling power.

2. A single assembly is apt to be avaricious, and in time will not

scruple to exempt itself from burdens, which it will lay, without compunction, on its constituents.

3. A single assembly is apt to grow ambitious, and after a time will not hesitate to vote itself perpetual. This was one fault of the Long Parliament; but more remarkably of Holland, whose assembly first voted themselves from annual to septennial, then for life, and after a course of years, that all vacancies happening by death or otherwise, should be filled by themselves, without any application to constituents at all.

4. A representative assembly, although extremely well qualified, and absolutely necessary, as a branch of the legislative, is unfit to exercise the executive power, for want of two essential properties, secrecy and despatch.

5. A representative assembly is still less qualified for the judicial power, because it is too numerous, too slow, and too little skilled in the laws.

6. Because a single assembly, possessed of all the powers of government, would make arbitrary laws for their own interest, execute all laws arbitrarily for their own interest, and adjudge all controversies in their own favor.

But shall the whole power of legislation rest in one assembly? Most of the foregoing reasons apply equally to prove that the legislative power ought to be more complex; to which we may add, that if the legislative power is wholly in one assembly, and the executive in another, or in a single person, these two powers will oppose and encroach upon each other, until the contest shall end in war, and the whole power, legislative and executive, be usurped by the strongest.

The judicial power, in such case, could not mediate, or hold the balance between the two contending powers, because the legislative would undermine it. And this shows the necessity, too, of giving the executive power a negative upon the legislative, otherwise this will be continually encroaching upon that.

To avoid these dangers, let a distinct assembly be constituted, as a mediator between the two extreme branches of the legislature, that which represents the people, and that which is vested with the executive power.

Let the representative assembly then elect by ballot, from among themselves or their constituents, or both, a distinct assembly, which, for the sake of perspicuity, we will call a council. It may consist of any number you please, say twenty or thirty, and should have a free and independent exercise of its judgment, and consequently a negative voice in the legislature.

These two bodies, thus constituted, and made integral parts of the legislature, let them unite, and by joint ballot choose a governor, who, after being stripped of most of those badges of domination, called prerogatives, should have a free and independent exercise of his judgment, and be made also an integral part of the legislature. This, I know, is liable to objections; and, if you please, you may make him only president of the council, as in Connecticut. But as the governor is to be invested with the executive power, with consent of council, I think he ought to have a negative upon the legislative. If he is annually elective, as he ought to be, he will always have so much reverence and affection for the people, their representatives and counsellors, that, although you give him an independent exercise of his judgment, he will seldom use it in opposition to the two houses, except in cases the public utility of which would be conspicuous; and some such cases would happen.

In the present exigency of American affairs, when, by an act of Parliament, we are put out of the royal protection, and consequently discharged from our allegiance, and it has become necessary to assume government for our immediate security, the governor, lieutenant-governor, secretary, treasurer, commissary, attorney-general, should be chosen by joint ballot of both houses. And these and all other elections, especially of representatives and counsellors, should be annual, there not being in the whole circle of the sciences a maxim more infallible than this, 'where annual elections end, there slavery begins'.

These great men, in this respect, should be, once a year,

> Like bubbles on the sea of matter borne,
> They rise, they break, and to that sea return.

This will teach them the great political virtues of humility, patience, and moderation, without which every man in power becomes a ravenous beast of prey.

This mode of constituting the great offices of state will answer very well for the present; but if by experiment it should be found inconvenient, the legislature may, at its leisure, devise other methods of creating them, by elections of the people at large, as in Connecticut, or it may enlarge the term for which they shall be chosen to seven years, or three years, or for life, or make any other alterations which the society shall find productive of its ease, its safety, its freedom or, in one word, its happiness.

A rotation of all offices, as well as of representatives and counsellors, has many advocates, and is contended for with many plausible arguments. It would be attended, no doubt, with many advantages; and if the society has a sufficient number of suitable characters to supply the great number of vacancies which would be made by such a rotation, I can see no objection to it. These persons may be allowed to serve for three years, and then be excluded three years, or for any longer or shorter term.

Any seven or nine of the legislative council may be made a quorum, for doing business as a privy council, to advise the governor in the exercise of the executive branch of power, and in all acts of state.

The governor should have the command of the militia and of all your armies. The power of pardons should be with the governor and council.

Judges, justices, and all other officers, civil and military, should be nominated and appointed by the governor, with the advice and consent of council, unless you choose to have government more popular; if you do, all officers, civil and military, may be chosen by joint ballot of both houses; or, in order to preserve the independence and importance of each house, by ballot of one house, concurred in by the other. Sheriffs should be chosen by the freeholders of counties; so should registers of deeds and clerks of counties.

All officers should have commissions, under the hand of the governor and seal of the colony.

The dignity and stability of government in all its branches, the morals of the people, and every blessing of society depend so much upon an upright and skilful administration of justice, that the judicial power ought to be distinct from both the legislative and executive, and independent upon both, that so it may be a check upon both, as both should be checks upon that. The judges, therefore, should be always men of learning and experience in the laws, of exemplary morals, great patience, calmness, coolness, and attention. Their minds should not be distracted with jarring interests; they should not be dependent upon any man, or body of men. To these ends, they should hold estates for life in their offices; or, in other words, their commissions should be during good behavior, and their salaries ascertained and established by law. For misbehavior, the grand inquest of the colony, the house of representatives, should impeach them before the governor and council, where they should have time and opportunity to make their defence; but, if convicted, should be removed from their offices, and subjected to such other punishment as shall be thought proper.

A militia law, requiring all men, or with very few exceptions besides cases of conscience, to be provided with arms and ammunition, to be trained at certain seasons; and requiring counties, towns, or other small districts, to be provided with public stocks of ammunition and intrenching utensils, and with some settled plans for transporting provisions after the militia, when marched to defend their country against sudden invasions; and requiring certain districts to be provided with field-pieces, companies of matrosses, and perhaps some regiments of light-horse, is always a wise institution, and, in the present circumstances of our country, indispensable.

Laws for the liberal education of youth, especially of the lower class of people, are so extremely wise and useful, that, to a humane and generous mind, no expense for this purpose would be thought extravagant.

The very mention of sumptuary laws will excite a smile. Whether our countrymen have wisdom and virtue enough to submit to them, I know not; but the happiness of the people might be greatly promoted by them, and a revenue saved sufficient to carry on this war forever. Frugality is a great revenue, besides curing us of vanities, levities, and fopperies, which are real antidotes to all great, manly, and warlike virtues.

But must not all commissions run in the name of a king? No. Why may they not as well run thus, 'The colony of   to A. B. greeting', and be tested by the governor?

Why may not writs, instead of running in the name of the king, run thus, 'The colony of   to the sheriff', &c., and be tested by the chief justice?

Why may not indictments conclude, 'against the peace of the colony of   and the dignity of the same'?

A constitution founded on these principles introduces knowledge among the people, and inspires them with a conscious dignity becoming freemen; a general emulation takes place, which causes good humor, sociability, good manners, and good morals to be general. That elevation of sentiment inspired by such a government, makes the common people brave and enterprising. That ambition which is inspired by it makes them sober, industrious, and frugal, You will find among them some elegance, perhaps, but more solidity; a little pleasure, but a great deal of business; some politeness, but more civility. If you compare such a country with the regions of domination, whether monarchical or aristocratical, you will fancy yourself in Arcadia or Elysium.

If the colonies should assume governments separately, they should be left entirely to their own choice of the forms; and if a continental constitution should be formed, it should be a congress, containing a fair and adequate representation of the colonies, and its authority should sacredly be confined to these cases, namely, war, trade, disputes between colony and colony, the post-office, and the unappropriated lands of the crown, as they used to be called.

These colonies, under such forms of government, and in such a union, would be unconquerable by all the monarchies of Europe.

You and I, my dear friend, have been sent into life at a time when the greatest lawgivers of antiquity would have wished to live. How few of the human race have ever enjoyed an opportunity of making an election of government, more than of air, soil, or climate, for themselves or their children! When, before the present epocha, had three millions of people full power and a fair opportunity to form and establish the wisest and happiest government that human wisdom can contrive? I hope you will avail yourself and your country of that extensive learning and indefatigable industry which you possess, to assist her in the formation of the happiest governments and the best character of a great people. For myself, I must beg you to keep my name out of sight; for this feeble attempt, if it should be known to be mine, would oblige me to apply to myself those lines of the immortal John Milton, in one of his sonnets: –

> I did but prompt the age to quit their clogs
> By the known rules of ancient liberty,
> When straight a barbarous noise environs me
> Of owls and cuckoos, asses, apes, and dogs.

NOTE

Copies of *Thoughts on Government* were sent by the author to many gentlemen with whom he had been in relations personal or political, and among others to Patrick Henry, of Virginia. The reply of Mr

Henry is on many accounts remarkable. It throws great light not only upon his own system at the commencement of the struggle, but upon the prevailing opinions of the time in the State to which he belonged.

Patrick Henry, Jr to John Adams, Williamsburgh, 20 May, 1776

My Dear Sir: – Your favor, with the pamphlet, came safe to hand. I am exceedingly obliged to you for it; and I am not without hopes it may produce good here, where there is among most of our opulent families a strong bias to aristocracy. I tell my friends you are the author. Upon that supposition, I have two reasons for liking the book. The sentiments are precisely the same I have long since taken up, and they come recommended by you. Go on, my dear friend, to assail the strongholds of tyranny; and in whatever form oppression may be found, may those talents and that firmness, which have achieved so much for America, be pointed against it.

Before this reaches you the resolution for finally separating from Britain will be handed to Congress by Colonel Nelson.[1] I put up with it in the present form for the sake of unanimity. 'Tis not quite so pointed as I could wish.

Excuse me for telling you of what I think of immense importance; 'tis to anticipate the enemy at the French Court. The half of our Continent offered to France, may induce her to aid our destruction, which she certainly has the power to accomplish. I know the free trade with all the States would be more beneficial to her than any territorial possessions she might acquire. But pressed, allured, as she will be – but, above all, ignorant of the great thing we mean to offer, may we not lose her? The consequence is dreadful.

Excuse me again. The confederacy; – that must precede an open declaration of independency and foreign alliances. Would it not be sufficient to confine it, for the present, to the objects of offensive and defensive nature, and a guaranty of the respective colonial rights? If a minute arrangement of things is attempted, such as equal representation, &c., &c., you may split and divide; certainly will delay the French alliance, which with me is every thing. The great force in San Domingo, Martinique, &c., is under the guidance of some person in high office. Will not the Mississippi lead your ambassadors thither most safely?

[1] This resolution was passed on the 15th. Force's *American Archives*, fourth series, vol. VI. c. 1524.

Our Convention is now employed in the great work of forming a constitution. My most esteemed republican form has many and powerful enemies. A silly thing, published in Philadelphia, by a native of Virginia, has just made its appearance here, strongly recommended, 'tis said, by one of our delegates now with you, – Braxton. His reasonings upon and distinction between private and public virtue, are weak, shallow, evasive, and the whole performance an affront and disgrace to this country; and, by one expression, I suspect his whiggism.[1]

Our session will be very long, during which I cannot count upon one coadjutor of talents equal to the task. Would to God you and your Sam Adams were here! It shall be my incessant study, so to form our portrait of government, that a kindred with New England may be discerned in it; and if all your excellencies cannot be preserved, yet I hope to retain so much of the likeness, that posterity shall pronounce us descended from the same stock. I shall think perfection is obtained, if we have your approbation. I am forced to conclude; but first, let me beg to be presented to my ever-esteemed S. Adams. Adieu, my dear sir; may God preserve you, and give you every good thing.

P.S. – Will you and S. A. now and then write?

[1] This refers to a small pamphlet published by Dunlap, at Philadelphia, and evidently designed as an answer to *Thoughts on Government*. Its title is *An Address to the Convention of the Colony and Ancient Dominion of Virginia, on the subject of Government in general, and recommending a particular Form to their Consideration, by a Native of that Colony*. The name of the writer has not been ascertained. Much interest attached to the proceedings of Virginia in framing a constitution, and an apprehension lest the popular features of the form recommended by Mr Adams should find favor, seems to have led to this effort to counteract it. The address was reprinted in the *Virginia Gazette*, at Williamsburgh, on the eighth of June, 1776, being the time fixed for the consideration of the declaration of rights by the Convention. The form recommended is in direct conflict with the first principles laid down in *Thoughts on Government*. A governor, during good behavior, elected by a house of representatives, renewed but once in three years; a council of twenty-four persons to serve for life, also chosen by the house; and a judiciary and military appointed by the governor, – constitute its main features. It is reprinted in the Great Collection made under the authority of Congress by Mr Force, fourth series, vol. v, cc. 748–54.

On the other hand, the tendency in Pennsylvania was to consider Mr Adams's theory as not popular enough. In the Collection alluded to, is to be found a paper entitled, 'The Interest of America', the purport of which is to recommend a single legislative branch, in which most of the powers are to be vested; a suggestion which was acted upon, as is well known, in the first constitution of Pennsylvania.

II Massachusetts

4.II.1 JOHN ADAMS' ACCOUNT OF THE DEVELOPMENT OF THE MOVEMENTS FOR INDEPENDENCE AND A STATE CONSTITUTION

From his 'Autobiography', in *The Works of John Adams*, ed. C. F. Adams (Boston, 1851) III 12–23

It is necessary that I should be a little more particular, in relating the rise and progress of the new government of the States.

On Friday, June 2d, 1775, 'The President laid before Congress a letter from the Provincial Convention of Massachusetts Bay, dated May 16th, which was read, setting forth the difficulties they labor under for want of a regular form of government, and as they and the other Colonies are now compelled to raise an army to defend themselves from the butcheries and devastations of their implacable enemies, which renders it still more necessary to have a regular established government, requesting the Congress to favor them with explicit advice respecting the taking up and exercising the powers of civil government, and declaring their readiness to submit to such a general plan as the Congress may direct for the Colonies, or make it their great study to establish such a form of government there as shall not only promote their advantage, but the union and interest of all America.'

This subject had engaged much of my attention before I left Massachusetts, and had been frequently the subject of conversation between me and many of my friends, – Dr Winthrop, Dr Cooper, Colonel Otis, the two Warrens, Major Hawley, and others, besides my colleagues in Congress, – and lay with great weight upon my mind, as the most difficult and dangerous business that we had to do; (for from the beginning, I always expected we should have more difficulty and danger, in our attempts to govern ourselves, and in our negotiations and connections with foreign powers, than from all the fleets and armies of Great Britain.) It lay, therefore, with great weight upon my mind, and when this letter was read, I embraced the opportunity to open myself in Congress, and most ernestly to entreat the serious attention of all the members, and of all the continent, to the measures which the times demanded. For my part, I thought there was great wisdom in the adage, 'when the sword is drawn, throw away the scabbard'. Whether we threw it away voluntarily or not, it was useless now, and would be useless forever. The pride of Britain, flushed with late triumphs and conquests, their infinite contempt of all the power of America, with an insolent, arbitrary Scotch faction, with a Bute and Mansfield at their head for a ministry, we might depend upon it, would force us to call forth every energy and resource of the country, to seek the friendship of England's enemies, and we had no rational hope, but from the *Ratio ultima regum et rerumpublicarum*. These efforts could not be made without government, and as I supposed no man would think of consolidating this vast continent under one national government, we should probably, after the example of the Greeks, the Dutch, and the Swiss, form a confederacy of States, each of which must have a separate government. That the case of Massachusetts was the most urgent, but that it could not be long before every other Colony must follow her example. That with a view to this subject, I had looked into the ancient and modern confederacies for examples, but they all appeared to me to have been huddled up in a hurry, by a few chiefs. But we had a people of more intelligence, curiosity, and enterprise, who must be all consulted, and we must realize the theories of the wisest writers, and invite the people to erect the whole building with their own hands, upon the broadest foundation. That this could be done only by conventions of representatives chosen by the people in the several colonies, in the most exact proportions. That it was my opinion that Congress ought now to recommend to the people of every Colony to call such conventions immediately, and set up governments of their own, under their own authority; for the people were the source of all authority and original of all power. These were new, strange, and terrible doctrines to the greatest part of the members, but not a very small number heard them with apparent pleasure, and none more than Mr John Rutledge, of South Carolina, and Mr John Sullivan, of New Hampshire.

Congress, however, ordered the letter to lie on the table for further consideration.

On Saturday, June 3d, the letter from the convention of the Massachusetts Bay, dated the 16th of May, being again read, the subject was again discussed, and then, '*Resolved*, That a committee of five persons be chosen, to consider the same, and report what in their opinion is the proper advice to be given to that Convention.'

The following persons were chosen by ballot, to compose that committee, namely, Mr J. Rutledge, Mr Johnson, Mr Jay, Mr Wilson, and Mr Lee. These gentlemen had several conferences with the delegates from our State, in the course of which, I suppose, the hint was suggested, that they adopted in their report.

On Wednesday, June 7th, 'On motion, *Resolved*, That Thursday, the 20th of July next, be observed throughout the twelve United Colonies as a day of humiliation, fasting, and prayer; and that Mr Hooper, Mr J. Adams, and Mr Paine, be a committee to bring in a resolve for that purpose.

'The committee appointed to prepare advice, in answer to the letter from the Convention of Massachusetts Bay, brought in their report, which was read and ordered to lie on the table for consideration.

'On Friday, June 9th, the report of the committee on the letter from the Convention of Massachusetts Bay being again read, the Congress came into the following resolution.

'*Resolved*, That no obedience being due to the Act of Parliament for altering the charter of the Colony of Massachusetts Bay, nor to a Governor or Lieutenant-Governor who will not observe the directions of, but endeavor to subvert, that charter, the Governor and Lieutenant-Governor of that Colony are to be considered as absent, and their offices vacant; and as there is no Council there, and the inconveniences arising from the suspension of the powers of government are intolerable, especially at a time when General Gage hath actually levied war, and is carrying on hostilities against his Majesty's peaceable and loyal subjects of that Colony; That, in order to conform as near as may be to the spirit and substance of the charter, it be recommended to the Provincial Convention to write letters to the inhabitants of the several places, which are entitled to representation in Assembly, requesting them to choose such representatives, and that the Assembly when chosen to elect Counsellors; and that such assembly or Council exercise the powers of government, until a Governor of His Majesty's appointment will consent to govern the Colony according to its charter.

'Ordered, That the President transmit a copy of the above to the Convention of Massachusetts Bay.'

Although this advice was in a great degree conformable to the New York and Pennsylvania system, or in other words, to the system of Mr Dickinson and Mr Duane, I thought it an acquisition, for it was a precedent of advice to the separate States to institute governments, and I doubted not we should soon have more occasions to follow this example. Mr John Rutledge and Mr Sullivan had frequent conversations with me upon this subject. Mr Rutledge asked me my opinion of a proper form of government for a State, I answered him that any form that our people would consent to institute, would be better than none, even if they placed all power in a house of representatives, and they should appoint governors and judges; but I hoped they would be wiser, and preserve the English Constitution in its spirit and substance, as far as the circumstances of this country required or would admit. That no hereditary powers ever had existed in America, nor would they, or ought they to be introduced or proposed; but that I hoped the three branches of a legislature would be preserved, an executive, independent of the senate or council, and the house, and above all things, the independence of the judges. Mr Sullivan was fully agreed with me in the necessity of instituting governments, and he seconded me very handsomely in supporting the argument in Congress. Mr Samuel Adams was with us in the opinion of the necessity, and was industrious in conversation with the members out of doors, but he very rarely spoke much in Congress, and he was perfectly unsettled in any plan to be recommended to a State, always inclining to the most democratical forms, and even to a single sovereign assembly, until his constituents afterwards in Boston compelled him to vote for three branches. Mr Cushing was also for one sovereign assembly, and Mr Paine was silent and reserved upon the subject, at least to me.

Not long after this, Mr John Rutledge returned to South Carolina, and Mr Sullivan went with General Washington to Cambridge, so that I lost two of my able coadjutors. But we soon found the benefit of their cooperation at a distance.

On Wednesday, October 18th, the delegates from New Hampshire laid before the Congress a part of the instructions delivered to them by their Colony, in these words: – 'We would have you immediately use your utmost endeavors to obtain the advice and direction of the Congress, with respect to a method for our administering justice, and regulating our civil police. We press you not to delay this matter, as its being done speedily will probably prevent the greatest confusion among us.'

This instruction might have been obtained by Mr Langdon, or Mr Whipple, but I always supposed it was General Sullivan who suggested the measure, because he left Congress with a stronger impression upon his mind of the importance of it, than I ever observed in either of the others. Be this, however, as it may have been, I embraced with joy the opportunity of haranguing on the subject at large, and of urging Congress to resolve on a general recommendation to all the States to call conventions and institute regular governments. I reasoned from various topics, many of which, perhaps, I could not now recollect. Some I remember; as,

1. The danger to the morals of the people from the present loose state of things, and general relaxation of laws and government through the Union.

2. The danger of insurrections in some of the most disaffected parts of the Colonies, in favor of the enemy, or as they called them, the mother country, an expression that I thought it high time to erase out of our language.

3. Communications and intercourse with the enemy, from various parts of the continent could not be wholly prevented, while any of the powers of government remained in the hands of the King's servants.

4. It could not well be considered as a crime to communicate intelligence, or to act as spies or guides to the enemy, without assuming all the powers of government.

5. The people of America would never consider our Union as complete, but our friends would always suspect divisions among us, and our enemies who were scattered in larger or smaller numbers, not only in every State and city, but in every village through the whole Union, would forever represent Congress as divided and ready to break to pieces, and in this way would intimidate and discourage multitudes of our people who wished us well.

6. The absurdity of carrying on war against a king, when so many persons were daily taking oaths and affirmations of allegiance to him.

7. We could not expect that our friends in Great Britain would believe us united and in earnest, or exert themselves very strenuously in our favor, while we acted such a wavering, hesitating part.

8. Foreign nations, particularly France and Spain, would not think us worthy of their attention while we appeared to be deceived by such fallacious hopes of redress of grievances, of pardon for our offences, and of reconciliation with our enemies.

9. We could not command the natural resources of our own country. We could not establish manufactories of arms, cannon, saltpetre, powder, ships, &c., without the powers of government; and all these and many other preparations ought to be going on in every State or Colony, if you will, in the country.

Although the opposition was still inveterate, many members of Congress began to hear me with more patience, and some began to ask me civil questions. 'How can the people institute governments?' My answer was, 'By conventions of representatives, freely, fairly, and proportionably chosen.' 'When the convention has fabricated a government, or a constitution rather, how do we know the people will submit to it?' 'If there is any doubt of that, the convention may send out their project of a constitution, to the people in their several towns, counties, or districts, and the people may make the acceptance of it their own act.' 'But the people know nothing about constitutions.' 'I believe you are much mistaken in that supposition; if you are not, they will not oppose a plan prepared by their own chosen friends; but I believe that in every considerable portion of the people, there will be found some men, who will understand the subject as well as their representatives, and these will assist in enlightening the rest.' 'But what plan of a government would you advise?' 'A plan as nearly resembling the government under which we were born, and have lived, as the circumstances of the country will admit. Kings we never had among us. Nobles we never had. Nothing hereditary ever existed in the country; nor will the country require or admit of any such thing. But governors and councils we have always had, as well as representatives. A legislature in three branches ought to be preserved, and independent judges.' 'Where and how will you get your governors and councils?' 'By elections.' 'How, – who shall elect?' 'The representatives of the people in a convention will be the best qualified to contrive a mode.'

After all these discussions and interrogatories, Congress was not prepared nor disposed to do any thing as yet. They must consider farther.

'*Resolved*, That the consideration of this matter be referred to Monday next.'

Monday arrived, and Tuesday and Wednesday passed over, and Congress not yet willing to do any thing.

On Thursday, October 26th, the subject was again brought on the carpet, and the same discussions repeated; for very little new was produced. After a long discussion, in which Mr John Rutledge, Mr Ward, Mr Lee, Mr Gadsden, Mr Sherman, Mr Dyer, and some others had spoken on the same side with me, Congress resolved, that a committee of five members be appointed to take into consideration the instructions given to the delegates of New Hampshire, and report their opinion thereon. The members chosen, – Mr John Rutledge, Mr J. Adams, Mr Ward, Mr Lee, and Mr Sherman.

Although this committee was entirely composed of members as well disposed to encourage the enterprise as could have been found in Congress, yet they could not be brought to agree upon a report and to bring it forward in Congress, till Friday, November 3d, when Congress, taking into consideration the report of the committee on the New Hampshire instructions, after another long deliberation and debate, – '*Resolved*, That it be recommended to the Provincial Convention of New Hampshire, to call a full and free representation of the people, and that the representatives, if they think it necessary, establish such a form of government, as in their judgment will best produce the happiness of the people, and most effectually secure peace and good order in the Province, during the continuance of the present dispute between Great Britain and the Colonies.'

By this time I mortally hated the words, 'Province', 'Colonies', and 'Mother Country', and strove to get them out of the report. The last was indeed left out, but the other two were retained even by this committee, who were all as high Americans as any in the house, unless Mr Gadsden should be excepted. Nevertheless, I thought this resolution a triumph, and a most important point gained.

Mr John Rutledge was now completely with us in our desire of revolutionizing all the governments, and he brought forward immediately some representations from his own State, when 'Congress, then taking into consideration of the State of South Carolina, and sundry papers relative thereto being read and considered,

'*Resolved*, That a committee of five be appointed to take the same into consideration, and report what in their opinion is necessary to be done. The members chosen, Mr Harrison, Mr Bullock, Mr Hooper, Mr Chase, and Mr S. Adams.'

On November 4th, 'The committee appointed to take into consideration the State of South Carolina, brought in their report, which being read,' a number of resolutions passed, the last of which will be found in page 235 of the Journals, at the bottom.

'*Resolved*, That if the Convention of South Carolina shall find it necessary to establish a form of government in that Colony, it be recommended to that Convention to call a full and free representation of the people, and that the said representatives, if they think it necessary, shall establish such a form of government as in their judgment will produce the happiness of the people, and most effectually secure peace and good order in the Colony, during the continuance of the present dispute between Great Britain and the Colonies.'

Although Mr John Rutledge united with me and others, in persuading the committee to report this resolution, and the distance of Carolina made it convenient to furnish them with this discretionary recommendation, I doubt whether Mr Harrison or Mr Hooper were, as yet, sufficiently advanced to agree to it. Mr Bullock, Mr Chase, and Mr Samuel Adams, were very ready for it. When it was under consideration, I labored afresh to expunge the words 'Colony', and 'Colonies', and insert the words 'State', and 'States', and the word 'dispute', to make way for that of 'war', and the word 'Colonies', for the word 'America', or 'States', but the child was not yet weaned. I labored, also, to get the resolution enlarged, and extended into a recommendation to the people of all the States, to institute governments, and this occasioned more interrogatories from one part and another of the House. 'What plan of government would you recommend?' &c. Here it would have been the most natural to have made a motion that Congress should appoint a committee to prepare a plan of government, to be reported to Congress and there discussed, paragraph by paragraph, and that which should be adopted should be recommended to all the States. But I dared not make such a motion, because I knew that if such a plan was adopted it would be, if not permanent, yet of long duration, and it would be extremely difficult to get rid of it. And I knew that every one of my friends, and all those who were the most zealous for assuming governments, had at that time no idea of any other government but a contemptible legislature in one assembly, with committees for executive magistrates and judges. These questions, therefore, I answered by sporting off hand a variety of short sketches of plans, which might be adopted by the conventions; and as this subject was brought into view in some way or other almost every day, and these interrogatories were frequently repeated, I had in my head and at my tongue's end as many projects of government as Mr Burke says the Abbé Sieyes had in his pigeonholes, not however, constructed at such length, nor labored with his metaphysical refinements. I took care, however, always to bear my testimony against every plan of an unbalanced government.

I had read Harrington, Sidney, Hobbes, Nedham, and Locke, but with very little application to any particular views, till these debates in Congress, and the interrogatories in public and private, turned my thoughts to these researches, which produced the *Thoughts on Government*, the Constitution of Massachusetts, and at length the *Defence of the Constitutions of the United States*, and the *Discourses on Davila*, writings which have never done any good to me, though some of them undoubtedly contributed to produce the Constitution of New York, the Constitution of the United States, and the last Constitutions of Pennsylvania and Georgia. They undoubtedly, also, contributed to the writings of Publius, called the Federalist, which were all written after the publication of my work in Philadelphia, New York, and Boston. Whether the people will permit any of these Constitutions to stand upon their pedestals, or whether they will throw them all down, I know not. Appearances at present are unfavourable and threatening. I have done all in my power according to what I thought my duty. I can do no more.

4.II.2 PROCLAMATION OF THE GENERAL COURT, JANUARY 23, 1776

American Archives, ed. Force, 4th series, IV 833–5

By the Great and General Court of the Colony of Massachusetts-Bay

A Proclamation

The frailty of human nature, the wants of individuals, and the numerous dangers which surround them, through the course of life, have, in all ages and in every country, impelled them to form societies and establish governments.

As the happiness of the people is the sole end of Government, so the consent of the people is the only foundation of it, in reason, morality, and the natural fitness of things; and, therefore, every act of Government, every exercise of sovereignty against, or without the consent of the people, is injustice, usurpation, and tyranny.

It is a maxim, that, in every Government there must exist, some where, a supreme, sovereign, absolute, and uncontrollable power; but this power resides, always, in the body of the people, and it never was, or can be delegated to one man or a few; the great Creator having never given to men a right to vest others with authority over them unlimited, either in duration or degree.

When Kings, Ministers, Governours, or Legislators, therefore, instead of exercising the powers intrusted with them according to the principles, forms, and proportions, stated by the Constitution, and established by the original compact, prostitute those powers to the purposes of oppression, to subvert, instead of supporting a free Constitution, to destroy, instead of preserving the lives, liberties, and properties of the people, they are no longer to be deemed magistrates vested with a sacred character, but become publick enemies, and ought to be resisted.

The Administration of *Great Britain*, despising equally the justice, humanity, and magnanimity, of their ancestors, and the rights, liberties, and courage of *Americans*, have, for a course of years, laboured to establish a sovereignty in *America*, not founded in the consent of the people, but in the mere will of persons a thousand leagues from us, whom we know not, and have endeavoured to establish this sovereignty over us against our consent, in all cases whatsoever.

The Colonies, during this period, have recurred to every peaceable resource in a free Constitution, by petitions and remonstrances, to obtain justice, which has been not only denied to them, but they have been treated with unexampled indignity and contempt, and, at length, open war, of the most atrocious, cruel, and sanguinary kind, has been commenced against them. To this, an open, manly, and successful resistance has, hitherto, been made. Thirteen Colonies are now firmly united in the conduct of this most just and necessary war, under the wise councils of their Congress.

It is the will of Providence, for wise, righteous, and gracious ends, that this Colony should have been singled out, by the enemies of *America*, as the first object both of their envy and their revenge, and, after having been made the subject of several merciless and vindictive statutes, (one of which was intended to subvert our Constitution by charter), is made the seat of war.

No effectual resistance to the system of tyranny prepared for us could be made, without either instant recourse to arms, or a temporary suspension of the ordinary powers of Government and tribunals of justice. To the last of which evils, in hopes of a speedy reconciliation with *Great Britain* upon equitable terms, the Congress advised us to submit; and mankind has seen a phenomenon without example in the political world: a large and populous Colony subsisting, in great decency and order, for more than a year, under such a suspension of Government.

But, as our enemies have proceeded to such barbarous extremities, commencing hostilities upon the good people of this *Colony*, and, with unprecedented malice, exerting their power to spread the calamities of fire, sword, and famine through the land, and no reasonable prospect remains of a speedy reconciliation with *Great Britain*, the Congress have resolved . . .[1]

In pursuance of which advice, the good people of this Colony have chosen a full and free representation of themselves, who, being convened in Assembly, have elected a Council, who, as the Executive branch of Government, have constituted necessary officers through the Colony. The present generation, therefore, may be congratulated on the acquisition of a form of Government more immediately, in all its branches, under the influence and control of the people, and, therefore, more free and happy than was enjoyed by their ancestors.

But, as a Government so popular can be supported only by universal knowledge and virtue in the body of the people, it is the duty of all ranks to promote the means of education for the rising generation, as well as true religion, purity of manners, and integrity of life, among all orders and degrees.

As an army has become necessary for our defence, and, in all free States the civil must provide for and control the military power, the major part of the Council have appointed magistrates and courts of justice in every County, whose happiness is so connected with that of the people, that it is difficult to suppose they can abuse their trust. The business of it is, to see those laws enforced, which are necessary for the preservation of peace, virtue, and good order. And the Great and General Court expects, and requires, that all necessary support and assistance be given, and all proper obedience yielded to them, and will deem every person who shall fail of his duty in this respect towards them, a disturber of the peace of this Colony, and deserving of examplary punishment.

[1] The Resolution is in John Adams' 'Autobiography', above, p. 407.

4.II.3 REASONS FOR AN INDEPENDENT CONSTITUTION

A Letter from the Chesterfield Committee of Correspondence, March 4, 1776, Hawley Papers, box I, New York Public Library

To the Chairman of the Committee of correspondence in Northampton –

At a Meeting of the Committee of Correspondence, inspection & Safety for the Town of Chesterfield, upon mature Deliberation, in consequence of the advice of our constituents, do desire of the Chairman of the Committee of Northampton that they immediately write Letters to the Committees of the Several Towns in the County that they be notifyed to meet on Monday next at three o'clock in the afternoon not exceeding the Time to consult on the following particulars and others that may be proposed to said convention –

I Whether it be not proper at present that the Court of Quarter Sessions be suspended or adjourned to some future Season –

II Whether the Justices of the County Shall in any Case act under their present Commissions –

Gentlemen the Reason of these Inquiries & of our urgent desire for this convention is, least, the People should be so inraged against the Setting of the Courts at present that it will be detrimental to the Common Cause, and if we do not suspend them, (without the advice of the Convention be to the contrary) we fear the Consequences will be very fatal

Chesterfield March 4, 1776
By order of the Committee of Chesterfield

From the Proceedings of a Convention in Hampshire, March 11, 1776, James R. Trumbull, *History of Northampton* (Northampton, 1902) II 389–90

Voted that it is inexpedient and improper that the Court of general Sessions of the Peace for the County of Hampshire should set at the Time of their Adjournment on the second Tuesday of March instant. [Adopted by a vote of 43 to 39.]

And that the reason why this Congress are of opinion that the Court aforesaid should not sit at the time & place aforementioned Is on account of their holding their commissions in the name of George the Third King of Britain, &c., and by the authority of the same. [On the second question raised by Chesterfield, the convention voted to let it 'subside'.]

Pittsfield Town Petition to the House of Representatives, May 29, 1776, Massachusetts Archives, CLXXXI 42–5

To the Honourable Council, & the Honourable House of Representatives of the Colony of Massachusetts Bay in General Assembly met at Watertown May 29th. 1776 –

The Petition & Memorial of the Inhabitants of the Town of Pittsfield in said Colony,

Humbly Showeth,

That they have the highest sense of the Importance of Civil & religious Liberty. – The destructive nature of Tyranny & lawless power, & the absolute necessity of legal Government to prevent Anarchy & Confusion.

That they, with their Brethren in other Towns in this County, were early & vigorous in opposing the destructive Measures of British Administration against the Colonies. – That they early signed the Non-Importation League & Covenant, raised Minute Men, agreed to pay them, ordered their public Monies to be paid to Henry Gardiner Esqr receiver General, cast in their mite for the Relief of Boston, & conformed in all things to the Doings of the Honourable Continental and Provincial Congresses.

That they met with the most violent opposition from an unfriendly party in this Town in every step in every Measure they pursued agreeable to the Common Councils of this Continent, which nothing but the most obstinate persevereance has enabled them to overcome & surmount; Which, together with the Inconveniences we have laboured under, affoard the true Reason why we have been so behind in the payment of our public Taxes. –

That they with the other Towns in this County, have come behind none in their Duty & attachment to their Countrys Cause & have exerted themselves much beyound their strength on all occasions. A fresh Instance of their Zeal was conspicuous on our late Defeat at Quebec, when a considerable Number of Men were raised & sent off in the Dead of Winter & lay dying with sickness before the walls of

Quebec before any one Man from this Colony had so much as left his own habitation for the Relief of our Distressed Friends in Canada. –

That from the purest & most disinterested Principles, & ardent Love for their Country, without selfish Considerations & in conformity to the Advice of the wisest Man in the Colony, they aided & assisted in suspending the executive Courts in this County in August 1774.

That on no Occasion have they spared either cost or Trouble, without hope of pecuniary reward, vigorously & unweariedly exerting ourselves for the support & in the Defence of our Countrys cause not withstanding the most violent Discouragements we have met with by open or secret Enemies in this Town & County & in a Neighbouring province.

That 'till last fall your Memorialists had little or no Expectation of obtaining any new previleges beyound what our defective Charter secured to us. –

That when they came more maturely to reflect upon the nature of the present Contest, & the Spirit & obstinacy of Administration – What an amazing Expence the united Colonies had incured? How many Towns had been burnt or otherwise damaged? what Multitudes had turned out to beg & how many of our valiant Heroes had been slain in the Defence of their Country & the Impossibility of our being ever again dependant on Great Britain or in any Measure subject to her Authority – When they further considered that the Revolution in England affoarded the Nation but a very imperfect Redress of Grievances the Nation being transported with extravagant Joy in getting rid of one Tyrant forgot to provide against another – & how every Man by Nature has the seeds of Tyranny deeply implanted within him so that nothing short of Ommipotence can eradicate them – That when they attended to the Advice given this Colony by the Continental Congress respecting the Assumption of our antient Constitution, how early that Advice was given, the Reasons of it & the principles upon which it was given which no longer exist, what a great Change of Circumstances there has been in the Views & Designs of this whole Continent since the giving said Advice – That when they considered, now is the only Time we have reason ever to expect for securing our Liberty & the Liberties of future posterity upon a permanent Foundation that no length of Time can undermine – Tho' they were filled with pain & Anxiety at so much as seeming to oppose public Councils yet with all these Considerations in our View, Love of Virtue freedom &

posterity prevailed upon us to suspend a second Time the Courts of Justice in this County after the Judges of the Quarter Sessions had in a pricipitate & clandestine Manner held one Court & granted out a Number of Licences to Innholders at the rate of six shillings or more each & divided the Money amongst themselves with this boast that now it was a going to be like former Times & had discovered a Spirit of Independance of the People & a Disposition triumphantly to ride over their heads & worse than renew all our former Oppressions. We further beg leave to represent that we were deeply affected at the Misrepresentations that have been made of us & the County in general, as Men deeply in Debt, dishonest, ungovernable, heady untractable, without principle & good Conduct & ever ready to oppose lawful Authority, as Mobbes disturbers of peace order & Union, unwilling to submit to any Government, or ever to pay our Debts, so that we have been told a former House of Representatives had it in actual Contemplation to send an armed force to effect that by violence which reason only ought to effect at the present Day. We beg leave to lay before your Honors our Principles real Views & Designs in what we have hitherto done & what Object we are reaching after, with this Assurance if we have erred it is thro' Ignorance & not bad Intention. –

We beg leave therefore to represent that we have always been persuaded that the people are the fountain of power. That since the Dissolution of the power of Great Britain over these Colonies they have fallen into a state of Nature. That the first step to be taken by a people in such a state for the Enjoyment or Restoration of Civil Government amongst them, is the formation of a fundamental Constitution as the Basis & ground work of Legislation.

That the Approbation of the Majority of the people of this fundamental Constitution is absolutely necessary to give Life & being to it. That then & not 'till then is the foundation laid for Legislation. We often hear of the fundamental Constitution of Great Britain, which all political Writers (except ministerial ones) set above the King Lords, & Commons, which they cannot change, nothing short of the great rational Majority of the people being sufficient for this.

That a Representative Body may form, but cannot impose said fundamental Constitution upon a people. They being but servants of the people cannot be greater than their Masters, & must be responsible to them. If this fundamental Constitution is above the whole

Legislature, the Legislature cannot certainly make it, it must be the Approbation of the Majority which gives Life & being to it. –

That said fundamental Constitution has not been formed for this Province the Corner stone is not yet laid & whatever Building is reared without a foundation must fall into Ruins. That this can be instantly effected with the Approbation of the Continental Congress & Law subordination & good government flow in better than their antient Channels in a few Months Time. – That till this is done we are but beating the air & doing what will & must be undone afterwards, & all our labour is lost & on divers Accounts much worse than lost.

That a Doctrine lately broached in this County by several of the Justices newly created without the Voice of the People, that the Representatives of the People may form Just what fundamental Constitution they please & impose it upon the people & however obnoxious to them they can obtain no relief from it but by a New Election, & if our Representatives should never see fit to give the people one that pleases them there is no help for it appears to us to be the rankest kind of Toryism, the self same Monster we are now fighting against.

These are some of the Truths we firmly believe & are countenanced in believing them by the most respectable political Writers of the last & present Century, especially by Mr Burgh in his political Disquisitions[1] for the publication of which one half of the Continental Congress were subscribers.

We beg leave further to represent that we by no Means object to the most speedy Institution of Legal Government thro' this province & that we are as earnestly desirous as any others of this great Blessing.

That knowing the strong Byass of human Nature to Tyranny & Despotism we have Nothing else in View but to provide for Posterity against the wanton Exercise of power which cannot otherwise be done than by the formation of a fundamental Constitution. What is the fundamental Constitution of this province, what are the unalienable Rights of the people the power of the Rulers, how often to be elected by the people &c have any of these things been as yet ascertained. Let it not be said by future posterity that in this great this noble this glorious Contest we made no provision against Tyranny amongst ourselves.

[1] James Burgh, *Political Disquisitions*, 3 vols. (London, 1774–5); a large collection of historical and literary references for Whig principles.

We beg leave to assure your Honors that the purest & most disinterested Love of posterity & a fervent desire of transmitting to them a fundamental Constitution securing their sacred Rights & Immunities against all Tyrants that may spring up after us has moved us in what we have done. We have not been influenced by hope of Gain or Expectation of Preferment & Honor. We are no discontented faction we have no fellowship with Tories, we are the staunch friends of the Union of these Colonies & will support & maintain your Honors in opposing Great Britain with our Lives & Treasure.

But if Commissions should be recalled & the Kings Name struck out of them, if the Fee Table be reduced never so low, & multitudes of other things be done to still the people all is to us as Nothing whilst the foundation is unfixed the Corner stone of Government unlaid. We have heared much of Governments being founded in Compact. What Compact has been formed as the foundation of Government in this province? – We beg leave further to represent that we have undergone many grievous oppressions in this County & that now we wish a Barrier might be set up against such oppressions, against which we can have no security long till the foundation of Government be well established. –

We beg leave further to represent these as the Sentiments of by far the Majority of the people in this County as far as we can Judge & being so agreeable to Reason Scripture & Common Sense, as soon as the Attention of people in this province is awakened we doubt not but the Majority will be with us.

We beg leave further to observe that if this Honourable Body shall find that we have embraced Errors dangerous to the safety of these Colonies it is our Petition that our Errors may be detected & you shall be put to no further Trouble from us but without an Alteration in our Judgment the Terrors of this World will not daunt us we are determined to resist Great Britain to the last Extremity & all others who may claim a similar Power over us. Yet we hold not to an Imperium in Imperio we will be determined by the Majority. –

Your Petitioners beg leave therefore to Request that this Honourable Body would form a fundamental Constitution for this province after leave is asked & obtained from the Honourable Continental Congress & that said Constitution be sent abroad for the Approbation of the Majority of the people in this Colony that in this way we may emerge from a state of Nature & enjoy again the Blessing of Civil Government in this way the Rights & Liberties of future Generations will be secured & the Glory of the present Revolution remain untarnished & future Posterity rise up & call this Honourable Council & House of Representatives blessed.

4.II.4 ESSEX COUNTY DEMANDS REFORM IN THE SYSTEM OF REPRESENTATION

Resolutions of an Essex County Convention, April 25, 1776, Massachusetts Archives, CLVI 192–6

To the Honourable the Council & the Honourable the House of Representatives for the Colony of the Massachusetts-Bay in General Court assembled April 1776. –

The Subscribers delegated, by the several Towns in the County of Essex to our Names affixed, to represent them in County Convention, to be held at Ipswich in said County on the twenty-fifth of this Instant April, for the Purposes appearing in this Memorial, beg Leave to Represent –

That, in the present Important Crisis, when every member of the community must be anxiously solicitous for the public Weal, and when a new, and we trust a glorious Empire is forming on the Basis of Liberty, the present State of Representation in this Colony has gained the Attention of the Towns from whence we are delegated, & we are chosen to meet in a County Convention for the Purpose of endeavoring to procure one more equal, than is at present enjoyed –

When the natural Rights which men possess are given up to Society, they ever expect to receive an equivalent, from the Benefits derived from a social State; Freemen submitting themselves to the Controul of others, and giving up the entire Right of Legislation and Taxation without reserving any Share to themselves, can receive no possible equivalent for the Concession; for they become absolute Slaves; But if they delegate a Number from themselves to conduct these important Articles of State, over whom they retain a suitable Controul, they enjoy a qualified Liberty, in many Respects preferable to what they relinquish –

If this Representation is equal, it is perfect; as far as it deviates from this Equality, so far it is imperfect and approaches to that State of

Slavery; & the want of a just Weight in Representation is an Evil nearly akin to being totally destitute of it – An Inequality of Representation has been justly esteem'd the Cause which has in a great Degree sapped the foundation of the once admired, but now tottering Fabric of the British Empire; and we fear that if a different Mode of Representation from the present, is not adopted in this Colony, our Constitution will not continue, to that late Period of Time, which the glowing Heart of every true American now anticipates –

In the early Period of our Settlement, when thirty or forty Families were first permitted to send each a Representative to the general Assembly, there can be no Doubt, but the proportionate Equality was duly adjusted; nor is there much more Doubt, but that, as just an equality took Place in the Representation of the several Corporations of the British Empire, when the Rule was first established there – That striking, that unjust Disproportion, which fills us with Disgust & Detestation, has arisen in Britain, chiefly from the great Increase of Numbers and Wealth in some Places of that Empire and a Decrease in others, & continued from a blind Attachment to the Forms of Antiquity in some, and a wicked Disposition in others, who found an effectual Way to turn this Inequality to their own Advantage, tho' to the Destruction of the State –

We cannot realize that, your Honours, our wise political Fathers have adverted to the present Inequality of Representation in this Colony, to the Growth of the Evil or to the fatal Consequences which will probably ensue from the Continuance of it – Each Town & District in the Colony is by some late Regulation permitted to send one Representative to the general Court, if such Town or District consists of thirty Freeholders & other Inhabitants qualified to elect, if one hundred & twenty to send two – No town is permitted to send more than two except the Town of Boston, which may send four – There are some Towns and Districts in the Colony in which there are between thirty and forty Freeholders & other Inhabitants qualified to elect only; there are others besides Boston, in which there are more than five hundred, – The first of these may send one Representative; – The latter can send only two, if these Towns as to Property are to each other in the same respective Proportion, is it not clear to a mathematical Demonstration, that the same Number of Inhabitants of Equal Property, in the one Town, have but an Eighth Part of the Weight in

Representation with the other, & with what colourable Pretext we would decently enquire –

If we regard Property as the Rule of Representation, it will be found that there are certain thirty Towns & Districts in the Colony, which altogether pay to the publick Expence, a sum not equal to what is paid by one other single Town in this County; yet the former may have a Weight in the Legislative Body, fifteen Times as large as the latter; nay it will be found by Examination, that a Majority of Voices in the Assembly may be obtained from the Members of Towns, which pay not more than one fourth Part of the publick Tax – The County of Essex, which we represent in Convention, pays more than one sixth part of the publick Tax; & they have not a Right to send one tenth Part of the Number of Representatives which may be by Law returned to the general Assembly; This County contains one or two thousand Polls more than any other County in the Colony – The Town of Ipswich is in Property (and we suppose in Numbers) nearly equal to the several Towns & Districts of Hadley, South Hadley, Amherst, Granby, Deerfield, Greenfield, Shelburne & Conway (and more than equal to the like Number of other Places in the Colony) who are or may be represented in the general Court; Ipswich can send only two Members; the other Towns and Districts above mentioned may send ten Members at the least; can the Division of two Towns into eight, Towns and Districts furnish an Argument for the disproportionate Representation which of Consequence has taken Place; if the Property and Numbers remain the same, the Reason is to us Paradoxical.[1] –

If a new System of Government, or any material alteration in the old is to be in the Contemplation of the next general Assembly; Is it not fitting that the whole Community should be equally concerned in adjusting this System –

The many evil Consequences that will naturally & must inevitably arise from this Inequality of Representation, we trust, we need not attempt to mark out to a wise and free House of Americans; the Delineation would be disagreeable as well as indecent – Nor would we arrogantly suggest, to your Honours, the Mode of Redress, we confide in your Wisdom and Justice, and if an Equality of Representation takes

[1] South Hadley and Amherst were districts created from Hadley; Granby was an incorporated town created from Hadley. Greenfield, Shelburne, and Conway were all districts created from Deerfield. All were in Hampshire County. [Robert J. Taylor, *Massachussetts*, *Colony to Commonwealth*, p. 39.]

Place in the Colony, we shall be satisfied whether it has Respect to Numbers, to Property or to a Combination of both.

4.II.5 FROM THE INSTRUCTIONS TO THE REPRESENTATIVES OF THE TOWN OF BOSTON, MAY 30, 1776

Boston Town Records, 1770 through 1777, in *A Report of the Record Commissioners of the City of Boston* (1887) pp. 237–8

Touching the internal Police of this Colony, it is essentially necessary, in Order to preserve Harmony among ourselves, that the constituent Body be satisfied, that they are fully & fairly represented – The Right to legislate is originally in every Member of the Community; which Right is always exercised of a State: But when the Inhabitants are become numerous, 'tis not only inconvenient, but impracticable *for all* to meet in One Assembly; & hence arose the Necessity & Practice of legislating by a few freely chosen by the many. – When this Choice is free, & the Representation, equal, 'tis the People's Fault if they are not happy: We therefore entreat you to devise some Means to obtain an *equal Representation* of the People of this Colony in the Legislature. But care should be taken, that the Assembly be not unweildy; for this would be an Approach to the Evil meant to be cured by Representation. The largest Bodies of Men do not always dispatch Business with the greatest Expedition, nor conduct it in the wisest manner –

It is essential to Liberty that the legislative, judicial & executive Powers of Government be, as nearly as possible, independent of & separate from each other; for where they are united in the same Persons, there will be wanting that natural Check, which is the principal Security against the enacting of arbitrary Laws, and a wanton Exercise of Power in the Execution of them. – It is also of the highest Importance that every Person in a Judiciary Department, employ the greatest Part of his Time & Attention in the Duties of his office. – We therefore farther instruct you, to procure the making such Law or Laws, as shall make it incompatible for the same Person to hold a Seat in the legislative & executive Departments of Government, at one & the same time: – That shall render the Judges in every Judiciary thro' the Colony, dependent, not on the uncertain Tenure of Caprice or Pleasure, but on an unimpeachable Deportment in the important Duties of their Station, for their Continuance in Office: And to prevent the Multiplicity of Offices in the same Person, that such Salaries be settled upon them, as Will place them above the Necessity of stooping to any indirect or collateral Means for Subsistence. –

We wish to avoid a Profusion of the public Monies on the one hand, & the *Danger of sacrificing our Liberties to a Spirit of Parsimony on the other*: – Not doubting of your Zeal & Abilities in the common Cause of our Country, we leave your Discretion to prompt such Exertions, in promoting any military Operations, as the Exigency of our public Affairs may require: And in the same Confidence in your Fervor & Attachment to the public Weal, we readily submit all other Matters of public Moment, that may require your Consideration to your own Wisdom & Discretion. –

The foregoing Draught of Instructions to our Representatives, having been read & considered, the Question was put – 'Whether the same shall be accepted, & given to our Representatives, as their Instructions' – Passed in the Affirmative unanimously. –

4.II.6 THE HOUSE OF REPRESENTATIVES SEEKS AUTHORITY TO DRAFT A CONSTITUTION, SEPTEMBER 17, 1776

Massachusetts Archives, CLVI 133

Resolved, That it be recommended to the Male Inhabitants of each Town in this State, being Free and Twenty One Years of Age, or upwards, that they assemble as soon as they can in Town-Meeting, upon reasonable previous Warning to be therefor given, according to Law, and that in such Meeting, they consider and determine whether they will give their Consent, that the present House of Representatives of this State of the *Massachusetts-Bay* in *New England*, together with the Council if they consent, in One Body with the House, and by equal Voice, should consult, agree on, and enact such a Constitution and Form of Government for this State, as the said House of Representatives & Council aforesaid, on the fullest and most mature Deliberation shall judge will most conduce to the Safety, Peace, and Happiness of this State, in all after Successions and Generations; and if they would direct that the same be made Public for the Inspection and Perusal of the Inhabitants, before the Ratification thereof by the Assembly. And that each Town as soon as may be after they have passed on the Question aforesaid, cause their Votes or Resolutions thereon to be certified into the Office of the Secretary of this State. And all Towns having a Right according to Law to a Representation in the General Assembly, and not having chose a Representative in Pursuance of the Precepts issued in *April* last, are at the Meeting aforementioned, impowered if they see Cause upon this Occasion, to return a Member or Members in the same Manner as they were by the Laws of this State impowered to do in Consequence of the Precepts aforesaid.

Also, Ordered, That *David Cheever*, Esq.; procure the foregoing Resolve to be Published in Hand-Bills, and sent to the Selectmen of each Town.

J. Warren, Speaker

4.II.7 BOSTON OBJECTS

From the Return of Boston (Suffolk County), 1776, *Boston Town Records, 1770–1777*, p. 248

1t. To form Government & establish a Constitution for the present & succeeding Generations, is a Task or Consideration the most important, it extends as much to our *Religious* as *Civil Liberties*, & includes our *All* – It effects every Individual; every Individual therefore ought to be consulting, acting & assisting.

2d. A Subject of such General, & indeed Infinite Concernment ought to be proceeded in with the greatest Caution & maturest Deliberation. – The Means or Channels of Information should all lay open to the People, & not restricted or confined to any particular Assembly however respectable. –

3d. Precipitancy is to be guarded against time & Opportunity should be taken by the people whose right it is to form Government, to collect the wisest Sentiments on this Subject; not of the present House only, but also of the Council, & every other Society, or Member

of the State, that would favor the Public with their Sentiments, In Order that they may possess themselves of such Principles, & wise Maxims sounded on the best Precedents, & thereby be enabled to form a judicious & happy Constitution of Government . . .
[This report was unanimously accepted by the town.]

4.II.8 ATTLEBOROUGH OBJECTS

The Return of Attleborough (Bristol County), October 28, 1776, Massachusetts Archives, CLVI 171

At a Town-meeting legally assembled at Attleborough, October the 14th 1776. In consequence of a Resolve of September 17th 1776 passed by the Honorable House of Representatives for the State of Massachusetts-Bay,
– The following Resolves were passed –

1st. Resolved that good Government is the Basis of Liberty, and absolutely necessary for the Safty & Welfare of a People –

2dly. Resolved, that as the End of Government is the Happiness of the People; so the Sole Power & right of forming a Plan thereof is essentially in the People –

3dly. Resolved, that as this State is at present destitute of a fixed & established form of Government, it is expedient & necessary that one be formed and established as soon as conveniently may be; agreeable to the Recommendation of the Continental Congress –

4thly. Resolved, that whereas the present honorable House of Representatives have passed a Resolve of September 17th 1776, referring to the Consideration & Determination of the male Inhabitants &c. of this State; whether they will impower the Said Honorable House with the Council &c, to agree on, and enact a Constitution & Form of Government for this State, we can by no means consent to give them such a Power, for two Reasons especially (viz) because we apprehend the present honorable House is not a fair Representation of the Inhabitants of this State, – many Towns (not having this important matter in view) having chosen and sent fewer than their just Proportion of Members to that Honorable Boddy, – and also because the right of the Inhabitants of the Said State by their Votes in Town-meeting to negative the Said form, or any Article in it when drawn is not expressly acknowledged in the Said Resolve. For –

5thly. it is resolved that it appears absolutely necessary for the Safty & Liberty of this State, that the Plan of Government when formed & published should be thoroughly examined & actually approved & consented unto by the good People of this State & convenient time for that Purpose be allowd before the establishment thereof – the establishment itself to be by a State Convention by them appointed for that Purpose

6thly. Resolved that the Honorable House be requested, to call upon the Several Towns in this State to chose one, or more Members for the purpose of draughting & publishing a Form of Government for this State, to be approved by the Several Towns, – in order to which Draught we would humbly purpose the following method (viz) that the Members so chosen for the Several Towns in each County, meet together in County Conventions & therein draught Said Forms –, which done, that they by themselves, or their Committee meet in a State Convention or Congress & compare their Several Forms together, whereby the Wisdom of the whole State may be collected & a Form extracted, to be published for the Inspection & approbation of the Several Towns, also that the time for the meeting of the Said County & State Conventions for carrying into execution the Said Prosess, be appointed by the Court; & finally that after the Said form Shall have been published, examined & consented to by the Several Towns in this State, or the major part of them – the Said State Convention to be impowered by their Constituents to establish the Same.

Dated at Attleborough
October the 28 – 1776 } test Jonathan Stanley { Town Clerk

4.II.9 CONCORD OBJECTS

The Return of Concord (Middlesex County), October 22, 1776, Massachusetts Archives, CLVI 182

At a meeting of the Inhabitents of the Town of Concord being free & twenty one years of age and upwards met by adjournment on the twenty first Day of October 1776 to take into Consideration a Resolve of the Honorable House of Representatives of this State on the 17th of September last the Town Resolved as followes –

Resolve 1st. That this State being at Present Destitute of a Properly established form of Government, it is absolutely necessary that one should be immediately formed and established –

Resolved 2 That the Supreme Legislative, either in their Proper Capacity, or in Joint Committee, are by no means a Body proper to form & Establish a Constitution, or form of Government; for Reasons following. first Because we Conceive that a Constitution in its Proper Idea intends a System of Principles Established to Secure the Subject in the Possession & enjoyment of their Rights and Privileges, against any Encroachments of the Governing Part – 2d. Because the Same Body that forms a Constitution have of Consequence a power to alter it. 3d. Because a Constitution alterable by the Supreme Legislative is no Security at all to the Subject against any Encroachment of the Governing part on any or on all of their Rights & privileges.

Resolve 3d. That it appears to this Town highly necesary & Expedient that a Convention, or Congress be immediately Chosen, to form & establish a Constitution, by the Inhabitents of the Respective Towns in this State, being free & of twenty one years of age, and upwards, in Proportion as the Representatives of this State formerly were Chosen; the Convention or Congress not to Consist of a greater number then the house of assembly of this State heretofore might Consist of, Except that each Town & District Shall have Liberty to Send one Representative, or otherwise as Shall appear meet to the Inhabitents of this State in General

Resolve 4th. that when the Convention, or Congress have formed a Constitution they adjourn for a Short time, and Publish their Proposed Constitution for the Inspection & Remarks of the Inhabitents of this State

Resolved 5ly. that the Honorable house of assembly of this State be Desired to Recommend it to the Inhabitents of the State to Proceed to Chuse a Convention or Congress for the Purpas abovesaid as soon as Possable –

A True Copy of the Proceeding of the Town of Concord at the General Town meeting above mentioned – attest Ephraim Wood Jr, Town Clerk

4.II.10 TOWNS OF WORCESTER COUNTY GIVE THEIR OPINIONS, NOVEMBER 26, 1776

Massachusetts Spy, December 4, 1776

At a meeting of the Committees of [S]afety &c. From a majority of the Towns in the County of Worcester, held by adjournment, at the Court House in said Worcester. November 26, 1776.

Voted,

THAT the Members inform the Convention what were the general sentiments of the inhabitants of their respective Towns, concerning a Resolve of the House of Representatives, on the 17th of September last, respecting the formation of a system of Government.

Lancaster, *Rutland*, *Harvard*, *Princeton*. *Paxton*, *Southborough*, *Hardwick*, *Uxbridge*, *New-Brantree*, *Oakham*, *Shrewsbury*, *Winchendon*, Consented, subject to the approbation or rejection of the people,

Oxford, Dissented by reason of unequal representation and brethen absent. *Sutton*, *Bolton Sturbridtge*, *Holden*, *Northbridge*, Dissented for unequal representation.

Worcester, Postponed acting on said resolve, till the third Monday in December next, to have the voice of their brethren in the Army.

Leicester, Dissented, presuming the people were excluded the right of approbation or rejection.

Dudley, *Charlton*, Objected to the present House.

Petersham, The same and against any Council.

Brookfield, Consented with right of approbation or rejection, and Government to be established by a future House.

Mendon, Not to comply with said resolve.

Spencer, The same, the Court not being in a proper situation,

Templeton, *Fitchburg*, *Douglas*, Objected to the present Court.

Northborough, *Upton*, *Westborough*, *Ashburnham*, Had no resolve, nor acted thereon.

Grafton, Did not act thereon.

Westminster, Had no resolve or acted thereon.

Voted,

That a system of Government is necessary to be established in this State so soon as it may be done with safety.

Whereas the Honorable the Continental Congress have thought fit, with the consent, and for the safety, peace and happiness of the American States to declare them free & independent on the Crown of Great-Britain &c. And have recommended to said States the forming such systems of Government as may be most agreeable to their respective situations and circumstances;

And whereas the present House of Representatives, to bring forward this important business have asked the consent of the people to impower that body with the Council, to form such a system of Government for this State; – The Committees of Safty &c. from a great majority of the Towns in the County of Worcester, convened at the Court House in said Worcester, on Tuesday the 26 of November 1776, for the purpose of reconciling the various sentiments of the inhabitants respecting said request, and preserving unanimity in the County; and also considering the loose and disjointed State, the people of the Massachusetts-Bay, have been in for divers years past, in which time, many errors have crept in and been supported with the remains of the late constitutions; that the evils are daily increasing and in all probability will continue till a fixed and permanent form of Government be established. Therefore to prevent, (as much as in themselves) anarchy and confusion, and the undue influence or power of individuals in monopolizing incompatible offices in the hands of particular persons, on the one hand and on the other to strengthen the hands of Government, against an unatural enemy, and lay a permanent foundation for safety, peace and happiness for this and succeeding generations; said Convention have come into the following votes, &c. with intention to lay the same before their respective Towns for their consideration.

Whereas an act passed in the late General Court. making the representation of the State very unequal and unsafe, this Convention is of opinion that the present General Court is not the most suitable body to form a system of Government for this State, moreover the business being of the greatest importance, will require more time and closeer attention than can be spared, by a house of representatives, from the ordinary and daily concerns of the State, Therefore voted, That a State Congress chosen for the sole purpose of forming a Constitution of Government is (in the opinion of this Convention) more eligible than an House of Representatives. Voted, That it be recommended to our respective Towns, that they instruct their Representatives, to exert their influence, that writs be issued from the General Court impowering and directing the Towns to chuse members, to form a State Congress, by a mode of representation agreeable to the last charter and as practised in the year 1775, for the purpose of forming a plan of Government, which, when formed, to be laid before the people for their inpection, approbation, rejection, or amendment, (if any they have to propose) and when approved by the people, that said Congress solemnly establish the same, issue out writs for convening a legislative body agreeable to said Constitution and dissolve.

Voted, That the proceedings of this Convention be submitted to the consideration of the other counties in this State, and request the favour of their sentiments on the subject.

Voted, To publish the foregoing in the Boston, Worcester and Hartford News-Papers, also in Hand Bills.

By order of the Convention
JOSEPH HENSHAW, Chairman

4.II.11 THE HOUSE OF REPRESENTATIVES RESOLVES TO GIVE THE GENERAL COURT POWER TO FORM A CONSTITUTION

State of Massachusetts Bay, in the House of Representatives, April 4, 1777, Massachusetts Archives, CLVI 200–2

That the happiness of Mankind depends very much on the Form of Constitution of Government they live under. that the only object and design of Government should be the good of the people are truths well understood at this day & truths taught by reason & Experience very clearly at all times and yet by far the greater part of Mankind are governed only for the advantage of their masters & are the miserable slaves of a single or a few despots whose Ideas or humanity never extend beyond the limits of their own [Grandeur?] or Interest and indeed among the Multitude of Mankind who have lived and the variety of people who have succeeded each other in the several ages of the world very few have ever had an oppertunity of choosing and forming a Constitution of Government for themselves. this is a great privilege & such an one the good People of this state by the distinguished favours of a kind Providence now Enjoy and which the Interst

& happiness of themselves & posterity loudly call upon them to improve with wisdom & prudence. the Infatuated Policy of Britain instead of destroying has in all probability (by the Goodness of God) promoted & accelerated the happiness of the people of the United States of America. the Cruelty and Injustice of Britain has driven u[s] to a declaration of Independence & a dissolution of our former Connections with them and made it necessary for each of the United States to form & constitute a mode of Goverment for themselves – and whereas by the suffrages of the good People of this State it has become more especially our duty to Consult & promote the happiness of our Constituents & haveing duly Considered the Advantages & necessity of immediately forming a fixed and permanent Constitution of Government & Conceiving it to be the Expectation of our Constituents that we should originate and recommend to them the most suitable method for Effecting this valuable and Important purpose. do Resolve – That it be & hereby is recommended to the several Towns & places in this State – Impowered by the Laws thereof to send members to the General Assembly that at their next Election of a Member or Members to represent them they make choice of men in whose Intigrity & Ability they can place the greatest Confidence & in addition to the Common & ordinary powers of Representation vest them with full powers to form such a Constitution of Goverment as they shall Judge best Calculated to promote the happiness of this State & when Compleated to Cause the same to be printed in all the Boston Newspapers & also in hand Bills one of which to be transmitted to the Selectmen of each town or the Committe of each plantation to be by them laid before their respective Towns or plantations at a regular meeting for that purpose to be called. to be by each Town & Plantation Considered. and a return of their approbation or disapprobation to be made to the Clerk of the House of Representatives specifiing the Numbers present in Such meeting voteing for & those voteing against the same at a reasonable time to be fixed on by said House and if upon a fair Examination of said returns it shall appear that said form of Goverment be approved of by at least two thirds of those who are Free & twenty one years of age within this State and present in the several meetings then the same shall be deemed and Established as the Constitution & form of Goverment of the state of Massachusetts Bay according to which the Inhabitants thereof shall be Governed in all succeeding Generations unless altered by their own Express direction or that of a fair Majority of them. and it is further recommended to the Selectmen of the several Towns in the return of their Precepts for the Choice of Representatives to signify their having Considered this resolve & their doings thereon

and it is also Resolved that Mr Storey, Mr Freeman & Capt. Page – be a committee to get these Resolves printed in hand Bills & sent to the several Towns & Plantations in this State as soon as may be & also to cause the same to be published in all the Boston Newspapers three weeks successively –

Sent up for Concurrence

4.II.12 THE CONSTITUTION OF 1778

Old South Leaflets, ed. Chester A. McLain no. 209 (Boston, n.d.) pp. 3–15

A CONSTITUTION AND FORM OF GOVERNMENT

For the State of Massachusetts Bay, agreed upon by the Convention of said State, February 28, 1778 – to be laid before the several towns and plantations in said State, for their aprobation or disaprobation.

State of Massachusetts Bay.
In Convention, February 28, 1778

Whereas, upon the Declaration of Independence, made by the Representatives of the United States, in Congress assembled, by which all connections between the said States and Great Britain, were dissolved, the General Assembly of this State thought it expedient that a new constitution of Government for this State, should be formed; and, apprehending that they were not invested with sufficient authority to deliberate and determine upon so interesting a subject, did, on the fifth day of May 1777, for the effecting this valuable purpose, pass the following Resolve:

'Resolved, That it be, and hereby is recommended to the several towns and places in this State, impowered by the laws thereof to send members to the General Assembly, that, at their next election of a member or members to represent them, they make choice of men, in whose integrity and abilities they can place the greatest confidence; and, in addition to the common and ordinary powers of representation, instruct them with full powers, in one body with the Council, to form such a constitution of government as they shall judge best calculated to promote the happiness of this State, and when compleated to cause the same to be printed in all the Boston news-papers, and also in hand-bills, one of which to be transmitted to the selectmen of each town, or the committee of each plantation, to be by them laid before their respective towns or plantations, at a regular meeting of the inhabitants thereof, to be called for that purpose, in order to its being by each town and plantation duly considered, and a return of their approbation or disapprobation to be made into the Secretary's office of this State, at a reasonable time to be fixed on by the General Court, specifying the numbers present in such meeting, voting for, and those voting against the same; and if upon a fair examination of the said returns, by the General Court or such a committee as they shall appoint for that purpose, it shall appear that the said form of government is approved of by at least two thirds of those who are free and twenty-one years of age, belonging to this State, and present in the several meetings, then the General Court shall be impowered to establish the same as the constitution and form of government of the State of Massachusetts-Bay; according to which the inhabitants thereof shall be governed in all succeeding generations, unless the same shall be altered by their own express direction, or that of at least two thirds of them. And it is further recommended to the selectmen of the several towns in the return of their precepts for the choice of Representatives to signify their having considered this resolve, and their doings thereon.'

And whereas the good people of this State, in pursuance of the said resolution, and reposing special trust and confidence in the Council and in their Representatives, have appointed, authorized and instructed their Representatives in one body with the Council, to form such a constitution of government as they shall judge best calculated to promote the happiness of this State, and when compleated, to cause the same to be published for their inspection and consideration.

We therefore the Council and Representatives of the people of the State of Massachusetts-Bay, in Convention assembled, by virtue of the power delegated to us, and acknowledging our dependence upon the all-wise Governor of the Universe for direction, do agree upon the following form of a constitution of government for this State, to be sent out to the people, that they may act thereon, agreeably to the afore-recited resolve.

I. – There shall be convened, held and kept a General Court, upon the last Wednesday in the month of *May* every year, and at all other times as the said General Court shall order and appoint; which General Court shall consist of a Senate and House of Representatives to be elected as this Constitution hereafter directs.

II. – There shall be elected annually a Governor and Lieutenant-Governor, who shall each have, by virtue of such election, a seat and voice in the Senate; and the stile and title of the Governor shall be *His Excellency*; and the stile and title of the Lieutenant-Governor shall be *His Honor*.

III. – No person shall be considered as qualified to serve as Governor, Lieutenant-Governor, Senator or Representative, unless qualified respectively at the time of their several elections as follows, viz: The Governor and Lieutenant-Governor shall have been inhabitants of this State five years immediately preceeding the time of their respective election; the Governor shall be possessed, in his own right, of an estate of the value of *one thousand pounds, whereof five hundred pounds* value, at the least, shall be in real estate, within this State; the Lieutenant-Governor shall be possessed, in his own right, of an estate of the value of *five hundred pounds, two hundred and fifty pounds* thereof, at the least, to be in real estate, within this State: A Senator shall be possessed, in his own right, of an estate to the value of *four hundred pounds, two hundred pounds* thereof, at least, to be in real estate, lying in the district for which he shall be elected: A Representative shall be possessed, in his own right, of an estate of the value of *two hundred pounds, one hundred pounds* thereof, at the least, to be in real estate, lying in the town for which he shall be elected. Senators and Representatives shall have been inhabitants of districts and towns for which they shall be respectively elected one full year immediately preceeding such election; provided that when two or more towns join in the choice of a Representative, they may choose an inhabitant of either of said towns, he being otherwise qualified as this article directs.

IV. – The Judges of the Superior Court, Secretary, Treasurer-General, Commissary-General, and settled Ministers of the Gospel, while in office; also all military officers while in the pay of this or of the United States, shall be considered as disqualified for holding a seat in the General Court; and the Judges and Registers of Probate for holding a seat in the Senate.

V. – Every male inhabitant of any town in this State, being free, and twenty-one years of age, excepting Negroes, Indians and molattoes, shall be intitled to vote for a Representative or Representatives, as the case may be, in the town where he is resident, provided he has paid taxes in said town (unless by law excused from taxes) and been resident therein one full year immediately preceeding such voting, or that such town has been his known and usual place of abode for that time, or that he is considered as an inhabitant thereof; and every such inhabitant qualified as above, and worth *sixty pounds* clear of all charges thereon, shall be intitled to put in his vote for Governor, Lieutenant-Governor and Senators; and all such voting for Governor, Lieutenant-Governor, Senators or Representatives, shall be by ballot and not otherwise.

VI. – Every incorporated town within this State shall be intitled to send one Representative to the General Court; any town having three hundred voters, may send three; having seven hundred and sixty, may send four, and so on; making the increasing number necessary for another member, twenty more than the last immediately preceeding increasing number, 'till the whole number of voters in any town are reckoned. And each town shall pay the expense of its own representative or representatives; and the inhabitants of any two or more towns, who do not incline to send a Representative for each town, may join in the choice of one, if they shall so agree.

VII. – The Selectmen of each town shall some time in the month of *April* annually, issue their warrant or warrants under their hands and seals, directed to some Constable or Constables within their towns respectively, requiring him or them to notify the inhabitants qualified to vote for a representative, to assemble in some convenient place in such town, for the choice of some person or persons, as the case may be, to represent them in the General Court the ensuing year: the time and place of meeting to be mentioned in the warrant or warrants for calling such meeting: And the selectmen of each town respectively, or the major part of them, shall make return of the name or names of the person or persons elected by the major part of the voters present, and voting in such meeting, to represent said town in the General Court the ensuing year, into the Secretary's office, on or before the last Wednesday of *May*, then next ensuing: And when two or more towns shall agree to join for such choice, the major part of the Selectmen of those towns, shall in the manner above directed, warn a meeting to be held in either of the said towns, as they shall judge most convenient, for that purpose, and shall make return as aforesaid, of the person chosen at such meeting.

VIII. – The number of Senators shall be twenty eight; (exclusive of the Governor and Lieutenant-Governor) Their election shall be annual, and from certain districts, into which the State shall be divided as follows, viz: The middle district to contain the counties of *Suffolk*, *Essex*, and *Middlesex*, within which ten Senators shall be elected: the southern district to contain the counties of *Plymouth*, *Barnstable*, *Bristol*, *Dukes' County* and *Nantucket*, within which six Senators shall be elected; the western district to contain the counties of *Hampshire*, *Worcester* and *Berkshire*, within which eight Senators shall be elected; the northern district to contain the counties of *York*, and *Cumberland*, within which three shall be elected; the eastern district to contain the county of *Lincoln*, within which one shall be elected: And as the numbers of the inhabitants in the several districts may vary from time to time, the General Court shall in the way they shall judge best, sometime in the year one thousand seven hundred and ninety, and once in twenty years ever after, order the number of the inhabitants in the several districts to be taken, that the Senators may be apportioned a new to the several districts, according to the numbers of the inhabitants therein. And the General Court may at such new apportionment increase the number of Senators to be chosen as they may see fit; provided that the whole number shall never exceed thirty six, exclusive of the Governor and Lieutenant-Governor.

IX. – The inhabitants of the several towns in this State qualified as this Constitution directs, shall on the first Wednesday in the Month of *November* annually, give in their votes in their respective towns, at a meeting which the Selectmen shall call for that purpose, for Senators for the year ensuing the last Wednesday in *May* then next. The votes shall be given in for the members of each district separately according to the foregoing apportionment, or such as shall be hereafter ordered; and the Selectmen and Town Clerk of each town, shall sort and count the votes, and by the third Wednesday in *December* then next, transmit to the Secretary's office, a list certified by the town-clerk, of all the persons who had votes as Senators for each district at such meeting, and the number each person had affixed to his name. The lists so sent in shall be examined by the General Court at their then next sitting, and a list for each district of those voted for, to the amount of double the number assigned such district (if so many shall have votes) taking those who had the highest numbers, shall be made out and sent by the first of *March*, the next after, to the several towns in this State, as a nomination list, from which said towns shall, at their meetings for the choice of Governor in the month of *May*, vote for the Senators assigned the respective districts; which votes shall be counted and sorted, and lists certified as before directed, made out and sent in to the Secretary's office, by ten o'clock in the forenoon of the last Wednesday in said *May*, and not afterwards; which lists shall be examined by the House of Representatives for the first time of the election of Senators, and ever afterwards by the Senate and House of Representatives on said last Wednesday of *May*, or as soon after as may be; and those persons in each district, equal to the number assigned such district, who have the greatest number of votes, shall be Senators for the ensuing year, unless it shall appear to the Senate that any member or members thereof were unduly elected, or not legally qualified; of which the Senate shall be the judges. And the Senate when so constituted shall continue in being 'till another Senate is chosen, and the members thereof gone through all the steps necessary to qualify them to enter on the business assigned them by this Constitution.

X. – There shall forever hereafter, on the first Wednesday in the month of *May* annually, to be held, in each town in this State, a meeting of the inhabitants of such towns respectively, to give or put in their votes for Governor, Lieutenant-Governor and Senators; which meeting the Selectmen shall cause to be notified in the manner before directed, for the meeting for the choice of Representatives: and the town-clerk shall return into the Secretary's office by ten o'clock in the morning of the last Wednesday of said *May*, and not afterwards, an attested list of all the persons who had votes for Governor and Lieutenant-Governor respectively, certifying the number of votes each person so voted for had, which lists shall be, on said last Wednesday of *May*, or as soon after as may be, examined by the Senate and House of Representatives; and the persons who on such examination, shall appear to have the greatest number of votes for those offices respectively, provided it be a majority of the whole number, shall be by the two Houses declared Governor and Lieutenant-Governor, and intitled to act as such the ensuing year: and if no person shall have such majority for Governor or for Lieutenant-Governor, the Senate and House of Representatives shall as soon as may be, after examining said lists, proceed by joint ballot to elect a Governor or Lieutenant-Governor, or both, as the case may require, confining themselves to one of those three who had the greatest number of votes collected in the several towns for the office to be filled.

XI. – If any person chosen Governor, Lieutenant-Governor, Senator or Representative, whose qualification shall be questioned by any one member of the Senate or House of Representatives, within twenty-four days after his appearing to enter upon the execution of his office, shall not make oath before a Senator, the Speaker of the House of Representatives, or some Justice of the Peace, that he is qualified as required by this Constitution, and lodge a certificate thereof in the Secretary's office, within ten days after notice given him of such questioning by the Secretary, whose duty it shall be to give such notice, his election shall be void; and any person claiming privilege of voting for Governor, Lieutenant-Governor, Senators, or Representatives, and whose qualifications shall be questioned in town-meeting, shall by the Selectmen be prevented from voting, unless he shall make oath that he is qualified as this Constitution requires; said oath to be administered by a Justice of the Peace, or the Town-Clerk, who is hereby impowered to administer the same when no Justice is present.

XII. – Whenever any person who may be chosen a member of the Senate, shall decline the office to which he is elected, or shall resign his place, or die, or remove out of the State, or be any way disqualified, the House of Representatives may, if they see fit, by ballot, fill up any vacancy occasioned thereby, confining themselves in the choice to the nomination list for the district to which such member belonged, whose place is to be supplied, if a sufficient number is thereon for the purpose; otherwise the choice may be made at large in such district.

XIII. – The General Court shall be the supreme legislative authority of this State, and shall accordingly have full power and authority to erect and constitute judicatories and Courts of record, or other Courts; and from time to time to make and establish all manner of wholesome and reasonable orders, laws, and statutes; and also, for the necessary support and defence of this government, they shall have full power and authority to levy proportionable and reasonable assessments, rates and taxes, and to do all and every thing they shall judge to be for the good and welfare of the State, and for the Government and ordering thereof; provided nevertheless, they shall not have any power to add to, alter, abolish, or infringe any part of this constitution. And the enacting stile in making laws shall be 'by the Senate and House of Representatives in General Court assembled, and by the authority of the same'.

XIV. – The Senate and House of Representatives shall be two separate and distinct bodies, each to appoint its own officers, and settle its own rules of proceedings; and each shall have an equal right to originate or reject any bill, resolve or order, or to propose amendments in the same, excepting bills and resolves, levying and granting money or other property of the State, which shall originate in the House of Representatives only, and be concurred or non-concurred in whole by the Senate.

XV. – Not less than sixty members shall constitute or make a quorum of the House of Representatives; and not less than nine shall make a quorum of the Senate.

XVI. – The Senate and House of Representatives shall have power to adjourn themselves respectively; provided such adjournment shall not exceed two days at any one time.

XVII. – The Governor shall be President of the Senate. He shall be General and Commander in Chief of the Militia, and Admiral of the Navy of this State; and impowered to embody the militia, and cause them to be marched to any part of the State, for the public safety, when he shall think necessary; and in the recess of the General Court, to march the militia, by advice of the Senate, out of the State, for the defence of this, or any other of the United States; provided always that the Governor shall exercise the power given by this constitution, over the militia and navy of the State, according to the laws thereof, or the resolves of the General Court. He shall, with the advice of the Senate, in the recess of the General Court, have power to prorogue the same from time to time, not exceeding forty days in any one recess of said Court; and in the sitting of said Court, to adjourn or prorogue the said Court to any time they shall desire, or to dissolve the same at their request, or to call said Court together sooner than the time to which it may be adjourned or prorogued, if the welfare of the State shall require the same. He shall have power at his discretion to grant reprieves to condemned criminals for a term or terms of time, not exceeding six months. It shall be the duty of the Governor to inform the legislature at every session of the General Court, of the condition of the State, and from time to time to recommend such matters to their consideration, as shall appear to him to concern its good government, welfare and prosperity.

XVIII. – Whenever the person, who may be chosen Governor shall decline the trust to which he is thereby elected, or shall resign, or die, or remove out of the State, or be otherwise disqualified, the Lieutenant-Governor shall have the like power during the vacancy in the office of Governor, as the Governor is by this Constitution vested with; and in case of a vacancy in the office of Governor and Lieutenant-Governor, the major part of the Senate shall have authority to exercise all the powers of a Governor during such vacancy; and in case the Governor and the Lieutenant-Governor are both absent from the Senate, the Senior or first Senator then present shall preside therein.

XIX. – All Civil officers annually chosen, with salaries annually granted for their services, shall be appointed by the General Court, by ballot; each branch to have a right to originate or negative the choice: All other Civil officers, and also all General, Field and Staff officers, both of the militia and of the troops, which may be raised by and be in the pay of this State, shall be appointed by the Governor and the Senate; Captains and Subalterns of troops raised by and in the pay of this State, to be also appointed by the Governor and Senate.

XX. – The Governor and Senate shall be a Court for the trial of all impeachments of any officers of this State, provided that if any impeachment shall be prosecuted against the Governor, Lieutenant-Governor, or any one of the Senate; in such case the person impeached shall not continue one of the Court for such trial. Previous to the trial of any impeachment, the members of the Court shall be respectively sworn, truly and impartially to try and determine the charge in question, according to evidence, which oath shall be administered to the members by the President, and to him by any one of the Senate; and no judgment of said Court shall be valid, unless it be assented to by two thirds of the members of said Court present at such trial; nor shall judgment extend further than to removal of the person tried from office, and disqualification to hold or enjoy any place of honor, trust or profit, under the State; the party so convicted shall nevertheless be liable and subject to indictment, trial, judgment and punishment, according to the laws of the State; and the power of impeaching all officers for malconduct in their respective offices, shall be vested in the House of Representatives.

XXI. – The Governor may, with the advice of the Senate, in the recess of the General Court, lay an embargo, or prohibit the exportation of any commodity for any term of time, not exceeding forty days in any one recess of said Court.

XXII. – The Governor shall have no negative as Governor, in any matter pointed out by this Constitution to be done by the Governor and the Senate, but shall have an equal voice with any Senator, on any question before them; provided that the Governor (or, in his absence out of the State, the Lieutenant-Governor) shall be present in Senate to enable them to proceed on the business assigned them by this Constitution, as Governor and Senate.

XXIII. – The power of granting pardons shall be vested in the Governor, Lieutenant-Governor and Speaker of the House of Representatives, for the time being, or in either two of them.

XXIV. – The Justices of the Superior Court, the Justices of the Inferior Courts of Common Pleas, Judges of Probate of Wills, Judges of the Maritime Courts, and Justices of the Peace, shall hold their respective places during good behavior.

XXV. – The Secretary, Treasurer-General, and Commissary-General, shall be appointed annually.

XXVI. – The Attorney-General, Sheriffs, Registers of the Courts of Probate, Coroners, Notaries-Public, and Naval-Officers, shall be appointed and hold their places during pleasure.

XXVII. – The Justices of the Superior Court, Justices of the Inferior Courts, Courts of General Sessions of the Peace, and Judges of the Maritime Courts, shall appoint their respective Clerks.

XXVIII. – The Delegates for this State to the Continental Congress shall be chosen annually by joint ballot of the Senate and House of Representatives, and may be superseded in the mean time in the same manner. If any person holding the office of Governor, Lieutenant-Governor, Senator, Judge of the Superior Court, Secretary, Attorney-General, Treasurer-General, or Commissary-General, shall be chosen a member of Congress, and accept the trust, the place which he so held as aforesaid shall be considered as vacated thereby, and some other person chosen to succeed him therein: And if any person serving for this State at said Congress, shall be appointed to either of the aforesaid offices, and accept thereof, he shall be considered as resigning his seat in Congress, and some other person shall be chosen in his stead.

XXIX. – No person unless of the Protestant religion shall be Governor, Lieutenant-Governor, a member of the Senate or of the House of Representatives, or hold any judiciary employment within this State.

XXX. – All Commissions shall run in the name of the 'State of *Massachusetts-Bay*', bear test, and be signed by the Governor or

Commander in Chief of the State, for the time being, and have the seal of the State thereunto affixed, and be attested by the Secretary or his deputy.

XXXI. – All writs issuing out of the Clerk's office of any of the Courts of law within this State, shall be in the name of the 'State of *Masachusetts-Bay*', under the seal of the Court from whence they issue, bear test of the Chief Justice, or senior or first Justice of the Court, where such writ is returnable, and be signed by the Clerk of such Court. Indictments shall conclude 'against the peace and dignity of the State'.

XXXII. – All the statute laws of this State, the common law, and all such parts of the English and British statute laws, as have been adopted and usually practised in the Courts of law in this State, shall still remain and be in full force until altered or repealed by a future law or laws of the legislature; and shall be accordingly observed and obeyed by the people of this State, such parts only excepted as are repugnant to the rights and privileges contained in this Constitution: and all parts of such laws as refer to and mention the Council shall be construed to extend to the Senate; and the inestimable right of trial by jury shall remain confirmed as part of this Constitution forever.

XXXIII. – All monies shall be issued out of the Treasury of this State, and disposed of by warrants under the hand of the Governor for the time being, with the advice and consent of the Senate, for the necessary defence and support of the Government, and the protection and preservation of the inhabitants thereof agreeable to the acts and resolves of the General Court.

XXXIV. – The free exercise and enjoyment of Religious profession and worship shall forever be allowed to every denomination of protestants within this State.

XXXV. – The following oath shall be taken by every person appointed to any office in this State, before his entering on the execution of the office; viz. *I, A. B. do swear* (or *affirm*, as the case may be) *that I will bear faith and true allegiance to the State of Massachusetts Bay, and that I will faithfully execute the business of the office of agreeably to the laws of this State, according to my best skill and judgment, without fear, favor, affection or partiality.*

XXXVI. – *And whereas it may not be practicable to conform to this Constitution in the election of Governor, Lieutenant Governor, Senators and Representatives for the first year:*

Therefore the present Convention, if in being, or the next General Assembly, which shall be chosen upon the present Constitution, shall determine the time and manner, in which the people shall choose said officers for the first year, and upon said choice, the General Assembly, then in being, shall be dissolved, and give place to the free execution of this Constitution.

By Order of the Convention,
JEREMIAH POWELL, President.

Attest. SAMUEL FREEMAN, Clerk

4.II.13 THE PURPOSES OF A CONSTITUTION: THE 'ESSEX RESULT' ON THE THEORY OF THE STATE

From 'The Essex Result', 1778

Result of the Convention of Delegates holden at Ipswich in the County of Essex, who were Deputed to take into Consideration the Constitution and Form of Government proposed by the Convention of the State of Masachusetts-Bay. Newbury-Port: Printed and Sold by John Mycall. 1778.

In Convention of Delegates from the several towns of Lynn, Salem, Danvers, Wenham, Manchester, Gloucester, Ipswich, Newbury-Port, Salisbury, Methuen, Boxford, & Topsfield, holden by adjournment at Ipswich, on the twenty-ninth day of April, one thousand seven hundred & seventy-eight.

Peter Coffin Esq.; in the Chair.

The Constitution and form of Government framed by the Convention of this State, was read paragraph by paragraph, and after debate, the following votes were passed.

1. That the present situation of this State renders it best, that the framing of a Constitution therefor, should be postponed 'till the public affairs are in a more peaceable and settled condition.

2. That a bill of rights, clearly ascertaining and defining the rights of conscience, and that security of person and property, which every member in the State hath a right to expect from the supreme power thereof, ought to be settled and established, previous to the ratification of any constitution for the State.

3. That the executive power in any State, ought not to have any share or voice in the legislative power in framing the laws, and therefore, that the second article of the Constitution is liable to exception.

4. That any man who is chosen Governor, ought to be properly qualified in point of property – that the qualification therefor, mentioned in the third article of the Constitution, is not sufficient – nor is the same qualification directed to be ascertained on fixed principles, as it ought to be, on account of the fluctuation of the nominal value of money, and of property.

5. That in every free Republican Government, where the legislative power is vested in an house or houses of representatives, all the members of the State ought to be equally represented.

6. That the mode of representation proposed in the sixth article of the constitution, is not so equal a representation as can reasonably be devised.

7. That therefore the mode of representation in said sixth article is exceptionable.

8. That the representation proposed in said article is also exceptionable, as it will produce an unwieldy assembly.

9. That the mode of election of Senators pointed out in the Constitution is exceptionable.

10. That the rights of conscience, and the security of person and property each member of the State is entitled to, are not ascertained and defined in the Constitution, with a precision sufficient to limit the legislative power – and therefore, that the thirteenth article of the constitution is exceptionable.

11. That the fifteenth article is exceptionable, because the numbers that constitute a quorum in the House of Representatives and Senate, are too small.

12. That the seventeenth article of the constitution is exceptionable, because the supreme executive officer is not vested with proper authority – and because an independence between the executive and legislative body is not preserved.

13. That the nineteenth article is exceptionable, because a due independence is not kept up between the supreme legislative, judicial, and executive powers, nor between any two of them.

14. That the twentieth article is exceptionable, because the supreme executive officer hath a voice, and must be present in that Court, which alone hath authority to try impeachments.

15. That the twenty second article is exceptionable, because the supreme executive power is not preserved distinct from, and independent of, the supreme legislative power.

16. That the twenty third article is exceptionable, because the power of granting pardons is not solely vested in the supreme executive power of the State.

17. That the twenty eighth article is exceptionable, because the delegates for the Continental Congress may be elected by the House of Representatives, when all the Senators may vote against the election of those who are delegated.

18. That the thirty fourth article is exceptionable, because the rights of conscience are not therein clearly defined and ascertained; and further, because the free exercise and enjoyment of religious worship is there said to be *allowed* to all the protestants in the State, when in fact, that free exercise and enjoyment is the natural and uncontroulable right of every member of the State.

A committee was then appointed to attempt the ascertaining of the true principles of government, applicable to the territory of the Massachusetts-Bay; to state the non-conformity of the constitution proposed by the Convention of this State to those principles, and to delineate the general outlines of a constitution conformable thereto; and to report the same to this Body.

This Convention was then adjourned to the twelfth day of May next, to be holden at Ipswich.

The Convention met pursuant to adjournment, and their committee presented the following report.

The committee appointed by this Convention at their last adjournment, have proceeded upon the service assigned them. With diffidence have they undertaken the several parts of their duty, and the manner in which they have executed them, they submit to the candor of this Body. When they considered of what vast consequence, the forming of a Constitution is to the members of this State, the length of time that is necessary to canvass and digest any proposed plan of government, before the establishment of it, and the consummate coolness, and solemn deliberation which should attend, not only those gentlemen who have, reposed in them, the important trust of delineating the several lines in which the various powers of government are to move, but also all those, who are to form an opinion of the execution of that trust, your committee must be excused when they express a surprise and

regret, that so short a time is allowed the freemen inhabiting the territory of the Massachusetts-Bay, to revise and comprehend the form of government proposed to them by the convention of this State, to compare it with those principles on which every free government ought to be founded, and to ascertain it's conformity or non-conformity thereto. All this is necessary to be done, before a true opinion of it's merit or demerit can be formed. This opinion is to be certified within a time which, in our apprehension, is much too short for this purpose, and to be certified by a people who, during that time, have had and will have their minds perplexed and oppressed with a variety of public cares. The committee also beg leave to observe, that the constitution proposed for public approbation, was formed by gentlemen, who, at the same time, had a large share in conducting an important war, and who were employed in carrying into execution almost all the various powers of government.

The committee however proceeded in attempting the task assigned them, and the success of that attempt is now reported.

The reason and understanding of mankind, as well as the experience of all ages, confirm the truth of this proposition, that the benefits resulting to individuals from a free government, conduce much more to their happiness, than the retaining of all their natural rights in a state of nature. These benefits are greater or less, as the form of government, and the mode of exercising the supreme power of the State, are more or less conformable to those principles of equal impartial liberty, which is the property of all men from their birth as the gift of their Creator, compared with the manners and genius of the people, their occupations, customs, modes of thinking, situation, extent of country, and numbers. If the constitution and form of government are wholly repugnant to those principles, wretched are the subjects of that State. They have surrendered a portion of their natural rights, the enjoyment of which was in some degree a blessing, and the consequence is, they find themselves stripped of the remainder. As an anodyne to compose the spirits of these slaves, and to lull them into a passively obedient state, they are told, that tyranny is preferable to no government at all; a proposition which is to be doubted, unless considered under some limitation. Surely a state of nature is more excellent than that, in which men are meanly submissive to the haughty will of an imperious tyrant, whose savage passions are not bounded by the laws of reason, religion, honor, or a regard to his subjects, and

the point to which all his movements center, is the gratification of a brutal appetite. As in a state of nature much happiness cannot be enjoyed by individuals, so it has been comformable to the inclinations of almost all men, to enter into a political society so constituted, as to remove the inconveniences they were obliged to submit to in their former state, and, at the same time, to retain all those natural rights, the enjoyment of which would be consistent with the nature of a free government, and the necessary subordination to the supreme power of the state. . . .

The freemen inhabiting the territory of the Massachusetts-Bay are now forming a political society for themselves. Perhaps their situation is more favourable in some respects, for erecting a free government, than any other people were ever favored with. That attachment to old forms, which usually embarrasses, has no place amongst them. They have the history and experience of all States before them. Mankind have been toiling through ages for their information; and the philosophers and learned men of antiquity have trimmed their midnight lamps, to transmit to them instruction. We live also in an age, when the principles of political liberty, and the foundation of governments, have been freely canvassed, and fairly settled. Yet some difficulties we have to encounter. Not content with removing our attachment to the old government, perhaps we have contracted a prejudice against some part of it without foundation. The idea of liberty has been held up in so dazzling colours, that some of us may not be willing to submit to that subordination necessary in the freest States. Perhaps we may say further, that we do not consider ourselves united as brothers, with an united interest, but have fancied a clashing of interests amongst the various classes of men, and have acquired a thirst of power, and a wish of domination, over some of the community. We are contending for freedom – Let us all be equally free – It is possible, and it is just. Our interests when candidly considered are one. Let us have a constitution founded, not upon party or prejudice – not one for to-day or to-morrow – but for posterity. . . .

A republican form is the only one consonant to the feelings of the generous and brave Americans. Let us now attend to those principles, upon which all republican governments, who boast any degree of political liberty, are founded, and which must enter into the spirit of a FREE republican constitution. For all republics are not FREE.

All men are born equally free. The rights they possess at their births are equal, and of the same kind. Some of those rights are alienable, and may be parted with for an equivalent. Others are unalienable and inherent, and of that importance, that no equivalent can be received in exchange. Sometimes we shall mention the surrendering of a power to controul our natural rights, which perhaps is speaking with more precision, than when we use the expression of parting with natural rights – but the same thing is intended. Those rights which are unalienable, and of that importance, are called the rights of conscience. We have duties, for the discharge of which we are accountable to our Creator and benefactor, which no human power can cancel. What those duties are, is determinable by right reason, which may be, and is called, a well informed conscience. What this conscience dictates as our duty, is so; and that power which assumes a controul over it, is an usurper; for no consent can be pleaded to justify the controul, as any consent in this case is void. The alienation of some rights, in themselves alienable, may be also void, if the bargain is of that nature, that no equivalent can be received. Thus, if a man surrender all his alienable rights, without reserving a controul over the supreme power, or a right to resume in certain cases, the surrender is void, for he becomes a slave; and a slave can receive no equivalent. Common equity would set aside this bargain.

When men form themselves into society, and erect a body politic or State, they are to be considered as one moral whole, which is in possession of the supreme power of the State. This supreme power is composed of the powers of each individual collected together, and VOLUNTARILY parted with by him. No individual, in this case, parts with his unalienable rights, the supreme power therefore cannot controul them. Each individual also surrenders the power of controuling his natural alienable rights, ONLY WHEN THE GOOD OF THE WHOLE REQUIRES IT. The supreme power therefore can do nothing but what is for the good of the whole; and when it goes beyond this line, it is a power usurped. If the individual receives an equivalent for the right of controul he has parted with, the surrender of that right is valid; if he receives no equivalent, the surrender is void, and the supreme power as it respects him is an usurper. If the supreme power is so directed and executed that he does not enjoy political liberty, it is an illegal power, and he is not bound to obey. . . .

Over the class of unalienable rights the supreme power hath no controul, and they ought to be clearly defined and ascertained in a

BILL of RIGHTS, previous to the ratification of any constitution. The bill of rights should also contain the equivalent every man receives, as a consideration for the rights he has surrendered. This equivalent consists principally in the security of his person and property, and is also unassailable by the supreme power: for if the equivalent is taken back, those natural rights which were parted with to purchase it, return to the original proprietor, as nothing is more true, than that ALLEGIANCE AND PROTECTION ARE RECIPROCAL. . . .

That state, (other things being equal) which has reposed the supreme power in the hands of one or a small number of persons, is the most powerful state. An union, expedition, secrecy and dispatch are to be found only here. Where power is to be executed by a large number, there will not probably be either of the requisites just mentioned. Many men have various opinions: and each one will be tenacious of his own, as he thinks it preferable to any other; for when he thinks otherwise, it will cease to be his opinion. From this diversity of opinions results disunion; from disunion, a want of expedition and dispatch. And the larger the number to whom a secret is entrusted, the greater is the probability of it's disclosure. This inconvenience more fully strikes us when we consider that want of secrecy may prevent the successful execution of any measures, however excellently formed and digested.

But from a single person, or a very small number, we are not to expect that political honesty, and upright regard to the interest of the body of the people, and the civil rights of each individual, which are essential to a good and free constitution. For these qualities we are to go to the body of the people. The voice of the people is said to be the voice of God. No man will be so hardy and presumptuous, as to affirm the truth of that proposition in it's fullest extent. But if this is considered as the intent of it, that the people have always a disposition to promote their own happiness, and that when they have time to be informed, and the necessary means of information given them, they will be able to determine upon the necessary measures therefor, no man, of a tolerable acquaintance with mankind, will deny the truth of it. . . .

Yet, when we are forming a Constitution, by deductions that follow from established principles, (which is the only good method of forming one for futurity,) we are to look further than to the bulk of the people, for the greatest wisdom, firmness, consistency, and perseverance. These

qualities will most probably be found amongst men of education and fortune. From such men we are to expect genius cultivated by reading, and all the various advantages and assistances, which art, and a liberal education aided by wealth, can furnish. From these result learning, a thorough knowledge of the interests of their country, when considered abstractedly, when compared with the neighbouring States, and when with those more remote, and an acquaintance with it's produce and manufacture, and it's exports and imports. All these are necessary to be known, in order to determine what is the true interest of any state; and without that interest is ascertained, impossible will it be to discover, whether a variety of certain laws may be beneficial or hurtful. From gentlemen whose private affairs compel them to take care of their own household, and deprive them of leisure, these qualifications are not to be generally expected, whatever class of men they are enrolled in.

Let all these respective excellencies be united. Let the supreme power be so disposed and ballanced, that the laws may have in view the interest of the whole; let them be wisely and consistently framed for that end, and firmly adhered to; and let them be executed with vigour and dispatch.

Before we proceed further, it must be again considered, and kept always in view, that we are not attempting to form a temporary constitution, one adjusted only to our present circumstances. We wish for one founded upon such principles as will secure to us freedom and happiness, however our circumstances may vary. One that will smile amidst the declensions of European and Asiatic empires, and survive the rude storms of time. It is not therefore to be understood, that all the men of fortune of the present day, are men of wisdom and learning, or that they are not. Nor that the bulk of the people, the farmers, the merchants, the tradesmen, and labourers, are all honest and upright, with single views to the public good, or that they are not. In each of the classes there are undoubtedly exceptions, as the rules laid down are general. The proposition is only this. That among gentlemen of education, fortune and leisure, we shall find the largest number of men, possessed of wisdom, learning, and a firmness and consistency of character. That among the bulk of the people, we shall find the greatest share of political honesty, probity, and a regard to the interest of the whole, of which they compose the majority. That wisdom and firmness are not sufficient without good intentions, nor

the latter without the former. The conclusion is, let the legislative body unite them all. The former are called the excellencies that result from an aristocracy; the latter, those that result from a democracy.

The supreme power is considered as including the legislative, judicial, and executive powers. The nature and employment of these several powers deserve a distinct attention.

The legislative power is employed in making laws, or prescribing such rules of action to every individual in the state, as the good of the whole requires, to be conformed to by him in his conduct to the governors and governed, with respect both to their persons and property, according to the several relations he stands in. What rules of action the good of the whole requires, can be ascertained only by the majority, for a reason formerly mentioned. Therefore the legislative power must be so formed and exerted, that in prescribing any rule of action, or, in other words, enacting any law, the majority must consent. This may be more evident, when the fundamental condition on which every man enters into society, is considered. No man consented that his natural alienable rights should be wantonly controuled: they were controulable, only when that controul should be subservient to the good of the whole; and that subserviency, from the very nature of government, can be determined but by one absolute judge. The minority cannot be that judge, because then there may be two judges opposed to each other, so that this subserviency remains undetermined. Now the enacting of a law, is only the exercise of this controul over the natural alienable rights of each member of the state; and therefore this law must have the consent of the majority, or be invalid, as being contrary to the fundamental condition of the original social contract. In a state of nature, every man had the sovereign controul over his own person. He might also have, in that state, a qualified property. Whatever lands or chattels he had acquired the peaceable possession of, were exclusively his, by right of occupancy or possession. For while they were unpossessed he had a right to them equally with any other man, and therefore could not be disturbed in his possession, without being injured; for no man could lawfully dispossess him, without having a better right, which no man had. Over this qualified property every man in a state of nature had also a sovereign controul. And in entering into political society, he surrendered this right of controul over his person and property, (with an exception to the rights of conscience) to the supreme legislative power, to be

exercised by that power, *when the good of the whole demanded it.* This was all the right he could surrender, being all the alienable right of which he was possessed. The only objects of legislation therefore, are the person and property of the individuals which compose the state. If the law affects only the persons of the members, the consent of a majority of any members is sufficient. If the law affects the property only, the consent of those who hold a majority of the property is enough. If it affects, (as it will very frequently, if not always,) but[1] the person and property, the consent of a majority of the members, and of those members also who hold a majority of the property, is necessary. If the consent of the latter is not obtained, their interest is taken from them against their consent, and their boasted security of property is vanished. Those who make the law, in this case give and grant what is not theirs. The law, in it's principles, becomes a second stamp act. Lord Chatham very finely ridiculed the British house of commons upon that principle. 'You can give and grant, said he, only your own. Here you give and grant, what? The property of the Americans.' The people of the Massachusetts-Bay then thought his Lordship's ridicule well pointed. And would they be willing to merit the same? Certainly they will agree in the principle, should they mistake the application. The laws of the province of Massachusetts-Bay adopted the same principle, and very happily applied it. As the votes of proprietors of common and undivided lands in their meetings, can affect only their property, therefore, the votes shall be collected according to the respective interests of the proprietors. If each member, without regard to his property, has equal influence in legislation with any other, it follows, that some members enjoy greater benefits and powers in legislation than others, when these benefits and powers are compared with the rights parted with to purchase them. For the property-holder parts with the controul over his person, as well as he who hath no property, and the former also parts with the controul over his property, of which the latter is destitute. Therefore to constitute a perfect law in a free state, affecting the persons and property of the members, it is necessary that the law be for the good of the whole, which is to be determined by a majority of the members, and that majority should include those, who possess a major part of the property in the state.

The judicial power follows next after the legislative power; for it

[1] *Editor's note:* Read 'both'?

cannot act, until after laws are prescribed. Every wise legislator annexes a sanction to his laws, which is most commonly penal, (that is) a punishment either corporal or pecuniary, to be inflicted on the member who shall infringe them. It is the part of the judicial power (which in this territory has always been, and always ought to be, a court and jury) to ascertain the member who hath broken the law. Every man is to be presumed innocent, until the judicial power hath determined him guilty. When that decision is known, the law annexes the punishment, and the offender is turned over to the executive arm, by whom it is inflicted on him. The judicial power hath also to determine what legal contracts have been broken, and what member hath been injured by a violation of the law, to consider the damages that have been sustained, and to ascertain the recompense. The executive power takes care that this recompense is paid.

The executive power is sometimes divided into the external executive, and internal executive. The former comprehends war, peace, the sending and receiving ambassadors, and whatever concerns the transactions of the state with any other independent state. The confederation of the United States of America hath lopped off this branch of the executive, and placed it in Congress. We have therefore only to consider the internal executive power, which is employed in the peace, security and protection of the subject and his property, and in the defence of the state. The executive power is to marshal and command her militia and armies for her defence, to enforce the law, and to carry into execution all the orders of the legislative powers.

A little attention to the subject will convince us, that these three powers ought to be in different hands, and independent of one another, and so ballanced, and each having that check upon the other, that their independence shall be preserved – If the three powers are united, the government will be absolute, *whether these powers are in the hands of one or a large number*. The same party will be the legislator, accuser, judge and executioner; and what probability will an accused person have of an acquittal, however innocent he may be, when his judge will be also a party.

If the legislative and judicial powers are united, the maker of the law will also interpret it; and the law may then speak a language, dictated by the whims, the caprice, or the prejudice of the judge, with impunity to him – And what people are so unhappy as those, whose laws are uncertain. It will also be in the breast of the judge, when grasping

after his prey, to make a retrospective law, which shall bring the unhappy offender within it; and this also he can do with impunity – The subject can have no peaceable remedy – The judge will try himself, and an acquittal is the certain consequence. He has it also in his power to enact any law, which may shelter him from deserved vengeance.

Should the executive and legislative powers be united, mischiefs the most terrible would follow. The executive would enact those laws it pleased to execute, and no others – The judicial power would be set aside as inconvenient and tardy – The security and protection of the subject would be a shadow – The executive power would make itself absolute, and the government end in a tyranny – Lewis the eleventh of France, by cunning and treachery compleated the union of the executive and legislative powers of that kingdom, and upon that union established a system of tyranny. France was formerly under a free government.

The assembly or representatives of the united states of Holland, exercise the executive and legislative powers, and the government there is absolute.

Should the executive and judicial powers be united, the subject would then have no permanent security of his person and property. The executive power would interpret the laws and bend them to his will; and, as he is the judge, he may leap over them by artful constructions, and gratify, with impunity, the most rapacious passions. Perhaps no cause in any state has contributed more to promote internal convulsions, and to stain the scaffold with it's best blood, than this unhappy union. And it is an union which the executive power in all states, hath attempted to form: if that could not be compassed, to make the judicial power dependent upon it. Indeed the dependence of any of these powers upon either of the others, which in all states has always been attempted by one or the other of them, has so often been productive of such calamities, and of the shedding of such oceans of blood, that the page of history seems to be one continued tale of human wretchedness.

The following principles now seem to be established.

1. That the supreme power is limited, and cannot controul the unalienable rights of mankind, nor resume the equivalent (that is, the security of person and property) which each individual receives, as a consideration for the alienable rights he parted with in entering into political society.

2. That these unalienable rights, and this equivalent, are to be clearly defined and ascertained in a BILL of RIGHTS, previous to the ratification of any constitution.

3. That the supreme power should be so formed and modelled, as to exert the greatest possible power, wisdom, and goodness.

4. That the legislative, judicial, and executive powers, are to be lodged in different hands, that each branch is to be independent, and further, to be so ballanced, and be able to exert such checks upon the others, as will preserve it from a dependence on, or an union with them.

5. That government can exert the greatest power when it's supreme authority is vested in the hands of one or a few.

6. That the laws will be made with the greatest wisdom, and best intentions, when men, of all the several classes in the state concur in the enacting of them.

7. That a government which is so constituted, that it cannot afford a degree of political liberty nearly equal to all it's members, is not founded upon principles of freedom and justice, and where any member enjoys no degree of political liberty, the government, so far as it respects him, is a tyranny, for he is controuled by laws to which he has never consented.

8. That the legislative power of a state hath no authority to controul the natural rights of any of it's members, unless the good of the whole requires it.

9. That a majority of the state is the only judge when the general good does require it.

10. That where the legislative power of the state is so formed, that a law may be enacted by the minority, each member of the state does not enjoy political liberty.

And

11. That in a free government, a law affecting the person and property of it's members, is not valid, unless it has the consent of a majority of the members, which majority should include those, who hold a major part of the property in the state.

It may be necessary to proceed further, and notice some particular principles, which should be attended to in forming the three several powers in a free republican government.

The first important branch that comes under our consideration, is the legislative body. Was the number of the people so small, that the

whole could meet together without inconvenience, the opinion of the majority would be more easily known. But, besides the inconvenience of assembling such numbers, no great advantages could follow. Sixty thousand people could not discuss with candor, and determine with deliberation. Tumults, riots, and murder would be the result. But the impracticability of forming such an assembly, renders it needless to make any further observations. The opinions and consent of the majority must be collected from persons, delegated by every freeman of the state for that purpose. Every freeman, who hath sufficient discretion, should have a voice in the election of his legislators. To speak with precision, in every free state where the power of legislation is lodged in the hands of one or more bodies of representatives elected for that purpose, the person of every member of the state, and all the property in it, ought to be represented, because they are objects of legislation. All the members of the state are qualified to make the election, unless they have not sufficient discretion, or are so situated as to have no wills of their own; persons not twenty one years old are deemed of the former class, from their want of years and experience. The municipal law of this country will not trust them with the disposition of their lands, and consigns them to the care of their parents or guardians. Women what age soever they are of, are also considered as not having a sufficient acquired discretion; not from a deficiency in their mental powers, but from the natural tenderness and delicacy of their minds, their retired mode of life, and various domestic duties. These concurring, prevent that promiscuous intercourse with the world, which is necessary to qualify them for electors. Slaves are of the latter class and have no wills. But are slaves members of a free government? We feel the absurdity, and would to God, the situation of America and the tempers of it's inhabitants were such, that the slave-holder could not be found in the land.

The rights of representation should be so equally and impartially distributed, that the representatives should have the same views, and interests with the people at large. They should think, feel, and act like them, and in fine, should be an exact miniature of their constituents. They should be (if we may use the expression) the whole body politic, with all it's property, rights, and priviledges, reduced to a smaller scale, every part being diminished in just proportion. To pursue the metaphor. If in adjusting the representation of freemen, any ten are reduced into one, all the other tens should be alike reduced: or if any

hundred should be reduced to one, all the other hundreds should have just the same reduction. The representation ought also to be so adjusted, that it should be the interest of the representatives at all times, to do justice, therefore equal interest among the people, should have equal interest among the body of representatives. The majority of the representatives should also represent a majority of the people, and the legislative body should be so constructed, that every law affecting property, should have the consent of those who hold a majority of the property. The law would then be determined to be for the good of the whole by the proper judge, the majority, and the necessary consent thereto would be obtained: and all the members of the State would enjoy political liberty, and an equal degree of it. If the scale to which the body politic is to be reduced, is but a little smaller than the original, or, in other words, if a small number of freemen should be reduced to one, that is, send one representative, the number of representatives would be too large for the public good. The expences of government would be enormous. The body would be too unwieldy to deliberate with candor and coolness. The variety of opinions and oppositions would irritate the passions. Parties would be formed and factions engendered. The members would list under the banners of their respective leaders: address and intrigue would conduct the debates, and the result would tend only to promote the ambition or interest of a particular party. Such has always been in some degree, the course and event of debates instituted and managed by a large multitude.

For these reasons, some foreign politicians have laid it down as a rule, that no body of men larger than a hundred, would transact business well: and Lord Chesterfield called the British house of commons a mere mob, because of the number of men which composed it.

Elections ought also to be free. No bribery, corruption, or undue influence should have place. They stifle the free voice of the people, corrupt their morals, and introduce a degeneracy of manners, a supineness of temper, and an inattention to their liberties, which pave the road for the approach of tyranny, in all it's frightful forms. . . .

The rights of representation should also be held sacred and inviolable, and for this purpose, representation should be fixed upon known and easy principles; and the constitution should make provision, that recourse should constantly be had to those principles within a very

small period of years, to rectify the errors that will creep in through lapse of time, or alteration of situations. The want of fixed principles of government, and a stated regular recourse to them, have produced the dissolution of all states, whose constitutions have been transmitted to us by history.

But the legislative power must not be trusted with one assembly. A single assembly is frequently influenced by the vices, follies, passions, and prejudices of an individual. It is liable to be avaricious, and to exempt itself from the burdens it lays upon it's constituents. It is subject to ambition, and after a series of years, will be prompted to vote itself perpetual. The long parliament in England voted itself perpetual, and thereby, for a time, destroyed the political liberty of the subject. Holland was governed by one representative assembly annually elected. They afterwards voted themselves from annual to septennial; then for life; and finally exerted the power of filling up all vacancies, without application to their constituents. The government of Holland is now a tyranny *though a republic.*

The result of a single assembly will be hasty and indigested, and their judgments frequently absurd and inconsistent. There must be a second body to revise with coolness and wisdom, and to controul with firmness, independent upon the first, either for their creation, or existence. Yet the first must retain a right to a similar revision and controul over the second.

Let us now ascertain some particular principles which should be attended to, in forming the executive power.

When we recollect the nature and employment of this power, we find that it ought to be conducted with vigour and dispatch. It should be able to execute the laws without opposition, and to controul all the turbulent spirits in the state, who should infringe them. If the laws are not obeyed, the legislative power is vain, and the judicial is mere pageantry. As these laws, with their several sanctions, are the only securities of person and property, the members of the state can confide in, if they lie dormant through failure of execution, violence and oppression will erect their heads, and stalk unmolested through the land. The judicial power ought to discriminate the offender, as soon after the commission of the offence, as an impartial trial will admit; and the executive arm to inflict the punishment immediately after the criminal is ascertained. This would have an happy tendency to prevent crimes, as the commission of them would awaken the attendant idea of

punishment; and the hope of an escape, which is often an inducement, would be cut off. The executive power ought therefore in these cases, to be exerted with union, vigour, and dispatch. Another duty of that power is to arrest offenders, to bring them to trial. This cannot often be done, unless secrecy and expedition are used. The want of these two requisites, will be more especially inconvenient in repressing treasons, and those more enormous offences which strike at the happiness, if not existence of the whole. Offenders of these classes do not act alone. Some number is necessary to the compleating of the crime. Cabals are formed with art, and secrecy presides over their councils; while measures the most fatal are the result, to be executed by desperation. On these men the thunder of the state should be hurled with rapidity; for if they hear it roll at a distance, their danger is over. When they gain intelligence of the process, they abscond, and wait a more favourable opportunity. If that is attended with difficulty, they destroy all the evidence of their guilt, brave government, and deride the justice and power of the state.

It has been observed likewise, that the executive power is to act as Captain-General, to marshal the militia and armies of the state, and, for her defence, to lead them on to battle. These armies should always be composed of the militia or body of the people. Standing armies are a tremendous curse to a state. In all periods in which they have existed, they have been the scourge of mankind. In this department, union, vigour, secrecy, and dispatch are more peculiarly necessary. Was one to propose a body of militia, over which two Generals, with equal authority, should have the command, he would be laughed at. Should one pretend, that the General should have no controul over his subordinate officers, either to remove them or to supply their posts, he would be pitied for his ignorance of the subject he was discussing. It is obviously necessary, that the man who calls the militia to action, and assumes the military controul over them in the field, should previously know the number of his men, their equipments and residence, and the talents and tempers of the several ranks of officers, and their respective departments in the state, that he may wisely determine to whom the necessary orders are to be issued. Regular and particular returns of these requisites should be frequently made. Let it be enquired, are these returns to be made only to the legislative body, or a branch of it, which necessarily moves slow? – Is the General to go to them for information? intreat them to remove an improper officer, and give him another they shall chuse? and in fine is he to supplicate his orders

from them, and constantly walk where their leading-strings shall direct his steps? If so, where are the power and force of the militia – where the union – where the dispatch and profound secrecy? Or shall these returns be made to him? – when he may see with his own eyes – be his own judge of the merit, or demerit of his officers – discern their various talents and qualifications, and employ them as the service and defence of his country demand. Besides, the legislative body or a branch of it is local – they cannot therefore personally inform themselves of these facts, but must judge upon trust. The General's opinion will be founded upon his own observations – the officers and privates of the militia will act under his eye: and, if he has it in his power immediately to promote or disgrace them, they will be induced to noble exertions. It may further be observed here, that if the subordinate civil or military executive officers are appointed by the legislative body or a branch of it, the former will become dependent upon the latter, and the necessary independence of either the legislative or executive powers upon the other is wanting. The legislative power will have that undue influence over the executive which will amount to a controul, for the latter will be their creatures, and will fear their creators.

One further observation may be pertinent. Such is the temper of mankind, that each man will be too liable to introduce his own friends and connexions into office, without regarding the public interest. If one man or a small number appoint, their connexions will probably be introduced. If a large number appoint, all their connexions will receive the same favour. The smaller the number appointing, the more contracted are their connexions, and for that reason, there will be a greater probability of better officers, as the connexions of one man or a very small number can fill but a very few of the offices. When a small number of men have the power of appointment, or the management in any particular department, their conduct is accurately noticed. On any miscarriage or imprudence the public resentment lies with weight. All the eyes of the people are converted to a point, and produce that attention to their censure, and that fear of misbehaviour, which are the greatest security the state can have, of the wisdom and prudence of its servants. This observation will strike us, when we recollect that many a man will zealously promote an affair in a public assembly, of which he is but one of a large number, yet, at the same time, he would blush to be thought the sole author of it. For all these reasons, the supreme executive power should be rested in the hands of one or of

a small number, who should have the appointment of all subordinate executive officers. Should the supreme executive officer be elected by the legislative body, there would be a dependence of the executive power upon the legislative. Should he be elected by the judicial body, there also would be a dependence. The people at large must therefore designate the person, to whom they will delegate this power. And upon the people, there ought to be a dependence of all the powers in government, for all the officers in the state are but the servants of the people.

We have not noticed the navy-department. The conducting of that department is indisputably in the supreme executive power: and we suppose, that all the observations respecting the Captain-General, apply to the Admiral.

We are next to fix upon some general rules which should govern us in forming the judicial power. This power is to be independent upon the executive and legislative. The judicial power should be a court and jury, or as they are commonly called, the Judges and jury. The jury are the peers or equals of every man, and are to try all facts. The province of the Judges is to preside in and regulate all trials, and ascertain the law. We shall only consider the appointment of the Judges. The same power which appoints them, ought not to have the power of removing them, not even for misbehavior. That conduct only would then be deemed misbehavior which was opposed to the will of the power removing. A removal in this case for proper reasons, would not be often attainable: for to remove a man from an office, because he is not properly qualified to discharge the duties of it, is a severe censure upon that man or body of men who appointed him – and mankind do not love to censure themselves. Whoever appoints the judges, they ought not to be removable at pleasure, for they will then feel a dependence upon that man or body of men who hath the power of removal. Nor ought they to be dependent upon either the executive or legislative power for their salaries; for if they are, that power on whom they are thus dependent, can starve them into a compliance. One of these two powers should appoint, and the other remove. The legislative will not probably appoint so good men as the executive, for reasons formerly mentioned. The former are composed of a large body of men who have a numerous train of friends and connexions, and they do not hazard their reputations, which the executive will. It has often been mentioned that where a large body of men are responsible for any

measures, a regard to their reputations, and to the public opinion, will not prompt them to use that care and precaution, which such regard will prompt one or a few to make use of. Let one more observation be now introduced to confirm it. Every man has some friends and dependents who will endeavor to snatch him from the public hatred. One man has but a few comparatively, they are not numerous enough to protect him, and he falls a victim to his own misconduct. When measures are conducted by a large number, their friends and connexions are numerous and noisy – they are dispersed through the State – their clamors stifle the execrations of the people, whose groans cannot even be heard. But to resume, neither will the executive body be the most proper judge when to remove. If this body is judge, it must also be the accuser, or the legislative body, or a branch of it, must be – If the executive body complains, it will be both accuser and judge – If the complaint is preferred by the legislative body, or a branch of it, when the judges are appointed by the legislative body, then a body of men who were concerned in the appointment, must in most cases complain of the impropriety of their own appointment. Let therefore the judges be appointed by the executive body – let their salaries be independent – and let them hold their places during good behaviour – Let their misbehaviour be determinable by the legislative body – Let one branch thereof impeach, and the other judge. Upon these principles the judicial body will be independent so long as they behave well and a proper court is appointed to ascertain their mal-conduct.

The Committee afterwards proceeded to consider the Constitution framed by the Convention of this State. They have examined that Constitution with all the care the shortness of the time would admit. And they are compelled, though reluctantly to say, that some of the principles upon which it is founded, appeared to them inconsonant, not only to the natural rights of mankind, but to the fundamental condition of the original social contract, and the principles of a free republican government. In that form of government the governor appears to be the supreme executive officer, and the legislative power is in an house of representatives and senate. It may be necessary to descend to a more particular consideration of the several articles of that constitution.

The second article thereof appears exceptionable upon the principles we have already attempted to establish, because the supreme executive officer hath a seat and voice in one branch of the legislative body, and

is assisting in originating and framing the laws, the Governor being entitled to a seat and voice in the Senate, and to preside in it, and may thereby have that influence in the legislative body, which the supreme executive officer ought not to have.

The third article among other things, ascertains the qualifications of the Governor, Lieutenant Governor, Senators and Representatives respecting property – The estate sufficient to qualify a man for Governor is so small, it is hardly any qualification at all. Further, the method of ascertaining the value of the estates of the officers aforesaid is vague and uncertain as it depends upon the nature and quantity of the currency, and the encrease of property, and not upon any fixed principles. This article therefore appears to be exceptionable.

The sixth article regulates the election of representatives. So many objections present themselves to this article, we are at a loss which first to mention. The representation is grossly unequal, and it is flagrantly unjust. It violates the fundamental principle of the original social contract, and introduces an unwieldy and expensive house. Representation ought to be equal upon the principles formerly mentioned. By this article any corporation, however small, may send one representative, while no corporation can send more than one, unless it has three hundred freemen. Twenty corporations (of three hundred freemen in each) containing in the whole six thousand freemen, may send forty representatives, when one corporation, which shall contain six thousand two hundred and twenty, can send but nineteen. One third of the state may send a majority of the representatives, and all the laws may be enacted by a minority – Do all the members of the state then, enjoy political liberty? Will they not be controuled by laws enacted against their consent? When we go further and find, that sixty members make an house, and that the concurrence of thirty one (which is about one twelfth of what may be the present number of representatives) is sufficient to bind the persons and properties of the members of the State, we stand amazed, and are sorry that any well disposed Americans were so inattentive to the consequences of such an arrangement.

The number of representatives is too large to debate with coolness and deliberation, the public business will be protracted to an undue length and the pay of the house is enormous. As the number of freemen in the state encreases, these inconveniences will encrease; and in a century, the house of representatives will, from their numbers, be a mere mob. Observations upon this article croud upon us, but we will

dismiss it, with wishing that the mode of representation there proposed, may be candidly compared with the principles which have been already mentioned in the course of our observations upon the legislative power, and upon representation in a free republic.

The ninth article regulates the election of Senators, which we think exceptionable. As the Senators for each district will be elected by all the freemen in the state properly qualified, a trust is reposed in the people which they are unequal to. The freemen in the late province of Main, are to give in their votes for senators in the western district, and so, on the contrary. Is it supposeable that the freemen in the county of Lincoln can judge of the political merits of a senator in Berkshire? Must not the several corporations in the state, in a great measure depend upon their representatives for information? And will not the house of representatives in fact chuse the senators? That independence of the senate upon the house, which the constitution seems to have intended, is visionary, and the benefits which were expected to result from a senate, as one distinct branch of the legislative body, will not be discoverable.

The tenth article prescribes the method in which the Governor is to be elected. This method is open to, and will introduce bribery and corruption, and also originate parties and factions in the state. The Governor of Rhode-Island was formerly elected in this manner, and we all know how long a late Governor there, procured his re-election by methods the most unjustifiable. Bribery was attempted in an open and flagrant manner.

The thirteenth article ascertains the authority of the general court, and by that article we find their power is limited only by the several articles of the constitution. We do not find that the rights of conscience are ascertained and defined, unless they may be thought to be in the thirty fourth article. That article we conceive to be expressed in very loose and uncertain terms. What is a *religious* profession and worship of God, has been disputed for sixteen hundred years, and the various sects of christians have not yet settled the dispute. What is a free exercise and enjoyment of religious worship has been, and still is, a subject of much altercation. And this free exercise and enjoyment is said to be *allowed* to the protestants of this state by the constitution, when we suppose it to be an unalienable right of all mankind, which no human power can wrest from them. We do not find any bill of rights either accompanying the constitution, or interwoven with it,

and no attempt is made to define and secure that protection of the person and property of the members of the state, which the legislative and executive bodies cannot withhold, unless the general words *of confirming the right to trial by jury*, should be considered as such definition and security. We think a bill of rights ascertaining and clearly describing the rights of conscience, and that security of person and property, the supreme power of the state is bound to afford to all the members thereof, ought to be fully ratified, before, or at the same time with, the establishment of any constitution.

The fifteenth article fixes the number which shall constitute a quorum in the senate and house of representatives – We think these numbers much too small – This constitution will immediately introduce about three hundred and sixty members into the house. If sixty make a quorum, the house may totally change its members six different times; and it probably will very often in the course of a long session, be composed of such a variety of members, as will retard the public business, and introduce confusion in the debates, and inconsistency in the result. Besides the number of members, whose concurrence is necessary to enact a law, is so small, that the subjects of the state will have no security, that the laws which are to controul their natural rights, have the consent of a majority of the freemen. The same reasoning applies to the senate, though not so strikingly, as a quorum of that body must consist of nearly a third of the senators. . . .

The judges by the twenty fourth article are to hold their places during good behaviour, but we do not find that their salaries are any where directed to be fixed. The house of representatives may therefore starve them into a state of dependence.

The twenty-eighth article determines the mode of electing and removing the delegates for Congress. It is by joint ballot of the house and Senate. These delegates should be some of the best men in the State. Their abilities and characters should be thoroughly investigated. This will be more effectually done, if they are elected by the legislative body, each branch having a right to originate or negative the choice, and removal. And we cannot conceive why they should not be elected in this manner, as well as all officers who are annually appointed with annual grants of their sallaries, as is directed in the nineteenth article. By the mode of election now excepted against, the house may choose their delegates, altho' every Senator should vote against their choice.

The thirty-fourth article respecting liberty of conscience, we think exceptionable, but the observations necessary to be made thereon, were introduced in animadverting upon the thirteenth article.

The Committee have purposely been as concise as possible in their observations upon the Constitution proposed by the Convention of this State – Where they thought it was non-conformable to the principles of a free republican government, they have ventured to point out the non-conformity – Where they thought it was repugnant to the original social contract, they have taken the liberty to suggest that repugnance – And where they were persuaded it was founded in political injustice, they have dared to assert it. . . .

[There follows a detailed scheme for the legislative, executive and judicial branches of government.]

The committee have only further to report, that the inhabitants of the several towns who deputed delegates for this convention, be seriously advised, and solemnly exhorted, as they value the political freedom and happiness of themselves and of their posterity, to convene all the freemen of their several towns in town meeting, for this purpose regularly notified, and that they do unanimously vote their disapprobation of the constitution and form of government, framed by the convention of this state; that a regular return of the same be made to the secretary's office, that it may there remain a grateful monument to our posterity of that consistent, impartial and persevering attachment to political, religious, and civil liberty, which actuated their fathers, and in defence of which, they bravely fought, chearfully bled, and gloriously died.

The above report being read was accepted.

Attest, PETER COFFIN, *Chairman.*

4.II.14 THE GENERAL COURT REQUESTS THE TOWNS TO SAY WHETHER THEY WANT A CONSTITUTIONAL CONVENTION[1]

State of Massachusetts-Bay, in the House of Representatives, February 19, 1779, Massachusetts Archives, CLX 32

WHEREAS *the Constitution or Form of Civil Government, which was proposed by the late Convention of this State to the People thereof, hath been disapproved by a Majority of the Inhabitants of said State:*

And whereas it is doubtful, from the Representations made to this Court what are the Sentiments of the major Part of the good People of this State as to the Expediency of now proceeding to form a new Constitution of Government:

Therefore, *Resolved*, That the Selectmen of the several Towns within this State cause the Freeholders, and other Inhabitants in their respective Towns duly qualified to vote for Representatives, to be lawfully warned to meet together in some convenient Place therein, on or before the last Wednesday of *May* next, to consider of and determine upon the following Questions.

First, Whether they chuse at this Time to have a new Constitution or Form of Government made.

Secondly, Whether they will impower their Representatives for the next Year to vote for the calling a State Convention, for the sole Purpose of forming a new Constitution, provided it shall appear to them, on Examination, that a major Part of the People present and voting at the Meetings called in the Manner and for the Purpose aforesaid, shall have answered the first Question in the affirmative.

And in Order that the Sense of the People may be known theron: Be it further *Resolved*, That the Selectmen of each Town be and hereby are directed to return into the Secretary's Office, on or before the first

1 [*Editor's note.*] The constitution proposed by the General Court was overwhelmingly rejected by the town meetings in 1778. Boston Town Meeting voted unanimously against it. One objection was to the absence of any declaration of rights; but the most general ground of opposition was that the General Court had no authority to make a constitution for the people. The question is discussed in Pole, *Political Representation*, 178–189, which contains an analysis of 'The Essex Result'.

Wednesday in *June* next, the Doings of their respective Towns on the first Question above mentioned, certifying the Numbers voting in the Affirmative, and Numbers voting in the Negative, on the said Question.

Sent up for Concurrence,

JOHN PICKERING, *Speaker*

In COUNCIL, February 20, 1779

Read and concurred, JOHN AVERY, *Dep. Sec'ry*

Consented to by the Major Part of the Council

4.II.15 THE GENERAL COURT CALLS A CONVENTION

State of Massachusetts-Bay, in the House of Representatives, June 15, 1779, Massachusetts Archives, CLX 125

WHEREAS *by the Returns made into the Secretary's Office from more than two thirds of the Towns belonging to this State, agreeably to a Resolve of the General Court of the 20th of* February *last, it appears that a large majority of the inhabitants of such Towns, as have made return as aforesaid, think it proper to have a new Constitution or Form of Government, and are of opinion that the same ought to be formed by a Convention of Delegates who should be specially authorized to meet for this Purpose:* Therefore,

RESOLVED, That it be and it hereby is recommended to the several Inhabitants of the several towns in this State to form a Convention for the sole purpose of framing a new Constitution, consisting of such Number of Delegates from each town throughout the State, as every different town is intitled to send Representatives to the General Court, to meet at *Cambridge*, in the county of *Middlesex*, on the first day of *September* next.

And the Selectmen of the several towns and places in this State, impowered by the laws thereof to send Members to the General Assembly, are hereby authorized and directed to call a Meeting of their respective towns at least fourteen days before the meeting of the said Convention, to elect one or more Delegates to represent them in said Convention, at which Meeting for the election of such Delegate or

Delegates, every Freeman, inhabitant of such town, who is twenty one years of age, shall have a right to vote.

Be it also *Resolved*, That it be and hereby is recommended to the inhabitants of the several towns in this State to instruct their respective Delegates to cause a printed copy of the Form of a Constitution they may agree upon in Convention, to be transmitted to the Selectmen of each town, and the Committee of each plantation, and the said Selectmen and Committees are hereby impowered and directed to lay the same before their respective towns and plantations at a regular meeting of the Male inhabitants thereof being free and twenty one years of age, to be called for that purpose, in order to its being duly considered and approved or disapproved by said towns and plantations; and it is also recommended to the several towns within this State to instruct their respective Representatives to establish the said Form of a Constitution as the Constitution and Form of Government of the State of *Massachusetts-Bay*, if upon a fair Examination it shall appear that it is approved of by at least two thirds of those who are free and twenty one years of age, belonging to this State, and present in the several Meetings.

Sent up for Concurrence,

JOHN HANCOCK, *Speaker*

In COUNCIL, June 21, 1779. Read and concurred.

JOHN AVERY, *Dep. Secr'y.*

Consented to by the Major Part of the COUNCIL.

4.II.16 ADDRESS ISSUED BY THE CONSTITUTIONAL CONVENTION, 1780

Massachusetts Archives, CCLXXVI 9

Friends and Countrymen,

Having had your Appointment and Instruction, we have undertaken the arduous Task of preparing a civil Constitution for the People of the Massachusetts Bay; and we now submit it to your candid Consideration. It is your *Interest* to revise it with the greatest Care and Circumspection, and it is your undoubted *Right*, either to propose such Alterations and Amendments as you shall judge proper, or, to

give it your own Sanction in its present Form, or, totally to reject it.

In framing a Constitution, to be adapted as far as possible to the Circumstances of Posterity yet unborn, you will conceive it to be exceedingly difficult, if not impracticable, to succeed in every part of it, to the full Satisfaction of all. Could the *whole Body* of the People have Conven'd for the same Purpose, there might have been equal Reason to conclude, that a perfect Unanimity of Sentiments would have been an Object not to be obtain'd. In a Business so universally interesting, we have endeavor'd to act as became the Representatives of a wise, understanding and free People; and, as we have Reason to believe you would *yourselves* have done, we have open'd our Sentiments to each other with Candor, and made such mutual Concessions as we could consistently, and without marring the only Plan, which in our most mature Judgment we can at present offer to you.

The Interest of the Society is common to all its Members. The great Enquiry is, wherein this Common Interest consists. In determining this Question, an Advantage may arise from a Variety of Sentiments offer'd to public Examination concerning it. But wise Men are not apt to be obstinately tenacious of their own Opinions: They will always pay a due Regard to those of other Men and keep their minds open to Conviction. We conceive, that in the present Instance, by accommodating ourselves to each other, and individually yielding particular and even favorite Opinions of smaller moment, to essential Principles, and Considerations of general Utility, the public Opinion of the Plan now before you may be consolidated. – But without such mutual Condescention in unimportant Matters, we may almost venture to predict, that we shall not soon, if ever, be bless'd with such a Constitution as those are intitled to, who have struggled hard for Freedom and Independence. You will permit us on this Occasion, just to hint to you our own Apprehension, that there may be amongst us, some Persons disaffected to that great Cause for which we are contending, who may be secretly instructed by our common Enemy to divide and distract us; in hopes of preventing our Union in any Form of Government whatever, and by this Means of depriving us of the most honorable Testimony, as well as the greatest Security of our Freedom and Independence. – If there be such Men, it is our Wisdom to mark them, and guard ourselves against their Designs.

We may not expect to agree in a perfect System of Government: This is not the Lot of Mankind. The great End of Government, is, to

promote the Supreme Good of human Society: Every social Affection should therefore be interested in the Forming of a Government and in judging of one when it is Formed. Would it not be prudent for Individuals to cast out of the Scale, smaller Considerations and fall in with an evident Majority, unless in Matters in which their Consciences shall constrain them to determine otherwise? Such a Sacrifice, made for the sake of Union, would afford a strong Evidence of public Affection; and Union, strengthened by the social Feeling, promise a greater Stability to any Constitution, and, in its operation, a greater Degree of Happiness to the Society. It is here to be remembered, that on the Expiration of Fifteen Years a new Convention may be held, in order that such Amendments may be made in the Plan you may now agree to, as Experience, that best Instructor, shall then point out to be expedient or necessary.

A Government without Power to exert itself, is at best, but an useless Piece of Machinery. It is probable, that for the want of Energy, it would speedily lose even the Appearance of Government, and sink into Anarchy. Unless a due Proportion of Weight is given to each of the Powers of Government, there will soon be a Confusion of the whole. An Overbearing of any one of its Parts on the rest, would destroy the Balance and accelerate its Dissolution and Ruin: And, a Power without any restraint is Tyranny. The Powers of Government must then be balanced: To do this accurately requires the highest Skill in political Architecture. Those who are to be invested with the Administration, should have such Powers given to them, as are requisite to render them useful in their respective Places; and such *Checks* should be added to every Branch of Power as maybe sufficient to prevent its becoming formidable and injurious to the Common wealth. If we have been so fortunate as to succeed in this point of the greatest Importance, our Happiness will be compleat, in the Prospect of having laid a good Foundation for many Generations. *You* are the Judges how far we have succeeded; and whether we have raised our Superstructure, agreeably to our profess'd Design; upon the Principles of a *Free Common Wealth*.

In order to assist your Judgments, we have thought it necessary, briefly to explain to you the Grounds and Reasons upon which we have formed our Plan. In the third article of the Declaration of Rights, we have, with as much Precision as we were capable of, provided for the free exercise of *the Rights of Conscience:* We are very sensible that

our Constituents hold those Rights infinitely more valuable than all others; and we flatter ourselves, that while we have considered Morality and the public Worship of GOD, as important to the happiness of Society, we have sufficiently guarded the rights of Conscience from every possible infringement. This Article underwent long debates, and took Time in proportion to its importance; and we feel ourselves peculiarly happy in being able to inform you, that though the debates were managed by persons of various denominations, it was finally agreed upon with much more Unanimity than usually takes place in disquisitions of this Nature. We wish you to consider the Subject with Candor, and Attention. Surely it would be an affront to the People of Massachusetts Bay to labour to convince them, that the Honor and Happiness of a People depend upon Morality; and that the Public Worship of GOD has a tendency to inculcate the Principles thereof, as well as to preserve a People from forsaking Civilization, and falling into a state of Savage barbarity.

In the form now presented to you; there are no more Departments of Government than are absolutely necessary for the free and full Exercise of the Powers thereof. The House of Representatives is intended as the Representative of the Persons and the Senate, of the property of the Common Wealth. These are to be annually chosen, and to sit in seperate Bodies, each having a Negative upon the Acts of other. This Power of a Negative in each must ever be necessary; for all Bodies of Men, assembled upon the same occasion and united by one common Interest of Rank, Honor, or Estate, are liable, like an individual, to mistake bias and prejudice. These two Houses are vested with the Powers of Legislation, and are to be chosen by the Male Inhabitants who are Twenty one Years of age, and have a Freehold of the small annual income of Three Pounds or Sixty Pounds in any Estate. Your Delegates considered that Persons who are Twenty one Years of age, and have no Property, are either those who live upon a part of a Paternal estate, expecting the Fee thereof, who are but just entering into business, or those whose Idleness of Life and profligacy of manners will forever bar them from acquiring and possessing Property. And we will submit it to the former Class, whether they would not think it safer for them to have their right of Voting for a Representative suspended for small space of Time, than forever hereafter to have their Privileges liable to the control of Men, who will pay less regard to the Rights of Property because they have nothing to loose.

The Power of Revising, and stating objections to any Bill or Resolve that shall be passed by the two Houses, we were of opinion ought to be lodged in the hands of some *one* person; not only to preserve the Laws from being unsystematical and innaccurate, but that a due balance may be preserved in the three capital powers of Government. The Legislative, the Judicial and Executive Powers naturally exhist in every Government: And the History of the rise and fall of the Empires of the World affords us ample proof, that when the Man or Body of Men enact, interpret and execute the Laws, property becomes too precarious to be valuable, and a People are finally borne down with the force of corruption resulting from the Union of those Powers. The Governor is emphatically the Representative of the whole People, being chosen not by one Town or County, but by the People at large. We have therefore thought it safest to rest this Power in his hands; and as the Safety of the Common wealth requires, that there should be one Commander in Chief over the Militia, we have given the Governor that Command for the same reason, that we thought him the only proper Person that could be trusted with the power of revising the Bills and Resolves of the General Assembly; but the People may if they please choose their own Officers.

You will observe that we have resolved, that Representation ought to be founded on the Principle of equality; but it cannot be understood thereby that each Town in the Commonwealth shall have Weight and importance in a just proportion to its Numbers and property. An exact Representation would be unpracticable even in a System of Government arising from the State of Nature, and much more so in a state already divided into nearly three hundred Corporations. But we have agreed that each Town having One hundred and fifty Rateable Poles shall be entitled to send one Member, and to prevent an advantage arising to the greater Towns by their numbers, have agreed that no Town shall send two unless it hath three hundred and seventy five Rateable Poles, and then the still larger Towns are to send one Member for every two hundred and twenty-five Rateable Polls over and above Three hundred and seventy-five. This method of calculation will give a more exact Representation when applied to all the Towns in the State than any that we could fix upon.

We have however digressed from this Rule in admiting the small Towns now incorporated to send Members. There are but a few of them which will not from their continual increase, be able to send one

upon the above plan in a very little Time. And a few who will never probably have that number have been heretofore in the exercise of this privilege, and will now be very unwilling to relinquish it.

To prevent the governor from abusing the Power which is necessary to be put into his hands we have provided that he shall have a Council to advise him at all Times and upon all important Occasions, and he with the advice of his Council is to have the Appointment of Civil Officers. This was very readily agreed to by your Delegates, and will undoubtedly be agreeable to their Constituents; for if those Officers who are to interpret and execute the Laws are to be dependent upon the Election of the people it must forever keep them under the Controul of ambitious, artful and interested men, who can obtain most Votes for them. – If they were to be Appointed by the Two Houses or either of them, the persons appointing them would be too numerous to be accountable for putting weak or wicked Men into Office. Besides the House is designed as the Grand Inquest of the Common Wealth, and are to impeach Officers for male Conduct, the Senate are to try the Merits of such impeachments; it would be therefore unfit that they should have the Creation of those Officers which the one may impeach and the other remove: but we conceive there is the greatest propriety in Vesting the Governor with this Power, he being as we have before observed, the compleat representative of all the People, and at all Times liable to be impeached by the House before the Senate for male Administration. And we would here observe that all the Powers which we have given the Governor are necessary to be lodged in the hands of one Man, as the General of the Army and first Magistrate, and none can be entitled to it but he who has the Annual and United Suffrages of the whole Common Wealth.

You will readily conceive it to be necessary for your own Safety, that your Judges should hold their Offices during good behaviour; for Men who hold their places upon so precarious a Tenure as annual or other frequent Appointments will never so assiduously apply themselves to study as will be necessary to the filling their places with dignity. Judges should at all Times feel themselves independent and free.

Your Delegates have further provided that the Supreme Judicial Department, by fixed and ample Salaries, may be enabled to devote themselves wholly to the Duties of their important Office. And for this reason, as well as to keep this Department seperate from the others

in Goverment have excluded them from a Seat in the Legislature; and when our Constituents consider that the final Desicion of their Lives and Property must be had in this Court, we conceive they will universally approve the measure. The Judges of Probate and those other officers whose presence is always necessary in their respective Counties are also excluded.

We have attended to the inconveniences suggested to have arisen from having but one Judge of Probate in each County; but the erecting and altering Courts of Justice being a mere matter of Legislation, we have left it with your future Legislature to make such Alterations as the Circumstances of the several Counties may require.

Your Delegates did not conceive themselves to be vested with Power to set up one Denomination of Christians above another; for Religion must at all Times be a matter between GOD and individuals: But we have, nevertheless, found ourselves obliged by a Solemn Test, to provide for the exclusion of those from Offices who will not disclaim those Principles of Spiritual Jurisdiction which Roman Catholicks *in some Countries* have held, and which are subversive of a free Government established by the People. We find it necessary to continue the former Laws, and Modes of proceeding in Courts of Justice, until a future Legislature shall alter them: For, unless this is done, the title to Estates will become precarious, Law-suits will be multiplied, and universal Confusion must take place. And least the Commonwealth for want of a due Administration of Civil Justice should be involved in Anarchy, we have proposed to continue the present Magistrates and Officers until new Appointments shall take place.

Thus we have, with plainess and sincerity, given you the Reasons upon which we founded the principal parts of the System laid before you, which appeared to us as most necessary to be explained: And we do most humbly beseech the Great Disposer of all Events, that we and our Posterity may be established in and long enjoy the Blessings of a well-ordered and free Government.

In the Name, and pursuant to a Resolution of the Convention,

JAMES BOWDOIN, *President,*

Attest

SAMUEL BARRETT, *Secretary.*

4.II.17 THE MASSACHUSETTS CONSTITUTION OF 1780

Constitution or form of government for the Commonwealth of Massachusetts, Massachusetts Archives, CCLXXVI 30

PREAMBLE.

THE end of the institution, maintenance and administration of Government, is to secure the existence of the body-politic; and to furnish the individuals who compose it, with the power of enjoying, in safety and tranquillity, their natural rights and the blessings of life: And whenever these great objects are not obtained, the people have a right to alter the Government, and to take measures necessary for their safety, prosperity and happiness.

THE body politic is formed by a voluntary association of individuals: It is a social compact, by which the whole people covenants with each citizen, and each citizen with the whole people, that all shall be governed by certain laws for the common good. It is the duty of the people, therefore, in framing a Constitution of Government, to provide for an equitable mode of making laws, as well as for an impartial interpretation, and a faithful execution of them; that every man may, at all times, find his security in them.

WE, therefore, the people of Massachusetts, acknowledging, with grateful hearts, the goodness of the Great Legislator of the Universe, in affording us, in the course of his providence, an opportunity, deliberately and peaceably, without fraud, violence, or surprise, of entering into an original, explicit and solemn compact with each other; and of forming a new Constitution of Civil Government, for ourselves and posterity; and devoutly imploring His direction in so interesting a design, DO agree upon, ordain and establish, the following *Declaration of Rights*, and *Frame of Government*, as the CONSTITUTION OF THE COMMONWEALTH OF MASSACHUSETTS.

MASSACHUSETTS.

PART THE FIRST,

A DECLARATION OF THE RIGHTS of the Inhabitants of the Commonwealth of Massachusetts.

Art. I. ALL men are born free and equal, and have certain natural, essential, and unalienable rights; among which may be reckoned the right of enjoying and defending their lives and liberties; that of acquiring, possessing, and protecting property; in fine, that of seeking and obtaining their safety and happiness.

II. IT is the right as well as the duty of all men in society, publicly, and at stated seasons, to worship the SUPREME BEING, the great creator and preserver of the universe. And no subject shall be hurt, molested, or restrained, in his person, liberty, or estate, for worshipping GOD in the manner and season most agreeable to the dictates of his own conscience; or for his religious profession or sentiments; provided he doth not disturb the public peace, or obstruct others in their religious worship.

III. AS the happiness of a people, and the good order and preservation of civil government, essentially depend upon piety, religion and morality; and as these cannot be generally diffused through a community, but by the institution of the public worship of GOD, and of public instructions in piety, religion and morality: Therefore, to promote their happiness, and to secure the good order and preservation of their government, the people of this Commonwealth have a right to invest their legislature with power to authorize and require, and the legislature shall, from time to time, authorize and require, the several towns, parishes, precincts, and other bodies politic, or religious societies, to make suitable provision, at their own expense, for the institution of the public worship of GOD, and for the support and maintenance of public protestant reachers of piety, religion and morality, in all cases where such provision shall not be made voluntarily.

AND the people of this Commonwealth have also a right to, and do, invest their legislature with authority to enjoin upon all the subjects an attendance upon the instructions of the public teachers aforesaid, at stated times and seasons, if there be any on whose instructions they can conscienciously and conveniently attend.

PROVIDED notwithstanding, that the several towns, parishes, precincts, and other bodies politic, or religious societies, shall, at all times, have the exclusive right of electing their public teachers, and of contracting with them for their support and maintenance.

AND all monies paid by the subject to the support of public worship, and of the public teachers aforesaid, shall, if he require it, be uniformly applied to the support of the public teacher or teachers of his own

religious sect or denomination, provided there be any on whose instructions he attends; otherwise it may be paid towards the support of the teacher or teachers of the parish or precinct in which the said monies are raised.

AND every denomination of christians, demeaning themselves peaceably, and as good subjects of the Commonwealth, shall be equally under the protection of the law; And no subordination of any one sect or denomination to another shall ever be established by law.

IV. THE people of this Commonwealth have the sole and exclusive right of governing themselves as a free, sovereign, and independent state; and do, and forever hereafter shall, exersice and enjoy every power, jurisdiction, and right, which is not, or may not hereafter, be by them expresly delegated to the United States of America, in Congress assembled.

V. ALL power residing originally in the people, and being derived from them the several magistrates and officers of Government, vested with authority, whether legislative, executive, or judicial, are their substitutes and agents, and are at all times accountable to them.

VI. NO man, nor corporation, or association of men, have any other title to obtain advantages, or particular and exclusive privileges, distinct from those of the community, than what arises from the consideration of services rendered to the public; and this title being in nature neither hereditary, nor transmissible to children, or descendents, or relations by blood, the idea of a man born a magistrate, lawgiver, or judge, is absurd and unnatural.

VII. GOVERNMENT is instituted for the common good; for the protection, safety, prosperity, and happiness of the people; and not for the profit, honour, or private interest of any one man, family or class of men: Therefore the people alone have an incontestable, unalienable, and indefeasible right to institute Government; and to reform, alter, or totally change the same, when their protection, safety, prosperity and happiness require it.

VIII. IN order to prevent those, who are vested with authority, from becoming oppressors, the people have a right, at such periods and in such manner as they shall establish by their frame of government, to cause their public officers to return to private life; and to fill up vacant places by certain and regular elections and appointments.

IX. ALL elections ought to be free; and all the inhabitants of this Commonwealth, having such qualifications as they shall establish by their frame of government, have an equal right to elect officers, and to be elected, for public employments.

X. EACH individual of the society has a right to be protected by it in the enjoyment of his life, liberty and property, according to standing laws. He is obliged, consequently, to contribute his share to the expense of this protection; to give his personal service, or an equivalent, when necessary: But no part of the property of any individual, can, with justice, be taken from him or applied to public uses, without his own consent, or that of the representative body of the people: In fine, the people of this Commonwealth are not controulable by any other laws, than those to which their constitutional representative body have given their consent. And whenever the public exigencies require, that the property of any individual should be appropriated to public uses, he shall receive a reasonable compensation therefor.

XI. EVERY subject of the Commonwealth ought to find a certain remedy, by having recourse to the laws, for all injuries or wrongs which he may receive in his person, property, or character. He ought to obtain right and justice freely, and without being obliged to purchase it; compleatly, and without any denial; promptly, and without delay; comformably to the laws.

XII. NO subject shall be held to answer for any crime or offence, until the same is fully and plainly, substantially and formally, described to him; or be compelled to accuse, or furnish evidence against himself. And every subject shall have a right to produce all proofs, that may be favourable to him; to meet the witnesses against him face to face; and to be fully heard in his defence by himself, or his council, at his election. And no subject shall be arrested, imprisoned, despoiled, or deprived of his property, immunities, or privileges, put out of the protection of the law, exiled, or deprived of his life, liberty, or estate, but by the judgment of his peers, or the law of the land.

AND the legislature shall not make any law, that shall subject any person to a capital or infamous punishment, excepting for the government of the army, and navy, without trial by jury.

XIII. IN criminal prosecutions, the verification of facts in the vicinity where they happen, is one of the greatest securities of the life, liberty, and property of the citizen.

XIV. EVERY subject has a right to be secure from all unreasonable searches, and seizures of his person, his houses, his papers, and all his possessions. All warrants, therefore, are contrary to this right, if the cause or foundation of them be not previously supported by oath or affirmation; and if the order in the warrant to a civil officer, to make search in suspected places, or to arrest one or more suspected persons, or to seize their property, be not accompanied with a special designation of the persons or objects of search, arrest, or seizure: and no warrant ought to be issued but in cases, and with the formalities, prescribed by the laws.

XV. IN all controversies concerning property, and in all suits between two or more persons, except in cases in which it has heretofore been otherways used and practised, the parties have a right to a trial by a jury; and this method of procedure shall be held sacred, unless, in causes arising on the high-seas, and such as relate to mariners wages, the legislature shall hereafter find it necessary to alter it.

XVI. THE liberty of the press is essential to the security of freedom in a state; it ought not, therefore, to be restrained in this Commonwealth.

XVII. THE people have a right to keep and to bear arms for the common defence. And as in time of peace armies are dangerous to liberty, they ought not to be maintained without the consent of the legislature; and the military power shall always be held in an exact subordination to the civil authority, and be governed by it.

XVIII. A FREQUENT recurrence to the fundamental principles of the constitution, and a constant adherence to those of piety, justice, moderation, temperance, industry, and frugality, are absolutely necessary to preserve the advantages of liberty, and to maintain a free government: The people ought, consequently, to have a particular attention to all those principles, in the choice of their officers and representatives: And they have a right to require of their law-givers and magistrates, an exact and constant observance of them, in the formation and execution of the laws necessary for the good administration of the Commonwealth.

XIX. THE people have a right, in an orderly and peaceable manner, to assemble to consult upon the common good; give instructions to their representatives; and to request of the legislative body, by the way of addresses, petitions, or remonstrances, redress of the wrongs done them, and of the grievances they suffer.

XX. THE power of suspending the laws, or the execution of the laws, ought never to be exercised but by the legislature, or by authority derived from it, to be exercised in such particular cases only as the legislature shall expressly provide for.

XXI. THE freedom of deliberation, speech and debate in either house of the legislature, is so essential to the rights of the people, that it cannot be the foundation of any accusation or prosecution, action or complaint, in any other court or place whatsoever.

XXII. THE legislature ought frequently to assemble for the redress of grievances, for correcting, strengthening, and confirming the laws, and for making new laws, as the common good may require.

XXIII. NO subsidy, charge, tax, impost, or duties ought to be established, fixed, laid or levied, under any pretext whatsoever, without the consent of the people, or their representatives in the legislature.

XXIV. LAWS made to punish for actions done before the existence of such laws, and which have not been declared crimes by preceeding laws, are unjust, oppressive, and inconsistent with the fundamental principles of a free government.

XXV. NO subject ought, in any case, or in any time, to be declared guilty of treason or felony by the legislature.

XXVI. NO magistrate or court of law, shall demand excessive bail or sureties, impose excessive fines, or inflict cruel or unusual punishments.

XXVII. IN time of peace no soldier ought to be quartered in any house without the consent of the owner; and in time of war such quarters ought not to be made but by the civil magistrate, in a manner ordained by the legislature.

XXVIII. NO person can, in any case, be subjected to law-martial, or to any penalties or pains, by virtue of that law, except those employed in the army or navy, and except the militia in actual service, but by authority of the legislature.

XXIX. IT is essential to the preservation of the rights of every individual, his life, liberty, property and character, that there be an impartial interpretation of the laws, and administration of justice. It is the right of every citizen to be tried by judges as free, impartial and independent as the lot of humanity will admit. It is therefore not only the best policy, but for the security of the rights of the people, and of every citizen, that the judges of the supreme judicial court should hold their offices as long as they behave themselves well; and that they should have honourable salaries ascertained and established by standing laws.

XXX. IN the government of this Commonwealth the legislative department shall never exercise the executive and judicial powers, or either of them: The executive shall never exercise the legislative and judicial powers, or either of them: The judicial shall never exercise the legislative and executive powers, or either of them: To the end it may be a government of laws and not of men.

PART the SECOND.

The Frame of Government.

THE people inhabiting the territory formerly called the Province of Massachusetts Bay, do hereby solemnly and mutually agree with each other, to form themselves into a free, sovereign, and independent body-politic or state, by the name of THE COMMONWEALTH OF MASSACHUSETTS.

CHAPTER I.

The Legislative Power

SECTION I.

The General Court

Art. I. THE department of legislation shall be formed by two branches, *a Senate* and *House of Representatives:* each of which shall have a negative on the other.

THE legislative body shall assemble every year on the last Wednesday in May, and at such other times as they shall judge necessary; and shall dissolve and be dissolved on the day next preceeding the said last Wednesday in May; and shall be styled, THE GENERAL COURT *of* MASSACHUSETTS.

II. NO bill or resolve of the Senate or House of Representatives shall become a law, and have force as such, until it shall have been laid before the Governor for his revisal: And if he, upon such revision, approve thereof, he shall signify his approbation by signing the same. But if he have any objection to the passing of such bill or resolve, he shall return the same, together with his objections thereto, in writing, to the Senate or House of Representatives, in which soever the same shall have originated; who shall enter the objections sent down by the Governor, at large, on their records, and proceed to reconsider the said bill or resolve: But if after such reconsideration, two thirds of the said Senate or House of Representatives, shall, notwithstanding the said objections, agree to pass the same, it shall, together with the objections, be sent to the other branch of the legislature, where it shall also be reconsidered, and if approved by two thirds of the members present, it shall have the force of a law: But in all such cases, the votes of both houses shall be determined by yeas and nays; and the names of the persons voting for, or against, the said bill or resolve, shall be entered upon the public records of the Commonwealth.

AND in order to prevent unnecessary delays, if any bill or resolve shall not be returned by the Governor within five days after it shall have been presented, the same shall have the force of a law.

III. THE General Court shall forever have full power and authority to erect and constitute judicatories and courts of record, or other courts, to be held in the name of the Commonwealth, for the hearing, trying, and determining of all manner of crimes, offences, pleas, processes, plaints, actions, matters, causes and things, whatsoever, arising or happening within the Commonwealth, or between or concerning persons inhabiting, or residing, or brought within the same; whether the same be criminal or civil, or whether the said crimes be capital or not capital, and whether the said pleas be real, personal, or mixt; and for the awarding and making out of execution thereupon: To which courts and judicatories are hereby given and granted full power and authority, from time to time, to administer oaths or affirmations, for the better discovery of truth in any matter in controversy or depending before them.

IV. AND further, full power and authority are hereby given and granted to the said General Court, from time to time, to make, ordain, and establish, all manner of wholesome and reasonable orders, laws, statutes and ordinances, directions and instructions, either with penalties or without; so as the same be not repugnant or contrary to this Constitution, as they shall judge to be for the good and welfare of this Commonwealth, and for the government and ordering thereof, and of the subjects of same, and for the necessary support and defence of the government thereof; and to name and settle annually, or provide by fixed laws, for the naming and settling all civil officers within the said Commonwealth; the election and constitution of whom are not hereafter in the Form of Government otherwise provided for; and to set forth the several duties, powers and limits, of the several civil and military officers of this Commonwealth, and the forms of such oaths or affirmations as shall be respectively administered unto them for the execution of their several offices and places, so as the same be not repugnant or contrary to this Constitution: and to impose and levy proportional and reasonable assessments, rates, and taxes, upon all the inhabitants of, and persons resident, and estates lying, within the said Commonwealth; and also to impose, and levy, reasonable duties and excises, upon any produce, goods, wares, merchandize, and commodities whatsoever, brought into, produced, manufactured, or being within the same; to be issued and disposed of by warrant, under the hand of the Governor of this Commonwealth for the time being, with the advice and consent of the Council, for the public service, in the necessary defence and support of the government of the said Commonwealth, and the protection and preservation of the subjects thereof, according to such acts as are or shall be in force within the same.

AND while the public charges of government, or any part thereof, shall be assessed on polls and estates, in the manner that has hitherto be practised; in order that such assessments may be made with equality, there shall be a valuation of estates within the Commonwealth taken anew once in every ten years at the least, and as much oftener as the General Court shall order.

CHAPTER I.

SECTION II.

SENATE

Art. I. THERE shall be annually elected by the freeholders and other inhabitants of this Commonwealth, qualified as in this Constitution is provided, forty persons to be Counsellors and Senators for the year ensuing their election; to be chosen by the inhabitants of the districts, into which the Commonwealth may from time to time be divided by the General Court for that purpose: And the General Court, in assigning the numbers to be elected by the respective districts, shall govern themselves by the proportion of the public taxes paid by the said districts; and timely make known to the inhabitants of the Commonwealth, the limits of each district, and the number of Counsellors and Senators to be chosen therein; provided that the number of such districts shall be never less than thirteen; And that no district be so large as to entitle the same to choose more than six Senators.

AND the several counties in this Commonwealth shall, until the General Court shall determine it necessary to alter the said districts, be districts for the choice of Counsellors and Senators, (except that the counties of Duke's County and Nantucket shall form one district for that purpose) and shall elect the following number for Counsellors and Senators, viz.

Suffolk	Six
Essex	Six
Middlesex	Five
Hampshire	Four
Plymouth	Three
Barnstable	One
Bristol	Three
York	Two
Duke's County and Nantucket	One
Worcester	Five
Cumberland	One
Lincoln	One
Berkshire	Two

II. THE Senate shall be the first branch of the legislature; and the Senators shall be chosen in the following manner, viz. There shall be a meeting on the first Monday in April annually, forever, of the inhabitants of each town in the several counties of this Commonwealth; to be called by the Selectmen, and warned in due course of law, at least seven days before the first Monday in April, for the purpose of electing persons to be Senators and Counsellors: And at such meetings every male inhabitant of twenty-one years of age and upwards, having a freehold estate within the Commonwealth, of the annual income of three pounds, or any estate of the value of sixty pounds, shall have a right to give in his vote for the Senators for the district of which he is an inhabitant. And to remove all doubts concerning the meaning of the word 'inhabitant' in this Constitution, every person shall be considered as an inhabitant, for the purpose of electing and being elected into any office, or place within this State, in that town, district or plantation, where he dwelleth, or hath his home.

THE Selectmen of the several towns shall preside at such meetings impartially; and shall receive the votes of all the inhabitants of such towns present and qualified to vote for Senators, and shall sort and count them in open town meeting, and in presence of the Town Clerk, who shall make a fair record, in presence of the Selectmen, and in open town meeting, of the name of every person voted for, and of the number of votes against his name; and a fair copy of this record shall be attested by the Selectmen and Town-Clerk, and shall be sealed up, directed to the Secretary of the Commonwealth for the time being, with a superscription, expressing the purport of the contents thereof, and delivered by the Town-Clerk of such towns, to the Sheriff of the county in which such town lies, thirty days at least before the last Wednesday in May annually; or it shall be delivered into the Secretary's office seventeen days at least before the said last Wednesday in May; and the Sheriff of each county shall deliver all such certificates by him received into the Secretary's office seventeen days before the said last Wednesday in May.

AND the inhabitants of plantations unincorporated, qualified as this Constitution provides, who are or shall be empowered and required to assess taxes upon themselves toward the support of government, shall have the same privilege of voting for Counsellors and Senators in the plantations where they reside, as town inhabitants have in their respective towns; and the plantation-meetings for that purpose shall be held annually on the same first Monday in April, at such place in the plantations respectively, as the Assessors thereof shall direct; which Assessors shall have like authority for notifying the electors, collecting and returning the votes, as the Selectmen and Town-Clerks have in their several towns, by this Constitution. And all other persons living in places unincorporated (qualified as aforesaid) who shall be assessed to the support of government by the Assessors of an adjacent town, shall have the privilege of giving in their votes for Counsellors and Senators, in the town where they shall be assessed, and be notified of the place of meeting by the Selectmen of the town where they shall be assessed, for that purpose accordingly.

III. AND that there may be a due convention of Senators on the last Wednesday in May annually, the Governor, with five of the Council, for the time being, shall, as soon as may be, examine the returned copies of such records; and fourteen days before the said day he shall issue his summons to such persons as shall appear to be chosen by a majority of voters, to attend on that day, and take their seats accordingly: Provided nevertheless, that for the first year the said returned copies shall be examined by the President and five of the Council of the former Constitution of Government; and the said President shall, in like manner, issue his summons to the persons so elected, that they may take their seats as aforesaid.

IV. THE Senate shall be the final judge of the elections, returns and qualifications of their own members, as pointed out in the Constitution; and shall, on the said last Wednesday in May annually, determine and declare who are elected by each district, to be Senators by a majority of votes: And in case there shall not appear to be the full number of Senators returned elected by a majority of votes for any district, the deficiency shall be supplied in the following manner, viz. The members of the House of Representatives, and such Senators as shall be declared elected, shall take the names of such persons as shall be found to have the highest number of votes in such district, and not elected, amounting to twice the number of Senators wanting, if there be so many voted for; and out of these, shall elect by a ballot a number of Senators sufficient to fill up the vacancies in such district: And in this manner all such vacancies shall be filled up in every district of the Commonwealth; and in like manner all vacancies in the Senate, arising by death, removal out of the State, or otherwise, shall be supplied as soon as may be, after such vacancies shall happen.

V. PROVIDED nevertheless, that no person shall be capable of being elected as a Senator who is not seized in his own right of a freehold within this Commonwealth, of the value of three hundred pounds at least, or possessed of personal estate to the value of six hundred pounds at least, or of both to the amount of the same sum, and who has not been an inhabitant of this Commonwealth for the space of five years immediately preceeding his election, and at the time of his election, he shall be an inhabitant in the district, for which he shall be chosen.

VI. THE Senate shall have power to adjourn themselves, provided such adjournments do not exceed two days at a time.

VII. THE Senate shall choose its own President, appoint its own officers, and determine its own rules of proceedings.

VIII. THE Senate shall be a court with full authority to hear and determine all impeachments made by the House of Representatives, against any officer or officers of the Commonwealth, for misconduct and mal-administration in their offices. But previous to the trial of every impeachment, the members of the Senate shall respectively be sworn, truly and impartially to try and determine the charge in question, according to evidence. Their judgment, however, shall not extend further than to removal from office, and disqualification to hold or enjoy any place of honour, trust, or profit under this Commonwealth: But the party so convicted, shall be nevertheless, liable to indictment, trial, judgment, and punishment, according to the laws of the land.

IX. NOT less than sixteen members of the Senate shall constitute a quorum for doing business.

CHAPTER I.

SECTION III.

House of Representatives.

Art. I. THERE shall be in the Legislature of this Commonwealth, a representation of the people, annually elected, and founded upon the principle of equality.

II. AND in order to provide for a representation of the citizens of this Commonwealth, founded upon the principle of equality, every corporate town containing one hundred and fifty rateable polls, may elect one Representative: Every corporate town, containing three hundred and seventy-five rateable polls, may elect two Representatives: Every corporate town, containing six hundred rateable polls, may elect three Representatives; and proceeding in that manner, making two hundred and twenty-five rateable polls the mean increasing number for every additional Representative.

PROVIDED nevertheless, that each town now incorporated, not having one hundred and fifty rateable polls, may elect one representative: but no place shall hereafter be incorporated with the privilege of electing a Representative, unless there are within the same one hundred and fifty rateable polls.

AND the House of Representatives shall have power from time to time to impose fines upon such towns as shall neglect to choose and return members to the same, agreeably to this Constitution.

THE expenses of travelling to the General Assembly, and returning home, once in every session, and no more, shall be paid by the government, out of the public treasury, to every member who shall attend as seasonably as he can, in the judgment of the House, and does not depart without leave.

III. EVERY member of the House of Representatives shall be chosen by written votes; and for one year at least next preceeding his election, shall have been an inhabitant of, and have been seized in his own right of a freehold of the value of one hundred pounds within the town he shall be chosen to represent, or any rateable estate to the value of two hundred pounds; and he shall cease to represent the said town immediately on his ceasing to be qualified as aforesaid.

IV. EVERY male person, being twenty-one years of age, and resident in any particular town in this Commonwealth for the space of one year next preceeding, having a freehold estate within the same town, of the annual income of three pounds, or any estate of the value of sixty pounds, shall have a right to vote in the choice of a Representative or Representatives for the said town.

V. THE members of the House of Representatives shall be chosen annually in the month of May, ten days at least before the last Wednesday of that month.

VI. THE House of Representatives shall be the Grand Inquest of this Commonwealth; and all impeachments made by them shall be heard and tried by the Senate.

VII. ALL money-bills shall originate in the House of Representatives; but the Senate may propose or concur with amendments, as on other bills.

VIII. THE House of Representatives shall have power to adjourn themselves; provided such adjournment shall not exceed two days at a time.

IX. NOT less than sixty members of the House of Representatives, shall constitute a quorum for doing business.

X. THE House of Representatives shall be the judge of the returns, elections, and qualifications of its own members, as pointed out in the constitution; shall choose their own Speaker; appoint their own officers, and settle the rules and orders of proceeding in their own house: They shall have authority to punish by imprisonment, every person, not a member, who shall be guilty of disrespect to the House, by any disorderly, or contemptuous behaviour, in its presence; or who, in the town where the General Court is sitting, and during the time of its sitting, shall threaten harm to the body or estate of any of its members, for any thing said or done in the House; or who shall assault any of them therefor; or who shall assault, or arrest, any witness, or other person, ordered to attend the House, in his way in going or returning; or who shall rescue any person arrested by the order of the House.

AND no member of the House of Representatives shall be arrested, or held to bail on mean process, during his going unto, returning from, or his attending, the General Assembly.

XI. THE Senate shall have the same powers in the like cases; and the Governor and Council shall have the same authority to punish in like cases. Provided that no imprisonment on the warrant or order of the Governor, Council, Senate, or House of Representatives, for either of the above-described offenses, be for a term exceeding thirty days.

AND the Senate and House of Representatives may try, and determine, all cases where their rights and privileges are concerned, and which, by the Constitution, they have authority to try and determine, by committees of their own members, or in such other way as they may respectively think best.

CHAPTER II.

Executive Power

SECTION I.

Governor

Art. I. THERE shall be a supreme executive Magistrate, who shall be styled, THE GOVERNOR OF THE COMMONWEALTH OF MASSACHUSETTS; and whose title shall be – HIS EXCELLENCY.

II. THE Governor shall be chosen annually: And no person shall be eligible to this office, unless at the time of his election, he shall have been an inhabitant of this Commonwealth for seven years next preceeding; and unless he shall, at the same time, be seized in his own right, of a freehold within the Commonwealth, of the value of one thousand pounds; and unless he shall declare himself to be of the christian religion.

III. THOSE persons who shall be qualified to vote for Senators and Representatives within the several towns of this Commonwealth, shall, at a meeting to be called for that purpose, on the first Monday of April annually, give in their votes for a Governor, to the Selectmen, who shall preside at such meetings; and the Town-Clerk, in the presence and with the assistance of the Selectmen, shall, in open town-meeting, sort and count the votes, and form a list of the persons voted for, with the number of votes for each person against his name; and shall make a fair record of the same in the town books, and a public declaration thereof in the said meeting; and shall, in the presence of the inhabitants, seal up copies of the said list, attested by him and the Selectmen, and transmit the same to the Sheriff of the county, thirty days at least before the last Wednesday in May; and the Sheriff shall transmit the same to the Secretary's office, seventeen days at least before the said last Wednesday in May; or the Selectmen may cause returns of the same to be made to the office of the Secretary of the Commonwealth seventeen days at least before the said day; and the Secretary shall lay the same before the Senate and the House of Representatives, on the last Wednesday in May, to be by them examined: And in case of an election by a majority of all the votes returned, the choice shall be by them declared and published: But if no person shall have a majority of votes, the House of Representatives shall, by ballot, elect two out of four persons who had the highest number of votes, if so many shall have been voted for; but, if otherwise, out of the number voted for; and make return to the Senate of the two persons so elected; on which, the Senate shall proceed, by ballot, to elect one, who shall be declared Governor.

IV. THE Governor shall have authority, from time to time, at his discretion, to assemble and call together the Counsellors of this Commonwealth, for the time being; and the Governor, with the said Counsellors, or five of them at least, shall, and may, from time to time, hold and keep a Council, for the ordering and directing the affairs of the Commonwealth, agreeably to the Constitution and the laws of the land.

V. THE Governor, with advice of Council, shall have full power and authority, during the session of the General Court, to adjourn or prorogue the same to any time the two Houses shall desire; and to dissolve the same on the day next preceeding the last Wednesday in May; and, in the recess of the said court, to prorogue the same from time to time, not exceeding ninety days in any one recess; and to call it together sooner than the time to which it may be adjourned or prorogued, if the welfare of the Commonwealth shall require the same: And in case of any infectious distemper prevailing in the place where the said court is next at any time to convene, or any other cause happening whereby danger may arise to the health or lives of the members from their attendance, he may direct the session to be held at some other the most convenient place within the State.

AND the Governor shall dissolve the said General Court on the day next preceeding the last Wednesday in May.

VI. IN cases of disagreement between the two Houses, with regard to the necessity, expediency or time of adjournment, or prorogation, the Governor, with advice of the Council, shall have a right to adjourn or prorogue the General Court, not exceeding ninety days, as he shall determine the public good shall require.

VII. THE Governor of this Commonwealth for the time being, shall be the commander in chief of the army and navy, and of all the military forces of the State, by sea and land; and shall have full power by himself, or by any commander, or other officer or officers, from time to time, to train, instruct, exercise and govern the militia and navy; and, for the special defence and safety of the Commonwealth, to assemble in martial array, and put in warlike posture, the inhabitants thereof, and to lead and conduct them and with them, to encounter, repel, resist, expel and pursue, by force of arms, as well by sea as by land, within or without the limits of this Commonwealth, and also to kill, slay and destroy, if necessary, and conquer by all fitting ways, enterprises and means whatsoever, all and every such person and persons as shall, at any time hereafter, in a hostile manner attempt or enterprise the destruction, invasion, detriment, or annoyance of this Commonwealth; and to use and exercise, over the army and navy, and over the militia in actual service, the law-martial, in time of war or invasion, and also in time of rebellion, declared by the legislature to exist, as occasion shall necessarily require; and to take and surprise by all ways and means whatsoever, all and every such person or persons, with their ships, arms, ammunition and other goods, as shall, in a hostile manner, invade or attempt the invading, conquering, or annoying this Commonwealth; and that the Governor be intrusted with all these and other powers, incident to the offices of Captain-General and Commander in Chief, and Admiral, to be exercised agreeably to the rules and regulations of the Constitution, and the laws of the land, and not otherwise.

PROVIDED, that the said Governor shall not, at any time hereafter, by virtue of any power by this Constitution granted, or hereafter to be granted to him by the legislature, transport any of the inhabitants of this Commonwealth, or oblige them to march out of the limits of the same, without their free and voluntary consent, or the consent of the General Court; except so far as may be necessary to march or transport them by land or water, for the defence of such part of the State, to which they cannot otherwise conveniently have access.

VIII. THE power of pardoning offences, except such as persons may be convicted of before the Senate by an impeachment of the House, shall be in the Governor, by and with the advice of Council: But no charter of pardon, granted by the Governor, with advice of the Council, before conviction, shall avail the party pleading the same, notwithstanding any general or particular expressions contained therein, descriptive of the offence, or offences intended to be pardoned.

IX. ALL judicial officers, the Attorney-General, the Solicitor-General, all Sheriffs, Coroners, and Registers of Probate, shall be nominated and appointed by the Governor, by and with the advice and consent of the Council; and every such nomination shall be made by the Governor, and made at least seven days prior to such appointment.

X. THE Captains and subalterns of the militia, shall be elected by the written votes of the trainband and alarm list of their respective companies, of twenty-one years of age and upwards: The field-officers of regiments shall be elected by the written votes of the Captains and subalterns of their respective regiments: The Brigadiers shall be elected in like manner, by the field-officers of their respective brigades: And such officers, so elected, shall be commissioned by the Governor, who shall determine their rank.

THE Legislature shall, by standing laws, direct the time and manner of convening the electors, and of collecting votes, and of certifying to the Governor the officers elected.

THE Major-Generals shall be appointed by the Senate and House of Representatives, each having a negative upon the other; and be commissioned by the Governor.

AND if the electors of Brigadiers, field-officers, Captains or subalterns, shall neglect or refuse to make such elections, after being duly notified according to the laws for the time being, then the Governor, with advice of Council, shall appoint suitable persons to fill such offices.

AND no officer, duly commissioned to command in the militia, shall be removed from his office, but by the address of both Houses to the Governor; or by fair trial in court-martial, pursuant to the laws of the Commonwealth for the time being.

THE commanding officers of regiments shall appoint their Adjutants and Quartermasters; the Brigadiers their Brigade Majors; and the Major-Generals their Aids; and the Governor shall appoint the Adjutant-General.

THE Governor, with advice of Council, shall appoint all officers of the continental army, whom by the confederation of the United States it is provided that this Commonwealth shall appoint, – as also all officers of forts and garrisons.

THE divisions of the militia into brigades regiment and companies, made in pursuance of the militia laws now in force, shall be considered as the proper divisions of the militia of this Commonwealth, until the same shall be altered in pursuance of some future law.

XI. NO monies shall be issued out of the treasury of this Commonwealth, and disposed of (except such sums as may be appropriated for the redemption of bills of credit or Treasurer's notes, or for the payment of interest arising thereon) but by warrant under the hand of the Governor for the time being, with the advice and consent of the Council, for the necessary defence and support of the Commonwealth; and for the protection and preservation of the inhabitants thereof, agreeably to the acts and resolves of the General Court.

XII. ALL public boards, the Commissary-General, all superintending officers of public magazines and stores, belonging to this Commonwealth, and all commanding officers of forts and garrisons within the same, shall once in every three months officially and without requisition, and at other times, when required by the Governor, deliver to him an account of all goods, stores, provisions, ammunition, cannon with their appendages, and small arms with their accoutrements, and of all other public property whatever under their care respectively; distinguishing the quantity, number, quality and kind of each, as particularly as may be; together with the condition of such forts and garrisons: And the said commanding officer shall exhibit to the Governor, when required by him, true and exact plans of such forts, and of the land and sea or harbour or harbours adjacent.

AND the said boards, and all public officers, shall communicate to the Governor, as soon as may be after receiving the same, all letters, dispatches, and intelligences of a public nature, which shall be directed to them respectively.

XIII. AS the public good requires that the Governor should not be under the undue influence of any of the members of the General Court, by a dependence on them for his support – that he should in all cases, act with freedom for the benefit of the public – that he should not have his attention necessarily diverted from that object to his private concerns – & that he should maintain the dignity of the Commonwealth in the character of its chief magistrate – it is necessary that he should have an honorable stated salary, of a fixed & permanent value, amply sufficient for those purposes, & established by standing laws: And it shall be among the first acts of the General Court, after the commencement of this Constitution, to establish such salary by law accordingly.

PERMANENT and honorable salaries shall also be established by law for the Justices of the supreme judicial court.

AND if it shall be found, that any of the salaries aforesaid, so established, are insufficient, they shall, from time to time, be enlarged as the General Court shall judge proper.

CHAPTER II.

SECTION II.

Lieutenant-Governor

Art. I. THERE shall be annually elected a Lieutenant-Governor of the Commonwealth of Massachusetts, whose title shall be HIS HONOR – and who shall be qualified, in point of religion, property, and residence in the Commonwealth, in the same manner with the Governor: And the day and manner of his election, and the qualifications of the electors, shall be the same as are required in the election of a Governor. The return of the votes for this officer, and the declaration of his election, shall be in the same manner: And if no one person shall be found to have a majority of all the votes returned, the vacancy shall be filled by the Senate and House of Representatives, in the same manner as the Governor is to be elected, in case no one person shall have a majority of the votes of the people to be a Governor.

II. THE Governor, and in his absence the Lieutenant-Governor, shall be President of the Council, but shall have no vote in Council: And the Lieutenant-Governor shall always be a member of the Council, except when the chair of the Governor shall be vacant.

III. WHENEVER the chair of the Governor shall be vacant, by reason of his death, or absence from the Commonwealth, or otherwise, the Lieutenant-Governor, for the time being, shall, during such vacancy, perform all the duties incumbent upon the Governor, and shall have and exercise all the powers and authorities, which by this Constitution the Governor is vested with, when personally present.

CHAPTER II.

SECTION III.

Council, and the Manner of settling Elections by the Legislature.

Art. I. THERE shall be a Council for advising the Governor in the executive part of government, to consist of nine persons besides the Lieutenant-Governor, whom the Governor, for the time being, shall have full power and authority, from time to time, at his discretion, to assemble and call together. And the Governor, with the said Counsellors, or five of them at least, shall and may, from time to time, hold and keep a Council, for the ordering and directing the affairs of the Commonwealth, according to the laws of the land.

II. NINE Counsellors shall be annually chosen from among the persons returned for Counsellors and Senators, on the last Wednesday in May, by the joint ballot of the Senators and Representatives assembled in one room: And in case there shall not be found upon the first choice, the whole number of nine persons who will accept a seat in the Council, the deficiency shall be made up by the electors aforesaid from among the people at large; and the number of Senators left shall constitute the Senate for the year. The seats of the persons thus elected from the Senate, and accepting the trust, shall be vacated in the Senate.

III. THE Counsellors, in the civil arrangements of the Commonwealth, shall have rank next after the Lieutenant-Governor.

IV. NOT more than two Counsellors shall be chosen out of any one district of this Commonwealth.

V. THE resolutions and advice of the Council shall be recorded in a register, and signed by the members present; and this record may be called for at any time by either House of the legislature; and any member of the Council may insert his opinion contrary to the resolution of the majority.

VI. WHENEVER the office of Governor and Lieutenant-Governor shall be vacant, by reason of death, absence, or otherwise, then the Council or the major part of them, shall, during such vacancy, have full power and authority, to do, and execute, all and every such acts, matters and things, as the Governor or the Lieutenant-Governor might or could, by virtue of this Constitution, do or execute, if they, or either of them, were personally present.

VII. AND whereas the elections appointed to be made by this Constitution, on the last Wednesday in May annually, by the two Houses of the legislature, may not be compleated on that day, the said elections may be adjourned from day to day until the same shall be compleated. And the order of elections shall be as follows; the vacancies in the Senate, if any, shall first be filled up; the Governor and Lieutenant-Governor shall then be elected, provided there should be no choice of them by the people: And afterwards the two Houses shall proceed to the election of the Council.

CHAPTER II.

SECTION IV.

Secretary, Treasurer, Commissary, &c.

Art. I. THE Secretary, Treasurer and Receiver-General, and the Commissary-General, Notaries Public, and Naval-Officers, shall be chosen annually, by joint ballot of the Senators and Representatives in one room. And that the citizens of this Commonwealth may be assured, from time to time, that the monies remaining in the public Treasury, upon the settlement and liquidation of the public accounts, are their property, no man shall be eligible as Treasurer and Receiver-General more than five years successively.

II. THE records of the Commonwealth shall be kept in the office of the Secretary, who may appoint his Deputies, for whose conduct he shall be accountable, and he shall attend the Governor and Council, the Senate and House of Representatives, in person, or by his deputies, as they shall respectively require.

CHAPTER III.

Judiciary Power.

Art. I. THE tenure, that all commission officers shall by law have in their officers, shall be expressed in their respective commissions. All judicial officers, duly appointed, commissioned and sworn, shall hold their offices during good behaviour, excepting such concerning whom there is different provision made in this Constitution: Provided nevertheless, the Governor, with consent of the Council, may remove them upon the address of both Houses of the Legislature.

II. EACH branch of the Legislature, as well as the Governor and Council, shall have authority to require the opinions of the Justices of the supreme judicial court, upon important questions of law, and upon solemn occasions.

III. IN order that the people may not suffer from the long continuance in place of any Justice of the Peace, who shall fail of discharging the important duties of his office with ability or fidelity, all commissions of Justices of the Peace shall expire and become void in the term of seven years from their respective dates; and upon the expiration of any commission, the same may, if necessary, be renewed, or another person appointed, as shall most conduce to the well-being of the Commonwealth.

IV. THE Judges of Probate of Wills, and for granting letters of administration, shall hold their courts at such place or places, on fixed days, as the convenience of the people shall require. And the Legislature shall, from time to time, hereafter appoint such times and places; until which appointments, the said courts shall be holden at the times and places which the respective Judges shall direct.

V. ALL causes of marriage, divorce and alimony, and all appeals from the Judges of Probate shall be heard and determined by the Governor and Council, until the Legislature shall, by law, make other provision.

CHAPTER IV.

Delegates to Congress.

THE delegates of the Commonwealth to the Congress of the United States, shall, sometime in the month of June annually, be elected by the joint ballot of the Senate and House of Representatives, assembled together in one room; to serve in Congress for one year, to commence on the first Monday in November then next ensuing. They shall have commissions under the hand of the Governor, and the great seal of the Commonwealth; but may be recalled at any time within the year, and others chosen and commissioned, in the same manner, in their stead.

CHAPTER V.

The University at Cambridge, and Encouragement of Literature &c.

SECTION I.

The University.

Art. I. WHEREAS our wise and pious ancestors, so early as the yea one thousand six hundred and thirty-six, laid the foundation of Harvard-College, in which university many persons of great eminence have, by the blessing of GOD, been initiated in those arts and sciences, which qualified them for public employments, both in Church and State: And whereas the encouragement of arts and sciences, and all good literature, tends to the honour of GOD, the advantage of the christian religion, and the great benefit of this and the other United

States of America – It is declared, That the PRESIDENT and FELLOWS of HARVARD-COLLEGE, in their corporate capacity, and their successors in that capacity, their officers and servants, shall have, hold, use, exercise and enjoy, all the powers, authorities, rights, liberties, privileges, immunities and franchises, which they now have, or are entitled to have, hold, use, exercise and enjoy: And the same are hereby ratified and confirmed unto them, the said President and Fellows of Harvard-College, and to their successors, and to their officers and servants, respectively, forever.

II. AND whereas there have been at sundry times, by divers persons, gifts, grants, devises of houses, lands, tenements, goods, chattels, legacies and conveyances, heretofore made, either to Harvard-College in Cambridge, in New-England, or to the President and Fellows of Harvard-College, or to the said College, by some other description, under several charters successively: IT IS DECLARED, That all the said gifts, grants, devises, legacies and conveyances, are hereby forever confirmed unto the President and Fellows of Harvard-College, and to their successors, in the capacity aforesaid, according to the true intent and meaning of the donor or donors, grantor or grantors, devisor or devisors.

III. AND whereas by an act of the General Court of the Colony of Massachusetts-Bay, passed in the year one thousand six hundred and forty-two, the Governor and Deputy-governor, for the time being, and all the magistrates of that jurisdiction, were, with the President, and a number of the clergy in the said act described, constituted the Overseers of Harvard-College: And it being necessary, in this new Constitution of Government, to ascertain who shall be deemed successors to the said Governor, Deputy-Governor and Magistrates: IT IS DECLARED, That the Governor, Lieutenant-Governor, Council and Senate of this Commonwealth, are, and shall be deemed, their successors; who, with the President of Harvard-College for the time being, together with the Ministers of the congregational churches in the towns of Cambridge, Watertown, Charlestown, Boston, Roxbury, and Dorchester, mentioned in the said act, shall be, and hereby are, vested with all the powers and authority belonging, or in any way appertaining to the Overseers of Harvard-College: PROVIDED, that nothing herein shall be construed to prevent the Legislature of this Commonwealth from making such alterations in the government of the said university, as shall be conducive to its advantage, and the interest of the republic of letters, in as full a manner as might have been done by the Legislature of the late Province of the Massachusetts-Bay.

CHAPTER V.

SECTION II.

The Encouragement of Literature, &c.

WISDOM, and knowledge, as well as virtue, diffused generally among the body of the people, being necessary for the preservation of their rights and liberties; and as these depend on spreading the opportunities and advantages of education in the various parts of the country, and among the different orders of the people, it shall be the duty of legislatures and magistrates, in all future periods of this Commonwealth, to cherish the interests of literature and the sciences, and all seminaries of them; especially the university at Cambridge, public schools, and grammar schools in the towns; to encourage private societies and public institutions, rewards and immunities, for the promotion of agriculture, arts, sciences, commerce, trades, manufacturers, and a natural history of the country; to countenance and inculcate the principles of humanity and general benevolence, public and private charity, industry and frugality, honesty and punctuality in their dealings; sincerity, good humor, and all social affections, and generous sentiments among the people.

CHAPTER VI.

Oaths and Subscriptions; Incompatibility of and Exclusion from Officers; Pecuniary Qualifications; Commissions; Writs; Confirmation of Laws; Habeas Corpus; The Enacting Stile; Continuance of Officers; Provision for a future Revisal of the Constitution, &c.

Art. I. ANY person chosen Governor, Lieutenant-Governor, Counsellor, Senator, or Representative, and accepting the trust, shall, before he proceed to execute the duties of his place or office, make and subscribe the following declaration, viz. –

'I, A.B. do declare, that I believe the christian religion, and have a firm persuasion of its truth; and that I am seized and possessed, in my own right, of the property required by the Constitution as one qualification for the office or place to which I am elected.'

AND the Governor, Lieutenant-governor, and Counsellors, shall make and subscribe the said declaration, in the presence of the two

Houses of Assembly; and the Senators and Representatives first elected under this Constitution, before the President and five of the Council of the former Constitution, and forever afterwards before the Governor and Council for the time being.

AND every person chosen to either of the places or offices aforesaid, as also any person appointed or commissioned to any judicial, executive, military, or other office under the government, shall, before he enters on the discharge of the business of his place or office, take and subscribe the following declaration, and oaths or affirmations, viz. –

'I, A.B. do truly and sincerely acknowledge, profess, testify and declare, that the Commonwealth of Massachusetts is, and of right ought to be, a free, sovereign and independent State; and I do swear, that I will bear true faith and allegiance to the said Commonwealth, and that I will defend the same against traiterous conspiracies and all hostile attempts whatsoever: And that I do renounce and abjure all allegiance, subjection and obedience to the King, Queen or Government of Great-Britain, (as the case may be) and every other foreign power whatsoever: And that no foreign Prince, Person, Prelate, State or Potentate, hath, or ought to have, any jurisdiction, superiority, pre-eminence, authority, dispensing or other power, in any matter, civil ecclesiastical or spiritual, within this Commonwealth; except the authority and power which is or may be vested by their Constituents in the Congress of the United States: And I do further testify and declare, that no man or body of men hath or can have any right to absolve or discharge me from the obligation of this oath, declaration or affirmation; and that I do make this acknowledgment, profession, testimony, declaration, denial, renunciation and abjuration, heartily and truly, according to the common meaning and acceptation for the foregoing words, without any equivocation, mental evasion, or secret reservation whatsoever,

So help me GOD.'

'I, A.B. do solemnly swear and affirm that I will faithfully and impartially discharge and perform all the duties incumbent on me as ; according to the best of my abilities and understanding, agreeably to the rules and regulations of the Constitution, and the laws of this Commonwealth.

'So help me GOD.'

PROVIDED always, that when any person chosen or appointed as aforesaid, shall be of the denomination of the people called Quakers, and shall decline taking the said oaths, he shall make his affirmation in the foregoing forms, and subscribe the same, omitting the words '*I do swear,*' '*and abjure,*' '*oath or,*' '*and abjuration,*' in the first oath; and in the second oath, the words '*swear and,*' and in each of them the words '*So help me GOD,*' subjoining instead thereof, '*This I do under the pains and penalties of perjury.*'

AND the said oaths or affirmations shall be taken and subscribed by the Governor, Lieutenant-Governor, and Counsellors, before the President of the Senate, in the presence of the two Houses of Assembly; and by the Senators and Representatives first elected under this Constitution, before the President and five of the Council of the former Constitution; and forever afterwards before the Governor and Council for the time being: And by the residue of the officers aforesaid, before such persons and in such manner as from time to time shall be prescribed by the Legislature.

II. NO Governor, Lieutenant-Governor, or Judge of the supreme judicial court, shall hold any other office or place, under the authority of this Commonwealth, except such as by this Constitution they are admitted to hold, saving that the Judges of the said court may hold the offices of Justices of the Peace through the State; nor shall they hold any other place or office, or receive any pension or salary from any other State or government or Power whatever.

NO person shall be capable of holding or exercising at the same time, more than one of the following offices within this state, viz. – Judge of Probate – Sheriff – Register of Probate – or Register of Deeds – and never more than any two offices which are to be held by appointment of the Governor, or the Governor and Council, or the Senate, or the House of Representatives, or by the election of the people of the State at large, or of the people of any county, military offices and the offices of Justice of the Peace excepted, shall be held by one person.

NO person holding the office of Judge of the supreme judicial court – Secretary – Attorney-General – Solicitor-General – Treasurer or Receiver-General – Judge of Probate – Commissary-General – President, Professor, or Instructor of Harvard-College – Sheriff – Clerk of the House of Representatives – Register of Probate – Register of Deeds – Clerk of the Supreme Judicial Court – Clerk of the Inferior Court of Common Pleas – or Officer of the Customs, including in this description Naval-Officers – shall at the same time have a seat in the Senate or House of Representatives; but their being chosen or appointed to, & accepting the same, shall operate as a resignation of their seat in the Senate or House of Representatives; and the place so vacated shall be filled up.

AND the same rule shall take place in case any Judge of the said Supreme Judicial Court, or Judge of Probate, shall accept a seat in Council; or any Counsellor shall accept of either of those offices or places.

AND no person shall ever be admitted to hold a seat in the Legislature, or any office of trust or importance under the government of this Commonwealth, who shall, in the due course of law, have been convicted of bribery or corruption in obtaining an election or appointment.

III. IN all cases where sums of money are mentioned in this Constitution, the value thereof shall be computed in silver at six shillings and eight pence per ounce: And it shall be in the power of the Legislature from time to time to increase such qualifications, as to property, of the persons to be elected to offices, as the circumstances of the Commonwealth shall require.

IV. ALL commissions shall be in the name of the Commonwealth of Massachusetts, signed by the Governor and attested by the Secretary or his Deputy, and have the great seal of the Commonwealth affixed thereto.

V. ALL writs issuing out of the clerk's office in any of the courts of law, shall be in the name of the Commonwealth of Massachusetts: They shall be under the seal of the court from whence they issue: They shall bear test of the first Justice of the court to which they shall be returnable, who is not a party, and be signed by the clerk of such court.

VI. ALL the laws which have heretofore been adopted, used and approved in the Province, Colony or State of Massachusetts-Bay, and usually practised on in the courts of law, shall still remain and be in full force, until altered or repealed by the Legislature; such parts only excepted as are repugnant to the rights and liberties contained in this Constitution.

VII. THE privilege and benefit of the writ of habeas corpus shall be enjoyed in this Commonwealth in the most free, easy, cheap, expeditious and ample manner; and shall not be suspended by the Legislature, except upon the most urgent and pressing occasions, and for a limited time not exceeding twelve months.

VIII. THE enacting stile, in making and passing all acts, statutes and laws shall be – 'Be it enacted by the Senate and House of Representatives in General Court assembled, and by the authority of the same.'

IX. TO the end there may be no failure of justice or danger arise to the Commonwealth from a change of the Form of Government – all officers, civil and military, holding commissions under the government & people of Massachusetts-Bay in New England, and all other officers of the said government and people, at the time this Constitution shall take effect, shall have, hold, use, exercise and enjoy all the powers and authority to them granted or committed, until other persons shall be appointed in their stead: And all courts of law shall proceed in the execution of the business of their respective departments; and all the executive and legislative officers, bodies and powers shall continue in full force, in the enjoyment and exercise of all their trusts, employments and authority; until the General Court and the supreme and executive officers under this Constitution are designated and invested with their respective trusts, powers and authority.

X. IN order the more effectually to adhere to the principles of the Constitution, and to correct those violations which by any means may be made therein, as well as to form such alterations as from experience shall be found necessary – the General Court which shall be in the year of our Lord one thousand seven hundred and ninety-five, shall issue precepts to the Selectmen of the several towns, and to the assessors of the unincorporated plantations, directing them to convene the qualified voters of their respective towns and plantations for the purpose of collecting their sentiments on the necessity or expediency of revising the Constitution, in order to amendments.

AND if it shall appear by the returns made, that two thirds of the qualified voters throughout the State, who shall assemble and vote in consequence of the said precepts, are in favour of such revision or amendment, the General Court shall issue precepts, or direct them to be issued from the Secretary's office to the several towns to elect delegates to meet in Convention for the purpose aforesaid.

THE said delegates to be chosen in the same manner and proportion as their Representatives in the second branch of the Legislature are by this Constitution to be chosen.

XI. THIS form of government shall be enrolled on parchment and deposited in the Secretary's office, and be a part of the laws of the land – and printed copies thereof shall be prefixed to the book containing the laws of this Commonwealth, in all future editions of the said laws.

JAMES BOWDOIN, *President* of the Convention.

Attest,

SAMUEL BARRETT, Secretary.

The Ratification of the Constitution of 1780: The Return of Boston, May 12, 1780, Boston Town Records, 1778–1783, 129–35

Wednesday May 10th. 9. O. Clock Forenoon – Met according to Adjournment

The Committee to whom was referred the consideration of the third Article in the Declaration of Rights – Reported the same with such alterations as they Judged most consonant to the Sense of the Town and is as follows – Vizt.

As the Happiness of a People and the Good Order; and Preservation of civil Government essentially depends upon Piety, religion and morality; and as these cannot be generally deffused through a Community, but by the Publick Worship of God, and Publick Instructions in Piety religion and morality, Therefore to promote their happiness and to secure the good order and preservation of their Government the People of this Commonwealth have a right to invest their Legislative with Power; to Authorize and require all the Inhabitants of this Commonwealth to make provision at their own expence for the Publick Worship of God and for the support and maintainance of Publick Protestant teachers of Piety, Religion and Morality who have not made such provision voluntary, or who have not made voluntary provision for some other Publick religious Teacher or for the support of some other Publick Worship within their commonwealth – And the several Towns Parishes Precincts and other Bodies politick or religious societies shall at all times have the exclusive right of electing their Publick teachers and of contracting with them for their support and maintainance; provided nevertheless that the minority of such Towns, Parishes Precincts and other Bodies Politick or religious Societies shall not be bound by the voice of the Majority in their electing their Publick Teachers or contracting with them for their support, but such Minority may if they see fit elect some other publick religious Teacher and Support him And all Monies Assessed upon the Subject for the support Of Publick Worship and of Publick religious

Teachers shall if he requires it be uniformely Applied to the support of the Publick Worship which he may chuse to support: provided however that such Teachers shall bonafide receive the same to his own Use Otherwise such sum shall be appropriated to the use of the Poor of any Parish or religious society that such Subject shall chuse if he makes his Election within twelve Months, and if not it shall be applied to the support of the Poor of the Parish or Precinct in which said Moneys were raised. And all Religious Sects and Denominations Whatsoever, demeaning themselves Peaceably and as good Subjects of the Commonwealth shall be equally under the Protection of Law – And no Subordination of any one Sect or denomination to another shall ever be established by Law

The foregoing Report having been read, it was moved, and Voted that a Question previous to the Report, being Acted upon. Vizt. Whether there shall be any thing further Added to the 2d. Article in the Declaration of Rights, which relates to Religion – And the Question being accordingly put – Passed in the Affermative, by a great Majority

The said Report being again taken up Paragraph by Paragraph – and amended the same was Accepted by the Town

It was moved and Voted that when this Meeting shall be Adjourned it be to 4. O.Clock P:M:

Moved that a Committee be appointed to bring in an Article in addition to the Article in the 43 Page – but the Motion was withdrawn

Adjourned to 4: O.Clock P:M:

4: O:Clock : P:M: Met according to Adjournment

It was moved and carried that the foregoing Clauses be added to the Report of the Committee on the 3d. Article in the Declaration of Rights Vizt. – The foregoing however is not to be so construed as to Nullify or infring any express voluntary Contract that hath been entered into between any Person or Persons, or any Town Parish, Precinct or Body of Men on the one Part and any Teacher or Minister of Religion on the other

The aforegoing Report of the Committee of the Committee [*sic*] on the 3d. Article, which had been accepted paragraph by paragraph – was put in the whole as amended – when it appeared that Four hundred and twenty were for accepting the Report – and one hundred and Forty against Receiving it

A Motion was then made that if the amendments proposed by the Town cannot be obtained by their Delegates, that they then shall be and hereby are Instructed to Vote for the 3d. Article in the Declaration of Rights, as it stands in the Form laid before the People – rather than the Article, should be lost at the next Meeting of the Convention – And the Question being put – it appeared that two hundred and seventy seven were in faviour of the Motion, and one hundred and forty against it

On a Motion, Voted, to appoint a Committee to draw up the reasons for the proposed Alterations in some Articles of the Frame of a Constitution presented by the Convention; and to draught Instructions to our Delegates in the said Convention

Voted, that Perez Morton Esqr.
Mr Samuel Eliot
William Tudor Esqr.
Mr John Sweetser
Mr Thomas Walley

be a Committee for the Purpose aforesaid

Adjourned to Fryday next. 3 O: Clock P: M:

Fryday May 12. 3 O: Clock P: M: met according to Adjourment

Mr Morton had leave to withdraw his dissent to the passing the Article which relates to the mode of electing Senators

The Preamble to the Constitution or Form of Government for the Commonwealth of Massachusetts, again read – whereupon the Question was put – Vizt. Whether the Town do approve and accept of the Same – passed in the Affermative

The Committee appointed to draw up reasons for the proposed alterations in some Articles of the Constitution or Form of Goverment laid before the Town, and also to draught Instruction to our Delagates in the Convention – Report as follows – Vizt. Gentlemen

The Town of Boston have Convened in a legal Meeting to consider the Constitution or Forms of Goverment agreed on by the Convention, & by them proposed to the People for their Approbation, rejection, or amendment, having had the same repeatedly read proposed to a discussion of the Several Articles theirein contained and having recommended amendments in the 16th. Article of the Declaration of Rights, in the 7th. Article of the 2d. Chapter in the 4th. Section of the 2d. Chapter & in the 7th. Article of the 6th. Chapter unanimously voted to accept said Constitution or Form of Goverment with the Amendments, the third Article in the Declaration of Rights excepted, provided by the most Strenious endeavours of their Delegates the said Amendments can be procured, otherwise to accept the said Articles as they were agreed to by the Convention, But the 3d. Article in the Declaration of Rights was refered to futer consideration; the meeting then consisting of eight hundred and eighty seven Voters – The Town then proceeded to consider the 3d. Article; which having been largely debated, was amended and Voted, 420 for & 51 against it. It was then moved and seconded, that if you could not obtain this Article as amended, you should be impowered to Vote for The 3d. Article as it originally stood rather than the Amendment should be the Means of postponing the establishment of the Constitution at the next Meeting of the Convention; as some Form was necessary to give Stability and force to Goverment. The Question being put the numbers were 277 for and 140 against it. Your utmost exertions are nevertheless earnestly enjoined to obtain the Amendments. A principle of respect to a Body of Men of such distinguished rank and Ability as the Convention would not assuredly have led the Town to Assign the reasons for any alterations they might make in a system they had formed and recommended. But as the Convention have requested the doing it, it is now to be performed on a higher Principle. In general it may be Observed that the Amendments proposed were made upon the idea that they would more effectually subserve the excuse of Civil and Religious Liberty, that great object of our endeavours, and the point to which all our efforts ought to tend, The Amendment of 16th. April [Article] of the Declerations of Rights, was made upon the strongest persuation, that Liberty of Speech, as it respected publick Men in their publick Conduct, was an essential and darling right of every member of a free State upon which in a very emenent Degree the preservation of their other reights depends; that nothing spoken with design to give information of the State of the Publick should be ever subject to the smalest restraint; and that any Attempt to oppose such restraint ought to excite an alarm in the People as it infered a consciousness of demerit on the part of those Attempting That such restraint was more degrading and more Strongly marked the Slaves than ever the privation of the Liberty of the Press; and that the latter, so absolutely necessary, and therefore so justly dear to every free State could not be maintained in its full force and vigour without the former. But while we hold up the Liberty of the Press, as essentially necessary to general Freedom, as it respects publick Men and Measures we reject with Abhorrence the idea of its abuse to the injury of private Characters. – The next amendment gives Power to the Governor, in the recess of the General Court, to march or transport, the Inhabitants of this State for the relief of a Neighbouring State invaded or threatened with immediate invation. This was judged incumbent on the general Principles of humanity, and absolutely necessary upon the Principles of Policy, A threatn'd invastion may be wholly prevented by the early appearance of a respectable Military force and Invation actually begun may be easally repeled, in many Instances by an immediate Opposition. In the former case, the Lives & Property of our Friends & Neighbours may be entirely saved & Secured; and in the Latter case fewer lives may be lost In all Probability, and less Property Destroyed, Besides delay may give oppertunity to an Enemy (so disposed) to take Post, and establish himself in such a manner as would require a very great force to remove him while an early force might be adequate to his immediate expulsion. Further the withholding immediate aid, may open a passage into our own State, and to bring the War to our own doors. – It was also suggested, that the Article, of Confederation bound us to grant immediate relief, which can only be Obtained by Vesting the Governor with such power, and was therefore Voted, – The next amendements respects the time of service of the Commissary General which is proposed to be limited to the Term of Five years. This was done because it was apprehended that a change or relation of Officers was necessary, in general to the preservation of Freedom. Persons longe in Office are apt to lose that sence of Dependance upon the People, which is essential to keep them within the Line of duty to the Publick. And especially may the good of the Community be promoted by the retirements of such Persons from Office at certain fixed periods, who have been largely intrusted with Publick Money or Stores – The next Article respects that important Write of Habeas Corpus. Many Reasons might be given for the Alterations made. It was judged best to confir the Suspension of this security of personal Liberty or freedom from Imprisonments to times of War, invation and rebellion, the terms urgent and pressing occations, being too indefinite and giving scope to the most powerfull Engine of Despotism, and Slavery. It was not conceived that any cause could possibly exist in time of peace, that could justify imprisonments without allegation or charge; and the granting a power in a season of tranquility liable to such gross abuse, and which might be attend with consequences destructive of the dearest priviledges and best interest of the Subject was deemed incompatable with every Principle of Liberty. Nay it was apprehended that it might Opperate as an incentive to Despotism; and to hold up a temtation to Tyranny while human Nature is constituted as we find it was judged to be wholy inexpedient. Confineing the suspencion won in time of War, invation and rebellion, to Six Months, was supposed a proper Limetation, as every purpose of an honest Goverment might be fully answered, in that period. A larger pereod might lead to a State of forgetfullness of the unhappy Subject of Suspission, and he might Drag on a Wretched being in the Dark abode of a Dungion, or within the gloomy walls of a Prison, without a Single Ray of hope to enlighten his cell or a single Friend to chear his Desponding spirit. Thus may his dreadfull Confinement when the Reason that operated to his Commitment have been long done away. Can a Power pregrant with such mighty Evils be too Strongly guarded; Or can we be too solicetious to confine it within the narrow limits that will comport with the Publick safety? – The only Article now to be attended to is the third in the Decleration of Rights, which Asserts that Piety, Religion and morality are essential to the happiness, Peace and Good order of a People and that these Principles are diffused by the Publick Instructions &c – and in Consequence makes provision for their support. The alterations proposed here which you will Lay before the Convention were designed to Secure the Reights of Consience and to give the fullest Scope to religious Liberty In support of the proposition it urged that if Publick Worship and Publick teaching, did certainly (as was allowed) defuse a general Sence of Duty & moral Obligations, and, so secured the safety of our Persons and Properties, we ought chearfully to pay those from whose agency we derived such Advantages. But we are Attempting to support (it is said) the Kingdom of Christ; It may as well be said we are supporting the Kingdom of God, by institution of a Civil Goverment, which Declared to be an Ordinance to the Deity, and so refuse to pay the civil magistrate. What will be the consequence of such refusal – The greatest disorders, if not a Dissolution of Society. Suspend all provision for the inculation of Morality, religion and Piety, and confusion & every evil work may be justly dreaded; for it is found that with all the Restraints of religion induced by the Preaching of Ministers, and with all the Restraints of Goverment inforced by civil Law, the World is far from being as quiet an abode as might be wished. Remove the former by ceasing to support Morality, religion and Piety and it will be soon felt that human Laws were feble barriers opposed to the uninformed lusts of Passions of Mankind. But though we are not supporting the kingdom of Christ may we not be permitted to Assist civil society by an addoption, and by the teaching of the best set of Morals that were ever offered to the World. To Object to these Morrals, or even to the Piety and Religion we aim to inculcate, because they are drawn from the Gospel, must appear very singular to an Assembly generally professing themselves Christians. Were this really our intention, no Objection ought to be made to it provided, as in fact the case that equal Liberty is granted to every religious Sect and Denomination Whatever, and it is only required that every Man should pay to the support of Publick Worship In his own way. But should any be so Conscientious that they cannot pay to the support of any of the various denominations among us they may then alott their Money to the support of the Poor – It remains only to fix the time when this Form of Goverment shall take place; But having had large experience of your Ability and Zeal in the course of the very lengthy Session of Convention, the last Winter we very Chearfully leave the Determination of this point to that prudence, Judgement and Integrity, which have so strongly marked your conduct in this Department and to the united Wisdom of the whole Body.

The foregoing Report of the Committee having been read and considered – the Question was put – Vizt. 'Whether the same shall be accepted, by the Town' – Passed in the Affermative, almost unanimously

The Resolves of the Convention, passed the 2d. March having been read and considered – whereupon

Voted, almost unanimously that the Selectmen of this Town be directed to transmit to the Secretary of the Convention the doings of this Town relative to the Form of Government agreeable to the Resolves of Convention; in order, to the Secretary of Convention laying the same before a Committee to be appointed for the purpose of examining and Arranging them for the Rivision and consideration of the Convention at the Adjournment; with the Number of Voters on each side of every Question, in order that the said Convention at the Adjournment may Collect the general sense of their Constituents on the several parts of the proposed Constitution; and if it do not appear to be two thirds, of their Constituents in faviour thereof, that the

Convention may alter it in such a manner as that it may be Agreeable to the sentiments of two thirds of the Voters throughout the State, also

Voted, almost unanimousley the Delegates of this Town be and hereby are impowered at the next Session of the Convention; to agree upon a time when this Form of Government shall take Place without returning the same again to the People: Provided that two thirds of the Male Inhabitants of the Age of twenty one years and upwards, Voting in the Several Towns and Plantations Meeting, shall agree to the Same, or the Convention shall conform it to the Sentements of two thirds of the People as aforesaid

A Motion made, that this Meeting be now dessolved

And the Meeting was accordingly dissolved.

III Virginia

4.III.1 THE VIRGINIA BILL OF RIGHTS, JUNE 12, 1776

Laws of Virginia, ed. W. W. Hening, IX 110

At a General Convention of Delegates and Representatives, from the several counties and corporations of Virginia, held at the Capitol in the City of Williamsburg on Monday the 6th May 1776.

A Declaration of Rights made by the representatives of the good people of Virginia, assembled in full and free Convention; which rights do pertain to them and their posterity, as the basis and foundation of government.

1. That all men are by nature equally free and independent, and have certain inherent rights, of which, when they enter into a state of society, they cannot by any compact deprive or divest their posterity; namely, the enjoyment of life and liberty, with the means of acquiring and possessing property, and pursuing and obtaining happiness and safety.

2. That all power is vested in, and consequently derived from, the people; that magistrates are their trustees and servants, and at all times amenable to them.

3. That government is, or ought to be instituted for the common benefit, protection, and security of the people, nation, or community; of all the various modes and forms of government, that is best which is capable of producing the greatest degree of happiness and safety, and is most effectually secured against the danger of maladministration; and that when any government shall be found inadequate or contrary to these purposes, a majority of the community hath an indubitable, unalienable and indefeasible right to reform, alter or abolish it, in such manner as shall be judged most conducive to the public weal.

4. That no man, or set of men, are entitled to exclusive or separate emoluments or privileges from the community, but in consideration of publick services; which, not being descendible, neither ought the offices of magistrate, legislator or judge to be hereditary.

5. That the legislative and executive powers of the state should be separate and distinct from the judiciary; and that the members of the two first may be restrained from oppression, by feeling and participating

the burthens of the people, they should, at fixed periods, be reduced to a private station, return into that body from which they were originally taken, and the vacancies be supplied by frequent, certain, and regular elections, in which all, or any part of the former members to be again eligible or ineligible, as the laws shall direct.

6. That elections of members to serve as representatives of the people in assembly, ought to be free; and that all men having sufficient evidence of permanent common interest with, and attachment to the community, have the right of suffrage, and cannot be taxed or deprived of their property for publick uses, without their own consent, or that of their representatives so elected, nor bound by any law to which they have not, in like manner, assented for the public good.

7. That all power of suspending laws, or the execution of laws, by any authority without consent of the representatives of the people, is injurious to their rights, and ought not to be exercised.

8. That in all capital or criminal prosecutions a man hath a right to demand the cause and nature of his accusation, to be confronted with the accusers and witnesses, to call for evidence in his favour, and to a speedy trial by an impartial jury of his vicinage, without whose unanimous consent he cannot be found guilty; nor can he be compelled to give evidence against himself; that no man be deprived of his liberty, except by the law of the land or the judgment of his peers.

9. That excessive bail ought not to be required, nor excessive fines imposed, nor cruel and unusual punishments inflicted.

10. That general warrants, whereby an officer or messenger may be commanded to search suspected places without evidence of a fact committed, or to seize any person or persons not named, or whose offence is not particularly described and supported by evidence, are grievous and oppressive, and ought not to be granted.

11. That in controversies respecting property, and in suits between man and man, the ancient trial by jury is preferable to any other, and ought to be held sacred.

12. That the freedom of the press is one of the great bulwarks of liberty, and can never be restrained but by despotick governments.

13. That a well-regulated militia, composed of the body of the people trained to arms, is the proper, natural and safe defence of a free state; that standing armies in time of peace should be avoided as dangerous to liberty; and that in all cases the military should be under strict subordination to, and governed by, the civil power.

14. That the people have a right to uniform government; and, therefore, that no government separate from, or independent of the government of Virginia, ought to be erected or established within the limits thereof.

15. That no free government, or the blessings of liberty, can be preserved to any people, but by a firm adherence to justice, moderation, temperance, frugality and virtue, and by frequent recurrence to fundamental principles.

16. That religion, or the duty which we owe to our Creator, and the manner of discharging it, can be directed only by reason and conviction, not by force or violence; and therefore all men are equally entitled to the free exercise of religion, according to the dictates of conscience; and that it is the mutual duty of all to practise Christian forbearance, love, and charity towards each other.

4.III.2 THE CONSTITUTION OF VIRGINIA, JUNE 29, 1776

Laws of Virginia, ed. W. W. Hening, IX 117

The Constitution, or Form of Government, agreed to and resolved upon by the Delegates and Representatives of the several counties and corporations of Virginia.

1. WHEREAS George the third [a digest of the Declaration of Independence follows].... By which several acts of misrule, the government of this country, as formerly exercised under the crown of Great Britain, is TOTALLY DISSOLVED.

2. WE, the Delegates and Representatives of the good people of Virginia, having maturely considered the premises, and viewing with great concern the deplorable conditions to which this once happy country must be reduced, unless some regular adequate mode of civil polity is speedily adopted, and in compliance with a recommendation of the General Congress, do ordain and declare the future form of government of Virginia to be as followeth:

3. The legislative, executive, and judiciary departments shall be separate and distinct, so that neither exercise the powers properly belonging to the other: nor shall any person exercise the powers of

more than one of them at the same time; except that the justices of the county courts shall be eligible to either House of Assembly.

4. The legislative shall be formed of two distinct branches, who, together, shall be a complete Legislature. They shall meet once, or oftener, every year, and shall be called the GENERAL ASSEMBLY OF VIRGINIA.

5. One of these shall be called the HOUSE OF DELEGATES, and consist of two representatives, to be chosen for each county, and for the district of West-Augusta, annually, of such men as actually reside in, and are freeholders of the same, or duly qualified according to law, and also of one delegate or representative to be chosen annually for the city of Williamsburg, and one for the borough of Norfolk, and a representative for each of such other cities and boroughs, as may hereafter be allowed particular representation by the legislature; but when any city or borough shall so decrease as that the number of persons having right of suffrage therein shall have been for the space of seven years successively less than half the number of voters in some one county in Virginia, such city or borough thenceforward shall cease to send a delegate or representative to the Assembly.

6. The other shall be called the SENATE, and consist of twenty-four members, of whom thirteen shall constitute a House to proceed on business; for whose election the different counties shall be divided into twenty-four districts, and each county of the respective district, at the time of the election of its delegates, shall vote for one Senator, who is actually a resident and freeholder within the district, or duly qualified according to law, and is upwards of twenty-five years of age; and the Sheriffs of each county, within five days at farthest after the last county election in the district, shall meet at some convenient place, and from the poll so taken in their respective counties return as a Senator the man who shall have the greatest number of votes in the whole district. To keep up this Assembly by rotation, the districts shall be equally divided into four classes and numbered by lot. At the end of one year after the general election, the six members elected by the first division shall be displaced, and the vacancies thereby occasioned supplied from such class or division, by new election, in the manner aforesaid. This rotation shall be applied to each division, according to its number, and continued in due order annually.

7. The right of suffrage in the election of members for both Houses shall remain as exercised at present, and each House shall choose its

own speaker, appoint its own officers, settle its own rules of proceeding, and direct writs of election, for the supplying intermediate vacancies.

8. All laws shall originate in the House of Delegates, to be approved or rejected by the Senate, or to be amended with consent of the House of Delegates; except money bills, which in no instance shall be altered by the Senate, but wholly approved or rejected.

9. A Governour, or chief magistrate, shall be chosen annually, by joint ballot of both Houses to be taken in each House respectively, deposited in the conference room, the boxes examined jointly by a committee of each House, and the numbers severally reported to them, that the appointments may be entered (which shall be the mode of taking the joint ballot of both Houses, in all cases) who shall not continue in that office longer than three years successively, nor be eligible until the expiration of four years after he shall have been out of that office. An adequate, but moderate salary shall be settled on him, during his continuance in office; and he shall, with the advice of a Council of State, exercise the executive powers of government according to the laws of this Commonwealth; and shall not, under any pretence, exercise any power or prerogative by virtue of any law, statute or custom of England. But he shall, with the advice of the Council of State, have the power of granting reprieves or pardons, except where the prosecution shall have been carried on by the House of Delegates, or the law shall otherwise particularly direct; in which cases, no reprieve or pardon shall be granted, but by resolve of the House of Delegates.

10. Either House of the General Assembly may adjourn themselves respectively. The Governour shall not prorogue or adjourn the Assembly during their sitting, nor dissolve them at any time; but he shall, if necessary, either by advice of the Council of State, or on application of a majority of the House of Delegates, call them before the time to which they shall stand prorogued or adjourned.

11. A Privy Council, or Council of State, consisting of eight members, shall be chosen by joint ballot of both Houses of Assembly, either from their own members or the people at large, to assist in the administration of government. They shall annually choose, out of their own members, a president, who, in case of death, inability, or absence of the Governour from the government, shall act as Lieutenant-Governour. Four members shall be sufficient to act, and their advice and proceedings shall be entered on record, and signed by the members present (to any part whereof, any member may enter his dissent)

to be laid before the General Assembly, when called for by them. This Council may appoint their own clerk, who shall have a salary settled by law, and take an oath of secrecy in such matters as he shall be directed by the board to conceal. A sum of money appropriated to that purpose shall be divided annually among the members, in proportion to their attendance; and they shall be incapable, during their continuance in office, of sitting in either House of Assembly. Two members shall be removed, by joint ballot of both Houses of Assembly, at the end of every three years, and be ineligible for the three next years. These vacancies, as well as those occasioned by death or incapacity, shall be supplied by new elections, in the same manner.

12. The Delegates for Virginia to the Continental Congress shall be chosen annually, or superseded in the meantime by joint ballot of both Houses of Assembly.

13. The present militia officers shall be continued, and vacancies supplied by appointment of the Governour, with the advice of the Privy Council, on recommendations from the respective county courts; but the Governour and Council shall have a power of suspending any officer, and ordering a court-martial, on complaint of misbehaviour or inability, or to supply vacancies of officers, happening when in actual service. The Governour may embody the militia, with the advice of the Privy Council; and when embodied, shall alone have the direction of the militia, under the laws of the country.

14. The two Houses of Assembly shall, by joint ballot, appoint Judges of the Supreme Court of Appeals, and General Court, Judges in Chancery, Judges of Admiralty, Secretary, and the Attorney-General, to be commissioned by the Governour, and continue in office during good behaviour. In case of death, incapacity, or resignation, the Governour, with the advice of the Privy Council, shall appoint persons to succeed in office, to be approved or displaced by both Houses. These officers shall have fixed and adequate salaries, and, together with all others holding lucrative offices, and all ministers of the Gospel of every denomination, be incapable of being elected members of either House of Assembly or the Privy Council.

15. The Governour, with the advice of the Privy Council, shall appoint Justices of the Peace for the counties; and in case of vacancies, or a necessity of increasing the number hereafter, such appointments to be made upon the recommendation of the respective county courts. The present acting Secretary in Viriginia, and clerks of all the county

courts, shall continue in office. In case of vacancies, either by death, incapacity, or resignation, a Secretary shall be appointed as before directed, and the clerks by the respective courts. The present and future clerks shall hold their offices during good behaviour, to be judged of and determined in the General Court. The sheriffs and coroners shall be nominated by the respective courts, approved by the Governour, with the advice of the Privy Council, and commissioned by the Governour. The Justices shall appoint Constables; and all fees of the aforesaid officers be regulated by law.

16. The Governour, when he is out of office, and others offending against the State, either by mal-administration, corruption, or other means by which the safety of the State may be endangered, shall be impeachable by the House of Delegates. Such impeachment to be prosecuted by the Attorney-General, or such other person or persons as the House may appoint in the General Court, according to the laws of the land. If found guilty, he or they shall be either forever disabled to hold any office under government, or be removed from such office *pro tempore*, or subjected to such pains or penalties as the law shall direct.

17. If all or any of the Judges of the General Court should on good grounds (to be judged of by the House of Delegates) be accused of any of the crimes or offences before mentioned, such House of Delegates may, in like manner, impeach the Judge or Judges so accused, to be prosecuted in the Court of Appeals; and he or they, if found guilty, shall be punished in the same manner as is prescribed in the preceding clause.

18. Commissions and grants shall run, *In the name of the* COMMONWEALTH *of* VIRGINIA, and bear test by the Governour, with the seal of the Commonwealth annexed. Writs shall run in the same manner, and bear test by the clerks of the several courts. Indictments shall conclude, *Against the peace and dignity of the Commonwealth.*

19. A Treasurer shall be appointed annually, by joint ballot of both Houses.

20. All escheats, penalties, and forfeitures, heretofore going to the King, shall go to the Commonwealth, save only such as the Legislature may abolish, or otherwise provide for.

21. The territories, contained within the Charters, erecting the Colonies of Maryland, Pennsylvania, North and South Carolina, are hereby ceded, released, and forever confirmed, to the people of these

Colonies respectively, with all the rights of property, jurisdiction and government, and all other rights whatsoever, which might, at any time heretofore, have been claimed by Virginia, except the free navigation and use of the rivers Potowmack and Pokomoke, with the property of the Virginia shores or strands bordering on either of the said rivers, and all improvements which have been, or shall be made thereon. The western and northern extent of Virginia shall in all other respects, stand as fixed by the Charter of King James the First in the year one thousand six hundred and nine, and by the publick treaty of peace between the courts of Britain and France, in the year one thousand seven hundred and sixty-three; unless by act of this legislature, one or more governments be established westward of the Allegheny mountains. And no purchases of lands shall be made of the Indian natives, but on behalf of the publick, by authority of the General Assembly.

22. In order to introduce this government, the representatives of the people met in Convention shall choose a Governour and Privy Council, also such other officers directed to be chosen by both Houses as may be judged necessary to be immediately appointed. The Senate to be first chosen by the people to continue until the last day of March next, and the other officers until the end of the succeeding session of Assembly. In cases of vacancies, the speaker of either House shall issue writs for new elections.

IV Pennsylvania

4 THE PENNSYLVANIA CONSTITUTION OF 1776

Federal and State Constitutions, ed. F. N. Thorpe (Washington, 1909) v 3081–92

The Constitution of the Commonwealth of Pennsylvania as established by the general convention elected for that purpose, and held at Philadelphia, 15 July 1776, and continued by adjournment, to 28 September 1776.

WHEREAS all government ought to be instituted and supported for the security and protection of the community as such, and to enable the individuals who compose it to enjoy their natural rights, and the other blessings which the author of existence has bestowed upon man; and whenever these great ends of government are not obtained, the people have a right by common consent to change it, and take such measures as to them may appear necessary to promote their safety and happiness. AND WHEREAS the inhabitants of this Commonwealth have, in consideration of protection only, heretofore acknowledged allegiance to the king of Great Britain; and the said king has not only withdrawn that protection, but commenced and still continues to carry on, with unabated vengeance, a most cruel and unjust war against them, employing therein not only the troops of Great Britain, but foreign mercenaries, savages and slaves, for the avowed purpose of reducing them to a total and abject submission to the despotic domination of the British Parliament (with many other acts of tyranny, more fully set forth in the Declaration of Congress) whereby all allegiance and fealty to the said king and his successors are dissolved and at an end, and all power and authority derived from him ceased in these colonies. AND WHEREAS it is absolutely necessary for the welfare and safety of the inhabitants of said colonies, that they be henceforth free and independent States, and that just, permanent and proper forms of government exist in every part of them, derived from and founded on the authority of the people only, agreeably to the directions of the honourable American Congress. WE, the representatives of the freemen of Pennsylvania, in general convention met, for the express purpose of framing such a government, confessing the goodness of the great Governour of the universe (who alone knows to what degree of earthly happiness mankind may attain by perfecting the arts of government) in permitting the people of this State, by common consent, and without violence, deliberately to form for themselves such just rules as they shall think best for governing their future society; and being fully convinced that it is our indispensible duty to establish such original principles of government as will best promote the general happiness of the people of this State and their posterity, and provide for future improvements, without partiality for or prejudice against any particular class, sect, or denomination of men whatever, do, by virtue of the authority vested in us by our constituents, ordain, declare and establish the following *Declaration of Rights* and *Frame of Government*, to be the Constitution of this Commonwealth, and to remain in force therein for ever unaltered, except in such articles as shall hereafter, on experience, be found to require improvement, and which shall by the same authority of the people, fairly delegated as this frame of government directs, be amended or improved for the more effectual obtaining and securing the great end and design of all government, herein before mentioned.

CHAPTER I

A Declaration of the Rights of the Inhabitants of the Commonwealth or State of Pennsylvania.[1]

I. [Virginia Bill of Rights, s. 1.]

II. That all men have a natural and unalienable right to worship Almighty God, according to the dictates of their own consciences and understanding; and that no man ought or of right can be compelled to attend any religious worship, or erect or support any place of worship, or maintain any ministry contrary to, or against, his own free will and consent; nor can any man, who acknowledges the being of a God, be justly deprived or abridged of any civil right as a citizen, on account of his religious sentiments or peculiar mode of religious worship; and that no authority can, or ought to be vested in, or assumed by any power whatever, that shall in any case interfere with, or in any manner controul the right of conscience in the free exercise of religious worship.

[1] Sections of the same purport as clauses of the Virginia Bill of Rights are replaced by a reference to that document.

III. That the people of this State have the sole, exclusive and inherent right of governing and regulating the internal police of the same.

IV. [Virginia, s. 2.]

V. [Virginia, s. 3.]

VI. [Virginia, s. 5.]

VII. [Virginia, s. 6.]

VIII. That every member of society hath a right to be protected in the enjoyment of life, liberty, and property, and therefore is bound to contribute his proportion towards the expense of that protection, and yield his personal service when necessary, or an equivalent thereto; but no part of a man's property can be justly taken from him, or applied to public uses, without his own consent or that of his legal representatives: Nor can any man who is conscientiously scrupulous of bearing arms be justly compelled thereto, if he will pay such equivalent; nor are the people bound by any laws, but such as they have in like manner assented to, for their common good.

IX. [Virginia, s. 8.]

X. [Virginia, s. 10.]

XI. [Virginia, s. 11.]

XII. That the people have a right to freedom of speech, and of writing, and publishing their sentiments; therefore the freedom of the press ought not to be restrained.

XIII. [Virginia, s. 13.]

XIV. [Virginia, s. 15.]

XV. That all men have a natural inherent right to emigrate from one State to another that will receive them, or to form a new State in vacant countries, or in such countries as they can purchase, whenever they think that thereby they may promote their own happiness.[1]

XVI. That the people have a right to assemble together, to consult for their common good, to instruct their representatives, and to apply to the legislature for redress of grievances, by address, petition, or remonstrance.

Plan or Frame of Government for the Commonwealth or State of Pennsylvania.

1. The Commonwealth or State of Pennsylvania shall be governed hereafter by an assembly of the representatives of the freemen of the

[1] [*Editor's note.*] S. E. Morison points out that this clause opposes the claim made in the Virginia Bill of Rights, section 14. Pennsylvania, unlike Virginia, had a defined Western boundary.

same, and a President and Council, in manner and form following –

2. The supreme legislative power shall be vested in a House of Representatives of the freemen of the Commonwealth or State of Pennsylvania.

3. The supreme executive power shall be vested in a President and Council.

4. Courts of justice shall be established in the city of Philadelphia, and in every county of this State.

5. The freemen of this Commonwealth and their sons shall be trained and armed for its defence, under such regulations, restrictions, and exceptions as the general assembly shall by law direct, preserving always to the people the right of choosing their colonels and all commissioned officers under that rank, in such manner and as often as by the said laws shall be directed.

6. Every freeman of the full age of twenty-one years, having resided in this State for the space of one whole year next before the day of election for Representatives, and paid public taxes during that time, shall enjoy the right of an elector: Provided always, that sons of freeholders of the age of twenty-one years shall be entitled to vote although they have not paid taxes.

7. The House of Representatives of the freemen of this Commonwealth shall consist of persons most noted for wisdom and virtue, to be chosen by the freemen of every city and county of this Commonwealth respectively, and no person shall be elected unless he has resided in the city or county for which he shall be chosen two years immediately before the said election, nor shall any member, while he continues such, hold any other office except in the militia.

8. No person shall be capable of being elected a member to serve in the House of Representatives of the freemen of this Commonwealth more than four years in seven.

9. The members of the House of Representatives shall be chosen annually by ballot, by the freemen of the Commonwealth, on the second Tuesday in October forever (except this present year), and shall meet on the fourth Monday of the same month, and shall be stiled, *The General Assembly of the Representatives of the Freemen of Pennsylvania*, and shall have power to choose their speaker, the treasurer of the State, and their other officers; sit on their own adjournments; prepare bills and enact them into laws; judge of the elections and qualifications of their own members; they may expel a member, but not a second time

for the same cause; they may administer oaths or affirmations on examination of witnesses; redress grievances; impeach state criminals; grant charters of incorporation; constitute towns, boroughs, cities, and counties; and shall have all other powers necessary for the legislature of a free state or commonwealth: but they shall have no power to add to, alter, abolish, or infringe any part of this Constitution.

10. A quorum of the House of Representatives shall consist of two-thirds of the whole number of members elected; and having met and chosen their speaker, shall each of them before they proceed to business take and subscribe as well the oath or affirmation of fidelity and allegiance hereinafter directed, as the following oath or affirmation, viz.:

'I——do swear (or affirm) that as a member of this Assembly, I will not propose or assent to any bill, vote, or resolution, which shall appear to me injurious to the people; nor do or consent to any act or thing whatever, that shall have a tendency to lessen or abridge their rights and privileges as declared in the Constitution of this State; but will in all things conduct myself as a faithful honest representative and guardian of the people, according to the best of my judgment and abilities.'

And each member, before he takes his seat, shall make and subscribe the following declaration, viz.:

'I do believe in one God, the Creator and Governour of the universe, the rewarder of the good and the punisher of the wicked, and I do acknowledge the Scriptures of the Old and New Testament to be given by Divine Inspiration.'

And no further or other religious test shall ever hereafter be required of any civil officer or magistrate in this State.

11. Delegates to represent this state in Congress shall be chosen by ballot by the future general assembly at their first meeting, and annually forever afterwards, as long as such representation shall be necessary. Any delegate may be superseded at any time, by the general assembly appointing another in his stead. No man shall sit in Congress longer than two years successively, nor be capable of re-election for three years afterwards; and no person who holds any office in the gift of the Congress shall hereafter be elected to represent this Commonwealth in Congress.

12. If any city or cities, county or counties shall neglect or refuse to elect and send Representatives to the General Assembly, two-thirds

of the members from the cities or counties that do elect and send Representatives, provided they be a majority of the cities and counties of the whole State, when met, shall have all the powers of the General Assembly, as fully and amply as if the whole were present.

13. The doors of the House in which the Representatives of the Freemen of this State shall sit in General Assembly, shall be and remain open for the admission of all persons who behave decently, except only when the welfare of this State may require the doors to be shut.

14. The votes and proceedings of the General Assembly shall be printed weekly during their sitting, with the yeas and nays, on any question, vote or resolution, where any two members require it, except when the vote is taken by ballot; and when the yeas and nays are so taken every member shall have a right to insert the reasons of his vote upon the minutes, if he desires it.

15. To the end that laws before they are enacted may be more maturely considered, and the inconvenience of hasty determinations as much as possible prevented, all bills of public nature shall be printed for the consideration of the people, before they are read in general assembly the last time for debate and amendment; and, except on occasions of sudden necessity, shall not be passed into laws until the next session of assembly; and for the more perfect satisfaction of the public, the reasons and motives for making such laws shall be fully and clearly expressed in the preambles.

16. The stile of the laws of this Commonwealth shall be, *Be it enacted, and it is hereby enacted by the Representatives of the Freemen of the Commonwealth of Pennsylvania in General Assembly met, and by the authority of the same.* And the General Assembly shall affix their seal to every bill, as soon as it is enacted into a law, which seal shall be kept by the assembly, and shall be called, THE SEAL OF THE LAWS OF PENNSYLVANIA, and shall not be used for any other purpose.

17. The city of Philadelphia and each county of this Commonwealth respectively, shall on the first Tuesday in November in this present year, and on the second Tuesday in October annually for the two next succeeding years, viz. the year 1777, and the year 1778, choose six persons to represent them in General Assembly. But as representation in proportion to the number of taxable inhabitants is the only principle which can at all times secure liberty, and make the voice of a majority of the people the law of the land; therefore the General Assembly shall cause complete lists of the taxable inhabitants

in the city and each county in the Commonwealth respectively, to be taken and returned to them, on or before the last meeting of the assembly elected in the year 1778, who shall appoint a representation to each, in proportion to the number of taxables in such returns; which representation shall continue for the next seven years afterwards, at the end of which, a new return of the taxable inhabitants shall be made, and a representation agreeable thereto appointed by the said Assembly, and so on septennially forever. The wages of the representatives in General Assembly and all other State charges shall be paid out of the State treasury.

18. In order that the Freemen of this Commonwealth may enjoy the benefit of election as equally as may be until the representation shall commence, as directed in the foregoing section, each county at his own choice may be divided into districts, hold elections therein, and elect their representatives in the county, and their other elective officers, as shall be hereafter regulated by the General Assembly of this State. And no inhabitant of this State shall have more than one annual vote at the general election for representatives in assembly.

19. For the present the Supreme Executive Council of this State shall consist of twelve persons chosen in the following manner. The freemen of the city of Philadelphia, and of the counties of Philadelphia, Chester, and Bucks., respectively, shall choose by ballot one person for the city, and one for each county aforesaid, to serve for three years and no longer, at the time and place for electing representatives in General Assembly. The freemen of the counties of Lancaster, York, Cumberland, and Berks., shall, in like manner elect one person for each county respectively, to serve as councillors for two years and no longer. And the counties of Northampton, Bedford, Northumberland and Westmoreland, respectively, shall, in like manner, elect one person for each county, to serve as councillors for one year, and no longer. And at the expiration of the time for which each councillor was chosen to serve, the freemen of the city of Philadelphia, and of the several counties in this state, respectively, shall elect one person to serve as councillor for three years and no longer; and so on every third year forever. By this mode of election and continual rotation, more men will be trained to public business, there will in every subsequent year be found in the Council a number of persons acquainted with the proceedings of the foregoing years, whereby the business will be more consistently conducted, and moreover the danger of establishing an inconvenient

aristocracy will be effectually prevented. All vacancies in the Council that may happen by death, resignation, or otherwise, shall be filled at the next general election for Representatives in General Assembly, unless a particular election for that purpose shall be sooner appointed by the President and Council. No member of the General Assembly or delegate in Congress, shall be chosen a member of the Council. The President and Vice-president shall be chosen annually by the joint ballot of the General Assembly and Council, of the members of the Council. Any person having served as a councillor for three successive years, shall be incapable of holding that office for four years afterwards. Every member of the Council shall be a justice of the peace for the whole Commonwealth, by virtue of his office.

In case new additional counties shall hereafter be erected in this State, such county or counties shall elect a councillor, and such county or counties shall be annexed to the next neighbouring counties, and shall take rotation with such counties.

The Council shall meet annually, at the same time and place with the General Assembly.

The treasurer of the state, trustees of the loan office, naval officers, collectors of customs or excise, judge of the admiralty, attornies general, sheriffs, and prothonotaries, shall not be capable of a seat in the General Assembly, Executive Council, or Continental Congress.

20. The President, and in his absence the Vice-president, with the Council, five of whom shall be a quorum, shall have power to appoint and commissionate judges, naval officers, judge of the admiralty, attorney-general, and all other officers, civil and military, except such as are chosen by the General Assembly or the people, agreeable to this Frame of Government, and the laws that may be made hereafter; and shall supply every vacancy in any office, occasioned by death, resignation, removal or disqualification, until the office can be filled in the time and manner directed by law or this Constitution. They are to correspond with other States, and transact business with the officers of government, civil and military; and to prepare such business as may appear to them necessary to lay before the General Assembly. They shall sit as judges, to hear and determine on impeachments, taking to their assistance for advice only, the Justices of the Supreme Court. And shall have power to grant pardons, and remit fines, in all cases whatsoever, except in cases of impeachment; and in cases of treason and murder, shall have power to grant reprieves, but not to

pardon, until the end of the next sessions of Assembly; but there shall be no remission or mitigation of punishments on impeachments, except by act of the Legislature; they are also to take care that the laws be faithfully executed; they are to expedite the execution of such measures as may be resolved upon by the General Assembly; and they may draw upon the treasury for such sums as shall be appropriated by the House: They may also lay embargoes, or prohibit the exportation of any commodity, for any time, not exceeding thirty days, in the recess of the House only: They may grant such licences, as shall be directed by law, and shall have power to call together the General Assembly when necessary, before the day to which they shall stand adjourned. The President shall be commander-in-chief of the forces of the State, but shall not command in person, except advised thereto by the Council, and then only so long as they shall approve thereof. The President and Council shall have a secretary, and keep fair books of their proceedings, wherein any councillor may enter his dissent, with his reasons in support of it.

21. All commissions shall be in the name, and by the authority of the Freemen of the Commonwealth of Pennsylvania, sealed with the State seal, signed by the President or Vice-president, and attested by the secretary; which seal shall be kept by the Council.

22. Every officer of state, whether judicial or executive, shall be liable to be impeached by the General Assembly, either when in office, or after his resignation or removal for mal-administration: All impeachments shall be before the President or Vice-president and Council, who shall hear and determine the same.

23. The Judges of the Supreme Court of Judicature shall have fixed salaries, be commissioned for seven years only, though capable of re-appointment at the end of that term, but removable for misbehaviour at any time by the General Assembly; they shall not be allowed to sit as members in the Continental Congress, executive council, or general assembly, nor to hold any other office civil or military, nor to take or receive fees or perquisites of any kind.

24. The Supreme Court, and the several courts of common pleas of this Commonwealth, shall, besides the powers usually exercised by such courts, have the powers of a court of chancery, so far as relates to the perpetuating testimony, obtaining evidence from places not within this state, and the care of the persons and estates of those who are *non compotes mentis*, and such other powers as may be found

necessary by future general assemblies, not inconsistent with this constitution.

25. Trials shall be by jury as heretofore: And it is recommended to the legislature of this State, to provide by law against every corruption or partiality in the choice, return, or appointment of juries.

26. Courts of sessions, common pleas, and orphans' courts shall be held quarterly in each city and county; and the legislature shall have power to establish all such other courts as they may judge for the good of the inhabitants of the State. All courts shall be open, and justice shall be impartially administered without corruption or unnecessary delay: All their officers shall be paid an adequate but moderate compensation for their services: And if any officer shall take greater or other fees than the law allows him, either directly or indirectly, it shall ever after disqualify him from holding any office in this State.

27. All prosecutions shall commence in the name and by the authority of the Freemen of the Commonwealth of Pennsylvania; and all indictments shall conclude with these words, *Against the peace and dignity of the same*. The style of all process hereafter in this State shall be, *The Commonwealth of Pennsylvania*.

28. The person of a debtor, where there is not a strong presumption of fraud, shall not be continued in prison, after delivering up, bona fide, all his estate real and personal, for the use of his creditors, in such manner as shall be hereafter regulated by law. All prisoners shall be bailable by sufficient sureties, unless for capital offences, when the proof is evident, or presumption great.

29. Excessive bail shall not be exacted for bailable offences: And all fines shall be moderate.

30. Justices of the peace shall be elected by the freeholders of each city and county respectively, that is to say, two or more persons may be chosen for each ward, township, or district, as the law shall hereafter direct: And their names shall be returned to the President in Council, who shall commissionate one or more of them for each ward, township, or district so returning, for seven years, removable for misconduct by the general assembly. But if any city or county, ward, township, or district in this Commonwealth, shall hereafter incline to change the manner of appointing their justices of the peace as settled in this article, the General Assembly may make laws to regulate the same, agreeable to the desire of a majority of the freeholders of the city or county, ward, township, or district so applying. No justice of the peace shall

sit in the General Assembly unless he first resigns his commission; nor shall he be allowed to take any fees, nor any salary or allowance, except such as the future legislature may grant.

31. Sheriffs and coroners shall be elected annually in each city and county, by the freemen; that is to say, two persons for each office, one of whom for each, is to be commissioned by the president in council. No person shall continue in the office of sheriff more than three successive years, or be capable of being again elected during four years afterwards. The election shall be held at the same time and place appointed for the election of representatives: And the commissioners and assessors, and other officers chosen by the people, shall also be then and there elected, as has been usual heretofore, until altered or otherwise regulated by the future legislature of this State.

32. All elections, whether by the people or in General Assembly, shall be by ballot, free and voluntary: And any elector who shall receive any gift or reward for his vote, in meat, drink, monies or otherwise, shall forfeit his right to elect for that time, and suffer such other penalties as future laws shall direct. And any person who shall directly or indirectly give, promise, or bestow any such rewards to be elected, shall be thereby rendered incapable to serve for the ensuing year.

33. All fees, licence money, fines and forfeitures heretofore granted, or paid to the governor, or his deputies for the support of government, shall hereafter be paid into the public treasury, unless altered or abolished by the future legislature.

34. A register's office for the probate of wills and granting letters of administration, and an office for the recording of deeds, shall be kept in each city and county; the officers to be appointed by the General Assembly, removable at their pleasure, and to be commissioned by the President in Council.

35. The printing presses shall be free to every person who undertakes to examine the proceedings of the legislature, or any part of government.

36. As every freeman to preserve his independence (if without a sufficient estate), ought to have some profession, calling, trade or farm, whereby he may honestly subsist, there can be no necessity for, nor use in establishing offices of profit, the usual effects of which are dependence and servility unbecoming freemen, in the possessors and expectants; faction, contention, corruption, and disorder among the

people: but if any man is called into public service, to the prejudice of his private affairs, he has a right to a reasonable compensation. And whenever an office, through increase of fees or otherwise, becomes so profitable as to occasion many to apply for it, the profits ought to be lessened by the Legislature.

37. The future Legislature by this State shall regulate intails in such a manner as to prevent perpetuities.

38. The penal laws as heretofore used shall be reformed by the future Legislature of this State, as soon as may be, and punishments made in some cases less sanguinary, and in general more proportionate to the crimes.

39. To deter more effectually from the commission of crimes, by continued visible punishments of long duration, and to make sanguinary punishments less necessary; houses ought to be provided for punishing by hard labour, those who shall be convicted of crimes not capital; wherein the criminals shall be imployed for the benefit of the public, or for reparation of injuries done to private persons: And all persons at proper times shall be admitted to see the prisoners at their labour.

40. Every officer, whether judicial, executive or military, in authority under this commonwealth, shall take the following oath or affirmation of allegiance, and general oath of office before he enters on the execution of his office:

'I—do swear (or affirm) that I will be true and faithful to the Commonwealth of Pennsylvania: And that I will not directly or indirectly do any act or thing prejudicial or injurious to the constitution or government thereof, as established by the convention.'

'I—do swear (or affirm) that I will faithfully execute the office of—for the—of—and will do equal right and justice to all men, to the best of my judgment and abilities, according to law,'

41. No public tax, custom, or contribution shall be imposed upon, or paid by the people of this State, except by a law for that purpose: And before any law be made for raising it, the purpose for which any tax is to be raised ought to appear clearly to the legislature to be of more service to the community than the money would be, if not collected; which being well observed, taxes can never be burthens.

42. Every foreigner of good character who comes to settle in this State, having first taken an oath or affirmation of allegiance to the same, may purchase, or by other just means acquire, hold, and transfer land

or other real estate; and after one year's residence, shall be deemed a free denizen thereof, and entitled to all the rights of a natural born subject of this state, except that he shall not be capable of being elected a Representative until after two years' residence.

43. The inhabitants of this State shall have liberty to fowl and hunt in seasonable times on the lands they hold, and on all other lands therein not inclosed; and in like manner to fish in all boatable waters, and others not private property.

44. A school or schools shall be established in each county by the legislature, for the convenient instruction of youth, with such salaries to the masters paid by the public as may enable them to instruct youth at low prices: And all useful learning shall be duly encouraged and promoted in one or more universities.

45. Laws for the encouragement of virtue, and prevention of vice and immorality, shall be made and constantly kept in force, and provision shall be made for their due execution: And all religious societies or bodies of men heretofore united or incorporated for the advancement of religion or learning, or for other pious and charitable purposes, shall be encouraged and protected in the enjoyment of the privileges, immunities, and estates which they were accustomed to enjoy, or could of right have enjoyed, under the laws and former constitution of this State.

46. The Declaration of Rights is hereby declared to be a part of the Constitution of this Commonwealth, and ought never to be violated on any pretence whatever.

47. In order that the freedom of the commonwealth may be preserved inviolate forever, there shall be chosen by ballot by the freemen in each city and county respectively, on the second Tuesday in October, in the year one thousand seven hundred and eighty-three, and on the second Tuesday in October, in every seventh year thereafter, two persons in each city and county of this State, to be called the Council of Censors; who shall meet together on the second Monday of November next ensuing their election; the majority of whom shall be a quorum in every case, except as to calling a convention, in which two-thirds of the whole number elected shall agree: And whose duty it shall be to enquire whether the Constitution has been preserved inviolate in every part; and whether the legislative and executive branches of government have performed their duty as guardians of the people, or assumed to themselves, or exercised other or greater

powers than they are intitled to by the constitution: They are also to enquire whether the public taxes have been justly laid and collected in all parts of this Commonwealth, in what manner the public monies have been disposed of, and whether the laws have been duly executed. For these purposes they shall have power to send for persons, papers, and records; they shall have authority to pass public censures, to order impeachments, and to recommend to the legislature the repealing such laws as appear to them to have been enacted contrary to the principles of the Constitution. These powers they shall continue to have, for and during the space of one year from the day of their election and no longer: The said Council of Censors shall also have power to call a Convention, to meet within two years after their sitting, if there appear to them an absolute necessity of amending any article of the Constitution which may be defective, explaining such as may be thought not clearly expressed, and of adding such as are necessary for the preservation of the rights and happiness of the people; but the articles to be amended, and the amendments proposed, and such articles as are proposed to be added or abolished, shall be promulgated at least six months before the day appointed for the election of such Convention, for the previous consideration of the people, that they may have an opportunity of instructing their delegates on the subject.

BENJ. FRANKLIN, *Prest.*

PART 5

America After the Revolution

5.1 THE VIRGINIA ACT ABOLISHING ENTAIL ON ESTATES

'An Act declaring tenants of lands or slaves in taille to hold the same in fee simple', *Laws of Virginia*, ed. W. W. Hening, vol. IX, ch. 26, pp. 226–7

I. WHEREAS the perpetuation of property in certain families, by means of gifts made to them in fee taille, is contrary to good policy, tends to deceive fair traders, who give a credit on the visible possession of such estates, discourages the holder thereof from taking care and improving the same, and sometimes does injury to the morals of youth, by rendering them independent of and disobedient to their parents; and whereas the former method of docking such estates taille by special act of assembly, formed for every particular case, employed very much of the time of the legislature, and the same, as well as the method of defeating such estates, when of small value, was burthensome to the publick, and also to individuals:

II. *Be it therefore enacted by the General Assembly of the commonwealth of Virginia, and it is hereby enacted by authority of the same*, That any person who now hath, or hereafter may have, any estate in fee taille, general or special, in any lands or slaves in possession, or in the use or trust of any lands or slaves in possession, or who now is or hereafter may be entitled to any such estate taille in reversion or remainder, after the determination of any estate for life or lives, or of any lesser estate, whether such estate taille hath been or shall be created by deed, will, act of assembly, or by any other ways or means, shall from henceforth, or from the commencement of such estate taille, stand *ipso facto* seized, possessed, or entitled of, in, or to such lands or slaves, or use in lands or slaves, so held or to be held as aforesaid, in possession, reversion, or remainder, in full and absolute fee simple, in like manner as if such deed, will, act of assembly, or other instrument, had conveyed the same to him in fee simple; any words, limitations, or conditions, in the said deed, will, act of assembly, or other instrument, to the contrary notwithstanding.

III. Saving to all and every person and persons, bodies politick and corporate, other than the issue in taille, and those in reversion and remainder, all such right, title, interest, and estate, claim, and demand, as they, every, or any of them, could or might claim if this act had never been made; and saving also to such issue in taille, and to those in reversion and remainder, any right or title which they may have acquired by their own contract for good and valuable consideration actually and bona fide paid or performed.

5.2 THE VIRGINIA ACT ON DESCENT OF ESTATES, ABOLISHING PRIMOGENITURE, 1785

'An act directing the course of descents', *Laws of Virginia*, ed. W. W. Hening, vol. XII, ch. 60, pp. 138–40

I. *Be it enacted by the General Assembly*, That henceforth when any person having title to any real estate of inheritance, shall die intestate as to such estate, it shall descend and pass in parency to his kindred male and female in the following course, that is to say:

II. To his children or their descendants, if any there be:

III. If there be no children nor their descendants, then to his father.

IV. If there be no father, then to his mother, brothers and sisters; and their descendants, or such of them as there be:

V. If there be no mother, nor brother, nor sister, nor their descendants, then the inheritance shall be divided into two moieties, one of which shall go to the paternal, the other to the maternal kindred, in the following course, that is to say:

VI. First to the grandfather:

VII. If there be no grandfather, then to the grandmother, uncles and aunts on the same side, and their descendants, or such of them as there be:

VIII. If there be no grandmother, uncle nor aunt, nor their descendants, then to the great grandfathers, or great grandfather if there be but one.

IX. If there be no great grandfather, then to the great grandmothers, or great grand mother if there be but one, and the brothers and sisters of the grandfathers and grandmothers, and their descendants, or such of them as there be:

X. And so on in other cases without end; passing to the nearest lineal male ancestors, and for the want of them to the lineal female ancestors in the same degree, and the descendants of such male and female lineal ancestors, or to such of them as there be.

XI. But no right in the inheritance shall accrue to any person whatever, other than to children of the intestate, unless they be in being and capable in law to take as heirs at the time of the intestates death.

XII. And where for want of issue of the intestate, and of father, mother, brothers and sisters, and their descendants, the inheritance is before directed to go by moieties to the paternal and maternal kindred, if there should be no such kindred on the one part, the whole shall go to the other part: And if there be no kindred either on the one part or the other, the whole shall go to the wife or husband of the intestate. And if the wife or husband be dead, it shall go to her or his kindred, in the like course as if such wife or husband had survived the intestate and then died, entitled to the estate.

XIII. And in the cases before mentioned where the inheritance is directed to pass to the ascending and collateral kindred of the intestate, if part of such collaterals be of the whole blood to the intestate, and other part of the half blood only, those of the half blood shall inherit only half so much as those of the whole blood; But if all be of the half blood, they shall have whole portions, only giving to the ascendants (if there be any) double portions.

XIV. And where the children of the intestate, or his mother, brothers, and sisters, or his grandmother, uncles, and aunts, or any of his female lineal ancestors living, with the children of his deceased lineal ancestors male and female in the same degree come into the partition, they shall take per capita, that is to say by persons; and where a part of them being dead, and a part living, the issue of those dead have right to partition, such issue shall take per stripes, or by stocks, that is to say, the share of their deceased parent.

XV. And where any of the children of the intestate, or their issue, shall have received from the intestate in his life-time any real estate by way of advancement, and shall choose to come into partition with the other parceners, such advancement shall be brought into hotchpot with the estate descended.

XVI. In making title by descent it shall be no bar to a demandant that any ancestor through whom he derives his descent from the intestate, is or hath been an alien. Bastards also shall be capable of inheriting or of transmitting inheritance on the part of their mother, in like manner as if they had been lawfully begotten of such mother.

XVII. Where a man having by a woman one or more children, shall afterwards intermarry with such woman, such child or children, if recognized by him, shall be thereby legitimated. The issue also in marriages deemed null in law shall nevertheless be legitimate.

XVIII. This act shall commence and be in force from and after the first day of January, one thousand seven hundred and eighty-seven.

'An act concerning wills; the distribution of intestates estates; and the duty of executors and administrators', ibid. vol. XII, ch. 61, pp. 140 and 146

I. *BE it enacted by the General Assembly*, That every person aged twenty-one years or upwards, being of sound mind, and not a married woman, shall have power, at his will and pleasure, by last will and testament in writing, to devise all the estate, right, title, and interest, in possession, reversion, or remainder, which he hath, or at the time of his death shall have, of, in, or to lands, tenements, or hereditaments, or annuities, or rents charged upon issuing out of them; so as such last will and testament be signed by the testator, or by some other person in his presence, and by his direction; and moreover, if not wholly written by himself, be attested by two or more credible witnesses subscribing their names in his presence. . . .

XXV. When any person shall die intestate as to his goods and chattels or any part thereof, after funeral, debts, and just expences paid, if there be no child, one moiety, or if there be a child or children, one-third of the surplus shall go to the wife, but she shall have no more than the use for her life of such slaves as shall be in her share, and the residue of the surplus, and after the wife's death, the slaves in her share, or if there be no wife, then the whole of such surplus shall be distributed in the same proportions, and to the same persons, as lands are directed to descend in, and by an act of general assembly, intituled 'An act directing the course of descents'. Nothing in this act contained, shall be understood so as to compel the husband to make distribution of the personal estate of his wife dying intestate. Where any children of the intestate, or their issue, shall have received from the intestate, in his life-time, any personal estate by way of advancement, and shall choose to come into the distribution with the other persons entitled, such advancement shall be brought into hotchpot with the distributable surplus.

XXVI. The general court, and the several courts, respectively, shall have the like jurisdiction to hear and determine the right of administration of the estates of persons dying intestate, as is herein before mentioned, as to the proof of wills, in respect to the intestate's place of residence, or death, or where the estate shall lie, and shall grant certificates for obtaining such administration to the representatives who apply for the same, prefering first the husband or wife, and then such others as are next entitled to distribution, or one or more of them, as the court shall judge will best manage and improve the estate.

5.3 THE VIRGINIA ACT FOR RELIGIOUS LIBERTY

October 1785, *Laws of Virginia*, ed. Hening, vol. XII, ch. 34, pp. 84–6

I. WHEREAS Almighty God hath created the mind free; that all attempts to influence it by temporal punishments or burthens, or by civil incapacitations, tend only to beget habits of hypocrisy and meanness, and are a departure from the plan of the Holy author of our religion, who being Lord both of body and mind, yet chose not to propagate it by coercions on either, as was in his Almighty power to do; that the impious presumption of legislators and rulers, civil as well as ecclesiastical, who being themselves but fallible and uninspired men, have assumed dominion over the faith of others, setting up their own opinions and modes of thinking as the only true and infallible, and as such endeavouring to impose them on others, hath established and maintained false religions over the greatest part of the world, and through all time; that to compel a man to furnish contributions of money for the propagation of opinions which he disbelieves, is sinful and tyrannical; that even the forcing him to support this or that teacher of his own religious persuasion, is depriving him of the comfortable liberty of giving his contributions to the particular pastor, whose morals he would make his pattern, and whose powers he feels most persuasive to righteousness, and is withdrawing from the ministry those temporary rewards, which proceeding from an approbation of their personal conduct, are an additional incitement to earnest and unremitting labours for the instruction of mankind; that our civil rights have no dependence on our religious opinions, any more than our opinions in physics or geometry; that therefore the proscribing any citizen as unworthy the public confidence by laying upon him an incapacity of being called to offices of trust and emolument, unless he profess or renounce this or that religious opinion, is depriving him injuriously of those privileges and advantages to which in common with his fellow-citizens he has a natural right; that it tends only to corrupt the principles of that religion it is meant to encourage, by bribing with a monopoly of wordly honours and emoluments, those who will externally profess and conform to it; that though indeed these are criminal who do not withstand such temptation, yet neither are those innocent who lay the bait in their way; that to suffer the civil magistrate to intrude his powers into the field of opinion, and to restrain the profession or propagation of principles on supposition of their ill tendency, is a dangerous fallacy, which at once destroys all religious liberty, because he being of course judge of that tendency will make his opinions the rule of judgment, and approve or condemn the sentiments of others only as they shall square with or differ from his own; that it is time enough for the rightful purposes of civil government, for its officers to interfere when principles break out into overt acts against peace and good order; and finally, that truth is great and will prevail if left to herself, that she is the proper and sufficient antagonist to error, and has nothing to fear from the conflict, unless by human interposition disarmed of her natural weapons, free argument and debate, errors ceasing to be dangerous when it is permitted freely to contradict them:

II. *Be it enacted by the General Assembly*, That no man shall be compelled to frequent or support any religious worship, place, or ministry whatsoever, nor shall be enforced, restrained, molested, or burthened in his body or goods, nor shall otherwise suffer on account of his religious opinions or belief; but that all men shall be free to profess, and by argument to maintain, their opinion in matters of religion, and that the same shall in no wise diminish, enlarge, or affect their civil capacities.

III. And though we well know that this assembly elected by the people for the ordinary purposes of legislation only, have no power to restrain the acts of succeeding assemblies, constituted with powers equal to our own, and that therefore to declare this act to be irrevocable would be of no effect in law; yet we are free to declare, and do declare, that the rights hereby asserted are of the natural rights of mankind, and that if any act shall be hereafter passed to repeal the present, or to narrow its operation, such act will be an infringement of natural right.

5.4 SLAVERY

(i) *Pennsylvania Act for the Gradual Abolition of Slavery*

Statutes at Large of Pennsylvania, 1780, vol. x, ch. 881, pp. 67–73

(Section I, P. L.) When we contemplate our abhorrence of that condition to which the arms and tyranny of Great Britain were exerted to reduce us, when we look back on the variety of dangers to which we have been exposed, and how miraculously our wants in many instances have been supplied and our deliverances wrought, when even hope and human fortitude have become unequal to the conflict, we are unavoidably led to a serious and grateful sense of the manifold blessings which we have undeservedly received from the hand of that Being from whom every good and perfect gift cometh. Impressed with these ideas, we conceive that it is our duty, and we rejoice that it is in our power, to extend a portion of that freedom to others, which hath been extended to us, and a release from that state of thraldom, to which we ourselves were tyrannically doomed, and from which we have now every prospect of being delivered. It is not for us to enquire why, in the creation of mankind, the inhabitants of the several parts of the earth were distinguished by a difference in feature or complexion. It is sufficient to know that all are the work of an Almighty Hand. We find in the distribution of the human species that the most fertile as well as the most barren parts of the earth are inhabited by men of complexions different from ours and from each other, from whence we may reasonably, as well as religiously infer, that He, who placed them in their various situations, hath extended equally His care and protection to all, and that it becometh not us to counteract His mercies:

We esteem it a peculiar blessing granted to us, that we are enabled this day to add one more step to universal civilization by removing as much as possible the sorrows of those who have lived in undeserved bondage, and from which by the assumed authority of the Kings of Britain, no effectual legal relief could be obtained. Weaned by a long course of experience from those narrow prejudices and partialities we had imbibed, we find our hearts enlarged with kindness and benevolence towards men of all conditions and nations, and we conceive ourselves at this particular period extraordinarily called upon, by the blessings which we have received, to manifest the sincerity of our profession and to give substantial proof of our gratitude:

(Section II, P. L.) And whereas the condition of those persons who have heretofore been denominated negro and mulatto slaves, has been attended with circumstances which not only deprived them of the common blessings that they were by nature entitled to, but has cast them into the deepest afflictions by an unnatural separation and sale of husband and wife from each other, and from their children, an injury the greatness of which can only be conceived by supposing that we were in the same unhappy case. In justice, therefore, to persons so unhappily circumstanced, and who, having no prospect before them whereon they may rest their sorrows and their hopes, have no reasonable inducement to render that service to society which they otherwise might, and also in grateful commemoration of our own happy deliverance from that state of unconditional submission to which we were doomed by the tyranny of Britain:

[Section I.] (Section III, P. L.) Be it enacted and it is hereby enacted by the Representatives of the Freemen of the Commonwealth of Pennsylvania in General Assembly met, and by the authority of the same, That all persons, as well negroes and mulattoes as others who shall be born within this state, from and after the passing of this act, shall not be deemed and considered as servants for life or slaves; and that all servitude for life or slavery of children in consequence of the slavery of their mothers, in the case of all children born within this state from and after the passing of this act as aforesaid, shall be and hereby is utterly taken away, extinguished and forever abolished.

[Section II.] (Section IV, P. L.) Provided always, and be it further enacted by the authority aforesaid, That every negro and mulatto child born within this state after the passing of this act as aforesaid who would in case this act had not been made, have been born a servant for years or life or a slave, shall be deemed to be and shall be, by virtue of this act the servant of such person or his or her assigns who would in such case have been entitled to the service of such child until such child shall attain unto the age of twenty-eight years, in the manner and on the conditions whereon servants bound by indenture for four years are or may be retained and holden, and shall be liable to like correction and punishment, and entitled to like relief in case he or she be evilly treated by his or her master or mistress, and to like freedom dues and other privileges as servants bound by indenture for four years are or may be entitled unless the person to whom the service of any such child shall belong shall abandon his or her claim to the same, in which case the overseers of the poor of the city, township or district, respectively where such child shall be so abandoned, shall [by indenture] bind out every child so abandoned as an apprentice for a time not exceeding the age hereinbefore limited for the service of such children.

[Section III.] (Section V, P. L.) And be it further enacted by the authority aforesaid, That every person who is or shall be the owner of any negro or mulatto slave or servant for life or till the age of thirty-one years, now within this state, or his lawful attorney shall, on or before the said first day of November next, deliver, or cause to be delivered, in writing to the clerk of the peace of the county or to the clerk of the court of record of the city of Philadelphia, in which he or she shall respectively inhabit, the name and surname and occupation or profession of such owner and the name of the county and township, district or ward wherein he or she resideth, and also the name and names of any such slave and slaves and servant and servants for life or till the age of thirty-one years, together with their ages and sexes severally and respectively set forth and annexed, by such person owned or statedly employed and then being within this state, in order to ascertain and distinguish the slaves and servants for life and years till the age of thirty-one years, within this state who shall be such on the said first day of November next, from all other persons, which particulars shall by said clerk of the sessions and clerk of said city court be entered in books to be provided for that purpose by the said clerks; and that no negro or mulatto now within this state shall, from and after the said first day of November, be deemed a slave or servant for life or till the age of thirty-one years unless his or her name shall be entered as aforesaid on such record except such negro and mulatto slaves and servants as are hereinafter excepted; the said clerk to be entitled to a fee of two dollars for each slave or servant so entered as aforesaid from the treasurer of the county, to be allowed to him in his accounts.

(Section VI, P. L.) Provided always, That any person in whom the ownership or right to the service of any negro or mulatto shall be vested at the passing of this act, other than such as are hereinbefore excepted, his or her heirs, executors, administrators and assigns, and all and every of them severally shall be liable to the overseers of the poor of the city, township or district to which any such negro or mulatto shall become chargeable, for such necessary expense, with costs of suit thereon, as such overseers may be put to through the neglect of the owner, master or mistress of such negro or mulatto, notwithstanding the name and other descriptions of such negro or mulatto shall not be entered and recorded as aforesaid; unless his or her master or owner shall, before such slave or servant attain his or her twenty-eighth year, execute and record in the proper county, a deed or instrument securing to such slave or servant his or her freedom.

[Section IV.] (Section VII, P. L.) And be it further enacted by the authority aforesaid, That the offenses and crimes of negroes and mulattoes as well slaves and servants and [sic] [as] freemen, shall be inquired of, adjudged, corrected and punished in like manner as the offenses and crimes of the other inhabitants of this state are and shall be enquired of, adjudged, corrected and punished, and not otherwise, except that a slave shall not be admitted to bear witness against a freeman.

[Section V.] (Section VIII, P. L.) And be it further enacted by the authority aforesaid, That in all cases wherein sentence of death shall be pronounced against a slave, the jury before whom he or she shall be tried shall appraise and declare the value of such slave, and in case such sentence be executed, the court shall make an order on the state treasurer, payable to the owner for the same and for the costs of prosecution, but in case of a remission or mitigation for the costs only.

[Section VI.] (Section IX, P. L.) And be it further enacted by the authority aforesaid, That the reward for taking up runaway and absconding negro and mulatto slaves and servants and the penalties for enticing away, dealing with or harboring, concealing or employing negro and mulatto slaves and servants shall be the same, and shall be recovered in like manner as in case of servants bound for four years.

[Section VII.] (Section X, P. L.) And be it further enacted by the authority aforesaid, That no man or woman of any nation or color, except the negroes or mulattoes who shall be registered as aforesaid shall at any time hereafter be deemed, adjudged or holden, within the territories of this commonwealth, as slaves or servants for life, but as free men and free women, and except the domestic slaves attending upon delegates in Congress from the other American states, foreign ministers and consuls, and persons passing through or sojourning in this state, and not becoming resident therein; and seamen employed in ships, not belonging to any inhabitant of this state nor employed in any ship owned by any such inhabitant: [Provided such domestic slaves be not aliened or sold to any inhabitant] nor (except in the case of members of Congress, foreign ministers and consuls) retained in this state longer than six months.

[Section VIII.] (Section XI, P. L.) Provided always, and be it further enacted by the authority aforesaid, That this act, nor anything in it contained, shall not give any relief or shelter to any absconding or runaway negro or mulatto slave or servant, who has absented himself or shall absent himself from his or her owner, master or mistress, residing in any other state or country, but such owner, master or mistress, shall have like right and aid to demand, claim and take away his slave or servant as he might have had in case this act had not been made. And that all negro and mulatto slaves now owned, and heretofore resident in this state, who have absented themselves or been clandestinely carried away, or who may be employed abroad as seamen, and have not returned or been brought back to their owners, masters or mistresses, before the passing of this act may, within five years be registered as effectually as is ordered by this act concerning those who are now within this state, on producing such slave before any two justices of the peace, and satisfying the said justices by due proof of the former residence, absconding, taking away or absence of such slave as aforesaid; who, thereupon, shall direct and order the said slave to be entered on the record as aforesaid.

(Section XII, P. L.) And whereas attempts may be made to evade this act by introducing into this state negroes and mulattoes bound by covenant to serve for long and unreasonable terms of years, if the same be not prevented:

[Section IX.] (Section XIII, P. L.) Be it therefore enacted by the authority aforesaid, That no covenant of personal servitude or apprenticeship whatsoever shall be valid or binding on a negro or mulatto for a longer term than seven years, unless such servant or apprentice were at the commencement of such servitude or apprenticeship under the age of twenty-one years; in which case such negro or mulatto may be holden as a servant or apprentice respectively according to the covenant, as the case shall be until he or she shall attain the age of twenty-eight years, but no longer.

[Section X.] (Section XIV, P. L.) And be it further enacted by the authority aforesaid, That an act of assembly of the province of Pennsylvania, passed in the year one thousand seven hundred and five, entitled 'An act for the trial of negroes',[1] and another act of assembly of the said province, passed in the year one thousand seven hundred and twenty-five, entitled 'An act for the better regulating of negroes in this province',[2] and another act of assembly of the said province passed in the year one thousand seven hundred and sixty-one, entitled 'An act for laying a duty on negro and mulatto slaves imported into this province',[3] and also another act of assembly of the said province, passed in the year one thousand seven hundred and seventy-three, entitled 'An act for making perpetual an act for laying a duty on negro and mulatto slaves imported into this province and for laying an additional duty on said slaves',[4] shall be and are hereby repealed, annulled and made void.

Passed March 1, 1780. See the Acts of Assembly passed October 1, 1781, ibid. ch. 953; March 29, 1788, ibid. ch. 1345; December 8, 1789, ibid. ch. 1476. Recorded L. B. no. 1, p. 339, &c.

(ii) *An Exchange between Luther Martin and John Rutledge*

August 21, 1787, *Records of the Federal Convention*, ed. Farrand, II 364

Mr. L. MARTIN, proposed to vary the Sect: 4. art VII. so as to allow a prohibition or tax on the importation of slaves. 1. as five slaves are to be counted as 3 free men in the apportionment of Representatives, such a clause wd. leave an encouragement to this trafic. 2. slaves weakened one part of the Union which the other parts were bound to protect: the privilege of importing them was therefore unreasonable. 3. it was inconsistent with the principles of the revolution and dishonorable to the American character to have such a feature in the Constitution.

[1] Passed January 12, 1705–6, *Statutes at Large of Pennsylvania*, ch. 143.
[2] Passed March 5, 1725–6, ibid. ch. 292.
[3] Passed March 14, 1761, ch. 467.
[4] Passed February 26, 1773, ch. 681.

Mr. Rutlidge did not see how the importation of slaves could be encouraged by this Section. He was not apprehensive of insurrections and would readily exempt the other States from the obligation to protect the Southern against them. – Religion & humanity had nothing to do with this question. Interest alone is the governing principle with nations. The true question at present is whether the Southn. States shall or shall not be parties to the Union. If the Northern States consult their interest, they will not oppose the increase of Slaves which will increase the commodities of which they will become the carriers.

5.5 THE SOCIAL ORDER: OPINIONS OF JOHN ADAMS

From *Defence of the Constitutions of Government of the United States*. See *Works*, ed. C. F. Adams, IV 391–5, 434

Let us now return to M. Turgot's idea of a government consisting in a single assembly. He tells us our republics are 'founded on the equality of all the citizens, and, therefore, "orders" and "equilibriums" are unnecessary, and occasion disputes'. But what are we to understand here by equality? Are the citizens to be all of the same age, sex, size, strength, stature, activity, courage, hardiness, industry, patience, ingenuity, wealth, knowledge, fame, wit, temperance, constancy, and wisdom? Was there, or will there ever be, a nation, whose individuals were all equal, in natural and acquired qualities, in virtues, talents, and riches? The answer of all mankind must be in the negative. It must then be acknowledged, that in every state, in the Massachusetts, for example, there are inequalities which God and nature have planted there, and which no human legislator ever can eradicate. I should have chosen to have mentioned Virginia, as the most ancient state, or indeed any other in the union, rather than the one that gave me birth, if I were not afraid of putting suppositions which may give offence, a liberty which my neighbors will pardon. Yet I shall say nothing that is not applicable to all the other twelve.

In this society of Massachusettensians then, there is, it is true, a moral and political equality of rights and duties among all the individuals, and as yet no appearance of artificial inequalities of condition, such as hereditary dignities, titles, magistracies, or legal distinctions; and no established marks, as stars, garters, crosses, or ribbons; there are, nevertheless, inequalities of great moment in the consideration of a legislator, because they have a natural and inevitable influence in society. Let us enumerate some of them: – 1. There is an inequality of wealth; some individuals, whether by descent from their ancestors, or from greater skill, industry, and success in business, have estates both in lands and goods of great value; others have no property at all; and of all the rest of society, much the greater number are possessed of wealth, in all the variety of degrees between these extremes; it will easily be conceived that all the rich men will have many of the poor, in the various trades, manufactures, and other occupations in life, dependent upon them for their daily bread; many of smaller fortunes will be in their debt, and in many ways under obligations to them; others, in better circumstances, neither dependent nor in debt, men of letters, men of the learned professions, and others, from acquaintance, conversation, and civilities, will be connected with them and attached to them. Nay, farther, it will not be denied, that among the wisest people that live, there is a degree of admiration, abstracted from all dependence, obligation, expectation, or even acquaintance, which accompanies splendid wealth, insures some respect, and bestows some influence. 2. Birth. Let no man be surprised that this species of inequality is introduced here. Let the page in history be quoted, where any nation, ancient or modern, civilized or savage, is mentioned, among whom no difference was made between the citizens, on account of their extraction. The truth is, that more influence is allowed to this advantage in free republics than in despotic governments, or than would be allowed to it in simple monarchies, if severe laws had not been made from age to age to secure it. The children of illustrious families have generally greater advantages of education, and earlier opportunities to be acquainted with public characters, and informed of public affairs, than those of meaner ones, or even than those in middle life; and what is more than all, an habitual national veneration for their names, and the characters of their ancestors described in history, or coming down by tradition, removes them farther from vulgar jealousy and popular envy, and secures them in some degree the favor, the affection, and respect of the public. Will any man pretend that the name of Andros, and that of Winthrop, are heard with the same sensations in any village of New England? Is not gratitude the sentiment that attends the latter, and disgust the feeling excited by the former? In the Massachusetts, then, there are persons descended from some of their ancient governors, counsellors, judges, whose fathers, grandfathers, and great-grandfathers, are remembered with esteem by many living, and who are mentioned in history with applause, as benefactors to the country, while there are others who have no such advantage. May we go a step farther, – Know thyself, is as useful a precept to nations as to men. Go into every village in New England, and you will find that the office of justice of the peace, and even the place of representative, which has ever depended only on the freest election of the people, have generally descended from generation to generation, in three or four families at most. The present subject is one of those which all men respect, and all men deride. It may be said of this part of our nature, as Pope said of the whole: –

> Of human nature, wit her worst may write,
> We all revere it in our own despite.

If, as Harrington says, the ten commandments were voted by the people of Israel, and have been enacted as laws by all other nations; and if we should presume to say, that nations had a civil right to repeal them, no nation would think proper to repeal the fifth, which enjoins honor to parents. If there is a difference between right and wrong; if any thing can be sacred; if there is one idea of moral obligation; the decree of nature must force upon every thinking being and upon every feeling heart the conviction that honor, affection, and gratitude are due from children to those who gave them birth, nurture, and education. The sentiments and affections which naturally arise from reflecting on the love, the cares, and the blessings of parents, abstracted from the consideration of duty, are some of the most forcible and most universal. When religion, law, morals, affection, and even fashion, thus conspire to fill every mind with attachment to parents, and to stamp deep upon the heart their impressions, is it to be expected that men should reverence their parents while they live, and begin to despise or neglect their memories as soon as they are dead? This is in nature impossible. On the contrary, every little unkindness and severity is forgotten, and nothing but endearments remembered with pleasure.

The son of a wise and virtuous father finds the world about him sometimes as much disposed as he himself is, to honor the memory of his father; to congratulate him as the successor to his estate; and frequently to compliment him with elections to the offices he held. A sense of duty, his passions and his interest, thus conspiring to prevail upon him to avail himself of this advantage, he finds a few others in similar circumstances with himself; they naturally associate together, and aid each other. This is a faint sketch of the source and rise of the family spirit; very often the disposition to favor the family is as strong in the town, county, province, or kingdom, as it is in the house itself. The enthusiasm is indeed sometimes wilder, and carries away, like a torrent, all before it.[1]

These observations are not peculiar to any age; we have seen the effects of them in San Marino, Biscay, and the Grisons, as well as in Poland and all other countries. Not to mention any notable examples which have lately happened near us, it is not many months since I was witness to a conversation between some citizens of Massachusetts. One was haranguing on the jealousy which a free people ought to entertain of their liberties, and was heard by all the company with pleasure. In less than ten minutes, the conversation turned upon their governor; and the jealous republican was very angry at the opposition to him. 'The present governor,' says he, 'has done us such services, that he ought to rule us, he and his posterity after him, for ever and ever.' 'Where is your jealousy of liberty?' demanded the other. 'Upon my honor,' replies the orator, 'I had forgot that; you have caught me in an inconsistency; for I cannot know whether a child of five years old will be a son of liberty or a tyrant.' His jealousy was the dictate of his understanding. His confidence and enthusiasm the impulse of his heart.

The pompous trumpery of ensigns, armorials, and escutcheons are not, indeed, far advanced in America. Yet there is a more general anxiety to know their originals, in proportion to their numbers, than in any nation of Europe; arising from the easier circumstances and higher spirit of the common people. And there are certain families in every state equally attentive to all the proud frivolities of heraldry. That kind of pride, which looks down on commerce and manufactures as degrading, may, indeed, in many countries of Europe, be a useful and necessary quality in the nobility. It may prevent, in some degree, the whole nation from being entirely delivered up to the spirit of avarice. It may be the cause why honor is preferred by some to money. It may prevent the nobility from becoming too rich, and acquiring

[1] The late election of a president in France, by the popular vote, will occur as a striking illustration of the force of these observations.

too large a proportion of the landed property. In America, it would not only be mischievous, but would expose the highest pretensions of the kind to universal ridicule and contempt. Those other hauteurs, of keeping the commons at a distance, and disdaining to converse with any but a few of a certain race, may in Europe be a favor to the people, by relieving them from a multitude of assiduous attentions and humiliating compliances, which would be troublesome. It may prevent the nobles from caballing with the people, and gaining too much influence with them in elections and otherwise. In America, it would justly excite universal indignation; the vainest of all must be of the people, or be nothing. While every office is equally open to every competitor, and the people must decide upon every pretension to a place in the legislature, that of governor and senator, as well as representative, no such airs will ever be endured. . . .

Ibid. IV 434

'All government is of three kinds, – a government of servants, a government of subjects, or a government of citizens. The first is absolute monarchy, as that of Turkey; the second, aristocratical monarchy, as that of France; the third, a commonwealth, as Israel, Rome, Holland. Of these, the government of servants is harder to be conquered and the easier to be held. The government of subjects is the easier to be conquered and the harder to be held. The government of citizens is both the hardest to be conquered and the hardest to be held.

'The reason why a government of servants is hard to be conquered, is, that they are under a perpetual discipline and command. Why a government of subjects is easily conquered, is on account of the factions of the nobility.

'The reasons why a government of citizens, where the commonwealth is equal, is hardest to be conquered, are, that the invader of such a society must not only trust to his own strength, inasmuch as, the commonwealth being equal, he must needs find them united; but in regard that such citizens, being all soldiers, or trained up to their arms, which they use not for the defence of slavery, but of liberty, a condition not in this world to be bettered, they have, more especially upon this occasion, the highest soul of courage, and, if their territory be of any extent, the vastest body of a well-disciplined militia that is possible in nature. Wherefore an example of such a one, overcome by the arms of a monarch, is not to be found in the world.'

In the art of lawgiving, chap. i. he enlarges still farther upon this subject; and instances Joseph's purchase of all the lands of the Egyptians for Pharaoh, whereby they became servants to Pharaoh; and he enlarges on the English balance, &c.

In America, the balance is nine tenths on the side of the people. Indeed, there is but one order; and our senators have influence chiefly by the principles of authority, and very little by those of power; but this must be postponed.

5.6 THE SOCIAL ORDER: OPINIONS OF WILLIAM PINKNEY OF SOUTH CAROLINA

June 25, 1787, *Records of the Federal Convention*, ed. Farrand, II 397–404

Resolution 4.[1] being taken up.

Mr PINKNEY spoke as follows – The efficacy of the System will depend on this article. In order to form a right judgmt. in the case, it will be proper to examine the situation of this Country more accurately than it has yet been done. The people of the U. States are perhaps the most singular of any we are acquainted with. Among them there are fewer distinctions of fortune & less of rank, than among the inhabitants of any other nation. Every freeman has a right to the same protection & security; and a very moderate share of property entitles them to the possession of all the honors and privileges the public can bestow: hence arises a greater equality, than is to be found among the people of any other country, and an equality which is more likely to continue – I say this equality is likely to continue, because in a new Country, possessing immense tracts of uncultivated lands, where every temptation is offered to emigration & where industry must be rewarded with competency, there will be few poor, and few dependent – Every member of the Society almost, will enjoy an equal power of arriving at the supreme offices & consequently of directing the strength & sentiments of the whole Community. None will be excluded by birth, & few by

1 [Relating to the second branch, and thus the crucial question of state equality.]

fortune, from voting for proper persons to fill the offices of Government – the whole community will enjoy in the fullest sense that kind of political liberty which consists in the power the members of the State reserve to themselves, of arriving at the public offices, or at least, of having votes in the nomination of those who fill them.

If this State of things is true & the prospect of its continuing probable, it is perhaps not politic to endeavour too close an imitation of a Government calculated for a people whose situation is, & whose views ought to be extremely different.

Much has been said of the Constitution of G. Britain. I will confess that I believe it to be the best Constitution in existence; but at the same time I am confident it is one that will not or can not be introduced into this Country, for many centuries. – If it were proper to go here into a historical dissertation on the British Constitution, it might easily be shewn that the peculiar excellence, the distinguishing feature of that Governmt. can not possibly be introduced into our System – that its balance between the Crown & the people can not be made a part of our Constitution. – that we neither have or can have the members to compose it, nor the rights, privileges & properties of so distinct a class of Citizens to guard. – that the materials for forming this balance or check do not exist, nor is there a necessity for having so permanent a part of our Legislative, until the Executive power is so constituted as to have something fixed & dangerous in its principle – By this I mean a sole, hereditary, though limited Executive.

That we cannot have a proper body for forming a Legislative balance between the inordinate power of the Executive and the people, is evident from a review of the accidents & circumstances which gave rise to the peerage of Great Britain. [Pinckney then briefly sketched the growth of the nobility and commons.]

I have said that such a body cannot exist in this Country for ages, and that untill the situation of our people is exceedingly changed no necessity will exist for so permanent a part of the Legislature. To illustrate this I have remarked that the people of the United States are more equal in their circumstances than the people of any other Country – that they have very few rich men among them, – by rich men I mean those whose riches may have a dangerous influence, or such as are esteemed rich in Europe – perhaps there are not one hundred such on the Continent; that it is not probable this number will be greatly increased: that the genius of the people, their mediocrity of situation &

the prospects which are afforded their industry in a Country which must be a new one for centuries are unfavorable to the rapid distinction of ranks. The destruction of the right of primogeniture & the equal division of the property of Intestates will also have an effect to preserve this mediocrity; for laws invariably affect the manners of a people. On the other hand that vast extent of unpeopled territory which opens to the frugal & industrious a sure road to competency & independence will effectually prevent for a considerable time the increase of the poor or discontented, and be the means of preserving that equality of condition which so eminently distinguishes us.

If equality is as I contend the leading feature of the U. States, where then are the riches & wealth whose representation & protection is the peculiar province of this permanent body. Are they in the hands of the few who may be called rich; in the possession of less than a hundred citizens? certainly not. They are in the great body of the people, among whom there are no men of wealth, and very few of real poverty. – Is it probable that a change will be created, and that a new order of men will arise? If under the British Government, for a century no such change was probable, I think it may be fairly concluded it will not take place while even the semblance of Republicanism remains. – How is this change to be effected? Where are the sources from whence it is to flow? From the landed interest? No. That is too unproductive & too much divided in most of the States. From the Monied interest? If such exists at present, little is to be apprehended from that source. Is it to spring from commerce? I believe it would be the first instance in which a nobility sprang from merchants. Besides, Sir, I apprehend that on this point the policy of the U. States has been much mistaken. We have unwisely considered ourselves as the inhabitants of an old instead of a new country. We have adopted the maxims of a State full of people & manufactures & established in credit. We have deserted our true interest, and instead of applying closely to those improvements in domestic policy which would have ensured the future importance of our commerce, we have rashly & prematurely engaged in schemes as extensive as they are imprudent. This however is an error which daily corrects itself & I have no doubt that a few more severe trials will convince us, that very different commercial principles ought to govern the conduct of these States.

The people of this country are not only very different from the inhabitants of any State we are acquainted with in the modern world;

but I assert that their situation is distinct from either the people of Greece or Rome, or of any State we are acquainted with among the antients. . . .

Our true situation appears to me to be this. – a new extensive Country containing within itself the materials for forming a Government capable of extending to its citizens all the blessings of civil & religious liberty – capable of making them happy at home. This is the great end of Republican Establishments. We mistake the object of our Government, if we hope or wish that it is to make us respectable abroad. Conquest or superiority among other powers is not or ought not ever to be the object of republican systems. If they are sufficiently active & energetic to rescue us from contempt & preserve our domestic happiness & security, it is all we can expect from them, – it is more than almost any other Government ensures to its citizens.

I believe this observation will be found generally true: – that no two people are so exactly alike in their situation or circumstances as to admit the exercise of the same Government with equal benefit: that a system must be suited to the habits & genius of the people it is to govern, and must grow out of them.

The people of the U. S. may be divided into three classes – *Professional men* who must from their particular pursuits always have a considerable weight in the Government while it remains popular – *Commercial men*, who may or may not have weight as a wise or injudicious commercial policy is pursued. – If that commercial policy is pursued which I conceive to be the true one, the merchants of this Country will not or ought not for a considerable time to have much weight in the political scale. – The third is the *landed interest*, the owners and cultivators of the soil, who are and ought ever to be the governing spring in the system. – These three classes, however distinct in their pursuits are individually equal in the political scale, and may be easily proved to have but one interest. The dependence of each on the other is mutual. The merchant depends on the planter. Both must in private as well as public affairs be connected with the professional men; who in their turn must in some measure depend upon them. Hence it is clear from this manifest connection, & the equality which I before stated exists, & must for the reasons then assigned, continue, that after all there is one, but one great & equal body of citizens composing the inhabitants of this Country among whom there are no distinctions of rank, and very few or none of fortune.

For a people thus circumstanced are we then to form a government & the question is what kind of Government is best suited to them.

Will it be the British Govt.? No. Why? Because G. Britain contains three orders of people distinct in their situation, their possessions & their principles. – These orders combined form the great body of the Nation. . . . Each therefore must of necessity be represented by itself, or the sign of itself; and this accidental mixture has certainly formed a Government admirably well balanced.

But the U. States contain but one order that can be assimilated to the British Nation, – this is the order of Commons. They will not surely then attempt to form a Government consisting of three branches, two of which shall have nothing to represent. They will not have an Executive & Senate (hereditary) because the King & Lords of England are so. The same reasons do not exist and therefore the same provisions are not necessary.

We must as has been observed suit our Governmt. to the people it is to direct. These are I believe as active, intelligent & susceptible of good Governmt. as any people in the world. The Confusion which has produced the present relaxed State is not owing to them. It is owing to the weakness & (defects) of a Govt. incapable of combining the various interests it is intended to unite, and destitute of energy. – All that we have to do then is to distribute the powers of Govt. in such a manner, and for such limited periods, as while it gives a proper degree of permanency to the Magistrate, will reserve to the people, the right of election they will not or ought not frequently to part with. – I am of opinion that this may be easily done; and that with some amendments the propositions before the Committee will fully answer this end.

No position appears to me more true than this; that the General Govt. can not effectually exist without reserving to the States the possession of their local rights. They are the instruments upon which the Union must frequently depend for the support & execution of their powers, however immediately operating upon the people, and not upon the States.

5.7 A DEBATE ON PROPERTY AND SUFFRAGE: WITH JAMES MADISON'S PROGNOSIS OF THE POLITICAL CONSEQUENCES OF ECONOMIC DEVELOPMENT

August 7, 1787, *Records of the Federal Convention*, ed. Farrand, II 201–8

Mr Wilson. This part of the Report was well considered by the Committee, and he did not think it could be changed for the better. It was difficult to form any uniform rule of qualifications for all the States. Unnecessary innovations he thought too should be avoided. It would be very hard & disagreeable for the same persons at the same time, to vote for representatives in the State Legislature and to be excluded from a vote for those in the Natl. Legislature.

Mr Govr. Morris. Such a hardship would be neither great nor novel. The people are accustomed to it and not dissatisfied with it, in several of the States. In some the qualifications are different for the choice of the Govr. & Representatives; In others for different Houses of the Legislature. Another objection agst. the clause as it stands is that it makes the qualifications of the Natl. Legislature depend on the will of the States, which he thought not proper.

Mr Elseworth. thought the qualifications of the electors stood on the most proper footing. The right of suffrage was a tender point, and strongly guarded by most of the State Constitutions. The people will not readily subscribe to the Natl. Constitution if it should subject them to be disfranchised. The States are the best Judges of the circumstances & temper of their own people.

Col Mason. The force of habit is certainly not attended to by those gentlemen who wish for innovations on this point. Eight or nine States have extended the right to suffrage beyond the freeholders, what will the people there say, if they should be disfranchised. A power to alter the qualifications would be a dangerous power in the hands of the Legislature.

Mr Butler. There is no right of which the people are more jealous than that of suffrage. . . .

Mr Dickinson. had a very different idea of the tendency of vesting the right of suffrage in the freeholders of the Country. He considered them as the best guardians of liberty; And the restriction of the right to them as a necessary defence agst. the dangerous influence of those multitudes without property & without principle with which our Country like all others, will in time abound. As to the unpopularity of the innovation it was in his opinion chemirical. The great mass of our Citizens is composed at this time of freeholders, and will be pleased with it.

Mr Elseworth. How shall the freehold be defined? Ought not every man who pays a tax, to vote for the representative who is to levy & dispose of his money? Shall the wealthy merchants & manufacturers, who will bear a full share of the public burdens be not allowed a voice in the imposition of them – taxation & representation ought to go together.

Mr Govr. Morris. He had long learned not to be the dupe of words. The sound of Aristocracy therefore had no effect on him. It was the thing, not the name, to which he was opposed, and one of his principal objections to the Constitution as it is now before us, is that it threatens this Country with an Aristocracy. The aristocracy will grow out of the House of Representatives. Give the votes to people who have no property, and they will sell them to the rich who will be able to buy them. We should not confine our attention to the present moment. The time is not distant when this Country will abound with mechanics & manufacturers who will receive their bread from their employers. Will such men be the secure & faithful Guardians of liberty? Will they be the impregnable barrier agst. aristocracy? – He was as little duped by the association of the words 'taxation & Representation.' The man who does not give his vote freely is not represented. It is the man who dictates the vote. Children do not vote . . . because they have no will of their own. The ignorant & the dependent can be as little trusted with the public interest. He did not conceive the difficulty of defining 'freeholders' to be insuperable. Still less that the restriction could be unpopular. 9/10 of the people are at present freeholders and these will certainly be pleased with it. As to Merchts. &c. if they have wealth & value the right they can acquire it. If not they don't deserve it.

Col Mason. We all feel too strongly the remains of antient prejudices, and view things too much through a British medium. A Freehold is the qualification in England, & hence it is imagined to be the only proper one. The true idea in his opinion was that every man having evidence of attachment to & permanent common interest with the Society ought to share in all its rights & privileges. Was this qualification restrained to freeholders? Does no other kind of property but land evidence a common interest in the proprietor? does nothing besides property mark a permanent attachment. Ought the merchant, the monied man, the parent of a number of children whose fortunes are to be pursued in his own Country, to be viewed as suspicious characters, and unworthy to be trusted with the common rights of their fellow Citizens.

Mr MADISON. the right of suffrage is certainly one of the fundamental articles of republican Government, and ought not to be left to be regulated by the Legislature. A gradual abridgment of this right has been the mode in which Aristocracies have been built on the ruins of popular forms. Whether the Constitutional qualification ought to be a freehold, would with him depend much on the probable reception such a change would meet with in States where the right was now exercised by every description of people. In several of the States a freehold was now the qualification. Viewing the subject in its merits alone, the freeholders of the Country would be the safest despositories of Republican liberty. In future times a great majority of the people will not only be without landed, but any other sort of, property. These will either combine under the influence of their common situation; in which case, the rights of property & the public liberty, will not be secure in their hands: or which is more probable, they will become the tools of opulence & ambition, in which case there will be equal danger on another side. . . .

Docr FRANKLIN. It is of great consequence that we shd. not depress the virtue & public spirit of our common people; of which they displayed a great deal during the war, and which contributed principally to the favorable issue of it. He related the honorable refusal of the American seamen who were carried in great numbers into the British Prisons during the war, to redeem themselves from misery or to seek their fortunes, by entering on board the Ships of the Enemies to their Country; contrasting their patriotism with a contemporary instance in which the British seamen made prisoners by the Americans, readily entered on the ships of the latter on being promised a share of the prizes that might be made out of their own Country. This proceeded he said from the different manner in which the common people were treated in America & G. Britain. He did not think that the elected had any right in any case to narrow the privileges of the electors. . . . He was persuaded also that such a restriction as was proposed would give great uneasiness in the populous States. The sons of a substantial farmer, not being themselves freeholders, would not be pleased at being disfranchised, and there are a great many persons of that description.

On the question for striking out as moved by Mr Govr. Morris, from the word 'qualifications' to the end of the III article.

N. H. no. Mas. no. Ct. no. Pa. no. Del. ay. Md. divd. Va. no. N. C. no. S. C. no. Geo. not prest. [Ayes, 1; noes, 7; divided, 1.]

Article IV, Section 1, after brief discussion on the following day, passed unanimously.

5.8 FRANKLIN ON THE STATE OF AMERICA AFTER THE REVOLUTION, 1786[1]

'The Internal State of America; being a true description of the Interest and Policy of that vast Continent', in *Franklin's Writings*, ed. Jared Sparks (Boston, 1856) II 461–7

There is a tradition, that, in the planting of New England, the first settlers met with many difficulties and hardships; as is generally the case when a civilized people attempt establishing themselves in a wilderness country. Being piously disposed, they sought relief from Heaven, by laying their wants and distresses before the Lord, in frequent set days of fasting and prayer. Constant meditation and discourse on these subjects kept their minds gloomy and discontented; and, like the children of Israel, there were many disposed to return to that Egypt, which persecution had induced them to abandon. At length, when it was proposed in the assembly to proclaim another fast, a farmer of plain sense rose, and remarked, that the inconveniences they suffered,

[1] [*Editor's note.*] For the accurate dating of this essay, see Verner W. Crane, 'Franklin's "The Internal State of America" (1786)', in *William and Mary Quarterly*, vol. XV, no. 2 (April 1958).

This essay was Franklin's reply to the prolonged criticisms of the United States in the British press. It is polemical, and should be read as a work of propaganda rather than a survey of ascertained facts; it is included here as a vivid example of the reasoning by which the most optimistic view of American prospects could be sustained.

and concerning which they had so often wearied Heaven with their complaints, were not so great as they might have expected, and were diminishing every day, as the colony strengthened; that the earth began to reward their labor, and to furnish liberally for their subsistence; that the seas and rivers were found full of fish, the air sweet, the climate healthy; and, above all, that they were there in the full enjoyment of liberty, civil and religious. He therefore thought, that reflecting and conversing on these subjects would be more comfortable, as tending more to make them contented with their situation; and that it would be more becoming the gratitude they owed to the Divine Being, if, instead of a fast, they should proclaim a thanksgiving. His advice was taken; and from that day to this they have, in every year, observed circumstances of public felicity sufficient to furnish employment for a thanksgiving day; which is therefore constantly ordered and religiously observed.

I see in the public newspapers of different States frequent complaints of *hard times*, *deadness of trade*, *scarcity of money*, &c. It is not my intention to assert or maintain, that these complaints are entirely without foundation. There can be no country or nation existing, in which there will not be some people so circumstanced, as to find it hard to gain a livelihood; people who are not in the way of any profitable trade, and with whom money is scarce, because they have nothing to give in exchange for it; and it is always in the power of a small number to make a great clamor. But let us take a cool view of the general state of our affairs, and perhaps the prospect will appear less gloomy than has been imagined.

The great business of the continent is agriculture. For one artisan, or merchant, I suppose, we have at least one hundred farmers, by far the greatest part cultivators of their own fertile lands, from whence many of them draw, not only the food necessary for their subsistence, but the materials of their clothing, so as to need very few foreign supplies; while they have a surplus of productions to dispose of, whereby wealth is gradually accumulated. Such has been the goodness of Divine Providence to these regions, and so favorable the climate, that, since the three or four years of hardship in the first settlement of our fathers here, a famine or scarcity has never been heard of amongst us; on the contrary, though some years may have been more, and others less plentiful, there has always been provision enough for ourselves, and a quantity to spare for exportation. And although the crops of last year were generally good, never was the farmer better paid for the part he can spare commerce, as the published price-currents abundantly testify. The lands he possesses are also continually rising in value with the increase of population; and, on the whole, he is enabled to give such good wages to those who work for him, that all who are acquainted with the old world must agree, that in no part of it are the laboring poor so generally well fed, well clothed, well lodged, and well paid, as in the United States of America.

If we enter the cities, we find, that, since the Revolution, the owners of houses and lots of ground have had their interest vastly augmented in value; rents have risen to an astonishing height, and thence encouragement to increase building, which gives employment to an abundance of workmen, as does also the increased luxury and splendor of living of the inhabitants, thus made richer. These workmen all demand and obtain much higher wages than any other part of the world would afford them, and are paid in ready money. This class of people therefore do not, or ought not, to complain of hard times; and they make a very considerable part of the city inhabitants.

At the distance I live from our American fisheries, I cannot speak of them with any degree of certainty; but I have not heard, that the labor of the valuable race of men employed in them is worse paid, or that they meet with less success, than before the Revolution. The whalemen indeed have been deprived of one market for their oil; but another, I hear, is opening for them, which it is hoped may be equally advantageous; and the demand is constantly increasing for their spermaceti candles, which therefore bear a much higher price than formerly.

There remain the merchants and shopkeepers. Of these, though they make but a small part of the whole nation, the number is considerable, too great indeed for the business they are employed in; for the consumption of goods in every country, has its limits; the faculties of the people, that is, their ability to buy and pay, being equal only to a certain quantity of merchandise. If merchants calculate amiss on this proportion, and import too much, they will of course find the sale dull for the overplus, and some of them will say, that trade languishes. They should, and doubtless will, grow wiser by experience, and import less. If too many artificers in town, and farmers from the country, flattering themselves with the idea of leading easier lives, turn shopkeepers, the whole natural quantity of that business divided among them all may afford too small a share for each, and occasion complaints, that trade is dead; these may also suppose, that it is owing to scarcity of money, while, in fact, it is not so much from the fewness of buyers, as from the excessive number of sellers, that the mischief arises; and, if every shop-keeping farmer and mechanic would return to the use of his plough and working-tools, there would remain of widows, and other women, shop-keepers sufficient for the business, which might then afford them a comfortable maintenance.

Whoever has travelled through the various parts of Europe, and observed how small is the proportion of people in affluence or easy circumstances there, compared with those in poverty and misery; the few rich and haughty landlords, the multitude of poor, abject, rack-rented, tythe-paying tenants, and half-paid and half-starved ragged laborers; and views here the happy mediocrity, that so generally prevails throughout these States, where the cultivator works for himself, and supports his family in decent plenty, will, methinks, see abundant reason to bless Divine Providence for the evident and great difference in our favor, and be convinced, that no nation known to us enjoys a greater share of human felicity.

It is true, that in some of the States there are parties and discords; but let us look back, and ask if we were ever without them? Such will exist wherever there is liberty; and perhaps they help to preserve it. By the collision of different sentiments, sparks of truth are struck out, and political light is obtained. The different factions, which at present divide us, aim all at the public good; the differences are only about the various modes of promoting it. Things, actions, measures, and objects of all kinds, present themselves to the minds of men in such a variety of lights, that it is not possible we should all think alike at the same time on every subject, when hardly the same man retains at all times the same ideas of it. Parties are therefore the common lot of humanity; and ours are by no means more mischievous or less beneficial than those of other countries, nations, and ages, enjoying in the same degree the great blessing of political liberty.

Some indeed among us are not so much grieved for the present state of our affairs, as apprehensive for the future. The growth of luxury alarms them, and they think we are from that alone in the high road to ruin. They observe, that no revenue is sufficient without economy, and that the most plentiful income of a whole people from the natural productions of their country may be dissipated in vain and needless expenses, and poverty be introduced in the place of affluence.

This may be possible. It however rarely happens; for there seems to be in every nation a greater proportion of industry and frugality, which tend to enrich, than of idleness and prodigality, which occasion poverty; so that upon the whole there is a continual accumulation. Reflect what Spain, Gaul, Germany, and Britain were in the time of the Romans, inhabited by people little richer than our savages, and consider the wealth they at present possess, in numerous well-built cities, improved farms, rich movables, magazines stocked with valuable manufactures, to say nothing of plate, jewels, and coined money; and all this, notwithstanding their bad, wasteful, plundering governments and their mad, destructive wars; and yet luxury and extravagant living have never suffered much restraint in those countries. Then consider the great proportion of industrious frugal farmers inhabiting the interior parts of these American States, and of whom the body of our nation consists; and judge whether it is possible, that the luxury of our seaports can be sufficient to ruin such a country. If the importation of foreign luxuries could ruin a people, we should probably have been ruined long ago; for the British nation claimed a right, and practised it, of importing among us, not only the superfluities of their own production, but those of every nation under heaven; we bought and consumed them, and yet we flourished and grew rich. At present, our independent governments may do what we could not then do, discourage by heavy duties, or prevent by heavy prohibitions, such importations, and thereby grow richer; if, indeed, which may admit of dispute, the desire of adorning ourselves with fine clothes, possessing fine furniture, with elegant houses, &c., is not, by strongly inciting to labor and industry, the occasion of producing a greater value, than is consumed in the gratification of that desire.

The agriculture and fisheries of the United States are the great sources of our increasing wealth. He that puts a seed into the earth is recompensed, perhaps, by receiving forty out of it; and he who draws a fish out of our water, draws up a piece of silver.

Let us (and there is no doubt but we shall) be attentive to these, and then the power of rivals, with all their restraining and prohibiting acts, cannot much hurt us. We are sons of the earth and seas, and, like Antæus in the fable, if, in wrestling with a Hercules, we now and then recieve a fall, the touch of our parents will communicate to us fresh strength and vigor to renew the contest.

5.9 AN AMERICAN LANGUAGE?

Preface to *An American Dictionary of the English Language*, Noah Webster (New York, 1828)

In the year 1783, just at the close of the revolution, I published an elementary book for facilitating the acquisition of our vernacular tongue, and for correcting a vicious pronunciation, which prevailed extensively among the common people of this country. Soon after the publication of that work, I believe in the following year, that learned and respectable scholar, the Rev. Dr. Goodrich of Durham, one of the trustees of Yale College, suggested to me, the propriety and expediency of my compiling a dictionary, which should complete a system for the instruction of the citizens of this country in the language. At that time, I could not indulge the thought, much less the hope, of undertaking such a work; as I was neither qualified by research, nor had I the means of support, during the execution of the work, had I been disposed to undertake it. For many years therefore, though I considered such a work as very desirable, yet it appeared to me impracticable; as I was under the necessity of devoting my time to other occupations for obtaining subsistence.

About twenty seven years ago, I began to think of attempting the compilation of a Dictionary. I was induced to this undertaking, not more by the suggestion of friends, than by my own experience of the want of such a work, while reading modern books of science. In this pursuit, I found almost insuperable difficulties, from the want of a dictionary, for explaining many new words, which recent discoveries in the physical sciences had introduced into use. To remedy this defect in part, I published my Compendious Dictionary in 1806; and soon after made preparations for undertaking a larger work.

My original design did not extend to an investigation of the origin and progress of our language; much less of other languages. I limited my views to the correcting of certain errors in the best English Dictionaries, and to the supplying of words in which they are deficient. But after writing through two letters of the alphabet, I determined to change my plan. I found myself embarrassed, at every step, for want of a knowledge of the origin of words, which Johnson, Bailey, Junius,

Skinner and some other authors do not afford the means of obtaining. Then laying aside my manuscripts, and all books treating of language, except lexicons and dictionaries, I endeavored, by a diligent comparison of words, having the same or cognate radical letters, in about twenty languages, to obtain a more correct knowledge of the primary sense of original words, of the affinities between the English and many other languages, and thus to enable myself to trace words to their source.

I had not pursued this course more than three or four years, before I discovered that I had to unlearn a great deal that I had spent years in learning, and that it was necessary for me to go back to the first rudiments of a branch of erudition, which I had before cultivated, as I had supposed, with success.

I spent ten years in this comparison of radical words, and in forming a synopsis of the principal words in twenty languages, arranged in classes, under their primary elements or letters. The result has been to open what are to me new views of language, and to unfold what appear to be the genuine principles on which these languages are constructed.

After completing this synopsis, I proceeded to correct what I had written of the Dictionary, and to complete the remaining part of the work. But before I had finished it, I determined on a voyage to Europe, with the view of obtaining some books and some assistance which I wanted; of learning the real state of the pronunciation of our language in England, as well as the general state of philology in that country; and of attempting to bring about some agreement or coincidence of opinions, in regard to unsettled points in pronunciation and grammatical construction. In some of these objects I failed; in others, my designs were answered.

It is not only important, but, in a degree necessary, that the people of this country, should have an *American Dictionary* of the English Language; for, although the body of the language is the same as in England, and it is desirable to perpetuate that sameness, yet some differences must exist. Language is the expression of ideas; and if the people of one country cannot preserve an identity of ideas, they cannot retain an identity of language. Now an identity of ideas depends materially upon a sameness of things or objects with which the people of the two countries are conversant. But in no two portions of the earth, remote from each other, can such identity be found. Even physical objects must be different. But the principal differences between the people of this country and of all others, arise from different forms of government, different laws, institutions and customs. Thus the practice of hawking and hunting, the institution of heraldry, and the feudal system of England originated terms which formed, and some of which now form, a necessary part of the language of that country; but, in the United States, many of these terms are no part of our present language, – and they cannot be, for the things which they express do not exist in this country. They can be known to us only as obsolete or as foreign words. On the other hand, the institutions in this country which are new and peculiar, give rise to new terms or to new applications of old terms, unknown to the people of England; which cannot be explained by them and which will not be inserted in their dictionaries, unless copied from ours. Thus the terms, *land-office; land-warrant; location of land; consociation* of churches; *regent* of a university; *intendant* of a city; *plantation*, *selectmen*, *senate*, *congress*, *court*, *assembly*, *escheat*, &c. are either words not belonging to the language of England, or they are applied to things in this country which do not exist in that. No person in this country will be satisfied with the English definitions of the words *congress*, *senate* and *assembly*, *court*, &c. for although these are words used in England, yet they are applied in this country to express ideas which they do not express in that country. With our present constitutions of government, *escheat* can never have its feudal sense in the United States.

But this is not all. In many cases, the nature of our governments, and of our civil institutions, requires an appropriate language in the definition of words, even when the words express the same thing, as in England. Thus the English Dictionaries inform us that a *Justice* is one deputed by the *King* to do right by way of judgment – he is a *Lord* by his office – Justices of the peace are appointed by the *King's commission* – language which is inaccurate in respect to this officer in the United States. So *constitutionally* is defined by Todd or Chalmers, *legally*, but in this country the distinction between *constitution* and *law* requires a different definition. In the United States, a *plantation* is a very different thing from what it is in England. The word *marshal*, in this country, has one important application unknown in England or in Europe.

A great number of words in our language require to be defined in a phraseology accommodated to the condition and institutions of the people in these states, and the people of England must look to an American Dictionary for a correct understanding of such terms.

The necessity therefore of a Dictionary suited to the people of the United States is obvious; and I should suppose that this fact being admitted, there could be no difference of opinion as to the *time*, when such a work ought to be substituted for English Dictionaries.

There are many other considerations of a public nature, which serve to justify this attempt to furnish an American Work which shall be a guide to the youth of the United States. Most of these are too obvious to require illustration.

One consideration however which is dictated by my own feelings, but which I trust will meet with approbation in correspondent feelings in my fellow citizens, ought not to be passed in silence. It is this. 'The chief glory of a nation,' says Dr. Johnson, 'arises from its authors.' With this opinion deeply impressed on my mind, I have the same ambition which actuated that great man when he expressed a wish to give celebrity to Bacon, to Hooker, to Milton and to Boyle.

I do not indeed expect to add celebrity to the names of *Franklin*, *Washington*, *Adams*, *Jay*, *Madison*, *Marshall*, *Ramsay*, *Dwight*, *Smith*, *Trumbull*, *Hamilton*, *Belknap*, *Ames*, *Mason*, *Kent*, *Hare*, *Silliman*, *Cleaveland*, *Walsh*, *Irving*, and many other Americans distinguished by their writings or by their science; but it is with pride and satisfaction, that I can place them, as authorities, on the same page with those of *Boyle*, *Hooker*, *Milton*, *Dryden*, *Addison*, *Ray*, *Milner*, *Cowper*, *Davy*, *Thomson* and *Jameson*.

A life devoted to reading and to an investigation of the origin and principles of our vernacular language, and especially a particular examination of the best English writers, with a view to a comparison of their style and phraseology, with those of the best American writers, and with our colloquial usage, enables me to affirm with confidence, that the genuine English idiom is as well preserved by the unmixed English of this country, as it is by the best *English* writers. Examples to prove this fact will be found in the Introduction to this work. It is true, that many of our writers have neglected to cultivate taste, and the embellishments of style; but even these have written the language in its genuine *idiom*. In this respect, Franklin and Washington, whose language is their hereditary mother tongue, unsophisticated by modern grammar, present as pure models of genuine English, as Addison or Swift. But I may go farther, and affirm, with truth, that our country has produced some of the best models of composition. The style of President Smith; of the authors of the Federalist; of Mr Ames; of Dr Mason; of Mr Harper; of Chancellor Kent; [the prose] of Mr Barlow; of the legal decisions of the Supreme Court of the United States; of the reports of legal decisions in some of the particular states; and many other writings; in purity, in elegance and in technical precision, is equaled only by that of the best British authors, and surpassed by that of no English compositions of a similar kind.

The United States commenced their existence under circumstances wholly novel and unexampled in the history of nations. They commenced with civilization, with learning, with science, with constitutions of free government, and with that best gift of God to man, the christian religion. Their population is now equal to that of England; in arts and sciences, our citizens are very little behind the most enlightened people on earth; in some respects, they have no superiors; and our language, within two centuries, will be spoken by more people in this country, than any other language on earth, except the Chinese, in Asia, and even that may not be an exception.

It has been my aim in this work, now offered to my fellow citizens, to ascertain the true principles of the language, in its orthography and structure; to purify it from some palpable errors, and reduce the number of its anomalies, thus giving it more regularity and consistency in its forms, both of words and sentences; and in this manner, to furnish a standard of our vernacular tongue, which we shall not be ashamed to bequeath to *three hundred millions of people*, who are destined to occupy, and I hope, to adorn the vast territory within our jurisdiction.

If the language can be improved in regularity, so as to be more easily acquired by our own citizens, and by foreigners, and thus be rendered a more useful instrument for the propagation of science, arts, civilization and christianity; if it can be rescued from the mischievous influence of sciolists and that dabbling spirit of innovation which is perpetually disturbing its settled usages and filling it with anomalies; if, in short, our vernacular language can be redeemed from corruptions, and our philology and literature from degradation; it would be a source of great satisfaction to me to be one among the instruments of promoting these valuable objects. If this object cannot be effected, and my wishes and hopes are to be frustrated, my labor will be lost, and this work must sink into oblivion.

This Dictionary, like all others of the kind, must be left, in some degree, imperfect; for what individual is competent to trace to their source, and define in all their various applications, popular, scientific and technical, *sixty* or *seventy thousand* words! It satisfies my mind that I have done all that my health, my talents and my pecuniary means would enable me to accomplish. I present it to my fellow citizens, not with frigid indifference, but with my ardent wishes for their improvement and their happiness; and for the continued increase of the wealth, the learning, the moral and religious elevation of character, and the glory of my country.

To that great and benevolent Being, who, during the preparation of this work, has sustained a feeble constitution, amidst obstacles and toils, disappointments, infirmities and depression; who has twice borne me and my manuscripts in safety across the Atlantic, and given me strength and resolution to bring the work to a close, I would present the tribute of my most grateful acknowledgments. And if the talent which he entrusted to my care, has not been put to the most profitable use in his service, I hope it has not been 'kept laid up in a napkin', and that any misapplication of it may be graciously forgiven.

New Haven, 1828

5.10 THE HISTORY OF THE REVOLUTION: A CONTEMPORARY ACCOUNT

David Ramsay, *The History of the American Revolution* (1790) II 314–25

The age and temperament of individuals had often an influence in fixing their political character. Old men were seldom warm whigs. They could not relish the great changes which were daily taking place. Attached to ancient forms and habits, they could not readily accommodate themselves to new systems. Few of the very rich were active in forwarding the revolution. This was remarkably the case in the eastern and middle States; but the reverse took place in the southern extreme of the confederacy. There were in no part of America, more determined whigs than the opulent slaveholders in Virginia, the Carolinas and Georgia, The active and spirited part of the community, who felt themselves possessed of talents, that would raise them to eminence in a free government, longed for the establishment of independent constitutions: But those who were in possession or expectation of royal favour, or of promotion from Great Britain, wished that the connexion between the Parent State and the colonies, might be preserved. The young, the ardent, the ambitious and the enterprising were mostly whigs, but the phlegmatic, the timid, the interested and those who wanted decision were, in general, favourers of Great Britain, or at least only the lukewarm inactive friends of independence. The whigs received a great reinforcement from the operation of continental money. In the year 1775, 1776, and in the first months of 1777, while the bills of Congress were in good credit, the effects of them were the same, as if a foreign power had made the United States a present of twenty million of silver dollars. The circulation of so large a sum of money, and the employment given to great numbers in providing for the American army, increased the numbers and invigorated the zeal of the friends to the revolution: on the same principles, the American war was patronised in England, by the many contractors and agents for transporting and supplying the British army. In both cases the inconveniences of interrupted commerce were lessened by the employment which war and a domestic circulation of money substituted in its room. The convulsions of war afforded excellent shelter for desperate debtors. The spirit of the times revolted against dragging to jails for debt, men who were active and zealous in defending their country, and on the other hand, those who owed more than they were worth, by going within the British lines, and giving themselves the merit of suffering on the score of loyalty, not only put their creditors to defiance, but sometimes obtained promotion or other special marks of royal favour.

The American revolution, on the one hand, brought forth great vices; but on the other hand, it called forth many virtues, and gave occasion for the display of abilities which, but for that event, would have been lost to the world. When the war began, the Americans were a mass of husbandmen, merchants, mechanics and fishermen; but the necessities of the country gave a spring to the active powers of the inhabitants, and set them on thinking, speaking and acting, in a line far beyond that to which they had been accustomed. The difference between nations is not so much owing to nature, as to education and circumstances. While the Americans were guided by the leading strings of the mother country, they had no scope nor encouragement for exertion. All the departments of government were established and executed for them, but not by them. In the years 1775 and 1776 the country, being suddenly thrown into a situation that needed the abilities of all its sons, these generally took their places, each according to the bent of his inclination. As they severally pursued their objects with ardor, a vast expansion of the human mind speedily followed. This displayed itself in a variety of ways. It was found that the talents for great stations did not differ in kind, but only in degree, from those which were necessary for the proper discharge of the ordinary business of civil society. In the bustle that was occasioned by the war, few instances could be produced of any persons who made a figure, or who rendered essential services, but from among those who had given specimens of similar talents in their respective professions. Those who from indolence or dissipation, had been of little service to the community in time of peace, were found equally unserviceable in war. A few young men were exceptions to this general rule. Some of these, who had indulged in youthful follies, broke off from their vicious courses, and on the pressing call of their country became useful servants of the public: but the great bulk of those, who were the active instruments of carrying on the revolution, were self-made, industrious men. These who by their own exertions, had established or laid a foundation for establishing personal independence, were most generally trusted, and most successfully employed in establishing that of their country. In these times of action, classical education was found of less service than good natural parts, guided by common sense and sound judgement.

Several names could be mentioned of individuals who, without the knowledge of any other language than their mother tongue, wrote not only accurately, but elegantly, on public business. It seemed as if the war not only required, but created talents. Men whose minds were warmed with the love of liberty, and whose abilities were improved by daily exercise, and sharpened with a laudable ambition to serve their distressed country, spoke, wrote, and acted, with an energy far surpassing all expectations which could be reasonably founded on their previous acquirements.

The Americans knew but little of one another, previous to the revolution. Trade and business had brought the inhabitants of their seaports acquainted with each other, but the bulk of the people in the interior country were unacquainted with their fellow citizens. A continental army, and Congress composed of men from all the States, by freely mixing together, were assimilated into one mass. Individuals of both, mingling with the citizens, disseminated principles of union among them. Local prejudices abated. By frequent collision asperities were worn off, and a foundation was laid for the establishment of a nation, out of discordant materials. Intermarriages between men and women of different States were much more common than before the war, and became an additional cement to the union. Unreasonable jealouses had existed between the inhabitants of the eastern and of the southern States; but on becoming better acquainted with each other, these in a great measure subsided. A wiser policy prevailed. Men of liberal minds led the way in discouraging local distinctions, and the great body of the people, as soon as reason got the better of prejudice, found that their best interests would be most effectually promoted by such practices and sentiments as were favourable to union. Religious bigotry had broken in upon the peace of various sects, before the American war. This was kept up by partial establishments, and by a dread that the church of England through the power of the mother country, would be made to triumph over all other denominations. These apprehensions were done away by the revolution. The different sects, having nothing to fear from each other, dismissed all religious controversy. A proposal for introducing bishops into America before the war, had kindled a flame among the dissenters; but the revolution was no sooner accomplished, than a scheme for that purpose was perfected, with the consent and approbation of all those sects who had previously opposed it. Pulpits which had formerly been shut to worthy men, because their heads had not been consecrated by the imposition of the hands of a Bishop or of a Presbytery, have since the establishment of independence, been reciprocally opened to each other, whensoever the public convenience required it. The world will soon see the result of an experiment in politics, and be able to determine whether the happiness of society is increased by religious establishments, or diminished by the want of them.

Though schools and colleges were generally shut up during the war, yet many of the arts and sciences were promoted by it. The Geography of the United States before the revolution was but little known; but the marches of armies, and the operations of war, gave birth to many geographical enquiries and discoveries, which other wise would not have been made. A passionate fondness for studies of this kind, and the growing importance of the country, excited one of its sons, the Rev. Mr Morse, to travel through every State of the Union, and amass a fund of topographical knowledge, far exceeding any thing heretofore communicated to the public. The necessities of the States led to the study of Tactics, Fortification, Gunnery, and a variety of other arts connected with war, and diffused a knowledge of them among a peaceable people, who would otherwise have had no inducement to study them.

The abilities of ingenious men were directed to make farther improvements in the art of destroying an enemy. Among these, David Bushnell of Connecticut invented a machine for submarine navigation, which was found to answer the purpose of rowing horizontally, at any given depth under water, and of rising or sinking at pleasure. To this was attached a magazine of powder, and the whole was contrived in such a manner, as to make it practicable to blow up vessels by machinery under them. Mr Bushnell also contrived sundry other curious machines for the annoyance of British shipping; but from accident they only succeeded in part. He destroyed one vessel in charge of Commodore Symonds, and a second one near the shore of Long-Island.

Surgery was one of the arts which was promoted by the war. From the want of hospitals and other aids, the medical men of America, had few opportunities of perfecting themselves in this art, the thorough knowledge of which can only be acquired by practice and observation. The melancholy events of battles, gave the American students an opportunity of seeing, and learning more in one day, than they could have acquired in years of peace. It was in the hospitals of the United States, that Dr Rush first discovered the method of curing the lock jaw by bark and wine, added to other invigorating remedies, which has since been adopted with success in Europe, as well as in the United States.

The science of government, has been more generally diffused among the Americans by means of the revolution. The policy of Great Britain, in throwing them out of her protection, induced a necessity of establishing independent constitutions. This led to reading and reasoning on the subject. The many errors that were at first committed by unexperienced statesmen, have been a practical comment on the folly of unbalanced constitutions, and injudicious laws. The discussions concerning the new constitution, gave birth to much reasoning on the subject of government, and particularly to a series of letters signed Publius, but really the work of Alexander Hamilton, in which much political knowledge and wisdom were displayed, and which will long remain a monument of the strength and acuteness of the human understanding in investigating truth.

When Great Britain first began her encroachments on the colonies, there were few natives of America who had distinguished themselves as speakers or writers, but the controversy between the two countries multiplied their number.

The stamp act, which was to have taken place in 1765, employed the pens and tongues of many of the colonists, and by repeated exercise improved their ability to serve their country. The duties imposed in 1767, called forth the pen of John Dickinson, who in a series of letters signed a Pennsylvania Farmer, may be said to have sown the seeds of the revolution. For being universally read by the colonists, they universally enlightened them on the dangerous consequences, likely to result from their being taxed by the parliament of Great Britain.

In establishing American independence, the pen and the press had merit equal to that of the sword. As the war was the people's war, and was carried on without funds, the exertions of the army would have been insufficient to effect the revolution, unless the great body of the people had been prepared for it, and also kept in a constant disposition to oppose Great Britain. To rouse and unite the inhabitants, and to persuade them to patience for several years, under present sufferings, with the hope of obtaining remote advantages for their posterity, was a work of difficulty: This was effected in a great measure by the tongues and pens of the well informed citizens, and on it depended the success of military operations.

To enumerate the names of all those who were successful labourers in this arduous business, is impossible. The following list contains in nearly alphabetical order, the names of the most distinguished writers in favour of the rights of America.

John Adams, and Samuel Adams, of Boston; – Bland, of Virginia; John Dickinson, of Pennsylvania; Daniel Dulany, of Annapolis; William Henry Drayton, of South-Carolina; Dr Franklin, of Philadelphia; John Jay, and Alexander Hamilton, of New-York; Thomas Jefferson, and Arthur Lee of Virginia; Jonathan Hyman, of Connecticut; Governor Livingston, of New-Jersey; Dr Mayhew, and James

Otis, of Boston; Thomas Paine, Dr Rush, Charles Thompson, and James Wilson, of Philadelphia; William Tennant, of South-Carolina; Josiah Quincy, and Dr Warren, of Boston. These and many others laboured in enlightening their countrymen, on the subject of their political interests, and in animating them to a proper line of conduct, in defence of their liberties. To these individuals may be added, the great body of the clergy, especially in New-England. The printers of news-papers, had also much merit in the same way. Particularly Eedes and Gill, of Boston; Holt, of New-York; Bradford, of Philadelphia; and Timothy, of South-Carolina.

The early attention which had been paid to literature in New-England, was also eminently conducive to the success of the Americans in resisting Great Britain. The university of Cambridge was founded as early as 1636, and Yale college in 1700. It has been computed, that in the year the Boston port act was passed, there were in the four eastern colonies, upwards of two thousand graduates of their colleges dispersed through their several towns, who by their knowledge and abilities, were able to influence and direct the great body of the people to a proper line of conduct, for opposing the encroachments of Great Britain on their liberties. The colleges to the southward of New-England, except that of William and Mary in Virginia, were but of modern date; but they had been of a standing sufficiently long, to have trained for public service, a considerable number of the youth of the country. The college of New-Jersey, which was incorporated about 28 years before the revolution, had in that time educated upwards of 300 persons, who, with a few exceptions, were active and useful friends of independence. From the influence which knowledge had in securing and preserving the liberties of America, the present generation may trace the wise policy of their fathers, in erecting schools and colleges. They may also learn that it is their duty to found more, and support all such institutions. Without the advantages derived from these lights of this new world, the United States would probably have fallen in their unequal contest with Great Britain. Union which was essential to the success of their resistance, could scarcely have taken place, in the measures adopted by an ignorant multitude. Much less could wisdom in council, unity in system, or perseverance in the prosecution of a long and self denying war, be expected from an uninformed people. It is a well known fact, that persons unfriendly to the revolution, were always most numerous in those parts of the

United States, which had either never been illuminated, or but faintly warmed by the rays of science. The uninformed and the misinformed, constituted a great proportion of those Americans, who preferred the leading strings of the Parent State, though encroaching on their liberties, to a government of their own countrymen and fellow citizens.

As literature had in the first instance favoured the revolution, so in its turn, the revolution promoted literature. The study of eloquence and of the Belles lettres, was more successfully prosecuted in America, after the disputes between Great Britain and her colonies began to be serious, than it ever had been before. The various orations, addresses, letters, dissertations and other literary performances which the war made necessary, called forth abilities where they were, and excited the rising generation to study arts, which brought with them their own reward. Many incidents afforded materials for the favourites of the muses, to display their talents. Even burlesquing royal proclamations, by parodies and doggerel poetry, had great effects on the minds of the people. A celebrated historian has remarked, that the song of Lillibullero forwarded the revolution of 1688 in England. It may be truly affirmed, that similar productions produced similar effects in America. Francis Hopkinson rendered essential service to his country, by turning the artillery of wit and ridicule on the enemy. Philip Freneau laboured successfully in the same way. Royal proclamations and other productions which issued from royal printing presses, were by the help of a warm imagination, arrayed in such dresses as rendered them truly ridiculous. Trumbull with a vein of original Hudibrastic humour, diverted his countrymen so much with the follies of their enemies, that for a time they forgot the calamities of war. Humphries twined the literary with the military laurel, by superading the fame of an elegant poet, to that of an accomplished officer. Barlow increased the fame of his country and of the distinguished actors in the revolution, by the bold design of an epic poem ably executed, on the idea that Columbus foresaw in vision, the great scenes that were to be transacted on the theatre of that new world, which he had discovered. Dwight struck out in the same line, and at an early period of life finished, an elegant work entitled the conquest of Canaan, on a plan which has rarely been attempted. The principles of their mother tongue, were first unfolded to the Americans since the revolution, by their countryman Webster. Pursuing an unbeaten track, he has made discoveries in the genius and construction of the English language, which had escaped the researches of preceding philologists. These and a group of other literary characters have been brought into view by the revolution. It is remarkable, that of these, Connecticut has produced an unusual proportion. In that truly republican state, every thing conspires to adorn human nature with its highest honours.

From the later periods of the revolution till the present time, schools, colleges, societies and institutions for promoting literature, arts, manufactures, agriculture, and for extending human happiness, have been increased far beyond any thing that ever took place before the declaration of independence. Every state in the union, has done more or less in this way, but Pennsylvania has done the most. The following institutions have been very lately founded in that state, and most of them in the time of the war or since the peace. A university in the city of Philadelphia; a college of physicians in the same place; Dickinson college at Carlisle; Franklin college at Lancaster; the Protestant Episcopal academy in Philadelphia; academies at York-town, at Germantown, at Pittsburgh and Washington; and an academy in Philadelphia for young ladies; societies for promoting political enquiries; for the medical relief of the poor, under the title of the Philadelphia Dispensary; for promoting the abolition of slavery, and the relief of free negroes unlawfully held in bondage; for propagating the gospel among the Indians, under the direction of the United Brethren; for the encouragement of manufactures and the useful arts; for alleviating the miseries of prisons. Such have been some of the beneficial effects, which have resulted from that expansion of the human mind, which has been produced by the revolution, but these have not been without alloy.

To overset an established government unhinges many of those principles, which bind individuals to each other. A long time, and much prudence, will be necessary to reproduce a spirit of union and that reverence for government, without which society is a rope of sand. The right of the people to resist their rulers, when invading their liberties, forms the corner stone of the American republics. This principle, though just in itself, is not favourable to the tranquillity of present establishments. The maxims and measures, which in the years 1774 and 1775 were successfully inculcated and adopted by American patriots, for oversetting the established government, will answer a similar purpose when recurrence is had to them by factious demagogues, for disturbing the freest governments that were ever devised.

War never fails to injure the morals of the people engaged in it. The American war, in particular, had an unhappy influence of this kind. Being begun without funds or regular establishments, it could not be carried on without violating private rights; and in its progress, it involved a necessity for breaking solemn promises, and plighted public faith. The failure of national justice, which was in some degree unavoidable, increased the difficulties of performing private engagements, and weakened that sensibility to the obligations of public and private honor, which is a security for the punctual performance of contracts.

In consequence of the war, the institutions of religion have been deranged, the public worship of the Deity suspended, and a great number of the inhabitants deprived of the ordinary means of obtaining that religious knowledge, which tames the fierceness, and softens the rudeness of human passions and manners. Many of the temples dedicated to the service of the most High, were destroyed, and these from a deficiency of ability and inclination, are not yet rebuilt. The clergy were left to suffer, without proper support. The depreciation of the paper currency was particularly injurious to them. It reduced their salaries to a pittance, so insufficient for their maintenance, that several of them were obliged to lay down their profession, and engage in other pursuits. Public preaching, of which many of the inhabitants were thus deprived, seldom fails of rendering essential service to society, by civilising the multitude and forming them to union. No class of citizens have contributed more to the revolution than the clergy, and none have hitherto suffered more in consequence of it. From the diminution of their number, and the penury to which they have been subjected, civil government has lost many of the advantages it formerly derived from the public instructions of that useful order of men.

On the whole, the literary, political, and military talents of the citizens of the United States have been improved by the revolution, but their moral character is inferior to what it formerly was. So great is the change for the worse, that the friends of public order are loudly called upon to exert their utmost abilities, in extirpating the vicious principles and habits, which have taken deep root during the late convulsions.

Bibliographical Guide

I. ORIGINAL SOURCES IN PRINT AND COLLECTIONS OF DOCUMENTS

i. *Politics, Central Government, Political Ideas*

John Adams, *Defence of the Constitutions of Government of the United States* (1787) in *Works*, ed. C. F. Adams, vol. IV, Boston, 1851.

The Adams Papers: *Diary and Autobiography of John Adams*, ed. L. H. Butterfield *et al.*, 4 vols., Cambridge, Mass., 1961.

Documents Illustrative of the Formation of the Union of the American States, Washington, D.C., 1927.

The Federal Convention and the Formation of the Union of the American States, ed. Winton U. Solberg with introduction, Indianapolis, 1958.

Letters of the Continental Congress, ed. Edmund C. Burnett, 8 vols., Washington, D.C., 1921–6.

Pamphlets of the American Revolution, ed. Bernard Bailyn, 4 vols., of which vol. I so far, Cambridge, Mass., 1965.

The Papers of Alexander Hamilton, ed. Harold C. Eyrett and J. E. Cooke, vol. I, New York, 1961.

The Papers of James Madison, ed. William T. Hutchinson and William M. E. Rachal, 5 vols. so far, Chicago, 1962–7.

Records of the Federal Convention, ed. Max Farrand, 4 vols., New Haven, Conn., 1937.

The Writings of George Washington, ed. J. C. Fitzpatrick, 39 vols., Washington, D.C., 1931–44.

ii. *Observations of social conditions, politics and prospects*

John Quincy Adams, *Life in a New England Town: 1787–1788*, Boston, 1903.

François, Marquis de Barbé-Marbois, *Our Revolutionary Forefathers*, New York, 1929. (Diary and letters of residence in U.S., 1779–85.)

J. P. Brissot de Warville, *Nouveau voyage dans les États-Unis, 1788*, 3 vols., Paris, 1791.

François Jean, Marquis de Chastellux, *Voyages dans l'Amérique septentrionale*, 1780–2, transl., London, 1787.

M. G. St Jean de Crèvecœur, *Letters from an American Farmer*, London, 1782; frequently reprinted.

Thomas Jefferson, *Notes on the State of Virginia*, ed. T. P. Abernethy, New York, 1964.

II. SECONDARY WORKS

i. *Politics, Central Government, Political Ideas*

John R. Alden, *The American Revolution: 1775–83*, New York, 1954.

Charles A. Beard, *An Economic Interpretation of the Constitution of the United States*, New York, 1913.

Carl L. Becker, *The Declaration of Independence*, New York, 1922.

Robert E. Brown, *Charles Beard and the Constitution*, Princeton, 1956.

Carl Van Doren, *The Great Rehearsal*, New York, 1948.

Max Farrand, *The Framing of the Constitution of the United States*, New Haven, 1913.

E. James Ferguson, *The Power of the Purse: A History of American Public Finance, 1776–1790*, Chapel Hill, 1961.

Alan Heimert, *Religion and the American Mind from the Great Awakening to the Revolution*, Cambridge, Mass., 1966.

John R. Howe, *The Changing Political Thought of John Adams*, Princeton, 1966.

Merrill Jensen, *The Articles of Confederation*, Madison, Wisconsin, 1948.

—— The New Nation, *A History of the United States during the Confederation*, New York, 1950.

Cecelia M. Kenyon, 'Republicanism and Radicalism in the American Revolution; an Old-fashioned Interpretation', *William and Mary Quarterly* (April, 1962).

—— 'Men of Little Faith: the Antifederalists on the Nature of Representative Government', *William and Mary Quarterly* (January, 1955).

Forrest McDonald, *We the People: the Economic Origins of the Constitution*, Chicago, 1958.

—— *E Pluribus Unum*, Boston, 1965.

Jackson T. Main, *The Antifederalists*, Chapel Hill, 1961.

—— 'The Origins of a Political Élite: the Upper Houses in the Revolutionary Era', *Huntington Library Quarterly* (February, 1964).

John C. Miller, *Origins of the American Revolution*, 2nd ed., Stanford, 1959.

Richard B. Morris, 'The Confederation Period and the American Historian', *William and Mary Quarterly* (April, 1956).

William M. Nelson, *The American Tory*, Oxford, 1961.

R. R. Palmer, *The Age of the Democratic Revolution*, vol. 1: *The Challenge*, Princeton, 1959.

J. R. Pole, 'An Anatomy of the American Whig' (review article on Bailyn's *Pamphlets*), *The Historical Journal* (1966).

—— 'Historians and the Problem of Early American Democracy', *American Historical Review* (April, 1962).

—— 'The Making of the Constitution', in *British Essays in American History*, ed. H. C. Allen and C. P. Hill, London, 1957.

—— *Political Representation in England and the Origins of the American Republic*, London and New York, 1966.

Clinton Rossiter, *Seedtime of the Republic*, New York, 1953.

Robert L. Schuyler, *The Constitution of the United States*, New York, 1928.

Clarence L. Ver Steeg, 'The American Revolution Considered as an Economic Movement', *Huntington Library Quarterly*, 1956–7.

—— *Robert Morris, Financier of the Revolution*, Philadelphia, 1954.

ii. *In the States: Constitution-making, Government, Economic Development*

John R. Alden, *The South in the Revolution*, Baton Rouge, 1957.

Anne Bezanson, *Prices and Inflation during the American Revolution: Pennsylvania 1770–1790*, Philadelphia, 1951.

Robert E. Brown, *Middle Class Democracy and the Revolution in Massachusetts, 1691–1780*, Ithaca, 1955.

Robert E. Brown and Katharine Brown, *Virginia 1705–1786; Democracy or Aristocracy?* E. Lansing, Mich., 1964.

Robert L. Brunhouse, *The Counter-Revolution in Pennsylvania, 1776–1790*, Harrisburg, 1942.

T. C. Cochran, *New York in the Confederation; an Economic Study*, Philadelphia, 1932.

Philip A. Crowl, *Maryland during and after the Revolution*, Baltimore, 1943.

Harry A. Cushing, *The Transition in Massachusetts from Province to Commonwealth*, Columbia University Studies in History, Economics and Public Law, VII, New York, 1896.

George Dangerfield, *Chancellor Robert R. Livingston of New York, 1746–1813*, New York, 1960.

Elisha P. Douglass, *Rebels and Democrats*, Chapel Hill, 1953.

Robert A. East, *Business Enterprise in the American Revolutionary Era*, New York, 1938.

—— 'Massachusetts Conservatives in the Critical Period' in *The Era of the American Revolution*, ed. Richard B. Morris, New York, 1939.

H. J. Eckenrode, *The Revolution in Virginia*, Boston, 1916.

E. James Ferguson, *The Power of the Purse: A History of American Public Finance, 1776–1790*, Chapel Hill, 1961.

Hugh Blair Grigsby, *The History of the Virginia Federal Convention of 1788, with some account of the eminent Virginians of that era, who were members of the body*, ed. R. A. Brock, 2 vols., Richmond, 1890, 1891.

Oscar and Mary F. Handlin, *Commonwealth: A Study of the Role of Government in the American Economy: Massachusetts, 1774–1861*, New York, 1947.

Samuel B. Harding, *The Contest over the Ratification of the Federal Constitution of Massachusetts*, New York, 1896.

Freeman H. Hart, *The Valley of Virginia in the American Revolution, 1763–1789*, Chapel Hill, 1942.

G. H. Haynes, *Representation and Suffrage in Massachusetts, 1620–1891*, Baltimore, 1894.

Merrill Jensen, *The New Nation, 1781–1789*, New York, 1950.

Charles R. Lingley, *The Transition in Virginia from Colony to Commonwealth*, New York, 1910.

Richard P. McCormick, *Experiment in Independence*, New Brunswick, 1950.

Forrest McDonald, *We the People*, Chicago, 1958.

David J. Mays, *Edmund Pendleton, 1721–1803*, 2 vols., Cambridge, Mass., 1952.

Richard B. Morris, *Government and Labor in Early America*, New York, 1946.

Allen Nevins, *The American States during and after the Revolution*, New York, 1924.

J. R. Pole, *Political Representation in England and the Origins of the American Republic*, London and New York, 1966.

J. Paul Selsam, *The Pennsylvania Constitution of 1776*, Philadelphia, 1936.

C. Page Smith, *James Wilson, Founding Father*, Chapel Hill, 1956.

—— *John Adams*, 2 vols., New York, 1962.

Ernest W. Spaulding, *New York in the Critical Period, 1783–1789*, New York, 1932.

Robert J. Taylor, *Western Massachusetts in the Revolution*, Providence, 1954.

Chilton Williamson, *American Suffrage from Property to Democracy*, Princeton, 1960.

Harry B. Yoshpe, *The Disposition of Loyalist Estates in the Southern District of the State of New York*, New York, 1939.

iii. *Public Lands – Society – America after the Revolution*

T. P. Abernethy, *From Frontier to Plantation in Tennessee*, Chapel Hill, 1932.

—— *Western Lands and the American Revolution*, New York, 1937.

C. W. Alvord, *The Mississippi Valley in British Politics*, 2 vols., Cleveland, Ohio, 1917.

Carl Bridenbaugh, *Cities in Revolt: Urban Life in America 1743–1776*, New York, 1955.

—— *Myths and Realities*, Baton Rouge, 1952.

Carl Bridenbaugh and Jessica Bridenbaugh, *Rebels and Gentlemen: Philadelphia in the Age of Franklin*, New York, 1962.

Wallace Brown, *The King's Friends*, Providence, R.I., 1966.

J. Franklin Jameson, *The American Revolution considered as a Social Movement*, Princeton, 1926.

Jackson T. Main, *The Social Structure of Revolutionary America*, Princeton, 1965.

Frederick B. Tolles, 'The Revolution as a Social Movement: a Re-evaluation', in *American Historical Review* (October, 1954).

Harry B. Yoshpe, *The Disposition of Loyalist Estates in the Southern District of the State of New York*, New York, 1939.

III. ADDITIONAL SOURCES

Federal and State Constitutions, ed. F. N. Thorpe, Washington, 1909.

Journals of the Continental Congress, 1774–89, ed. W. C. Ford *et al.*, 34 vols., Washington, 1904–37.

Laws of Virginia, W. W. Hening, comp., 13 vols., Richmond, Virginia, 1809–23.

David Ramsay, *The History of the American Revolution*, 2 vols., 1790.

Revolutionary Diplomatic Correspondence of the United States, ed. F. Wharton, 6 vols., Washington, 1889.

Sources and Documents Illustrating the American Revolution, 1764–1788 and the Formation of the Constitution, Oxford, 1923.

Tracts of the American Revolution, 1763–76, ed. Merrill Jensen, Indianapolis and New York, 1967.

Noah Webster, *An American Dictionary of the English Language*, New York, 1828.

Works of Benjamin Franklin, ed. Jared Sparks, 1856.

Index